I0824363

Buddha Śākyamuni

Guru Padmasambhava

Longchen Rabjam
(Longchenpa, 1308–1364)

༄། །རྒྱལ་བ་ཀློང་ཆེན་རབ་འབྱམས་ཀྱིས་མཛད་པའི་
མན་ངག་རིན་པོ་ཆེ་མཛོད་དང་
དིལ་མགོ་མཁྱེན་རྩེ་རིན་པོ་ཆེས་མཛད་པའི་
མན་ངག་མཛོད་ཀྱི་དོན་ཁྲིད་རབ་གསལ་ཟླ་བའི་བདུད་རྩི་བཞུགས་སོ།།

པདྨ་ཀ་རའི་སྒྲ་བསྒྱུར་མཐུན་ཚོགས་ནས་
སྒྲ་བསྒྱུར་ཞུས།

The Padmakara Translation Group gratefully acknowledges the generous support of the Tsadra Foundation in sponsoring the translation and preparation of this book.

The Precious Treasury of Essential Instructions

Longchen Rabjam

with *The Nectar of Brilliant Moon*, a commentary by
Dilgo Khyentse Rinpoche

TRANSLATED BY THE
Padmakara Translation Group

FOREWORDS BY
Shechen Rabjam Rinpoche and Jigme Khyentse Rinpoche

TRANSLATOR'S INTRODUCTION BY
Matthieu Ricard

SHAMBHALA

Shambhala Publications, Inc.
2129 13th Street
Boulder, Colorado 80302
www.shambhala.com

Cover art: Thangka courtesy of Eric Colombel's Private Collection
Cover design: Meredith Jarett

9 8 7 6 5 4 3 2 1

First Edition
Printed in the United States of America

Shambhala Publications makes every effort to print on acid-free, recycled paper.
Shambhala Publications is distributed worldwide by Penguin Random House, Inc., and its subsidiaries.

LIBRARY OF CONGRESS CATALOGING-IN-PUBLICATION DATA
Names: Rab-gsal-zla-ba, Dil-mgo Mkhyen-brtse, 1910–1991
author |Shechen Rabjam Jigme Chokyi Senge, 1966–writer of foreword |
Klong-chen-pa Dri-med-'od-zer, 1308–1363. Theg pa chen po'i man ngag gi
bstan bcos yid bzhin rin po che'i mdzod. English. | Comité de traduction
Padmakara, translator.
Title: The Precious Treasury of Essential Instructions. / Dilgo Khyentse
Rinpoche; translated by the Padmakara Translation Group; foreword by
Shechen Rabjam Rinpoche; translator's introduction by Matthieu Ricard.
Other titles: Man ngag mdzod kyi don khrid rab gsal zla ba'i bdud rtsi.
English Description: First edition. | Boulder: Shambhala, 2026. |
Includes bibliographical references and index. |
Identifiers: LCCN 2025010824 | ISBN 9781645474791 trade paperback
Subjects: LCSH: Klong-chen-pa Dri-med-'od-zer, 1308–1363. Theg pa chen po'i
man ngag gi bstan bcos yid bzhin rin po che'i mdzod | Rnying-ma-pa
(Sect)—Doctrines | Spiritual life—Buddhism
Classification: LCC BQ7950.K6673 R3313 2025 | DDC 294.3/61—dc23/eng/20250911
LC record available at https://lccn.loc.gov/2025010824

The authorized representative in the EU for product safety and compliance is eucomply OÜ, Pärnu mnt 139b-14, 11317 Tallinn, Estonia, hello@eucompliancepartner.com.

Contents

Foreword

The Treasury of Essential Instructions stands apart from the other of the Seven Treasuries composed by the omniscient Longchen Rabjam, which are precisely structured and complemented with autocommentaries. This Treasury is essentially a series of profound and direct spiritual instructions. One could imagine Longchenpa waking up in the morning and penning the advice that arose in his mind on that day—whether on renunciation to worldly affairs, doing retreat in a mountain solitude, or the sublime view of the Great Perfection.

In the same vein, whether Kyabje Dilgo Khyentse Rinpoche was teaching the foundational aspects of the path or the most profound tenets of the Great Perfection, he invariably emphasized the vital importance of merging the Dharma with one's mind through dedicated practice.

I recall vividly an instance in Bhutan in 1985 when Rinpoche said to me, "Matthieu has served me with dedication, but he came to receive teachings, so I want to give him some specific instructions." It was particularly precious that Rinpoche chose to give explanations on *The Treasury of Essential Instructions*. Each afternoon, over the course of nearly a month, a small group of us were fortunate to receive these teachings. His teachings flowed effortlessly from the very depths of his realization, spoken in a continuous, unbroken stream, without pause or hesitation, as if reading from an unseen book within his wisdom mind.

I am especially glad that these teachings were recorded on Matthieu's worn-out tape recorder, later transcribed, published, and translated into several languages. I chose to name this commentary *The Nectar of the Brilliant Moon*, in homage to the name Rabsel Dawa (Brilliant Moon) given to Khyentse Rinpoche in his youth when he received his novice vows.

I pray that these invaluable instructions may shine like a full moon on the path of liberation and enlightenment and that they may serve to preserve and propagate the Buddhadharma in general and the Khyentse lineage in particular, bringing benefit to countless sentient beings.

Shechen Rabjam
Thekchog Chökyi Gatsel
Paro, Bhutan

Foreword

This book is a commentary on a poem by Longchenpa, one of Tibet's most prolific and revered masters. In the ancient translation tradition, Longchenpa is honored as the equal of the Buddha, embodying not only vast scholarship across the sciences and Buddhist philosophy but also profound realization. His writings, some of which have been lost, reflect a union of learning and lived experience, making him not merely a scholar but a living expression of awakened wisdom and compassion. For this reason, my teachers referred to him as the Omniscient One, a title reserved for the Buddha himself.

Longchenpa did not theorize; he completely embodied the teachings. His writings distill the path of awakening into essential instructions that guide us in realizing the Buddha's own qualities within ourselves. These texts are not just literary treasures, they are vibrant manifestations of the Dharmakaya, the true nature of reality, kept alive through the unbroken lineage of masters like Jigme Lingpa and, in our time, Kyabje Dilgo Khyentse Rinpoche.

I have heard accounts of my teachers conversing directly with Longchenpa and Jigme Lingpa through visions—such is the extraordinary living continuity of this tradition. I am profoundly grateful to Venerable Konchog Tenzin (Matthieu) for making available this translation: a feast for all sincere seekers of the Dharma.

Kyabje Dilgo Khyentse Rinpoche gave these teachings kindly and without reservation over one month in Bhutan, out of boundless compassion for all beings.

For those drawn to the Buddha's teachings, from foundational teachings to the Great Perfection, this book offers precise and potent guidance, the distilled essence of awakening.

Jigme Khyentse Rinpoche | 2025

Translator's Introduction

The Precious Treasury of Essential Instructions (*Man ngag rin po che'i mdzod*), translated in this volume, was composed by Longchen Rabjam Drime Özer (*Kun mkhyen klong chen rab 'byams dri med 'od zer*, 1308–1364), commonly known as Longchenpa. He is considered the greatest exponent of the Nyingma tradition in the lineage of Guru Padmasambhava, Vimalamitra, and the other great vidyādharas.

By all accounts, Longchenpa attained the highest level of learning and spiritual realization while still a young man. His writings, especially the Seven Treasuries, are revered as the expression of the wisdom of the primordial Buddha Samantabhadra and the essence of the Seventeen Tantras of the Great Perfection (*Rdzogs chen rgyud bcu bdun*). In his *Exhortation to Read Longchenpa's Seven Treasuries*[1] Patrul Rinpoche wrote,

> Just hearing one sentence of such excellent texts
> Can shatter samsaric existence into pieces.
> So if you have the good fortune to read them in full
> Yet choose to discard them, what can you possibly be thinking?

One of these Treasuries, *The Precious Treasury of Essential Instructions*, is translated in the present volume together with a commentary by Kyabje Dilgo Khyentse Rinpoche (1910–1991). In terms of subject matter, the text follows a general progression, beginning with the most basic principles of Buddhist teaching and leading to instructions that enable direct realization of the three *kāya*s and the highest state of enlightenment. Throughout the text, however, Longchenpa constantly returns to the fundamentals, repeatedly reminding us of the importance of disenchantment with samsaric existence, conditioned as it is by ignorance and suffering. He urges us to be determined to escape samsara and to wish for buddhahood in order to free all beings from suffering.

Longchenpa conveys this straightforwardly, leaving no doubt about the need to focus on spiritual practice, to let go of self-clinging and the eight worldly concerns, and to rely on qualified spiritual masters from an authentic lineage. *The Treasury of Essential Instructions* is thus regarded as an invaluable companion on the spiritual path. Indeed, some practitioners customarily read one or more sets of instructions every day, working through the text from start to finish and beginning again when they reach the end, continually drawing new inspiration from Longchenpa's instructions.

The Treasury of Essential Instructions encompasses the teachings of all nine vehicles.* Initially, according to the vehicle of gods and humankind, one abandons the ten unvirtuous actions and practices their virtuous contraries. One next renounces the worldly attitudes that are the causes of suffering and pursues the goal of liberation from samsara, according to the lesser vehicle of the listeners* (*śrāvaka*s) and the solitary realizers* (*pratyekabuddha*s). This attitude gives way to the vast motivation of wanting to attain buddhahood for the sake of all beings, wishing to free them from suffering and bring them to the state of enlightenment. Then, as a means of swiftly progressing on this path, one adopts the Secret Mantra's skillful methods, leading to the realization of the view of the Luminous Great Perfection, the view that directly reveals the ultimate nature of reality as the immutable, pristine awareness of primordial purity.

When Khenchen Pema Sherab commented on the four-hundred-and-sixth set of six points, which he regarded as one of the text's most profound, he noted that the loftiest view of the Great Perfection, as expounded for example in *The Treasury of the Dharmadhātu* (*Chos dbyings mdzod*, another of the Seven Treasuries), lies for the moment beyond the direct experience of most practitioners. By contrast, *The Treasury of Essential Instructions* provides us with the tools to progress gradually from the foundation of the path to the summit of the highest teachings. In this connection, Dilgo Khyentse Rinpoche once said, "If a teaching pertains to the Great Perfection but the disciple is not at that level, it will not be beneficial. Just as a newborn cannot digest the food of a one-year-old, a one-year-old child cannot digest an adult's food." As Khyentse Rinpoche also says in his commentary on the sixty-third set of instructions, "You may expound the essence and the variety of the teachings, but whatever you say remains confined to the realm of the intellect and does not serve to transform your mind. Turn inward and practice."

As a skilled and insightful teacher, Longchenpa crafted his writing—here as elsewhere in his Seven Treasuries and other texts—to address his readers' varying needs, not as a reflection of his own intellectual development. In our humble opinion, it is a waste of time to venture to trace such an evolution in the case of a master of vast learning and unfathomable realization, who appears to have attained the ultimate result at the beginning, rather than at the end, of his career.

Concerning *The Treasury of Essential Instructions*, Longchenpa clearly expresses his intention at the beginning of the text:

> For the fortunate ones who aspire to liberation,
> I have condensed the essence of the sutras, tantras, and pith instructions
> And will teach these crucial and eminently profound points in verses of six instructions:
> Listen to them with respect.

Dilgo Khyentse Rinpoche comments upon this verse as follows: "For their benefit, here is the essence of innumerable instructions gathered and offered in the manner of excellent food. These instructions, in which many vital points are condensed in few words, represent the very heart of spiritual instructions. While there is a vast array of teachings, the most profound ones, able to fulfill all the needs of those who practice them, will be presented here in verses of six points." Longchenpa also reminds us of the purpose of the text as he concludes,

> Even a single six-point set from this precious treasury of teachings, brimming with spiritual qualities,
> Will enable you to achieve the ultimate goal.
> I have explained this wish-fulfilling jewel, these essential instructions,
> For the benefit of sincere practitioners aspiring for liberation.

This verse is commented upon by Khenpo Jamyang Drupa Lodrö in his word commentary *The Torch That Illuminates the Meaning*:[2]

> These instructions are like a precious treasury from which all the immense and wondrous qualities of the kāyas and wisdoms of the victorious ones arise. Not only the entire body of this text but every one of its sets of six points will, if understood and practiced

> correctly, bring about the manifestation of the ultimate fruition of the essence of the state of buddhahood, the dharmakāya, which fulfills the aspirations of all sentient beings according to their needs. Even though nothing in this world can adequately compare to the worth of these essential instructions, in order for people to understand, they may be likened to an array of beautifully arranged heaps of precious gems.

The Treasury of Essential Instructions is the only one of the *Seven Treasuries* for which Longchenpa did not write an autocommentary—perhaps because he thought that each of its six-part instructions constituted a single self-sufficient piece of heart advice. Moreover, there is no discernible order in the arrangement of the instructions contained in the collection. And given that Longchenpa could obviously have created one had he so wished, we may imagine that he wrote these various pieces of spiritual counsel for the sake of earnest practitioners, as they came into his wisdom mind, often alternating fundamental teachings on renunciation with the highest aspects of the Great Perfection.

In October 1985, at his residence in Bhutan, Kyabje Dilgo Khyentse Rinpoche, mindful of the needs of practitioners in this degenerate age, gave a small number of his disciples, including Shechen Rabjam Rinpoche, Jigme Khyentse Rinpoche, and myself, an extensive oral explanation of Longchenpa's verses, lasting over three weeks. Bestowed with immense kindness, his profound exposition on the text focused on the implementation of Longchenpa's instructions in one's own practice. We recorded Khyentse Rinpoche's teachings and they were recently transcribed and printed in an 820-page volume.[3]

The Seven Treasuries

Various catalogs[4] of Longchen Rabjam's writings list up to three hundred texts. His main writings are gathered into several collections: the Seven Treasuries (*Mdzod bdun*), which present the entire scope of Buddhist philosophy and practice; the Trilogy of Rest (*Ngal gso skor gsum*), which presents the graded path of practice; the Trilogy of Natural Freedom (*Rang grol skor gsum*), focused on the practice of the Great Perfection; the Trilogy of Dispelling Darkness (*Mun sel skor gsum*), consisting of commentaries on the *Guhyagarbha Tantra*; and the Heart Essence in Four Parts (*Snying thig ya bzhi*),[5] a comprehensive presentation of the two great streams of Great Perfection teachings deriving from Vimalamitra and from Guru Rinpoche. Two volumes of miscellaneous writings (*gsung thor bu*) have also survived, as well as many other texts that can be found in the catalogs of Longchenpa's works.

Among Longchenpa's writings, the Seven Treasuries occupy a position of special importance. The partial catalog created by Longchenpa himself at Tharpa Ling, during his exile in Bhutan, mentions six of the seven works, as no mention is made of *The Precious Treasury of the Fundamental Nature*. Moreover, the catalog lists the remaining works in a rather disconnected manner according to their subject matter and without suggesting any specific relation between them. This may lead one to suppose that Longchenpa himself may have regarded them as individual compositions in their own right and did not think of them as an integrated series. Be that as it may, owing no doubt to the similarity of their titles, scholarly tradition has come to regard the Seven Treasuries as a fully rounded collection and, as such, one of Longchenpa's greatest masterpieces. We find for example that Mipham Rinpoche (*Mi pham 'jam dbyangs rgya mtsho*, 1846–1912) composed in 1908 an extensive table of contents (*dkar chag*) together with a biography of Longchenpa for the xylographs of the Seven Treasuries carved at the Derge Great Printing Press.[6] Mipham Rinpoche mentions that he based his work on another extensive account of Longchenpa's life, works, and spiritual legacy written by the Second Shechen Rabjam, Gyurme Kunzang Namgyal (*Zhe chen rab 'byams 'Gyur med kun bzang rnam rgyal*, 1713–1769),[7] presented as a table of contents of the xylographs carved at Dzogchen Monastery, which are ordered slightly differently than those of the Derge edition.

These arrangements of the Seven Treasuries do not intend to reflect their chronological order, as the dates of their composition are mostly unknown, even though educated guesses can be made for some of them.[8] Instead, they serve as a guide to help students deepen their understanding and progress along the path of the nine vehicles. Many teachers—including Khenpo Jigme Phuntsok (*Mkhan po 'Jigs med phun tshogs*, 1933–2004) from Larung Gar philosophical college—have used this order to teach the Seven Treasuries to their students.

These two eminent masters summarize the descriptions of the Seven Treasuries as follows. The vast and profound *Precious Wish-Fulfilling Treasury* (*Yid bzhin rin po che'i mdzod*) enables one to establish with certainty—through study, reflection, and meditation—the meaning and key points of the various treatises pertaining to the sutras and the tantras. It is arranged in twenty-two chapters and is accompanied by a detailed autocommentary, *The White Lotus* (*Padma dkar po*), together with a guide for meditation titled *The Profound Meaning of the Adamantine Essence* (*Zab don rdo rje snying po*).

Whereas *The Wish-Fulfilling Treasury* and its commentary expound the Buddhist and non-Buddhist philosophical views, covering the various views that emerged in India, *The Precious Treasury of Philosophical Views* (*Grub mtha' rin po che'i mdzod*) engages in a more detailed presentation of the various views in eight chapters. It sets out the vehicles of the sutras and tantras of the first and second periods of translation into Tibetan of Buddhist texts from India.

The Precious Treasury of Essential Instructions (*Man ngag rin po che'i mdzod*), translated in the present volume, presents the essential teachings of the sutras and tantras in 413 series of six points. It lays the foundations for the Adamantine Essence of the Great Perfection in a profound way and exposes the vital points of the path and the fruit in the form of sets of advice for fortunate beings wishing to embark on the path to liberation and enlightenment.

The Precious Treasury of the Dharmadhātu (*Chos dbyings rin po che'i mdzod*) is considered by several authorities (including Chödrak Sangpo, Longchenpa's first biographer;[9] the Second Shechen Rabjam Rinpoche; and Mipham Rinpoche) to be an exposition of the essential instructions of the space class (*klong sde*) of the Great Perfection teachings. In thirteen chapters, it presents the ultimate wisdom (*dgongs pa*) of the primordial Buddha, the great natural perfection of all phenomena, explaining their nature in terms of primordial purity (*ka dag*) according to the view and practice of Trekchö,* or "cutting through solidity" (*khregs gcod*). The text is accompanied by an autocommentary, *A Treasury of Scriptural Transmission* (*Lung gi gter mdzod*), in which Longchenpa supports his exposition with a wealth of quotations from the tantras.

The Precious Treasury of the Fundamental Nature (*Gnas lugs rin po che'i mdzod*) is also an exposition of the meaning of primordial purity (*ka dag*) according to the view of Trekchö. It presents the true nature of spontaneously arising luminous wisdom according to the teachings of the class of pith instruction (*man ngag sde*). It takes the form of a song of spontaneous realization (*dohā*, *nyams mgur*) presented from the perspective of the Great Perfection's four vajra principles, or *four samayas*,* which are said to be beyond transgression and are thus "primordially kept." These four principles are the samaya of the nonexistence of phenomena (*med pa'i dam tshig*), the samaya of their single nature (*gcig pu'i dam tshig*), the samaya of their evenness (*phyal ba'i dam tshig*), and the samaya of their spontaneous presence (*lhun grub kyi dam tshig*). These four adamantine principles are united in the sphere of suchness, transcending the notions of cause and effect.[10] As Dilgo Khyentse Rinpoche once remarked, in such a context, "samaya" refers to the unmoving primordial wisdom of the ultimate expanse, and "since everything is the display of this wisdom, this samaya cannot be transgressed." The text is composed of five parts and sixteen sections and is supported by an autocommentary. While both *The Treasury of the Dharmadhātu* and *The Treasury of the Fundamental Nature* describe the realization of primordial purity according to the view and practice of Trekchö, the former focuses primarily on how to rest within primordial purity, while the latter concentrates on obtaining a definitive conviction concerning the ultimate nature of all things.

The Precious Treasury of the Supreme Vehicle (*Theg mchog rin po che'i mdzod*) is an extraordinary text that expounds the meaning of the Seventeen Tantras and the Hundred and Nineteen Essential Instructions (*Man ngag brgya bcu dgu*) of the Great Perfection's pith instruction class. It does this in twenty-five sections, beginning with an explanation of how the three kāyas appear and culminating with a presentation of the spontaneous accomplishment of the fruit. This treatise discusses the vast array of the tantras and pith instructions of the heart essence of luminosity in terms of the ground, path, and fruit and elucidates in detail the profound meaning of both Trekchö and Thögal (*thod rgal*),* or "direct crossing." Chödrak Sangpo recorded that in 1343, when Longchenpa was at Gangri Thökar, he had a dream indicating that his master Kumārāja had passed into *parinirvāṇa*. It is said that to preserve the Great Perfection teachings and to secure his master's legacy, Longchenpa composed this *Treasury of the Supreme Vehicle*.[11] While he was doing so, the three main protectors of the Great Perfection teachings—Mamo Ekajaṭī, Za Rāhula, and Damchen Dorje Lekpa—are said to have appeared in person and assisted Longchenpa in composing his treatise, with Ekajaṭī making the paper, Rāhula the ink, and Dorje Lekpa the bamboo pens.

The Precious Treasury of Words and Meaning (*Tshig don rin po che'i mdzod*) is a summary of part of *The Treasury of the Supreme Vehicle*, from the sixth through the final section. It focuses on direct experience of the practice and is arranged in eleven vajra points, leading to the ultimate fruition of perfect enlightenment. This work is also known as *The Treasury of Luminosity* (*'Od gsal mdzod*) and is accompanied by a profound autocommentary.

A Short Biography of Gyalwa Longchen Rabjam

Longchenpa (1308–1364) was born in Tödrong, the Upper Dra Valley, in Central Tibet. His mother was Drokza Sönam Gyen (*'Brog bza' bsod rnam rgyan*) and his father Lopön Tenpa Sung (*Slob dpon Bstan pa srung*),[12] a descendant of Gyalwa Chöyang, one of Guru Padmasambhava's twenty-five main disciples. When he was conceived, his mother dreamed of two suns on a lion's head illuminating the world before merging with her. At his birth, the dharma protectress Rematī appeared as a black woman. She held the baby, promised to protect him, returned him to his mother, and vanished. He was named Dorje Gyaltsen.

Longchenpa is considered the incarnation of Lhacham Pemasel, a daughter of King Trisong Detsen to whom Guru Padmasambhava entrusted the teachings of *The Heart Essence of the Ḍākinīs*. His mother passed away when he was nine, and his father when he was twelve. He then went to Samye Monastery, where Khenpo Samdrub Rinchen gave him novice vows and the name Tsultrim Lodrö.[13]

At sixteen, he had a vision of the goddess of learning, Sarasvatī, who placed him on her palm and took him to visit Mount Meru and the four continents for seven days. She prophesied that he would effortlessly master all the Buddha's teachings. He received numerous instructions and empowerments in the outer and inner tantras from various masters of the Ancient and the New Traditions, including his father; Tashi Rinchen (*Bkra shis rin chen*); Lama Dampa Sönam Gyaltsen (the throne holder of Sakya, *Bla ma dam pa bsod nams rgyal mtshan*, 1312–1375); and the Third Karmapa, Rangjung Dorje (*Karma pa rang byung rdo rje*, 1284–1339). With the master Zhönnu Döndrub (*Slob dpon gzhon nu don grub*) he studied *The One Hundred Thousand Nyingma Tantras* (*Rnying ma'i rgyud 'bum*), *The Embodiment of the Realization of All Buddhas* (*Mdo dgongs pa 'dus pa*), *The Magical Net, or Emanations* (*Rgyud sgyu 'phrul drva ba*), and the Mind Section of the Great Perfection (*Rdzogs chen sems sde*).

At nineteen, Longchenpa entered the renowned philosophical college of Sangphu Neutok, an ancient Kadampa monastery known for its high-quality studies. Over six years, he became well versed in Buddhist philosophy, valid cognition, grammar, poetry, and Sanskrit.

Disheartened by the rude attitude of some scholars from Kham, Longchenpa decided to leave Neutok and seek solitude, much to the great dismay of his fellow students and teachers. He then spent eight months in "dark retreat" (in complete darkness) in the Chokla cave, above Cha Valley in Uru. In the fifth month of his retreat, he had a vision of a sixteen-year-old *ḍākinī* adorned with a golden veil, colorful silks, and gold and jewel ornaments, riding a horse adorned with brocades and small bells. She placed her diadem upon Longchenpa's head and foretold that he would soon meet his root master, Rigdzin Kumārāja[14] (*Rig 'dzin Kumārādza, Gzhon nu shes rgyal po*, 1266–1343). Following this vision, Longchenpa spent a month immersed in experiences of bliss, clarity, and freedom from discursive thoughts.

At twenty-seven, the moment Longchenpa met Rigdzin Kumārāja in the highlands of Yartökyam above Samye, he felt boundless devotion and knew that he had found his root guru. He saw Kumārāja as the great pandita Vimalamitra in person. Kumārāja was a disciple of the *mahāsiddha* Melong Dorje (*Sgrub chen Me long rdo rje*, 1243–1303) and the lineage holder of *The Heart Essence of Vimalamitra.*

The night before Longchenpa's arrival, Kumārāja dreamed of a divine bird leading a large flock carrying his books away in all directions. He interpreted this as a sign that someone would spread his teachings far and wide. Later, Vimalamitra appeared in a dream, confirming that Longchenpa would become the primary holder of his teachings.

Together with Karmapa Rangjung Dorje, Longchenpa accompanied Kumārāja and his other disciples for two years, receiving all the essential instructions of the Great Perfection and various transmissions of Nyang Ral Nyima Özer's revealed treasures, including the Kagye Deshek Dupa (*Bka' brgyad bde gshegs 'dus pa*). The disciples lived ascetically in tents, in harsh conditions, as Kumārāja kept moving from place to place to avoid attachment to any particular area. Longchenpa had very little food and used a ragged bag as both mattress and blanket during the cold winter. Eventually, after imparting to him all the Heart Essence teachings, Kumārāja proclaimed Longchenpa his spiritual successor.

For the next seven years, Longchenpa lived in seclusion in various caves near Chimphu, above Samye Monastery. During this time, along with profound meditative experiences, he had numerous visions, including peaceful and wrathful forms of Guru Padmasambhava, the Eight Herukas, and a week-long vision of Black Vārāhī. He often returned to Kumārāja for guidance, and on five occasions, despite owning very little, he gave his master all his possessions as a sign of complete renunciation and devotion.

At thirty-one, while still in retreat, Longchenpa began bestowing empowerments and instructions on *The Heart Essence of Vimalamitra* to his own disciples.

Soon after, his close disciple Özer Gocha found a copy of *The Heart Essence of the Ḍākinīs*, the Dzogchen cycle transmitted by Guru Rinpoche to Yeshe Tsogyal in Drigung Titro cave. *The Heart Essence of the Ḍākinīs* had been revealed as a spiritual treasure by Longchenpa's previous incarnation, Pema Ledrel Tsal. The dharma protectress Shenpo Sodrubma also presented Longchenpa with the same text. To stress the importance of receiving teachings through an unbroken lineage, Longchenpa went as well to receive *The Heart Essence of the Ḍākinīs* transmission from Gyalse Lekpai Gyaltsen, a disciple of Pema Ledrel Tsal.

At thirty-three, when he gave the transmission of *The Heart Essence of the Ḍākinīs*, some disciples saw Longchenpa appearing in saṃbhogakāya form, amid a rain of flowers, while beams and circles of lights were visible all over the mountain. Longchenpa himself had a vision of Guru Padmasambhava and his consort Yeshe Tsogyal bestowing empowerments and entrusting him once more with *The Heart Essence of the Ḍākinīs* lineage. Guru Rinpoche gave Longchenpa the initiation name Orgyen Trime Özer (*O rgyan dri med 'od zer*), while Yeshe Tsogyal gave him the name Dorje Ziji (*Rdo rje gzi brjid*).

Following the exhortation of the dharma protectress Yudrönma, Longchenpa then went to stay in a cave at Kangri Thökar, high above the Kyichu River, south of Lhasa. There he achieved the ultimate realization of the Great Perfection and composed many of his most important treatises, including several of the famed Seven Treasuries.

At Kangri Thökar, Longchenpa had a vision of Kumārāja, who was pointing his fingers in the subjugation mudra. He felt that he had thus received an empowerment from his teacher. Moreover, he had visions of the primordial Buddha Samantabhadra and of Vimalamitra. The latter urged him to extract the quintessence of the *Heart Essence of Vimalamitra* teachings. Accordingly, Longchenpa composed *The Quintessence of the Guru*, which subsequently served as the core practice of many generations of dedicated Great Perfection practitioners. In addition, Vimalamitra asked Longchenpa to restore the Uru Shayi Lhakhang temple that was built by Nyang Tingdzin Zangpo, one of the main disciples of both Guru Rinpoche and Vimalamitra.

Nearby, at Drigung, a powerful leader named Gompa Kunrin was threatening the authority of Tai Situ Changchub Gyaltsen (*T'ai si tu Byang chub rgyal mtshan*, 1302–1371), who ruled Central Tibet. A prediction stated that a son of demons, with a sword-like birthmark, would go to hell unless an emanation of Mañjuśrī subdued him. Gompa Kunrin saw himself in this prophecy and believed Longchenpa to be this emanation. He invited him and became his disciple. Soon, thanks to Longchenpa's influence, Gompa Kunrin abandoned his plans to wage war against Changchub Gyaltsen. However, Changchub Gyaltsen suspected that Longchenpa was taking sides against him and sent troops to eliminate him.

Facing such a threat, Longchenpa chose to seek refuge in Bhutan. He had many disciples and had established eight hermitages[15] and monasteries throughout the country, with his main seat at Tharpa Ling, high above the Bumthang valley. In Bhutan, Longchenpa had a daughter and a son with his spiritual consort, the Bhutanese Kyipala (*Skyid pa lags*). His son, Gyalse Jamyang Trakpa Özer (*Rgyal sras 'jam dbyangs grags pa 'od zer*, 1356–1409), became a respected scholar, and the latter's son Se Dawa (*Sras zla ba*, b. 1413) founded Samten Ling monastery in the valley below Tharpa Ling. Both continued spreading Longchenpa's teachings and became respected masters in their own rights.[16]

Later, Tai Situ Changchub Gyaltsen recognized that Longchenpa had done well by stopping Gompa Kunrin from going to war. He apologized, requested Longchenpa to return to Tibet, and became his devoted disciple. Longchenpa then taught in various places across Central and Southern Tibet, including Lhodrak, Yamdrok, and Gongkar, where a thousand devotees gathered. Over the course of a month, he also gave teachings to a large crowd in Lhasa.

Longchenpa then announced that he would not remain in this world much longer.[17] At the age of fifty-six, he returned to the hermitages of Samye Chimphu, saying that it was a perfect place to leave his illusory body. Though he had become very weak, he gave his disciples an unelaborate empowerment (*spros med kyi dbang*) related to the Great Perfection. At midday on the eighteenth day of the twelfth lunar month of the female water-hare year (January 30, 1364), he asked those around him to prepare some offerings and then leave the room. As they were reluctant to leave, he told them, "Don't insist or make any commotion. Simply remain in meditative evenness." He then assumed the dharmakāya posture and departed, entering the state of the primordial exhaustion of phenomena.[18]

While his body was preserved for twenty-five days, it emitted a fragrant scent of sandalwood and camphor, and many miraculous signs appeared.

When the body was finally cremated, the earth trembled three times and a loud noise sounded seven times. In the ashes, his heart, eyes, and skull were found together, unburned by the flames.

Longchenpa had countless disciples and is said to have reincarnated at various times in history, notably as the great Bhutanese tertön Pema Lingpa (*Padma gling pa*, 1450–1521).

A Short Biography of Dilgo Khyentse Rinpoche

Dilgo Khyentse Rinpoche (*Dil mgo mkhyen rtse rin po che*) was born in 1910 into the Dilgo family at Sakar, on the banks of the Drichu (Yangse River), in the Denkhok valley of eastern Tibet. He was blessed at birth and given the name Tashi Paljor by the great master Mipham Rinpoche, who was spending the last years of his life in a hermitage above Sakar. From his early childhood, Tashi Paljor manifested a deep desire to devote himself to spiritual life. His father, Tashi Tsering, a local dignitary, whose two elder sons had become monks (one of whom was recognized as the incarnation of Sangye Nyenpa Rinpoche), wanted his youngest son to take care of family affairs. But a serious accident occurred when young Tashi Paljor fell into a large pot of boiling soup in the communal kitchen, leaving him bedridden for six months. This incident put an end to his father's stubbornness, since lamas whom he respected predicted that the child would not survive if he was not allowed to follow his aspirations. In desperation, his father also asked Tashi Paljor what could help him recover. The child requested to be covered with monks' robes, and soon after his health began to improve.

During a visit to the Dilgo family, the great Sakya master Jamyang Loter Wangpo (*Ngor dpon slob 'jam dbyangs blo gter dbang po*, 1847–1914) had recurring dreams indicating that Tashi Paljor was the reincarnation of his own teacher, Jamyang Khyentse Wangpo (*'Jam dbyangs mkhyen brtse'i dbang po*, 1820–1892).

Yet, Tashi Tsering remained reluctant to let anyone recognize his son as an incarnate lama, until Shechen Gyaltsab Pema Namgyal (*Zhe chen rgyal tshab 'gyur med padma rnam rgyal*, 1871–1926), whom he respected immensely, officially recognized and enthroned Tashi Paljor as the reincarnation of the wisdom mind of Jamyang Khyentse Wangpo and gave him the principal teachings of the Nyingma tradition. After Shechen Gyaltsab's death, Dilgo Khyentse Rinpoche considered Dzongsar Khyentse Chökyi Lodrö (*Rdzong gsar 'Jam dbyangs mkhyen brtse chos kyi blo gros*, 1893–1959) as his main teacher. He also studied extensively with the very learned Khenpo Shenga (1871–1927)[19] and Khenpo Thubga (1886–1956).[20]

Dilgo Khyentse Rinpoche visited Dzongsar frequently to receive teachings from Khyentse Chökyi Lodrö, who treated him with great respect. After receiving the transmission of the sixty volumes of *The Precious Collection of Revealed Treasures*, the *Rinchen Terdzö* (*Rin chen gter mdzo chen mo*), Dilgo Khyentse Rinpoche expressed his wish to spend the rest of his life in solitary retreats. However, Chökyi Lodrö told him that it was time to pass on to others the precious teachings he had received. He also told Khyentse Rinpoche, "Your spiritual treasures will greatly benefit others. I had a dream last night. There were clouds in the shapes of the eight auspicious symbols and with them in the sky were many buddhas and bodhisattvas. From those clouds fell an abundant rain of nectar, benefiting beings. I understood this as a sign that you must spread your treasure teachings." He then asked Dilgo Khyentse Rinpoche to give him the empowerments for some of these treasures.[21]

At the request of Khyentse Chökyi Lodrö, Kyabje Dilgo Khyentse Rinpoche traveled to Amdo in 1952 to confer the Rinchen Terdzö transmission, which lasted four months. During his visit, he went to Yama Tashikhyil, a small monastery on a wooded hilltop surrounded by hermitages, where Shabkar Tsok Druk Rangdrol (*Zhabs dkar tshogs drug rang grol*, 1781–1851) spent the last twenty years of his life. There Shabkar would sit on a stone seat under a juniper tree in the forest, where he taught and sang some of the realization songs that illuminate his autobiography. When Dilgo Khyentse Rinpoche visited the place, the hermits invited him to sit on that seat and asked him to teach. As he improvised songs of spiritual realization, a rainbow appeared, and fine snowflakes fell gently like a shower of flowers. Witnesses felt that Dilgo Khyentse Rinpoche must be a reincarnation of Shabkar. Dilgo Khyentse Rinpoche remarked, "There must be some truth in this supposition."

By the late 1950s, as the war intensified in Kham, Khyentse Rinpoche and his family narrowly escaped to Central Tibet, leaving everything behind, including Rinpoche's precious books and many of his writings. They embarked on an extensive pilgrimage in U and Tsang. For six months, Khyentse Rinpoche sat before the famous Crowned Buddha statue in Lhasa, reciting one hundred thousand long mandala offerings. During an epidemic in Lhasa, he performed many ceremonies and prayers for the sick and dying, despite his family's fears of him becoming infected. During this time, his mother and his elder brother Shedrub passed away.

From Tsurphu, the seat of the Karmapa northwest of Lhasa, Khyentse Rinpoche, his family, and a few disciples decided to go into exile. With hardly any provisions left, they reached the Bhutanese border, where the Bhutanese government offered them hospitality. In Wangdi Podrang, they heard on a small radio that Khyentse Chökyi Lodrö had died in Sikkim. By then, Dilgo Khyentse Rinpoche was forty-nine. He went to Sikkim to perform Khyentse Chökyi Lodrö's cremation. In Kalimpong and Darjeeling, he met Dudjom Rinpoche and Kangyur Rinpoche, with whom he exchanged teachings.

At the queen's request, Khyentse Rinpoche moved to Bhutan and became a schoolteacher at Simtokha, near the capital, Thimphu. His inner perfection soon attracted many disciples, and over the years, he became the most eminent Buddhist teacher in Bhutan, revered by everyone, from the royal family to the humblest farmer.

Several times a year, Khyentse Rinpoche performed large ceremonies called *drubchen*, or "great accomplishment," lasting from eight to fourteen continuous days and nights. Once, he spent two weeks at the Tiger's Nest Cave in Paro Taktsang, offering one hundred thousand butter lamps and giving many teachings and empowerments. While there, he had a vision of Rigzin Jigme Lingpa (*Rig 'dzin 'Jigs med gling pa*, 1729–1798), who placed his hand on Khyentse Rinpoche's head and said, "You are the heir of my teachings, the Heart Essence of the Vast Expanse (*Klong chen snying thig*)." He also instructed that to maintain peace and preserve the Buddhist teachings in Bhutan, four large stūpas should be built, each containing one hundred thousand miniature clay stūpas. This was done accordingly.

In India, Khyentse Rinpoche became one of the Fourteenth Dalai Lama's main teachers. He had met His Holiness in Lhasa on several occasions, and over the years, Khyentse Rinpoche offered him most of the major teachings of the Nyingma tradition. The Dalai Lama said, "Khyentse Rinpoche is one of my most important gurus. Since our first meeting, I have felt a special karmic connection with him. I particularly appreciate his nonsectarian attitude. Despite his fame, he always remains very gentle and humble. The Buddha explained in detail the qualities of an authentic teacher, and I found all of these qualities in Khyentse Rinpoche."

During his life, inside and outside Tibet, Khyentse Rinpoche gave the empowerments of *The Collection of Revealed Treasures* (*Rin chen gter mdzo chen mo*, seventy volumes in the new Shechen edition) five times. In India, Nepal, and Bhutan, he gave *The Oral Teachings of the Nyingma* (*Rnying ma bka' ma*) four times, *The Treasury of Precious Instructions* (*Gdams ngag rin po che'i mdzod*) three times, the *Revealed Treasures* of Chogyur Lingpa and of Pema Lingpa once, the treasures of Jatshön Nyingpo four times, and numerous times the empowerments of Longchenpa's *Heart Essence in Four Parts*, as well as Jigme Lingpa's *Heart Essence of the Vast Expanse*. He gave also the empowerments of the *Compendium of Sadhanas* (*Sgrub thabs kun btus*) and many others. As for reading transmissions, he twice gave the 103 volumes of the Kangyur, twice Mipham Rinpoche's *Collected Writings*, and once *The One Hundred Thousand Nyingma Tantras* (*Rnying ma rgyud 'bum*), as well as the Collected Writings of Jigme Lingpa, Patrul Rinpoche, and Shechen Gyaltsab.

He gave all these transmissions to eminent masters, including the Fourteenth Dalai Lama, Dza Trulshik Rinpoche (who became his main Dharma heir), Kangyur Rinpoche, Khamtrul Rinpoche, Penor Rinpoche, Drigung Kyabgön Chetsang, and many others. He received empowerments and rare transmissions from the Fourteenth Dalai Lama, the Sixteenth Karmapa, Dudjom Rinpoche, Kangyur Rinpoche, Trulshik Rinpoche, Jé Khenpo Yeshey Sengué, Penor Rinpoche, Tenga Rinpoche, Taklung Tsetrul Rinpoche, Taklung Shabdrung, Sengdrak Rinpoche, and others.

Khyentse Rinpoche's achievements in various fields could each have filled an entire lifetime. He spent over twenty years in retreat, possessed an astonishing depth and breadth of knowledge, taught ceaselessly, wrote twenty-five large volumes, and oversaw numerous major projects to preserve and disseminate Buddhist teachings in many countries.

He taught during every free moment, tirelessly responding to all requests for instruction and spiritual guidance, sometimes to a handful of disciples, sometimes to thousands. Anyone who heard Khyentse Rinpoche teach was struck by his remarkable delivery. Once in 1984, at the end of a teaching he gave at Tibet House in Delhi, Doboom Rinpoche, who had invited him, mentioned, "It says in the sutras that the Buddha delivered his teachings like the continuous flow of a river. I felt the same when listening to Dilgo Khyentse Rinpoche." Khyentse Rinpoche always matched his teachings to the audience's level of understanding. Even a few simple words from him could lead to a succession of fresh insights into the spiritual life.

Wherever he was, Khyentse Rinpoche would rise well before dawn to pray and meditate for several hours before embarking on an uninterrupted flow of activities until late into the night. He accomplished a tremendous daily workload with total serenity and apparent effortlessness. Profoundly gentle and patient though he was, Khyentse Rinpoche's presence, his vastness of mind and magnificent appearance, inspired awe and respect.

In early 1991, while teaching in Bodhgaya, Khyentse Rinpoche began to show the first signs of ill-health. He then traveled to Dharamsala, spending a month giving important empowerments and transmissions to His Holiness the Dalai Lama. Back in Nepal, as spring progressed, his health steadily deteriorated. He spent much of his time in silent prayer and meditation, setting aside only a few hours a day to meet those in need. He was obliged to cancel a fourth journey to Tibet, where he had planned to visit Shechen Monastery one last time. Instead, he chose to spend three and a half months in retreat opposite the Tiger's Nest, Paro Taktsang, in Bhutan, one of the most sacred places Padmasambhava blessed.

After his retreat, Rinpoche seemed to be in better health. He visited several of his disciples who were in retreat and spoke to them of the ultimate teacher, beyond birth and death or any physical manifestation. However, soon after, he showed signs of illness again. On the evening of September 27, 1991, he asked his attendants to help him sit upright and went into a peaceful sleep. In the early hours of the morning, his breathing ceased and his mind dissolved in the absolute expanse.

Thus, Khyentse Rinpoche's extraordinary life came to an end, a life spent from an early age entirely in study, practice, and teaching. Wherever he was, day or night, in the same uninterrupted flow of kindness, humor, wisdom, and dignity, his every effort had been directed to the preservation and expression of all forms of Buddhist teaching.

At the request of disciples from Tibet and all over the world, his body was preserved for a year using traditional embalming methods. It was taken from Bhutan to Shechen Monastery in Nepal for several months, allowing more people to pay their respects. Each Friday, the anniversary of his death, one hundred thousand butter lamps were offered at the Bodhnath Stupa near Shechen Monastery. The entire Tibetan community joined the monks in preparing and lighting the lamps.

Finally, in November 1992, Khyentse Rinpoche's remains were cremated near Paro in Bhutan. The three-day ceremony was attended by over a hundred prominent lamas, members of the royal family, Bhutanese ministers, five hundred Western disciples, and a crowd of about fifty thousand devotees—a gathering unprecedented in Bhutan's history.

Many great individuals, despite brilliance in science or the arts, may not always be good human beings. Khyentse Rinpoche, however, was someone whose greatness was totally in accord with the teachings he professed. However unfathomable his inner realization was, outwardly he was an extraordinarily good human being. His only concern was the present and ultimate benefit of others. Here was a living example of what lay at the end of the spiritual path and an inspiration for all.

Khyentse Rinpoche's life story has been recounted in much detail by Khyentse Rinpoche himself and by some of his close students in *Brilliant Moon: The Autobiography of Dilgo Khyentse.*[22] His story is also illustrated in several photography books, beginning with *Journey to Enlightenment: The Life and World of Dilgo Khyentse, Spiritual Teacher from Tibet.*[23]

The Translation

As mentioned earlier, Dilgo Khyentse Rinpoche gave the commentary presented in this volume in Bhutan in 1985. When receiving it, I formed the aspiration to translate it from the recordings I made at the time. Yet, I was carried away by chronic distraction. I finally turned to the translation three years ago, after requesting the learned Khenpo Gyurme Dorje, also called Gyakar Khenpo, from Shechen to transcribe the recording into writing. Rabjam Rinpoche carefully checked this transcript, and it was published by Shechen Publications.

The translation of Gyalwa Longchen Rabjam's root verses was done by Khenpo Sönam Tsewang in close collaboration with Judith Amtzis and myself. Khyentse Rinpoche's commentary was translated by me and edited by Judith and Wayne Amtzis. Together, we brought this endeavor to completion in a wonderful spirit of friendship and collaboration.

I simultaneously did the French translation of both the root text and the commentary, with the precious editorial help of Carisse Busquet, Anne Tardy, and Witty Wahida Léon. For clarity, I have given each set of instructions a title and prepared the endnotes and the glossary. (Note that an asterisk (*) in the text indicates that the term is explained in the glossary.)

We owe an immense debt of gratitude to Khenchen Pema Sherab for most kindly giving teachings on *The Precious Treasury of Essential Instructions* between 2018 and 2024, two or three weeks annually, completing them as he turned eighty-eight years old. His teachings were orally translated into English by Khenpo Sönam Tsewang and into French by myself.

As a support for the teachings, Khenchen used a detailed word commentary, *The Mirror That Illuminates the Meaning* (*Man ngag mdzod kyi 'bru 'grel don gsal me long*), composed in 2010 by Khenpo Jamyang Drupai Lodrö ('Jam dbyangs grub pa'i blo gros, 1939–2015).[24]

We also consulted a two-volume transcription of oral explanations on *The Treasury of Essential Instructions* by Dzogchen Tulku Pema Kalsang (*Rdzogs chen sprul sku pad ma skal bzang*, b. 1943), published in Tibet in 2011.[25]

Acknowledgments

To clarify many points in the commentary, I was fortunate to consult with Khenchen Pema Sherab, Jigme Khyentse Rinpoche, Khenpo Sönam Tsewang, Khenpo Gyurme Dorje (Gyakar Khenpo) of Shechen Monastery, and a few others, all of whom answered my questions with great generosity. I also sincerely thank Helena Blankleder and Wulstan Fletcher for their insights during our many conversations and for helping me to improve the formulation of some difficult passages.

I express my gratitude to Richard Barron for his translation of the root text, *The Precious Treasury of Pith Instructions*, published by Padma Publishing in 2006, which I studied attentively. I also thank David Germano for sharing an early draft of his own translation of the same root text, which he had studied in eastern Tibet with Khenpo Jigme Phuntsok, and for encouraging me to translate Khyentse Rinpoche's commentary. My gratitude also goes to Anne Benson for sharing the draft of her French translation of the root text and the clarifications she received from Pema Wangyal Rinpoche and Jigme Khyentse Rinpoche.

I offer my heartfelt gratitude to Nikko Odiseos for wholeheartedly embracing the publication of this volume and to Anna Wolcott Johnson for her precious guidance and careful editing of the final manuscript.

Finally, we are infinitely grateful to the Tsadra Foundation for supporting the transcription, publication, translation, and editing of this precious text.

Matthieu Ricard
Ngenlung Drechaling, Phobjika
(One of the eight places where Longchenpa lived in Bhutan)

Structure of the Text

The root text of *The Precious Treasury of Essential Instructions* is not divided into explicit sections, as is often the case with elaborate treatises. However, according to the commentaries, the text can be presented in three parts:

I. The "virtuous beginning" includes the title, the homage paid by the author to all the buddhas and bodhisattvas, and the pledge he made when composing it.

II. The "virtuous middle" consists of two sections.

   A. The instructions upon the various stages of the path condensed into 413 sets of six crucial points. These are themselves divided into three subsections.

      1. 409 sets of instructions that distill the essential points of practicing the lower, the superior, and the extraordinary aspects of the path, beginning with laying the foundations for entering the path and culminating with the full realization of the enlightened mind of the buddhas.

      2. Three sets of instructions describing how beings of superior, medium, and limited faculties can achieve liberation.

         Verses 410 explain how beings of superior faculties find liberation in this life, at the moment of death, or during the *bardo*.

         Verses 411–412 show how individuals with average and limited faculties can become liberated in the intermediate state of the bardo.

      3. A final set of six points, verse 413, which describes the attainment of ultimate fruition, where six qualities of perfect enlightenment manifest.

   B. Heart advice on why these beneficial instructions should be practiced.

In the final section of the text, from verse 395 onward, several sets are further subdivided into subsets of six points, bringing the total number to 438 sets. In those expanded sets, Gyalwa Longchenpa uses analogies to guide us to the deepest levels of the teachings.

III. The "virtuous conclusion" is a final declaration of the text's purpose, followed by a prayer dedicating the merits of composing this text to all beings, and ending with a colophon.

Dilgo Khyentse Rinpoche (1910–1991)

The Nectar of the Brilliant Moon

Explanations on
The Precious Treasury of Essential Instructions
of Gyalwa Longchen Rabjam

—Dilgo Khyentse Rinpoche

Homage

In the language of India:[26] *Upadeśaratnakoṣanāma*
In the language of Tibet: *Man ngag rin po che'i mdzod ces bya ba*
In English: *The Precious Treasury of Essential Instructions*

In Sanskrit, *upadeśa*[27] means "instructions," *ratna* means "jewels," *koṣa* means "treasure," and *nāma* means "named."

I prostrate in homage to all the buddhas and bodhisattvas!

> **On the great ship of supreme wisdom* and compassion**
> **You have crossed the ocean of the three worlds:**
> **I pay homage to the captains—the buddhas and bodhisattvas,* their offspring,**
> **Who, according to their aspirations, have reached ultimate realization.**

Having crossed the ocean of the three worlds of samsaric existence, the supreme buddhas and bodhisattvas spontaneously accomplish the twofold aim of benefiting others and themselves. We pay homage to those who have attained first the highest states of existence and ultimately the definite excellence of enlightenment, thus becoming wish-fulfilling jewels for this world.

> **For the fortunate ones who aspire to liberation,***
> **Having condensed the essence of the sutras,* tantras,* and pith instructions,**
> **I will each these crucial and eminently profound points in verses of six instructions:**
> **Listen to them with respect.**

It is a great fortune to have respect for the Dharma* and a supreme fortune to study it, reflect, and meditate upon it with perseverance.

The sutras of the perfect Buddha and the vast and profound aspects of the many sections of the tantras are readily available to all. Yet, because of their weak intelligence, feeble perseverance, and strong attraction to the distractions of ordinary life, those who aspire to travel the path of liberation and attain the precious level of buddhahood fail to integrate these teachings into their mind streams.

For their benefit, here is the essence of innumerable instructions gathered together and offered in the manner of excellent food. These instructions, in which many vital points are condensed in few words, represent the very heart of spiritual instructions. While there is a vast array of teachings, the most profound ones, which can fulfill all the needs of those who practice them, will be presented here in verses of six points.

–1–

Entering the Path

At the onset, here are six entry points (on the path):
Persevere in the three trainings,* the foundations of the path.
Engage in nonsectarian listening to the various teachings and reflect upon their content.
Train your body, speech, and mind and master them.
Curb your negativities and magnify your virtues.
Cultivate a sense of shame and modesty[28] and generate confidence.
Rely upon a spiritual master and virtuous friends.
These points are very important for beginners.

Anyone taking their first steps on the path must fully observe six recommendations. What are they?

The three trainings—discipline, concentration, and wisdom—serve as the support and foundation of the path. Practice them properly, without letting them decline.

Regardless of the specific path you practice, if you have neglected to study extensively, you are likely to stray from the correct path. Therefore, make sure to study assiduously.

If the meaning of what you have studied is limited to the words, it is nothing more than reverberations of echoes. Hence, you must properly integrate the meaning of the teachings into your mind stream.

Furthermore, if you do not study a wide range of teachings, without narrow-mindedness, and limit yourself to one perspective, you will be like a one-eyed yak grazing. If you become infatuated with one particular tradition and look down on others, you will be unable to grasp the essence of the path.

Through study and reflection, you may gain a correct understanding and experience of the view, meditation, and conduct according to the ultimate meaning. But if you tell yourself, "I have studied a lot! I am a fine scholar now!" and become contaminated by pride, remember that "the water of qualities does not stay on the peak of pride." Tame and pacify your body, speech, and mind like kneading a cotton ball.

When studying and reflecting, refrain from scrutinizing the faults of others; otherwise, you will keep finding faults in them without even noticing the flaws on your own face. This will lead you to a situation where you use what you have studied and contemplated to generate wrong opinions about others and to slander them profusely,[29] while remaining blind to your own defects. Instead, look into the mirror that reflects your own flaws back to you; by looking at your face in the mirror, you can improve your imperfections, shave if necessary, and give yourself a neat appearance.

In general, Dharma study aims at continually transforming your mind with mindfulness and circumspection.[30] If not, what's the point of studying? The goal of extensive studies is a mind free of defects. As it is said, "The sign of having studied is to have pacified and mastered your mind; the sign of having meditated is to be free from afflictive mental states* (*kleśa*s)."

Therefore, avoid all negative actions and anything that contradicts the precepts of the *prātimokśa** (the vows of individual liberation), the bodhisattva vows, and the vows of Secret Mantra, while properly cultivating the various wholesome aspects of your mind. In the best case, a Dharma practitioner will progress every day; in the middle case, every month; and in the lesser case, at least every year.

Guard against negativity and magnify virtuous actions, thus becoming a disciple of our teacher, the Munīndra,[31] with some of you donning the saffron robes, the victory banner of the teachings. Engaging in negative acts would be shameful; uphold the precepts with caution, for if you indulge in drinking or any other reckless behavior, how can you not feel embarrassed when you think of the wisdom deities, your spiritual master, and the supreme Dharma? Maintain moral awareness, fearing justified disapproval. Have a clear, ardent, and confident faith.

Ask yourself, "Will I be able to generate the supreme qualities of liberation?" and follow a spiritual master like his shadow. As said, "Even a common log, lying in a sandalwood grove, will eventually become permeated with the fragrance of sandalwood."[32]

So, entrust yourself to a spiritual guide, or if you cannot live near such a virtuous teacher, at least associate with virtuous friends who will encourage you to practice Dharma with your body, speech, and mind so that you align your conduct with the supreme Dharma. As a beginner who crosses the door of Dharma, cherish these recommendations.

–2–

Preparing for Solitary Places

Then, if you wish to stay alone in a secluded place,
It is important to prepare yourself in six ways:
Before you part from your spiritual guide,
You must be able to rely on your own abilities.
You must have cleared up your doubts, learned how to overcome obstacles, and have no more questions to ask.
You must be free of diseases, negative influences, and other obstacles.
You must have completely removed yourself from your place in society,
Have all the instructions you need to accomplish the twofold aim [of others and yourself],
And have a clear conviction in the realization of the view.

To enter the Dharma, you must first have a spiritual master. Before you dedicate yourself to practice in a peaceful, secluded place, away from distractions and scattering activities, just as empowerment* requires a preparatory ritual, here six preparations are necessary to ensure you are free from adverse conditions and ready for a mountain retreat. What are these preparations?

Once away from your spiritual master, being self-reliant means that even when you no longer live constantly in his presence, which allowed you to ask questions and resolve your doubts, even if obstacles arise and you risk deviating from your practice, you know how to overcome these challenges using the essential instructions received from your master. If you do not have the intimate conviction that you can do this,[33] as soon as you find yourself far from your master in a solitary place, doubts will arise and deviations will occur, hindering your spiritual practice. You must therefore be able to rely on your own resources, having received from your master all the necessary explanations on the practices you are undertaking, having clarified your doubts and uncertainties, without any unresolved questions, and being equipped with the tools to overcome any obstacle.

You should be able to tell yourself, "By listening to my master's instructions, I have resolved all my uncertainties and received answers to all my questions. I have received all the instructions, including the single instruction that can ensure reaching buddhahood, and those needed to dispel hindrances. I can now face them on my own."

In a lonely place, you must also protect yourself from illness. Normally, when you become ill, you go to a doctor, but if you are far from everything, you must do your best to prevent obstacles from health issues, including mental disturbances associated with the "wind in the heart,"[34] and external threats from humans, gods, and demons. In fact, as a practitioner, you will face many external, internal, and secret challenges and you must guard against them.

Someone who goes far away to trade at a village fair may run into assailants, bandits, or thieves. Likewise, there will be many obstacles in the way of the practitioner who strives to attain enlightenment: external obstacles such as enemies or thieves, internal obstacles such as the five poisons* that disturb the mind, or secret obstacles such as the proliferation of wandering thoughts. Do whatever it takes to avoid these obstacles.

How can you best extricate yourself from your place in society? As you practice the supreme Dharma, direct your mind to the Dharma, your Dharma to a renunciant life, your renunciant life to death, and your death to an uninhabited cave. So it is said.

Otherwise, if you go on retreat in a mountain hermitage, become known as a *lama*,* and indulge in religious possessions and other inappropriate means of livelihood, nothing good will come of it.

Remove yourself in the best possible way from your position in human society. Then, for your own good and the good of others, foster meditative experiences and realization. Clear away beings' obscurations, karmic debts, and misuse of religious offerings. This will lead to the dual achievement of benefiting others and yourself. In particular, through direct experience, you will gain a clear conviction about the view.

–3–

An Appropriate Place to Retire

Six features of a suitable retreat place:
A place of solitude with all the desirable qualities,
Blessed by accomplished masters,
Free from the defilement caused by broken *samayas*,* which allows the oath-bound protectors to gather.
Free of distractions and agitation,
With favorable conditions, and easy access to basic necessities.
A place free of nuisances caused by humans and nonhumans.

Regarding the attributes of a suitable place, first of all, it must be free of distractions and activities of all kinds that cause a lack of attention, your stay being dedicated to the practice of meditative concentration (*samādhi**). In a place where many people congregate, or a region rife with thieves ready to rob you, everything will hinder your spiritual practice.

Finding Rest in Meditation[35] describes criteria for choosing an appropriate retreat place. In winter, take shelter in a forest or in caves and hermitages at low altitudes where the temperature is milder, while in spring, places where the heat and cold are balanced are recommended. During the heat of summer, which induces drowsiness, proceed to higher altitudes, near mountain peaks and glaciers. In autumn, choose a place from which you can see a vast and open sky.

The ideal place is one blessed by the presence of Guru Padmasambhava or other accomplished masters. If the blessings of these masters remain intact, the deities and ḍākinīs[36] will gather and dispel obstacles. Conversely, if many samaya breaches have contaminated the place, your meditative experiences and realization will fail to take birth and the oath-bound Dharma protectors will remain distant.

You must remain free of distraction and busyness. If causes of distraction abound—for instance, if you must frequently meet visitors and benefactors—you will be diverted from your practice.

Regarding provisions and other means of living, avoid any extreme. If, like a great lama or a dignitary, you burden yourself with endless preparations, your practice will be constantly delayed. But if you take too little, wanting to emulate Jetsun Milarepa[37] and the yogis* of his time, living there might prove to be too harsh. Avoiding both extremes of abundance of delicious and fancy food and of deprivation of basic needs, seek a place where it is easy to obtain what you need to live, where you are safe from human dangers, thieves in particular, and free from obstacles created by nonhuman beings.

–4–

Six Favorable Conditions

Six favorable conditions regarding material facilities:
Avoid extremes regarding nourishment, food, and drink.
Gather the offerings and the consecrated substances needed for your practice.
Have with you the necessary texts with the profound instructions.
Obtain whatever is required to create the right conditions for removing the obstacles.
In short, prepare everything you need to practice,
Without accumulating wealth or possessions.

To settle into a mountain retreat, it is wise to have all the right conditions in place. Unless you have unshakable confidence from your meditative experiences and realization, a confidence that can strengthen those experiences and realization in the face of adversity—that is, as long as you are a beginner—you must gather all the favorable conditions, just as you would collect dry twigs to start a fire easily.

What are these favorable conditions? As mentioned earlier, it is inappropriate to hoard excessive amounts of food and drink as though you were a notable preparing a feast. Nor is it desirable to be so severely short of provisions that you suffer from hunger. As the saying goes, "If this human body—difficult to obtain and easy to destroy—has sufficient food, it will remain healthy." We beings of the *kamadhatu*, the "world of desire," require food to survive.

Similarly, when you retire to solitude, you should have gathered everything required to make offerings and perform your sādhana practice, such as amrita and rakta, purifying incense, and other substances related to the practice of your chosen wisdom deity, the *yidam.**

Of all these, the most important are the texts containing spiritual instructions for the creation and perfection phases, or for whatever practice you are engaged in. They will enable you to overcome obstacles and to progress while clearing hesitations and doubts.

Also have the necessary supplies to remove hindrances, including substances and weapons to deter enemies, and medicines to treat diseases. In case nonhuman entities create obstacles, you should have on hand the ritual substances to establish favorable conditions through the visualization and recitation of Vajrakīlaya.[38]

For all these reasons, if you leave for a retreat without having gathered the main necessities, such as proper clothing and food, you risk failing to keep your commitment to spiritual practice. So, make sure you have everything you need.

If, however, driven by your past habits, overflowing with ideas and plans, you seek treasure in a jewel island, run a business, accumulate goods, and crave making a profit, you will be lost in the circle of existences, samsara.* Avoid pursuing material wealth.

–5–

Virtuous Friends

Six positive qualities to look for in your noble spiritual friends:
They come from a respected lineage and have a gentle nature.
They have sincere faith, ardent diligence, and great wisdom.
They share the same Dharma practice and are easy to be with.
They are humble and in control of their minds.
They maintain their sacred commitments (samayas) are intact,
and they are endowed with pure perception.
They are kindhearted and caring and know how to keep the
profound teachings secret.
These are the friends you can rely upon.

During a mountain retreat, if you share the company of friends who live in harmony with the Dharma, as it is said, "One friend in harmony with the Dharma is a support for virtuous practice; three, four, or more are a source of attachment or discord."

In India, women wear on their wrists many glass bangles that jingle against each other. If they take most them off and wear only one, there will be no noise. Similarly, if you stay alone in a mountain retreat, you will be free of distractions and busyness. A friend in tune with the teachings, however, can help you clear away obstacles and advance in your practice by being available to clarify points in the oral instructions received from your master. Other than that, whenever many people are around, as the saying goes, "The mouth is a box of mischief and an open door to all negative behavior." Especially when you devote yourself primarily to mantra* recitation, talking is a distraction.

If you associate with bad companions, thieves, and cheats from a swindling background, their company will contaminate you. Befriend respectable people who have pacified and mastered their minds.[39] Otherwise, as the masters say, "Those who lean on the poisonous tree of bad friends will perish. Those who rely on the medicinal tree of virtuous friends will thrive." If those you befriend are calm and peaceful, you will naturally master your own mind.

Those who strive to follow the Dharma must have the threefold faith: clear, ardent, and confident.[40] They should develop confidence in all the virtuous activities; otherwise, they will practice in vain.

But faith alone is insufficient; you must persevere diligently in your practice. Our teacher, the Buddha, pursued the accumulation (of merit and wisdom) for three immeasurable *kalpa*s,* enabling him to be reborn two thousand times as a universal monarch,[41] and soon after to become the fully enlightened Buddha. Jetsun Milarepa attained the level of perfect union [with the fundamental nature of mind] in a single lifetime. They mastered these accomplishments through great effort, without which no spiritual quality can arise.

You must also acquire the threefold wisdom generated by study, reflection, and meditation, or else you will remain ignorant and stupid, which leads nowhere. In addition to having attained a sound knowledge, if you have a virtuous spiritual friend, he or she should be a disciple of the same master and have received the same instructions. If you have different masters, asking such a friend about points in your practice that should be kept secret is inappropriate. But if you befriend someone who has received the same teachings and is pursuing the same practice as you, accompanying him or her over time will be easy and pleasant.

Such a friend should not be arrogant—for no one appreciates the proud—but humble and calm. Befriending someone who likes entertainment, distractions of all kinds, and needs to have fun, you will be tainted by these defects. Instead, seek the company of those who have mastered their senses.

Above all, if you are dealing with someone whose spiritual lineage is flawed regarding the samayas, you will be contaminated naturally, just as one frog with a skin disease will infect all the other frogs in the pond. A disciple who fails to preserve the purity of his sacred commitments is like a drop of rancid milk, which, when poured into a jar, makes all the milk go bad.

Therefore, associate with people with impeccable samaya, who see the Dharma and the spiritual masters purely. Someone without an ounce of faith, even if he saw Śākyamuni Buddha flying in space, will be of no help to you.

Imbued with pure vision, you must consider all disciples connected to the same master and within the same mandala* as vajra brothers and sisters, as children of the same parents. Until you reach buddhahood, with great affection, feel as close to them as light is to a flame.

Keep secret the deeper aspects of view, meditation, and conduct, as well as your meditative experiences and realization. To divulge them before you have attained stable accomplishment* will be a source of obstacles and hindrances to yourself and to others. Know how to maintain secrecy.

–6–

Bringing Your Practice to Its Ultimate Point

Six sublime teachings to bring your practice to its peak:
Rely on the scriptures.
Establish the ultimate reality through reasoning and logic.
Strike the crucial points of the instructions.
Follow the steps of the gradual path.
Guide all beings, whatever their levels,[42] **and**
Free yourself from the belief in extremes.

Anyone who engages in the Dharma needs these six instructions to bring their practice to its ultimate point.

The spiritual instructions you practice must not contradict the words of the Buddha or the scriptural authority of the great scholars. Therefore, you need to familiarize yourself with the fundamental texts. Also, if needed, you should be able to validate with logic and reasoning the essential instructions of accomplished beings of the past and the present that are rooted in their direct experience.

If you hit the crucial point with instructions such as the Three Sentences That Strike the Vital Points,[43] the effect will be comparable to poking a pig in the nose with a stick: it will quickly turn around and never come back. The same will happen with any thought of desire, animosity, or stupidity: if you hit it with the stick of instructions, it will disappear like dry wood vanishing in a fire.

When you put into practice your spiritual master's instructions, you must first understand them, then experience them directly, and ultimately actualize the wisdom born from realization. As your inner certainty grows, so will your determination, enthusiasm, and diligence, leading you to complete all the stages, paths, and *bhūmis*.*

Once your mind stream is liberated, you will be able to guide all beings, high or low, on the path of liberation with unfailing benevolence.

If you are only concerned with your own well-being, you will fail to walk in the footsteps of the bodhisattvas. Unfettered by the subject-object duality, you must bring all beings onto the path. Finally, having actualized ultimate realization, you will be free of all hope and fear.

–7–

Six Forms of Resilience

Six forms of resilience to bring Dharma practice to perfection:
Even if your life is threatened, never turn your back on the supreme Dharma.
Even when faced with illness, never generate adverse views.
Do not let others' expectations destroy your determination to practice Dharma.
Know how to blend the meditative[44] and the post-meditative states.

> **Maintain your diligence until reaching your goal.**
> **Realize simultaneously the equal taste of what is to be discarded and its antidote.**

A traveler heading to a distant land may face great difficulties, but with resilience, he or she will reach their desired destination. Likewise, when you study, reflect, and meditate on the supreme Dharma, whatever obstacles arise from illness, evil influences, or other disturbances, persevere to the end without falling under their sway.

What qualities must you bring to their optimum point?

If someone threatens to take your life unless you renounce your spiritual master and his teachings, without thinking for even a moment that your life depends on it, you should never turn away from the supreme Dharma.

You need to practice the instructions you have received for a long time. All along the way, whatever acts of pacification, augmentation, attraction, or subjugation your spiritual master undertakes,[45] do not dwell on negative thoughts and views. Be like Jetsun Milarepa, who never perceived the slightest flaw in his master, Marpa of Lodrak.

Once you have committed yourself to a particular teaching, keep your promise, even if it means risking your life or physical danger. If benefactors or any other important people come to your door, letting them into your retreat would be breaking your pledge and many obstacles would follow. Do not allow these disruptions!

Merge meditation and post-meditation. Otherwise, the little experience you gain during meditative evenness will be carried away by distraction in the post-meditation periods and lost. On the other hand, if during breaks you do not let your meditation drift into ordinary states of mind, the deep concentration (*samādhi*) born during meditation will be strengthened rather than squandered. If you are unable to merge meditation and post-meditation, you will be equally unable to link the practice done in this life with that of the next. But if you can achieve such a fusion, no interval between meditations will be wasted. If, for example, your meditative experience was particularly good today and you do not let it be lost in distraction and delusion during the post-meditation period, when you begin your evening meditation session, the progress you made during the day will still be present and you will have seamlessly merged these various periods.

If you are practicing a supreme wisdom deity and are determined not to give up until accomplishment, persevere one-pointedly in visualizing the deity and reciting the mantra. If after only a few days of practice, you think with annoyance, "Oh, I do not have any sign of accomplishment!" and stop in order to move on to another practice, it will not help you. Remember to persevere relentlessly until you reach spiritual accomplishment.

Whatever undesirable and disturbing state of mind arises, immediately apply the proper antidote. For example, if you become seriously ill due to an imbalance of wind, bile, or phlegm, you will promptly take an appropriate medicine, lest you die. Similarly, as soon as any undesirable state of mind arises, drive it away by applying the antidote without delay. By repeating this process again and again and succeeding each time in eliminating a particular afflictive state of mind, you can be confident that you will not relapse. Sustain this training over time.

For a genuine Dharma practitioner, all joys and sorrows have the same flavor. If you can only practice when the conditions are good, you will struggle to accomplish the Dharma.

If you begin by encountering difficulties with food and clothing, face hardships of all kinds, and your meditative experiences and realization do not come about easily, but you persevere, you will eventually become completely at ease, bring your spiritual experience to consummation, and enjoy the flavor of "equal taste."[46]

–8–

Six Topics for Reflection

Six things to reflect upon:
All problems arise from yourself.
All suffering comes from your past actions.
Karma* depends on multiple circumstances.
Adversity is the result of mental constructs.
That takes shape when you pursue delusive objects.
Think, "This is how the path to liberation becomes obscured."
If you are committed to long-term spiritual practice, consider these six points.

When undesirable events occur, you have your share of responsibility. People often say, "This house does not suit me, I'm not happy in this place, this food does not agree with me. . . ." Once you have committed yourself to the Dharma, blaming your unhappiness on your surroundings is not helpful.

When illnesses and sufferings affect you, think of them as karmic consequences of your past actions. If meditative experiences and realization are slow to manifest, this is due to your obscurations. If the commendable intention of doing good for others blooms only slowly in your mind stream, this results from harmful mental dispositions generated by fixation on your selfish interests. The fault for all this lies squarely with yourself.

When you are faced with illness, denigration or slander, or when you find yourself ruined—whatever hardship arises, do not think, "How can this be? I practice the Dharma and trust in the Three Jewels. This shouldn't happen to me!" Rather, tell yourself, "In my past lives I accumulated considerable bad karma by harming others. What is happening now is simply the karmic maturation of my actions. May my illness stand for all similar illnesses affecting other beings and may they be free of them! May the suffering that is mine today substitute for what all similar suffering sentient beings endure. May the obstacles and adverse circumstances I encounter in practicing the Dharma replace the obstacles others encounter and may they be free of them!" With such aspirations, confess your negative deeds.

Concerning past karma, for example, the combination of the impure aggregates* of your present life (form, feeling, perception, conditioning factors, and consciousness) and the karma you accumulated in the past is like the meeting of very dry wood and a flame that generates a fire. Your fate also depends on momentary conditions and circumstances. If you can succeed in bringing onto the path both favorable conditions—food, clothing, wealth, and other pleasant experiences—and unfavorable conditions, such as criticism and slander, instead of becoming obstacles, they will enhance your spiritual progress, as when a forest begins to burn and the wind rises, fanning the fire instead of extinguishing it.

When favorable conditions such as possessions, wealth, and pleasurable experiences come to you, avoid becoming attached to them. Offer the first part to the spiritual masters and the Three Jewels. Otherwise, if you incline toward pride and attachment when favorable circumstances of power, high position, and fame arise, many obstacles will follow.

Conversely, when adverse conditions arise—illnesses, negative influences, and instigators of obstacles—think, "Now that difficult circumstances have befallen me, may they serve to purify my bad karma and all my past negative actions!" Thus, bring both good and bad circumstances onto the path.

In this regard, practitioners who have gained some stability in their practice will be able to cope with unfavorable circumstances but will find bringing good circumstances onto the path more difficult. Being distracted by pleasant sensations and becoming attached to food and clothing is very easy. Therefore, to remain free from grasping is important. As for adversity, it comes from the countless discursive thoughts that have led you astray. Once these mental fabrications cease, obstacles will no longer arise.

The more your desire grows, the more female evil spirits harm you. The more your animosity—your hatred—grows, the more male evil spirits harm you.[47] The more your jealousy increases, the more the eight classes of malicious spirits harm you. All these nuisances are creations of your mind. If by dint of persistence you succeed in transforming your mind, no god or demon can harm you, for they are merely mental constructs.

What is the nature of the hallucinations deluded thoughts bring forth? The illusory samsaric activities of the ordinary world lack true existence. If you are convinced that illusions and dreams really exist and that a dream is more than just a dream, you cling strongly to the solidity of things. Even when a fatal disease strikes, you continue thinking you will live for a long time. This happens because the understanding of impermanence and death has not been born in your mind. Moreover, it also reveals that no matter how many teachings you have heard, you still long for samsaric enjoyment. The feeling of renunciation has not taken hold within you.

All this results from the error of chasing after external objects. If you cannot correct these mistakes, the path to liberation and enlightenment will be obscured. But if you work on clearing away these obscurations, large and small, they will eventually be purified.

–9–

Creating Your Own Suffering

Six points showing that you are responsible for your own troubles:
The sufferings of birth and death arise from yourself.
You suffer from not getting what you want,
And struggle as well to preserve and protect what you have gained; much suffering is thus self-created.

> **Attached to your loved ones and filled with anger toward your enemies,**
> **The suffering born of confrontation with your enemies and separation from your loved ones is created by yourself.**
> **Even the immense suffering of the three lower destinies**
> **Has no other origin than your own actions.**

All the evils you experience in the three worlds of samsara result from your own actions and eventually lead to your own destruction. Once caught in delusion, you are like a madman who jumps into icy water in the dead of winter or stands under the scorching sun at summer's peak, barely aware of the torment he is inflicting on his own body.

In the eyes of a noble being,[48] we ordinary beings are only harming ourselves. How is this possible? The main sufferings in the three worlds of samsara are those of birth, death, and the *bardo**—the intermediate state between death and rebirth. The suffering of death has nothing to do with punishment by any ruler: as soon as this body conditioned [by ignorance] enters samsara, it is doomed to the sufferings of birth and death. The source of all this lies in sentient beings falling into the delusion that prevails in the three samsaric worlds. If you examine closely the nature of this delusion, you will find that all these sufferings related to birth, death, and the bardo are generated by your mental fabrications.

If you analyze your thoughts, you will see that they have no real origin, no real cessation, and no location in between. Without understanding this, your mind will be filled with the five mental poisons, leading to endless wandering thoughts and constant suffering.

No matter how many possessions and riches you may have, it will never be enough. Even if were you born as a universal monarch, you would always want more and better. As for wealth and possessions, you suffer first from being unable to obtain them, then from having to protect them, and finally from losing them to others. As the popular wisdom says, "With power comes vice; with wealth comes torment." In *The Words of My Perfect Teacher*[49] and other texts, you can read, "If you own a horse, your suffering will be the size of a horse; if you own a bird, your suffering will be the size of a bird." You thus create your own torments. Give up your attachments, and the corresponding suffering will cease at the same time.

You consider anyone who harms your body, speech, mind, and general well-being as an enemy. You hold grudges and try to retaliate as much as you can. In this way, you accumulate a lot of negative karma, which leads you to suffer the infernal realms in your next lives.

Believing that you must favor your parents and all who are dear to you, you engage in negative actions, conduct business, and sometimes even take lives. But it is on you that the suffering will mature. There is no point in trying to reassure yourself that you have done all this to benefit your loved ones and that you will therefore be able to lay at their door the negative acts accumulated in their name.

The hostility you feel toward your enemies and the attachment you have for your loved ones result from your mental fixations. By overcoming them, you will become an exalted being who realizes emptiness. Then, as the Buddha said, if someone applied sandalwood ointment to your right side while a fierce enemy slashed your left side with an axe, you would have no attachment to the one and no hatred for the other. Until that time, while your mind remains gripped by desire and aversion, it will continue to harm you. Overcome these fixations or you will constantly fear meeting enemies and being separated from loved ones. In short, as long as you hold on to such mental projections, fear will never end, whereas liberating yourself from them frees you from all apprehension.

Moreover, hatred leads you to endure hellish suffering and desire-attachment to the painful state of constant lack experienced by the *preta*s, the "tortured spirits." Ignorance causes you to experience the suffering of animals. No powerful ruler imposes these sorrows upon you; you are responsible. As the Kadampa masters' *Seven-Point Mind Training*[50] teaches, "Knowing that all faults accrue to us, the blame is ours alone."

–10–

Deluded Thoughts That Manifest as Suffering

Six types of deluded thoughts that result in suffering:
Your untamed mind creates endless annoyance.
Your impure perceptions* make you experience everything as harmful.
You interpret sounds, which are empty by nature, as positive or negative.

Fixating on wandering thoughts makes you accept some and reject others.
You take for certain the uncertainties of happiness and suffering.
You burn your mind stream with the fire of anger and feed your resentment.

All harmful perceptions of the outer world come from your inner delusion, fabricated by discursive thoughts. This happens in six ways, and it is crucial to understand these points.

A yogi who has mastered his mind can turn both happiness and suffering into parts of his spiritual path. Until then, as Padampa Sangye[51] says,

> Hate for enemies is samsara's hallucination, caused by actions;
> People of Tingri, transmute your hatred and your hostile mind.

Until you subdue the hatred in your own mind, you will never see the end of external enemies: one, two, and more and more—this is unavoidable. All the harm that seems to come from others, whether humans, nonhuman entities, *deva*s, or evil forces, actually originates from your impure perceptions, nothing else. Once you develop pure perception, you will find these evil forces do not exist at all. Understand that they arise solely from your impure, distorted perceptions.

The same is true of fame and reputation, which are nothing more than echoes of emptiness. When the melodious sounds of a lute reach your ear, they are devoid of substance. Similarly, if you take pride in hearing people say, "You are very learned, you are an accomplished being, you are a master . . . ," you will only bring about your own downfall. As soon as you enjoy a bit of fame, you want more; as soon as you are somewhat respected, you chase after even more respect. This process is as endless as ripples on the surface of water. Beware of encouraging such a hubbub of empty noise.

The more you let your mind follow its whims, the more it will act like a restless monkey or an unruly child. The ordinary mind does not know how to be content. We beings of the world of desire, the *kāmadhātu*, are said to be like insatiable dogs. In fact, we humans seem to be never satisfied and to never have enough. This feeling of dissatisfaction triggers a series of reactions: you think you absolutely must repel adverse conditions, losses, criticism, and malice, and that you must by all means gather favorable circumstances, gain, praise, and fame.

If you persist in this way, as the saying goes, "These activities are like children's games: pursue them and they will never end; abandon them and they will be done with." All this arises comes from indulging your mind's whims. Conversely, by controlling your mind through mindfulness, vigilance, and circumspection, attraction and rejection will naturally loosen their grip.

Just because things are good now does not mean they will stay that way throughout your life. Nor does suffering mental or physical torment today mean that you will suffer forever. When you enjoy physical and mental well-being, if you assume this will last and use these good times for pursuing business and accumulating wealth, feeding a multitude of desires, aversions, and unreasonable thoughts, the corresponding karmic maturation will ensue, and happiness will elude you.

Just as a king who constantly intrigues and forges alliances with other rulers is likely to end up losing his kingdom,[52] everywhere in this world, all births end in deaths, all that is raised will fall, all that is gathered will separate, and all accumulation will become exhausted. But, as happened for Jetsun Milarepa, who encountered the Dharma because of suffering created by the iniquities and criticism he experienced, those facing serious trouble may develop a deep sense of weary renunciation and a strong desire to escape samsara.

Otherwise, you delude yourself if you become entrenched in the belief that absolute and nearly eternal happiness and suffering will be yours almost forever. Let go of attachment to the duality of happiness and suffering. Otherwise, if someone wrongs you, you may become resentful and say to yourself, "If I can't harm him this month, let's see if I can harm him this year, or at least later in life!" Ruminating on your desire for revenge will only inflame your mind stream with negative emotions. One thing is certain: you will never get over your "enemies" and will end up burning yourself.

–11–

Getting Rid of Deluded Perceptions

Six meaningful practices to counter your deluded perceptions:
Exercise patience and compassion toward those who harm you.
Do not see enemies as demons, but as your parents and as deities.

> **Train yourself to apprehend the lack of true existence of the deluded appearances you cling to.**
> **Cut off the root of delusion—the ordinary mind.**
> **Whatever happens, use it on the path.**
> **Do not be distracted by ordinary thoughts, apply the antidotes.**

Deluded perceptions cause your downfall. Here are six relevant ways to avoid them:

First, when an enemy wrongs you, practice patience as much as you can instead of being driven by resentment and seeking revenge. This will purify your deluded perceptions related to animosity.

As the omniscient Jigme Lingpa[53] said, "Being mistreated by enemies can lead to progress for your practice. Slander and criticism are spurs that exhort you to virtue and serve as teachers that destroy your attachments and fixations. You can never fully repay the debt of gratitude you owe these so-called enemies."

For those who are loving and compassionate, the more enemies, the swifter they will complete the twofold accumulation [of merit and wisdom]. Instead of letting enemies trigger animosity, let them encourage you to cultivate patience: "Evil spirits will harm me! Samaya breakers will harm me! This evil influence will harm me!" Avoid demonizing harmful forces, and instead cultivate kindness and compassion toward them. Offer them your body and think of them as your own parents. By showing them kindness and compassion, you will subdue these demons. Moreover, perceiving the demons as deities renders them harmless.

Clinging to the reality of your illusory perceptions, good or bad, lays the foundation for delusion. The troubles that you face today arise from believing in the true existence of things.

Train yourself to see praise and glory as illusory as a dream and understand that perceptions, no matter how varied, have no real existence. This training will be like spring rain that makes vegetation lush, naturally nourishing your meditative experiences and spiritual realization.

What is the root of this delusion? Nothing other than the mind. What is the root of the mind? Emptiness. Investigate this. Without establishing with certainty that the root of the mind is emptiness, you will keep getting misled and carried away by discursive thoughts. Use everything that arises and all of life's situations to progress on the path. A true Dharma practitioner turns adverse circumstances into allies.

How? If blessed with favorable circumstances and respect, do not become attached. Do not tell yourself that this must last forever and that you must do whatever it takes to ensure it.

When faced with adverse circumstances that make you angry or generate feelings of attraction or rejection, use them as opportunities to meditate on patience as best you can. When food and clothing come to you, offer them as sacred feasts,[54] or in other ways, and maintain nonattachment. This will naturally bring you closer to liberation.

As it is said, "So-called great meditators who get lost in ordinary behavior will never free their minds." Therefore, be mindful and vigilant at all times, both during meditation and in daily life. This will help your meditative experiences and realization to grow.

If you lack attention and vigilance—even if you have recited millions of mantras and spent many years in retreat but complain about your austerities, your discomfort, and how little you have—this shows that you have not truly transformed your mind. This only adds to the causes of wandering in samsara. Therefore, avoid falling into the ordinary and apply the necessary antidotes.

–12–

The Torments of Samsara

Six[55] characteristics of samsara that cause your own suffering:
Since your body and mind are entangled with suffering, you enjoy no peace.
Because you run toward suffering in this life, you will never part from it.
Not having mastered your body, there will be no happiness.[56]
Suffering being lasting and pervasive, happiness has no chance.
Until and unless your karma is exhausted, samsara will be full of suffering.

The three worlds of samsara can only bring suffering. This major flaw has six aspects.

Everyone endures physical ailments and mental pain. It is said that an irascible person attracts numerous troubles and has little chance of finding happiness.

When facing suffering, such as illness, you may tell yourself these problems will eventually pass. If you are wealthy, you may convince yourself you will be spared the worries of safeguarding your riches and keep on amassing more. But doing this will never overcome your sorrows.

Your body, composed of the four elements,* is like an illusion or a dream and is beyond your control. If you become too attached to it, happiness and liberation have no chance.

You may enjoy wealth, possessions, influence, power, and fame for a long time, but you will encounter suffering of equal magnitude. No matter how many people work for you, no matter how extensive your activities, true happiness will remain elusive. Until your negative karma is exhausted, the sufferings of the three worlds of samsara will never end. Let go of all these burdens!

–13–

Six Useless Things

Six totally useless things for practitioners:
All practices are useless if you have not entered the path.
Everything you do is useless if you do not engage in virtuous activities.[57]
A long life is useless if you do not practice Dharma.
Your good deeds are useless if not guided by Dharma.
Possessions are useless if not used to gather the two accumulations.
Whatever does not lead you to supreme enlightenment is useless.

Thus, six things can be abandoned, once you understand that you do not need them. What are they?

Until you have correctly entered the path, all activities you undertake are pointless. Throughout beginningless existences up to this day, the countless samsaric endeavors aimed at defeating your rivals and aiding your kin have borne no appreciable fruit; they only generated more desire and aversion. You do not need these kinds of activities!

When you fail to act in a genuinely virtuous way, anything else you do—such as amassing wealth through business, obtaining high social rank, or surrounding yourself with many subordinates—will prove entirely futile.

As a Dharma practitioner, if you live a long life, the best use of your time is to practice day after day. Conversely, if you live an unvirtuous life, going to war for example, and you do not practice Dharma in any way, as Jetsun Milarepa said to the hunter Chirawa Gönpo Dorje, "We talk about precious human life, but when I look at your life, I do not see anything precious about it."

Why use a long life to accumulate negative actions? Only Dharma brings immediate and ultimate benefit. The so-called benefits of wealth, possessions, and power are useless at the time of death. Prioritizing the hoarding of possessions over the accumulation of merit and wisdom turns you into a ghost tormented by scarcity while jealously guarding a treasure. You do not need that at all!

Practicing the path of liberation and enlightenment correctly and with tenacity imbues every day and every hour with meaning. Otherwise, worldly pursuits are meaningless.

–14–
The Qualities of Spiritual Guides

Six qualities of spiritual guides, captains on the path to liberation:
They light the lamp of wisdom for those who wander in darkness.
They lead to the right path those who are lost at the bottom of a deep ravine.
They rescue those who are swept away by the river [of samsaric existence] with the boat of great bliss.
They lead to freedom for those who are imprisoned.
They bring to the dry land of liberation the unfortunate ones mired in suffering.
With the sword of primordial wisdom* they cut through the bonds of duality that fetter sentient beings.
Consider spiritual masters as buddhas in person!

If you wish to embark properly on the path of liberation, without relying upon a genuine spiritual master who is like a ship's captain, you will be unable to reach buddhahood. Here are six benefits of following a qualified master.

We all wander in darkness, uncertain what to do and what to avoid [to progress on the path]. A spiritual teacher lights the torch that illuminates our understanding—acquired through study, reflection, and meditation—of what should be accomplished and what should be avoided.

Your spiritual teacher protects you from the abyss of samsara's lower destinies, where you wander endlessly, and enables you to reach nirvana,* the perfect peace that transcends all suffering.

The supreme master places you on the ship of great bliss and accompanies you on the journey to freedom, after you have wandered for so long in the three worlds of samsara, carried away by the waves of birth, old age, sickness, and death.

You were like a prisoner cast into jail by a tyrant, bound hand and foot, with no means of escape. But with the help of a spiritual master, you now have the opportunity to break free from the chains of your karma and the shackles of your afflictive mental states and be guided from samsara's delusion to ultimate freedom.

The beings of the six destinies of the three worlds of samsara are mired in the ever-expanding swamp of immeasurable suffering, including the suffering of change and the underlying suffering [that persists as long as one is blinded by ignorance]. Once again, it is the rope of the spiritual master that can lift them from these muddy waters and onto the firm ground of deliverance and omniscience.

We ordinary people are ensnared by our dualistic clinging to the concepts of subject and object. Thus, we wander in delusion and, in doing so, harm ourselves. With the sword of primordial wisdom, the spiritual master cuts through the bonds of karma and afflictive states of mind and guides us to liberation and bliss. Therefore, while the spiritual master is no different from the Buddha in terms of qualities, he surpasses the Buddha in the kindness he shows us in this life.

–15–

Six Aspects of Impermanence

Six disintegrating factors of ever-changing conditioned phenomena:
Born from the meeting of causes and conditions, they are destined to destruction.

Beings are certain to die: aren't all those who lived in the past dead?
The universe and its contents, in perpetual change, are certain to disintegrate.
Life is unpredictable and will be shattered by death.
Moment after moment, days and nights pass and are no more.
Birth ends inevitably with death.
Think about impermanence!

Caught up in distraction, if you practice Dharma without stimulating your mind by remembering the impermanence of all compounded phenomena, you will remain bound to samsara. Here are six ways to contemplate the transience of all things:

First, samsara's illusory phenomena result from the interaction of multiple interdependent causes and conditions. Just as a tent collapses when the interconnected sections of its frame are removed one by one, all phenomena that arise from the meeting of causes and conditions disintegrate as, one after the other, these causes and conditions, impermanent by nature, fall apart.

Until now, countless beings have been born in an immense variety of worlds: all these births have ended or will end in death. Whether it is the king of the gods, Brahmā; Indra; or even Buddha Śākyamuni, adorned with the major and minor marks of enlightenment; the *arhats*,* who had exhausted all defilement; the great rishis of India, gifted with the five kinds of clairvoyance* and able to fly through the sky; the [great panditas known as the] Six Ornaments of the World and the Two Supreme Ones;[58] and all other learned and spiritually accomplished beings—all of them displayed the appearance of passing into parinirvāṇa once their activities for the benefit of beings were accomplished. None lived forever.

As for us, from the moment we were born from our mother's womb, we have been approaching death, the flame of our life diminishing moment after moment, to finally and ineluctably go out.

Consider the universe, phenomena's coarse aspect: it will eventually be consumed by the seven fires at the end of the kalpa. The seasons—spring, summer, autumn, and winter—come and go without interruption. As for the subtle aspect of phenomena, nothing remains the same for two consecutive moments; each moment is destroyed while yielding to the next.

Consider the beings who populate this universe, whether they are supreme or ordinary beings, even gods like Brahmā, their lifespan is uncertain and ephemeral. No one can say, "I will die on this date, after such and such tasks are accomplished." The time of death is uncertain and each day, each night, each instant brings us closer to death, just as each step brings an animal led to the slaughterhouse closer to its end. Born into this perishable world, the inherent nature of life is that every birth ends in death. Thus, contemplating the fragility of all things, let the thought of impermanence spur your diligence.

–16–

Six Benefits of the Teachings

Six ways to benefit from the teachings:
Be interested in Dharma, listen to the teachings,
Appreciate and praise them,
Enter the path and practice, even in a small way.
These are all seeds of liberation that can end samsara.

Even if you cannot actively practice the Dharma, merely hearing it brings great benefits.

Recognizing the vast and profound qualities of the Dharma, if you aspire to follow the path to liberation and attain omniscience, not only the Dharma itself but even the sound of the drum or gong calling you to the teachings can close the doors to the lower realms of samsara.

When you reflect on the meaning of Dharma, you become aware of the qualities of the buddhas, bodhisattvas, liberation, and omniscience. You will rejoice and instill clear faith in your mind.

Moreover, everyone, including the worldly gods, praises those who have listened to Dharma, saying of them, "Here is someone who has received many teachings!"

Once you have gained some understanding of the teachings, you will enter the path of one of the three vehicles, and as you progress along the path of liberation, you will no longer be in danger of taking a wrong path that leads to the precipice.

Among gold nuggets, white gold is considered the most precious. Likewise, practicing Dharma even a little suffices to end the cycle of the three worlds of samsara for you and prevent you from falling into a bottomless abyss. The seed of liberation has now been planted.

As the sutras explain, simply hearing the sound of Dharma closes the doors of lower destinies to any sentient being, even those who, like animals, cannot understand the words themselves.

–17–

Six Benefits of Dharma Practice

The six[59] benefits of practicing Dharma properly:
Respected and praised by all, you will also be protected by the gods.
You will enjoy much happiness in this life, and after death will be born into higher realms of existence.
Finally, you will achieve perfect buddhahood.

If, in addition to hearing the Dharma, you combine listening, thinking, and meditating in the right way, six additional benefits will follow.

When, as a Dharma practitioner, you travel to an unknown country, the inhabitants will say, "Here is someone who practices Dharma." They will show you respect and kindness.

Living a life true to the Dharma, you will enjoy a good reputation, and the devas who abide on the side of virtue and of the Dharma will protect you from diseases, harmful influences, and other obstacles.

Even considering the scope of this current life, practicing Dharma makes you aware of its qualities and guides you onto the path that leads first to liberation and ultimately to omniscience, thus allowing you to go from bliss to bliss. By frequently listening to Dharma in this life, you will also hear it in future lives and will assimilate its meaning. Ultimately, you will attain perfect enlightenment. These are the benefits of committing to Dharma practice.

–18–

The Defects of Lacking the Dharma

Six disadvantages of not practicing Dharma:
Like an elderly blind person, you will be obscured by ignorance.
Like a courtesan, you will be skilled at luring others into samsara.
Like an onlooker at a fair, you will be distracted by meaningless activities.
Like a baby amused by its nanny, you will be easily seduced by appearances.
Like a small child effortlessly fooled while playing, your experience of awareness* will remain vulnerable.
Like a fish caught in a net, you will find it difficult to free yourself from deluded perceptions.
Thus, you will waste your life in meaningless activities.

If you fail to practice the supreme Dharma authentically, six defects will ensue.

Being ignorant of what to adopt and what to reject, you are like an elderly blind person with no idea of the right or wrong path, the easy or the difficult one, who is in danger of walking straight off of a precipice. People who believe that killing and other deviant behavior are virtuous, and who allow themselves to be consumed by the affairs of this life, are compared to this sightless elder.

Like an alluring courtesan, the eight worldly concerns* within the three worlds of samsara entice you to acquire food, clothing, wealth, possessions, power, and social standing. They are masters at luring you, causing you to squander your life in vain distractions, rather than giving its existence meaning.

Even the few qualities you may have acquired will vanish. You will be like someone who, distracted by the stalls at a large market, neglects everything else he has to do. Moreover, lacking vigilance and circumspection, the experiences pertaining to the six aspects of consciousness* will surely deceive you.

An adult who knows how to deal with children also knows how to mystify them. Likewise, without training in mindfulness and vigilance, your mind, as credulous as a child, will be easily deceived.

Children are readily distracted by their games. If you allow yourself to be similarly caught up in distraction, you will find yourself immersed in samsara's deluded appearances.

Severing the bonds of illusion is very difficult. A fish exploring the river, irresistibly drawn to bait on a hook, will soon be pulled out of the water onto dry land and lose its life. Your mind is likewise constantly distracted by illusory appearances, and you waste your life in endeavors as futile as they are endless, squandering your human existence endowed with freedoms* and possibilities.

–19–

Degeneration of the Practice

Six evils afflicting those whose practice degenerates:
Even your juniors will despise you.
You will be criticized throughout the realms of gods and humans.
The noble ones will avoid you as they would a filthy vessel.
Abandoned by the protectors, you will encounter many obstacles.
Your wishes will not be fulfilled, and your merits and good fortune will decline.
In the next life, you will suffer in the lower realms.

Even though you practice the Dharma, if you fail to do so correctly or if your practice deteriorates, it will lead to six unfortunate consequences.

First, you will experience a decline, much like someone losing their status. People will criticize you for abandoning the Dharma and will hold you in low regard. Gods and men will decry your lack of perseverance in your practice. Such faltering in your Dharma practice may lead you to drift into samsara's lower realms, leading to widespread disapproval.

If a vessel crafted from gold or another precious material is filled with filth, it is deemed unclean and perceived as less valuable. In the same way, if your mind harbors only faults and flaws, spiritual masters and virtuous friends will distance themselves from you. Seeing that you indulge in negative behavior contrary to the Dharma, the devas who stand on the side of virtue will cease to care for you, and the protecting deities will abandon you. In this life, you will suffer from innumerable obstacles and negative influences.

Though you may momentarily succeed in your greed, hostility, or deceit, ultimately you are only harming yourself. Your aspirations will be thwarted and the little merit you have will evaporate like water in a parched pond. Once you have allowed your Dharma to degenerate, in future lives you will have no other destination than the lower realms, where you will suffer greatly.

–20–

The Disadvantages of Delaying Spiritual Practice

Six disadvantages of placing all your hopes in a distant future:
If you do not practice Dharma while you enjoy freedoms and favorable conditions,
You will squander your human life on the paths of distraction.
Death, unpredictable, will crush you.
Once you pass the threshold of death, you will fall into the lower realms,
Where your body and mind will suffer intensely.
Even if you feel bitter remorse, you will have no choice but to suffer.
There you will languish without seeing the time of liberation coming.

When a task comes to mind, if you do not complete it right away and instead delay it, six defects will follow.

While you are enjoying a human existence endowed with freedoms and good potential, if you do not engage day and night in meaningful endeavors—even if only for the briefest moment—if you are not practicing Dharma properly and instead indulge in laziness and idleness, know that your life will soon be exhausted. When death suddenly strikes, you will bitterly regret not having trained. In the throes of agony, however, you will be unable to practice and death will overwhelm you.

When death comes, on top of having neglected to practice Dharma, you will have accumulated bad karma in samsara through craving, hostility, and lack of discernment. You will sink into the lower realms, where you will endure the scorching heat or the piercing cold of the hells, the thirst and hunger of the tortured spirits, and the bondage and exploitation of animals, all of which will afflict you physically and mentally with intense suffering.

At that point, you may feel deep regret for your failure to practice Dharma, but it will be too late. Burdened with remorse, you will suffer in the three worlds of samsara with no end in sight.

–21–
Fear Samsara

Six things to fear in samsara:
How sad to think of human suffering!
How frightening to think of the suffering of demigods!
What anguish to think of the gods' suffering!
How painful to think of the suffering of animals!
How distressing to think of the suffering of tortured spirits!
What terror to think of the suffering of hell beings!
The time for escaping samsara's six realms has come!
Not only has the time come, it is getting late . . .

Observe the condition of beings in the three worlds of samsara, and you will find no possibility of lasting happiness anywhere. Humans endure the pains of birth, old age, sickness, and death, along with the torments of encountering enemies and being separated from loved ones. Myriad dreadful things occur, and their desires remain unfulfilled. Thus, they are continually afflicted with various troubles, with little prospect of finding true happiness.

The demigods perish in battles against the gods. The gods, due to their superior merits, dwell in space, shielded by impenetrable armor and wielding powerful weapons. Moreover, when the demigods recount their battles to their wives, the terror they evoke causes expectant mothers to lose their unborn children. You can only be horrified when contemplating this suffering.

The gods enjoy the miraculous wish-fulfilling tree and feast on ambrosia. Their lives are spent in constant frivolity and sensual pleasures, leaving no room for the supreme Dharma. Yet the torment of falling into the lower realms awaits them. Dread this state as if you were standing at the edge of a vertiginous abyss.

Consider the plight of animals in the depths of the ocean: large creatures devour the small, and many small ones feed on the larger. On the surface of the earth, beasts of prey hunt and consume other wild species. Domestic animals are enslaved—some burdened with heavy loads, others with pierced noses, their milk taken, subjected to castration, and enduring terrible abuse. Reflecting on their fate can only bring you to tears.

The tortured spirits suffer—depending on the causes and conditions—from external or internal obstacles, or other specific obstructions [that prevent them from eating].[60] For twelve long years, they do not even hear the word "water," and their existence becomes a crucible of unslaked thirst and gnawing famine. Imagining such suffering, you can only be anguished.

Consider the agony of the eight hot hells, the eight cold hells, the outlying hells, and the ephemeral hells. Take time to visualize this suffering, and remember that during the time of Śākyamuni Buddha and Śāriputra, the arhats made the hells visible. Those who witnessed this were so terrified that they lost their appetites, while others who had already eaten were overcome with nausea, as narrated in the *jātaka* tales, the accounts of the Buddha's previous lives.

For all these reasons, the various destinies within the six realms are like prison sentences. The time to seek escape has come. Not only has the time come, but it is already very late! Without a moment to waste, practice Dharma diligently as soon as possible!

–22–

Freedom from Samsara

Six ways to free yourself from samsara:

Banishing the extreme of eternalism, overcome procrastination and laziness.

Putting nothing aside to secure your future, devote everything to the Dharma.

Abandon ordinary activities and embrace the tradition of the Buddha's teachings.

Using the antidote of the four powers,[61] purify your negative acts and bad karma.

Accumulate as much merit and wisdom as possible by engaging in the ten virtuous Dharmic activities.*
With the help of the supreme preparation, main part, and conclusion, transform everything you do into the path of Dharma.
In this way, you will quickly be liberated from samsara.

It is long overdue that we liberate ourselves from the six realms of samsara. How can this be achieved? The root lies in our attachment to eternalism. By uprooting the belief in the permanence of things, abandon the habit of postponing your practice.

Let go of any intention to engage in negative behavior and to indulge in frivolous entertainments such as ordinary music; discard all forms of laziness. Stop telling yourself, "Not yet, but next year." Now, right now, dedicate all your actions, words and thoughts wholeheartedly to the Dharma, day after day.

Once you have earnestly engaged in Dharma practice, drop all ordinary mundane pursuits—be they defeating your enemies, protecting your kin, obsessing over the eight worldly concerns, engaging in business, farming, hoarding goods, or participating in village ceremonies. Instead, devote yourself to the traditional paths: the paths of prātimokṣa, the bodhisattva path, and the Secret Mantra, persevering in study, reflection, and meditation.

Furthermore, combining the power of the support, the power of regret, the power of the antidote, and the power of taking a pledge, make amends for your shortcomings by reciting three times a day and three times a night *The Sūtra of the Three Heaps*,[62] along with any confession prayer of your choice from the Secret Mantra Vehicle, making every effort to purify your mind of negativity.

Commit to the ten Dharmic activities,[63] which include writing and reading, with diligence and determination and without distraction, and boundless benefits will ensue. Engage as much as you can in the twofold accumulation of merit associated with formal representations and in wisdom that transcends all representation.

It is also essential to combine the three supreme methods[64] using skillful means*: the supreme preparation of generating bodhicitta*; the supreme main practice free of representations, which protects the accumulated merit from further deterioration; and the supreme dedication that multiplies these merits. If you do this, all of your actions of body, speech, and mind will naturally align with the path of Dharma.

By correctly practicing these six dharmas, you will swiftly attain liberation from the three worlds of samsara. Therefore, exert every effort to apply these skillful means.

–23–
Six Mistakes

Six mistakes that hinder the Dharma:
The mistake of powerful and high-ranking people is intoxication with pride.
The mistake of ordained individuals is indulging in worldly activities.
The mistake of scholars is to spend their lives arguing about words.
The mistake of Secret Mantra practitioners is to let the five poisons consume their mind streams.
The mistake of ignorant meditators is to rely upon inappropriate means of livelihood.
The mistake of ordinary people is to trust their deluded perceptions.
Abandon these mistakes and strive to practice the Dharma.

Practicing the Dharma incorrectly can lead you to accumulate various wrongdoings. This obstructs the path of Dharma and constitutes a serious error.

Coveting a high rank, you crave power and influence, pride and arrogance grow in your mind, and you relentlessly strive to chase personal ambition. Since this has nothing to do with accomplishing the supreme Dharma, you are going astray from the true path. This is the first mistake.

Celebrated and praised for worldly achievements centered on this life—whether admired for being clever and influential or for your skill in managing domestic affairs and strategizing about ordinary activities—you actually stand in opposition to the precepts of prātimokṣa, the bodhisattva vow, and the Secret Mantra pledges. This is a source of delusion for anyone who has taken any vows.

If you immerse yourself in the study of the five traditional sciences,* without grounding your understanding in reflection and meditation, but rather focusing solely on elucidating words and expressions, you risk wasting your entire life. Teachers are vulnerable to this error.

Whatever state of mind perturbs you most among the five poisons, counteract it with the appropriate antidote. If you do not neutralize the five mental toxins as soon as they arise—just as you would quickly extinguish the first flames of a fire—these poisons will reduce the life force of liberation to ashes. Therefore, if *ngakpa*s—the practitioners of the Vajrayāna, the adamantine path of the Secret Mantra—are running around seeking sexual gratification, drinking alcohol, or casting spells, while their mind streams are still ensnared by ordinary afflictive mental states marred by the five poisons, this is a grave mistake.

Therefore, if practitioners of the Vajrayāna, the adamantine path of the Secret Mantra, indulge in seeking sexual pleasure, drinking alcohol, or casting spells while their minds are still entangled in ordinary afflictive states marred by the five poisons, this is a grave mistake.

With the intention of duping the naive, some may proclaim, "I am a mountain hermit. I have had profound meditative experiences and have attained high realization," or "I am a lama," "I am a *siddha*!" and live by misusing spiritual possessions. Such so-called great meditators are sorely mistaken.

Those who cling to deluded, ordinary worldly activities as if they were real, immersing themselves in this illusion and placing all their hopes in it, are misguided. Abandon this delusion and commit yourself to practicing the supreme and authentic Dharma.

–24–

Six Right Attitudes

Six unmistaken and beneficial attitudes:
Listen to the words of the teacher, his instructions given out of compassion.
Study the teachings of the Victorious One; they are worthy of trust.
Day and night, in meditation and in post-meditation, keep track of your positive and negative actions.
Reflect on the interdependence* of cause and effect in order to determine where you will be born in the next life.

Abandon clinging and attachment to your body and possessions.
Establish in your mind an understanding of the sutras, tantras, and pith instructions.
Doing this, you will swiftly attain buddhahood.

If you aspire to walk the path to liberation and omniscience, follow the guidance of your spiritual teacher. It will protect you from going astray. Otherwise, even the well-intentioned advice from your parents and loved ones will be at odds with the Dharma. By practicing instructions kindly imparted by your spiritual master, you will progress along the journey to liberation.

In whom should you place your trust and hope? Rely upon the teachings of the Buddha, the Bhagavān.* Rest assured that his words are unmistaken and his omniscience never errs.

In addition, regularly examine your conscience, both day and night: "Have my actions, words, and thoughts been virtuous? Have I committed any negative deeds?" Reflect deeply on your conduct. If you have acted virtuously, cultivate and amplify those actions. If you have strayed into negativity, confess and thoroughly purify your mind.

By assessing your current behavior, you gain insight into your future rebirths. Perfectly practiced major virtues will lead you to the pure lands, while lesser virtues will result in a rebirth within the higher realms of samsara. Conversely, the most serious negative acts will cast you into the infernal realms, while the lesser ones will cause rebirth among *asuras* (demigods) or in other difficult situations. Always keep in mind the inescapable law of interdependent cause and effect.

Discard all attachment and excessive cherishing of your body and possessions, and learn to be content with just enough to sustain yourself—food to satisfy hunger and clothing to shield against the elements. In doing so, you will remain in harmony with the Dharma. Discard attachment that drives you to pamper your body, amass belongings, and adorn yourself with ornaments.

Study the scriptures, tantras, and profound instructions; reflect and meditate upon them, and most importantly, internalize their essence. If you succeed in blending your mind with Dharma, the many teachings you have received on sacred texts, tantras, and profound instructions will have served their purpose by transforming your mind. Acting like this, you will quickly attain buddhahood.

–25–
SIX POINTS TO CONSIDER DEEPLY

Six points to consider appropriately and perfectly:
Investigate whether worldly activities are beneficial.
Consider how you will leave behind your accumulated wealth and possessions.
Observe how often evil is returned for good.
Notice how you will go alone, even if you have a great entourage.
Realize how, at the moment of death, you will have no power over what you painstakingly harvested and gathered.
See how the powerful and famous leave their power and glory behind when they pass away.
Considering these points, absorb them into your mind.

With attention and vigilance, carefully examine your mind in the following six ways.

Begin by examining worldly activities confined to this life—such as the pursuit of praise and fame, wealth and possessions, power and social standing. Are these truly beneficial? See how everything that rises eventually falls, all gatherings eventually disperse, all accumulations are ultimately exhausted, and every birth ends in death. Even if your wealth equals that of King Vaiśravaṇa, on the day of your death, you will leave behind not only your riches, but your own body as well. At that crucial moment, only the supreme Dharma will be of any use—the true treasure to accumulate.

Today we live in the dark age of the five types of degeneracy.* Whether it is children toward their parents, siblings toward each other, or disciples toward spiritual masters, instead of showing gratitude, people too often return evil for good, as happens when food is given to aggressive monkeys. Consider this situation.

Whether you live among many people, command an army of a hundred thousand, or preside as the abbot of a community of a thousand monks and nuns, at the moment of death, you have no choice but to go alone. Therefore, consider carefully what is truly in your best interest, for ultimately you will face death on your own.

If you continually expand your worldly activities—such as farming or accumulating wealth—you will gather negative actions upon negative actions until events spiral beyond your control. Remember, when death comes, you cannot take even a grain of wheat or a speck of gold with you. Contemplate this truth.

Your social standing and power may be unrivaled, and your fame may reach the furthest corners of the universe, but in death, you must leave it all behind. Only a few words of praise might remain.

Acknowledging the transitory nature of worldly affairs, taking support of mindfulness and vigilance, foster a powerful sense of renunciation—the resolve to escape samsara—and a deep disenchantment with the eight worldly concerns. As it is said, "Whoever is free from the eight worldly dharmas is a noble being; whoever has reduced them is a noble being in the making." The authenticity of your Dharma practice can be measured by the diminishing grip of these eight worldly concerns.

–26–

Having No Regret

Six[65] perfect and meaningful situations where you are free from regret:
Even should you die from the difficulties encountered in practicing Dharma, have no regret.
Choose to remain humble, even if scorned, and have no regret.
Even if people consider you irresponsible for leaving your homeland, have no regret.
Even if you starve after giving away all you have for Dharma, have no regret.
As long as you abandon negative actions, have no regret even if you take rebirth in the lower realms.

If you act in excellent ways, in accordance with the Dharma, and accomplish worthy goals, you have no reason for regret.

In your pursuit of the Dharma, even if you were to die from a lack of food or clothing, there would be nothing to regret. Consider the austerities endured by the bodhisattva known as Noble Dharma[66] and Jetsun Milarepa in their practice of the Dharma.

Free from arrogance, you remain very humble, wearing patched rags. If people call you pitiable, pointing out your various faults, and yet you feel no regret, this is a sign that you have shed vanity and conceit.

In your native land, you are constantly besieged by desire, aversion, and delusion. Realizing this, you leave your homeland and find yourself at the mercy of strangers for your livelihood. Even if you are called a fool at home, there is no need to feel regret.

If you dedicate all your wealth and possessions to the Dharma, you may suffer poverty. However, knowing that you have accumulated merit for many future lives and are advancing toward liberation, you have no reason for regret.

If you purify your negative actions using the antidote of the four powers, and refrain from repeating them, you will be spared from the lower realms. Yet even if residual past karma causes you to be reborn there, you still have nothing to regret.[67]

–27–

Unsuitable Vessels

Six unsuitable vessels that keep you away from Dharma:
If, like swine, you eat everything you see, practicing Dharma will be difficult.
If, like a peacock, you only have eyes for yourself, you will be unable to get along with others.
If, like a rock, you are rigid and stuck in one place, you will have fewer opportunities to practice.
If, like a thornbush,[68] you prick everyone who comes near, you will fail to respect your samayas.
If, like a snake, you are irritable and threatening, you have not mastered your mind.
If, like a monkey, you are hyperactive, you will fail to focus on your practice.
If, like an ox, you are dim-witted, you will not understand the teachings.
Abandon these shortcomings and prioritize practice.

Six faults make you unfit to receive the Dharma and keep you from it.

A pig will eat anything it comes across, clean or unclean. Similarly, if you hoard all the kinds of religious possessions and adopt unseemly ways of living, you will have no chance to attain liberation and accomplish the Dharma.

If you consider yourself very handsome and strut like a peacock, exuding youth and might, such arrogance will keep you from getting along with anyone.

Convinced of the excellence of your detestable ways, you shut the door to all progress and cannot develop pure perception of your master and fellow spiritual companions. You will resemble a massive boulder that cannot be demolished without major effort and will thus forestall any possibility of attaining liberation.

If you go out of your way to harm others, becoming like a thorny plant, you will be unable to keep your vows and samayas properly.

If animosity rages in your mind, and you behave like a venomous, aggressive snake—remember, "There is no greater sin than hatred." The time to master your mind will never come.

A monkey is a restless animal, never staying still, always busy. Similarly, if you lack focus and are constantly entangled in countless pursuits, you will be unable to strike the right balance in your spiritual practice.

If despite having your questions answered about how to act and what to avoid, you still fail to grasp the essential points of conduct, you are as dull as an ox that cannot distinguish between right and wrong. In such a state, how can you understand the Dharma? As said, "Ignorance begets suffering."

Therefore, abandon these defects and cherish the practice of Dharma.

–28–

Become an Excellent Recipient

Six ways to avoid becoming an unsuitable receptacle for the Dharma:
Cast off the curse of attachment to the things of this life.
Enthusiastically practice virtue: make it your glory and ultimate goal.
Expel the evil demon of pride and self-aggrandizement.
Maintain a low profile: humility is an early indication of *siddhi*.*

Holding the antidote to be paramount invites hordes of demons. Abandon this!
Turn adversities into good fortune by turning conceptual thoughts into allies.
Doing all of this makes you receptive to the sublime Dharma.

These six teachings help you to avoid faults that make you an unsuitable vessel and an unfortunate being.

Just as an evil spell burdens a household, if your mind is consumed by worldly affairs, you become preoccupied only with concern for them and neglect the supreme Dharma. However, if you let go of preoccupations with ordinary activities and remain unaffected by them when they arise, you will find boundless energy and determination in your pursuit of virtuous activities and the supreme Dharma.

By practicing the sublime Dharma to the best of your ability and dedicating yourself entirely to spiritual practice, you will be filled with virtue. This treasure, once stored within you, cannot be stolen by enemies and will accompany you throughout your future lives.

Becoming intoxicated with pride—thinking that you are replete with excellent qualities, such as having a high status or rank—is like being possessed by an evil demon. Just as you would do all in your power to expel a malicious spirit that crept into your home, expel pride and self-admiration from your mind in the same way.

Adopting the lowest position without the slightest trace of pride is a sign of both ordinary and supreme achievements. Therefore, practice humility.

When meditative experiences and realization arise in your mind, bringing insight and other signs of accomplishment, if you become vain and cling to these qualities as supreme, you are being deceived by Devaputra Māra, the arrogant demon of the "son of the gods."[69] This demon, along with all others, must be driven from your mind.

If you fail to let all thoughts, good or bad, liberate themselves as they arise, and instead give free rein to all your negative mental patterns, they will continue to mislead you, as they did for so long. By employing the three methods of liberating thoughts,[70] you will become friends with these thoughts and, as the saying goes, know how to "transform bad omens into good fortune." Even if illnesses, harmful spirits, and obstacle makers appear, they will serve as catalysts for your progress toward enlightenment and will enhance your meditative experiences and realization.

If you do all this, your Dharma will become supreme and you will be an excellent recipient of the teachings.

–29–

Bringing Your Practice to Its peak

Six ways to focus your attention to bring your practice to its ultimate point:
Fear the Lord of Death as though a murderer were chasing you.
Feel as much disenchantment toward samsara as a wife toward an abusive husband.
Feel the same revulsion for deluded appearances as a nauseous person seeing food.
Feel the same disgust for worldly activities as for a partner who betrays you.
Have as little enthusiasm for farming as someone with only infertile land prone to frost.
Feel the same weariness toward your kin as when you remember ungrateful children who turned against you.
If you generate these thoughts, your Dharma practice will reach perfection.

Even if you are determined to practice the supreme Dharma, it must be practiced correctly to achieve the ultimate fruition. Six methods can guide you:

Just as a frog caught in the jaws of a poisonous snake thinks only, "When will it kill me?" so too should you constantly fear the Lord of Death, Yamarāja. Ask yourself, "When will the Lord of Death come for me?" with the same intensity as if a killer were chasing you. Thus, let the thoughts of impermanence and death spur your Dharma practice.

At all times, feel sadness for the three worlds of samsara engulfed by suffering, much like a woman trapped in a marriage with a cruel spouse, her mind constantly troubled and never at peace. Likewise, if on hearing of the tribulations of the three worlds of samsara, you feel only sadness and sorrow, you are well on the way to liberation.

Just as a jaundiced person has no appetite for rich food, feel disgust for activities that serve only this present life—defeating your enemies, protecting your relatives, and other deluded behavior driven by the eight worldly concerns, which you will never be able to fully complete anyway.

"He is an expert in worldly affairs!" "He is famous!" "He's a brave man!"... so many empty accolades. Disengage yourself from all this. When friends betray you, recalling them brings sadness and erodes trust. Similarly, do not place your trust in the fickle ways of the world.

As for working in the fields and other ordinary activities, first you accumulate goods, then you have to protect them, and finally you lose them. View such worldly efforts as vain and endless. Be wary and discouraged by all worldly pursuits. If, for example, you have land at a high altitude, the crops will constantly be ruined by frost. In such a case, what is the use of sowing your field? The same holds true for the affairs of this life.

Do not entertain strong attachments to your kin, as such attachments bind you perpetually to samsara. Consider how heartbroken parents feel when, despite all their nurturing, their child shows no gratitude. Think of your relatives in the same way.

By observing these six points, you will bring the supreme Dharma to its culmination.

–30–

The Consequences of Not Following Six Key Points

Failing to develop these six qualities will lead to these six consequences:
Even if they study, they just argue about words.
Even if they teach, they put their eloquence at the service of jealousy.
Even if they meditate, they are attracted to discursive thoughts.
Even if they contemplate the teachings, they remain greedy for food, wealth, and profit.
Even if they abide in solitude, they entertain their negative emotions.
Even if they observe the precepts, they reinforce their afflictive mental states;
Look at these six situations and keep them at a distance!

As just mentioned, the absence of six qualities can give rise to defects that hinder the flourishing of Dharma in your mind.

You may have studied many teachings, yet if you fail to elucidate their meaning through reflection and meditation and instead spend your time engaging in futile debates over words, you are like some verbose politicians, full of talk but devoid of substance. This neither frees the minds of others nor brings certainty to your own practice concerning view, meditation, and conduct. It may even foster destructive jealousy.

Even if you are capable of speaking eloquently, if genuine meditative experiences and realizations do not arise in your mind through practice, you are merely chasing discursive thoughts, while counting on some future result. Unless you stabilize your practice in this lifetime, all this is mere wishful thinking.

If you succeed in clearly elucidating the ultimate meaning of Dharma through reflection but then use your spiritual qualities for worldly purposes—such as acquiring food and possessions, gaining renown as a great scholar, or attracting followers—no true benefit will arise beyond fleeting material gains.

If you live alone in a mountain hermitage but bring along all your mental poisons, you will dwell on past habits and future expectations. In the present, no matter what thoughts arise from awareness, delusion will dominate your mind. Though your body may remain in the retreat, you will be no different from the wild animals around you. This brings no true benefit.

If you observe the precepts of prātimokṣa, the bodhisattva vows, and the pledges of the Secret Mantra without applying them as remedies to your afflictive mental states, this facade will fool only the naive. Even if others shower you with praise and you start to think that you are "somebody," it is ultimately worthless.

Examine your mind for these six tendencies. If you find them, reject such flaws as far as possible.

–31–

Six Self-Examinations

Six kinds of self-examination:
Examine yourself: Are you disconnected from samsaric phenomena?

Examine yourself: Do you nurture attachment to your friends and aversion for your enemies?
Examine yourself: Will you have a wealth of virtue when you depart this world?
Examine yourself: Have you brought the signs of accomplishment to perfection through meditation?
Examine yourself: When you try to benefit others, does their faith weaken?
Examine yourself: Are you sure that pure visions will manifest at the time of death?
Such self-examination will allow you to fulfill your highest aspirations.

You must examine your mind stream with the help of mindfulness and vigilance.

Ask yourself: "To what extent have I severed my entanglements in the three worlds of samsara?" "To what extent have I abandoned my clinging?" and "How deeply have I generated a sense of renunciation?" Reflect on where you stand.

Has your animosity toward your enemies and your attachment to your dear ones decreased over time? Are you able to eliminate these as you continue to receive teachings?

As you move from place to place, evaluate how much spiritual qualities in harmony with the supreme Dharma have grown in your mind stream.

When meditating wholeheartedly in solitary places, assess the signs of your progress in meditative experiences and realization. Is your view stable? How is your meditation faring? Examine all of this thoroughly.

When working for the benefit of others, ask yourself whether your altruistic activities increase their confidence and faith or cause them to decline. Consider whether your efforts are free from the eight worldly considerations.

Ask yourself: "If someone like me dies today, will the pure visions manifest?" "Will I get through the bardo with ease?" Examine these points repeatedly, and your aspirations will be fulfilled.

–32–

The Flaws That Prevent You from Progressing

Six defects caused by distancing yourself from Dharma:
Failing to accomplish your main purpose is caused by not being mindful of death.
Craving power and high position results from ignorance of their deceptive nature.
Attachment to friends and relatives derives from not understanding that you will be separated from them.
Thirst for sense pleasures comes from failing to recognize their many faults.
Accumulating wealth and possessions stems from forgetting that you must leave them behind.
Procrastination in meditation practice is caused by ignorance of impermanence.
Abandon these faults!

When we talk about failing to achieve the highest goal, we are referring to the ultimate stage of the bodhisattva path. Such failure usually happens when you forget that the time of death is unpredictable and that the circumstances that will bring it about are uncertain and can occur at any time.

Strength, status, influence, power, wealth, abundance of possessions, and fame—striving for them pertains to the eight worldly concerns. Like illusions and dreams, they seduce and deceive you. Failing to recognize this is a serious flaw.

You have strong emotional ties to your parents, family, and friends, and you spend your life providing them with food and clothing. Amid these activities, you drift away from the Dharma. As it is said,

> Families are as fleeting as a crowd on market day;
> Don't bicker or fight, people of Tingri.[71]

Your attachments stem from not realizing that like a crowd in a marketplace, your loved ones will be dispersed by the Lord of Death.

Beautiful forms, harmonious sounds, delightful fragrances . . . You are endlessly drawn to sense pleasures, much like someone who, drinking salt water, becomes increasingly thirsty. Indulging in the objects of the five senses is a folly, born from countless defects accumulated over time, all stemming from an inability to recognize the absurdity of this condition.

With your hands tied by greed, you hoard possessions and wealth as though they were hidden treasure. Yet, when death comes, you will have to leave even your own body behind; how much more so your possessions and wealth? Yet, unaware of this truth, you act as though you could take everything with you and continue to accumulate more.

You may meditate at your leisure, without achieving any sign of accomplishment, consoling yourself with thoughts like, "If not this year, it will be next year or the one after." In doing so, you keep procrastinating, ignoring the reality that all compound phenomena are impermanent, and that this impermanence will inevitably catch up with you! This highlights the failing of succumbing to laziness without even realizing it. If these faults manifest, overcome them!

–33–

Merging Your Mind with Dharma

Six signs that your mind has blended with Dharma:
You are seized with the same natural revulsion [for worldly affairs] as for the rags of a corpse thrown into a ravine.
Your mind is saturated with compassion, like that of a mother for her only child.
Your spiritual qualities blossom like fields in the summertime.
Your joyful perseverance is relentless, like the spinning wheel of swords.[72]
Your deluded perceptions liberate themselves, like a knot in a snake's body.
You return to your ultimate nature, like a ship's captain returning to port.
Such an authentic being can be considered a supreme one.

Here are six essential instructions for blending your mind with Dharma:

First, you must feel the same aversion to the sufferings of samsara as a jaundiced person who has lost all appetite for rich food. To take another example, no one wants to wear the clothes of a corpse found in a graveyard. Feeling such aversion lays the foundation for Dharma practice.

Always and in every situation, cultivate an immense and unwavering compassion for all beings, similar to that of a mother separated from her only child, who never ceases to worry over the child's fate. Excluding no one from your heart, generate unfailing compassion for all beings.

Repeatedly generate joyful and persevering enthusiasm that allows all the qualities of abandoning [all obscurations*] and realizing [all qualities] to be born in your mind. For the best practitioners, progress will be noticeable day by day. If you can practice like this, all the major and minor qualities of your body, speech, and mind will blossom like summer vegetation: trees rooted in the warm, moist earth, bushes between the rocks, and a multitude of other plants. Your joyful perseverance in practicing the supreme Dharma must be uninterrupted. Don't just make efforts one day and not the next; maintain your diligence continually, like the wheel of swords that turns without the slightest interruption and can clear from the path trees of all kinds without difficulty.

Once your enthusiastic perseverance becomes steady, you will need no further antidote to counteract the deluded perceptions associated with attachment to dualistic thinking. They will free themselves like a snake naturally unwinding its own coils.

As deluded perceptions are spontaneously liberated, you will naturally establish yourself in the view of the primordial nature and conquer the blissful citadel of meditative experiences and spiritual realization, like a ship's captain who brings back jewels from a treasure island and returns to port with joy in his heart.

Whoever applies these teachings is a genuine practitioner, and the qualities they manifest are in harmony with the lives of perfect liberation of the masters of past and present. Please practice with wholehearted dedication!

–34–

Six Deluded States Contrary to Dharma

Six delusions incompatible with Dharma:
Attachment to samsara, which is difficult to overcome;
Insufficiently rooted awareness, which is easily deceived;
The deceptive objects of the six consciousness, which are utterly enticing;
The vain activities of samsara, which are difficult to abandon and proliferate endlessly;
Life, which quickly exhausts itself with the passing of days and nights;
The numberless people who waste their lives in futility—
Contemplate this and engage in sublime Dharma.

Six worldly delusions contradict the supreme Dharma:

A mind that continually craves food and clothing and fixates on the fluctuating fortunes of the three worlds of samsara will find it difficult to perceive worldly things as insignificant, like the rags of a corpse abandoned in a ravine. While cultivating such a view is highly desirable, it remains elusive until a profound sense of renunciation takes root in your mind.

Many people pose as Dharma practitioners but are consumed by mundane pursuits, as trivial and fleeting as children's games—one ends only for another to begin. Under such conditions, [for beginners] the experience of awareness is easily lured and has little chance to break free from delusion.[73] You may strive to apply antidotes to your attachments, particularly to the objects perceived by six aspects of consciousness, especially the visual ones, but without constant vigilance, you will find yourself easily deceived by the countless attachments and aversions that bind themselves to these objects.

In any case, accomplishing all the trivial activities of the threefold samsaric world is impossible. If you persist in these pursuits, you will be carried away by habitual tendencies. Even if you think you should abandon them, you might find yourself unable to break free from these patterns and will keep perpetuating them.

As days and nights pass, you will find that after a year, three hundred and sixty-five days of your life have been consumed. If you are not aware of the exhaustion of your lifespan, you will fail to understand that you are getting closer and closer to death.

In essence, you are squandering your life in futility and distraction. Very few people use the months and years of life they are given in accord with what is truly meaningful—the Dharma.

Considering all this, apply yourself with one-pointed concentration to the supreme Dharma. Do not fall under the sway of adverse circumstances!

–35–

Six Questions to Consider

Six questions to encourage you to practice the sublime meaning:
Attachment and aversion will undoubtedly deceive you, but when?
Your body and your consciousness will definitely separate, but when?
[This body] that you borrowed from the four elements will inevitably be claimed, but when?
The appearances of this life will inexorably vanish, but when?
You will unavoidably have to leave your illusory possessions behind, but when?
The Lord of Death will inevitably manifest and strike you down, but when?
Day and night, ask yourself these questions from the core of your heart.

In samsara, ordinary activities limited to this present life, such as attachment to your loved ones and enmity toward foes, have misled you from time immemorial and may continue to do so for a long time to come. Knowing that they are ever ready to deceive you, remain as vigilant as a ruler wary of his enemies.

Your body and your consciousness have come together for a short while, like a bird resting on a treetop. When you see them, you wonder when they will separate, knowing that it will be soon. Your body and mind can also part at any time. Keep in mind this impeding separation and understand that practicing Dharma while you still can is essential.

Consider your body: its solid components, flesh and bones, correspond to the earth element; its liquid components, blood and bodily fluids, to the water element. Its heat corresponds to the fire element; the mouth, nostrils, and other cavities, as well as the breath, correspond to the air element. Yet, these four elements are not truly yours; they are borrowed from the world. You must constantly ask yourself, "When will they be reclaimed? When that time comes, will I be able to continue using them?" The answer is that you do not know. Always keep in mind that while enjoying this loan, you should make the best use of it.

From the moment your mother gave birth to you, your life has been ebbing away like the sun following its course toward the mountains of the sunset. Death approaches like the shadows of the mountains at twilight. The day death finally strikes, the joys and happiness that illuminated your life will fade. Moreover, you cannot say with certainty that your life will end at a particular time, or when you have completed a certain task. Once you reach the point of extinction, nothing in this life, not even as much as a sesame seed, will be of any use.

When the Lord of Death blows out the flame of your life, your family, power, happiness, wealth, large home, and all the illusory possessions you have accumulated without realizing their illusory nature will be left behind and you will depart. So, if you have possessions, do not cling to them.

Always be on the alert, wondering when the Lord of Death will inevitably force you to leave everything. But, if you are wisely concerned, the contemplation of death and impermanence will encourage you to keep Dharma constantly at the forefront of your mind. In doing so, you will remember these six considerations day and night and earnestly practice Dharma.

–36–

Blending Your Mind with the Dharma

Six ways of blending your mind with the Dharma:
If you want to overcome craving, develop contentment.
If you want to rise above aversion toward enemies, tame animosity within.
If you want to benefit others, infuse your mind stream with bodhicitta.
If you want to transform the perceptions of others, ignite the blessings in your mind.

If you want to train in the pure lands,[74] familiarize yourself with your own self-luminous awareness.
If you want to pacify suffering, kindle the great bliss within.
If you do all this, the inner auspicious interdependence will manifest externally.

If you sincerely aspire to blend your mind with the supreme Dharma, when they do unite, qualities will flourish and defects will fade. Now, you intertwine your mind with the ordinary activities of this life and keep failing to align it with the Dharma, thus drifting further and further away from it. Here are six ways to infuse your mind stream with the supreme Dharma:

In the realm of sensory enjoyments, your primary concern is the need for food and possessions. This world of desire, though devoid of any essence, is said to be a world that ignores contentment, like an unsatiable dog. True contentment is knowing how to be satisfied with food sufficient to quell your hunger and clothing that protects you from cold. As we are reminded, "Abundance stands at the door of someone who knows how to be content." Such a person is always satisfied, regardless of circumstances. You would do well to cultivate this precious quality at all times.

When your enemies seek to harm, slander, denigrate, or even sue you, do not consider retaliation. When you feel anger toward your detractors, tame that anger within your own mind. Then, even if the three worlds were to stand as enemies, you would harbor no animosity and could disarm those enemies by the sheer power of benevolence. Use this antidote to tame your resentment as often as necessary.

If you aspire to benefit others in various ways, consider all beings as your parents or children and repeatedly generate the altruistic intention to attain enlightenment for their sake. Once you have developed bodhicitta, as it is said, "we who cultivate the altruistic mind of enlightenment are the beloved of the world." Bodhicitta has the power to conquer the hearts of all beings and allows you to benefit them continually.

While others entertain various perceptions, good and bad, if you wish to master your own perceptions of the outer world and of the beings in it, allow the blessings of the spiritual masters to penetrate your mind. Without these blessings, even if you engage in all sorts of activities to pacify, increase, attract, and subjugate, you will not attain any sign of accomplishment. For these blessings to permeate your body, speech, and mind, constantly cultivate respectful devotion.

If you aspire to be reborn in a pure land, you must prepare for it. To do this, recognize the luminous nature of your awareness in its pristine simplicity, and you will realize that the pure lands are nothing other than the manifest aspect of such awareness. They do not exist anywhere else. Therefore, constantly familiarize yourself with the nature of your awareness.

To alleviate all the bodily and mental suffering endured in samsara, you must learn how to bring all adversity onto the path. To this end, meditate on seeing illnesses, evil influences, and obstacles as means of exhausting your negative karma. If evil spirits harm you, consider that they are collecting karmic debts incurred in your past lives. Integrate all these difficulties into the path with the help of selfless love and compassion, while knowing that their ultimate nature is nothing other than great bliss.

If you understand that all the countless torments and nuisances you experience have no intrinsic existence, you can fine-tune inner interdependence. Once this has been done within your mind, the interdependence of external phenomena will also be fine-tuned and will manifest as an ally. As it is said, "If you master your own perceptions, you will naturally transform those of others."

–37–

Wasting Human Existence

Even if you have obtained the freedoms and advantages, six actions can rob them of their meaning:
Abandoning listening and contemplating, the antidotes to ignorance;
Abandoning your spiritual master, the root of blessings;
Abandoning your yidam deity, the source of spiritual attainments;
Postponing meditative concentration, the root of all accomplishments;
Remaining attached to negative actions and obscurations, yet hoping to be free from disease and harmful influences;
Wishing to transform others' perceptions while behaving contrary to the Dharma—
Thoughtless individuals will attract these defects like a magnet draws iron.

To have obtained the favorable freedoms and conditions, encountered the Dharma, and met a spiritual master yet fail to extract the essence of the teachings leads to six defects.

The remedies to ignorance are study, reflection, and meditation. If you cannot wholeheartedly and with perseverance devote yourself to these pursuits, if you cannot devote yourself to these pursuits wholeheartedly and with perseverance, and instead indulge in trivial activities such as dancing, singing, playing profane music, and other superficial distractions while neglecting study and reflection, the time to dispel ignorance will never come.

Unless, inspired by the immense benevolence of your spiritual master, you pray to him at all times with the devotion and confidence that perceives him as the Buddha in person, blessings will penetrate your mind no more than sunlight penetrates a north-facing cave.

If you hope to achieve both common and supreme siddhis,* the only path is through dedicated meditation, recitations, and practices related to your chosen deity, the yidam. Without such dedication, you have no chance of seeing your aspirations fulfilled.

The root of these ordinary and supreme accomplishments is familiarity with a samādhi free from both torpor and restlessness. Without cultivating such concentration, your practice will remain mired in laziness and procrastination and the qualities of concentration, calm abiding (*śamatha**) and deeper insight (*vipaśyana**) will not be born in you.

If you transgress the precepts of individual liberation, of the bodhisattvas, and of the Secret Mantra, and blithely indulge in the ten unvirtuous actions and other causes of obscuration, it is unrealistic to expect to be spared by disease and evil influences! Diseases and harm from evil spirits result from your negative deeds and obscurations. If you persist in harmful behavior and desires, take pleasure in taking life, revel in meat and blood, and chase women or men, there is no way you will overcome these afflictive emotions and demons.

As for the way others experience the world and perceive you, they will only trust you if you have mastered your own ways of perceiving the world and conduct yourself in accordance with Dharma. Otherwise, if you indulge in worldly activities without having realized the view and behave in disorderly ways, or if you are distracted in your meditation while boasting of your achievements, you have no chance of positively transforming the perceptions of others.

One who lacks sincerity and authenticity will attract these six defects, just as a magnet attracts iron.

–38–

Six Mistakes

Six mistakes everyone should avoid:
Engaging in many projects without completing them because of lacking determination;
Failing to break free from the chains of desire and aversion because of excessive attachment to friends and relatives;
Becoming the servant of food and clothing because of craving;
Blabbering about the view while letting the ultimate meaning slip away;
Failing to immediately act upon the intention to practice, so the time to practice never comes;
Neglecting to familiarize yourself with the practice now and simply hoping to overcome the forces of karma in the bardo—
You must watch out for these six mistakes and abandon them.

We would all improve by eliminating six errors that result from failing to integrate the Dharma into our mind stream. What are they?

If you do not make firm and stable resolutions, any efforts you undertake in listening, reflecting, and meditating will be in vain, as you will fail to carry them out.

If, swayed by your personal biases, you harbor strong likes and dislikes toward your surroundings, you will be unable to break free from these fetters and miss the opportunity to practice the supreme Dharma with enthusiasm.

If you keep indulging in meat, blood, and alcohol, you will become a slave to your appetites and will never have the liberty to practice Dharma at your leisure.

If you claim to have realized emptiness, accomplished your wisdom deity, and attained clairvoyance, when in reality you have nothing more to offer than grand speeches about the view, you may succeed in fooling the people around you, but in doing so, you corrupt your own mind. All this is entirely without substance, and you miss the core of the teachings.

The moment you conceive the intention to practice the supreme Dharma and to seek a spiritual master, if you fail to act on this aspiration immediately and instead think, "I will take my time to prepare," the time to practice Dharma may never arrive.

Now, while you are free from physical illness and mental suffering, if you do not immediately and persistently familiarize yourself with the view, meditation, and conduct, when death is imminent and you find yourself between two worlds, even if you hope to rely on the view, meditation, and conduct, your failure to integrate them when you had the chance will result in being carried away by the power of your karma.

Thus, examine carefully and vigilantly whether these six defects are present in your mind stream. If they are, strive to neutralize them with antidotes.

–39–

Six Ways to Transform Your Experience

Six methods of observation to transform your mind:
When you fixate on the true existence of things, observe the changes of the four seasons.
When you cling to life as permanent, look at a dewdrop on a blade of grass.
When you are confused about cause and effect, observe how seeds germinate into sprouts.
If you do not understand that appearances arise in the mind, examine the nature of dreams.
When you fail to recognize one taste, try a few pieces of molasses of various shapes.
When you do not understand nonduality, look at water and ice.
Each of these observations is a powerful antidote to ignorance.

Six ways to discern whether the supreme Dharma has truly transformed your way of thinking:

If you believe that the objects perceived by your senses are permanent and solid, look at how summer turns to autumn and winter to spring. Notice how everything changes from moment to moment, day and night. See how the lush foliage of summer gives way to the dry and frozen earth of winter. From this, you will easily understand that nothing lasts, nothing is fixed.

Avoid clinging to the permanence of things, assuming that you will live forever. Observe how, after a heavy rain, the countless waterdrops hanging onto blades of grass fall at the first breath of wind. The same will happen to your life.

If you are confused about the laws of cause and effect and doubt their validity, consider the natural world: when you plant rice seeds, it is rice that grows; when you sow other seeds, they grow according to their nature.[75] Understand that all phenomena are governed by the infallible laws of causality.

All appearances, all your perceptions, are mental constructs. If this eludes you, reflect on last night's dreams, whether good or bad: Are they anything other than products of your mind? Upon waking, you realize that these dreams have no existence outside your mind. The same is true of the joys and sufferings of life: you attribute real existence to them because you have not scrutinized them, but they are merely creations of your mind. You believe them to be real and permanent, but if you examine their nature, you will find that this belief stems from blissful ignorance. Therefore, it is wise to ponder the example of the dream.

If you wish to know the vital point of all the teachings, the antidote that can transform your mind, it is the practice of "equal taste." Molasses can be made into many shapes—spherical, cubic, or elongated—but when eaten, its sweetness is always the same. Similarly, whatever studies, reflections, and meditations you have done, if you have integrated them well into your mind stream [you will experience the singularity of their taste] just as the sweetness of molasses remains consistent regardless of its shape.

If you do not understand nonduality, consider the relationship between water and ice: during the cold winter months, water turns into ice, solid enough for yaks and horses to walk on. When spring arrives, the ice melts back into water, the two merging inseparably, as they are not distinct entities. Perceive in the same way the unity of all phenomena.

Reflect on these analogies repeatedly, and their meaning will become clear to you. As it is said, "If you read the outside world like a book, you need not read books written in black and white." These reflections serve as powerful antidotes to the various delusions to which they apply.

–40–

Six Analogies

Using the six analogies on the path:
Think of your supreme master as a doctor.
Think of your spiritual companions as caregivers.

> **Think of your practice as the way to recovery.**
> **Think of yourself as a patient**
> **And of the Dharma as medicine.**
> **Think of the fruit of practice as healing.**
> **Avoid wrong views.**

If you consistently adopt these six considerations, you will succeed in putting the supreme Dharma into practice along the path.

Consider the example of a patient who consults an expert doctor and carefully follows all their recommendations. Such a patient can swiftly recover from illness. Similarly, if you wonder, "Can I attain enlightenment?" the answer is that fully practicing according to your spiritual master's guidance will lead you away from samsara and bring you closer to buddhahood.

Regard your vajra brothers and sisters—the companions in your practice of the sublime Dharma—as caregivers who assist the sick person that you are. In return, treat them with gratitude and kindness. Cherish them as you would the heart in your chest and consider them as precious as your own eyes.

Think of practicing the teachings as taking medicine prescribed by a doctor. Some remedies may be sweet, but even if others are bitter and hard to swallow, you take them willingly to recover. Some treatments may involve discomfort, like moxibustion or bloodletting, yet you endure these procedures to be cured. In the same way, when practicing Dharma, bear the austerities and hardships as necessary treatments for your spiritual ailments.

You suffer relentlessly from the disease of the five poisons, the afflictive states of mind. Unless you consult a good doctor, you risk wasting your life.

View yourself as a patient in dire need of the Dharma, and regard the teachings given by your spiritual master as remedies that you must take in sufficient quantity to be cured. This is the mindset with which you should study, reflect, and continually meditate on the sublime Dharma. The fruit of listening, reflecting, and integrating the teachings through meditation is like recovering from an illness, resulting in optimal physical and mental well-being, your greatest joy. Likewise, through study, contemplation, and meditation, you will develop supreme spiritual qualities and attain the excellence of enlightenment.

Cultivate these six attitudes and avoid their opposites, which include attraction to pernicious worldly activities and disregarding your master's instructions.

–41–

Six Certainties

Six excellent types of behavior leading to six certain outcomes:
Relying upon your spiritual master, you will certainly receive blessings.
Meditating on your yidam deity, you will certainly achieve the accomplishments.
Guarding the samayas, the oath-bound protectors will certainly gather around you.
Diligent in your practice, spiritual experiences and realization will certainly occur.
Resting in the fundamental nature, the two obscurations will certainly be purified.
Continuing to practice without distraction, you will certainly develop positive qualities.

If you embrace these excellent approaches in accord with the Dharma, you are certain to attain six significant benefits:

First, delight the heart of your spiritual master, at best by practicing, in the intermediate case by serving him with your actions and words, and at the very last by making offerings, and you can be confident that the blessings of his enlightened body, speech, and mind will permeate you.

Devote yourself to recitations and meditation focused on your supreme tutelary deity, and you will not be disappointed. You will achieve ordinary and extraordinary accomplishments.

Preserve the sacred commitments perfectly, the root samayas and their branches. If you transgress them slightly, make amends by confessing. The sworn Dharma protectors will then accompany you like your shadow. As it is said, "A perfectly pure samaya is the life stone of the protectors."[76]

Practice uninterruptedly day and night, with unflagging diligence, and you will keep your meditation, your post-meditation, and all your perceptions always on the path. Consequently, meditative experiences and realization are bound to arise.

Properly uphold the view of Mahāmudrā and the Great Perfection regarding the absolute nature of all phenomena, and the two veils*—the veil formed by afflictive mental states and the veil that obscures all that can be known—will dissipate as surely as dirt is washed from a garment.

Practice in this way at all times, with undivided attention and vigilance, and you can be assured that the qualities resulting from removing obscurations and from obtaining realization will manifest.

–42–

Six Sources of Fear

Six situations that trigger fear when you become aware of them:
Attachment to worldly activities is like a cool swamp where elephants become stuck.
Relatives and friends you are attached to are like prison guards.
The pleasures of this life are like an old dog gnawing a bone.
Engaging in negative acts out of ignorance is like a blind person walking over the edge of a precipice.
Afflictive states of mind, the five poisons, are like the bites of poisonous snakes.
Grasping to the six sense objects is like a bee stuck in honey.
Fearing these situations and avoiding them is very important.

When you grasp the true nature of the three worlds of samsara, you will lose interest in them and experience six distinct fears.

Defeating enemies, protecting loved ones, trading, farming, accumulating religious possessions by participating in village ceremonies: these worldly activities will entrap you. It is like an elephant seeking relief from the heat in a swamp, only to become mired and perish. Worldly activities have the same effect.

When you forge strong emotional ties with your relatives and friends, it is like being held in a mighty king's prison with guards who make sure you do not escape. Aren't you similarly kept in a jail guarded by your relatives?

If you insatiably crave the pleasures, comforts, and enjoyments of this life, you are like a hungry old dog who keep gnawing on a bone with toothless jaws until they bleed. Likewise, if you pursue the pleasures of this life without ever finding contentment, you will eventually bring about your own ruin.

Doubting the laws of cause and effect, lacking perseverance in study, reflection, and meditation, and remaining clouded by ignorance, you keep committing negative actions and resemble a blind man who walks off a cliff to an instant death.

Unless you quickly apply the appropriate antidotes to your mental afflictions, you are like a walker who unwittingly irritates a venomous snake, and so faces imminent death. In that situation, the antidotes come too late to be of any use.

With eyes fascinated by shapes and ears by sounds, you are like a bee drawn to the taste of honey, only to become stuck and perish. Similarly, if you become attached to the objects of enjoyment associated with the six aspects of consciousness, you too will be trapped.

Fearing these outcomes, avoid these situations and take care to distance yourself from them.

–43–

Six Drawbacks

Six drawbacks of ordinary life:[77]
Attachment to a large home? The burning iron houses of hell.
Children and a spouse? A forest of trees covered with sword-like leaves.
Jewels and fine clothes? Blazing tongues of fire.
Food and drink? Burning lumps of red-hot iron.
Servants and attendants? The guardians of the infernal kingdoms.
Anger and conflict? A hail of burning embers.
Know that these circumstances destroy virtue and excellence.

If you are engaged in worldly affairs, be mindful that they have many flaws and no substantial qualities.

Striving to acquire land and build grand mansions only sows the seeds for finding yourself confined in an iron house in hell in your next life.

Providing endlessly for your spouse and children—working tirelessly to supply them with food, clothing, and material possessions—is like venturing into a forest where the trees have blades for leaves. When the wind stirs those blades, your body is slashed and your life is imperiled, bringing nothing but trouble.

Adorning yourself with gold and silver jewels, brocades, and other ornaments and becoming increasingly attached to them is like being burned alive.

Constantly craving meat, liquor, and other delicacies, behaving like a swine, will one day lead you to swallow red-hot iron balls, igniting your mouth in flames and leaving your teeth helpless to crush them. Likewise, all sensory pleasures, including food and drink, are various ways to engulf yourself in improper lifestyles.

Surrounding yourself with servants and subordinates who toil for you is like being surrounded by the guards and workers of hell, reinforcing your attachment and aversion.

If endless quarrels and acrimony plague your relationships, whether between spouses or between masters and servants, it is like being caught under a downpour of burning embers from the sky, consuming both your body and mind.

In these situations, overcome desire and hatred and recognize phenomena's fundamental nature, in which all virtues and forms of excellence are gathered.

–44–

Defects of Desire

Six defects of the desire for sense pleasures that you must recognize:
Desire torments your body and mind in this life,
Leads you to the lower realms in the next,
And makes you wander in samsara for a long time.
It leads to conflict with everyone and exacerbates nonvirtue
While diminishing virtue. That is why noble ones denounce desire.

Avoid being carried away by attachment and desire for sense pleasures and recognize the flaws inherent in them.

Often you indulge in the pursuit of sensory pleasures without a second thought. This desire leaves neither your body nor your mind at peace during the day and keeps you restless at night. Your cravings drive you to engage in farming and other activities that bring nothing but hardship. In doing so, you kill countless animals, further fueling your attachment and aversion. As a result, you will be reborn in the lower realms of hell, or as a hungry ghost, or as an animal, wandering through samsara with no hope of liberation in sight.

In your quest for wealth, possessions, power, and social status, driven by the spirit of competition, you may find yourself embroiled in lawsuits and conflicts with others.

As you quarrel, your negative deeds motivated by attachment and dislike will naturally increase and virtue will be obscured in your mind stream. Such behavior is decried by noble beings. Therefore, it is wise to abandon the ordinary pursuits of this life.

–45–

Defects Associated with Attachment to the Body

Six defects of being bound by physical desire:
The body is a container of all impurities.
It is a web of veins, tendons, and bones,
A cesspool of pus, lymph, vomit, urine, and excrement.
It has nine orifices with their respective ducts.
It is a city of microorganisms inhabiting six hollow organs and five viscera[78]
And is innately the source of all physical ailments.
Those who are ignorant of all this are attached to the body and are thus lured.

We, the beings of the three worlds of samsara, are particularly attached to our bodies and possessions.

Yet, upon close examination, one will find that the body is a mere vessel for thirty-six kinds of impurities. Imagine a crystal vase filled with filth—who would desire it?

The body is essentially a network of veins, tendons, and bones. Stripped of flesh and blood, it is but a skeleton that hardly stirs any desire.

Inside, it is a pool of pus, lymph, vomit, urine, feces, and other repulsive substances, which flow in and out through the body's nine orifices and their channels. The body also contains six hollow organs and five vital organs—such as the heart, lungs, and liver—which harbor a teeming metropolis of eighty thousand different microorganisms.

This gross body of flesh and blood is an ephemeral combination of the five elements—earth, water, fire, wind, and space. Yet, unaware of this, we remain attached to the body, foolishly cherishing, cleansing, and pampering it. Understand that this body is nothing but a collection of impurities.

–46–

The Illusory Nature of Phenomena

Six ways in which phenomena are meaningless and devoid of essence:
The infinite variety of phenomena that appear as objects
Are evanescent and fragile like water bubbles;
Like banana trees, whose trunks lack substance;
Like mirages, deceiving beings naive as children;
Like magical illusions, which appear in myriad ways without actually existing;
Like dreams, which manifest through the force of habitual tendencies;
Like lightning, which is fleeting and changing.
Those who understand this will reach the other shore of existence.

If you closely examine the myriad phenomena within the three worlds of samsara, you will find that the notion of their true existence does not make sense. Though phenomena may appear enticing, they are ultimately devoid of true essence, as illustrated by the following six examples.

First, consider the vast array of phenomena labeled as "good" or "bad." They are similar to the contents of last night's dreams. If it was a good dream, when you wake up, none of its attractive qualities remain. If it was a nightmare in which you were thrown in jail or faced execution by soldiers, no harm has been done to you in reality.

All activities in this world are doomed to rapid destruction, like transient bubbles on water.

The worldly affairs to which you devote so much energy—defeating your enemies, siding with your relatives, fretting about your social status—are fundamentally hollow, like a reed, solid in appearance but empty at the core.

If you believe that the fantasies of ordinary life can be fully realized and strive to achieve them, you are one of those childish people who are easily deceived. When the sun shines under certain conditions on a vast plain, a mirage of water may appear. Yet, if you chase this mirage, you will not find water to quench your thirst.

All the phenomena of this world appear while being devoid of existence, as a rainbow shimmers in the sky or as a magician, with the help of twigs or pebbles, conjures horses, oxen, and entire armies that seem real enough to inspire fear.

Why do all these appearances of samsara manifest in such ways? They are expressions of habitual tendencies formed in the past, no more real than last night's dreams, changing as rapidly as lightning in the sky.

By letting go of all these attachments, you will be able to cross samsara's ocean of suffering and reach the other shore.

All the phenomena of this world appear without true existence, much like a rainbow that shimmers in the sky or the illusions of a magician who, with mere twigs or pebbles, conjures horses, oxen, or entire armies that leave onlookers in awe.

How do the appearances of samsara arise? They are manifestations of habitual patterns formed in the past. Yet they are no more real than last night's dreams and vanish as swiftly as lightning flashing across the sky.

If you release your attachment to these illusions, you will traverse the ocean of samsaric suffering and reach the far shore of liberation.

–47–

Six Useful Tips for Unskilled Beginners

Six ways for less gifted beginners to enter the path:
Having seen the suffering of samsara, strive to enter the spiritual path.

Knowing that all worldly activities are futile, lose interest in gain and fame.
Reducing your pride and desires, embrace humility.
Accompanying friends who have faith and are diligent, develop your enthusiasm for the practice.
Having been born in the lineage of the Great Vehicle* (Mahāyāna), do not be satisfied with a limited motivation.
Interested in all fields of knowledge, practice what inspires you.
These are the foremost prerequisites for noble practitioners to enter the spiritual path.

The path for beginners to engage in the practice has six gateways.

Searching for an entry point into the path of liberation, first understand that the three worlds of samsara are inherently fraught with suffering and that, until now, you have been mired in samsara, which is devoid of any essence. Once you have found this entrance, dedicate all your efforts to the path.

Whatever the ordinary activities of this life are, you will never have time to complete them, and moreover, they have little lasting significance. You may secure food and clothing, yet worldly activities have no end. Ceasing to worry about them and minimizing your appetite for gain and recognition, you will find true contentment.

When content, if you remain without pride or vanity and always choose humility, supreme spiritual qualities will spontaneously blossom in you.

Free from haughtiness, if you associate with friends who have faith in the supreme Dharma and persevere in their practice, they will inspire you to diligence. As the saying goes, "With two legs, you can travel far." Apply yourself with such diligence.

If you strive to practice the supreme Dharma, you will encounter the basic and the Great Vehicle. The latter is characterized by the excellent attitude of altruism and the vast accumulation of merit and wisdom. The basic vehicle* includes the vehicle of gods and men, which emphasizes observance of the laws of cause and effect and prudence in one's behavior. Without becoming infatuated with the vehicle of the listeners, bring forth in yourself the qualities of the path of the Great Vehicle.

If you earnestly engage in study, reflection, and meditation in all spheres of traditional knowledge and sciences, you will fulfill your aspirations on the path to liberation and omniscience. This is the gateway for becoming a noble being.

–48–

Six Activities Necessary for Intermediate-Level Practitioners to Avoid

Six activities intermediate-level practitioners should avoid:
Avoid engaging in farming, such as plowing, irrigation, and protecting the boundaries of your land.
Do not waste your youth by taking on the burden of a profit-oriented business.
Avoid clinging to friends and relatives or acting on their behalf to please them.
Avoid quarrels generated by animosity and partiality.
Avoid future worldly plans such as building homes and preserving and protecting wealth.
Avoid the demon of worldly activities that lead to involvements and distraction such as being acquainted with and meeting influential people.
These are important commitments for practitioners of the intermediate level.

Once on the path, practitioners of the supreme Dharma should dispense with certain activities. Why are they unnecessary?

Plowing, irrigation, profit-oriented ventures, and the difficulties encountered in protecting the boundaries of your land—all these secular endeavors are devoid of true essence.

Do not be overly concerned with the glamour of youth nor burden[79] yourself with the profit and loss of trade, as these pursuits involve all ten negative acts and are all ultimately senseless.

Striving to please patrons, acting as an intermediary for others, becoming overly attached to your loved ones—you will fail to fulfill these undesirable involvements that lead you away from Dharma.

Swayed by attraction and animosity, you idolize your own group while demonizing others, igniting endless and unfortunate arguments. As it is said, "There is no greater negativity than hatred," for it brings forth much harmful karma.

You hoard your wealth and possessions, believing in a long life ahead. Give up all those future plans, such as building houses and the like.

Understand that the distractions rooted in sensory pleasures are the work of demons. Do not seek the company of the powerful of this world, and do not strive to please them.

This is the second level of commitment for all practitioners of the supreme Dharma.

–49–

The Qualities of Yogis with Superior Abilities

Six qualities of yogis of higher capacities who practice in charnel grounds:[80]
They do not associate with worldly people to avoid being contaminated by their mediocrity.
They keep their activities of body, speech, and mind hidden from human eyes.
They do not seek ordinary food and clothing but survive on food offered to the dead and wear their clothing.
Without fear, they engage in the practice of *ḍākas*, heroic ones.
Cultivating the spiritual experiences of secret conduct, they abandon mundane behavior.
Resting in the *dharmatā*,* they realize great bliss.
Those who tread the path of liberation follow this conduct as the third entrance level for practitioners.

A yogi with superior abilities, who has developed a deep conviction in the view and meditation, and attained perfect stability in the practice of the supreme Dharma, will wander in charnel grounds and solitary places.

If you associate with ordinary people who indulge in deplorable behavior, you risk contamination by the degeneration of samayas. Instead of seeking their company, remain alone, like a wounded animal in hiding.

Whatever your activities of body, speech, and mind, do not flaunt them or seek to gain advantages by courting others. Whatever you do, go to places of solitude, away from human eyes, and live in a hidden way.

Do not spend your time searching for delicious food and fancy clothes. Be content with the food left as an offering to the dead in charnel grounds and wear the clothes found there.

If you venture into frightening places or mountain solitudes, you will overcome the difficulties encountered there through the deep concentration of your view and your meditation, becoming free from fear and anxiety. In charnel grounds, in the company of *mamos*[81] and ḍākinīs, you will engage in the practices of union.

To deepen your view and meditation of the path of the Adamantine Vehicle of the Secret Mantra, set aside all worldly activity and as soon as inner realization arises, the great bliss inherent in the ultimate nature of reality, the dharmatā, will manifest.

This is the practice of those who have attained perfect stability by traveling the path of liberation, the third level of access.

–50–

The Supreme Yogis

Six qualities of the supreme yogis free of preferences:
They are unattached to their home place or to anywhere else.
They are free from the two extremes: eternalism and nihilism.
Neither friends nor strangers know them any longer.
No more than a passing cloud are they attached to any place.
All perceptions of their six consciousnesses manifest as allies.
They do not judge anything as "good" or "bad."
This is the fourth entrance level to the noble path to liberation.

A yogi of the highest caliber, whose view and realization are unwavering, will leave behind his homeland and, without the slightest attachment, wander like a vagabond in uncharted places.

Concerning the nature of the view, such a yogi becomes familiar with the primordial wisdom free of mental elaborations, dwelling in the sphere of the nature of ultimate reality, beyond the two extremes of real existence (eternalism), and of nonexistence (nihilism).

Living inconspicuously, this yogi goes unrecognized by friend or foe, while those who remain in one place inevitably form an ever-increasing web of likes and dislikes. It is preferable not to settle anywhere but to wander without a particular destination, moving from one solitary place to another, without attachment, like clouds floating freely across the sky.

Whatever perceptions arise within the six aspects of consciousness, good or bad, remain free of fixation. As Jetsun Milarepa said,

> When I move,
> I bring all phenomena onto the path.
> When I stay, I dwell in pristine simplicity.
> This is my way of resting in the nature of ultimate reality.

Equalize all experience without hope or fear, without rumination, without being attached to success if you obtain all you desire—such as fame, power, or high rank—and without loathing the undesirable, such as slander, malicious gossip, or sanctions imposed by justice.

This is the fourth way a yogi enters the path.

–51–

Don't Worry, Be Carefree

Six fears to abandon if you want to accomplish the Dharma:
Do not conform to expected behavior in order to please others for fear of being rejected.
Do not accumulate wealth and possessions for fear of future deprivation.
Do not make all kinds of plans for fear of future suffering.
Do not strive to secure a high position for fear of a diminished status.
Do not aspire to worldly success for fear of downfall.
Do not disturb the minds of others for fear of being surpassed.

If you wish to practice Dharma authentically, you must release both hope and fear, for a mind plagued by anxiety will find itself in constant conflict with the Dharma.

In particular, free yourself from the worry that "If I act this way, my patrons will not like it," or "The local chief will not be pleased." Abandon any contrived behavior designed to win others' approval. Thinking, "come what may," free yourself of the burden of living up to others' expectations.

Do not think, "If I live long, I may struggle to secure food and clothing," and do not start accumulating possessions and wealth out of fear of destitution.

Let go of the apprehension that makes you brood, "I might face difficulties and suffer in the future, so I need to stock up on supplies and medicine." Do not waste your time planning for the future in anticipation of the suffering you might endure.

Avoid thoughts like, "I will always be a nobody, and important people disdain me," which might lead you to seek power, status, or even a position as a spiritual leader. Refrain from such pursuits, and cast aside any intention to involve yourself in worldly strategies out of fear of harm from others.

Fearing that others will surpass you, do not harbor spiteful thoughts such as "If I gain a high position, I could dominate all these people." Strive not to cloud your mind with such apprehensions.

–52–

Setting Boundaries

Six crucial boundaries to establish in your spiritual practice:
By freeing yourself from attachment and aversion, you establish the outer boundary.
By ceasing to accumulate material possessions, you establish the inner boundary.
By freeing yourself from the duality of subject and object, you establish the secret boundary.
By freeing yourself from desiring the best, you establish the higher boundary.
By freeing yourself from fearing the worst, you establish the lower boundary.
By letting go of fixation on physical and mental activities, you establish the intermediate boundary.
Those who have established these boundaries will be immune to obstacles.

Should you decide to go for retreat into mountain solitude, it is good to set six types of boundaries.

First, by freeing yourself from excessive attachment to loved ones and animosity toward your foes, you will set the outer boundary of your retreat.

If you are not only content with not accumulating possessions, but do not even think about it and do not accept anything, you set the inner boundaries.

If you avoid succumbing, even slightly, to the power of deluded thoughts that cling to the duality of subject and object, you establish the secret boundaries.

If you refrain from longing for future excellence—meditative experiences, realization, or advancing on the paths and bhūmis and other signs of accomplishment—expectations indicating the intrusion of demonic forces in your mind, you set the upper boundaries.

When, without letting yourself fear the worst, you avoid wondering whether you will ultimately accomplish anything, along with the fear that by staying in retreat for a long time you may run out of food and clothing, you are setting the lower boundaries.

Finally, if you leave entirely all the activities and tasks that you are engaged in and stop contemplating the countless projects that you expected to complete in the future, you set the intermediate boundaries.

It is inconceivable that a practitioner who respects these six boundaries will face obstacles. After establishing these limits, the great translator Rinchen Sangpo[82] spent twelve years in retreat, at the end of which he ascended with his body for the heavenly field of Kecara.[83] Karak Gomchung[84] went into retreat for the rest of his life, inscribed these six boundaries on the post marking the boundary of his retreat, and vowed to observe them. If you do the same, your retreat will live up to its name.

–53–

Six Points Needed to Reach Buddhahood

Achieving buddhahood depends on six points:
The ideal support for Dharma practice depends upon [a human birth endowed with] the right freedoms and conditions.
Without practice, you will not achieve liberation since liberation depends on practice.
Practice itself depends on knowing what and how to practice.

This in turn depends on listening to the teachings.
For study to be effective, it must be supported by reflection.
And these all depend upon a spiritual guide.

If you want to reach buddhahood, six points are indispensable:

If you possess a human existence with the eighteen freedoms and favorable conditions, you are ready to practice the supreme teachings of any of the three vehicles. So, everything depends on having a human existence, free and endowed the right conditions.

When you practice wholeheartedly without respite, day and night, erecting the citadel of the life force of practice and persevering with constancy, you must have a clear understanding of the crucial points of your practice. Marmots and other wild animals also live in secluded places, but this leads them nowhere [in terms of liberation]. Therefore, true accomplishment depends on a sound knowledge of the essentials of practice.

Clarifying all your doubts and misunderstandings about what you have studied depends in turn on having comprehended the meaning of the teachings. To do this, you must intimately blend these teachings with your mind. Also, to fully assimilate the essential points of Dharma, you must engage in ongoing study and contemplation.

Ultimately, the root of these six points depends on having an authentic spiritual guide. Make sure you satisfy all six requirements.

–54–

Qualities of Excellence

The six qualities of excellence:
Thanks to the accumulation of merits, you are born to an excellent family and your nature is calm and controlled.
Because your wisdom and discernment are vast, you are an adept in the various fields of knowledge.
Because your insight is excellent, you realize the nature of ultimate reality, boundless.
Because of your diligent practice, spiritual experiences, realization, and signs of accomplishment manifest.
Because of your compassion and skillful means, you never tire of benefiting others.

Because you have the crucial instructions, you are capable of guiding others on the path.
Supreme among humans, such noble beings are always virtuous.

There are six indispensable characteristics of beings who are knowledgeable, virtuous, and good-natured.

By having abundantly accumulated merits, they are reborn in a respected lineage, royal or otherwise, in all their lives. Peaceful by nature, they are self-controlled and have gentle and pleasant manners, unlike rough people who do not get along with anyone.

Those who possess fine discernment, both innate and acquired, and who have studied and reflected exhaustively will realize the ultimate nature of reality without bias.

If they practice diligently and with full focus, meditative experiences, realization, and signs of accomplishment will arise in their mind streams.

Upon the emergence of these signs, their boundless compassion prevents them from feeling discouraged or weary, regardless of the efforts they make to transform beings through skillful means.

Having themselves mastered the essential and supreme points of the path of liberation, they become adept at guiding beings committed to the path.

The manners of noble and exalted beings endowed with these six excellences are consistently virtuous, making them perfectly suited to serve as spiritual mentors.

–55–

Six Qualities to Cultivate

Six positive qualities authentic disciples should cultivate:
Disenchanted by samsara, they renounce deluded appearances.
Uninterested in non-Dharmic activities, they see them as meaningless.
Just as they shun their enemies, they avoid involvements and distractions.
They have no desire or hope for fame.
They cut the ties of grasping at dear ones and are free from concerns about pleasing them.

They abandon the discrimination that fuels attachment to kin and aversion to adversaries.
They renounce the world to devote themselves to the sublime Dharma.

Authentic disciples must have six qualities:

As they feel nothing but sadness and weariness toward the three worlds of samsara, the distinctive signs of the supreme Dharma will manifest.

They tell themselves, "All these ordinary worldly activities, all these deceptive appearances, lack any essence!" and the determination to be free from them grows in their minds.

They have the courage to disdain and renounce activities contrary to Dharma, such as taking life, appropriating religious property, or engaging in village ceremonies.

They do not fall into feverish agitation or distraction, which they dismiss as harmful to their bodies and minds.

They remain indifferent to the lure of fame in this life and do not bother to achieve it.

They are not preoccupied with pleasing their kin by all means and sever social ties centered on this life. They do not discriminate between so-called friends and enemies, overcoming both attachment and aversion.

In short, by freeing their minds from all worldly concerns, they are blessed with the good fortune to practice the sublime Dharma.

–56–

Maintaining Independence

Six situations where you avoid leaving the reins of your life in others' hands:
Not born into servitude, you are spared the demands that fall upon the powerless.
Not being a householder, you are free from the bondage of married life.
Not born as an important person, you are free to practice Dharma as you wish.
You have no ties of attachment that discourage you from [practicing Dharma] whenever and however you wish.

You have no unrealistic promises to keep.
The lake of suffering caused by the torrents of your negative actions does not overflow.
Those with such freedoms have every reason to rejoice.

If a Dharma practitioner gives others a tether to lead him by the nose, he will be at their mercy and his practice will be considerably delayed. There are six such situations to avoid:[85]

If you become the servant of a local chief or a religious leader, you have no choice but to do their bidding. You hand them control over your life and will never feel at ease.

If you live with a partner or marry, you will be fully preoccupied with your spouse and children. When two people are thus bound to each other by their mutual attraction, they have little time to practice the sublime Dharma and will struggle to progress on the path to liberation.

Being born into an influential family—such as that of a king, dignitary, or other prominent person—will entangle you in a web of duties and distractions, hindering your ability to practice freely.

Conversely, if you are not deterred by the demands of your parents, siblings, and friends to delay your practice, you will enjoy the freedom to practice the Dharma according to your aspirations.

There's no point in making many pledges if you cannot fulfill them. So, avoid committing to too many things at once and only undertake what you can bring to fruition.

Because of negative actions in your past lives, you may face various afflictions in this life, such as illnesses, imprisonment, or other calamities. Similarly, your karma might lead you to be conscripted into an army, leaving you with no choice but to follow orders.

However, if you are spared the overflow of the lake of suffering caused by the downpour of your bad karma and are free to choose to practice Dharma, you have much to rejoice about.

–57–

Lifestyles Conducive to Spiritual Practice

Six conducive lifestyles for meditation and spiritual practice:
Have just enough for your needs, without falling into the two extremes.
Eat moderately,[86] neither overeating nor going hungry.
Avoid illness caused by imbalance of the elements.
Do not become overweight by eating too much rich food.
Do not weaken your system by eating nonnutritious food.
Respect the cycle of day and night and avoid eating at untimely hours.
Such a lifestyle is crucial and conducive to virtuous activities.

If you live in solitude and dedicate yourself to meditative concentration, there are six lifestyles that align harmoniously with the supreme Dharma:

Excessive wealth and too many possessions will lead you to be busy with trade, farming, amassing religious wealth, and participating in village ceremonies. Conversely, if you become destitute, you may starve to death. Avoid both extremes and be content with just enough to keep yourself warm and healthy.

If you do not know how to satisfy yourself with the essentials for your health and eat without measure, you will suffer from the ills of excess. You will tend to become drowsy, and the imbalance of the elements, winds, bile, and humors will result in various illnesses. Know how to find the right amount of nourishing food that suits your body, avoiding both overindulgence and inadequate, poor-quality food. If your health declines, you may struggle to maintain your practice and risk starvation.

While practicing, respect the natural cycle of day and night. Avoid eating at random times, which exacerbates negative emotions and promotes drowsiness.

These guidelines will help you find the right balance in your practice.

Second, if you do not know how to moderate your intake of essential foods and eat without restraint, you will suffer from the ills of excess. This can lead to drowsiness and an imbalance of the elements, winds, bile, and humors, resulting in various illnesses. Seek to find the right amount of nourishing food that suits your body, avoiding both excess that leads to gaining weight or having too little food of poor quality. If your health declines, you will be unable to persevere in practice and may even risk starvation.

While practicing, respect the natural cycle of day and night. Avoid eating at random times, as this aggravates negative emotions and increase drowsiness.

These recommendations will help you find the right balance in your practice.

–58–

Circumstances That Encourage Practice

Six circumstances that inspire faith and perseverance:
Experiencing adversity makes you aware of impermanence.
Understanding the law of cause and effect encourages you to avoid negative actions as poison.
Filled with devotion and respect, you perceive your spiritual master as the Buddha in person.
Confidence in the teachings inspires you to practice virtue joyfully.
Trust in the virtuous community, the *sangha*,* encourages you to rely upon it to escort you to the higher states.
Yearning to achieve enlightenment motivates you to strive as much as you can.
This is the tradition of the noble and fortunate ones.

Anyone eager to practice the sublime Dharma must embody fervent devotion and unwavering diligence. Six particular circumstances encourage practitioners to enhance these qualities:

Adversities such as illness, demons, malevolent spirits, and obstacle makers can become allies in your Dharma practice, for they remind you that everything is impermanent and devoid of essence.

Convinced of the ineluctability of the laws of cause and effect, you will avoid negative actions and faults as you would avoid food laced with poison.

A mind infused with devotion and respect will perceive the spiritual master as the Buddha himself.

Developing a deep conviction in the supreme Dharma, even if you practice day and night, you will never think you have done enough. You will persist with joy and enthusiasm.

If the members of the noble sangha, the virtuous community, uphold the three levels of precepts impeccably,[87] they will be regarded as Dharma ornaments by the faithful, strengthening their trust. This will inspire the faithful to practice mindfulness, vigilance, and circumspection, taking the sangha as a guide to lead them out of the realms of samsara.

If you aspire to attain buddhahood with the same yearning as a thirsty person seeks water, you will persevere in cultivating all the desired qualities. Thus, you will have the good fortune to accomplish the Dharma and follow the tradition of noble beings.

–59–

Mastering the Mind with Dharma

Six attributes of those who have trained their minds in Dharma:
Their minds are neither perverted nor wild and they maintain an unwavering confidence in Dharma.
They are determined and resilient in the face of unbearable hardships.
Seeing the defects of samsara, they renounce it out of fear.
Their mind stream is pure, stainless, and receptive.
Through extensive study and reflection, they understand the teachings that reveal the ultimate truth.
They are worthy vessels of the profound empowerments and samayas.
Such beings seem to be as rare as an island of jewels.

As your mind stream is being transformed by the supreme Dharma, there are six ways to control your afflictive mental states with mindfulness and vigilance.

Doubting your spiritual guide, lacking confidence in the supreme Dharma, succumbing to laziness and indolence—you are free of such defects and devote yourself to spiritual practice with the same eagerness as a hungry person seeks food.

Once you are resolved to practice Dharma, remain steadfast and resilient, whether you are facing illness, mental torment, or suffering from thirst and hunger. Uphold your commitment regardless of the circumstances.

Clearly seeing the defects inherent in the sufferings of the three worlds of samsara and telling yourself it would be wonderful to be free from the delusion of these three worlds, you aspire to escape samsara with the desperate energy of a person thrown alive into a fire.

Once you are resolved to practice Dharma, remain steadfast and resilient, whether you are facing illness, mental torment, or suffering from thirst and hunger. Uphold your commitment regardless of the circumstances.

Whatever vast and profound aspects of the Dharma you contemplate, never telling yourself that they are beyond your mental capacities, being free from false views and other flaws that would make you a defective vessel, your mind stream remains perfectly pure.

Having clarified all doubts and hesitations about the essential points of view, meditation, and action, not taking wrong paths or straying into deviations, you correctly realize the ultimate essence of the Dharma.

Having received the transmission of an empowerment and the corresponding sacred commitments (samayas), you uphold them impeccably. The purity of your samayas makes you a suitable vessel for the accomplishments of the profound path.

Just as an explorer cannot find the jewel island on the great ocean unless he has accumulated sufficient merit in the past, even rarer are the practitioners who are truly qualified to receive the supreme Dharma.

–60–

Six Qualities in the Face of Adversity

Six kinds of resilience toward adverse circumstances that result from practice:
You can endure all kinds of physical pain.
You can refrain from pernicious talk and meaningless chatter.
You manage to mindfully experience joy and suffering, good and bad situations.
You can brave the melancholy and anxiety that may arise in lonely places far from your fellow humans.
You can rely on the antidote of mindfulness in the clamor of cities.

You can protect your vows and precepts by standing firm in the face of unfavorable situations.
Those who possess these qualities will advance with ease on the path of Dharma.

Here are six qualities of a practitioner whose mind is not easily disturbed and whose Dharma practice withstands adverse circumstances:

He bears all forms of physical discomfort, such as hunger and thirst, with fortitude for the sake of the supreme Dharma, and remains resolute in the face of hardships.

He understands the importance of avoiding negative speech. As the saying goes, "The mouth is the reservoir of vice, the gateway from which all faults and transgressions flow." Joy and suffering alike stem from our words. Thus, a good practitioner is able to refrain from foolish talk that fosters mundane attachment and aversion.

He can bring to the path all the joy and suffering that arises in his mind. Having applied himself to the practices explained in the teachings on training the mind (*lojong*)[88] even if suffering is deliberately inflicted upon him, he remains undisturbed and avoids pride or vanity in moments of happiness, demonstrating resilience in all circumstances.

In solitary places, despite a lack of human contact and external distractions, he remains perfectly content without sadness or anxiety.

He maintains his focus even amid the distractions of populated areas, numerous benefactors, or a large monastic community, showing strength in resisting external influences.

He integrates all joy and suffering into his practice. Having applied himself to the teachings of mind training, he remains undisturbed by inflicted suffering.

Whatever vows and precepts he has received from an abbot or a spiritual master, he can observe them without being swayed by afflictive states of mind and challenging conditions.

The practitioner who embodies these qualities will traverse the path of liberation with ease, wherever he or she is on that path.

–61–

Blending Your Mind with Dharma

Six[89] ways of blending your mind with the qualities of the path to liberation.
Blend your mind with the general teachings (the sutras), and you will attain enlightenment in the distant future.
Blend your mind with the teachings of the Secret Mantra, and you can walk the path of the three *kāyas*.*
Blend your mind with the crucial instructions on ultimate reality, and you will cut through the erroneous path of clinging to extreme views.
Blend your mind with the Mahāyāna teachings, and whatever you do will benefit others.
Blend your mind with the teachings of the listeners and the solitary realizers, and you will abandon samsaric activities.
Whoever has done so can be considered to have blended their mind with Dharma.

If you progress correctly on the path, the qualities of liberation will become an intimate part of yourself, enabling you to dispel all defects and will counteract negative emotions.

When the four changes of attitude[90] and other considerations merge with your mind, you will avoid engaging in activities driven by the eight worldly concerns. Think of your future lives and focus solely on achieving buddhahood for future lives.

Thoroughly assimilating the teachings of the Vajrayāna Secret Mantra, you will accomplish the pure lands of the three kāyas and understand that these bodies are not external entities but simply facets of the fundamental nature of your mind, the *tathāgatagarbha.** With this understanding at the core of your practice, the three kāyas become your path even as you engage in the phases of development and perfection.

Integrate in your mind the key points of the ultimate truth. With the supreme view, meditation, and action, you will avoid falling into the extremes of eternalism and nihilism, steering clear of these two polarities.

When the teachings of the Great Vehicle permeate your mind, all your positive actions of body, speech, and mind will be infused with the excellent altruistic attitude of the bodhisattvas, aligning with their conduct.

Having perfectly assimilated the teachings of the listeners and the solitary realizers, you will see the three worlds of samsara as adversaries and abandon all samsaric activities.

These six qualities are signs than those who practice these methods have intimately blended their minds with the Dharma.

–62–

Dismantle Grasping

Six ways to eliminate the tenacious belief [in the solidity of phenomena]:
Generate the conviction that the six sense objects[91] are deceptive and lead you astray.
Generate the conviction that ordinary activities mislead you, since they are meaningless.
Generate the conviction that believing phenomena to be real is illusory and deceptive.
Generate the conviction that fame, praise, and honors are delusory.
Generate the conviction that "enemy" and "friend" are illusory as they are subject to change.
If you can realize the lack of true existence [of phenomena], deceptive appearances and their grasp will collapse.

Whatever activities you undertake, whether spiritual or secular, as soon as you grasp them, you are enslaved by attachment to the seeming solidity of things. This can foster pride, vanity, and conceit. To dismantle such attachments, there are six instructions:

Understand that your perceptions of sense objects—shapes, sounds, smells, tastes, and textures—no matter how beautiful and attractive they may seem, are as deceptive as fantasies and dreams, and they will no longer be able to arouse grasping or repulsion in your mind. With a clear conviction that all these objects and circumstances are inherently deceptive, your mind will no longer be drawn into their wake.

Engaged in the countless activities of ordinary life, you will never see their conclusion and will perpetually delay your Dharma practice. Be convinced that these pursuits are simply misguided. Therefore, disregarding all these physical, verbal, and mental activities, devote yourself solely to the supreme Dharma.

If you cling to and take pride in worldly qualities, your mind will become distracted and lead you astray. Understand clearly that such attachments are fundamentally illusory and deceptive.

Do you enjoy worldly fame and are you the recipient of praise and respect? These only serve to increase your distraction and busyness and hinder your contemplation. Your Dharma practice will be delayed and you will be defiled by dubious means of livelihood, including the misuse of religious resources. You can be sure that these are only deceptive illusions. So, do not care about recognition and avoid adopting improper ways of life.

You blindly cling to those you perceive as friends and feel animosity toward those you consider enemies. Knowing that these distinctions are transient and comparable to optical illusions and dreams, embrace all beings in unconditional benevolence and refrain from exaggerated affection for loved ones and disproportionate hostility toward adversaries.

Ultimately, recognize that, like dreams, neither samsara nor nirvana exist in their own right. By dismantling your reifying attachment to the reality of illusory appearances, your path will remain stainless.

–63–

Giving Meaning to Your Life

Six activities that give full meaning to the freedoms and favorable conditions [of a precious human life]:
Even though you may be wealthy, wealth has no value, since it is deceptive. So, strive in practice.
You might study a lot but be trapped by the play of words. So, strive in practice.
You might be learned, but you miss the essence. So, strive in practice.
You might reflect [upon the teachings], but you only multiply your concepts. So, strive in practice.
You might teach, but you get stuck in mere intellectual understanding. So, strive in practice.
Without practicing, you cannot actualize [buddhahood]. So, devote yourself to practice.

Even if you have correctly developed spiritual qualities associated with the supreme Dharma, you should continually enhance them. To do this, six instructions help you make your existence meaningful when you enjoy the necessary freedoms and favorable conditions.

If you have accumulated wealth and material possessions, recognizing that they are devoid of essence, do not worry about preserving and augmenting them. Far more important is to be diligent about what is essential: your spiritual accomplishment.

You have listened to teachings encompassing the ten branches of traditional sciences, but by just following the words, you squander their deeper meaning. That is why one-pointedly practicing the core teachings is important.

If you have learned the various branches of knowledge correctly but fail to distill their single essence, you have not fulfilled their purpose. Limiting yourself to the general aspects of the teachings[92] will not suffice. You must concentrate fully on practice.

If your mind is full of ideas and you undertake a multitude of activities, the only result will be a proliferation of wild thoughts. Instead, try to eliminate activities altogether.

Opening your mouth, you may expound the essence and the variety of the teachings, but whatever you say remains confined to the realm of the intellect and does not serve to transform your mind. Turn inward and practice.

Persevering in your practice without actualizing meditative experiences and spiritual realization reduces you to merely the semblance of a practitioner, which is fruitless. Therefore, you must devote yourself wholeheartedly to spiritual practice.

–64–

Giving Up Samsara

Six points of mind training for renouncing samsara:
Ordinary activities are deceptive and meaningless: renounce them!
Craving sense pleasures intensifies your desire: renounce them!
In the end, negative aims and objectives lack any purpose:
renounce them!
Eventually, you must leave everything behind: renounce
attachment to wealth and possessions.

All that is conditioned is doomed to separation: renounce longing for friends and relatives.

Attraction and aversion, grasping to subject and object, are the roots of ruin: renounce them!

Those who renounce all these will naturally accomplish the supreme Dharma.

If you wish to leave all the activities of the three worlds of samsara behind, know that the supreme Dharma is the main antidote to the circle of existences. There are six instructions for training and transforming your mind in excellent ways by relying on the supreme Dharma:

Whether you are defeating enemies, protecting loved ones, or engaging in other samsaric pursuits, recognize that these actions are ultimately in vain. They will deplete your life and continually delay your Dharma practice. Clear your mind of worldly concerns.

No matter what goods, food, and clothing you obtain, if you entertain strong attachments and fixations, nothing will ever satisfy you, since you have the mindset of a being from the world of desire, the *kāmaloka*. Clear your mind of all cravings.

Long-term worldly ambitions, such as political aspirations, pale in comparison to the quest for perfect buddhahood. Abandon all such mediocre goals.

When the time of death comes, you will have to leave everything behind, including your cherished body. Therefore, cast aside any plans to accumulate possessions and free yourself from greed.

All compounded phenomena arise from a combination of causes and conditions. When this assemblage breaks down, its elements can only disperse. Nothing escapes this. That is why it is said that "everything that has come together will fall apart."

Abandon your infatuations. Excessive emotional attachment to family will cause you to delay your Dharma practice. Avoid such a situation and disentangle your mind from clinging.

Attraction and aversion are the wellspring of all the suffering of samsaric existence. These two impulses arise from the belief in the duality of subject and object. If you can free yourself from this dualistic clinging, the Dharma will naturally be accomplished, even without a conscious effort to practice it.

–65–

Trust in the Laws of Causality

Six methods to develop conviction in the law of cause and effect:
Study the *piṭakas ("baskets" of the teachings) and trust the law of causality.**
Reflecting upon the example of drops of water filling a pot, gather the two accumulations [of merit and wisdom].
Reflect upon the example of a single spark reducing an entire forest to ashes and abandon all negative actions.
All happiness and pain result from your past actions: engage in meritorious activities.
You cannot perfect the accumulations in one instant: accumulate merit little by little.
Be certain that as long as there is self-grasping,* there will be karma.

Six instructions for gaining certainty about the infallibility of the laws of causation:

Study carefully the words of the Tathāgata, the Buddha, our teacher, as recorded in the sutras, especially *The Sūtra of the Hundred Karmas*[93] and *The Sūtra of the Application of the Mindful Presence of the Supreme Dharma*,[94] and you will gain an intimate conviction concerning the infallibility of the laws of cause and effect.

Just as a vase slowly fills with water drop by drop, do not underestimate the significance of even the smallest accumulation of merit and wisdom. Diligently engage in the twofold accumulation of merit and wisdom, persevering in your practice.

No matter how small a spark falls on dry wood, it can start a fire that may consume an entire forest. With this example in mind, do not be discouraged by thinking that you will not be able to purify yourself of negative actions accumulated in your past lives, with the help of antidotes. Know that even a small amount of virtuous practice, if done correctly, can truly eliminate the effect of negative actions.

The joys and sorrows of your current life do not depend only on the extent of your courage or on your ingenuity. They result in a large way from your deeds in past lives. Therefore, if you aspire for happiness in future lives, you must constantly engage in the twofold accumulation [of merit and wisdom] and perform positive acts. But you will not achieve this twofold accumulation in a day or a month: you must persevere, day after day, night after night.

No matter how much you have glimpsed emptiness, until attachment to the notion of "I" is eradicated, even noble beings will have to suffer retribution for past acts [committed before they have reached that level], since his body is composed of impure aggregates and no one escapes the laws of causality. Karma will continue to operate as long as attachment to the self remains. Therefore, you must trust the laws of causality.

Even if you have glimpsed the nature of emptiness, attachment to the notion of "I" persists, and a noble being will still experience retribution for actions committed prior to their realization. The body, composed of impure aggregates, is subject to the laws of causality. Karma will continue to operate as long as self-attachment remains.

–66–

The Defects of the Vessel

Six defects of the recipient that should be discarded when receiving teachings:
To receive teachings prematurely is to be like an unbaked earthen pot.
Not paying attention is to be like an upside-down pot.
Not retaining what you have heard is to be like a pot with a hole.
To listen with negative intentions is to be like a pot containing poison.
Listening that does not fulfill its function is like food mixed with dirt.
Listening to the teachings with pride is like receiving them in a filthy pot.
Avoid all these defects when listening to teachings.

The teachings are like ambrosia, the nectar of immortality. They are thus appropriately received in a vessel free of six defects. These instructions are for those who wish to listen to the teachings properly:

The Buddha gave step-by-step teachings on the preliminaries, the main part, and the subsequent stages [on the path to enlightenment] to individuals of higher, intermediate, and lower abilities. If you try to engage in the main practices prematurely without first preparing your mind with foundational practices, it is like attempting to fill an unbaked clay pot with water—it will crumble. Similarly, if the vessel of your mind is not ready, it will not be able to perform its function.

When you are about to receive the teachings, listen with your full attention. An inattentive mind is like an upside-down vase: no matter how much nectar is poured in, none will enter. In this case, you could receive many teachings without them serving as antidotes to self-grasping and afflictive mental states.

Continually refresh the teachings in your memory. Then establish with certainty the meaning of what you have heard through study, reflection, and meditation.

Continuously refresh your memory of the teachings and establish with certainty their meaning through study, reflection, and meditation.

Yet, if a vase has a leak, it cannot be filled, regardless of how long the nectar is poured. Similarly, teachings heard in great numbers but not retained through diligent listening, reflection, and meditation will never be assimilated.

Whether you listen to the teachings, reflect on them, or meditate on them, if you harbor attachment, animosity, or competitiveness, it is like eating delicious food mixed with poison, thus causing your own death. Maintain a pure motivation at all times!

Whatever path of supreme Dharma you have been taught, you must follow it properly without confusing the progressive levels of the path or corrupting them.[95] Even a brand-new garment will lose its charm if stained.

Remember that "the water of qualities does not remain on the summit of pride." Aware of this, do not get caught in the trap of words, failing to grasp the crucial points of the meaning. Otherwise, the water of qualities related to abandonment [of obscurations] and realization will not accumulate in your mind.

Avoid these six defects and listen to the supreme Dharma in an excellent way.

–67–

Qualities of Noble Beings

Six qualities of noble beings who listen perfectly to the teachings:
Endowed with supreme wisdom, they are eager to learn and are unbiased.
They realize they will never tire of following spiritual masters or of learning.
They rely upon and please many learned ones.
Through extensive learning, they distinguish the teachings' various aspects.
Studying continually, they gain certainty again and again.
Having learned a lot, they question and debate [on key points].
Thus, they uphold the ocean-like treasure of Dharma.

To begin with, after listening to the Dharma, you must engage in study. Otherwise, you will not become a suitable recipient of the teachings. There are six qualities associated with listening to the Dharma:

Endowed with innate intelligence and wisdom gained through training, immerse yourself in learning, reflection, and meditation. Examine and understand the various philosophical views with an open and impartial mind.

Once under the guidance of a qualified spiritual master, whatever he or she teaches will contribute to your progress toward liberation and omniscience [of buddhahood]. Seek instructions from as many authentic spiritual masters as possible. Remember the example of bodhisattva Norsang (Maṇibhadra), who studied with 112 bodhisattvas. Even if your knowledge is already as vast as an ocean, never consider it sufficient: no matter how many rivers flow into the ocean, it is never too much for the ocean. If you never think that you have acquired enough knowledge, you will eventually succeed in freeing your mind perfectly.

Having relied upon many learned and accomplished spiritual masters (a hundred million, if need be!) and pleasing them with your progress, you will travel the path appropriately and without error. Having heard a broad array of teachings, in all their breadth and depth, you will gain a comprehensive understanding of the nine vehicles.

Anyone who has studied extensively will gain an ever-deeper conviction about the teachings, will assimilate them in full, and further examine, clarify, and elucidate their meaning through listening, reflection, and meditation. If the vast ocean was yours, you would also inherit the treasure of jewels it contains. To hold the treasure of the Dharma is essential.

–68–

How to Think

Six perfect methods of studying [a Dharma text]:
Ask yourself: What do these words really mean?
What are the classifications and how do I summarize them?
What are the particular details and to which category do they relate?
How do I condense the teachings in order to practice?
Carefully studying in this way will open the door to the precious Dharma.

Through reflection, you must establish with certainty the meaning of the teachings you have heard. There are six methods for refining your understanding of the subject of your reflection.

Consider the word "buddha" for example, [in Tibetan, *sangs rgyas*, pronounced *sang gye*]. [The first syllable,] *sang*, "awakened," means that the Buddha has awakened from the sleep of ignorance, the ignorance associated with the two obscurations. [The second syllable,] *gye*, "developed," means that all the qualities of his mind have fully blossomed as a result of having first removed the two veils that concealed his buddha nature* and then realized all that needs to be realized. Every word can hold many profound meanings. Therefore, continually ask yourself, "What do these words teach? What do they mean?" If their meaning eludes you, seek the guidance of learned scholars and retain their insight.

In general, the eighty-four thousand aspects or sections of the Buddha's teachings can be categorized into nine or three graded vehicles, advanced, intermediate, and basic. If you want to categorize them further, consider which view, meditation, and conduct correspond to each of these vehicles. You may also ask, what the quintessential points of each vehicle are if their meaning is condensed.

You can further examine which teachings pertain to the profound—those concerning emptiness—and which ones to the vast—encompassing the ten bhūmis and five paths.* Also, ask yourself, to which of the Three Baskets* [vinaya, sutra, and abhidharma] do the teachings you have heard and reflected upon belong.

You may possess a wealth of knowledge, but how do you extract its essence to put it into practice? To refine and elucidate your practice, regard the canonical writings as profound spiritual instructions. Just as opening the door of a treasure room reveals precious wish-fulfilling gems, by clearly establishing the meaning of the teachings you have heard through reflection, you will open wide the doors of the bountiful treasure of the Dharma.

–69–

How to Meditate

Six qualities of perfect meditation:
It should not be ignorant of the ultimate reality and should be free from the extremes of eternalism and nihilism.
It relates to emptiness and compassion, the path of the Great Vehicle.
It abides in the dharmatā, the ultimate nature of reality, free from the distractions of lethargy and agitation.
It unites calm abiding and deeper insight, enhancing spiritual experiences and realization.
It is free from hope and fear, subject and object, fixation and concepts.
It is the antidote to negative emotions and obscurations.
Meditation like this leads you to the other shore.

Once you have established with certainty the meaning of the teachings through listening and reflection, you must become familiar with such meaning through meditation. There are six methods of generating a perfect meditation:

Not remaining ignorant of the fundamental nature of all phenomena, and gaining a correct and intimate realization of that nature, you will understand the view of the Middle Way, which avoids the extremes of eternalism and nihilism held by non-Buddhists, the *tīrthikas*.*

Next, recognize the vital force of the Great Vehicle by uniting the wisdom of emptiness with the skillful means of great compassion. Through this union, all your actions, words, and thoughts will guide you along the path of the Great Vehicle, the supreme practice.

If you perfectly realize the view of the ultimate nature, emptiness, and your concentration in this view neither sinks into torpor nor is distracted by restlessness, both of which are traps, you will obtain a deeper insight combined with calm abiding, enabling you to destroy afflictive mental states.

First, cultivate calm abiding, and as it says, "Free from attachment to the mundane world, you will accomplish the Pure Land of Manifest Joy."[96] Begin with an inner stillness free from distraction. This, however, should not be an ordinary, or "worldly," śamatha, but must be united with vipaśyanā, the wisdom that realizes the absence of self (*anātman*). Through this union, all the qualities of meditative experience and spiritual realization will flourish.

Based on this śamatha, when the qualities of the path—such as infallible memory and insight—manifest, avoid pride in these achievements, attachment to them, hope for more, or fear of not achieving them. As a result, the characteristics of attachment to the subject-object duality, fixations, and goals will dissipate.

Realizing the view of the ultimate nature of reality, in which subject-object and all other attributes and clinging are dissolved, serves as a natural antidote to the two obscurations, the one formed by afflictive mental states and the one that veils all that can be known.

Contemplatives who meditate in this way will reach the other shore of the ocean of suffering of the three worlds of samsaric existence. Be diligent in this practice!

–70–

Coping with Circumstances

Six qualities of not being defeated by circumstances:
You consider words of praise and blame to be mere echoes.
You aspire to reconcile those involved in conflicts over attachment and aversion.
Your actions do not contradict the Dharma.
Knowing that your possessions result from your past generosity, you do not seek to accumulate wealth.
Understanding diseases and demons as inspirations for your practice, you do not try to avoid them.

You constantly maintain pure perception, devotion, and respect.
Whoever can transmute adverse circumstances in this way is a hero.

When you embark on a long journey, you may face enemies or thieves, endure the trials of the four elements, or find yourself at the edge of a precipice—many obstacles lie in wait. The same holds true when you set out on the path to liberation and enlightenment. All kinds of favorable and unfavorable circumstances will arise. If you can skillfully bring them onto the path, they will serve as catalysts for your spiritual practice. Here are six qualities of those who do not succumb to adversity:

Even if you are praised and enjoy a good reputation, do not feel superior or become conceited. Do not think with smugness, "I am famous!" Conversely, if you are disparaged or slandered, do not lose heart. Rely on the support of mind training, the lojong teachings. Do not bury yourself in anxiety. View all circumstances as insubstantial as an echo.

Unswayed by the endless advice of ordinary people driven by attachment and aversion, constantly align your conduct with the supreme Dharma.

Examine whether your actions, words, and thoughts accord with the Dharma. If they contradict it, discard them; if not, act on them while reinforcing the antidotes.

If you have everything you need to live and you enjoy some possessions, remember that they are the fruits of your generosity in past lives. Do not hoard them—give freely and make offerings from the finest portion of what you own.

If you are affected by illness, negative influences, or any other obstacles, do not attempt to reject them: these adversities help spur your spiritual practice. In the long run, they allow you to distinguish between mere meditative experiences and true realization, and they strengthen your sense of renunciation and weariness with samsara. Therefore, welcome these difficulties.

With pure vision and deep trust, recognize these hardships as manifestations of Buddha's activities. With unwavering devotion, guard against reacting with attraction and repulsion. Even if multiple obstacles arise, utilize them on the path. Just as a forest fire intensifies when the wind picks up, if a practitioner knows how to integrate difficult circumstances into the path, they will accelerate his progress in meditation and realization and invigorate his spiritual practice.

If you possess all that you need and enjoy your belongings, remember that they are the fruits of your generosity in past lives. Do not hoard them

If you are affected by illness, negative influences, or any other obstacles, do not attempt to reject them. These adversities help propel your spiritual practice forward. In the long run, they allow you to distinguish between mere meditative experiences and true realization, and they strengthen your sense of renunciation and weariness with samsara.

With pure vision and deep trust, recognize these hardships as manifestations of the Buddha's activities. With unwavering devotion, guard against reacting with attraction and aversion. Even if numerous obstacles arise, utilize them on the path.

–71–

Six Bad Ideas

Six polluting and harmful ideas to abandon:
The negative thought of attaining great fame;
The unwholesome thought of accumulating gain and wealth;
The mistaken belief in the true existence of phenomenal appearances;
The intention to exploit your body and speech for sense pleasures;
The wish to secure a livelihood for this life;
The aspiration to achieve liberation only for yourself—
The wise will abandon such concepts, products of the "blessings" of the demons.

If you want to practice the path correctly, beware of six bad ideas or concerns that diminish and contaminate the path:

A yogi or renunciate who practices Dharma diligently in secluded places is called *chadral,* meaning "free from activity." In such a case, aspiring for fame is a negative idea that you had better eschew.

The pursuit of profits and possessions indicates that the demon of distraction is at work. Give up the unwholesome idea of engaging in such activities.

As long as you perceive external appearances, whether attractive or not, as truly existing, and as long as you strive to attain what seems pleasant and avoid what seems unpleasant, liberation from attachment and aversion will remain out of reach. View all external phenomena as devoid of inherent existence, like illusions or dreams.

When your body and speech are captivated by desires for food, clothing, wealth, women or men, and other objects of craving, you are no longer your own master and will keep on postponing your Dharma practice. Forsake such concerns.

If, engulfed by the worldly affairs of this life, you strive to secure abundant sustenance and need all manner of material things, you will be endlessly distracted. Cast off this desire.

If, instead of aspiring to liberate all beings from the sufferings of conditioned existence, you seek only your own liberation, you are adopting the approach of the lower vehicle.

If these unwholesome thoughts arise in your mind, it is a sign of the "blessings," in other words the obstacles of the demons. Therefore, the wise will cast them aside.

–72–

Do Not Run after External Objects

Six states in which the senses do not chase external objects:
The poison of attachment or aversion to your homeland does not harm you.
Intense desire for sense pleasures does not grip you.
The weapons of the eight worldly concerns do not injure you.
The impurity of deceit does not stain your conduct.
The winds of busyness and distraction do not blow you about.
You spend your days and nights in virtuous activities.
Like this, adopt the conduct of the noble ones!

As you practice Dharma, your senses can be enticed by the external world. When objects engage your consciousness through the five sense organs, attachment [or rejection] arises, and with it, the primary cause of wandering in the three worlds of samsara. How can you free yourself from this?

In your homeland, you keep strengthening attachment to your loved ones and aversion toward others, turning your surroundings into a prison ruled by the demon of afflictive emotions. To avoid being ensnared by this poisonous attitude, it is best to leave your homeland or, at least, discard any bias driven by attraction or repulsion.

If you indulge in pleasures in the ordinary way, your thirst for them will never be quenched and you will constantly delay your spiritual practice. Break free from the inclination to pursue sense pleasures.

If you strive to act on the eight worldly concerns, you are like a person mortally wounded by gunfire—death is imminent. Avoid falling under the sway of these concerns.

If your actions are not genuinely honest and straightforward, if they are tainted by deception or hypocrisy, motivated by a desire to fool others, and you pretend to be mindful in your behavior when you are not—or to have a high view, meditation, and conduct when you do not—you are deceiving not only others but also yourself. Do not degrade yourself by misleading others because you have not mastered your own mind.

Being distracted by the desire to please your benefactors, manage religious property, participate in village ceremonies, or build houses will leave you as restless as one carried away by the wind. Such pursuits will hinder your concentration.

If you devote your days and nights to practicing the teachings in an excellent manner without corrupting your conduct with wrongdoing, you will remain in harmony with the supreme Dharma and truly uphold the tradition.

–73–

Six Types of Faith

Six types of faith that can heal the mind:
With devotional faith, pray to spiritual masters and meditate upon them.
With respectful faith, strive to make offerings to the Three Jewels.
With confident faith, engage in meditation practice upon your primary deity, the yidam.
With inspired faith, abide in meditation on ultimate reality.
With irreversible faith, transform adversity into an ally.
With ultimate faith, blend your mind with Dharma.
Engaging in this way on the path to liberation is crucial.

As it is said, "Faith opens the door to the light of the Dharma, faith is the wealth, the treasure, and the supreme legs. It is also the hand that gathers all virtues."

Faith is the first of the seven spiritual treasures. Cultivate perfectly pure faith: it will heal your mind stream and regenerate your strength when you encounter difficulties in your practice. There are six aspects to such faith:

By learning of the lives of perfect liberation of the unsurpassed spiritual masters, you develop an aspiration to attain the qualities of meditative experience and realization associated with buddhahood and continually strive toward this ideal. Praying with ardent aspiration, meditate on the master constantly and, to the best of your ability, practice guru yoga,* the "union with the nature of the master."

If your body, speech, and mind act with respect for the Three Jewels, you will accumulate both merit and wisdom. Without ever turning away from the Three Supreme Jewels, keep them constantly in mind, diligently make offerings, and, in particular, dedicate the first part of your food and drink to them. This forms the foundation of your commitment to Dharma practice.

When your faith is based on unwavering conviction, free from doubt, and you affirm to yourself, "These are the laws of causality, the benefits of *dhāraṇīs*[97] and mantras, the result of meditating upon wisdom deities," these deities will support you. In order to obtain all the ordinary and extraordinary accomplishments, with a perfectly concentrated mind, commit yourself to meditation and to accomplishing the yidam.

When you hear about the many qualities associated with the bhūmis and paths (of the bodhisattvas), you will develop a joyful faith. To obtain all these qualities, meditate single-mindedly on the meaning of emptiness, the ultimate nature of reality.

If you are prepared to give your life for the Dharma and cannot imagine abandoning it, you have an "irreversible" faith. In this case, all adverse circumstances will manifest as allies of your practice.

At all times, keep your mind from running wild, maintain an attentive presence and unwavering circumspection, and as the effect of such faith, your mind stream will naturally blend with the Dharma.

Treasure these six aspects of faith as precious gems on your path to liberation and enlightenment.

–74–

Keeping the Precepts

Six ways to observe moral discipline without hypocrisy:
Know that moral discipline is the root of the Buddha's teachings.
Know that negative actions lead to the lower realms,
That if you do not keep your vows, the root of Dharma practice will rot.
Know that [moral discipline] is the foundation of all positive qualities,
The ladder that allows you to climb to the higher realms of existence.
Know that [moral discipline] is the mount that carries you on the path to liberation.
Therefore, you must consistently take care to maintain pure moral discipline.

To practice the supreme Dharma, one takes vows relating to prātimokṣa, bodhicitta, and the Secret Mantra. If you not only take these vows but also keep them flawlessly, without hypocrisy, you lay the foundation for all spiritual qualities.

The Buddha's teachings are rooted in perfectly pure moral discipline. Just as the earth supports mountains, continents, and all living beings, moral discipline forms the foundation of all the supreme qualities born of eliminating [all veils] and realizing [all that is to be realized to attain enlightenment]. Guard this discipline like you would the apple of your eye.

If you damage your discipline and transgress the samayas, you have no other destination than samsara's lower realms. Know how to reject as poison every form of negative and unvirtuous action, large or small. Constantly control your mind stream with the help of mindfulness and vigilance, guarding yourself against any wrongdoing.

If you do not control your mind, the root of the Dharma will rot, and if the roots rot, even the mightiest tree can be toppled by the wind. Likewise, know that if your vows are damaged, the root of your Dharma will decay.

With your mind focused single pointedly, recognize that perfectly pure moral discipline is the foundation of all spiritual qualities.

To begin with, individuals who observe perfect discipline will be reborn in the higher realms of existence, never in the lower ones. Regard such discipline as a jeweled ladder that leads you to the higher destinies.

It is the same perfect discipline that takes you to the levels of liberation and ultimately to omniscience. Like riding an excellent horse, you will arrive in no time at your destination, no matter how distant.

If you keep your vows impeccably, the gods who abide on the side of virtue will protect you and the exalted beings will keep you in their thoughts. Therefore, guard your vows and precepts with sincerity and resolve.

–75–

Overcoming Adverse Circumstances

Six[98] ways of ensuring that antidotes triumph over adverse circumstances, [negative emotions]:
Repel [negative emotions] by considering them as enemies, like the listeners do.
Purify yourself of them completely by relying on the vehicle of the six perfections (the way of the bodhisattvas).
Transform them into the path through skillful means, as does the Secret Mantra.
Let them naturally subside through the most profound essential instructions.
Let them naturally dissolve in the state free of extremes.
Arrive at the clear conviction that there is no need to do anything about them.
No matter what method you adopt that suits your mental abilities,
The crucial point is to ensure that you do not let the enemy of negative emotions defeat you.

If your mind perfectly assimilates the supreme Dharma, the appropriate antidotes will always be ready to tame the "three poisons"—craving, hostility, and ignorance. These remedies will counteract the adverse effects of these poisons in six distinct ways.

As you embark on the path of the listeners and the solitary realizers, you will perceive afflictive mental states as adversaries. You will counteract desire with disgust, overcome animosity with benevolence, and dispel ignorance through an understanding of interdependence, both in its direct and reverse aspects, enabling you to conquer these three poisons.

As you progress in your training and develop the excellent attitude of benevolence according to the six transcendent perfections* of the Great Vehicle, you will understand that afflictive mental states are devoid of true existence, much like illusions and dreams. Understanding their true nature, you will purify them within emptiness.

Then, when you commit yourself to the Vajrayāna path of the Secret Mantra, you become like an expert doctor who can transmute a poison so that it no longer endangers life and may even enhance your health. As this example shows, the methods of the Secret Mantra allow you to transform mental poisons into the path itself, recognizing them as manifestations of primordial wisdom.

At the level of the fourth initiation, the deepest aspect of the Adamantine Vehicle of the Secret Mantra, afflictive mental states are liberated in their true nature, just as a knot in a snake's body spontaneously unties and ceases to constrain it.

Freed from all afflictive mental states that cling to the four extremes,[99] eternalism and nihilism in particular, appearances and meditative experiences will constantly arise as the play of primordial wisdom, and you will let them rest in their true nature, emptiness.

Ultimately, the very notions of afflictive mental states to be eliminated and antidotes to be deliberately applied disappear. You will forever transcend all effort, with striving resolved in the sphere of the four samayas* of the Great Perfection that are primordially kept: "one" [nature], "nonexistence," "spontaneous presence," and "all-embracing evenness."

Thus, according to your abilities, you can apply these six decisive resolutions and practice the great, the small, and the intermediate vehicle, according to what best suits your mental dispositions. The essential point is not to fall under the power of afflictive mental states or allow them to hinder you. In this way, these negative states of mind will no longer manifest as enemies but as allies.

–76–

Good Disciples

Six qualities of perfect students who are worthy recipients of Dharma teachings:
They are good-natured and possess a sense of shame and modesty.
They follow their teacher's words and have excellent faith and devotion.
They practice with great diligence, even at the cost of their bodies and lives.
They are loving and caring toward their fellow students and their minds are steeped in compassion.
They are tireless, patient, and helpful, bringing happiness to others.
Their three doors (body, speech, and mind) are pacified, and they uphold their samayas and vows.
Such fortunate beings are suitable receptacles for the nectar of Dharma.

To receive and follow the teachings of the supreme Dharma, you must be a fitting vessel, just as a snow lioness's milk can only be collected in a golden vessel, for ordinary ones would break under its potency. Similarly, if disciples are suited for the teachings, their minds will have the capacity to embrace both the vast and the profound aspects of the supreme Dharma.

As you pursue your Dharma practice, remember the words of the Kadampa masters [to teachers], "You may succeed in correcting the defects of your disciples, yet you may not be able to change their temperament." Keep this in mind. A good temperament enables you to live in harmony with everyone, remain humble, and maintain confidence in your spiritual guide. But disciples with negative dispositions may be easily led astray by deceitful and malicious individuals. They may follow the spiritual master like hunters going after a musk deer and take the Dharma as if it were musk. Reveling in their trophies, they will throw away their samayas.

Once you have received teachings and follow a spiritual master, if you commit negative acts, you should feel ashamed of yourself. You should also wonder what your spiritual masters and wisdom deities will think of you and feel embarrassed by how others might perceive you.

Whatever your spiritual guide instructs you to do, accomplish it tirelessly. If you develop an unwavering trust and devotion to the teachings received from your teacher, your practice will flourish continually.

Practicing in accordance with your teacher's instructions and behaving in accordance with the Dharma, whatever physical hardships and mental difficulties you may encounter, let go of attachment and fixations to your body and even your life, and you will practice wholeheartedly with courage and perseverance.

When you follow a master, you should be easy to live with, like a belt worn without discomfort. You should adapt easily to all situations, like salt that dissolves in any type of water. You should feel a mutual affection for your vajra brothers and sisters, your companions until enlightenment.

At all times, avoid focusing on selfish interests. Instead, infuse your mind with altruism and compassion, the best of all mental states, and persevere in cultivating the qualities of the Mahāyāna path.

No matter how difficult it may seem to listen to teachings, reflect on them and integrate them through meditation. Never tell yourself these practices are beyond your capacities. Ignore weariness, remain free from discouragement, and show fortitude. By doing so, be assured that you will first enjoy the well-being of humans and devas and ultimately reach the state of buddhahood naturally.

As it is said, "The sign of genuine study is mastery of the mind, and the sign of genuine meditation is freedom from negative emotions." You must therefore pacify your body, speech, and mind and behave in harmony with Dharma. By upholding the integrity of your vows and samayas, you will become a fortunate being, a worthy recipient of the ambrosia of Dharma and of the qualities that arise from abandoning [all defects] and realizing [all that is to be realized]. This is the proper way to practice.

–77–

Six Difficult-to-Find Freedoms

Six points to reflect upon concerning the freedoms that are':
Birth as a human being is not easy to achieve. Make efforts in Dharma now.
Meeting a spiritual master is difficult. Harvest the fruits of his positive qualities.

Encountering the Dharma is difficult. Practice it diligently.
The opportunity to hear teachings with profound meaning is not easy to find. Practice the essence of the oral transmission.
Cutting the flow of deceptive appearances is difficult to accomplish. Train your mind in the teachings of nonduality.
Gathering the perfect circumstances is not easy. When you have them, focus on practice.
These are the endeavors that bring happiness in this and future lives.

If you enjoy the freedom to practice the supreme Dharma, recognize its immense value and rarity. Appreciating how difficult it is to obtain, you will enhance your diligence to practice tenfold. Six considerations will help you in this process:

The precious human body is the support for practicing the supreme Dharma. But whether we consider it from the perspective of its causes, various analogies, or sheer probabilities,[100] obtaining such a vessel is exceedingly rare. Therefore, once it is yours, be diligent and fully focused on your spiritual practice.

Since the chance to follow a true master and to receive teachings across the three vehicles of the sublime Dharma is equally rare, do not remain idle during the day and do not sleep too long at night. Practice diligently!

Moreover, receiving the extraordinary and profound instructions repeatedly is quite difficult. Therefore, you should practice the essential oral instructions imparted by the spiritual master. Like clarified butter, these teachings represent the very essence of the Dharma, enabling you to interrupt the flow of deluded perceptions and avoid any form of deviation. This is not an easy task. Seize this opportunity to diligently train yourself in uniting emptiness—in which skillful means and wisdom have merged—with compassion.

Favorable circumstances—enjoying a human existence, meeting a spiritual master and the supreme Dharma, and taking full monastic vows—are not easily obtained. So, when you have them, do not waste your time. Instead, persevere properly in Dharma practice, the best thing you can do to secure happiness in this life and to go from bliss to bliss in future lives.

–78–

Six Points for Beginners

Six important points for those embarking on the path of Dharma:
You have many lives ahead of you, hence generosity is important.
Moral discipline is the ladder that leads to higher realms of existence, hence its importance.
Wearing the armor and weapon of patience is important for endurance.
Perseverance is the source of all qualities, hence its importance.
Meditative concentration allows you to be undistracted from its object, hence its importance.
Wisdom enables you to spontaneously accomplish the [two] benefits, hence its importance.
Those who practice these important points will quickly travel the path to liberation.

When embarking on the path of Dharma, six essential points must be considered:

Future lives span a far greater duration than your present existence. To ensure material comfort in these future existences, use whatever resources you possess now—no matter their size—for acts of generosity and offerings.

You cannot ascend to the upper floors of a beautiful house without a staircase. Likewise, if you wish to be reborn into the relatively happy modes of existence of humans and gods, the proper staircase to climb is observing the moral discipline associated with the vows of prātimokṣa, bodhicitta, and the Secret Mantra.

In your Dharma practice, you will face difficulties, fatigue, weariness, and discouragement. Bear these with fortitude. It is crucial not to be overwhelmed by physical or mental afflictions but to show resilience.

Diligence in study, reflection, and meditation is the source of all spiritual qualities, hence the importance of perseverance.

Once this perseverance is in place, to practice with a perfectly focused mind you need to maintain an unwavering concentration, not letting the mind drift into excitement or dullness. Sustain attentive presence and alertness at all times.

The root of this guidance is wisdom born from listening, reflection, and meditation, which teaches to overcome obstacles on the paths and bhūmis. All the qualities of the spiritual path will manifest in your mind and you will understand the essential instructions given by your teacher. Wisdom is the root of the accomplishment of the double goal of self and others. Hence its great importance.

Keeping these six important points constantly in mind, you will quickly travel the path to liberation and buddhahood.

–79–

Negative Consequences for Those Who Fail to Practice the Pāramitās

Six negative consequences for those who fail to undertake the following points:
The world of tortured spirits awaits those who do not practice generosity.
The animal kingdom awaits those who do not observe moral discipline.
The hell realms await those who do not practice patience.
The abyss of the states deprived of freedom awaits those who do not practice diligence.
The hordes of the four demons[101] await those who do not train in meditative concentration.
Samsara always awaits those who do not cultivate wisdom.
These consequences await them and they are likely to succumb.

Six misfortunes that await those who lack the important qualities (related to the six *pāramitās*):

If you do not give away your possessions and wealth in this life in a well-chosen manner, you will likely find yourself reborn among the pretas—the spirits tortured by insatiable need. Their realm is closer than you might think, and will be your next destination.

Once you have properly received the vows of individual liberation, bodhisattvas, and the Secret Mantra, if you transgress them, the animal kingdom awaits you in your next life.

Frequent outbursts of hatred lead to rebirth in the underworld. Without cultivating patience, the infernal realms will lie in your path.

If hatred frequently overcomes you, this is the unmistaken cause of rebirth in the underworld. Therefore, unless you cultivate patience, the infernal realms lie in your path.

If you do not engage in Dharma practice with joyful enthusiasm, you risk falling in the eight abysses of places deprived of freedom and favorable conditions. These states are contrary to the freedoms and conditions needed for practicing Dharma. Moreover, you do not even know in which place you will end up.

If you do not practice the concentration that combines calm abiding with deeper insight, the four classes of demons (*māras**) lie in ambush: the demons of the kleśas, the eighty-four thousand afflictive mental states; the demons of the aggregates tainted by ignorance who magnetize suffering and support karma and negative mental states; the demon of death, who is bound to strike you; and the demons called *devaputras*, "sons of the gods," who appear as soon as you are distracted by sense pleasures. The hordes of these four māras await and you will fall into their hands.

Unless you genuinely cultivate wisdom through listening, reflection, and meditation, you will not only fail to attain the realm of unchanging bliss by practicing as taught in the tradition, but will keep wandering in a predictably endless samsara, the state of conditioned existence.

Thus, the enemies of the six perfections are lurking nearby: avoid falling into their power and being stained by the flaws just described.

–80–

Six Endeavors of No Interest

Six irrelevant things for those whose mind stream is imbued with the profound teachings:
There is no need to retreat into solitude if your positive qualities are flourishing wherever you are.
There is no need to abandon samsara if your conceptual thoughts naturally liberate in their own place.
There is no need to care about other people's opinions if you are careful in your behavior.

There is no need to read the scriptures if you realize mind's natural simplicity.
There is no need to give up attachment if you realize that all appearance is illusory.
There is no need to seek buddhahood if you realize the true face of the fundamental nature.
Those with these qualities are truly sublime beings.

When you integrate in your mind the essential and profound instructions of the supreme Dharma, six things become unnecessary:

Whether you live in the country, reside in a monastery, or retire to a mountain retreat, if your virtuous practices are flourishing in an excellent way, you need not confine yourself to the solitude of a hermitage.

If all your deluded thoughts are liberated by themselves, you will no longer be under their control. Whether you call this "abandoning samsara" or something else, is of little importance.

Once you have trained your mind to be alert and watchful, you are protected from any misconduct caused by carelessness. Regardless of others' poor opinions or criticisms, and whether or not you agree with them, you have no reason to be ashamed or concerned about their judgment.

If you rest in the pristine simplicity of the nature of mind, this is the dharmakāya, the absolute body of buddhahood. Having realized this, you do not need to further consult any scripture. As said, "Once you have realized the nature of mind, the ultimate point of the Dharma, you can leave the books where they are" and you need not read them anymore.

Whatever perceptions you have of the six aspects of consciousness, by seeing them as illusions, as dreams, you will neither covet what you considered to be "good" nor dislike the "bad" and will worry anymore about discarding fixations.

If you recognize for yourself the natural and fundamental simplicity of mind, it is none other than the buddha nature, tathāgatagarbha, or dharmatā, the ultimate nature of reality. Since this is buddhahood itself, what is the point of looking for an imaginary buddhahood elsewhere or in some distant future?

Embodying these six kinds of simplicity, free from fabrication, you are truly noble among beings.

–81–

Supports of the Practice

Six supreme supports in your Dharma practice:
Honor the spiritual master and the Three Jewels as the supreme objects of veneration.
Give up the activities of this life as the supreme generosity.
Rely on faith, listening, and contemplation as the supreme wealth.
Recognize the true face of the nature of mind as your supreme friend.
Sever the attachment of selfish grasping as the supreme bodhicitta.
Seeing the spiritual master as the Buddha in person is the supreme sign of accomplishment.
With these six supports, you will spontaneously accomplish the two purposes.

Six factors serve as extraordinary allies for those who practice the supreme Dharma:

Do not honor just anyone. With firm faith, pray to the spiritual master and the Three Jewels, the supreme objects of veneration, and they will help you close the door to rebirths in the lower realms and plant the seed of liberation. Honor them at all times and place them reverently upon your crown.

The ultimate generosity is to let go of your grip on the eight worldly concerns. As it is said, "If you free yourself from self-clinging, there is no greater transcendent generosity." In accordance with these words, abandon all worldly pursuits centered on this life. As for the supreme wealth, it lies in the seven riches* of the noble beings, which include listening to the teachings and reflecting on their meaning, and cultivating faith as an aspiration and faith as a conviction, through which the qualities of the path of noble beings will manifest. In contrast, gold, silver, and other ordinary riches that you may accumulate only create bonds that hinder your progress.

Your closest and most loving friend is the fundamental nature of your mind. By recognizing it and understanding the key points of its natural simplicity, whatever you do, you will remain in bliss and enjoy a spacious, perfectly at ease mind. Apprehending this nature of mind is essential.

Where does bodhicitta come from? From the aspiration to attain enlightenment in order to benefit sentient beings. It also implies severing the ties of egocentric attachment and self-cherishing, while nurturing the remarkable altruistic attitude, which indicates the presence of bodhicitta in your mind, something to honor sincerely.

Signs of accomplishment can take many forms, such as flying through space or leaving footprints in rocks, which are also displayed by non-Buddhist tīrthikas. But the true hallmark of supreme accomplishment is the birth in your mind of an uncommon confidence in your spiritual teacher, seeing him as the Buddha himself.

With this supreme sign, you will naturally achieve the dual goal: the benefit of others and yourself.

–82–

Six Inappropriate Actions

Six negative actions to be given up:
Avoid scolding and denigrating people since you do not know their level of realization.
Do not hurt the faithful by living off the gains of wrong livelihood.
Do not engage in careless, crude, or unruly behavior.
Do not be dismissive of others or denigrate them for fear of being outdone.[102]
Do not abandon the sublime Dharma for food and clothing.
Do not disregard the profound interdependence of cause and effect.
If you give up such conduct, you will become a noble person.

Six types of behavior contrary to the Dharma that must be avoided:

Unless you are gifted with clairvoyance and the ability to objectively assess others impartially, it is improper to judge people as good or bad. As the Buddha himself said, "Except for those who, like me, have attained enlightenment, it is inappropriate for an ordinary person to judge others." Therefore, criticizing and disparaging others is a grave fault.

Do not upset the faithful by resorting to unsuitable ways of living, soliciting gains and honors, or burdening other with all kinds of demands.

If you claim to have realized the view when you have not and indulge in various foolish acts, such as drinking to excess, you are belittling the Buddha's teachings. Therefore, avoid behaving recklessly like a madman.

All beings, even dogs and insects, possess the buddha nature, the necessary basis for attaining enlightenment. Therefore, it is vital to respect them and never despise any of them. Even if others' qualities seem inferior to yours, do not belittle them out of fear they might surpass you.

Lacking food and clothing is not a reason to abandon your Dharma practice. If you were to forsake the Dharma, what good would there be in obtaining all that you need?

Concerning the laws of causality, it is said, "Even if your view is higher than the sky, your observance of the laws of cause and effect must be as fine as flour." These laws are unfailing; hence, conscientiously avoid every negative action and accomplish every positive action, even the smallest.

By eradicating these six mistakes, you will become a truly noble being.

–83–

Six Recommended Activities for a Practitioner

Six activities for Dharma practitioners:
Keep your spiritual master, meditation deity, and ḍākinī on the crown of your head.
Transform the virtue of your three doors into a path to enlightenment.
Entirely cast out self-grasping and fixation on phenomena as truly existent and permanent.
Vanquish thoughts focused on this particular life whenever they arise.
With the antidotes, uproot the five poisonous disturbing emotions triggered by certain objects.
Enrich your mind with a wealth of listening, contemplation, and meditation.
These activities will bring perfection for oneself and others.

Six kinds of activities of body, speech, and mind required for Dharma practitioners:

The spiritual master is the root of blessings; the yidam is the root of accomplishments; and the ḍākinīs, alongside the Dharma protectors, are the roots of enlightened action. Therefore, with deep reverence, visualize them above the crown of your head, make offerings, and focus your prayers, recitations, and spiritual practice upon them.

Whatever virtuous activities you undertake with your body, speech, and mind, do not regard them as solely for your personal benefit. Instead, consistently uphold the excellent altruistic attitude, infusing your thoughts, words and actions with the resolve to serve others. In this way, everything you do will contribute to your progress on the path of enlightenment.

Ignorance of death and the transient nature of all things leads to the mistaken belief in a self, which in reality does not exist. Having frozen this notion in your mind, you cling to the permanence of phenomenal appearances and crave pleasures, comfort, and fame. If you could let go of such concepts entirely, your interest in Dharma would blossom spontaneously.

If your aspirations for this life center on seeking fame and greatness, you will be drawn into countless activities and will keep postponing going into retreat. Do not fall prey to such thoughts and suppress them the moment they arise.[103]

When one of the five mental toxins surges in your mind, if it is animosity, meditate on patience; if it is desire, meditate on the repulsive aspects of the object of attraction; if it is a lack of discernment, contemplate the links of dependent arising, both in their order of appearance and in reverse order; if it is jealousy, rejoice in the [virtuous] deeds of others as well as your own; [and if it is pride, meditate on humility]. Thus, without letting these afflictive mental states develop, sever them at the root to prevent them from growing again.

What you really need is the wealth accrued through listening, reflecting, and meditating. Gather this as best you can, and even if you do not become highly learned in this life, sincere study will ensure rebirth as a scholar. As you develop the qualities of reflection and meditation, you will distance yourself from samsara. Practitioners who hold the wealth of study, reflection, and meditation in their minds will excel in benefiting both themselves and others. Be diligent in your practice.

–84–

Six Imperatives

Six imperatives at the time of practicing Dharma:
Death is swift and inevitable: give up non-Dharmic activities.
You are never far from falling into indolence: avoid procrastination.
Diligence is vulnerable to circumstances: use antidotes.
Faith and respect are easily diminished: avoid taking things for granted because of being overly familiar [with the spiritual master].
Deceptive appearances are difficult to cut through: recognize the lack of true existence of phenomena.
Bad habits are contagious: avoid the company of ill-mannered people.

Those who undertake Dharma practice need six allies:

You and all beings are guaranteed to die, perhaps sooner than anticipated. Keep this in mind so that the awareness of impermanence becomes deeply rooted within you, compelling you to practice Dharma. Therefore, constantly remind yourself of the transient nature of everything and repel as enemies every action, word, and thought that runs counter to the Dharma.

Even if you feel neither strong attachment to loved ones nor hostility toward others, do not succumb to indifference or stagnate in an apathy that inclines neither toward virtue nor nonvirtue, content merely with indolently eating and sleeping. Cast off such lethargy, as it will not bring you any spiritual qualities.

Consider what hinders the blossoming of consummate diligence in your mind. Distractions, overactivity, and the taste for secular entertainment, like singing, dancing, and music. Show restraint and cultivate the antidote of disenchantment toward those diversions.

Even if you hold respectful trust in your spiritual master and the Three Jewels, this trust can easily be swept away by circumstances. Sometimes, after becoming familiar with the teachings you have received, you may grow jaded, thinking that having heard so many teachings, what you hear now is of little importance. You have also met many teachers, but instead of developing confidence, you find faults in them and have no faith or respect. Guard against these attitudes.

It is very difficult to sever the root of clinging to the deceptive perceptions of the ordinary world, built on the duality of subject and object. Develop the perfect view that sees phenomena as being devoid of intrinsic existence.

If you keep bad company, contaminated by distraction and busyness, you may indulge in drink and lust, or even in taking lives, thus engaging in all kinds of reprehensible actions. Avoid the company of those who conduct themselves in a vile manner.

–85–

Entering the Gate of Buddhism

Six ways to take refuge that make you a Buddhist:
Take refuge in the Buddha in order to accomplish the three kāyas.
Take refuge in the Dharma of the three vehicles as the path.
Take refuge in the listeners, solitary realizers, and bodhisattvas as companions on the path.
Take refuge in the learned and accomplished masters as the objects to rely upon.
Take refuge in the assembly of wisdom deities, the [root of] siddhis.
Take refuge in the wisdom ḍākinīs, the [root of] blessings.
These are important for undertaking the preliminary practices.

In order to follow the path of Buddhism, you must take refuge in six ways:

The three kāyas of the Buddha constitute the ultimate refuge: the dharmakāya, the absolute body, is the ultimate nature of the mind; the saṃbhogakāya, the body of perfect enjoyment, is endowed with ten powers, four fearlessnesses, eighteen distinct qualities, thirty-two major signs, and eighty minor marks; while the nirmāṇakāya, the body of manifestation, is the source of benefit and happiness for all beings.

If you learn how to accomplish the level of the three Buddha bodies, you will understand that they are fully present in the buddha nature, the tathāgatagarbha, which innately abides in you. At present, this nature is veiled [by ignorance]. Take refuge in the three kāyas of the Buddha, and through their transformative power you will recognize that the primordial nature of the vajra-like refuge is present within you. These three bodies represent the ultimate accomplishment that you can achieve.

If you want to go to India, for example, on the way you will pass through many countries without losing sight of your ultimate destination. Likewise, when you apply yourself to practicing the supreme Dharma, the ultimate destination you should fervently keep in mind is accomplishing the three kāyas of the Buddha.

Without firm perseverance on the path of the three vehicles—of the listeners, the solitary realizers, and the bodhisattvas—you cannot reach buddhahood. Just as you complete a long journey step by step, through study, reflection, and meditation you must continuously engage in study, reflection, and meditation, assimilating the insights of both the scriptural Dharma and the Dharma of realization through the three trainings.

When you travel far away, without an escort or other support, you risk falling prey to enemies, thieves, or the four natural elements. Likewise, on the path to enlightenment, you should regard the sangha, the virtuous community of the vehicle of listeners, and the sangha of the Mahāyāna, the bodhisattvas, as your companions, your brothers and sisters. With unwavering loving-kindness, take refuge in them.

A spiritually accomplished and learned master imparts the extraordinary instructions on taking refuge in the Three Jewels. Through receiving these instructions, the master's qualities will be transferred to you. Therefore, you should also take refuge in the spiritual master who appears in the form of a manifested body, the nirmāṇakāya.

When a master gives you an empowerment, he manifests himself as the infinite number of peaceful and wrathful wisdom deities. By relying on these deities, you will obtain the common siddhis, or accomplishments, and the extraordinary one. Thus, practicing the "approach" and the "accomplishment" stages,[104] take refuge in your tutelary deity.

If you aspire to generate in your mind the qualities of the Secret Mantra pertaining to the Vajrayāna, the Adamantine Vehicle, unless you rely on the support of the ḍākas and ḍākinīs, you will fail. Take refuge in them and their blessings and enlightened activities will swiftly manifest.

Refuge is thus the indispensable preliminary and initial point of entry on the path, the gateway to Buddhism. Without knowing its significance, one cannot truly be a Buddhist. Therefore, prepare for the Dharma with deep faith and confidence in this foundational practice.

–86–

What Needs to Be Recognized

Devoted practitioners should recognize six points:
Aware that you will have to depart, practice Dharma for your own sake.
Aware that you will leave everything behind, discard attachment to delusive appearances.
Aware that you need to listen, receive instructions from a master.
Aware of what you must give up, abandon the negative actions of the three doors.
Aware that you must engage [in Dharma], practice the profound teachings.
Aware that you must recognize the view, observe the nature of your mind.
Acting in this way, you come closer to the ultimate meaning.

If you take refuge in the Three Jewels from the bottom of your heart and with complete confidence, it is crucial to recognize six defects and as many qualities:

First, understand that once born, all beings, including yourself, wander endlessly through the three worlds of samsara, unable to escape death. While you are free from physical illness and mental torments, seize this precious opportunity to practice Dharma as much as you can, thus achieving your own good.

When death comes, you will have to leave behind the joys and happiness of this life, your possessions and wealth, your relatives and friends, even your own body, departing alone like a hair pulled from a lump of butter. Nothing lasts indeed.

Knowing that you will have to abandon everything, discard all attachment and clinging to the deceptive appearances of this life's affairs as you would dispose of trash.

When you listen to the supreme Dharma correctly, even a single stanza of teaching, know that the master's words are all profound instructions. Having thus identified the path of liberation, welcome your master's instructions with full attention.

After hearing the teachings, it is essential to put them into practice, for they offer you the means to eliminate all negativity and delusion associated with your body, speech, and mind. No matter how great your negative actions may be, they are merely compounded phenomena, none of which are indestructible. Aware that you must free yourself from them, give up all negative conduct, in deeds, words, and thoughts.

To practice Dharma properly, you must cultivate perfect attention and vigilance. In all your practices, strive to grasp the deeper meaning directly—the ultimate essence of the eighty-four thousand teachings of the Dharma.

Recognizing the view, the true way of being of all things, you will recognize the fundamental nature of your mind, free from fabrications. Emancipated from delusion, contemplate this nature.

Proceeding in this way, rest assured that you are drawing closer to the ultimate meaning of the authentic path to liberation. Be diligent!

–87–

Become Familiar with Six Key Points

Six vital points with which fortunate beings must become familiar:
As the fundamental nature is beyond action, the key point is the absence of elaborations.
As meditation is total lucidity, the key point is the absence of distraction.
As conduct is illusory, the key point is phenomena's lack of true existence.
As the fruition is spontaneously accomplished, the key point is its natural presence.
As adverse circumstances are naturally liberated, the key point is nongrasping.
Since happiness and suffering are the work of your mind, the key point is to train your mind.
Those who hold these crucial points will achieve all their goals while remaining in nonaction.

Fortunate beings who follow a spiritual master and are diligent in the Dharma should familiarize themselves with six key points:

The fundamental nature of phenomena is emptiness. It is originally present in you like oil in sesame seeds, without the need for external causes and conditions. Therefore, feverish activity is unnecessary. Simply allow everything to rest in its fundamental nature, free of elaborations.

If you directly realize the meaning of emptiness as it is, your meditation will become perfectly clear and lucid, free from the amorphous fog of ignorance and the nebulous stupor that characterizes the concentration of the gods at the peak of samsara.[105] Therefore, with vigilance and undivided focus, contemplate the fundamental nature free of action. In doing so, you will recognize the face of luminosity and understand that all phenomena arise from it, unobscured—this is the key point.

Whatever actions you undertake, good or bad, whether you make generous donations and offerings or perform any other positive activity, know them to be like dreams and illusions. The object of your virtuous actions has no real existence, so self-satisfaction is irrelevant. Whatever your deeds, words, and thoughts, and the joys and sufferings associated with them, recognize their illusory and dreamlike nature and do not cling to them.

The ultimate fruition of view, meditation, and action is buddhahood, which is spontaneously present in your mind and does not need to be obtained as something new. Recognize the key point of the primordial presence of such fruition within you.

The objects of your virtuous actions have no inherent existence. In all your deeds, words, and thoughts, as well as the associated joys and sufferings, recognize their illusory, dreamlike nature and avoid clinging to them.

The ultimate fruition of view, meditation, and action is buddhahood, which is already spontaneously present within your mind and does not need to be acquired anew. Recognize the key point that this fruition has been primordially present within you all along.

Whatever good or bad circumstances you encounter, when met with proper antidotes, will naturally unravel, like a snake untangling its own knots. Thus, adverse circumstances will not become obstacles. Conversely, you fall into delusion by believing that these adverse circumstances have an existence of their own. If you know how to apply the key point of nongrasping, you will bring adverse circumstances onto the path, turning them into your allies.

All your joys and sufferings are merely manifestations of your mind. If you dreamed last night that you inherited a kingdom, you will wake up empty-handed. And if you dreamed that an enemy was about to kill you, on waking you will be safe and sound. In the same way, all your happiness and misfortunes are mere products of the mind: you imagine that they really exist when they do not. The key point is to know how to use all joys and sorrows to progress in your spiritual practice.

In doing so, you will spontaneously and effortlessly accomplish your own benefit as well as the benefit of others, discreetly, without seeking any notoriety, all while remaining discreet and without seeking recognition.

–88–

Judicious Advice

Six sensible pieces of advice to yourself:
Lifespan being uncertain, it makes sense to be diligent.
Samsara being nothing but suffering, it makes sense to feel sad about it.
Considering the beings of the six realms, it makes sense to care for them with immeasurable compassion.
It is appropriate to develop unceasing devotion and respect for the spiritual master.
It is wise to put the profound instructions into practice.
When you realize the nature of the mind, it makes sense to stay in solitary places.
Those who follow these wise pieces of advice are supreme practitioners.

Some logical reasoning will provide you with valuable insights and spur you to action:

As for your ordinary plans, given the inevitability of death and the unpredictability of its circumstances, it is only wise to dedicate yourself wholeheartedly to study, reflection, and meditation, without squandering even a single hour or moment.

All the activities and tribulations of samsara are inherently infused with suffering, either as the legacy of past actions or as seeds for future torments. It is logical, therefore, to feel nothing but weariness and disgust toward the various activities and features of samsara.

Contemplate the suffering endured by sentient beings across the six realms of samsara: the extreme heat and cold of the hells, the torment of thirst and hunger among tortured spirits, the bondage of animals, the pain of birth, aging, sickness, and death in the human realm, the conflicts of demigods, and the ultimate fall of gods. All these beings, who suffer constantly, have been your parents in former lives. It is only right to care for them with a compassion that never turns a blind eye to their grievous suffering.

Feeling respectful fervor for your spiritual master only once and for a fleeting moment is insufficient, as is having devotion when all goes well and losing it when suffering or other adversities arise. Your ardent devotion must be uninterrupted, like the flow of a river, keeping the presence of your master vividly in your thoughts continuously—whether in activity, stillness, or rest—invoking him or her from the depths of your heart.

A momentary feeling of respect for your spiritual master is insufficient, as is devotion that wavers with the tides of fortune and adversity. Your devotion must be unbroken, like the flow of a river, keeping the presence of your master vividly in your thoughts at all times, invoking them from the depths of your heart.

After receiving many profound instructions from your teacher, what sense does it make to leave them confined to the pages of books? It is far more meaningful to integrate them into your mind stream and persevere in your practice until you experience the warmth.

Thanks to your master's kind guidance, you may have glimpsed the nature of ultimate reality, but a mere recognition is not enough: you must refine your experience until it reaches perfect stability. To achieve this, dedicating yourself fully to practice in the solitude of a mountain hermitage is a wise step.

These six insights embody sound logic, and by following them, you can become a spiritually noble being, endowed with the abilities and good fortune essential for practicing the path of the supreme vehicle.

–89–

The Principles of the Various Vehicles

Six main points to know, summarizing the various vehicles of teaching:
You should know the defects of negative emotions as ordinarily experienced.

You should know that abandoning afflictive negative emotions is the particular way of the listeners and solitary realizers.
You should know that purifying them is the particular way of the bodhisattvas.
You should know that transforming them is the particular way of the Secret Mantra.
You should fully realize the nature of these negative emotions through self-arisen primordial wisdom.
You should know that you do not need to search for [antidotes] to be liberated from acceptance and rejection.
If you know all these points, you will not be stained by negative emotions.

To understand the teachings, you must know six key principles that encapsulate the practices across the various vehicles.

You can neutralize the five mental poisons or transform them on the path, but if you leave them unchecked in their ordinary state, be aware that even a minute dose of poison, as small as a sesame seed can take your life. Afflictive mental states, or negative emotions, the root of all defects, are the very foundation of the three worlds of samsara. Therefore, consider them as your foes.

On the path of the listeners and solitary realizers, afflictive mental states are confronted with antidotes, treated as enemies to be vanquished on the battlefield of the mind. This approach, specific to the Fundamental Vehicle, is vital for those new to the practice.

For those following the way of the bodhisattvas, the spiritual heirs of the buddhas, afflictive mental states are purified into emptiness, their true nature. These states are recognized as mere illusions, appearing real only because we attribute inherent existence to our deluded perceptions. In reality, they are entirely devoid of such intrinsic existence. This understanding allows these hindrances to dissolve naturally into their true nature. To perceive all phenomena and beings as illusory and dreamlike is the way of the bodhisattva.

Just as poison can be detoxified through medicinal substances or powerful mantras and its essence used to foster health and vitality, in the Vajrayāna tradition of the Secret Mantra, one can learn to take afflictive mental states onto the path and turn poison into medicine.

If you accurately and perfectly recognize the nature of the five mental poisons, you will understand that their fundamental nature is none other than the five wisdoms associated with the five buddha families.[106] These wisdoms do not result from the application of antidotes or from a process of transformation similar to dyeing a piece of cloth but arise primordially by themselves.

When you gain perfect confidence in your ability to transmute afflictive mental states into their respective primordial wisdoms, you no longer need to strive incessantly to achieve the positive and to avoid the negative. You will know how to perfect the path effortlessly.

By understanding and applying these various methods—initially viewing mental poisons as enemies, then applying antidotes, and eventually transforming them, using the various methods offered along the gradual path—practitioners can engage appropriately with afflictive mental states in a way that is attuned to their evolving capacities, ensuring they remain uninfluenced and untainted by these poisons.

–90–

Six Wishes and Analogies

Six types of aspirations Dharma practitioners should have:
The wish to know the true colors of samsara should be like investigating the faults of an evil person.
The wish to flee samsara should be like the soldiers of a routed army.
The wish not to get caught again should be like a fox that has escaped from a trap.
The wish to escape samsara should be like a servant who longs to be free from a cruel master.
The fear of wandering in samsara should be like a traveler who seeks the right path after having gone astray.
The wish to free yourself from samsara should be like ice melting into water.

Dharma practitioners should cultivate six attitudes:

The three worlds of samsara are filled with suffering and any samsaric activity is inevitably tainted with hidden defects and vices. These defects must be exposed, much like revealing the ignominy, greed, and aggression of wicked people, thus unearthing their deepest flaws.

You must escape the evils of these three worlds of samsara, as a soldier from a defeated army who runs away, avoids detection, and persevering through every hardship, marching day and night without rest, distances himself as far as possible.

Once you have set forth on the path of liberation, you must never turn back, like a fox who, after narrowly escaping from a snare, will cautiously avoid the noose of any other trap he may encounter on his way.

If you have the opportunity to abandon samsara, you must act with the same urgent resolve as the servant of a tyrannical master who has suffered many punishments and wonders anxiously when he will succeed to free himself. Likewise, ask yourself with dread when you will succeed in emancipating yourself from samsara.

The fear of getting lost here refers to the dread of drifting away in meaningless distraction or harmful behavior. Devious individuals who behave inappropriately will follow improper paths and whatever activities they undertake will reflect wrong ways of life. Be alert to this.

Constantly ask yourself, "When shall I be able to free myself from the suffering of samsara's three worlds?" Wish for this liberation to occur as naturally as chunks of ice melting in the warmth of spring, regardless of their size.

–91–

Uniting Dharma and Your Mind

Six mental attitudes that lead your mind into Dharma:
After studying, adhere to the teachings like a bee to nectar.
Contemplate them as though you were searching for gold among earth and rocks.
Obtain a realization of the teachings as though you were receiving a gold coin in your hand.
Become familiar [with such realization] as though you were polishing that gold coin.
Develop inner qualities as though you were turning that gold into ornaments.
Actualize the result as though you were fulfilling all of your aspirations.

If you strive to assimilate the supreme Dharma and blend it into your mind stream, six attitudes will help you:

Lest you forget the spiritual qualities of the supreme Dharma that you have listened to and reflected upon, train your mind to fully absorb the teachings, like a foraging bee drawn by the sweetness of nectar tirelessly returns to gather more.

Aspiring to practice the Dharma and generate the qualities of abandonment [of the obscurations that need to be removed] and realization [of all that is to be apprehended], you must be like a gold miner who searches for the precious metal in a deposit and digs day and night in spite of all difficulties, fatigue, cold, and hunger. Working with equal determination to study, reflect, and meditate upon the teachings of the supreme Dharma is quite fitting.

Realizing the meaning and key points of the view, meditation, and action of the Dharma is like mining a large quantity of gold and holding in your hands a chest brimming with nuggets, giving you full confidence that you will not be left destitute.

Constantly strengthen your conviction in the teachings you have received. For this, you must not only assiduously familiarize yourself with the Dharma but also keep it faithfully in mind, just as a beautiful young woman makes up her face before going out, even for a short time, and is always conscious of her appearance.

Just as the same young woman adorns herself with her finest and most precious jewels, you too should strive to enhance the spiritual qualities derived from study, reflection, and meditation. Among these qualities, give special emphasis to those that are most essential.

Once these qualities are fully actualized, they are worthy of being placed atop your head like a tiara adorned with the wish-fulfilling gem. This is what you must cultivate.

–92–

Six Alliances

Six combinations related to the Mahāyāna teachings (required for practitioners):

To destroy your grasping to the reality of things, you must combine the view with your experience.

To overcome your laziness, you must combine faith and perseverance.
To protect yourself from drifting into the lesser vehicles, you must combine skillful means with wisdom.
To root out animosity, you must acknowledge your faults, as well as recognize the qualities of others.
To tread the path of exalted beings, you must combine respectful devotion with tenacity.
To avoid straying from the path, you must combine study and practice.
These combinations are imperative yet rarely found.

Within the teachings of the Great Vehicle, six important connections should be established:

To dissolve the belief in the solid reality of the ordinary things of this life concerning yourself and others, adopt the view of the Middle Way, which is free from the conceptual extremes of existence and nonexistence. This will naturally lead to a direct realization of emptiness within your mind.

If you feel the need to shake off the indolence that keeps you entangled in worldly affairs centered on this life's interests, apply unwavering diligence—day and night—uniting your confidence in the Dharma with the path of liberation.

The method to avoid straying into the lesser vehicle of the listeners and solitary realizers, whose aim is only personal peace and happiness, is to seamlessly unite the skillful means of great compassion with the wisdom of emptiness.

To eradicate all hostility from your mind stream, among all the practical applications of mind training, implement the one that repeatedly proclaims the smallest of your own faults while granting others the benefit of the doubt, even when you perceive their shortcomings. By allowing others to take the victory, you will naturally cultivate patience.

To gradually ascend the steps of the path trodden by exalted beings, unite respectful fervor with tenacious perseverance. These two qualities are like the wings that enable a bird to soar through the skies.

To perfectly accomplish the path of liberation, overcome interruptions and prevent any conceivable deviations by combining exhaustive study of the teachings with direct experience of the practice. Reflection will help you to assimilate the meaning of view, meditation, and action.

These six connections are highly necessary, yet it is rare for individuals to fully integrate them into their mind stream.

–93–

Six Insurpassables Instructions

Six unsurpassable instructions:
"No learning" surpasses understanding the fundamental nature.
No reflection is better than the one that cuts [ignorance] at the root.[107]
No skill is greater than actualizing primordial wisdom.
No blessing is greater than turning your mind to Dharma.
No accomplishment is greater than realizing the unborn and undying nature of things.
No inner confidence is greater than realizing that there is nothing to achieve.
If you master all this, buddhahood will arise from within.

If you bring your inner confidence about the view and the conduct to its consummate point, you do not need anything else. Here are six instructions on this point:

Understanding emptiness as the fundamental nature of all phenomena is the highest form of study and reflection, while cutting delusion at its root is the supreme form of contemplation.

The most effective way to practice the Secret Mantra path of skillful means is to realize the true nature of things, allowing the fundamental nature of primordial wisdom to manifest in your mind in its unaltered simplicity.

The best way to receive the blessings of your spiritual master is to bring your body, speech, and mind as close as possible to the Dharma, as you would steer a horse with a bit and reins.

No ordinary or extraordinary achievement surpasses realizing the nature of absolute space, the Dharmadhātu. By recognizing that buddhahood is perfectly present in your mind, you will gain unsurpassed confidence in understanding that nothing truly needs to be attained and that buddhahood is not to be sought externally but realized within.

–94–

Six Undesirable Influences

Six states of freedom needed to accomplish spiritual practice:
Not to fall under the influence of friends because of emotional attachment;
Not to fall under the influence of flattery and good food;
Not to fall under the influence of socializing and distraction;
Not to fall under the influence of your relatives out of affection;
Not to fall under the influence of instructors who train you in arts and crafts.[108]
Not to fall under the influence of accumulating wealth and possessions.
Practitioners free of these six influences will successfully accomplish Dharma practice.

If you aspire to bring your Dharma practice to its ultimate point, you must avoid succumbing to six obstacles and deviations:

If you seek the company of many friends and do everything to gain their approval, your Dharma practice will drift away and be neglected. Therefore, do not come under the influence of others.

If people praise you as knowledgeable, accomplished, clairvoyant, and showing signs of achievement, be careful not to succumb to such flattery and take yourself too seriously, seeking respect and favor from others.

If you live in a mountain retreat, stay alone like a wounded animal in hiding. Meeting acquaintances and old friends make you fall prey to distraction and busyness. Avoid this!

Fostering strong emotional bonds with your kin can entangle you in endless activities to care for and protect them. Do not be trapped in such a situation.[109]

If you wish to diligently practice a perfectly pure Dharma, seek out a qualified spiritual master rather than dispersing your efforts in learning various forms of crafts, such as sacred painting or carving. Otherwise, worldly activities will carry you away.

If you enjoy some wealth and possessions, use them to make offerings and donations. Accumulating personal riches only sows the seed for rebirth as a tortured spirit, a spirit tormented by insatiable need. Avoid succumbing to this kind of influence.

By freeing yourself from these six kinds of influence, you will be able to travel the path of Dharma to its ultimate destination.

–95–

Six Defects of Character

Six character flaws should be abandoned after examining yourself:
You are constantly upset, you denigrate others, and your five poisonous emotions are blatant.
You are gullible, fickle, and unstable.
You enjoy engaging in frivolous activities and associating with others.
You are boorish, stubborn, and difficult to encourage.
You are a sycophant, always thirsty for something new, and procrastinate in your practice.
You are deceitful, dishonest, and vindictive.
Those who want to practice the supreme Dharma need to examine their faults and qualities and then abandon the former.

To encourage themselves to practice the Dharma, disciples must cultivate good character and avoid six flaws. Constantly ask yourself if these faults are affecting you. If they do, seek out the appropriate antidote and apply it.

Constantly embroiled in disputes, you are never at peace and keep unsettling your own mind. Engaging in incessant criticism of others and highlighting their faults prevents you from having pure vision. Such afflictive and poisonous mental states will only proliferate and grow more powerful.

You constantly busy yourself with all sorts of activities. Restless as a monkey that never stops moving, your thoughts scatter in all directions. Afflicted with an overflow of ideas, you complete none of your projects and fail to achieve your objectives.

Worldly affairs have no meaningful outcome, yet, by being constantly distracted by them, you deprive yourself of the fruits of the sublime Dharma. Eager to maintain multiple acquaintances, one distraction follows another.

If you are as stiff as a hardened yak-hide pouch, you will struggle to get along with others. Boorish and rough-talking, you will find it difficult to persevere in practicing the spiritual instructions you have received. Longing for status, you may covet fame and seek to associate with influential people. Fickle in nature, you will always be looking for fresh acquaintances, forsaking old friends, and thereby constantly postponing your Dharma practice.

You deceive others with various tricks and silently harbor deep-seated resentment when wronged.

Examine repeatedly whether you are affected by these blemishes indicative of a bad character, which hinder your practice of the exalted Dharma. If you find such defects within yourself, you must overcome them by applying the proper antidotes with perseverance.

–96–

Poor Conduct

Six defects of the misconduct of unfortunate ones:
Ungrateful for the support received, you return bad for good.
Instead of judging yourself, you dare to judge others.
Capricious, your mind is pathologically unstable.
Moving like a willow leaf,[110] you are flattering and hypocritical.
Ignorant of what gives purpose, your mind is full of fanciful concepts, and loves to gossip.
Doing nothing beneficial for others, you are nevertheless hopeful of receiving support.
Such unfortunate people are at odds with the sublime Dharma: avoid them as much as possible!

Unworthy recipients of the supreme Dharma, burdened by adverse karmic propensities, exhibit six defects:

When treated well, they lack the capacity for gratitude. When you treat them as well as you can, they return bad for good.

Unable to be circumspect and vigilant about themselves or to recognize their own faults, they dare to examine the faults of others again and again.

Unstable, prone to mood swings, they may appear cheerful from afar but reveal distress at close range. Perpetually narrow-minded and easily offended, they suffer from chronic mental instability, even without reason to be upset.

Their faces change as easily as willow leaves, with various contrived expressions and manners of speaking, all smiles before one person and very different before another. Their words are often at odds with their thoughts. In these ways, they continually delay their Dharma practice.

Incapable of accomplishing anything meaningful, they waste all their time in idle chatter and worldly distractions.

–97–

Bringing the Practice to Completion

Six flawless qualities of an individual that ensure perfection in Dharma practice:
You are mentally stable, virtuous in your thoughts, and less engaged in (worthless) activities.
You have perseverance, strong determination, and patience.
You are indomitable and not overcome by adverse circumstances.
You are steadfast in friendship and your faith and respect are sincere.
You are wise, give good advice, and are skillful.
Instead of pointing out the faults of others, you expose your own weaknesses.
Such a supreme individual is a friend until enlightenment.

Here are six instructions on how to bring Dharma practice to its ultimate point, free from the six defects that plague those with negative inclinations:

Such practitioners have stable minds and unwavering resolve. Their minds naturally turn to the Dharma; they are virtuous, good company, and unburdened by worldly activities and projects.

They practice the supreme Dharma with persistence, diligently studying, reflecting, and meditating. As for their character, having made a commitment, they remain steadfast, and no difficulty will cause them to abandon their promise. Whatever efforts are required and whatever difficulties they encounter to accomplish the Dharma, they endure these trials with fortitude.

Not easily overcome by obstacles created by others, they never turn away from the supreme Dharma, no matter what circumstances, good or bad, befall them.

Such practitioners are reliable and consistent. Time spent in their company, be it months or years, will not erode the quality of your relationship. Imbued with faith and fervent respect toward their spiritual master and the Three Jewels, they are free from pretense.

Gifted with an excellent frame of mind nurtured through study, reflection, and meditation, they remain resolutely focused on the Dharma. They are skilled in giving sound advice and guiding disciples.

Even if they clearly see the defects of others, they are not inclined to expose and proclaim them widely. Instead, they concentrate on amending their own hidden flaws by applying the necessary antidotes and methods for their eradication.

Such is the supreme friend in virtue, whose company is beneficial all the way to enlightenment.

–98–

The Flaws of Jealousy

Six defects related to jealousy that practitioners develop:
You want more profit, wealth, and possessions than others.
You want your followers and disciples to increase.
You want to accumulate more merit and riches than others.
You want the flag of your fame and renown to fly around the world.
You want to attain superiority over all other practitioners.
You want everything for yourself and nothing for others.
Such practitioners will succumb to the flowery arrows of the god of desire.[111]

Dharma practitioners can be prone to six defects stemming from jealousy:

Driven by the desire to be unrivaled, they endeavor to outshine everyone with their wealth. No matter how many people surround them, they yearn for a greater number of children and followers, though they lack an altruistic motivation and bodhicitta.

They seek more possessions than anyone else, a higher status, greater power, grandeur, and fame. In short, they want their privileges and good fortune to outmatch everyone else and strive to attract an ever-growing circle of people by capitalizing on their merits.

Hoping their names will resonate across the world, they devote all their energy to the pursuit of fame.

They get along with no one, constantly seeking to assert their superiority. Particularly, as they cannot bear the thought of anyone surpassing them, they succumb to the flowery arrows shot by the king of the demons, one of the gods of desire, and drift further and further away from the supreme Dharma.

–99–

The Warning Signs of These Defects

Six signs of sprouts that develop from such defects:
You are inspired by those who are privileged (with worldly prosperity) and who are entertained by many people.
You denigrate past Dharma practitioners and masters.
You boil with anger at the sight of other people's prosperity or qualities.
You mock the loving and caring people who benefit others.
You slander meditators and accomplished beings.
You support the ignorant and those who hold false views.

In line with what has been explained earlier, six signs indicate that you are falling into Māra's snare.

You plot to attract the largest number of followers and undertake countless activities but have scant enthusiasm to put the teachings of your spiritual lineage into practice.

Many learned, accomplished, and virtuous practitioners have preceded you, but you denigrate them out of a fear of being overshadowed, projecting a litany of faults onto them.

When you see others who are richer, more powerful, and more celebrated, or hold a higher position than yourself, you become infuriated, seething with anger.

You adopt a sarcastic attitude toward those who strive for the well-being of others with benevolence and compassion and attribute many faults to them.

Those who have achieved ordinary and extraordinary siddhis through their meditative practice you label as frauds, power-hungry, and other disparaging names, slandering them profusely.

You pride yourself on false views and ally yourself with those who ignorantly uphold such fallacious views. All such behavior must be avoided!

–100–

The Unfortunate Consequences of Relying upon Negative Individuals

Six disadvantages of relying upon negative individuals:
Just seeing them diminishes renunciation and faith.
Just listening to them leads you away from the path of liberation.
Just recalling them sows the seeds of samsara.
Just touching them causes blessings and accomplishments to evaporate.
Just conversing with them reduces pure perception and respectful devotion.
Just by making a spiritual connection with them, you are "blessed" by Māra
And eventually fall into the hell of ultimate torment.
Therefore, avoid such beings with bad karmic dispositions.

Becoming acquainted with negative individuals has six unfortunate consequences:

The mere sight of such individuals diminishes your resolve for renunciation, diminishes your yearning to escape the three worlds of samsara, and clouds your faith.

Simply hearing about their actions and behavior can divert you from the path of liberation.

Thinking about them and recalling their manners and actions sows the seeds for endless wandering in the three worlds of samsara.

Enjoying their company or merely interacting with them causes blessings and accomplishments to vanish like a rainbow fading in space.

Converse with them frequently, and your pure vision and faith will wither.

Receive teachings from them, thereby establishing a spiritual bond, and their bad behavior will contaminate you.

These consequences are nothing less than the "blessings" of demons that will propel you toward rebirth in the lower realms, beginning with the hell of unceasing agony.

Avoid at all costs the company of those with bad karma.

–101–

Characteristics of Bad Practitioners

Six obvious characteristics of unwholesome practitioners:
Their attitude is even inferior to ordinary people's, let alone spiritual individuals.
Their conduct is even worse than the worst, let alone those who have entered the path.
Their view is even worse than that of non-Buddhists, let alone that of the Mahāyāna path.
Their meditation is even worse than those who are attached to evil, let alone those practicing the Secret Mantra.
Their actions are even worse than the most wicked, let alone those who practice Dharma.
Their view and meditation are as far from the Dharma as E arth is from heaven.
Such impostors are mere thieves of the teachings.
Stay away from them, because they lead the faithful to the wrong path and to the lower realms.

If you associate with unworthy individuals, you risk being tainted by six distinct flaws:

Without even comparing them to practitioners who are in perfect harmony with the supreme Dharma, if they do not practice the Dharma properly, as it is advised, "Do not rely on people with a blasé attitude toward the Dharma, who have only an intellectual grasp of it." They fall short of even ordinary people of the secular world, and their thinking continuously distances their minds from the Dharma.

Not even comparing them to practitioners who have entered the path of Dharma, they are more wretched than people who engage in negative behavior, such as barbarians, butchers, or sex workers.

They are clearly far removed from the Great Vehicle and do not even compare favorably with non-Buddhist tīrthikas, who observe ethical precepts and, in some cases, refrain from taking life.

Without even comparing them to Vajrayāna followers of the Secret Mantra, they are worse than the most depraved with respect to lust, hostility, and ignorance.

Without even comparing them to genuine Dharma practitioners, they are more appalling than hunters and other dismaying individuals who constantly indulge in killing and the like.

There is no point in comparing their view, meditation, and action to those who practice them correctly, as theirs are as distant from the Dharma as the sky is from the earth. They are therefore nothing than spiritual impostors.

Although they may look like practitioners, they are the very antithesis of the Dharma. When sincere devotees follow such individuals, they are drawn into wrong paths by force of circumstances. Therefore, avoid them at all costs.

–102–

Six Shortcomings Leading to Failure

Six shortcomings that lead to failure in spiritual accomplishment:
Though you may have bodhicitta, without making aspirations,
You will not sow the seed for purifying the obscuration to the rūpakāya.
Though you may have compassion, without extinguishing selfishness,
You will not belong in the line of Mahāyāna practitioners who benefit others.
Though you may strive to act in harmony with everyone, if the time is not ripe,
Far from accomplishing others' good, you will only be mocked.
Though you may stay in mountain retreat, without renouncing samsara,
You will find it difficult to abandon attachment, aversion, and the propensity to conform to others' behavior.

> **No matter how many thousands of prayers you may make, if they lack faith and respect,**
> **Not even a single raindrop of blessings will fall on you.**
> **Though you may be greatly learned, without being free from conceptual elaborations,**
> **You will be unable to distinguish samsara from nirvana and will be trapped in the net of philosophical tenets.**
> **Address such shortcomings by incorporating these instructions into your mind.**

If you separate wisdom and skillful means, you will not properly accomplish the fruit of the supreme Dharma within your mind stream.

You may recite many times the stanza used to generate bodhicitta, but as it is said, "What matters is not merely conceiving the supreme bodhicitta but actualizing it." Therefore, unless you repeatedly generate the resolve to work for others' sake, as expressed in *The Prayer of Excellent Deeds*,[112] you will fail to purify the obscurations that keep you from acquiring the spiritual qualities of the form body (*rūpakāya*) and not even plant the seed for such purification.

You may feel compassion, but unless you have fully shed the shackles of self-importance, you will not join the ranks of those who benefit others on the Mahāyāna path.

Conforming to the customs of ordinary people, no matter what skillful means you deploy, if you lack the maturity to truly benefit others, you might be "skillful but in the manner of a child" and will become a laughingstock.

You may stay in a mountain hermitage for a long time, but unless you turn your mind from the activities centered on this life, and from samsara as a whole, by dwelling in a secluded place you will only be trading a large home for a small one[113] and will find it difficult to definitively sever the fetters of attraction and aversion that abound in the sphere of worldly concerns.

If you recite all manner of prayers and accumulate various recitations without faith and respect, not a drop of the spiritual master's blessings will enter you.

You may be very learned in the teachings of the sutras and the Secret Mantra, but unless you realize the meaning of the ultimate nature of reality free from elaboration, you will fail to escape samsara and attain nirvana and will remain trapped in the intellectual views of erroneous doctrines.

Therefore, take to heart the wisdom and methods of all essential instructions.

–103–

Six Essential Attitudes

Six requisites for Dharma practitioners:
Fear samsara as though you were being chased by an assassin.
Be as diligent in practicing virtuous activities as you are in cultivating crops.
Apply the antidotes like a patient undergoing treatment.
Sincerely undertake the benefit of others as you would care for a small child.
Be as skilled at taming your mind as a tanner at softening leather.
Annihilate self-grasping like someone who avenges his father's murder.
These are requisites to adopt at all times.

All Dharma practitioners are expected to adopt six indispensable attitudes.

Frightened by the sufferings of the three worlds of samsara, be like a convict fleeing from prison. Aware that an executioner is chasing him, he will not rest until he has put a great distance between them. Fear equally the three worlds of samsara, your formidable enemy.

Farmers who tend their fields do not slacken their efforts but persist until they reap a bountiful harvest. Likewise, engage in spiritual practices without relaxing your diligence until meditative experiences and ultimate realization are born.

At all times, apply antidotes to afflictive mental states and deluded perceptions, just as you take treatments prescribed by an expert physician to cure ailments associated with wind, bile, or phlegm—using treatments like bloodletting, moxibustion, and other methods.

At all times, with pure benevolence, dedicate yourself to the welfare of beings, just as parents who lovingly care for small children weather their moods and shoulder the myriad concerns that arise in their upbringing.

Tame and transform your mind stream with persistence, attention, vigilance, and discernment, just as an experienced tanner begins by moistening the leather and then patiently works and softens it, curing its original stiffness.

The root cause of your wandering in the three worlds of samsara is none other than self-clinging: consider it your worst enemy and never forget this.

Maintain the same relentless resolve as someone who, in the ordinary world, having sworn to kill his hereditary enemy, refuses to be satisfied until he has claimed his foe's very heart.

Constantly integrate these indispensable attitudes into your mind.

–104–

Taming Your Thoughts

Six ultimate points to tame your mind stream:
The ultimate imprisonment is attachment to your homeland: give it up.
The ultimate farming is to persevere in virtuous action: cultivate this.
The ultimate residence is the fundamental nature: settle there.
The ultimate protection is to abandon self-grasping and self-cherishing.
The ultimate enemies are the actual five poisons: tame them.
The ultimate practice is to abide in mindfulness without distraction.
If you practice these points, all your aspirations will be fulfilled.

If Dharma practitioners adhere to these six ultimate points, their spiritual practice will reach its highest attainment.

The ultimate renunciation and weariness with samsara is to abandon attachment and infatuation with friends and relatives in your homeland. This will free you from the distractions and busyness that come with socializing.

Cultivating your land provides you with food and clothing for a while, but persevering in virtuous practices yields the ultimate harvest.

Just as people take up residence in the ordinary world, establish yourself in the fundamental nature of reality. Strive to dwell in this most permanent of abodes, leaving behind this illusory and ever-changing samsara.

The ultimate protection is freeing yourself from self-centeredness. Any other defense, such as visualizing protective domes[114] and other methods, may shield you momentarily from negative ailments and influences, but they do not provide lasting sanctuary. Thus, free yourself from self-grasping and an exaggerated sense of self-importance.

The afflictive mental states, the five mental poisons, are your most serious enemy. If you subdue them, you will never need to worry about defeating external enemies.

Therefore, the ultimate practice is to master the mental states that disturb and obscure your mind, and free yourself from them by maintaining vigilant attention and introspection, steering clear of distraction.

If you master these six ultimate points, the immediate benefits and ultimate bliss will naturally unfold.

–105–

Six Potential Dangers

Six dangers that can divert practitioners:
If you have faith without giving up gain and fame,
Beware, because you may end up losing yourself in ordinary concerns.
If you remain in solitude without firm determination,
Beware, because you may end up by falling into distraction.
If you show signs of accomplishment without abandoning pride,
Beware, for in time you may be enchanted by the demons.
Though you may gather oath-bound protectors, if you lack compassion,
Beware, because over time you may commit unvirtuous actions.
If your realization is high, but you have not freed yourself from attachment,
Beware, because over time you may become impervious to the teachings.
If you engage in benefiting others, but remain entangled in selfishness,
Beware, because over time you risk becoming a charlatan.

Six obstacles and deviations threaten practitioners of the supreme Dharma.

You may have faith in your spiritual master and in the Three Jewels, but unless you have the courage to abandon the lure of gain and fame in daily life, you may drift away, becoming adept only in secular matters, seeking power and status. Beware of this ever-present danger!

If you settle down in a solitary mountain retreat without making a firm resolution to practice during the four periods of the day, whatever your practices might be, you may fall into distraction by engaging in various diversions and lapse into a comfortable inertia. Do things properly.

You may manifest signs of accomplishment, such as soaring through the skies, leaving footprints in rocks, or displaying clairvoyance, but if you take pride in these spiritual achievements, consider them supreme, and do nothing to eliminate such erroneous attitudes, these marks of progress will turn into hindrances and prevent you from fulfilling your life's aspirations. You risk becoming a charlatan and being swept away by Māra.

Without a deep concern for preserving the Buddha's teaching and lacking compassion for sentient beings, even if Dharma protectors accompany you like your shadow, you risk accumulating negative and perverse karma by invoking them to annihilate enemies and demons.

Your view and realization might be lofty, but if you are complacent about your achievements and remain attached to the ordinary things of this life, you may become resistant to the Dharma and your mind will not be transformed. Be aware of this danger!

If you engage in ceaseless benevolent acts to maintain a facade, amassing followers, making grand offerings, and dispensing charity in a variety of ways, but lack genuine benevolence, all this will amount to nothing more but the pursuit of your own interests. In the end, you turn into an impostor, amassing wealth and opulence. Beware of such folly!

–106–

Six Obscurations

Six obscurations to be removed:
Not retaining the sublime teachings and abandoning them is an obscuration.
Not recognizing the machinations of the demons is an obscuration.
Lacking devotion and respect for your spiritual master is an obscuration.
Lacking pure perception for your spiritual companions is an obscuration.

> **Denigrating practitioners who have entered the supreme vehicle is an obscuration.**
> **Engaging your three doors in negative and deceptive acts is an obscuration.**
> **Take to heart abandoning these obscurations and practice the path of liberation.**

Being content to practice Dharma merely in appearance, you turn your back on the path of liberation. Recognize here the influence of Māra. Otherwise, six insidious veils will cast their shadow over your Dharma.

To be satisfied with minimal studies instead of exploring the Dharma in all its depth and breadth is an obscuration akin to forsaking the Dharma, the greatest mistake of all.

Distraction, busyness, and the thirst for gain and fame are inspired by Māra. Unaware of this, you take pride in your renown and in your efforts to benefit beings on a grand scale. This will obscure your Dharma practice.

If you lack the devotion and respect to see your benevolent master as the union of all buddhas, this is an obscuration that prevents the emergence of any qualities of the path to liberation and enlightenment.

If you do not regard all vajra companions with affection and pure vision, seeing them as your brothers and sisters, fathers and mothers, you will generate adverse views about them, damaging your samaya—a grievous fault.

If, at the sight of a practitioner of the supreme vehicle, you denigrate, despise, and repeatedly deride her or him, this is a serious fault that obscures your pure vision.

If you engage in misconduct with your body, speech, and mind while pretending *to* behave flawlessly, posing as a practitioner who has pacified and mastered his mind and forsaken ordinary activities, you will be marred by hypocrisy.

Abandon such behavior and practice the path of liberation.

–107–

Six Invaluable Qualities

The six priceless qualities free from obscuration are:
Giving impartially without expectation of return;
Observing pure moral discipline with no worldly aspirations;
Arousing loving-kindness and compassion that never forsakes sentient beings;
Never being satisfied with your learning of the sublime Dharma, no matter how much you know;
Providing teachings without expecting any gain or respect;
Being equally kind to all beings with no partiality.
Noble conduct like this is truly virtuous.

In accordance with what has been previously said, once all veils are cleared, infinitely precious spiritual qualities will manifest themselves, including these six:

When acting for the benefit of others, you harbor no expectation that they will do something for you in return. Unrestricted, unbiased generosity is a sign that you are free of such veils.

In keeping moral discipline and precepts flawlessly, you are not motivated by the hope of rebirth as a deva or a human being, but by the aspiration to attain the omniscience of buddhahood. In this way, you are free from the obscuration associated with the observance of discipline.

Never losing interest in beings, you remain benevolent at all times and in all circumstances. You cultivate loving-kindness—the wish for beings to find happiness—and compassion—the wish for them to be forever free from suffering [and its cause]. By doing so, you are free from the obscurations that otherwise tarnish the path of the Great Vehicle.

Just as the ocean is never too full, no matter how many rivers flow into it, you cannot say that you had enough, no matter how many teachings you have received, how deep your spiritual experience is, or how well you grasp the meaning and key points of the supreme Dharma. By fully realizing the essential points of the Dharma, you will finally reach the other shore, free from all obscurations.

When transmitting the Dharma, you do not think about receiving any gain, services, respect, offerings, or any other benefits. Teaching the Dharma perfectly in this way, you will be free from deceit.

Not discriminating between your allies and adversaries and without preference or aversion for the various philosophical views, you cultivate unbounded impartiality toward all beings. This demonstrates that you are free of your veils.

If you have these six indications of freedom from obscurations, you are endowed with supreme virtue and conduct.

–108–

The Qualities of a Great Vehicle Practitioner

Six virtues of relying upon the Mahāyāna teachings:
You follow your spiritual master without laziness.
You dedicate yourself to benefiting beings without feeling weary or sad.
You do not develop any pride, even if you realize the fundamental nature.
You accept no gain that does not serve a meaningful purpose.
You are not frightened by the profound meaning [of the truth].
You are never satisfied, even if you have accumulated a wealth of virtue.

Based on the Three Baskets of the teachings, six spiritual qualities will manifest once you have entered the path of the Great Vehicle:

When you entrust yourself to a spiritual master, you remain tireless in body, speech, and mind. Even at the cost of your life, you follow your master like a shadow and delight him or her in all three ways.* Free from indolence, you never consider you have done enough.

In your endeavors to aid others, even when met with ingratitude, whatever fatigue and difficulties you endure, you dedicate yourself exclusively to their benefit, with enthusiasm and without weariness or discouragement.

Even if you truly realize the fundamental nature of dharmatā and emptiness, you are not complacent, telling yourself you have a lofty view and are an accomplished practitioner.

You have no interest in gain and respect of any kind unless you use them to make offerings and donations, or for some other noble purpose. Otherwise, they will only increase your distraction and busyness.

The more you consider the profound meaning of emptiness, as well as the view, meditation, and conduct of the Secret Mantra, the more your openness, conviction, and aspirations flourish, free from fear.

No matter the extent of your accumulation of virtue—with or without representations—you will never be satisfied, thinking that you have done enough, and you will continue to persevere.

These are the six qualities of the Great Vehicle that are developed by pursuing that path.

–109–

Overcoming Disruptive Mindsets

Six ways to subdue your great enemies, negative emotions:

A few days of meritorious activities cannot destroy the negative emotions;
Thus, you must practice continuously without settling for short-term efforts.

Afflictive states of mind originating from beginningless time are very difficult to tame:
Thus, you must skillfully use the most profound antidotes.

Self-grasping is difficult to destroy, and the duality of subject and object is widely pervasive,
Thus, you must strengthen the army of two accumulations and persevere in virtue.
The chronic disease of samsara is unremitting and difficult to cure:
Thus, you must always rely upon the spiritual master, your doctor.

The inferno of the five mental poisons is difficult to extinguish completely:
Thus, you must cultivate the ocean-like mind of bodhicitta.

**The path (of samsara), where you accumulate negative karma,
easily leads you downward:
Thus, you must ascend the ladder of liberation.**

Six antidotes can neutralize your arch enemies, the afflictive mental states.

If you strive for a few days and then give up, you will not be able to reduce the influence of afflictive mental states and eliminate your obscurations. Thus, you should persist in practice for the duration of your life. As said, "Do not hope for quick signs of accomplishment, meditate until your final breath."[115] Dedicate yourself to the Dharma for the long term and avoid practicing for a few months or years and then slacking off and falling back into distraction.

For countless lifetimes, until now, you have perpetuated the eighty-four thousand kinds of afflictive mental states. You cannot tame them by counteracting them only once or twice. You must persistently use the most powerful antidotes at every emergence of an undesirable mental state.

It is challenging to fully realize the emptiness of the self while still believing in and cherishing it, since the obscurations formed by the duality of subject and object are as powerful as the waves of the great ocean. Thus, you must deploy unwavering diligence in spiritual practice and perfect the dual accumulation of merit and wisdom.

In samsara, from beginningless time until now, the evils of karma and afflictive mental states have plagued you. To cure such a chronic disease, long neglected, is arduous and requires an excellent doctor skilled in dealing with both karma and negative emotions. This doctor is none other than the lama, the spiritual master, who can correctly apply the therapy of Dharma. Entrust yourself to him or her.

Equally difficult is extinguishing once and for all the fierce blaze of the five mental poisons. The proper antidote is bodhicitta, vast as the ocean, which has the power to transform all afflictive mental states into allies for cultivating altruism.

Throughout innumerable rebirths, individuals who have accumulated negative karma by committing the five heinous crimes with immediate retribution and the ten unvirtuous actions, as well as by transgressing the precepts of individual liberation, the bodhisattvas, and the Secret Mantra, only fall to lower and lower rebirths, with none rising. Therefore, strive to climb the staircase that leads first to higher destinies and, ultimately, to liberation from samsara.

–110–

Six Aspects of the Three Baskets and the Three Practices

Six distinct features of the Three Baskets and the three trainings:
The listeners approach the Three Baskets by following the words of the Teacher (the Buddha).
Solitary realizers naturally realize dependent origination from within.
Bodhisattvas achieve the boundless wisdom both by themselves and with the help of others.
The listeners practice (the three) trainings with a one-sided approach of (protecting) their own mind streams.
The solitary realizers' approach is at an intermediate level of striving primarily for their own purposes (yet benefiting others in a small way).
The bodhisattvas' approach is definitely based on compassion.

If you correctly practice the Three Baskets (sutras, abhidharma, and vinaya) alongside the three trainings, you will find that each of the three vehicles—the superior, intermediate, and foundational—offers teachings related to the Three Baskets. Understand that each vehicle has its own particularities that can be practiced harmoniously without contradicting the others, while honoring their specificity.

The basket of the listeners is so called because they listen to the teachings of the Teacher—the perfect Buddha—or their spiritual master, and then pass them on to others. These practitioners, also known as "listeners and proclaimers," adhere closely to the literal meaning of the Buddha's words. By eliminating the veil of afflictive mental states, they attain the state of an arhat.

According to the basket of solitary realizers, practitioners attain realization for their own sake. They understand the lack of individual identity but do not fully comprehend the lack of inherent identity in all phenomena.[116] They explore the inescapable aspect of external and internal interdependence.

Bodhisattvas, on the other hand, are wholly dedicated to awakening the primordial wisdom of emptiness, infused with great compassion, both within themselves and in all sentient beings.

The primary focus of the listeners' training is the taming of their own minds, which they do for their own benefit. This self-centered motivation thus limits them, preventing them from extending their intent boundlessly.

The view and meditation of the solitary realizers are slightly more expansive than those of the listeners, yet they, too, primarily seek their own welfare and lack the unconditional benevolence of the bodhisattvas.

The bodhisattvas' training, according to their basket, is driven by an unwavering commitment to the welfare of others, a motivation that inspires all their actions, words, and thoughts.

You must therefore take the best of each of these vehicles and integrate it into your mind stream, while skillfully avoiding their respective limitations.

–111–

The Defects of Ordinary Life

Six ways of looking at the shortcomings of the ordinary world:
Fame is like the rumble of thunder: stop reveling in it.
Riches are like clouds: do not try to catch them.
Relatives are like wishing for a child when you have grown old: give up all hopes.
Homes are like guesthouses: wander through mountain solitudes.
Happiness and comfort are like dreams: do not grasp to them as real.
You will leave everything behind: give up your attachment to things.
If you do so, your happiness will increase many times.

After pondering the inherent flaws of the ordinary activities of samsara as a whole and the futility of the eight worldly concerns in particular, it becomes evident that abandoning them is a wise choice. Ask yourself, what is truly wrong with samsara?

Fame and reputation are like the loud, yet hollow, rumbling of thunder. Even when achieved, notoriety is but fleeting and soon fades away. Avoid reveling in fame.

Wealth and possessions are as transient as clouds, forming briefly in the sky before dissipating moments later. Let them pass without grasping to them. Understand that possessions are impermanent and resist the urge to hoard.

Having no children of your own, even if you have many relatives and friends, you might think, when you see elderly people, that children could have taken care of you, especially at the end of your life. But why dwell on such an unattainable wish? Give up any attachment to the idea that your loved ones will look after you.

Consider your country, village, and home as mere inns in which you briefly dwell. Do not become attached to them; instead, wander freely in solitude, finding refuge in caves and beneath natural shelters.

The happiness and joys of this life are like last night's dreams—happy one moment, full of suffering the next. Beware of forging stubborn attachments to the comforts of this life.

In the end, regardless of your efforts, you will leave behind your body, your beliefs, your wealth, your land, and all the projects and activities of this life. You will enter the next life alone.

Free your mind from the eight worldly preoccupations and proceed joyfully toward the omniscience of buddhahood.

–112–

Six Duties of a Dharma Practitioner

Six actions Dharma practitioners must perform:

Wherever you are born, you need to work for the benefit of others:
Thus, train extensively in generating bodhicitta and making aspirations.

When experiencing happiness, you must recognize this as the blessing of the Dharma:
Thus, considering the benefits [of Dharma praxis], practice with perseverance.

When you suffer, you must understand this as the result of your past actions:

Thus, considering cause and effect, let mind training be the heart of your practice.

When you fall ill, you must consider this as training in meritorious action,
And when you are not ill, nurture your intrinsic awareness.

When you are old, be serene, and anticipating that,
Engage in accumulating (merit) and purifying (negativity) during your youth.

At the moment of death, you must be done with all your activities and projects:
Therefore, before you die, sever all worldly ties.

These, I feel, are the practices you must carry out with all your heart.

Here are six essential practices that every Dharma practitioner must cultivate over time:

Regardless of whether you are born into higher or lower realms, if you aspire to fully dedicate yourself to the welfare of others, you must engage in the entire range of bodhisattva activities. To do so, cultivate boundless benevolence, generate bodhicitta, and fervently pray to be able to work for the benefit of all beings on a vast scale, emulating the bodhisattvas Samantabhadra and Mañjuśrī.

In times of well-being, recognize that this is due to the Dharma and its blessings. Reflect on the benefits of practicing the teachings and, with eagerness, persevere in study, reflection, and meditation.

Should afflictions beset you—whether in the form of illness, malevolent influences, hindrances, disruptions, slander, or rumors—understand that these are the karmic consequences of harm you have inflicted on others in past lives. Do not resist them. Instead, use them to practice taking upon yourself the suffering of all beings. Experiencing suffering like this is the ultimate way to purify your past karma by allowing its consequences to ripen. Therefore, focus on the essence of mind training.

If illness strikes, view it as an opportunity to perfect your practice of virtue. Consider illness as a broom that sweeps away your obscurations, and integrate this trial into your spiritual path.

In the throes of suffering, you may lack the strength to practice Dharma properly. So, now, while you are healthy, is the time to bring the Dharma into your life experience. With genuine dedication to your practice, day after day, immerse yourself in awareness without wasting a single moment in idleness.

As you age, continue to practice the supreme Dharma and remain fearless in the face of death. As the incomparable physician from Dagpo, Gampopa, reminds us, at the time of death the best practitioner will be purified of attachment to birth and death, the average practitioner will be perfectly serene, and even the lesser practitioner will find peace in knowing that they have practiced diligently. Following this guidance, while you are still young, dedicate yourself with determination to the dual accumulation of merit and wisdom.

Finally, when you die, it is wise to let go of any lingering desires and ensure that you depart without regrets of unfinished endeavors. Before death arrives, sever all ties to mundane, worldly activities, and dedicate yourself entirely to the direct experience of the supreme Dharma.

I sincerely believe that this is the proper way to train in the Dharma and I urge you to pursue it with unwavering diligence.

–113–

Getting to the Point

Six instructions that strike the vital points:

Family members are like crowds gathered at a fair:
Who knows when you will be separated? Practice the ultimate meaning instead.

Relatives and friends are like a flock of birds gathered on a willow tree:
Who knows when they will scatter? Let go of attachment and longing.

Life is fragile like a dewdrop on a blade of grass:
Work hard on your meditation and Dharma practice.

> **By talking too much—like a parrot—your enemy, delusion, will arise:**
> **Avoid gossip and useless chatter. Remain silent.**
>
> **Dharma practice is like seeking gems on an island of precious stones:**
> **Avoid indiscriminate disclosure of oral transmissions and instructions.**
>
> **If you spend too much time with people, you will end up finding faults in everyone, even in the Buddha!**
> **Therefore, do not live together with others.**
>
> **These are pieces of supreme heart advice: listen to them with respect.**

If you know how to bring all phenomenal appearances onto the spiritual path, the entire world will manifest as a book of teachings. Six crucial instructions guide us in achieving this:

Though parents, family members, friends, and acquaintances may share our lives for a time, they will eventually part ways. Consider, for instance, a large fair where a crowd gathers briefly, only to disperse after a few hours. Similarly, when thinking of your loved ones, ask yourself, "Who knows when we will be separated?" Avoid conflicts and instead dedicate yourself to pursuing the path of enlightenment in solitude, always keeping the ultimate meaning in mind.

Even if you feel great affection for your family and friends, remember that you are like a flock of birds perched on a willow tree, and will soon scatter in all directions. Nothing guarantees that you can stay together for your whole life. You have no idea when the Lord of Death will take one or the other away. It is wiser to cut the ties of affection that bind you to your kin.

Moreover, your life expectancy and vitality are as fleeting as a dewdrop on a blade of grass. Exposed to the wind, it may fall at any moment. Aware of the fragility of existence, wise practitioners will sincerely dedicate all their energies to the Dharma of meditation and accomplishment.

If you tend to talk a lot, remember the saying, "The mouth is the reservoir of vice, the door to all faults and declines." Inconsiderate speech is a true enemy that fuels attraction and repulsion, causes much dissension, and leads others astray. Abandon all idle chatter and meaningless talk; do not be like a parrot that never stops talking.

When you practice the Dharma authentically, be like an explorer who embarks on a journey across the ocean in search of the fabled jewel island, persevering through all difficulties until he finds the wish-fulfilling gem, which he then cherishes with utmost care. In the same way, dedicate your mind to the instructions of the oral tradition. Use them to reach the vital points of your own practice but refrain from divulging them indiscriminately.

If you linger in the company of many people, you will end up finding fault with them. Some people even found faults in the Buddha himself! Therefore, it is best to avoid mingling with too many people and sharing your residence for too long. Let go of attachment, dislike, and resentment, and seek the quiet solitude of a mountain retreat.

This is profound advice from the heart for all those who wish to practice in harmony with the teachings. Listen to it with great care.

–114–

Timely Actions

Six timely actions for Dharma practitioners:

When you meet authentic masters,
This is the time to clarify your doubts and cut through intellectual fabrications. Ask questions.

When your awareness encounters difficult circumstances,
This is the time to blend your mind with practice. Train in it.

When you receive profound oral transmissions and instructions,
This is the time to destroy delusion. Strike at it.

When you are striving hard to practice Dharma,
This is the time when obstacles arise. Watch out for the māras!

When you accomplish your practice and the siddhis are close,
Obstacles created by the māras will arise. Be extremely vigilant.

When you are refining your view of the fundamental nature.
This is when the veil of deviation manifests. Rely upon the spiritual master.

These are crucial profound instructions. Keep them in your mind.

These six pieces of advice highlight crucial times when Dharma practitioners must act:

You have met genuine masters and have been graced with the nectar of their oral instructions: now is the time to put these instructions into practice and sever at the root any lingering doubts about the supreme Dharma. After asking all the necessary questions, you can retreat to the solitude of a mountain hermitage, no longer needing to seek further guidance from your kind master on these points.

When your awareness is confronted with adversity, distractions, and consuming activities, when desires or aversion flare up, confident in the stability of your practice, apply the appropriate countermeasures with a fully focused mind. Just as you seek treatment when ill, apply appropriate countermeasures when attraction and hostility arise, without yielding to them. Strengthen your resilience and refine your ability to integrate these challenges into your meditation.

When you rely on a spiritual master and receive profound oral transmissions, ensure that whatever practices you undertake swiftly dismantle your deluded perceptions. Persevere day and night, without making errors.

When you engage fully in practicing the supreme Dharma with fierce determination, the māras are said to redouble their efforts. Stay vigilant against these potential hindrances. Do not fall under their influence and make diligent use of skillful means to overcome them.

As you approach the pinnacle of your practice and the siddhis are within reach, the māras will intervene in force, just as they attempted to hinder Śākyamuni Buddha on the verge of his enlightenment. Be very careful not to be overwhelmed by them.

Finally, when the realization of the view of the fundamental nature of all things dawns in your mind and you bring your spiritual practice to culmination, the risk of deviation increases as various ultimate obscurations manifest. In such moments, relying on your spiritual master, clear any remaining doubt and mental projections, overcome obstacles, and guard against straying from the path.

Condensed to the essentials, these vital points of the profound instructions will benefit you. Practice them persistently.

–115–

Six Appropriate Types of Conduct

Six types of conduct to adopt to practice Dharma correctly:
Do not associate with those whose vile behavior is contagious.
Training in perfect conduct is difficult, so rely upon a spiritual master.
Appearances are skilled at deceiving you, so do not be distracted by objects.
When your experience of awareness is still unstable, ensure it does not follow delusion.
Attachment and dislike are intense, so ensure you do not become partial.
Delusory experiences easily carry you away, so cut attachment at the root.

When you want to practice the supreme Dharma correctly, you must avoid becoming entangled in six undesirable situations.

First, steer clear of those who constantly engage in negative actions, particularly those who take lives. Likewise, distance yourself from revelers in dance and song, or those who excessively pursue romantic conquests. Otherwise, you will be contaminated by their errors and leave the excellent path of Dharma for the path of unwholesome actions.

Embracing impeccable conduct is a challenging endeavor, as it requires a state of attentive presence, alertness, and careful discernment. To succeed in this, remain close to your spiritual guide, accompanying them like a shadow.

The senses, experienced through the six aspects of consciousness, are adept at deceiving your awareness. Guard the threshold of your senses with mindfulness and vigilance, ensuring that external stimuli do not distract your mind. When these objects are poised to mislead you, and your awareness is still vulnerable—like that of a child—be cautious not to form bad habits in relation to external perceptions.

If you become strongly attached to your loved ones while harboring deep-seated hostility toward your enemies, you will never be in harmony with your fellow beings. Do not fall into the bias of excessive fondness and aversion.

From beginningless existences until now, you have nurtured deluded perceptions and have become accustomed to them. Consequently, your mind clings to an object the moment it perceives it. Cut attachment and grasping at the root!

–116–

At the Least, Be without Regret at the Time of Death

Six states of freedom from regret for the lowest level of practitioners:
Possessing a sense of shame and modesty, you will have no regret even if you die.
Having committed no negative actions, you will have no regret even if you die.
Having distributed food and wealth for the purposes of the Dharma, you will have no regret even if you die.
Having maintained the purity of the three trainings, you will have no regret even if you die.
Having always persevered in virtuous actions, you will have no regret even if you die.
With no guilt or remorse in your heart, you will have no regret even if you die.
Thus, it is essential to have these qualities.

Even a modestly gifted practitioner can die without regret in six ways:

First, if you receive Dharma teachings and follow a spiritual master yet engage in many negative acts, you have good reasons to be ashamed and embarrassed in front of wisdom deities, spiritual masters, and Dharma friends, who will surely disapprove of your misconduct. Conversely, if at the moment of death you are imbued with a sense of moral decency and self-restraint, confident that you will naturally be reborn in higher realms and continue your path to liberation, you will die without regrets. The same is true if you have refrained from committing any negative action.

If you dedicated all your possessions to the Dharma and generously provided food and other necessities to those in need, even if you were to die a pauper, you would rejoice knowing that your wealth has been of true benefit to others, leaving you with no regrets.

If you practice impeccably the three trainings of ethical discipline, concentration, and wisdom according to the tradition, this treasure will never be lost, even across lifetimes. Moreover, if you have consistently made every effort to practice virtue diligently, even if death were to come right now, your conscience should remain clear.

With these reasons for having no regrets at the time of death, you will not be torn by remorse, thinking, "I have not been able to give up negative actions and continue to wander in samsara. I have not practiced the Dharma!"

–117–

In the Middle Case, Six Reasons to Rejoice at the Time of Death

Six things that average practitioners can delight in:
Rejoice! By relying on the Three Jewels, you are protected from samsara.
Rejoice! Having gathered the two accumulations, your happiness will grow [from life to life].
Rejoice! Having observed the samayas, you will be welcomed by the ḍākinīs.
Rejoice! Your tutelary deity, the yidam, will guide you through the intermediate state, the bardo.
Rejoice! You are forever inseparable from the supreme master.
Rejoice! Having familiarized yourself with the nature of mind, luminosity will manifest.
These are profound instructions that bring joy at the moment of death.

Even average practitioners have ample reason to rejoice, with six ways to enhance their joy:

If you take refuge in the three precious jewels from your heart, at all times and on all occasions, you will eventually see the end of samsara. Merely hearing the name of the Three Jewels can keep you from falling into the lower realms. You will be filled with joy, having gained certainty that the refuge offered by the Three Jewels is unfailing and supreme.

If you persevere in perfecting the dual accumulation of merit and wisdom, your excellence and bliss will increase throughout your successive lifetimes—something to celebrate.

Properly uphold the samayas of the Vajrayāna of the Secret Mantra—which are the "life stone"[117] of the ḍākinīs and the Dharma protectors. Thinking that at the time of death these ḍākinīs will come to invite and escort you to a pure land, you have much reason to rejoice.

Be diligent, fully focusing your mind on recitation and accomplishment practices centered on your tutelary wisdom deity, the yidam. This will allow you to train yourself to navigate birth, death, and the intermediate state between death and rebirth. Thus, when faced with the various and often terrifying apparitions of the bardo, the yidam will guide you to a pure buddha field, giving you much to rejoice about.

By relying unwaveringly on the supreme spiritual master, never separating from him or her, and practicing according to their instructions with trust, respect, and devotion, you will always meet such a master in future lives who will impart the teachings to you. This is truly cause for rejoicing!

Finally, through your teacher's kindness, you have recognized the fundamental nature of the mind and continue to familiarize yourself with this recognition. As a result, you will come to understand with joy that the ultimate nature of birth and death is nothing other than the clear light.

These six profound instructions are a source of joy at the time of death, which you will welcome without fear, even if it were to occur today.

–118–

Aspects of Immortality

Six states of deathlessness of yogis with higher capacities:
The realization of your own awareness transcends death.
Self-cognizing wisdom is primordially beyond death.
The naturally arising primordial wisdom is beyond death from the beginning.
The luminous nature of ultimate reality is primordially beyond death.
Awareness devoid of ignorance and self-grasping is primordially deathless.
Transcending cause and effect, [the nature of mind] is primordially liberated and deathless.
The space-like [nature of mind] is free from hope and fear and is thus deathless.
Those who realize this are free from the māra of death.

If you apprehend with certainty the nature of ultimate reality, you need not fear the sufferings of birth and death. Why is this so?

The nature of your own awareness—the source of the ground, path, and fruition—is none other than the ultimate nature of reality, the unchanging tathāgatagarbha in which there is nothing to eliminate and nothing to add, and which is beyond death.

Realizing the nature of the self-arisen primordial wisdom, as it is said, "Death, death is the doorway for the yogi to attain the lesser state of buddhahood."[118] Within the nature of reality, such a yogi can only ascend to perfect freedom and is no longer bound by death.

If, in all circumstances, you maintain the stable realization of the luminous ultimate nature, the dharmatā, everything that arises is the play of primordial wisdom, free of distraction and wandering. Such awareness never strays from dharmatā, in meditation or in post-meditation.

Having severed attachment to the self at its root, unerringly realizing the nature of awareness, you transcend the cycle of birth and death, for these exist only as long as the belief in the self exists. When this belief is eradicated, its consequences vanish as well. If you realize the meaning of the ultimate nature that transcends causality, the ultimate nature in which there is nothing to reject or to obtain, you will realize the primordial and perfect freedom that cannot be bound by negativity.

If you recognize that the fruit, the state of buddhahood, is naturally perfect in the nature of your own mind, vast as the sky, you will transcend hope and fear and realize the state of deathlessness.

Thus, practitioners who reach stable certainty in the ultimate nature of reality will feel not the slightest fear, even as the Lord of Death approaches. They are liberated into the continuum of dharmatā.

–119–

Six Defects Related to Attachment to the Reality of Things

Six defects from ignorantly grasping to things as real:
Discarding what you already have, you seek it elsewhere.
"Great meditators" are trapped by characteristics as they do not realize the ultimate truth.
Not recognizing objective appearances as deceptive in nature, you grasp to them as real.
You see objects as separate, failing to realize their oneness in the ultimate expanse of reality (*dharmadhātu*).
Not realizing the essence of your own self-cognizing [awareness], you discriminate between high and low (nirvana and samsara) while treading the path.
Unable to cut through delusion and grasping, the māras lure you.
Examine these defects of ignorance and let go of them.

If the realization of the view of the immutable dharmatā eludes you, your belief in the inherent existence of phenomena will intensify, and result in six flaws:

The unchanging nature of reality is present in your own mind. But if you ignore this presence and seek it afar, you are like someone who does not see the elephant in his house, declares it missing, and sets off to seek it in the forest.

Some so-called great meditators remain unaware that the perfectly pure fundamental nature is present within them. At times, they think it has a solid existence; at other times, they believe it does not exist at all. Sometimes they consider it to be luminosity, and at other times, emptiness. They become ensnared by these characteristics and remain captive to samsara's delusive appearances.

You should recognize that all appearances, whether deemed good or bad, arising as external objects in the field of the six aspects of consciousness, have the fictitious nature of illusions and dreams. If you believe in their intrinsic existence, once this grasping has crystallized, you will cling to what attracts you and reject what you dislike.

Failing to realize the oneness of samsara and nirvana within the absolute expanse, you view samsara as something to be discarded—yet remain unable to it go—and nirvana as something to be achieved—yet cannot reach it either. Understand that samsara and nirvana are not two separate entities but manifestations of reality's single ultimate nature.

If you genuinely realize the nature of awareness, the ups and downs of your experiences will no longer lure you. Rather, you will understand that the state of dharmatā is innately yours and proceed on the path of liberation in the continuum that transcends notions of "high" and "low."

If you cling to the reality of your thoughts, good or bad, and of various signs of accomplishment; and if you fail to uproot the three mental poisons, delusion, and belief in the solidity of things, even if meditative experiences and realization dawn, you will hold them to be supreme and, filled with conceit, fall under the sway of the māras. Eliminate all misconceptions that result from not having correctly realized the nature of reality.

–120–

Do Not Fall Back into Ordinary Concerns

Six instructions that prevent falling back:
Relying on a spiritual master, you will not fall back into worldly dharmas.
Contemplating the defects of sense objects, you will not fall back into worldly dharmas.
Reflecting on pleasure and pain, you will not fall back into worldly dharmas.

Contemplating the flaws of (the eight) ordinary concerns, you will not fall back into worldly dharmas.
Observing delusion, you will not fall back into worldly dharmas.
Contemplating the quagmire of suffering, you will not fall back into worldly dharmas.
Reflecting like this, you will be freed from these worldly dharmas.

When you undertake pure Dharma practice, until you bring your practice to its ultimate point, you need six instructions to avoid regressing:

Follow a spiritual guide in a proper manner and abide by his instructions. As this master will have enjoined you to leave behind the tumult of worldly life, do not be swayed back into ordinary activities under any circumstances.

Ponder carefully how sensory perceptions apprehended by the six aspects of consciousness have misled you thus far and the flaws that have resulted, and you will be less likely to revert to the eight worldly concerns.

Meditate constantly on the illusory and dreamlike nature of samsaric joys and sorrows. Knowing how to integrate them on the path, you will not fall back into secular entanglements.

The various behaviors arising from the eight worldly concerns may bring you some temporary satisfaction, but ultimately lead to complications, like licking honey off the edge of a sword. Feel a deep revulsion toward them and you will not fall back into ordinary concerns.

Realize that in the three worlds of samsara, every deed, word, and thought keeps you mired in illusion. Clearly understand that lingering in samsara is like eating food with poison and you will not return to it.

This samsara is a great quagmire of suffering in which you have been mired from beginningless existences until now. Contemplating such defects, you will not return to worldly affairs.

–121–

SIX SENTINELS

Six sentinels to post as antidotes:
(Worldly) activities day and night rob you of your life, so be watchful and apply antidotes.
The five poisons consume your mind stream, so be watchful and apply antidotes.
Sense pleasures are insatiable, so be watchful and apply antidotes.
Be watchful of violent behavior and apply antidotes.
Be watchful of worthless activities and apply antidotes.
Be watchful of whatever actions of the three doors you may perform and apply antidotes.
If you act like this, the rogue enemy of negative emotions will not defeat you.

In everyday life, the rich and powerful hire bodyguards to protect themselves from harm. Likewise, those earnestly who practice the Dharma must use six antidotes as their protectors.

Your Dharma practice will inevitably face obstacles, one of the most significant ones being impermanence, as your life slips away day by day, night by night. Spurred on by your awareness of impermanence, an antidote [to laziness], constantly post the sentry of diligence at the threshold [of your practice] of the supreme Dharma.

Perpetuating afflictive states of mind burns the seed of liberation within your mind. Therefore, at all times, post the sentinel of antidotes in your mind to clear it of the five poisons.

No matter how much food, clothing, possessions, and wealth you acquire, you are never satisfied, and fritter your life away in futile pursuits. Appoint contentment with what you have as the essential guard against this insatiable craving.

If you cast spells on your enemies, visualize wrathful deities and recite their mantras, and practice the triad of "protecting, repelling, and annihilating,"[119] and similar activities—unless your realization is high enough to enable you, among other things, to bring back to life those you have slain—you will be tainted with very serious faults. As an antidote, place the sentinel of kindness and compassion at the portal of your mind.

Until now you have been relentlessly engaged in samsaric affairs without yielding any meaningful harvest, not even as much as a sesame seed. For example, were you to collect all the anguished tears you have shed in samsara since time immemorial, they would surpass the expanse of the oceans. Moreover, if the limbs from your lifetimes just as an ant were amassed, they would rise higher than Mount Meru. Recognizing that all this (effort) has been utterly devoid of essence, as an antidote, post in your mind the sentinel of deep weariness toward samsara.

Ask yourself whether all your actions of body, speech, and mind are consistent with the Dharma. Then, as an antidote, post a sentinel who tirelessly repels all that contradicts the Dharma.

A person of very great wealth is always on guard, never knowing when enemies or thieves might strike. Your adversaries are the afflictive mental states: therefore, at all times, post a sentry, as an antidote, to prevent them from plundering you.

Heed this crucial advice.

–122–

Lost Opportunities

Six opportunities lost by those who do not practice:
Lazy people waste their lives in worthless (activities).
Those who yearn for fame squander their lives pursuing celebrity.
Those who crave food exhaust their lives in fear of starvation.
Those who are clever and crave wealth squander their lives pursuing profit in business.
Those who engage in study and reflection, but lack faith, waste their lives in the mere acquisition of knowledge while remaining resistant [to the Dharma].
Those who are less learned waste their lives in stupid meditation and thus fall into the wrong path.
It is extremely important not to fall into these six situations.

You may intend to practice the Dharma properly, but if you fail to grasp the essential points of practice, you may go astray in six ways.

Those of limited capacity achieve little in both ordinary life and the Dharma, squandering their existence in the mere pursuit of sustenance and clothing.

Those renowned for their skill in the intrigues of public life, and who devote long years of their lives to worldly affairs, miss the opportunity to practice the Dharma.

Those who continually think about food, meat, and alcohol keep succumbing to their insatiable desires and end up dying haunted by the fear of scarcity.

Those swept up in business and diversions, who lack vigilance and circumspection and constantly seek profit, and do not hesitate to cheat and swindle others, live under the burden of trade and gain. Perpetually hunting for a lucrative deal, they waste their entire lives.

Those who lack faith in the sublime Dharma, who do not cultivate fervent aspiration and unwavering trust, waste the treasure of study, reflection, and meditation. They grow jaded, and the Dharma does not blossom in their minds. Avoid falling into such traps.

Remember these words as well: "Without proper instruction, meditation is as futile as throwing pebbles [into water]."[120] If you have meditated for a long time without reducing your negative emotions and without experiencing the blossoming of meditative experiences and realization, you have gone astray.

Recognize these six lost opportunities and take the necessary steps to stay clear of such situations.

–123–

Eliminate Defects

Six solutions when defects manifest (on the path):
If you lose devotion and respect, consider the difficulty of developing inner qualities without them.
If you are carried away by distractions, transform conceptual thoughts into allies.
If you make no progress even though you meditate, strive (to improve) by using various skillful means.

If you become ill due to imbalances of the internal elements,
understand that this results from causes and conditions.
If what has been gathered dissipates, diligently make offerings
of sacred feasts and of torma.
If your bodhicitta diminishes, as an antidote, renew the
bodhisattva vows.
All this will counter whatever obstacles arise.

When defects contrary to your Dharma practice arise, there are six antidotes to eliminate them.

When devotion and respect for your spiritual masters decline, think of their qualities, achieved by eliminating [all obscurations] and realizing [all enlightened qualities]. Reflect as well on the great kindness they have shown in freeing you from samsara since they first held you with their compassion. This reflection will naturally reignite fervent devotion in your heart.

When you are carried away by distraction and mindless endeavors, recognize that your thought patterns are allowing these defects to build up bad habits. Through heightened awareness and vigilance, your wandering thoughts can turn into allies, just as an elephant becomes a supportive companion when tamed.

If your Dharma practice stagnates despite your efforts to meditate, stimulate it with a variety of profound and skillful means. Dispel obstacles and disruptions, and make your practice flourish. Then you will progress.

When the elements that constitute your body become imbalanced, illnesses occur. Perceive these ailments as karmic retribution for past misdeeds: cultivate selfless love and compassion in response.

If your entourage, disciples, and all that you have gathered begin to fade away, offer gaṇacakra feasts and ritual offerings (*tormas*) to the ḍākinīs and Dharma protectors and your activities will again thrive.

If the excellent mindset of benevolence and the intention to attain enlightenment for the sake of others declines, think of the flaws of self-centeredness, which have only brought calamities in your past lives. Repeatedly generate the mind of enlightenment, bodhicitta.

These are the natural ways to remove obstacles.

–124–

Six Key Points

Six outer and inner crucial points to integrate into your mind:
Inwardly, cutting through the fetters of self-clinging is crucial.
Outwardly, knowing objective appearances to be dharmakāya is crucial.
In between, accepting conceptual thoughts as allies is crucial.
At the highest level, exhausting views and realization [in dharmatā] is crucial.
At the lowest level, engaging in virtuous activities according to the scriptures is crucial.
In between, cultivating vigilant introspection without straying into distraction is crucial.
Gathering these conditions, you will swiftly tread the path to liberation.

If you aspire to blend the supreme Dharma with your mind, you can harmonize the inner and outer factors of interdependence in six ways:

Inwardly, if you sever the root of self-clinging, benevolence and bodhicitta will naturally blossom in your mind. Take this to heart to eradicate egocentricity.

Outwardly, in relation to the objects of the six aspects of consciousness, neither being seduced by those you deem good nor repulsed by those you deem bad, apprehend all as manifestations of the dharmatā. Free from likes and dislikes, integrate them on the path of spontaneous liberation into the dharmakāya, the absolute dimension. Doing so, the six types of perceptions will no longer deceive you.[121]

In between, within the natural liberation of all concepts of "good" and "bad," assimilate the three modes of liberating thoughts as they arise: liberation of thoughts through recognizing their true nature; liberation as natural as the knot unraveling in a snake's body; and liberation like a thief in an empty house [who can cause no harm]. You should practice in this way.

Looking upward, no matter the quality of your view and your realization, enhancing your meditative experiences and realization neither improves nor degrades the ultimate nature of reality, the dharmatā. When these are exhausted [in the dharmatā], you will reach the pinnacle of the path. This is crucial.

Looking down, at the beginner's level, gradually improve your conduct while progressing upward. To do this in accordance with the texts of the supreme Dharma, accumulate merit, cleanse obscurations, and engage in virtuous practices with or without representations. Never presume that you have practiced enough.

At the intermediary stage, free of distractions, guard your mind with attentive presence and vigilant introspection.

Nothing is more crucial than these six points. Fully integrate them into your mind stream and you will swiftly travel the path to its highest level.

–125–

Six Actions toward Buddhahood

Six precious actions for those who wish to attain buddhahood:
Even though you have realized the illusoriness of [phenomena], you must respect the law of cause and effect.
Even though you have achieved certainty, you must not denigrate others.
Even though all phenomena arise as allies, you must retreat in solitude.
Even though you understand nonmeditation, you must master your thoughts.
Even though meditation and post-meditation are not different, do not let your thoughts fall back into the ordinary.
Even though you have realized the fundamental nature, you must refine your scriptural knowledge and logical reasoning.
No matter how high your level of accomplishment, you must act upon these six points.

Six instructions to cherish particularly if you aspire to reach buddhahood:

Even if you realize the illusory nature of all phenomena—the universe and beings, samsara and nirvana—your observance of the laws of cause and effect must remain as fine as ground flour. Exercise the utmost caution in this regard.

"This is my view and my meditation. Even were I to consult a hundred virtuous scholars, a thousand siddhas, ten thousand spiritual masters, and a hundred thousand essential instructions, I have no remaining doubt to dispel." Even having developed such certainty, take no pride in it and do not look down on others.

Even if all phenomena arise as friends, remain steadfast in a mountain retreat, emulating the lives of perfect liberation of the great masters of the lineage of spiritual accomplishment.

Even if you master the state of nonmeditation during meditative equality, as well as during the intervals between sessions, regularly check whether or not you are succeeding in liberating deluded thoughts. Take control of your mental fabrications.

Even if the distinction between meditation and daily life fades, make sure you never fall into ordinariness.

Even if you have correctly realized the fundamental nature of everything, make sure that you remain in accord with the words of the Buddha, the commentaries of his followers, the logical reasoning of the great scholars, and the essential instructions of spiritual masters. Otherwise, taking pride in thinking that you have attained realization and that you are practicing the direct path is futile.

Even if you had many spiritual experiences and reached a high level of realization, do not fail to cherish these six instructions. Never abandon them, and you will succeed in freeing yourself from the six bonds of clinging to extreme views.

–126–

Clinging to Extremes

Six situations showing that any form of extremism is bondage:
Attachment, even to your yidam deity, is a cause of bondage.
Even the highest philosophical views, if you cling to them, are a cause of bondage.
Grasping, even to compassion, is a cause of bondage.
Being proud, even of profound realization, is a cause of bondage.
Being attached, even to spiritual experiences and realization, is a cause of bondage.
Grasping, even to the experience of nonduality, is a cause of bondage.

What need is there to mention ordinary self-grasping and attachment to wealth and property?
This is why freedom from attachment to anything is essential.

Even if your view of the nature of reality reaches its peak, it remains incomplete unless you are aware of six potential hindrances:

If you cling to your supreme chosen deity, the yidam, while discarding others, paradoxically your deity can become a source of bondage.

Even if your philosophical views are very high and belong to the Great Perfection or the Great Seal, the belief that your view is superior and all others are deficient becomes a hindrance in itself.

Even if you generate unconditional compassion for all beings of the three worlds, boasting that no one equals you in compassion, binds you to the chains of vanity.

If you achieve some signs of accomplishment, such as clairvoyance, meditative experiences, or realization, yet succumb to infatuation with these achievements, your profound insights become fetters.

If you have many kinds of contemplative experiences, realizations, and lucid insights, yet become attached to them, such attachment is well known for opening the door to the "demon" and thus becoming a cause of bondage.

If you have reached a level of certainty in your experience of the view but still lack the full realization of nonduality, you remain ensnared in the three worlds of samsara.

It goes without saying that ordinary attachments, including self-clinging, will enslave you. But you should also understand that clinging to the view, meditation, and conduct associated with the supreme Dharma is equally a hindrance. Be careful not to conceive any form of attachment.

–127–

Cutting Ties

Instructions to sever the six tethers:
Obsessed with wealth and possessions, you are bound by the tether of increasing and protecting them.
Obsessed with your family lineage, you are bound by the tether of prestige and fame.

Obsessed with distractions, you are bound by the tether of activities.
Obsessed with designations and words, you are bound by the tether of vanity.
Obsessed with spiritual experiences and realization, you are bound by the tether of pride.
Obsessed with virtuous practices, you are bound by the tether of antidotes.
Finding practitioners free of these tethers is difficult.

Six bonds hold you captive. Until you sever them, you will remain unable to walk the path to liberation and will remain like a horse tethered to its post.

In the grip of attachment to wealth and possessions, you toil to acquire what you do not yet have and fiercely cling to what you have, in this way making yourself a slave to greed.

Infatuated with your ancestry, whether you come from nobility, an influential family, or a respectable lineage, you are preoccupied with activities associated with your rank, your reputation, and the status of those you meet. Abandon this vain pursuit of prestige.

Caught by the activities associated with attraction and rejection, which completely distract your mind, your inability to meditate on a samādhi free from mind-wandering will hinder you.

Interested only in definitions and literal knowledge of the texts, indulging in your own erudition, you become a slave of your vanity.

If you are attached to and proud of your meditative experiences and realization, that is none other than the work of māra, which keeps you trapped.

If you persevere in spiritual practices day and night yet tell yourself that you have no equal in meditation practice, the antidotes themselves become chains of arrogance.

Authentic practitioners have freed themselves from all these ties, but nowadays such practitioners are very rare!

–128–

Results of Spiritual Practice

Six achievements of a practitioner:

Run away from situations that lead to attachment and aversion, and
Dharma-related virtuous activities will naturally flourish.

Do not be too irritable or emotional,
And your relationships with others will be long-lasting and less conflicted.

Respectfully follow the words of your noble spiritual masters,
And they will remember you and bless you to achieve the siddhis.

Do not give the reins to others,
And you will be joyous and successful in Dharma practice.

Discard aggressive behavior and be gentle and tamed,
And you will be in harmony with everyone and appreciated by all.

Give up partiality and cultivate kind-heartedness,
And everyone will regard you as genuine and praise you.

When spiritual qualities flourish in Dharma practitioners, six features naturally emerge.

If you fully disengage from situations that give rise to attachment and aversion—such as leaving your homeland—your spiritual practices and virtuous Dharma activities will flourish effortlessly.

When besieged by resentment, spite, and jealousy, you react in a confrontational manner. Avoid such behavior at all costs and your relationships with others will be harmonious, enduring, and devoid of discord.

If you faithfully and respectfully apply all the advice given by your supreme spiritual masters, they will rejoice in your practice and keep you in their thoughts. The blessings of ordinary and supreme siddhis will come effortlessly.

Don't give a tether to others to lead you by the nose.[122] Preserve your ability to freely accomplish your goals, and you will succeed in everything you do and bring your practice to its peak.

If you have mastered your mind through practicing the supreme Dharma and yet remain humble, you will maintain pleasant relations with others and bring joy to all those you meet.

Give up the bias that fosters constant discrimination between members of your group and outsiders. Instead, cultivate benevolence and generate the mind of enlightenment, and you will be recognized as a genuine practitioner.

–129–

Six Hopes to Surrender

Six expectations of the wicked to be abandoned:
Without helping others, they expect benefit.
Without working hard, they expect to achieve happiness.
Without practicing, they expect to attain siddhis.
Without abandoning mundane concerns, they hope the sacred Dharma will flourish.
Without practicing Dharma, they hope to teach others and benefit them.
Without having done much for others, they expect service and respect.
Such attitudes keep them as far from the path of liberation as an ocean's eastern and western shores.

Six vain hopes of people afflicted with a flawed disposition:

Doing nothing for others—not even as much as the magnitude of a single sesame seed—and yet entertaining expectations about them, hoping they will feed you and shower you with wealth, you can rest assured that they will not.

Without conquering the citadel of meditative experiences and realization with tenacity and hard work, the sun of bliss will not rise and you will be tossed back and forth between happiness and sorrow.

Unless you fully concentrate on developing the stronghold of your spiritual practice's life force, do not expect to attain ordinary siddhis, let alone the supreme one.

Unless you eschew the eight worldly concerns, you will never be in tune with the scriptures of the sublime Dharma.

You have not sincerely practiced the teachings you have received and yet imagine you can benefit others in a grand way with mere eloquence. How could you transform others without first transforming yourself?

Having practiced for a few months or even a few years, you may declare yourself a Dharma practitioner and expect others' respect and attention. However, this is not the way to progress on the path of liberation.

Realization of all these ambitions is as distant as are a vast ocean's eastern and western shores. Abandon such vain hopes!

–130–

Deplorable Behavior

Six kinds of misconduct of ill-natured individuals:
When food and drink are distributed, they want the largest share.
When they engage in business, they want all the profit.
When it comes to clothing, they want the warmest and softest.
They keep the best items and leave the inferior quality to others.
Even when they stay overnight at someone's home, they ask for the best place.
They expect the Dharma and the teachers to take care of their relatives.
For such individuals, the sprout of liberation will wither.

People with bad dispositions exhibit six defects:

They always want the best food and drink, but in the end they seldom get all they want.

When they engage in business, they try to take all the profit for themselves but have a hard time succeeding.

When choosing clothes, they covet the warmest and softest items and cannot bear to let others have them. With such behavior, they cannot expect much from others.

Whatever they do, they are convinced of their superiority, carrying an air of self-importance and looking down on others, wishing them no good.

If they ask for hospitality, even for a single night, they want the most comfortable bed, driven solely by the pursuit of personal ease.

While doing nothing for others, they expect the Dharma, their spiritual masters, friends, and family to support them, which is unlikely to happen.

For those who live in this manner, the shoot of liberation withers and fades.

–131–

Exemplary Behavior

Six unerring ways to enter the path:
Settle into solitary retreat but do not focus on "me" and "mine."
Gather the means of sustenance, but do not grasp it.
Maintain the conduct of a scholar and a disciplined person, but do not hold a high position.
Abandon behavior that diminishes the faith of others and act without pretense in front of them.
Benefit others with compassion, not protecting your life partner and your possessions alone.
Give generously without partiality or bragging, and do not expect anything in return.

There are six correct ways to enter the path of liberation.

If you settle in a mountain retreat avoid declaring, "This is my place, and that is his place." Having few attachments and demands, make nothing your own.

Keep only the bare necessities to protect yourself from hunger and bad weather. Without becoming fixated on notions of "me" and "mine," know how to be content with little and walk the path to liberation.

Even if you have acquired some qualities of learning and spiritual accomplishment, avoid yearning for a high position, a throne, or any other distinction, and you will be fine.

Root out any flaws that might cause others to lose faith, yet do not adopt artificial behavior merely to please everyone, thus compromising the accomplishment of your spiritual aspirations.

Cultivate compassion, aiming to do as much good as possible to others, rather than busying yourself with garnering wealth for your life partner and your home and cultivating a large number of social relationships for that purpose.

Make offerings to the Three Jewels and provide assistance to those in need without bias. Be generous without expecting that those you help will be useful to you in return. This is how bodhisattvas practice generosity and dedicate merit.

–132–

Be Autonomous in Your Practice

Six ways to become self-reliant in your practice:
Practice ethical discipline without hypocrisy and it will withstand adverse circumstances.
Clarify all confusion within the instructions so you will know how to perform all kinds of practices.
Be skillful in removing obstacles and obstructions, in curing diseases, and pacifying demonic forces.
Gain certainty through study and reflection so you will have no questions to ask.
Develop a clear understanding of the obscurations and deviations, and you will know the gradation of the various vehicles.
Don the armor [of protection] so you become invincible by the māras.

Six instructions for practitioners to become able to stand on their own feet.

If you preserve perfectly pure moral discipline, without concealing anything, no adverse circumstances will be able to overpower or hinder your integrity.

If you have fully understood and assimilated the essential instructions you have received, whether you engage in the preliminary or the main practice, you will remain free of confusion.

Freeing yourself from hope and fear regarding overcoming obstacles and interruptions, all such interferences will be liberated into their true nature [emptiness], while diseases and harmful influences will vanish of their own accord.

Once you have your study and reflection have reached their consummation, you no longer need to ask questions to anyone and can walk the path to liberation on your own.

If you have overcome all the obstacles that may stand in your way, you will know how to distinguish the view, meditation, and conduct of the supreme vehicle from those of the lesser ones.

To prevent the demon of ordinary life activities from invading your mind, don the armor of diligence, and your practice will naturally gain strength and resilience.

–133–

Dispensing with Shameful Situations

Instruction on six types of shameful activities to abandon:
Accumulating wealth and property is a source of shame.
Reveling in expensive clothes and glamour is a source of shame.
Adorning yourself with ornaments and indulging in coquetry is a source of shame.
Engaging in the distracting activities of pursuing wealth is a source of shame.
Engaging in many activities unrelated to the Dharma is a source of shame.
Pride and arrogance about your superiority is a source of shame.
From the bottom of my heart, I request all Dharma practitioners to abandon these activities.

Six behaviors should shame those who practice the supreme Dharma and ought to be abandoned.

Exemplary practitioners must relinquish their wealth and possessions. If they persist in amassing riches and material goods, only to die with such attachment, they have cause for profound regret.

Practitioners who flaunt themselves in fine clothing, women practitioners who adorn themselves with all kinds of jewels have every reason to feel ashamed.

When practitioners wear a lot of ornaments, make up their faces, or engage in flirtatious behavior, it is embarrassing.

If practitioners dedicate their time to material possessions, thereby falling into distraction, they are neglecting the Dharma and have good reason for shame.

A practitioner who covets a high position and constantly displays pride and vanity has much to be ashamed of.

Practitioners who follow a spiritual guide yet engage in all kinds of negative behavior contrary to the Dharma should be ashamed.

From the bottom of my heart, I implore all practitioners to abandon these six sources of shame.

–134–

The Life Example of Noble Beings

Six attitudes that illustrate the life of perfect liberation of the sublime masters:
Always mindful of impermanence and death, they encouraged themselves [to practice the Dharma].
Having recognized the suffering of samsara, they cast it away.
They gave up the luxuries of the kingdom as worthless as spit.
With pure faith and effort, they entered the gateway of the Dharma path.
They sought out spiritual masters, received and contemplated [their instructions], and cut through conceptual thoughts.
They endured great austerities and put their bodies and lives at stake.
Acting thus, they achieved accomplishment.
Accept them as role models and persevere in Dharma practice.

Six qualities exemplified in past and present masters' lives of perfect liberation, which you should integrate into your mind stream.

Undistracted, with unwavering focus, vigilance, and careful thought, these masters contemplated the transient nature of all things again and again. This is how they urged themselves to practice the supreme Dharma.

They had no interest in samsaric activities and left them far behind, having seen that they bring nothing but suffering across the three worlds.

Even when offered kingdoms as universal monarchs and enjoyment of all the wealth in the treasury of Vaiśravana, the god of fortune, they saw these as without essence and had no more interest in them than for spittle in the dust.

With consummate confidence and diligence, they entered the door of the Buddha's teachings and continuously cultivated their spiritual qualities.

They first sought authentic spiritual masters, endowed with all the necessary qualifications; then, they never considered that they had studied, reflected, and meditated sufficiently, eventually cutting off all conceptual elaboration.

They retreated to secluded places far from the crowds, settled there, and persevered in their practice, enduring great austerity with no concern for their bodies or even their lives.

If you can follow the example of these masters' lives of perfect liberation, your own life can reflect theirs. Take them as models and diligently engage in spiritual practice.

–135–

Six Benefits for Others

Six benefits brought to others through practicing as above:
Cultivating compassion, you care for all, far and near.
Attaining perfect realization, you dismantle the delusion of self-grasping.
Knowing the mental dispositions of others, you skillfully create favorable conditions.
All appearances and perceptions arise as friends, as they are liberated into the dharmatā.
Imbued with blessings, you can transform the perceptions of others.
When the time to transform others has come, faithful beings will gather.

At this stage, outer and inner auspicious circumstances have come together.

If you acquire the qualities mentioned above, six ways to help others will naturally arise:

When your mind is suffused with great compassion, you will extend profound kindness toward all beings, near and far, without the slightest trace of partiality. As a result, numerous disciples will naturally come to you.

By attaining the ultimate realization of view and meditation, you will eradicate the delusion of clinging to the belief in a self, the root cause of bondage in samsara.

Possessing the ability to assess both your own and others' capabilities, you will confidently maintain a steady practice and knowing how to act with caution and discernment, you will skillfully navigate the links of interdependence.

Freeing your attachments into the ultimate nature of reality, taking support of the view, meditation, and action, all appearances and experiences will manifest as friends instead of hindering your progress to liberation.

As the blessings of the spiritual master permeate your being, your ability to subtly transform the perceptions of others will flourish.

When the time comes to serve sentient beings, even if you initially turn them away, they will come back to you.

By embodying these qualities, you will have perfectly established the favorable inner and outer interdependent connections.

–136–

Failing to Assimilate Spiritual Qualities

Six defects of failing to assimilate virtue in your mind:
If you have not practiced, even though you know the Dharma, you will wander in samsara.
It is like shooting an arrow away from the target in front of you.
It is like chasing on the western side of the hill a robber who has escaped to the east.
It is like looking on a sand dune for the footprints of a thief who ran into the forest.

It is like running on the riverbank looking for something carried away by the stream.
It is like reciting an entire [ransom] ritual with no idea of where to put the thread-cross ransom.[123]
Acting like this, you remain distant from the state of great bliss.

Six examples illustrate the consequences of these misguided actions:

Without wholehearted dedication to practice, even if you become an expert in many areas of knowledge, you have little hope of ending your wandering in the three worlds of samsara.

Before shooting an arrow, you must locate the target. If you don't, even when the target is right before you, you will never hit the mark by shooting randomly into the distance. Likewise, if instead of freeing your mind from afflictive mental states, you turn your attention elsewhere, your efforts will be in vain.

Chasing a thief who has fled to the eastern hill by racing up the western slope, you have little chance of recovering your belongings. The same will happen if the bandits of the five poisons invade your mind and you fail to counteract them with the proper antidotes.

If the thief has fled to the forest and you look for his tracks on the sandy banks of a river, you will not catch him. The same will be true if you fail to recognize the thieves who have crept into your mind: distraction and restlessness.

If someone is swept away by a river and needs rescue, but you run around looking for him on the banks, you will not bring them to safety out of the water. Likewise, when you are immersed in the ocean of samsara's three worlds, owing to your karma and mental poisons, without practicing the Dharma, you have hardly any hope of reaching dry land.

When you have performed a ransom ritual, prepared tormas and other offerings, and are ready to place them somewhere on the nearby mountain, but have no idea about the mountain spirits (*tsen*) and regal spirits (*gyalpo*)[124] to whom you are making the offerings, the patient you are trying to heal through this ritual will hardly benefit.

Likewise, if you are enslaved by your thirst for sensual pleasures, while being oblivious of the key points of authentic Dharma practice, the practice will yield little benefit.

–137–

Six Difficulties

Six defects that can bring about difficulties:
For those who cling to samsara, having pure faith is difficult.
For those who lack shame or restraint, preserving the three trainings is difficult.
For those who do not meet authentic masters, entering the path to liberation is difficult.
For those who do not employ the path of skillful means,[125] giving rise to primordial wisdom is difficult.
For those who have not freed themselves from extreme views, realizing the [correct] view is difficult.
For those without clairvoyance, benefiting others is difficult.
These difficulties are such that practitioners who overcome them are rare.

While you are practicing the supreme Dharma, six undesirable defects can prevent the birth of spiritual qualities. You must eliminate them.

True and pure confidence can only blossom within you if you fully abandon your fascination for samsara and your attachment to it.

If you have never met a single qualified master, you will not know how to practice on the path of liberation and enlightenment, making it challenging even to begin the journey.

If you do not use the skillful means of the Adamantine Vehicle of the Secret Mantra, it will be difficult for the primordial wisdom essential to spiritual realization to arise in your mind.

If you do not emancipate yourself from the polarities of eternalism and nihilism, yet presume that you have achieved a perfectly pure view, remember the saying, "Where there is grasping, there is no view."[126] If that is the case, realizing the view will be very difficult.

Attempting to benefit others before becoming endowed with insight, you will be unable to accurately assess their capacities and dispositions and will find it very difficult to help them meaningfully.

Aware of these difficulties, do your best to overcome them and accomplish the Dharma. But these days, those who can achieve this are extremely rare.

–138–

Tackling Distraction

Six outcomes of habituation that protect you from distraction during your practice:
By remembering the freedoms and advantages [of a precious human life], you will abandon meaningless activities.
Never being distracted from nonconceptuality, you will be free from the enemy of laziness.
Because you have achieved the siddhis, your enthusiasm will be uninterrupted.
The growth of your spiritual experience and realization brings joy in meditation practice.
By mastering[127] pristine awareness, all distracting conditions manifest as dharmatā.
Your mind stream will blend with the teachings of the sutras and tantras.

When your practice has become perfectly stable, six trainings will allow you to withstand all the circumstances that typically cause distraction:

By earnestly pondering the difficulty of obtaining a human existence endowed with the proper freedoms and conditions, you will not need to purposefully disengage from the futile activities of this world, for they will vanish by themselves.

If awareness of impermanence is born in your mind, and you repeatedly remind yourself that the time of death is uncertain, your enemy—laziness—will no longer have power over you.

Having attained the ordinary and the supreme siddhis, when contemplating all the qualities that arise from them, you will be filled with joy and your diligence will flow uninterrupted.

When meditative experiences and realization arise in your mind stream, and you are aware that you have reached an optimal stability, your joy in practice will expand spontaneously.

Once you have fully mastered experiential awareness, all the circumstances that normally lead to distraction and delusion will dissolve into the continuum of the ultimate nature of reality.

When your mind has fully integrated the qualities of the sutra and the tantra teachings, these six indications of mastery over circumstances will manifest.

–139–

What to Count On

Six supports to rely upon until you have perfected your Dharma practice:
Do not rely on your family or ordinary relationships but on excellent Dharma friends.
Avoid evil friends, and place your trust in learned and disciplined spiritual masters.
Abandon discussion of (worldly) plans but instead deliberate on the goal of ultimate happiness.
Rely on study and contemplation and accustom your mind to them as much as possible.
Avoid populated areas and settle in solitary places in the mountains.
Seek spiritual instructions and practice them with diligence.
If you act like this, you will swiftly achieve the siddhis.

Until you have reached the highest point of the supreme Dharma, you must rely on six supports.

Forsake your attachments to your loved ones and instead rely on the support of virtuous friends who are in harmony with the Dharma. As the saying goes, "Friends who are in accord with the Dharma support your spiritual practice." Such friends constantly clarify and invigorate your spiritual practice.

At all times, stay away from those who misbehave, who accumulate all kinds of negativity and harbor wrong views against the Dharma and spiritual masters. If you rely on learned, wise, and virtuous mentors, their wisdom and virtuous qualities will flourish in your own mind.

Forget any plans concerning ordinary life, such as overcoming your opponents or favoring your loved ones. Instead, direct all your energy toward attaining lasting bliss through Dharma practice.

With the support of study and reflection, transform your mind as much as you can, applying what you have learned, using every available means to blend your mind with the Dharma.

No longer wander in crowded places but remain steady in mountain solitudes.

Seek out a wide range of instructions from spiritual masters, and be diligent in studying, reflecting, and integrating them in your mind stream through meditation.

By adopting these practices, you will attain the ordinary and the supreme accomplishments.

–140–

Mixing Benefit and Harm

Six situations where benefit and harm are mixed:
Relying upon a spiritual master who cannot help you develop positive qualities,
Nurturing students who do not conform to the established path of Dharma,
Practicing Dharma without abandoning the eight worldly concerns,
Attempting to benefit others while profiting from improper livelihood,
Taking the vows of discipline without intending to keep them,
Engaging in Secret Mantra conduct [inappropriately] while confusing vice with virtue.
Such situations where you mix harm and benefit show you to be just a facade of a Dharma practitioner.

There are six situations in which benefits and mistakes become entangled:

If you follow a spiritual master without developing any spiritual qualities and your sole interest is to receive material gifts, the master's qualities will not be transferred to you.

If you do not know how to properly practice according to an authentic lineage, gathering disciples will not help them achieve inner transformation.

If you pretend to practice the Dharma without forsaking the eight worldly concerns, you will remain bound by the chains of ordinary life.

If you meet your needs through unethical means, such as by misusing religious property under the guise of benefiting others, this will make a mockery of your activities and you will not be helping others in any way.

You may claim to observe discipline and precepts properly, but if—while taking many vows pertaining to individual liberation, the Great Vehicle of the bodhisattvas, and the Secret Mantra—you do not carefully discard what should be discarded and abide by what should be respected, you will open yourself to many faults.

If, confusing wrong with right, you fail to shun what must be abandoned and to perform what must be done,—boasting that you are a practitioner of the Secret Mantra and proclaiming, "Virtue is emptiness, vice is emptiness"—this will only lead to the proliferation of evil.

Those who thus blur the lines between what is beneficial and what is detrimental are mere facades of true practitioners.

–141–

Countermeasures

The six countermeasures that can be used like nails:[128]
Because harmful enemies increase when you vanquish them, the countermeasure is to subdue the evil of self-grasping.
As indulgence in sensory pleasures only exacerbates your desires, the countermeasure is to vigorously cut through craving.
Because chatter proliferates in the company of idlers, the countermeasure is to remain alone and keep silent.
Because the more you need to satisfy every wish of others, the more they multiply, the countermeasure is to let go of your tendency [to attend to others' needs] and let the situation follow its own course.
Because the more you force your mind to focus, the more it tightens, the countermeasure is to relax the mind in its natural state.[129]
Because your elaborate activities multiply the more you engage in them, the countermeasure is to freely rest in the natural state.
If you apply these countermeasures, the duality of hope and fear falls apart.

If you are practicing the Dharma in mistaken ways, here are six countermeasures:

If you are consumed by the urge to destroy at all costs the enemies who harm you and, full of animosity toward them, use all means to finish them off, you will only fuel the fire of hatred, increasing your enemies. The countermeasure is to sever the bonds of self-clinging and practice forbearance with your foes.

The more you indulge in the pleasures of the five senses, the more insatiable they become, leaving you perpetually unsatisfied. The countermeasure is to put aside these pleasures, treating them as your adversaries, and to resolutely cut off nagging desires.

If you succumb to chronic idleness and engage in endless gossip about the myriad likes and dislikes in this world, chatter will only multiply. The countermeasure is to remain silent and stay in the solitude of a mountain hermitage.

The more you attempt to meet the expectations of others, the more those expectations will grow. As a countermeasure, no matter what others may think of you, remain free of hopes and fears, and let things follow their own course.

The more you constrain your mind, the more tense it becomes, like a rope twisted into knots, causing you to become increasingly uptight. The countermeasure is to free your mind into its natural state and keep the flow of your virtuous practices going with a mind that is relaxed and perfectly at ease.

The more you drift into elaborations, the more intricate and convoluted things will become. The countermeasure is to let go and rest in natural bliss of simplicity.

By applying these countermeasures, the duality of hope and fear will gradually fade, allowing you to rest in an open and serene state of mind.

–142–

Uniting Your Mind with the Dharma

Six indications that your mind stream is at home with the Dharma.
To perceive sense pleasures as māras is a sign you have detachment from samsara.

To transform all your activities into the path is a sign of having received blessings.
To be able to gain mastery over pristine awareness is a sign of having obtained the supreme siddhi.
Not being swayed by circumstances is a sign of having realized the view.
To be filled with joy when seeing your spiritual master is a sign of devotion and respect.
To be able to give up the pursuits of this life is a sign that Dharma has benefited you.
Those who possess these great signs can be considered noble beings.

Six indications that you have succeeded in transforming your mind with the sublime Dharma:

Recognizing all attachment to sense pleasures as the workings of Māra indicates that you have grown weary of the fascination with the three worlds of samsara.

When all your physical, verbal, and mental activities are in accord with Dharma, it is a sign that the blessings of your spiritual master have taken root within you.

Mastering the experience of pristine awareness is a sign that you have achieved both the ordinary and the supreme siddhis.

Remaining undisturbed by torpor, restlessness, or distraction is a sign that you have reached the peak of insight and realization.

Even after attending your spiritual masters for a long time, if you continue to meet them frequently, contemplate their faces, and insatiably receive their instructions, it is a sign that respectful fervor is born in your mind.

Becoming increasingly disenchanted with worldly affairs and succeeding in transforming your mind stream are signs of the benefits of the Dharma.

If these six major signs have manifested in your mind, you can take your place among the supreme beings. Therefore, give them the importance they deserve.

–143–

Fearlessness

Six indispensable kinds of fearlessness:
By practicing the profound meaning [of the teachings], you will not fear the enemy of negative thoughts.
By contemplating the fundamental nature of the mind, you will not fear the enemy of the eight worldly concerns.
By refining your experience of the dharmakāya, you will not fear the enemy of dualism.
By taking groundlessness as the path, you will not fear the enemy of the two obscurations.
By training in great bliss, you will not fear the enemy of suffering.
By training in being unbiased, you will not fear the enemy of hope and fear.
Whoever possesses these six kinds of fearlessness will accomplish great purposes in whatever activities they undertake.

Six kinds of confidence that will help you to not fear obstacles on the path.

When you experience the profound meaning of the Secret Mantra, you need not fear the enemy of deluded and negative thoughts that disrupt your deep concentration.

When you have correctly realized the ultimate nature of mind—its primordial simplicity—you need not fear the enemy who urges you to chase after the eight worldly concerns.

When you have perfected your ability to experience thoughts as dharmakāya, you need not fear your enemy, the deceptive thoughts of duality that conceive of a subject and an object.

If you bring on the path the realization of dharmatā, the ultimate nature of reality, which has no [truly existing] basis or root, you need not fear your enemies—the veil formed by afflictive mental states and the veil that obscures all that can be known.

When you become familiar with the fundamental nature and nurture great bliss, you need not fear your enemy, the suffering of samsara's three worlds.

When you practice without being influenced by any bias, you need not fear the enemies of hope of success and fear of failing.

When you are free of these fears, you will accomplish a major goal.

–144–

Adopt and Discard

Six points on what to adopt and what to discard for those who have entered Dharma.
Without vigilance, your conduct will not accord with Dharma.
Without abandoning conformity with the ways of the world, your virtuous activities will remain incompatible with the path.
Without applying the crucial points, the warmth of the spiritual experience will not arise.
Seeking to benefit others before you are ready will not help.
If you have not achieved spiritual power and strength, you will not be able to overcome obstacles and adverse circumstances.
If you do not apply the crucial point of union [of wisdom and method], you will not attain enlightenment in one lifetime.
Therefore, you must ensure that your virtuous practices are effective.

For those on the path of Dharma, there are six defects to eliminate and six antidotes to apply.

Without unwavering vigilance over your actions of body and mind, you will lack circumspection and your conduct will inevitably stray from the Dharma.

If you do not let go of the desire to remain in harmony with the things of the ordinary world and to seek the approval of others [by complying with all their wishes], your spiritual practice will wither like a plant touched by frost and fail to achieve proper balance.

If you do not know how to harness your body, speech, and mind by applying the crucial points of the practice, the warmth born from mastering meditative experiences and realization will not manifest in your mind.

If you prematurely attempt to benefit others, believing it to be necessary, you will not truly be able to help them.

Until you have achieved a stable confidence in abilities born from yidam practice, even if you think you can clear obstacles, you will fail.

If you do not actualize the path that unites wisdom and method, you will not attain buddhahood in this lifetime.

Therefore, it is vital that your spiritual practice focuses on these key points: rely on attentive presence, give up the hope of pleasing everyone else, revive your practice by applying the key points, check whether the time has truly come [to help others] by assessing whether you have sufficiently developed your abilities and achieved the state of the union of wisdom and method. All this is very important.

–145–

Six Deplorable Attitudes

Six negative attitudes to discard:
To see your spiritual teacher as an ordinary person is a negative attitude because it deprives you of blessings.
To perceive your spiritual companions as rivals is a negative attitude because it tears your samayas.
To (engage in Dharma) for your vanity is a negative attitude because it distances you from the path of Dharma.
To sell Dharma instructions like merchandise is a negative attitude because you become tainted with wrong livelihood.
To use your yidam practice merely to prevent adverse circumstances is a negative attitude as you miss the entrance to the path.
To engage in Dharma activities to earn money is a negative attitude as you lose your path of liberation.
It is most imperative to avoid these six negative attitudes in your practice.

If you lack the respectful devotion that makes you see your spiritual masters as buddhas in person, and instead perceive them as ordinary beings, you drive all the blessings from your mind.

If, instead of considering your vajra brothers and sisters as children of the same family, you harbor feelings of rivalry, attachment, or aversion, you will break your sacred samayas. How deplorable!

Taking pride in your power, status, family lineage, or any other attribute of greatness will only distance you from liberation and from the Dharma. How deplorable!

If, instead of practicing the instructions you have received, you trade them as commodities to the masses, you misuse the Dharma for monetary gain and will be contaminated by an inappropriate livelihood. How deplorable!

If, instead of being diligent in recitations and accomplishment focused on your tutelary deity, the yidam, you spend your time performing rituals to ward off obstacles from your benefactors and protect them, or to subdue malevolent forces, you stray from the path that leads to accomplishments through yidam practice. How deplorable!

If, while posing as a genuine Dharma practitioner, you are merely gathering wealth, you destroy the path to liberation by accumulating religious possessions. How deplorable!

These six deplorable forms of conduct must be completely abandoned.

–146–

Forgetting the Path to Liberation

Six ways of forgetting the attributes of the path to liberation:
Distracted by sense objects, you forget respectful devotion;
Constantly seeking food like a beggar, you forget the Three Jewels;
Because of having a bad character and imprudent behavior, you forget samaya;
Turning a blind eye and being heartless, you forget the suffering of others;
Thirsty for and seeking wealth and material things, you forget virtue;
Poisoned by hatred and malice, you forget bodhicitta;
Carried away by meaningless activities, you forget the lower realms.
Those who forget these six points will wander for a long time.

If you want to practice the path of liberation correctly, but forget the qualities of the supreme Dharma, six defects will hamper your progress toward deliverance.

If your mind is constantly drawn to the five sense objects and succumbs to distraction, you will forget your respect for your spiritual master and your devotion will be obscured.

If you are constantly preoccupied, like a hungry beggar looking everywhere for food, you will forget the qualities of the Three Jewels.

If you are afflicted with a bad disposition, and are narrow-minded and impulsive, you will neglect the proper observance of the samayas with your spiritual master and spiritual companions, falling prey to hostility, greed, and jealousy.

Those who are unreflective of their past, inattentive to their future, and become trapped in the trivialities of the present, who are faint-hearted and forget how much they suffered in their youth and later in life, will be unable to urge themselves to practice Dharma.

If you are consumed by a feverish thirst for wealth and possessions, and obsessed with obtaining them, you will neglect your daily prayers and other spiritual practices.

If hatred sets your mind on fire, you will completely forget the noble attitude of benevolence.

Engulfed in the pursuits of this life and thinking of nothing but eating and drinking, you will forget the sufferings of the lower realms.

If you are affected by these six kinds of neglect, the path to liberation will remain distant and you will continue to wander in samsara for a very long time.

–147–

Six Exhortations

Six instructions in the form of exhortations:
The practices of the noble ones are your inheritance:
I beseech you not to postpone your practice out of laziness.

The conceptual thoughts that arise in your mind are meditation and serve as firewood for the wisdom fire:

I beseech you not to consider meditation with references and fixations to be supreme.

> **Suffering and adverse circumstances are encouragement to virtuous actions:**
> **I beseech you not to be saddened by them, nor to lament or reject them.**
>
> **The surge of the five poisons is the secret path to primordial wisdom:**
> **I beseech you not to misapprehend them as a horde of harmful enemies.**
>
> **Different kinds of obstacles are early signs of siddhis:**
> **I urge you not to doubt that, not to harbor negative thoughts about these obstacles, and not to become irritated by them.**
>
> **The appearances of samsara are the pure realms of the buddhas:**
> **I beseech you not to cling to the true existence of delusive appearances and dualistic thoughts.**

To master the key points of these six instructions will prompt you to practice the supreme Dharma without delay.

All supreme beings have dedicated themselves, in solitary places, to yogic practices that you must take to heart. Practice without delay as soon as they come to mind, avoiding procrastination driven by indolence and laziness.

Attempting to block the source of arising thoughts, you are obstructing the manifesting power of awareness and risk falling into an amorphous, indeterminate calm abiding (*śamatha*). Conversely, when you understand that the source these thoughts arise from is none other than the creativity of awareness itself, they become like wood that fuels the fire of wisdom. Therefore, I urge you not to consider single-pointed concentration and focusing on the characteristics of an object as supreme practices, for they belong to the meditation [of the formless gods] of the summit of samsaric existence.

When you are disturbed by unfavorable circumstances, illnesses, evil influences, interruptions, or vicious enemies, view these hindrances as catalysts for your virtuous Dharma practice. Therefore, do not grieve and lament over such tribulations, wondering why a Dharma practitioner should endure such torments. Feel no aversion to them but consider them as exhortations to virtue.

As for the manifestations of the five poisons—the afflictive states of mind—recognize that these poisons are, in truth, the secret path to the five primordial wisdoms, their true nature. Therefore, using these five mental toxins, you can revitalize your path to liberation.[130] So, I urge you not to misunderstand them as a horde of wicked enemies.

If obstacles accumulate, it is a sign that the attainment of siddhis is near. Do not harbor doubts, worries, or negative thoughts about them, and do not blame the eight classes of nonhuman evil spirits,[131] telling yourself that they bring about māra's obstacles. It is better to take these obstacles on the path.

If you correctly realize the true nature of the sufferings of the three worlds of samsara, they will all appear as the Pure Lands of the Victorious Buddhas. It is essential, therefore, that you do not take the impure perceptions arising from the subject-object duality as real.

–148–

Six Distortions

Six types of corruption that compel you to stray from the dharmatā:

The fundamental nature is unfettered and beyond partiality;
It is corrupted, however, by the mind's whims and conceptual thoughts.

The dharmatā is beyond words, thoughts, and expressions;
It is corrupted, however, by the extreme views of existence and nonexistence, and of exaggeration and denial.

The nature of the mind is nondual, beyond arising and ceasing;
It is corrupted, however, by clinging to the notions of birth and death.

The objects of your perceptions appear in the mirror of the empty nature of mind;

This mirror is clouded, however, by attachment and aversion,
duality, and the belief in true existence.

The ultimate truth is free from conceptual elaborations;
It is corrupted, however, by clinging to true existence and
doubting the ultimate meaning.

The fundamental nature, the ground of all, is impartial and
interdependent;
It is corrupted, however, by habitual tendencies formed by
delusion and dualism.

When qualities are mixed with defects, they are corrupted and lose their excellence. Six types of distortions lead to such corruptions:

Like space, the fundamental nature of phenomena is vast and does not lean in any direction. It encompasses both samsara and nirvana. Yet, if you superimpose onto it your mental fabrications and biases, distinguishing between a subject and an object, if you set appearances apart from emptiness, labeling appearances as "luminous," "flawed," or otherwise, you distort this fundamental nature and entangle it in a web of intellectual constructs.

The ultimate nature of reality, the dharmatā, is the inexpressible self-cognizant primordial wisdom within pristine awareness. But if you attach extraneous concepts to it, either by asserting its real existence (eternalism) or denying any form of existence (nihilism), you corrupt this nature by either misrepresenting what exists or misrepresenting what does not.

Methods and wisdom are perfectly united in the true nature of mind, which is devoid of beginning, dwelling, and cessation. But if you cling to notions of a true beginning and, consequently, of a true end, you are misconstruing reality.

The perceptions of the objects of the six senses appear in the mirror of mind's empty nature. It is important to liberate dualistic clinging to subject and object in their own nature, since even though they are devoid of true existence, they give rise to attraction to what is perceived as "good" and to rejection of what is perceived as "bad." If you attribute a true existence to phenomena by attaching to them your fixations and dualistic beliefs, and discriminate between good and bad, you will be deluded by your own perceptions.

The ultimate nature of reality, or the "ultimate truth in itself,"[132] is devoid of conceptual elaborations, such as the attributes of existence and nonexistence. Yet, it is corrupted by the misgivings that forge the concepts of true existence or nothingness and take them as real.

The fundamental nature of phenomena, the universal basis of samsara and nirvana, is none other than all-encompassing emptiness. It does not lean in any direction and unfolds through the play of interdependent arising, while remaining united with emptiness. Yet, the habitual tendencies formed by attachment to the subject-object duality distort and corrupt the experience of this nature, causing it to lose its impartiality.

–149–

Inappropriate Livelihoods

Six wrong livelihoods to abandon:
To achieve gains by deceiving others through hypocrisy is wrong livelihood.
To achieve gains by deceiving others through flattery is wrong livelihood.
To try to get something by asking indirectly is wrong livelihood.
To induce generosity in others through Dharma or to engage in calculated generosity are wrong livelihoods.
To listen and contemplate Dharma to earn worldly gains is wrong livelihood.
To use wealth for trivial purposes is wrong livelihood.
Those who wish to practice Dharma genuinely should abandon all these instances of wrong livelihood.

If, to practice Dharma, you secure your livelihood through dubious means, you create obstacles on your path to liberation and will be greatly defiled by the unethical use of goods and wealth meant for spiritual practice.

In the presence of a benefactor, you pose as a renunciant who has given up all activity; you act as though inspired by a strong sense of renunciation and disillusionment with samsara, appearing to be very attentive to the laws of cause and effect. You boast in various ways, all to project the image of an exemplary practitioner. If this leads the benefactor to support you generously, you have engaged in wrong livelihood.

If you repeatedly refer to past gifts from benefactors, extolling how their help came at a crucial time when you needed it most, and thereby secure further assistance by flattering them, this is another form of wrong livelihood.

When, motivated by the desire to obtain this or that, you use all kinds of tricks, such as saying, "Oh, I only have this thing of very bad quality," subtly solicitating favors in various way. If the person ends up giving you what you seek, this too is a form of wrongful living.

If you claim to be practicing Dharma while engaging in various questionable activities, this is wrong livelihood.

If you take advantage of the few qualities you have acquired through study, reflection, and meditation to teach Dharma solely for the sake of obtaining food, clothing, and other gains, this is wrong livelihood.

If you enjoy wealth and material possessions but do not use them for offerings and donations, and instead persist in accumulating even more, this is yet another aspect of wrong livelihood.

To genuinely practice the sublime Dharma, forsake all such behaviors associated with improper livelihood.

–150–

Six Pieces of Advice on Dharma in General

Six instructions on Dharma in general:
To sustain flawless conduct as you ascend from the basic level is my instruction.
To generate bodhicitta by cultivating the four immeasurables is my instruction.
In all practices, to maintain the view of union [of method and wisdom] is my instruction.
To look for the crucial points of the profound stages and paths is my instruction.
To preserve the view of the nature of mind free from extremes is my instruction.
To listen and contemplate the teachings without partiality is my instruction.

Six extraordinary instructions, which are like the heart treasure of the Buddha's teachings in general and embody the Dharma in its purest form:

Your view must be as high as possible, while your conduct must remain firmly grounded. Accordingly, you should begin by modeling your conduct on that of the listeners and the solitary realizers, being extremely attentive, vigilant, and cautious about the law of cause and effect. As one cannot ascend to the upper levels of an edifice without starting from the ground floor, so too must you begin your spiritual ascent by adhering to a life of purity, steering clear of intoxicants and sensual excesses.

With your heart filled with benevolence, continually apply the four immeasurable thoughts: altruistic love that wishes all beings to find happiness and its causes, compassion that wishes them freedom from suffering and its causes, sympathetic joy that wishes them not to be separated from their present happiness, and impartiality that extends these wishes to all beings, near and far, without being influenced by like and dislike. This is my heart advice, for it is the very root of the Mahāyāna path.

To remain in meditative equality that unites the methods of great compassion with the wisdom of emptiness is my spiritual advice.

To recognize that the profound and vital points of the five paths and the ten bhūmis are fully present within the nature of mind is my spiritual advice.

To free yourself from all extremes, such as eternalism and nihilism, by realizing the view of the fundamental and ultimate nature of mind, is my spiritual advice.

To combine study, reflection, and meditation with the zeal of a one-eyed yak grazing in a meadow [always fixing his single eye on the next patch of grass] and to engage in these three practices without sectarian bias to clarify all your doubts is my spiritual advice.

–151–

Six Grim Situations

Six instructions on when to give up hope:
Do not hope for an immodest person to observe vows.
Do not hope for a person who lacks diligence to practice [Dharma].
Do not hope for a person who lacks faith and respect to receive blessings.

Do not hope for a person who lacks wisdom to attain realization.
Do not hope for a lazy person to achieve any sign of accomplishment.
Do not hope for a wicked person to be kind.

You need to sever all expectations at the root by refraining from harboring all sorts of hopes and doubts about whether you will soon achieve buddhahood. Moreover, if you wish to acquire the spiritual qualities of the past and present masters but are tainted by any of the six defects detailed below, you have no chance to succeed.

Those with no sense of self-shame and who are also not embarrassed in front of others have little hope of observing the precepts of individual liberation, of the bodhisattvas, and of the Secret Mantra and will thus lead unruly lives.

Those who do not show tenacity and diligence are hopelessly incapable of attaining spiritual accomplishment.

Those who lack trust, faith, and respect for the Three Jewels and for spiritual masters have no hope of receiving their blessings.

Those who have not succeeded in developing consummate wisdom through study, reflection, and meditation have no hope of recognizing the fundamental nature of phenomena.

Those who squander their lives in idleness, indulging in eating and slumbering with the abandon of swine, have no hope of obtaining swift signs of accomplishment.

Those whose minds are not filled with the desire to benefit others but instead are full of hostility to everyone have no chance to be imbued with benevolence.

–152–

The Stages of Dharma Training

Six sequential steps for training yourself in Dharma:
The first step for entering the path is to learn reading, writing, grammar, logic, and epistemology.
The second step is to observe ethical discipline, listen to the teachings of the Three Baskets, and contemplate them.

> **The third step is to rely upon a sublime master to enter the path.**
> **The fourth step is to please your master and receive the sublime oral transmissions.**
> **The fifth step is to be diligent to bring your Dharma practice to perfection.**
> **The sixth step is to tirelessly work for the sake of others.**
> **Such is the tradition of the sublime followers of the path.**

As we transition from infancy to childhood, to adulthood and old age, at each stage we must consume food that suits our physical constitution at each age. Otherwise, we will not be able to digest it. Similarly, those who train in practicing Dharma should practice the path of the various vehicles gradually, allowing the corresponding spiritual qualities to flourish in the best possible way.

When approaching the Buddha's teachings, you must first master the basic skills of reading and writing. To ensure that your learning is free from flaws, you must then dedicate yourself to the study of grammar and logical reasoning.

Second, once these foundational steps have been completed in the best possible way, you should take great care to preserve the various aspects of the discipline of individual liberation, of the bodhisattvas, and of the Secret Mantra, as ethical discipline is the foundation of all spiritual qualities. You must also establish with certainty the meaning of what you have heard, contemplated, and assimilated through meditation.

Third, to fully enter the path of liberation, it is essential to follow supreme spiritual masters, *kalyāṇamitra*s, or "friends in virtue," in the proper way.

Fourth, you should gladden the hearts of your spiritual masters, in the best case by your spiritual practice, in the medium case by serving them in various ways with your body and speech, and in the least case by making material offerings. Then, you must receive with undivided attention the instructions of the oral lineage that they hold in their hearts.

Fifth, after having received these instructions, you should then put them into practice in conformity with the tradition and persevere with unbroken diligence until you achieve accomplishment.

Sixth, once meditative experiences and realization have blossomed in your mind, you will have accomplished your own good. At that point, you must work extensively for the benefit of others and serve the Buddha's teachings without any lassitude or discouragement.

By doing so, you will remain in harmony with the lives of consummate liberation led by the great masters of the past.

–153–

Taking Care of Disciples

Six ways to take care of fortunate students:
You should know how to cater to the varied interests of devoted students.
You should know how to establish diligent students on the path and not encourage them to engage in less important virtuous activities.
Do not let students who are studying and contemplating become addicted to words, but direct them to the path of practice.
Do not let students study to gain wealth, but guide them to engage in virtuous actions.
Do not teach students to accumulate possessions but rather to develop contentment.
Do not guide students in worldly pursuits, but encourage them to succeed in life by dedicating it to Dharma.
These are the ways of a skillful and kind teacher.

Six guidelines for teachers on how to care for fortunate disciples who are suitable vessels for the Dharma:

To disciples who perceive their spiritual masters as the Buddha in person and have full confidence in their instructions, it is appropriate to impart the teachings of the three vehicles that best suit their aspirations.

When guiding particularly diligent disciples, do not advise them to engage in ordinary activities or practice various crafts. Instead, allow them to focus entirely on the path of liberation. Consequently, the signs of the birth of the spiritual qualities of such a path will soon manifest.

For students who engage in an exhaustive exploration of the teachings through study and contemplation, do not let them be content with mere knowledge of the words. Encourage them to intimately assimilate the meaning of what they have studied and to dedicate their entire minds to contemplative practice.

Steer those with favorable spiritual inclinations away from the pursuit of material gain. Prompt them to train diligently in the higher qualities of abandonment [of obscurations] and realization [of enlightenment].

Inspire disciples to resist accumulating possessions over time, to have few desires, and to find contentment with the amount of food that satisfies their hunger and clothing that protects them from the weather.

Advise them not to aspire to worldly success through the defeat of adversaries or the preferential treatment of kin, nor through the gathering of wealth and similar pursuits. Instead, inspire them to focus their enthusiasm on practicing the supreme Dharma and show them how to succeed in their practice.

Spiritual friends who are experts in these various ways of guiding disciples are exemplary guides who will know how to best look after their students.

–154–

The Sentinels of Introspection

Six ways of mindful introspection:
Mindfully examine whether you are carried away by the ordinary pursuits of this life.
Mindfully examine whether you are distracted by laziness.
Mindfully examine whether you are affected by deviations and obscurations.
Mindfully examine whether you are carried away by delusive thoughts.
Mindfully examine whether you are caught up in idle gossip.
Mindfully examine whether you are remaining ordinary.

It is essential that the sentinel of mindful introspection and vigilance stands guard at the door of your mind to ensure that it will continue in the direction of the supreme Dharma.

Are you preoccupied with gain, respect, wealth and possessions, and other goals of ordinary life? If the sentinel of introspection alerts you that such concerns are on your mind, apply the antidote of contentment.

If you find yourself careless and lazy, distracted by the affairs of ordinary life—such as food, clothing, and the like—remember impermanence and death and let the sentinel of vigilance and mindful introspection lead you back to the heart of the supreme Dharma.

When meditative experiences and realization begin to dawn in your mind, enlist the sentinel of vigilant introspection to detect any deviations or obscurations that may arise. If such obstacles appear, apply the essential instructions that will remove obstacles and foster spiritual progress.

If countless afflictive thoughts of attachment and aversion continue to arise, you will find yourself enslaved by the three worlds of samsara. Therefore, call upon the sentinel of vigilance to activate the antidotes to desire and aversion.

If you fritter your life away in idle and meaningless chatter, you are merely wasting it. Use vigilant introspection to ensure you maintain quiet composure, avoiding conversations that revolve around attachment and hostility.

If you are not constantly diligent in practicing the supreme Dharma properly with your body, speech, and mind, you will stagnate in the most ordinary state. To remedy this, call upon the sentinel of vigilant introspection.

Free yourself from the grip of these defects by infusing all your actions with vigilant introspection, and you shall swiftly progress on the path of liberation.

–155–

Six Imperatives for Practitioners

Six things that Dharma practitioners should do:
Life dissipates without pausing, so be prepared to leave at any time.
Adopt virtue and discard nonvirtue, understanding the major and minor aspects of cause and effect.
Benefiting others is difficult, so make sure you do not lose your own sense of purpose.
Knowledge is limitless, so make sure you do not get carried away by words.
Do not drift into the ignorance of foolish meditation.
Do not let pride overtake your aspiration to become learned, disciplined, and virtuous.

To practice the supreme Dharma properly, you must fulfill six imperatives in all circumstances:

You do not know when you will die or under what circumstances. Therefore, you must remind yourself that death may come at any time and make unwavering efforts to travel the path to liberation.

The law of cause and effect is inescapable. Thus, even if your realization is as high and vast as the sky, remember that the intricate web of causality operates infallibly. It is therefore critical to avoid negative actions and to carry out virtuous ones.

It is very difficult for ordinary people to benefit others in a significant way right from the start. They must first earnestly transform their minds; otherwise they might even fail to accomplish their own good.

Concerning the entire scope of what can be known about the Dharma, as it is said,

> As countless as the stars in the night sky,
> Boundless is the domain of the knowable!
> As for now, the best for you is the essential meaning
> That enables you to conquer the immutable citadel.[133]

Therefore, without chasing mere words, focus on properly assimilating the vital points of spiritual practice.

If you ignore the key points of profound spiritual instructions and instead become mired in stupid meditation, it is like shooting arrows in the dark, with little chance to hit the target. Therefore, do what it takes to avoid slipping into foolish meditations.

Scholars, even if you behave virtuously and serve the Buddha's teachings, do not become inflated with pride, full of the satisfaction of having such and such expertise, as this would hinder the flourishing of your spiritual qualities.

Be diligent on all these points!

–156–

Considerations for Those Who Aspire to the Dharma

Six points to be carefully examined by those who wish to practice the Dharma.
If you do not give up the pursuits of this life, you will not be able to let go of your homeland.
If you do not give up craving for pleasures, you will not be able to stay in solitary places.
If you do not free yourself from philosophical constructs, even the teachings will bind you.
If you do not develop meditative concentration, you will not be able to sit on your cushion.
If you do not apply antidotes, you will not be able to overcome distraction.
If you cling to the superiority of your yogic practices, you will turn the antidote into poison.
Contemplating these points carefully is important.

To practice the supreme Dharma properly, six excellent qualities are required:

If you do not forsake attachment and animosity, and clear up ignorance, the desire to leave your native place is futile.[134] As long as your mind is ruled by attraction and repulsion, such aspiration will remain an empty wish.

If you cling too tightly to family, friends, neighbors, and acquaintances, you will not be able to give up the charm of this life, or abandon the eight worldly concerns and other vain samsaric activities. As a result, just as a monkey cannot stay still, you will be unable to abide in solitary mountain retreats.

Philosophical views often become artifices that entangle you. If you are not able to dissolve them into the ultimate nature of reality, the dharmatā, you will remain convinced that the views of your spiritual lineage are superior, while others are flawed. Under such circumstances, the Dharma will only serve to accumulate bad karma and will end up hindering instead of liberating you.

If the concentrations of calm abiding and deeper insight do not take birth in your mind, even if you aspire to rest in meditative evenness, you will not be able to sit on your cushion in meditation for long.

If you have not engendered a deep sense of renunciation and weariness toward samsara—the antidote to distraction and busyness—you may wander aimlessly into distant lands yet remain ensnared by distractions.

If Secret Mantra practitioners are believed to be great siddhas, highly accomplished practitioners, and pride themselves on being immune to negative emotions thanks to their advanced practices, this is like believing they have the capacity to ingest poison with impunity. Such delusion will only lead to their death. In this manner, they turn their back on the path of liberation.

Check carefully whether these defects are present, and if they are, abandon them.

–157–

The Signs of a Good Practitioner

Six outer and inner signs [of good practitioners] clearly elucidated:
Like an intelligent person, whatever tasks they undertake are completed.
Like a realized person, their words withstand scrutiny.
Endowed with understanding and intelligence, they can grasp the meaning of everything.
Having developed confidence, they can endure hardships.
Having mingled their minds with Dharma, they are disciplined.
As they are wise, they never tire of learning.
These are inner signs that manifest outwardly.

It is important to regularly and carefully observe your actions, words, and thoughts. If you keep doing so, you will bring your outer behavior and inner attitude into harmony, which is excellent.

Before undertaking any action with your body, speech, or mind, consider its appropriateness with great care. Once you have committed to an action, it is important to see it through to completion.

As realized beings have done, persistently study and reflect upon the spiritual instructions you have received and implement them in meditation. By doing so, you will master their key points, and when needed, you will be able to explain them to others following the proper order and progression.

Those gifted with intelligence are able to fathom the vast domains of knowledge and master the meaning of the many teachings of the sutras and tantras.

Once you have gained a firm confidence in your practice of the view, meditation, and conduct, and engage in ascetic practice with resolve and persistence, you will be able to endure with fortitude any hardship, physical ailments, or mental challenges that you may encounter.

By checking whether the Dharma has merged with your mind, you will cultivate such vigilance and circumspection that your mind will remain free from afflictive mental states. Applying the teachings, you will gain mastery over your mind.

No matter how many teachings you have heard, you will never feel that you have received enough, just as the vast ocean is never too full to receive more water.

These are the signs of inner qualities that manifest themselves on the outside.

–158–

Untie the Knot of Duality

Six means to untie the knot of subject-object duality:
When attachment and aversion arise, liberate them by looking at your mind.
When the five mental poisons manifest, liberate them by looking at their true nature.
When pain grips you, liberate it by meditating on great bliss.
When conceptual thoughts proliferate, liberate them by recognizing their nature.
When weariness sets in, liberate it by relaxing into ease.
When sluggishness and stagnation manifest, liberate them by intensifying the clarity and limpidity of pristine awareness.

Here are six criteria to determine whether you have successfully unraveled the knots of duality in your mind using antidotes:

When besieged by numerous thoughts of attachment toward allies and aversion toward adversaries, make sure that you do not surrender to these states of mind. Remain vigilant and discerning, and the bonds of attraction and repulsion will loosen.

When afflictive mental states—the five poisons—arise, contemplate their true nature, the dharmatā, which is devoid of beginning, dwelling, and ceasing. Using the essential instructions on the means of liberation according to the Great Perfection, recognize that the nature of the five poisons is none other than that of the five primordial wisdoms

If you are afflicted by pain due to illness or adverse circumstances, meditate on the pain as an expression of the wisdom of great bliss, and your torments will dissipate.

When myriad thoughts swarm in your mind, develop a clear conviction that the nature of these thoughts is no different from dharmatā, emptiness, and they cannot but be liberated.

When, with perfect concentration, you meditate on calm abiding and deeper insight, if your mind becomes fatigued from exertion, release it into a vast and serene ease, and your difficulties will dissolve.

When you meditate on calm abiding, you will sometimes become drowsy or lethargic. It is then important to refresh the clarity and transparency of pristine awareness and you will be freed from this torpor.

–159–

Six Things That Must Come Together

Six combinations necessary for Dharma practice:
The profound instructions must be combined with the introduction [to the nature of mind].
Such an introduction must be combined with the practical guidance [of the masters] of the lineage.
This practical guidance must be combined with spiritual experience.
Spiritual experience must be combined with warmth and signs [of progress].
The warmth and signs must be combined with the results that need to be achieved.
These results must be combined with activities that benefit others.

Separating these combinations leads to deviations from the path.

Those who engage in Dharma practice should take six instructions particularly to heart:

The profound spiritual instructions imparted by your masters must be combined with an introduction to your true nature, dharmatā.

This introduction to your own nature must be done according to the tradition of masters who hold an unblemished spiritual lineage—one that is free from impediments, deviations, and errors.

These masters must have practiced and fully experienced such a tradition themselves, enabling them to guide their disciples effectively and help them progress on the path.

The direct experience required of these masters who confer the introduction to the nature of mind should have manifested signs of spiritual "warmth" associated with superior, medium, or lesser practice. Such signs include a mind of renunciation and weariness toward samsara, respectful devotion, realization, and clairvoyance.

Once these signs of the warmth of the practice manifest in the practitioners' minds, they should lead to the ultimate and definitive fruition.

Once this fruition is actualized, it must naturally express itself through benefiting sentient beings as infinite as space itself.

If you separate what should be so united on the path, you will stray into deviations.

–160–

Six Instructions of Great Importance

Six essential instructions:
It is essential, whatever your practice might be, not to deviate from regular sessions.
It is essential to blend your mind stream with the teachings.[135]
It is essential for your concentration to endure disturbances so that your mind does not become agitated.
It is essential that your view be unbiased and free of extremes.

It is essential for you to remain in the state of dharmatā, beyond meeting and parting.
It is essential, from the aspect of method, to use whatever appears to generate wisdom.

Here are six instructions you should take to heart:

Whatever spiritual practices you engage in with your body, speech, and mind, seamlessly unite meditation and post-meditation, maintaining a consistent schedule of four or six daily sessions, without fail, and you will be able to sustain the flow and progress of your practice.

If you are listening to many teachings based on the Buddha's words and their commentaries, once you have apprehended the qualities of the Dharma, intimately blend them with your mind.

If your mind enters a state of concentration associated with calm abiding (*śamatha*), let this concentration remain undisturbed by distraction, lethargy, or the feverishness caused by desire and aversion.

If you realize the view of dharmatā—the ultimate nature of reality that transcends the extremes of existence and nonexistence—such a view will be free from bias and fixation on either appearances or emptiness.

Remain continuously in the view of dharmatā, free from the fluctuations caused by distraction and delusion.

Whatever appearances arise, rely on the essential instructions that make you an expert in skillful means: it is crucial to apply these teachings so that primordial wisdom, united with great bliss, can manifest.

–161–

Six Things to Do

Six things to do while engaging in authentic Dharma practice:
Look at samsara's defects until you become disgusted with them.
Familiarize yourself with the lack of intrinsic existence of phenomena and recognize their illusory nature.
Arouse bodhicitta and benefit others unconditionally.
Maintain the view beyond thought and differentiate samsara and nirvana.

Realize that whatever thoughts arise are naturally liberated as primordial wisdom.
Let the blessings blaze naturally from within, and you will transform the thoughts of others.

If you aspire to practice the Dharma in its purest form, six things should be accomplished:

Contemplating repeatedly the flaws of the three worlds of samsara, feel a deep sense of revulsion.

Cultivate the understanding that all the joys and sufferings of this life are devoid of intrinsic existence. Recognizing the dreamlike and illusory nature of all phenomena, free yourself from the shackles of desire and aversion.

Once the precious mind of enlightenment has been born in your mind stream, if you happen to be able to benefit others in large or small ways, never think that you have done enough for them and leave it at that. Persist in helping them unconditionally, expecting nothing in return.

When abiding in meditative evenness, the realization of the view that transcends the intellect, take it to heart to clearly distinguish the delusions of samsara from the qualities of nirvana.[136]

Whatever thoughts arise, do not attempt to forcibly suppress them. Allow them to dissolve naturally, as a snake untying its own knot, and primordial wisdom will emerge.

In response to fervent devotion toward your spiritual master, blessings will rain down of their own accord. Your perceptions will be transformed, and you will naturally begin to transform the perceptions of others.

–162–

Six Potential Deviations

Six potential errors in meditation that need to be discarded:
Do not be carried away by distraction and agitation; remain in the ultimate state of unelaboration.
Do not sink into sluggishness; intensify the clarity of pristine awareness.
Do not drift into distraction; hold [your awareness] with the glue of mindfulness.

Do not slip into an empty state of mind; infuse your experience with bliss and clarity.
Do not fall into hope and fear; maintain a state of spontaneous and luminous presence.
Do not sink into narrow-mindedness; maintain a state of spaciousness and elevation.

If you follow this advice, your path will be without error and supreme.

When fully engaged in the practice of meditation, six instructions will allow you to cut off the stream of deviations.

When caught up in the turbulence of thoughts, you may lose sight of the true meaning of dharmatā, the ultimate nature of reality. Remain in a state of perfect equality free of mental constructions.

When you cultivate calm abiding, avoid sinking into a dull, amorphous drowsiness. Revive clarity with the help of deeper insight.

Whatever you do, say, or think, do not be indifferent or complacent about what should and should not be done. Strengthen your vigilance, infusing it with the elixir of mindfulness.

Leaning single-mindedly toward the view of emptiness may lead to a vacant state of mind. Cultivate the experiences of bliss and clarity alongside it.

Do not allow hope or doubt to sway your aspiration to acquire the spiritual qualities that arise from meditative experiences and realization. Simply acknowledge the spontaneous presence of the ultimate nature of reality and it will shine forth as naturally as rays emanating from the sun.

Sometimes you practice, sometimes not. Avoid falling into a state of indecision or constriction. Instead, cultivate a state of mind as vast and lofty as the sky.

–163–

Six Destinations to Avoid

Six directions that those entering the spiritual path must avoid:
Do not let your unchanging faith stray into dualism.
Do not let your sadness about samsara stray into despair.
Do not let the spaciousness of the wisdom [born from] listening and contemplation stray into dry intellect.

Do not let your determination in Dharma practice stray into wishful thinking for happiness.
Do not let your bodhicitta aimed at benefiting others stray into fixation.
Do not let your lofty view stray into pride.
These pieces of advice are extremely essential, but very few apply them.

Those who embark on the path must keep clearly in mind the key points concerning the deviations to avoid.

If you possess unwavering faith and trust in the spiritual masters and the Three Jewels, be very careful not to fall into the trap of dualistic clinging that makes you discriminate between your side and the others.

When a deep sense of disillusionment with the three worlds of samsara wells up within you, do not let it descend into depression and despair.

The purpose of acquiring extensive knowledge through listening and reflecting is to assimilate it and to master your own mind. Do not be satisfied with mere dry words and conventional designations.

When you go to a solitary place to persevere resolutely in your practice, resist the temptation to use this opportunity for mere physical ease, indulging in nothing more than food and sleep in a completely ordinary way.

It is indispensable to generate bodhicitta, the altruistic wish to attain enlightenment for the sake of all beings. But do not let this aspiration turn into partiality and bias shaped by your personal attachments.

Even if you attain a high view and realization, do not become infatuated with pride and self-importance, imagining yourself to be a siddha, a spiritually accomplished being who has realized the ultimate nature of reality.

It is essential to cherish these six points, yet those who have avoided straying in these six directions are exceedingly rare!

–164–

Six Extremely Profound Instructions

Six extremely profound instructions that strike the vital points:
Slay the "I" and always accept defeat for yourself.
Do not brag about having benefited others.[137]

> **If you want to be efficient, give up meaningless and distracting chatter.**
> **If your learning is very vast, you will have the good fortune to remain in the non-elaborated nature of mind.**
> **If you want to cut your bondage [to samsara], do not follow the footprints of subject and object.**
> **Abandon the dense grasping (of ignorance) and uphold the ultimate unchanging domain of dharmatā.**
> **By doing so, you will swiftly accomplish your purpose.**

If you want to eliminate the fixation that makes you think "me!" here are six instructions that get to the heart of the matter:

As it is said,

> Offer gain and victory to others.
> Take loss and defeat upon yourself.[138]

Clinging to the idea of an "I" is the very cause of your wandering in samsara from beginningless time until this present life. If you seek to break free from the grip of ego, learn how to systematically take defeat upon yourself.

Moreover, do not boast about how helpful you have been to others, how you have imparted them with such and such qualities, and how kind you have been to them. In short, avoid glorifying your virtuous deeds as if they were inherently real.

Whatever vital insights you have gained from the Dharma, blend them with your mind stream and forgo all trivial and distracting conversations.

If you have heard various teachings and have studied them, make sure to have the good fortune to remain in the nature of mind, free from conceptual elaboration.

To sever the bonds of distraction and overactivity, do not chase after external phenomena—forms, sounds, scents, flavors, and tactile sensations—with a dualistic grasping on subject and object.

Leaving the murky darkness and foolish meditations that amount to throwing stones in the dark, experience the immutable citadel of the ultimate nature of reality.

By following these instructions, you will swiftly achieve your purpose.

–165–

Six Ways of Being

Six ways of being, clearly explained:
Rely upon a spiritual master for the best advice so that you will not be mistaken.
Do not postpone your engagement in virtuous activities so that you have no regrets even when death comes.
Stop discriminating between friends and enemies so that you remain in harmony with all.
Reciprocate the kindness of others and you will find kindness everywhere.
Abandon jealousy and harm so that you master your mind.
Preserve the legacy of noble beings, and you will accomplish whatever you wish.

Spiritual masters are your best source of advice. By following their instructions, you will be protected from delusion, and they will lead you perfectly on the path to liberation.

Do not postpone your practice by saying to yourself, "Later, later . . ." The very moment the thought of practicing the Dharma comes to your mind, begin at once and you will have no regret at the time of death.

Without clinging to discrimination between enemies to harm and loved ones to favor, cultivate impartiality, and you will be in harmony with all.

When people benefit you, repay them with as much kindness as possible, and everyone will regard you as a person of integrity and virtue.

In turn, you will not feel any jealousy or malice toward those who possess great qualities. Your mind will be peaceful, controlled, and at ease.

If you model yourself on the lives of perfect liberation of the learned, virtuous, and benevolent masters, all your aspirations will be fulfilled.

–166–

Free the Mind

Six extremely profound practices that liberate the mind:
The view is the nature of your mind: recognize it.
Meditation is its luminosity: perfect the state of lucidity.
Conduct is illusory: bring whatever appears onto the path.
Spiritual experience is regarding all that appears as dharmatā: uproot grasping and fixation.
The fruition is naturally present: let go of clinging to hope and fear.
Enlightened activity is to benefit others: guide sentient beings with compassion.

Six instructions enable you to free your mind from afflictive mental states and accomplish the profound essence of the Dharma.

What is called "view" is nothing other than the realization of the fundamental nature of your mind. Therefore, recognize this pristine view within yourself, and do not seek it externally.

Meditation is the process of taking your inner experience to its ultimate point. To achieve this, you must realize the true, luminous nature of your mind, dharmatā, a lucid and pristine awareness untainted by lethargy, excitement, and any other defect.

Conduct involves recognizing the illusory nature of all your actions, whether virtuous or not. Understand that positive actions arise through interdependence, and engage in them as much as you can, even as you perceive their illusory nature. When food, clothing, and wealth come your way, without clinging to them, see them as dreams and illusions, and bring them onto the path.

As the experience of realization dawns in your mind, uproot any biased attachment, conceit, and all other shortcomings.

The fruition, the state of buddhahood, has always been within you. There is no need to look for it elsewhere. Let go of all hope and fear about a fruition you could obtain in the future.

Enlightened activity is about benefiting others. Therefore, out of compassion, bring to the path of liberation all beings with whom you have established a connection.

–167–

There Is a Reason for Everything

Six aspects of the nature of practitioners:

Having generated bodhicitta for the sake of others, they will be kind to you;
Yet if you happen to become the object of their animosity, you must know that this is a support for cultivating patience.

If loving-kindness inspires you to be generous, followers will gather around you;
And if they do not, you must know that their absence is a support for increasing virtuous activities.

If you have attained realization, oath-bound protectors will gather like clouds;
And if they do not, you must know that this indicates that the samayas have been damaged.

If revulsion [for samsara] arises from the depths of your heart, wealth and possessions will gather;
And if they do not, you must know that this is the result of your past karma.

When you are about to attain the siddhis, all kinds of obstacles will appear;
And if they do not, you must know that this is due to the blessings of your spiritual masters.

Diligent practitioners will be the target of the māras.
And if this does not happen, you must know that this is a sign you have hit the key points of spiritual practice.

If you do not understand all these considerations, you are in danger of falling into wrong views.

If you generate bodhicitta—the wish to attain enlightenment for the sake of all beings—since you have an innate goodness, it will naturally inspire kindness in others. However, if you encounter individuals who respond with hostility or harm, do not react with anger. Instead, return good for evil, and use such situations as opportunities to strengthen your practice of patience.

When motivated by benevolence, you provide for the needy and feed the hungry, your qualities will attract many people to you. But if, despite your generosity, no one reaches out to you, embrace solitude as your best friend, for it allows you to focus entirely on progressing in your spiritual practice, free from distractions or involvements.

If you reach a certain level of realization, the Dharma protectors will naturally be drawn to you, like clouds gathering in the sky. However, if, despite your realization of dharmatā, the protectors do not appear, this may indicate a deterioration of your samayas. To remedy this, engage in confession, accumulation of merit, purification of negativity, and rituals of repair.

If you sincerely renounce all attachment to food, dwellings, and even your own body, remember the saying, "Wealth comes to the door of one who knows contentment." Abundance will find its way to you, even without wishing for it. If this does not happen, know that this is the karmic consequence of having stolen, beaten, or molested others.

As you are about to obtain the siddhis, the spiritual accomplishments, you may face a surge of obstacles. But if all goes well and no hindrances occur, know that this is the effect of the blessings and compassion of the masters of the spiritual lineage.

When practitioners intensify their efforts, the māras strive equally to interfere and cause mental distress and physical ailments. If these negative forces remain absent, however, it is a sign that you have touched the crucial points of the practice.

Without awareness of these points, there is a danger of developing false views, such as thinking that the practice of the supreme Dharma yields no results or that the laws of causality concerning virtuous and unvirtuous acts can be misleading.

–168–

The Ultimate Meaning

Six instructions on the ultimate meaning:
If you want to realize the view, search for the one who realizes.
When you do not find anyone, you will be free from the
limitations of the four extremes.

If you want to practice meditative concentration, search for the
meditator.
When you do not find anyone, you will realize that the
movement of thought is nonexistent.

If you decide to engage in the conduct, search for the one who
engages.
When you do not find anyone, you will naturally be liberated in
the state of inseparability.

If you want to accomplish the result, look for the one who
accomplishes.
When you do not find anyone, you will know that the three
kāyas are naturally complete within you.

If you want to carry out enlightened activities, search for the
one who carries them out.
When you do not find anyone, you will know that these
activities are spontaneously and effortlessly accomplished.

If you want to tread the paths and reach the bhūmis, search for
the one who treads the paths.
When you do not find anyone, you establish the fundamental
and ultimate nature of reality.

These are instructions on the ultimate and essential meaning.
Know that everything is the creative power of pristine
awareness.

Here are six instructions on the ultimate meaning, the culminating point of view, meditation, and action:

If you wish to realize the view of the dharmatā directly—and find yourself thinking with some attachment, "I have realized the view!"—then question who it is that has realized it. If you look repeatedly, you will not find any tangible agent—no form, no substance, or defining attributes that would confirm its existence. Yet, you cannot conclude either that it does not exist at all. Recognizing this, you will transcend the subject-object duality.

If you seek to cultivate the meditative concentration of samādhi, search for the attributes of the meditating mind itself. If this investigation leads you to conclude that no attributes can be found, you will understand the insubstantiality of mind's movements. Consequently, the mental fabrications associated with delusion will no longer proliferate.

If you wish to benefit beings, look for the agent that brings about such benefits. Like a dream or an illusion, it is elusive. If you cannot find it, it becomes liberated into the indivisibility [of subject, object, and action], its true nature.

If you aspire to obtain the fruition of buddhahood, look for the one who strives for it. You will find no separate doer and you will come to realize that the three kāyas are inherent in your mind. The ultimate nature of mind is emptiness, the dharmakāya; its expression is luminosity, the saṃbhogakāya; and its ceaseless cognitive potency[139] is the nirmāṇakāya.

If you wish to engage in enlightened activities, repeatedly ask yourself who is performing these actions. You cannot find any identifiable entity that would allow you to declare, "Here is the agent," and you cannot put such an agent to work like a servant. The truth is that enlightened activities are performed spontaneously and effortlessly.

If you wish to ascend the paths and levels, examine who is walking these paths. You will find no one and will naturally arrive at the true nature of all things. In this way, paths and levels will be spontaneously accomplished.

In essence, the phenomena of the ground, the path, and the fruition are none other than the magical display of awareness.

–169–

Controlling Your Mind

Six ways to perfectly tame your mind:
Demolish the mountain of pride and arrogance.
When you are jealous of others, revere them as wisdom deities.
When you are attached to benefiting others, sever such attachment with the sword of wisdom.
When you ignore the law of causality, remind yourself to clearly differentiate virtue and nonvirtue.
When others denigrate and slander you, be heedful, calm, and restrained.
When your mind becomes upset pondering the faults of others, consider that this comes from your impure perception.
When you practice in this way, your mind stream will blend with Dharma.

Here are six instructions to perfectly transform your mind:

If your pride and self-importance rise as high as a mountain, it is important to level them down to the ground.

If you become jealous of someone, place that person respectfully above your head, as you would do for your yidam, your tutelary deity.

If, after benefiting others, you tell yourself with some attachment, "Oh, I have truly benefited them!" remember that all actions totally lack intrinsic existence—they are like dreams and illusions. Sever your attachment with the sword of wisdom and discernment, thus destroying all forms of clinging.

Know that disregarding the laws of cause and effect will lead to erratic behavior. Develop trust in the inevitability of the consequences of good and evil, and distinguish them clearly. This is of utmost importance.

There may be times when you will face disparagement and slander. Resist the urge to reacting with bitterness. Instead, maintain a lucid and serene mind, staying master of yourself.

If you are perturbed by the faults of others, know that this stems solely from your impure perception [of phenomena and beings]. If your mind is disturbed, others are not to blame.

Embracing these attitudes indicates that you have successfully integrated the supreme Dharma into your mind stream.

–170–

Six Distinctions

Six introductions that lead to clear distinctions:

Pristine awareness, pure and limpid, is free from all philosophical constructs.
This is the introduction to the view: gain confidence in this.

The naturally pristine great bliss is free from reference points, grasping, and dualism.
This is the introduction to the meditation: abide naturally in this.

Unite method and wisdom and take all experiences onto the path to enlightenment.
This is the introduction to the conduct: train in the illusory nature of all things.

Be free from attachment to ordinary perceptions by perceiving all that appears and exists as a pure realm.
This is the introduction to the samayas: maintain perfect purity in this.

Whatever appears, abide in the bliss of self-arising primordial wisdom.
This is the introduction to the four empowerments:* tread the paths and bhūmis.

Those who practice like this are great yogis of the Secret Mantra.

If you correctly keep in mind the nature of pure and luminous awareness, the philosophical tenets of the various vehicles will be liberated in their true nature. Achieving this liberation constitutes the true introduction to the view. Ensure that you obtain definite certainty about such a view.

The natural radiance of the view is primordial wisdom, great bliss. Allow it to be liberated into its true nature. Free it from attachment to the duality of subject and object, from all notions of goal and references, and from tainted bliss. This natural liberation in the true nature of mind is the direct introduction to meditation; preserve it in the continuum of fundamental simplicity.

To perfectly unite the method of compassion and the wisdom of emptiness is the correct way to practice the path to enlightenment: this is the introduction to the conduct. Train yourself to perceive all appearances as dreamlike and illusory.

When you transcend all ordinary fixations on the notions of friend and foe and perceive your environment as a pure realm, this is the introduction to the sacred commitments. Preserve them immaculately.

Examine the perceptions of the six aspects of consciousness and continue your investigation until you are certain that they arise from the creativity of the great bliss of primordial, self-arisen wisdom. The phenomenal aspect corresponds to the vase empowerment; the emptiness aspect to the secret empowerment; the union of the two to the wisdom empowerment; and the realization of the fundamental and ultimate nature of mind to the fourth empowerment.

If you tread the path in this way, you are an authentic yogi of the Secret Mantra of the Adamantine Vehicle. This is an essential point.

–171–

Six Criteria of Authenticity

Six perfect qualities of those who engage in genuine Dharma practice:
Those who are free from attachment and grasping have a perfect generosity.
Those whose mind streams are stainless have perfect ethical discipline.
Those who are not perturbed by anger have perfect patience.
Those who experience weariness [toward samsara] with a mind of renunciation have perfect joyful effort.
Those who continually abide in meditative insight have perfect concentration.
Those who have realized the nature of mind have perfect wisdom.

The following are qualities exemplified in the practice of the most gifted practitioners:

When you have no attachment or craving for wealth and food, for your body and mind, your generosity is perfect and is aligned with the transcendent perfection[140] of giving.

When your mind stream remains unpolluted by karmic impurities and disruptive states of mind, your moral discipline is flawless.

When your mind is never carried away by anger, your patience is supreme.

When you feel a deep sense of renunciation toward the three worlds of samsara and feel heartsick when thinking of impermanence and death, you will surely be diligent. This is the perfection of enthusiastic effort toward virtue.

If you do not waver, even for an instant, from the realization of dharmatā, the ultimate nature of reality, this is the ideal meditative concentration.

If you realize the fundamental nature of mind, as it is, this is the ultimate wisdom that apprehends the nonexistence of the self (*anātman*).

–172–

The Mahāyāna Principles

Six instructions on the general Mahāyāna teachings:
Remember death at all times and crack the whip of perseverance.
Whatever [virtuous activities] you do, familiarizing yourself with them is of primary importance. Hence, train in the pursuit of Dharma.
Keeping count of your [virtuous activities], revitalize your merits and purify negativity.
Within the framework of the three supreme points,[141] make offerings and constantly strive to perfect the two accumulations.
Find the right balance in your spiritual practice and attune your perceptions to the Dharma.
Whatever you do, make sure to benefit others and seal your actions with the view of selflessness.
The practitioner who does this penetrates the essence of the supreme vehicle.

Of the many vast and profound instructions of the Great Vehicle, six general points can be highlighted:

Impermanence being manifest at every moment, the time of death is unpredictable and its circumstances uncertain. You have no assurance of being alive tonight. Think about this and with your body, speech, and mind practice virtue with fierce diligence, like a horse spurred into a gallop. Let the awareness of death spur you on to practice Dharma with the same intensity as that horse gallops.

Everything you do repeatedly with your body, speech, and mind generates habits. Since time immemorial to this very day, you have perpetuated the delusion of samsara, mistakenly attributing real existence to phenomena, thus reinforcing these habitual tendencies. That is why today your delusion persists. However, through diligent study, reflection, and meditation on the Dharma, you can come to perceive all phenomena as mere illusions or dreams. By continuously familiarizing yourself with the supreme Dharma's benefits and qualities, your actions, words, and thoughts will naturally incline toward it.

Every day, assess the virtuous acts and practices you have enacted. In particular, at night, before sleep, tally the day's actions, both positive and negative. Confess and purify any misdeed and if you undertook positive actions, resolve to amplify them the next day. In this way, practice the enhancement of virtue and the purification of faults.

Whatever meritorious acts you undertake, begin with the supreme preparation of bodhicitta, continue with the supreme main practice free of conceptual representations, and conclude with the supreme dedication of merit, thus strengthening your practice with these three supreme methods. For this, accumulate merit through the exercise of generosity, the observance of ethical discipline, and other virtuous practices; perfect the accumulation of wisdom through the view of emptiness, free from representations; and persevere by inseparably uniting these two accumulations.

Whatever spiritual practices you are engaged in, consider them like the two pans of a finely balanced scale, and check whether the virtuous practices you carry out with your body, speech, and mind are in equilibrium. Let spiritual practice permeate your three doors, and your perceptions will naturally align with the Dharma.

As for these actions of body, speech, and mind, do not aim solely at accomplishing your personal interests; rather, engage in them to benefit others.

Free from self-clinging and self-cherishing, embracing the excellent attitude of benevolence, know that the essence of the path of the Great Vehicle is contained entirely in these six points. Make this your primary focus. Understand that if you practice the complete set of six-point instructions presented in *The Treasury of Essential Instructions*, they contain the complete preliminary and main practices you need in this life.

–173–

Six Faulty Separations

Avoid six faulty separations:

Do not part from the support of an authentic master;
Otherwise, you will not find the path to liberation.

Do not separate your mind stream from trust in the teachings;
Otherwise, you will not realize the ultimate nature of all things.

Do not part from the profound instructions on spiritual practice;
Otherwise, the sprout of enlightenment will not grow.

Do not part from the wisdom born from listening and contemplation when engaging in elaborated practices;
Otherwise, you will not be freed from the fetters of doubt.

Do not part from mountain solitudes;
Otherwise, you will be consumed by clamor and distraction.

Do not part from the pledge of enthusiastic effort and endeavor;
Otherwise, the time to achieve spiritual qualities will never come.

Thus, it is very important not to part from any of these attributes.

Whatever spiritual practice you undertake, all elements of the path must converge harmoniously. Separating them would be as ineffective as attempting a journey by hopping on a single leg. Accordingly, there are six points that should always remain united, as their separation can lead to negative consequences. How can such dissociations be avoided?

Do not distance yourself from authentic spiritual masters on whom you rely: accompany them as closely as a shadow and strive to rejoice them in three ways. Otherwise, you will drift away from renunciation, lose your weariness of samsara, and diminish your interest in Dharma, ultimately preventing you from entering the path of liberation.

Strengthen your mind and be diligent in your spiritual practice, sparing neither your body nor even your life. Moreover, do not part from the various aspects of faith—clear faith, yearning faith, and confident faith. Without these, you will never attain the perfect realization of emptiness, the ultimate nature of reality.

Any practice you engage in must be based upon profound instructions received from a spiritual master belonging to an authentic spiritual lineage. Otherwise, even if you have heard many teachings and are well versed in various traditional sciences, without the essential instructions you will miss the crucial points and the seed of enlightenment will not take root in the field of your experience.

Regardless of how many elaborate practices you engage in, do not separate them from the wisdom born of study, reflection, and meditation. Practicing without the view acquired through listening and contemplation will leave your understanding vague, unable to free you from the fetters of doubt.

In the long run, it is good to reside in the solitude of a mountainside hermitage, where, free from diversions and involvements, everything you do will naturally tend toward virtue. Otherwise, if you abandon solitary places to frequent fairs, markets, and crowded areas, you will be carried away by their tumultuous distractions.

When practicing the Dharma, be diligent, do not slack off during the day or overindulge in sleep by night. Face sickness and suffering with resilience, and never abandon the practices you have committed to. If your resolve weakens and you forget your commitments, the spiritual qualities of the lineage masters will not be born in your mind.

Thus, do not allow any of these elements to be dissociated; they must to be practiced in unison.

–174–

Thwarting the Māras

Six things you must never part from in order to counteract six māras:
When relying on your spiritual master, never let the demon that makes you impervious to the Dharma enter your mind.
When relying on the Three Jewels, never let the demon of disrespect enter your mind.
When staying in a secluded place, never let the demon of laziness enter your mind.
When studying and contemplating, never let the demon of complacency enter your mind.
When meditating, never let the demon of stagnation enter your mind.
When benefiting others, never let the demon of distraction enter your mind.
These measures seem necessary to me, but [those who apply them] are as rare as stars in the daytime.

Now come six points needed to safeguard yourself against demons and not be vulnerable to them. These demons, or *māra*s, are not some kind of gods, malevolent forces, or local spirits who come to haunt you in real life with glaring eyes and wide-open mouths, baring their fangs in a threatening manner. Rather, a demon is anything or anyone that causes you to endlessly delay your spiritual practice.

When you rely upon a spiritual master, it is crucial to perceive the excellence of all his deeds with respectful devotion and to trust the validity of his words. After hearing many teachings, if you do not generate any confidence and if your mind remains unchanged, as it is said, "the Dharma cannot transform those who are resistant and unresponsive." This is a clear sign of a māra's influence.

After taking refuge in the Three Jewels, you must place complete trust in them. If you simply open your mouth to say, "I take refuge in the Three Jewels and the spiritual master!" without sincere respect and conviction, merely counting your repetitions of the name of the Three Jewels, you are not genuinely taking refuge. Such a lack of confidence is the sign of the demon's presence.

When residing in a solitary mountain retreat, practice to the best of your ability. Otherwise, if you simply indulge in eating and sleeping in the most ordinary way, taking your ease, it is a sign that the demon of indolence has taken hold.

Proper study and contemplation of the teachings should gradually transform your mind, fostering a sense of renunciation and disillusionment with samsara, while cultivating spiritual qualities associated with the various aspects of the path. Conversely, if after hearing countless teachings, you merely shrug away and say, "Well, the master said many things," and become indifferent to the Dharma, it is a sign that māra has made you jaded and resistant to the Dharma.

Once you engage in meditative concentration in a solitary retreat, the most gifted practitioners will see daily progress, while others may notice progress monthly. But if, after years of practice, your attachments, animosities, and lack of insight remain unchanged, and all you can do is count the years of meditation and list the practices you have undertaken, then your efforts have been in vain, thwarted by the demon's influence.

As said, "When benefiting others, do not succumb to the demon of distraction." Sometimes, in your eagerness to help others, you allow your contemplative practice to wither, allowing yourself to be carried away by the demon of restlessness and losing command of your mind, even for a short while. In such a case, your practice becomes nothing more than a facade.

It is imperative to counteract these demons, but nowadays those who do not fall victim to them are as rare as stars in broad daylight.

–175–

Six Allies

Six precepts of the ultimate training[142] you should take as allies:
Take as your ally your confidence in the supreme view;
Without it, you will not reach the heights of dharmatā.
Take as your ally the foundation of the pure precepts of the three trainings;
Without it, you will not be able to attain the desired siddhis.
Take as your ally the supreme conduct that knows the appropriate time;

Otherwise, you will not be able to reach the other shore of samsara.
Take as the ally of your practice confidence in the self-arisen primordial wisdom;
Without it, you will not be able to cut off the shackles of dualism and negative emotions.
Take as your ally the training in enhancing and advancing your spiritual experience;
Otherwise, you will not be able to ward off the legions of afflictive mental states.
Take as your ally all the profound and wide-ranging instructions;
Without them, you will not be able to fulfill your aspirations.
Accordingly, train in these instructions that are imbued with the meaning of the supreme essence.

The three trainings in discipline, concentration, and wisdom enable you to devote yourself to the supreme Dharma. Keep them as your allies and let them accompany you as your shadow throughout your life until you have fully perfected and completed the six precepts of training.

To practice, you must establish a level of authenticity and certainty that leaves no room for doubt. This requires a perfectly pure and unmistaken view. If you hold onto wrong views, as if you were blind, you cannot walk the path of liberation. Without such an unerring view, you will remain as distant from the realization of dharmatā as the earth is from the sky.

To realize this view, you must first lay the foundation by flawlessly adhering to the precepts of the three trainings of ethical discipline, concentration, and wisdom. Corrupting these precepts is like mixing poison with delicious food. Just as everyone would avoid such food, you too will be unable to attain the ordinary and supreme siddhis to which you aspire.

There is an appropriate time for every type of conduct. Therefore, you must fine-tune your practice as you progress through the application of the teachings of individual liberation, of the bodhisattva path, and of the Secret Mantra, according to your capacity to comprehend the view, the meditation, and the conduct. If your behavior is not attuned to the appropriate time and circumstances—if you indulge in drinking, promiscuity, gorge yourself on meat, and behave like any dissolute layperson—you will not reach the other shore of the ocean of samsara.

By weaving spiritual practice into your mind stream, primordial wisdom will spontaneously shine from within like a rising sun. When spiritual practice permeates your mind, primordial wisdom will naturally emerge, shining from within like the rising sun. Just as the sun illuminates all things on earth, large and small, allowing you to see them clearly, so too will the realization of primordial wisdom reveal the ultimate nature of reality, dispelling naturally the false perceptions rooted in dualistic thinking.

But if you do not gain the inner certainty that comes with the direct experience of primordial wisdom, you will not be able to cut through the ropes of dualistic fixations and afflictive states of mind. You will have spent many years ostensibly meditating, only to see your attachment to duality and your mental poisons remain untouched.

To foster spiritual growth and progress, you must be diligent and show devotion, respect, and trust in your spiritual master. Without harnessing your capacity to progress, you will be unable to ward off the army of negative emotions, which will continue to dominate you time and again.

Meditate on the profound and essential instructions. Do so without partiality, remaining in harmony with the various approaches available, just as a bee visits each flower in a beautiful meadow, collecting their nectar. The multitude of vast and deep instructions can also be compared to fine and deep ornaments engraved by a goldsmith's steady hand. If you do not apply these profound instructions in a nonsectarian way, you will fail to attain the ordinary and supreme accomplishments to which you aspire.

Therefore, practice these six excellent and essential points properly.

–176–

Six Priorities

Instructions on six priorities:
For a place to live, make the solitude of a mountainside your priority. Rely on it.
Other than that, populated places will be causes of suffering.
The foremost path is to revere your spiritual master as the Buddha;
Other than this, the signs of the path and the auspicious connections will be perturbed.

The foremost samaya is to apply the view of inseparable union in all situations;
Other than this, in separation, nothing can be accomplished.
The foremost spiritual experience and realization is transforming conceptual thoughts into primordial wisdom;
Other than this, you will not be able to defeat the armies of what must be discarded.
The foremost intention is to abandon all attachment to samsara;
Other than this, you will be carried away by the pursuits of this life.
The foremost aim is to free the subject who realizes the view in its true nature;
Other than this, you will not be free from the extremes of eternalism and nihilism.
These are the precious treasures that you must care for respectfully.

Six points are paramount for all practices on the path:

The priority regarding your dwelling place is to remain steadfast in a solitary mountain retreat. In such a setting you will have few distractions, will not be carried away by the bustle of everyday life, and your activities in harmony with Dharma will thrive. In contrast, residing in villages and other populated areas where many gather will only fuel your attachments and aversions, leading to countless distractions that culminate in suffering.

At the heart of the path lies guru yoga, the "union with the awakened nature of the master." With unwavering devotion, you must regard your spiritual master as the Buddha himself. This is the essential point of the path and the surest way to progress and remove obstacles. If you act otherwise, the auspicious conditions that lead to signs of progress will be disrupted.

The main point of samayas is to unite the means [of compassion] and the wisdom of emptiness. Failing to experience this union, and instead separating the means and wisdom, will prevent you from accomplishing your aims.

The priority of meditative experiences and realization is to transform conceptual thoughts so that they arise having the nature of primordial wisdom and are naturally liberated into their true nature at the moment they occur. If you do not allow these thoughts to be liberated, you will not be able to clear away the veil formed by afflictive states of mind and the veil that obscures all that can be known.

A central priority must be to develop a deep sense of disgust for the three worlds of samsara. Without this, you will remain entangled in the ordinary concerns of this life.

The fundamental purpose of the view is to liberate the object of realization and the subject who realizes it in their true nature (*dharmatā*). Otherwise, you cannot free yourself from the extremes of eternalism and nihilism.

These instructions are a precious treasure that you must cherish and care for with respect.

–177–

Six Things That Happen by Themselves

Six things that are accomplished naturally:
If you give up worldly activities, meritorious deeds will naturally follow.
If your three trainings are pure, oath-bound protectors will spontaneously gather around you.
If you cultivate compassion, benefiting beings will naturally happen.
If you carry out the approach and accomplishment practices, enlightened activities will come about automatically.
If you relax perfectly, you will directly perceive dharmatā quite naturally.
If you attain the supreme siddhi, ordinary ones will come by themselves.

If you practice the heart of the path, favorable outcomes will ensue without any particular effort on your part.

If you put the affairs of ordinary life out of your mind, virtuous activities and spiritual practices will come about naturally, since you will have no other concern than practicing the Dharma.

By fully and authentically cultivating the three trainings—ethical discipline, concentration, and insight—the Dharma protectors will naturally support you. As it is said, "A pure and perfect samaya is the life stone of the oath-bound protectors."[143]

If you nurture a kind heart and great compassion for all beings under the sky, the very power of that compassion, will spontaneously bring about the benefit of others, without any deliberate effort on your part.

When you have completed multiple times the various cycles of recitation and accomplishment centered on supreme wisdom deities, accumulating a significant number of recitations, the enlightened activities of pacification, augmentation, attraction, and subjugation will naturally be accomplished, requiring no additional effort.

If you completely relax your body, speech, and mind, the dharmatā, the true nature of reality, will reveal itself effortlessly, whereas excessive exertion will only obscure your understanding of this ultimate nature.

Once you have achieved the supreme siddhi with one-pointed concentration, the ordinary siddhis associated with pacifying, increasing, attracting, and subjugating will naturally arise, without the need for further effort.

–178–

Six Multitudes to Flee

Six multitudes to avoid:
Many are those who go astray in the pursuits of this life for not having given up their attachments.
Many are those who die ordinary deaths for having neither studied nor practiced.
Many are those who destroy the three trainings for not applying the proper antidotes.
Many are those who err in meditation for not having listened to [the teachings] and reflected [upon them].
Many are those who fall into the lower realms for disregarding the law of cause and effect.
Many are those whose spiritual practice is deceived by the demon of restlessness.
Therefore, it is advisable not to be one of them.

If you mix with some of these six groups, many defects will follow:

If you fail to relinquish your attachments to the pursuits of ordinary life, you will lose your way, consumed by the endless chase for food, clothing, and other material needs, just as many others do.

If you do not devote yourself to study, reflect, and meditate properly on the teachings that ought to be known, and practice only a superficial form of Dharma, you will achieve nothing and join the multitude of those who die in the ordinary way.

If you do not wisely apply the antidotes to afflictive states of mind, you will succumb to their influence and end up breaking the precepts and vows associated with the three trainings, having failed to uphold these commitments purely. This happens to many people!

If you have not done your best to listen to the teachings and ponder them, you risk becoming one of the many who meditate blindly, as if casting stones in the dark.

By failing to carefully and thoroughly observe the law of cause and effect, many people find themselves falling into lower destinies.

Many people are lured by distractions, entertainment, and fleeting thrills. Were they not trapped by these diversions, they would be deeply sickened by such pursuits.

I urge you not to join these multitudes, for if you do, your Dharma practice will inevitably decline.

–179–

VICTORY OVER DEMONS

Six states in which you are victorious over the demons:
The best encouragement to practice is mindfulness: do not cast it away to the demon of laziness.
The supreme mind training is to consider others as most important: do not cast it away to the demon of self-cherishing.
The [summit of the view] is certainty about the fundamental nature: do not cast it away to the demon of doubt.
The ultimate meditative practice is to be free of extremes: do not cast it away to the demon of partiality.
The supreme accomplishment practice is to strike the vital points: do not cast it away it to the demon of talkativeness.
The supreme realization is to be free of all extremes: do not cast it away to the demon of philosophical systems.

If you adhere to these six instructions in the following situations, you will overcome the obstacles posed by demons:

If you urge yourself to practice the Dharma with attentive presence and introspective vigilance, as long as you sustain these two qualities without distraction, you will not be overpowered by the demon of laziness.

The quintessential mind training is to cultivate benevolence. Once you possess this admirable quality, you will be protected from the demon of selfishness.

When you achieve unwavering certainty in the view of the fundamental nature, you will be free of the demon of doubt which leads you to wonder, "Is this the correct view or not?" or "Is this the right meditation or not?" thus preventing such doubts from creating obstacles.

If your meditative experience transcends all extremes, the demons of partiality and of belief in solid existence, which make you fall into eternalism, as well as the demon of nothingness, which draws you into nihilism, will have no hold on you.

If you strike the vital points of practice, your words and thoughts will remain in harmony with the Dharma. In this way, you will have escaped the grip of the demon who compels you to ramble about the highest view as if you had realized it, or makes you allude that you possess clairvoyance.

The ultimate realization stands beyond extremes: do not surrender it to the demon that incites you to discriminate between "your" philosophical system and "theirs," leading you to cling to various doctrinal positions.

–180–

Six Measures of Authenticity

Perfectly establishing the six measures of authenticity:
Your thoroughness in observing the law of cause and effect
indicates the strength of your conviction.
Your circumspection is measured by your fear of useless chatter.
The nobility of a friend is measured by the influence of their
positive qualities.
The quality of your meditation is measured by your ability to
remain in the nature of the mind, free of object.
An accomplished practice is measured by your ability to not be
carried away by either negative or positive qualities.

Reaching the state of exhaustion [of phenomena in the dharmatā][144] is the measure of your taking the three kāyas on the path.
Those who meet these criteria are supremely noble beings.

When engaged in Dharma practice, there are six indicators that reveal whether you have struck the vital points.

Scrupulously observing the law of causality in its subtlest aspects, avoiding even the slightest negative deeds and engaging in the smallest positive actions, demonstrates a deep conviction in this fundamental law.

If you beware of indulging in excessive talk and choose to speak little, this is a sign of cautiousness and restraint.

The extent of the desirable qualities that you have acquired by associating with spiritual friends reflects their positive influence on your way of being.

To fathom the nature of mind, which transcends any notion of a meditator and an object of meditation, is devoid of any fixed target or goal and is a mark of excellent meditation. As it is said, "the authentic view is to be free from fixation."

When the balance of your practice never wavers and is not destabilized by either new positive qualities or flaws, enabling you to integrate all experiences into the path, this signifies a mature and stable practice.

The emptiness aspect of the nature of mind is the dharmakāya, its luminous character is the saṃbhogakāya, and its unimpeded cognizance is the nirmāṇakāya. Integrating the three kāyas on the path all along your journey indicates that you have reached the state where phenomena are exhausted within the dharmatā.

Any practitioner who fulfills these six criteria is a true custodian of the Buddha's teachings and embodies all the hallmarks of authenticity.

–181–

Six Mistakes to Avoid

Six mistakes to avoid:
After taking the three vows, do not burden yourself with transgressions.
Do not discard the essential meaning to follow the words.

Do not embrace the eight worldly dharmas while forsaking supreme enlightenment.
Do not return empty-handed after obtaining the precious human rebirth.
Do not follow a lesser path after finding the profound meaning.
Do not fail to practice even after being well versed in the teachings.

At all times, avoid falling into six pitfalls:

After taking the vows of individual liberation, of the bodhisattvas, and of the Secret Mantra, avoid faults and downfalls. Should they occur, confess them, and purify yourself promptly.

If you ignore the crucial points of the practice of the essential meaning, even if you know many definitions and concepts, this will not guide you to the heart of meditative experience. Do not become ensnared in the pursuit of mere words.

Never set aside the accomplishment of enlightenment, of buddhahood, in favor of the eight worldly concerns.

Now that you have obtained this precious human existence with its rare freedoms and favorable conditions, make it meaningful by practicing diligently. Having crossed the threshold of the Dharma, do not leave empty-handed by squandering your life in distraction and busyness.

After realizing the meaning of profound emptiness through direct experience, do not get lost in the lesser vehicles.

You may become proficient in expounding the entirety of the Buddha's teachings to others, but remember that it is essential to have direct experience of the teachings through practice. Without this, all these scholarly discourses will not bring any benefit. Do not forget the practice!

–182–

Avert Obstacles

Six means to avert hindrances to Dharma practice:
When obstacles are rife, dismantle the wall of mundane conventions.
If revulsion for samsara does not arise, think of the urgency [to practice Dharma].

> **If compassion does not arise, put yourself in the shoes of the suffering beings.**
> **If the blessings fade away, generate devotion and perseverance.**
> **If many people are hurting you, examine yourself critically again and again.**
> **If you aspire to benefit others, cultivate bodhicitta and make aspiration prayers.**
> **If you do so, you will be free of these difficulties.**

The practice of the sublime Dharma is fraught with obstacles. It is crucial to recognize them and resist falling under their influence.

When faced with numerous challenges, break free from the barriers of worldly preoccupation that revolve around food, clothing, currying favor with the influential, and other trivialities. What a relief to leave all that behind!

If you fail to maintain a persistent interest in the practice of the sublime Dharma, think about impermanence: you have so little time in this life! If you do so, the yearning to practice the Dharma will inevitably surge in your mind.

If your compassion does not readily arise within you, think of your inability to bear even the sting of a thorn, and your pleasure when someone compliments you. Understand that all beings are like you. Put yourself in their place and do not harm anyone in any way.

If blessings seem to vanish from your mind stream, be diligent in invigorating the respectful devotion that makes you regard your spiritual masters as the Buddha in person and by appreciating the excellence of all their actions.

When confronted with harmful people and negative forces, use this as an opportunity to examine your meditative experience and realization. Consider all who are malevolent toward you as incentives to virtue. Take responsibility for the suffering that you encounter.

If you wish to benefit others, foster bodhicitta, the mind of enlightenment, nurture benevolence, and ardently aspire to gain the ability to help others.

By doing so, you will free yourself from all these defects.

–183–

Six Criteria of Authenticity

Six criteria for authenticity of the sublime Dharma you practice:
The authentic words of the Buddha are based on the sutras and tantras.
Authentic instructions emanate from an unbroken lineage.
Authentic blessings are untainted by broken samayas.
Authentic instructions are not contaminated by incompatible teachings.
Authentic spiritual experiences are based on integrating [the teachings] into your mind stream.
Authentic logical reasoning is based upon valid cognitions of direct perception and inference.
Meeting these six criteria is essential [for Dharma practice].

Six spiritual qualities result from authentic Dharma practice:

The teachings on which you focus your practice must originate from an authentic source—words indisputably spoken by the Buddha, which can be validated by canonical texts of the sutras and tantras.

Authentic pith instructions are passed down through a genuine lineage and transmission, replete with blessings, and have been transmitted without interruption from the primordial Buddha Samantabhadra to your root teacher.*

Blessings will quickly penetrate the mind of those who apply themselves to these teachings, provided they maintain an impeccably pure and undamaged samaya.

Given the similarity among many instructions, it is vital not to confuse them and to practice with flawless precision the instructions coming from an authentic and untainted lineage.

"To what extent have I applied antidotes to my afflictive mental states? At what point did the yearning for renunciation arise in my mind? How much has my meditative practice progressed?" To ensure the authenticity of your spiritual experience, it is indispensable to reflect on such questions.

Your Dharma practice will be authentic if it withstands the scrutiny of valid cognition—whether through direct perception, as when witnessing something with your own eyes or through logical inference.

Meeting these six criteria is essential to authenticate your Dharma practice.

–184–

Exposing Your Shortcomings

Six instructions to dig into your hidden flaws:
Do not fool yourself with your hypocritical moral discipline.
Do not bring devastation upon yourself with your negative and harmful actions.
Do not bring ruin upon yourself by succumbing to your own demons: attachment and grasping.
Do not disturb your own mind stream with the emotion of anger.
Do not let distraction and busyness divert you from your sense of purpose.
Do not throw yourself into the abyss of samsara.
If you listen to these pieces of advice, your future will be bright.

Identify your own flaws. It is important to seek them out from the depths of your being.

Hypocrisy, in this context, refers to deceiving others by pretending to be a genuine Dharma practitioner when, in reality, you are not. If you have not transformed your mind stream and yet claim otherwise, you are misleading both yourself and others.

By engaging in wrongful behavior, you bring ruin upon yourself. Therefore, refrain from committing negative acts, whether in plain sight or in secrecy.

If you harbor all sorts of attachments and fixations for the ordinary pursuits of this life, you are inviting the demon of ruin to settle in your mind stream. Do not foster attachment and fixations.

As soon as anger flares up, tranquility deserts your mind and unease takes its place. Do not let anger cloud your mind.

At first glance, distractions and involvements may seem appealing. But in the long run, they delay your spiritual practice and prevent you from achieving your aspirations.

Being in the three worlds of samsara resembles falling into a great abyss. Do not run to your doom in the abyss of samsaric activities.

Heeding this advice will help you cultivate a sincere aspiration to practice the sublime Dharma.

–185–

Linking the Levels

Six practices that combine the higher and the lower [objects of merit]:
Upward, make offerings to spiritual masters, wisdom deities, and ḍākinīs.
Downward, cut the bonds with possessions and pleasures related to sentient beings and their environment.
In between, develop an understanding of the union of appearances and emptiness.
For others, dedicate the merits for the benefit of all beings.
For yourself, cultivate the qualities of the Three Jewels.
In between, bring your meritorious actions and those of others into a nonreferential state.
Doing so, you will accomplish the essence of the profound path of the sublime Dharma.

The ideal way to transform your mind is by integrating and uniting the highest practices—that lead to spiritual experience and realization—with those suited for beings of lesser capacity.

Upwardly, meditate on guru yoga with devotion that sees the spiritual master—the root of blessings—as the Buddha himself. Engage in recitations, the practices of accomplishment, and activities associated with the yidam, the wisdom deity—the root of siddhis. Offer sacred feast and tormas to the ḍākinīs—the root of enlightened activities.

Downward, cut at the root any craving and urge for worldly pleasures and possessions, related to other beings in samsara and to the world around them.

In between, recognize that all perceptions related to this life are like colorful rainbows. Do not take them as concrete reality, but instead, uproot all forms of grasping and train yourself to unite the emptiness of their ultimate nature with their illusory, dreamlike appearance.

For the benefit of others, dedicate all the merits you have accumulated to all beings, instead of rather than keeping their benefit for yourself. In doing so, the impact of your positive actions will be multiplied, and you will fulfill the bodhisattva activities.

For your own growth, enhance the qualities associated with the Buddha, the Dharma, and the sangha that are already present in your mind, and generate those that have yet to arise.

Throughout all this, persistently encourage every form of positive action and spiritual practice, both in yourself and in others. Do not complacently congratulate yourself, however, for having accomplished many good deeds. Be diligent while remaining free of conceptualization.

This is the essential and profound way to practice the Dharma in an excellent way.

–186–

Six Deplorable Situations

Six deplorable situations that lead us away from the Dharma:
It is deplorable to commit negative actions after having obtained a human rebirth.
It is deplorable not to practice Dharma after having encountered it.
It is deplorable to break your vows after having received them.
It is deplorable to practice Dharma while breaking samayas.
It is deplorable to earn a wrong livelihood acquired by using the Dharma.
It is deplorable to claim to benefit others when you even fail to accomplish your own good.
Many disgrace themselves in these ways and thinking of them makes me feel depressed.

To stray from the Dharma means that your mind is becoming dissociated from it. As for the expression "*ya re cha*,"[145] it refers to something both deplorable and frightening and there are six situations that are cause for such dismay:

When those who have obtained this precious human existence do not give full meaning to their freedoms and favorable conditions by practicing the Dharma but engage in negative actions, it is truly disgraceful.

If you have encountered authentic Dharma and you are following a spiritual guide, yet, do not put the teachings into practice, showing as little interest in them than a dog has in a tuft of grass, it is deeply disheartening.

After properly receiving the vows of individual liberation, the precepts of the bodhisattvas, and those of the Secret Mantra, if you fail to uphold them with vigilance and circumspection and let them degenerate and be broken, it is truly lamentable.

Those who have damaged their samayas will find that their spiritual practice yields no results, despite their perseverance. This is truly appalling.

Using the Dharma to obtain material goods and benefits is an inappropriate way to secure your livelihood. Such improper use of religious possessions brings great defilements and is truly disgraceful.

While you are not even able to accomplish your own benefit, if you prematurely embark on benefiting others, you might become driven by desires for personal gain, respect, and fame, while doing no true good for others, which is truly a disgrace.

"When I think of these six deplorable behaviors and I see so many people engaging in them, I feel deeply depressed," Gyalwa Longchenpa tells us.

–187–

Becoming Resistant

Six causes of becoming resistant to the Dharma:
Associating with bad friends will make you resistant to virtuous activities.
Looking for faults in your spiritual masters will make you resistant to devotion and respect.
Giving up your effort to meditate will make you resistant to spiritual experience.
Staying on the path of distraction will make you resistant to the sublime Dharma.
Scrutinizing the faults of others will make you resistant to pure perception.
Letting your experience of awareness get lost in bad habits makes you slip into delusion.
Abandon these six causes and practice the sublime Dharma.

You begin by listening to the Dharma, then as you hear more teachings, you may lose your initial awe and fail to develop deep conviction. This is a sign that you have become jaded[146] or have slipped away from the Dharma. This can manifest in six ways:

If you keep bad company and lack dedication to the Dharma, your spiritual practices will falter.

If you focus on finding faults in your spiritual masters instead of contemplating their qualities, your respectful fervor will decline, and you will become resistant to devotion.

If you do not persevere in your practice, taking little rest during the day and sleep at night, any spiritual experience you gain will quickly dissipate, offering little benefit.

If you constantly stray into the paths of distraction, whatever study, reflection, and meditation you undertake will be plagued by lethargy. You will make no progress and become resistant to the Dharma.

If you fail to cultivate pure vision toward others, dwelling instead on their imperfections, your pure perception will decline.

Lacking a sense of urgency and imagining a long life ahead, you will engage in countless activities, which will become your way of living. As a result, your experience of awareness will be led astray in the three worlds of samsara.

Reject these six ways of becoming resistant to the Dharma. Strive to practice in the purest manner possible.

–188–

Defeating Six Enemies

Six instructions for driving away six enemies:
Do not surrender your precious human birth, with its freedoms and advantages, to the enemies: the ordinary things in life.
Do not surrender your altruism and bodhicitta to the enemy: the basic vehicle.
Do not surrender the precious gem, the nature of mind, to its enemy: delusion.
Do not deliver the wish-fulfilling gem of the two accumulations to its enemies: worldly pursuits.
Do not surrender your essential practice to its enemy: laziness.
Do not hand over your devotion and respect to their enemies: wrong views.

Six enemies oppose the practice of the sublime Dharma. Overcome them, and your practice will be flawless.

If, after obtaining this human life, graced with the freedoms and conditions conducive to practicing Dharma, you exhaust yourself in the futile chase for food and clothing, it means that you have surrendered to the enemies that the comforts of life represent, thus wasting an invaluable opportunity.

If you abandon bodhicitta—the altruistic resolve to attain enlightenment for the sake of all beings—in favor of seeking individual liberation alone, you are surrendering bodhicitta to its enemy, the lesser path of the listeners onto which you have strayed.

If you are not well focused on the direct experience of the jewel of the nature of mind and deliver it to delusion, your archenemy, the opportunity to realize the ultimate nature of reality will slip away.

Pursuing the twofold accumulation of merit and wisdom is like holding a precious wish-fulfilling gem in your hands. Do not forsake this accumulation nor forfeit this gem to your enemies: the eight worldly concerns entangled in this life's affairs.

If instead of dedicating yourself wholeheartedly to the essential practice, you only aspire to a cozy comfort while assuming the appearance of a practitioner, you abdicate before your enemy: laziness. Do not allow this to happen!

Persist in generating reverent devotion and powerful fervor. Do not capitulate to the enemy who makes you see faults in your spiritual master and companions, leading you to slander them and harbor adverse views.

–189–

Six Deceptive Attractions

Six dire consequences of overindulging in the sense objects:
Like a moth [attracted by] the flame of a lamp, your eyes are enchanted by forms.
Like a deer [enraptured by the melody] of a flute, your ears are enchanted by sounds.
Like a bee [attracted to] sandalwood, your nose is enchanted by smells.
Like fish [caught by] bait, your tongue is enchanted by taste.

Like elephants caught in a mud pool, your body is enchanted by touch.
Like a mother camel [obsessed by] the death of her offspring, your mind is enchanted by phenomena.
Therefore, make sure you do not overindulge in the six sense objects!

If you do not associate skillful means with the enjoyment of sensory pleasures, and experience them in ordinary ways, six unfortunate consequences will follow:

Fascinated by the flame of a lamp, the moth flies toward it and burns to death. It will be the same if you are seduced by form.

Captivated by sounds, you are like a deer, irresistibly attracted by the sweet melody of a hunter's flute—only to be struck down by an arrow as it draws near.

Enamored with of exhilarating scents, you are like a bee drawn to a fragrant tree, only to become impaled on thorns and perish.

Obsessed with flavors, you are like a fish attracted by the taste of the bait on a hook. Caught, pulled onto dry land, the fish chokes to death.

As for touch, consider the elephants in India during the hot season, seeking the coolness of mud pools. Once stuck, unable to escape, they eventually die.

The mind, for its part, lured by phenomena and consumed by fanciful projects, becomes obsessed with them like a mother camel who has just lost her child. More than any other animal, she grieves, sometimes to the point of death.

Therefore, be careful not to cling in ordinary ways to the objects of the six aspects of consciousness.

–190–

Taking Adversity onto the Path

Six ways to bring adversities onto the path:
When thoughts focused on this life arise, develop disgust from the depth of your heart.
Whenever you experience diseases and malignant forces, consider them as a broom that sweeps away your negativities and obscurations.

> **Whenever adversities and obstacles arise, consider them as encouragement to virtue.**
> **When you are harmed by your enemies' animosity, consider it as an opportunity to practice patience.**
> **Whatever conceptual thoughts arise, consider them as reminders of primordial wisdom.**
> **Look at the appearances of the universe and its contents as the pure realms of the buddhas.**
> **By doing so, all adversities will turn into the path of enlightenment.**

When Dharma practitioners are faced with six difficult circumstances, if they know how to bring them onto the path, they will turn into allies.

When a yearning for success in business, fame, and other worldly pursuits arises in your mind, remind yourself of the unpredictable nature of death, the impossibility of fulfilling every worldly ambition, the eventual exhaustion of all accumulations, and the inevitable separation of all that comes together. Contemplating these truths will naturally diminish your appetite for such trivial pursuits. This reflection is essential.

When afflicted by illness and beset by negative forces, rather than deeming the situation unbearable, envision yourself taking on the illnesses and adverse conditions of others, thereby relieving their suffering. This practice transforms obstacles into opportunities for purifying your own negativities and obscurations, thereby enhancing your spiritual practice.

When enemies display hostility, rulers impose punishments, or other misfortunes and obstacles arise, use these adversities as incentives to dedicate yourself to spiritual practice. Become disenchanted with samsara and determined to escape it, thus losing any taste for the ordinary affairs of this life.

Whatever thoughts arise, learn to liberate them as they appear. When you do so, no matter how many thoughts there are, they will only serve to make the primordial wisdom shine more brightly.

Perceive the universe and its inhabitants as pure realms, such as the Glorious Copper-Colored Mountain (Sandok Palri) or the Land of Bliss (Sukhāvatī) and pure vision will spontaneously manifest.

These six instructions guide you in transforming adverse circumstances into the path of enlightenment.

–191–

Six Misunderstandings

Failure to understand the above leads to the following six misunderstandings:
[Unlike a realized being] you will discriminate between qualities and defects,
And between the higher and lower states of the six realms of existence.
You will consider awareness (*rigpa*) to be arising and ceasing.
You will consider that pristine simplicity has elements that need to be discarded with the help of antidotes.
You will consider that awareness requires training and progression.
You will consider that the fruition will be achieved from elsewhere.
Failing to understand the supreme meaning of awareness,
Fools with limited intellect engage in the worldly preoccupations.

If you do not know how to bring the six aforementioned mistakes onto the path, you will struggle with all other flaws as well.

If you cultivate spiritual qualities to the best of your capacity, you will have understood the nature of qualities and defects, but you might also believe that they should be inherently pursued or rejected.

Among the six states of existence, if you develop a strong attachment to the so-called higher realms, thinking that the happiness and enjoyments of gods and humans are truly desirable, you will be unable to free yourself from samsara as a whole.

Awareness, by its very nature, is without beginning; it does not reside anywhere and does not cease. By assuming that it has an origin, a location, and an end, you are entertaining wrong views.

If you fathom the transparent simplicity of the mind, simply preserve it without rejecting anything or resorting to antidotes, and your practice will naturally progress. But if you indulge in all sorts of mental elaborations, your view will remain purely intellectual.

If you correctly realize the meaning of awareness, there is neither obscuration to purify nor path to travel. Failing to understand this will leave you wandering aimlessly.

Harboring a lot of hopes and doubts about attaining some fruition in the future will hinder your meditative experiences and realization. The fruition, buddhahood, is already present within you as the buddha nature (*tathāgatagarbha*). You err if you seek this buddha nature somewhere outside yourself.

If you ignore the Great Perfection, the summit of the view and of realization, and carry on with the ordinary affairs that beings pursue childishly, you merely embrace the worldly concerns that will continue to lure you.

–192–

Shameful Situations

Six shameful situations for Dharma practitioners:
Having entered the door of Dharma, engaging in unvirtuous actions is shameful.
Being attached to words and conventions [of Dharma] while not achieving your purpose is shameful.
After taking the bodhisattva vow, self-cherishing is shameful.
Mixing Dharma with worldly conventions is shameful.
Engaging in conflict, driven by attachment and aversion, is shameful.
Slandering the Dharma and those who practice it is shameful.
And yet, it is very rare to find people who avoid these shameful behaviors.

There are six reasons a practitioner who does not conform to the teachings should feel embarrassed in the presence of buddhas and bodhisattvas:

Engaging in improper conduct after you have entered the door of the teachings of individual liberation, the path of the bodhisattvas, and the Secret Mantra reflects a disrespect for the teachings of the Buddha. You have good reason to be ashamed of such behavior before the wisdom deities and ḍākinīs.

If you do not wholeheartedly engage in the practice of the quintessential meaning but instead merely ramble on about the meaning of words and cling to theories, you will fail to accomplish your essential purpose. This is embarrassing.

After taking the supreme vow of the bodhisattvas to attain enlightenment for the sake of all beings, if you then focus solely on your own welfare, you should be ashamed for failing to abandon self-clinging.

Attempting to combine the Dharma and worldly affairs is like trying to mix fire and water—they cannot coexist and one of the two is bound to disappear. Seeking to do both simultaneously is embarrassing.

When, overpowered by attachment and aggression, Dharma practitioners engage in constant quarreling, it is deeply regrettable and shameful.

If you keep criticizing fellow practitioners, slander the practice of the sublime Dharma itself, or defame both, it is quite disgraceful.

Avoid these various ways of behaving shamefully. Nowadays very few people do so.

–193–

Six Authentic Instructions

Six authentic and essential instructions:
Distraction is the work of demons: sever the bonds that enslave you to it.
Merits can become obstacles: do not over-rejoice in them.[147]
Power and fame are the trappings of demons: be humble on all occasions.
Biased views lean toward eternalism or nihilism: unite everything in the single absolute space.
Lacking the crucial points (in your practice) is a painful burden: look for pith instructions.
If you lack spiritual experience, the teachings remain mere empty words: blend your mind with practice.
By following [this advice], you will accomplish spiritual qualities.

If you practice the authentic path with resolve, consider these six meaningful instructions:

In the midst of a crowd, you are easily carried away by distractions and excitement: recognize this as the work of demons. Resist temptation and sever all involvements.

Abundance of possessions, wealth, influence, and a high status are marks of social success, but the more you become attached to them, the further you drift from the Dharma. Let go of any inclination for these trivialities.

The exercise of power is governed by māra. At all times and in all circumstances, keep to the most unassuming position and be humble.

If you keep discriminating between your philosophical views and those of others and being attached to your views, you will end up falling into one of the two extremes, nihilism or eternalism, without even noticing it. Instead, unite everything in the single expanse of the dharmadhātu, the absolute dimension.

If you miss the key points of the practice, even if you are diligent, you are just burdening yourself with hardship. Seek above all the instructions that convey the vital points of spiritual practice.

Beware of a view that is all talk. Merely professing theories is fruitless; instead, earnestly integrate the ultimate view into your mind stream.

By following these instructions, the highest spiritual qualities will naturally flourish.

–194–

The Time Has Come

Six instructions indicating the appropriate time:

For too long you have been wandering in the cycles of birth,
death, and bardo:
Today the time has come to conquer the unchanging citadel.

For too long you have been trapped in the machinery of
suffering:
Today the time has come to walk toward the Land of Great
Bliss.

For too long you have taken and discarded bodies through births and deaths:
Today the time has come to attain the unchanging absolute body, dharmakāya.

For too long you have remained confused in the darkness of ignorance:
Today the time has come to light the torch of primordial wisdom.

For too long you have been defeated by the army of the four demons:
Today the time has come to repel the hordes of samsara.

For too long you have been at the service of your desires:
Today the time has come to cultivate the crop of the ultimate harvest.

Not only is it the right time: it is getting late!

When practicing the exalted Dharma, it is important to assess your abilities and know the right time to act. Six instructions will guide you:

From beginningless births to this day, you have wandered from death to rebirth in the three worlds of samsara. Only an omniscient buddha could enumerate the multitude of your past existences. Today the time has come to seize the immutable citadel [of enlightenment] and end the relentless sufferings of birth and death. Conquer this citadel!

For so long and down to this very day, you have been caught up in the grinding wheels of the torments of samsara's three worlds. Piling up all the bodies that were yours just from your lifetimes as an ant would form a heap higher than Mount Meru. Now the time has come to claim the citadel of great bliss, the kingdom of the great and immutable bliss.

Throughout your countless lives and deaths, you have borrowed an immeasurable number of bodies. From this moment onward, ensure that every birth is liberated in the nirmāṇakāya, every death in the dharmakāya, and every bardo in the saṃbhogakāya—uniting them all within the dharmakāya.

For endless lives, you have been veiled in the ignorance of what should be accomplished and what must be avoided. Today, with unwavering focus, let the torch of primordial wisdom illuminate your mind!

The legions of the four māras are formidable foes, and you have succumbed to them countless times. Today the time has come to gather all your strength and repel the forces of the three worlds of samsara.

Never content, you have been enslaved by sense pleasures. Now is the time to break free from their grip and to reap the perennial and ultimate harvest.

For all of this, not only is it high time to act but it is also quite late. Get to the task right away!

–195–

Six Crucial Points

Examining six points that prove to be crucial:
If you do not know the [ultimate] nature of suffering to be bliss,
Desiring happiness in itself can be a painful disease.
If you do not apprehend the equality of attachment and aversion within your self-cognizing awareness,
Rejecting some and seeking others is a great sickness.
If you do not understand that, by nature, adverse circumstances are allies,
Relying on other methods, you will be tightly entangled in their net.
If you are not able to transform inauspiciousness into good fortune,
Even siddhis will turn into demons and become harmful.
If you do not tame your mind stream with the Dharma,
Even knowing myriad words [of teachings] will be no more than a parrot's prayer.
If your virtuous actions are not guided by bodhicitta,
They will either stray toward the paths of the listeners and the solitary realizers or to mere worldly merits.
Therefore, it is essential to take these crucial points into account.

Six points are required for authentic practice:

All the sufferings you endure in the three worlds of samsara should magnify your compassion and act as a broom, sweeping away your negative deeds and obscurations. Embrace them, knowing that their true nature is none other than bliss and understanding that fleeting happiness associated with wealth, possessions, and comfort only leads to further suffering and cannot bring about true felicity.

Know how to equalize animosity toward your enemies and affection for your loved ones within the fundamental equality of all phenomena. As soon as you cease to engage in attraction and repulsion, you disentangle yourself from the endless pursuit of acquiring everything you want and trying to discard what bothers you.

If you are unable to bring adverse circumstances—illnesses, harmful forces, or obstacles—onto the path and turn them into allies and instead resort to all sorts of irrelevant methods, they will not serve your purpose, and you will find yourself caught in their net.

When faced with adversity and undesirable events, if you do not see them as auspicious occasions to advance in your practice, even the attainment of the ordinary and supreme siddhis can turn into demons.

If you cannot control your mind through the application of the teachings, even if you mumble countless words, you will be like a parrot reciting the *Mani* without any idea of what it means.

If you do not imbue all the positive actions that you undertake with the intent to help others and with the noble attitude of bodhicitta, you will stray onto the lesser path of the listeners and the solitary realizers. The benefits of such acts will be minimal, and the associated merits will, at best, lead you to take rebirth among humans or devas, only to continue wandering in samsara once these merits are exhausted.

A good understanding of the Dharma must therefore lead you to take these crucial points into account so you can tread the path in the best possible way.

–196–

Six Outcomes

Six outcomes of Dharma practice:
If you stay in solitude, your virtuous activities will flourish.
If you praise others, they will naturally trust you.
If you master your mind, your virtues will increase.
If you gather the seven spiritual riches, you will never face poverty.
If you develop positive qualities, you may uphold the lineage of the victorious ones.
If you take care of the beings of the six realms, your activities will become like that of the bodhisattvas.
Despite these possibilities, those who strive in such ways are very rare.

Six outcomes naturally occur when you practice the Dharma, requiring no extra effort:

Seek solitude in the serenity of the mountains, and your spiritual qualities will blossom effortlessly. Everything you do will turn to virtue.

Avoid criticizing others. Instead, cultivate pure vision and praise them as much as possible. In return they will trust you and appreciate your qualities.

Master your mind to the fullest and you will no longer feel the urge to reform others. As a result, your meditative experiences, realization, and qualities will flourish.

Persevere in accumulating the seven noble qualities* and in all your future lives, you will never be impoverished in spiritual qualities nor suffer material destitution.

Seize every opportunity to enhance the qualities resulting from study, reflection, and meditation, and you will become an heir to the spiritual kingdom of the buddhas.

By contemplating the sufferings of all sentient beings and letting waves of compassion arise within you, you will effortlessly perform the activities of the bodhisattvas.

All this is certain, yet so few people choose to act this way.

–197–

Generate Inspiration

Six important points to generate inspiration:
It is difficult for devotion, respect, and faith to arise from the depth of your heart;
Hence the importance of deliberately and persistently bringing them to mind.

It is difficult for various conceptual thoughts to emerge as allies;
Hence the importance of being mindful in liberating whatever thoughts arise.

It is difficult to perceive the universe and its contents as pure realms;
Hence the importance of recognizing that all phenomena are like illusions and dreams.

It is difficult for the mind to reach a state where liberation occurs simultaneously with realization;
Hence the importance of practicing meditation with persistence.

It is difficult to truly benefit others;
Hence the importance of practicing bodhicitta as an aspiration.

It is difficult to become free from attachments and fixations;
Hence the importance of gradually reducing your desires and of knowing how to be content.

By training in this way, you will quickly reach the supreme state.

Six important points will enable you to generate joy and enthusiasm in the practice of the sublime Dharma:

It is challenging to feel a completely natural faith and reverence from the outset. Therefore, begin by deliberately generating these qualities, even if it feels somewhat artificial at first, by reflecting on the lives of perfect liberation of your spiritual masters, evoking the kindness they have shown you, and acknowledging the excellence of their actions. Persist in cultivating such devotion as best you can. Even though at first it may be artificial, over time a natural and genuine devotion will spontaneously arise.

For beginners, it is very difficult to liberate all thoughts, whether good or bad, at the moment they arise and transform them into allies. Thus, start by recognizing whatever thoughts arise, positive or negative, then learn to liberate them, and finally let them dissolve without a trace.

Perceiving the universe and all beings as pure realms of the buddhas is undoubtedly challenging. Begin by understanding that all phenomena and appearances of the universe, both good and bad, including sentient beings, entirely lack intrinsic existence and appear like dreams and magical illusions.

Achieving immediate realization of the ultimate nature of all things and liberation from afflictive states of mind in one stride, as exceptional beings have done, is difficult.[148] Therefore, make your practice a lifelong commitment. Summon your diligence!

At your current level, it may be very difficult to extend vast benefit to all sentient beings. Begin by generating bodhicitta as an aspiration, determined to accomplish the welfare of others through your own strength, and persistently nurture benevolence. This is of upmost importance!

Resisting the allure and entanglement of worldly pleasures is very difficult. Therefore, at the outset, aim to have as little desire as possible. Knowing how to always be content, your desire and grasping will naturally fade away.

By practicing these six points in this manner, you will swiftly reach supreme enlightenment.

–198–

Reinforcing Your Troops

Six strategies of Dharma practitioners for reinforcing their troops:
Reinforce your troops upward by deciding upon the view.
Reinforce your troops downward by recognizing the right time to act.
Reinforce your troops in the vanguard by knowing the illusory nature of all appearances.

Reinforce your forces at the back by abandoning your clinging to subject and object.
Reinforce your troops outwardly by engaging in listening and contemplating in a nonsectarian manner.
Reinforce your troops internally by taming the five mental poisons.
Acting in this way, you can repel the armies of samsara.

There are six strategies for Dharma practitioners to deploy their forces:

Reinforcing them upward refers to the view, which should be as high as possible. You should decisively elucidate the highest view.

Reinforcing them downward refers to adopting the conduct appropriate to your spiritual level. Whether you act as a beginner, a listener, a bodhisattva, or in any other way, your conduct should correspond to your level of meditative experience and gradually advance from the lowest to the highest.

Reinforce your vanguard by apprehending all appearances, good and bad, perceived through your senses as mere dreams and illusions.

Reinforce your rear guard to push away the dualistic clinging that has seized hold of your mind and enslaved it to subject-object duality. By doing so, your mind will then naturally regain its inherent freedom.

Reinforce your forces outwardly by severing your attachments to Buddhist and non-Buddhist views, as well as to any erroneous view, and by engaging in comprehensive, unbiased listening and contemplation. Doing so, you will free yourself from the shackles of ignorance of the various fields of knowledge and your understanding will expand.

Reinforce your troops inwardly by calling upon all the countermeasures necessary to subdue as best you can the five mental poisons that disturb and cloud your mind. With such strategies, you will rout all the armies of the three worlds of samsara!

–199–

Six Ignorant Hopes

Six ignorant and false hopes:
Without taming your own mind, you hope to tame others.
Through a mere intellectual understanding, you hope to realize the fundamental nature.
By meditating within a conceptual framework, you hope to purify negative emotions.
With biased views, you hope to tread the path of liberation.
Without engaging in virtuous actions, you hope to attain higher rebirths.
Without abandoning non-virtuous actions, you hope not to fall into the lower realms.
Those who entertain such false hopes will miss their goals.

As long as your mind remains under the yoke of afflictive mental states, your hopes will be dashed, whatever they may be.

In the first place, without having transformed your own mind with the help of Dharma, you will remain unable to transform that of others, even if you recognize the need for it.

If the realization of the fundamental nature of phenomena has not itself arisen in your mind, a mere literal understanding of the teachings will not bring about perfect realization.

Practicing various meditations associated with mental representations will hardly counteract afflictive mental states. Only primordial, nondual wisdom can transform them.

Harboring a range of biases about your own and other people's views will only create obstacles on the path to liberation. It is crucial to adopt an impartial, nonsectarian perspective.

Hoping to be reborn in the higher realms of existence—among humans or devas—while continuing to engage in negative actions has no chance to succeed, as the seed of such a rebirth has not been properly sown.

Similarly, hoping to escape the lower realms in your next life without forsaking negative actions in this life will not succeed.

Those who cling to such unrealistic hopes are only deceiving themselves. Their actions are at odds with their goals, leading them to die in delusion.

–200–

Losing Mindfulness

Six situations in which individuals lose their mindfulness without even realizing it:

By spending your entire life under the influence of the five poisons of negative emotions,
You lose your mindfulness and do not even notice that you are led to the lower realms of existence.

Entangled by your relationship with your spouse and children,
You lose your mindfulness and do not even notice that you are drowning in the ocean of suffering.

Living your life with a biased attitude of attachment to your friends and aversion to your enemies,
You lose your mindfulness and do not even notice that your karma is leading you to the lower realms.

Without abandoning any activities of your three doors of body, speech, and mind,
You lose your mindfulness while hoping to rest in the nature of mind.

Without forsaking the mundane activities of this life,
You lose your mindfulness yet hope to reach the path of liberation.

Being attached to mere words on the view of emptiness, without making any effort to practice it,
You lose your mindfulness yet hope for the signs of the warmth of spiritual experience and realization.

In such ways, so many people lose their mindfulness without even realizing it.

If the level of your practice does not match your capacities, you may remain unaware of both your faults and your qualities. This lack of mindfulness leads to six types of disappointments.

If you spend your life in the grip of the afflictive mental states, as long as they control your mind, you will be bound to experience the lower realms of samsara. Unaware, having lost all caution, not knowing how to avoid negative acts, you will constantly accumulate the causes for rebirth in these undesirable states.

Once you have let yourself be ruled by family ties—caring for a spouse and children—you will be hampered in many ways, including by being responsible for caring for them, feeding and clothing them. Hardly aware of it, you will find yourself repeatedly adrift in the ocean of samsara.

If you constantly feed your attachment to loved ones and aversion to those you dislike, you have no destination other than the lower realms of samsaric existence, neither knowing the way out nor understanding the causes that have propelled you into these unhappy states of existence.

Having put aside all physical, verbal, and mental activities, if you realize correctly the unaltered, primordial nature of mind, meditative experiences and ultimate realization will arise. But if you are caught up in countless activities, you will lose sight of this primordial nature, without even noticing.

If you continue to engage in a multitude of activities prompted by the eight worldly concerns of this life while hoping to attain liberation, you might as well expect to harvest fruit without planting seeds.

Without paying attention to the law of cause and effect and without even being aware of it, you may glimpse the realization of the view, but, acting in this way, you are indulging in mere words. Having lost your mindfulness, you have little reason to expect meditative experiences, realization, and other signs of accomplishment to arise in your mind.

If you lose your mindfulness to the extent of not recognizing these defects, you are falling into the fault of contradicting the Dharma.

–201–

Six Accomplishments Necessary to All

Six accomplishments we should all possess:
By contemplating the suffering of samsara, we urge ourselves to practice the Dharma.
By constantly cultivating faith and respect, we tame our minds.
By striving in restoration and purification practices, we cleanse our obscurations and those of others.
By generating an authentic bodhicitta, we accomplish the twofold aims of ourselves and others.
By receiving the empowerments that mature and the instructions that liberate, we lead ourselves and others to virtuous activities.
By persevering in practice, we eliminate our delusion and that of others.

Six accomplishments everyone should pursue, yourself and others:

Reflecting on the pervasive suffering within samsara will help you recognize the flaws of remaining in this vicious cycle. This understanding will inspire you to earnestly practice the sublime Dharma

Constantly cultivate faith and respect. Relying on these two qualities, vigorously carry your recalcitrant mind onto the path of liberation.

Be diligent in the methods of restoring your virtuous actions and purifying unvirtuous ones, thus dispelling your obscurations and aiding in dispelling those of others.

Cultivate benevolence and bodhicitta toward all sentient beings—the most excellent attitude, so you can effortlessly accomplish the dual goal of benefiting others and yourself.

By receiving empowerments that mature your mind stream and instructions that liberate it, you can naturally join the path of wholesome practices and guide others to it.

Persist in dedicating your entire mind to the direct experience of spiritual practice and you will naturally overcome your obscurations and those of others. These practices are of utmost importance.

–202–

Six Key Points

Six vital points clearly stated:
It is essential not to pursue wrong goals in this life and the next.
It is essential not to be mixed up with the conduct of ordinary people.
Everything depending on past karma, it is essential to observe the law of cause and effect meticulously.
It is essential to unite wisdom and compassion.
It is essential to take sense pleasures onto the path by using skillful means.
It is essential to conquer the lasting citadel (of the ultimate) by realizing the inseparability [of the two truths].
Those who are capable of all this are consummate yogis.

There are many aspects of the supreme Dharma, among which you should take six crucial points to heart:

Ensure that the supreme Dharma is your primary goal in this life and future lives. The crucial point is not to direct your mind to anything negative, vile, or unvirtuous.

It is vitally important that you act in accordance with the Dharma, without conforming to the conduct of ordinary people, especially those who indulge in negative behavior.

Recognize that your joys and sorrows are the fruit of your past actions. It is therefore essential that, from now on, you develop a deep conviction in the law of cause and effect, accomplishing all that is beneficial and discarding all that is harmful.

To unite wisdom and compassion inseparably is the extraordinary characteristic of the Mahāyāna path. Give it the importance it deserves.

Experts in the skillful means of the Adamantine Vehicle of Secret Mantra experience sensory experiences as aids rather than delusions.

Understanding the indivisibility of appearances and emptiness, of wisdom and method, conquer the citadel [of the ultimate nature of reality].

Those who observe these six vital points are consummate yogis.

–203–

Escape Distraction

Six ways to maintain attentive presence on the path:
Beginners [in spiritual practice] should avert distraction by first relying on artificial mindfulness.
Those who engage in meditative and post-meditative practices should not be distracted from the ultimate nature of reality, the dharmatā.
Those with a certain degree of familiarization should not let thoughts and appearances distract them from the primordial wisdom.
Those who have achieved perfection [in meditation] no longer have any object of distraction or subject to be distracted.
For those who have attained ultimate stability, the objects of distraction are not different from dharmatā.
Those who have reached the state of exhaustion of phenomena [in dharmatā] have gone beyond references and expressions.
Hence, I urge you all to reach such a state of perfection.

Six instructions to maintain your attentive presence and help you bring any circumstances onto the path:

As a novice, you should constantly monitor your mind for distractions, practice virtue, and avoid negative actions. Rely on a mindfulness that is attentive yet still somewhat contrived.

When you aspire, with a perfectly attentive mind, to merge meditative equality and post-meditation while in contemplation of the ultimate nature, it is vital to use the authentic mindfulness associated with dharmatā and to recognize the nature of awareness in its pristine simplicity.

As you become familiar with the inseparability of meditation and post-meditation, it is vital that all you perceive and experience manifest as primordial wisdom.

When your realization of the ultimate nature becomes as vast as space, there is neither a state of nondistraction nor any subject susceptible to distraction. At this stage, it is vital to experience all your perceptions and practices as nothing but the display of primordial wisdom.

Upon achieving perfect stability, no matter the number of distractions associated with the six types of sensory experiences, they will only deepen your realization of primordial wisdom and cannot fool you, as you now understand that they all pertain to the ultimate nature of reality, the dharmatā.

If you reach the exhaustion of phenomena, including mindfulness itself, this ineffable state is the culminating point of meditative experiences and the epitome of the Great Perfection's realization. This is a most vital point.

–204–

Six Things Not to Be Confused

Examining six similarities that can be confused:
The discomfort felt when yearning for the Dharma and saddened by samsara
Should not be confused with the discomfort felt in the face of adversity.
Unlimited devotion and respect born from the depths of your heart
Should not be confused with an artificial faith that is nothing but words,
Even though at first glance they may look the same,
Freeing yourself from attachment to friends, relatives, and all perceptions at large
Should not be confused with a lack of love and a distant indifference.
The supreme siddhis bestowed by the yidam deity
Should not be confused with māra's magical hallucinations that are just obstacles.
A compassion that inspires you to guide all sentient beings without exception
Should not be confused with a mere show of benevolence motivated by the eight worldly concerns.
An immersion in the luminosity of the ultimate nature, the dharmatā,
Should not be confused with drifting in a blank meditative state.

Six defects arise from confusing similar but distinct situations:

Inspired by your spiritual teachers and filled with faith, you may become overwhelmed with sadness and disillusionment about your negative behavior. At other times, you might be unsettled by illness and malignant influences and upset by adversity. While these two feelings may appear similar, they should not be mistaken for one another.

Boundless, respectful devotion for your spiritual masters arises from the depths of your being, ensuring that they remain at the heart of your thoughts and aspirations. But this should not be confused with a superficial faith, a mere facade that does not go beyond beautiful words. These two types of faith might look alike at first glance, so beware of confusing them.

Neatly cutting through attachment associated with your subjective perceptions of your loved ones should not be confused with withdrawing from them out of indifference and lack of love.

If you fully rely on your yidam, your tutelary deity, you will actualize the supreme accomplishment. But be careful not to confuse this with spurious prophecies that mandate you to benefit others on a grand scale—these are mere tricks of the demons.

Nor should you confuse a vast compassion that can free all beings through seeing, hearing, touching, and remembering, with a mere display of altruistic activities motivated by the eight worldly concerns.

Immerse yourself continuously in the luminosity of the ultimate nature, free from distraction and delusion, but do not misconstrue this state as a nihilistic denial of the law of cause and effect, an amorphous, blank state.

–205–

Examine These Six Similarities

Examining further the nature of these similarities:

Unhappiness due to sadness will dissipate after meeting with supreme beings,
While the upset due to adverse circumstances lingers on as there is no joy in it.

Devotion and respect born from the heart transform the body and mind,

Whereas faith just from the mouth will not enhance the glow of your faculties.

Cutting off your attachments, you will understand that you do not need anything,
Whereas a mere mental distancing will fluctuate [between joy and sadness] depending on circumstances.

Being bestowed with the supreme siddhis gathers joy and blessings,
While the obstacles of the demons bring fear and mental disturbances.

By guiding sentient beings, you will be liberated from the attachment of self-cherishing,
Whereas helping others driven by the eight worldly concerns aims at selfish gains and respect.

Remaining immersed in dharmatā brings clarity and radiance to your sense faculties,
Whereas a meditative state of blankness wraps you in darkness.

It is therefore essential to understand these differences without confusion.

Six ways to further elucidate the differences between the confusions outlined earlier:

The distress felt when contemplating the suffering inherent to the activities of the three worlds of samsara will naturally be dispelled by meeting spiritual masters and by the instructions they impart. In contrast, adversity, disease, malignant influences, and obstacles of all kinds will never result in any joy.

Reverent fervor from within brings joy to the mind, raises goose bumps, fills the eyes with tears of devotion, and makes you glow. On the other hand, trying to please the master with empty flattery—a mere pretense of faith—will not bring about any of the signs associated with sincere confidence.

By cutting off at the root the bonds of attachment to food and other comforts, to possessions of all kinds, you will realize that, in truth, you do not need much. By keeping the ordinary affairs of this life at a distance, you will be free of covetousness in all circumstances.

When supreme accomplishments are born in your mind, the spiritual qualities of the bhūmis and the paths will blossom. Endowed with insight and meditative concentration, you will abide in joy and receive a shower of blessings. On the other hand, if your meditative experiences are nothing more than traps set by māra, you will be plagued by anxiety and perpetual instability.

By devoting yourself to guiding beings to liberation, you will remain free from the shackles of selfishness. In contrast, if you undertake all kinds of activities ostensibly to benefit others while remaining under the influence of the eight worldly concerns, you are merely seeking benefits, honors and recognition for personal gain.

As you immerse yourself in the continuum of the ultimate nature of reality, dharmatā, your faculties will become increasingly clear and radiant. If not, you will stagnate in the darkness of an apathetic, murky vacuum.

Recognize these distinctions clearly and without error.

–206–

Six Self-Sufficient Purposes

Instructions to accomplish six all-sufficient purposes:
One lifetime is enough: this time, cut off once and for all [the cycle of existences].
One accumulation [of merits and wisdom] is enough: respect your spiritual masters by considering them as buddhas.
One practice is enough: meditate upon your master as the Buddha in person.
One precept is enough: give up unvirtuous activities.
One introduction [to the nature of mind] is enough: understand the movement of thoughts as dharmatā, the ultimate nature of reality.
One meditative experience is enough: abide in the suchness of phenomena.
Those who can accomplish these will swiftly achieve great bliss.

There are six instructions that are sufficient on their own:

Your present existence is sufficient to achieve liberation and there is no need for you to continue the chain of samsaric lives: once you have left your body behind in this life, you will have cut off the cycle of existences once and for all.

One accumulation and one purification are sufficient: entrusting yourself to a spiritual master ensures a perfect accumulation of merit and wisdom and the purification of your obscurations. This essential practice is the source of immense benefits.

A single activity is sufficient: taking the example of your spiritual master's life of perfect liberation will naturally lead you to authentic enlightenment.

One precept or training is sufficient: master your mind with mindfulness and vigilance, while discarding any activity contrary to the Dharma.

A single introduction to the nature of mind is sufficient: recognize the delusion associated with the movement of thoughts, which actually occurs within the space of the ultimate nature of all things, and all thoughts will be liberated the very moment they arise.

One experiential practice is sufficient: remain in the pristine simplicity and continuity of the fundamental nature.

If you listen[149] to these instructions and put them into practice, you will quickly reach the state of great bliss.

–207–

Six Key Instructions

Six profound and crucial instructions:
If you want the Dharma to benefit you, focus upon the teachings that benefit your mind.
If you wish to transform your mind, give yourself the right advice.
If you wish to actualize the dharmakāya, recognize the spontaneously arising movement of thoughts.
While nurturing your spiritual experience, do not become distracted from the nature of mind, but look inward.
If you wish to cut through the stream of conceptual thoughts, abandon the grasping associated with the mind-energy.
If you wish to reach the ultimate, rest in the simplicity of the unfabricated natural state.
These are extremely profound and essential instructions.

Here are six vital and profound instructions:

Wishing to transform your mind, whether through the words of the Buddha or the instructions of your spiritual master, focus on improving your mind by nurturing renunciation, devotion, and respect and make this your primary practice.

Wishing to pacify and tame your mind stream, continually give yourself wise counsel, eliminate your faults as you become aware of them, while adopting and nurturing all positive qualities.

Aspiring to actualize the level of the unborn dharmakāya, rest in meditative equality, free from identification with the movement of thoughts.

As your spiritual experience takes birth from within, train in the crucial practice of abandoning all forms of external distraction.

Aspiring to cut through the delusion associated with the movement and proliferation of discursive thoughts, rely on the crucial connection between mind and *prāṇa* by holding your breath in the "vase,"[150] and the whirlwind of thoughts will naturally subside.

The most profound and essential instruction for those who aspire to the ultimate destination, buddhahood, is to abide in the continuum of the pristine simplicity of the fundamental nature.

It is crucial to diligently practice in this way.

–208–

Outer and Inner Interdependence

Instructions on six outer and inner auspicious signs of interdependence:
Giving up worldly activities indicates the emergence of trust.
Developing humility is a sign that blessings have entered your mind.
Benefiting others through whatever you do is a sign of an altruistic mind.
Indifference to the eight worldly concerns is a sign of the reversal of grasping.
A natural weakening of duality is a sign of realizing the ultimate truth.

> **Unceasing diligence in virtue is a sign of having given yourself good advice.**
> **Those who exhibit these signs will reach the other shore of samsara.**

The outer and inner links of interdependence share the same nature. Therefore, when, inwardly, certainty in the direct experience of the Dharma arises in your mind, the outer links of interdependence will naturally harmonize themselves. This is evidenced by six signs:

Your lack of interest in the affairs of ordinary life signifies the birth of confidence in your mind, freeing you from cravings and attachments.

Humility, which consists of having no pride and never placing yourself above others, indicates that the blessings of spiritual masters have penetrated your mind

When whatever you do, say, or think benefits others, it is a sign that the altruistic thought of enlightenment, bodhicitta, has been born within you.

Indifference to the eight worldly concerns—neither harboring various hopes and fears about them nor doing anything to accomplish them—indicates that you have renounces your attraction to worldly affairs.

The spontaneous weakening of delusions associated with the duality of subject and object indicates that you are assimilating the view of absolute truth.

Perseverance in spiritual practice, day and night, indicates that you have given yourself sound and unerring advice.

Those in whom these six indications manifest will reach the other shore of the ocean of suffering of the three worlds of samsara.

–209–

Six Adamantine Slogans of the Great Perfection

Six adamantine slogans of the Great Perfection:
At the level of the ground, the Great Perfection establishes the nature of mind.
At the level of the path, the Great Perfection strikes the vital point of liberation from extremes.
At the level of the fruition, the Great Perfection leads to a state of extinction of hope and fear.
The Great Perfection related to objects consists of liberating all appearances in nongrasping.
The Great Perfection related to mind consists of experiencing thoughts as friends.
The ultimate Great Perfection lets the movement of thoughts vanish of its own accord.
Whoever knows this is the great king of yogis.

When speaking of the Great Perfection, what do we mean by "perfection"? Six points explain this unerringly:

At the level of the ground, [from the perspective of practitioners still clouded by delusion], the ultimate nature of the Great Perfection is veiled by obscurations.

At the level of the path, practitioners experience a mix of pure and impure perceptions.

At the level of fruition, the Great Perfection is achieved when only pure perceptions remain, signifying ultimate accomplishment.

Returning to the ground Great Perfection, once you have established with certainty the union of primordial purity and spontaneous presence, of emptiness and luminosity, this recognition constitutes the Great Perfection at the level of the ground.[151]

On the path, when a practitioner approaches the nature of this union of primordial purity and spontaneous presence through direct experience and reaches the crucial point of unobstructed realization free from the extremes of existence and nonexistence, eternalism and nihilism, it indicates the realization of the Great Perfection at the level of the path.

The Great Perfection at the level of the fruit is free from hope of achieving a result and fear of failure, a state that is accompanied by the recognition that all the qualities of the three kāyas are "perfect" or "complete" (*dzogs*) in the ultimate nature of mind and in the exhaustion of phenomena within dharmatā.

As for the Great Perfection related to phenomena (the objects), whatever perceptions of the six aspects of consciousness arise, any attachments to phenomena deemed to be "good" and any aversion those deemed to be "bad," will naturally be liberated into their true nature.

Recognizing the Great Perfection at the level of the mind (the subject), allows you to distinguish the ordinary mind—the stream of thoughts—from the true and ultimate nature of mind. This makes it possible to transform discursive thoughts into allies of your practice. When thoughts no longer pollute or hinder spiritual experience, this is the Great Perfection from the perspective of the mind.

Once the movement of thoughts has subsided in its true nature, which is devoid of beginning, abiding, and cessation, this is the ultimate Great Perfection.

Understanding all this is the sign that one has become an accomplished yogi of the Great Perfection.

–210–

Inner Confidence

Six signs that occur when you have achieved inner confidence:
The natural pacification of apparitions in the bardo is like having a perfect escort.
The natural purification of obscurations resembles the limpidity of a pristine gem.
The natural blazing of spiritual experience is like the fermentation of barley grains.
The natural blazing of great bliss evokes drinking strong beer.
Naturally retaining the recognition of the nature of mind is like a bee stuck in honey.
The natural manifestation of blessings is like a bountiful harvest.
Those who show these signs are great yogis.

Six indications that you have reached stability in the six aspects of the Great Perfection previously mentioned:

The luminosity you currently experience is called "child luminosity." If, during the bardo, you are able to merge it seamlessly with the ground luminosity, known as "mother luminosity,"[152] you will be spared the delusive phantasmagoria that usually arises in the bardo, just as a traveler who passes through a land rife with bandits and foes is protected by a valiant escort without fear or danger.

A pure and precious wish-fulfilling gem is immaculate inside and out, unlike ordinary clay, stones, and rocks. Similarly, when you realize the ultimate nature of reality, the two obscurations—the obscuration of afflictive emotions and the cognitive obscuration—are naturally dispelled. Once purified, these obscurations vanish of their own accord.

Spiritual experiences will arise spontaneously, without having to be deliberately generated, just as when you add a fermenting agent to soaked barley the flavor and potency of the beer manifest naturally without any further effort required on your part.

When spiritual experiences set your mind ablaze, you will dwell continually in great bliss and in a vast and perfect ease, much like a person intoxicated by strong alcohol who becomes wide-eyed, loquacious and fearless.[153]

Once you have taken possession of the kingdom of the nature of mind, you are like a bee drawn to a honey-coated object: it lands on it, savors it, digs in, and cannot bear to leave. Once you have grasped this nature of mind, you will stay with it and will not return to discursive thoughts.

Just as in autumn the ears of corn ripen and the chaff forms naturally without further intervention, when the blessings of the spiritual master naturally enter your mind, meditative experiences and realization spontaneously manifest.

Those who receive all these signs are great yogis.

–211–

Moving Away from the Dharma

Six situations in which Dharma practitioners fail to come closer [to the Dharma]:
If you practice generosity toward your kin and dear ones, you will not come closer to completing the twofold accumulation.
Being relaxed in your practice will not bring you closer to spiritual accomplishments.
Engaging in virtuous activities merely to avert adverse circumstances will not bring you closer to enlightenment.
Mixing ordinary conversations with mantra and prayer recitations will not bring you closer to achieving spiritual strength and power.
Being proud of your knowledge will not bring you closer to the fundamental nature.
Practicing for mundane reasons will not bring you closer to authentic Dharma.
Therefore, practitioners must be wary of such situations.

Six mistakes leads you away from genuine Dharma practice:

Driven by your inclinations toward your parents and relatives, if you direct your generosity to them alone, favoring them in many ways, you will fail to perfect the twofold accumulation of merit and wisdom.

Sometimes you practice a lot, sometimes just a little, thus diluting your practice's effectiveness. By frittering away your efforts, both ordinary and extraordinary siddhis will remain out of reach.

Undertaking various practices primarily to protect your benefactors, repel obstacles, or annihilate evil forces is not the way to create the causes for common siddhis or the supreme siddhi of buddhahood. You will not even come close to achieving them.

Intermingling your recitation of mantras and prayers with ordinary conversations is like mixing wholesome food with refuse: it diminishes the potency and efficacy of your recitations.

Having acquired some spiritual qualities, you consider them supreme and become proud. This is not the way to realize the view of the fundamental nature. It is said that the water of qualities cannot collect atop the rock of pride.

Whatever activities you undertake, if your only purpose is to flatter your benefactors and comply with their expectations, you will turn your back on the sublime Dharma and distance yourself further from it.

Be vigilant not to fall into these mistakes.

–212–

Six Risks

Six instructions that highlight situations in which there is more harm than good:
To befriend wild people,
To make Dharmic connections with evil-minded people,
To take vows and precepts without being equipped with antidotes,
To meditate without having studied and contemplated,
To practice the Secret Mantra with broken samayas,
Or for a captain, to embark into the high sea in search of precious gems.
These are situations that cause more harm than good. It is therefore important to examine them thoroughly.

By engaging in certain activities, if everything goes well, you will quickly attain buddhahood, but incorrect practice exposes you to six perils:

Associating with individuals of bad disposition, who are unsuitable vessels for the Dharma and whose minds are clouded by the five poisons, will contaminate you with their defects and distance you from the Dharma. This puts you at great risk.

Forming spiritual connections with unqualified teachers—those who have not internalized the sublime Dharma, and who are devious, proud, and jealous—will cause your spiritual qualities to wither.

You may have taken the vows and precepts of individual liberation, of the bodhisattvas, and of the Secret Mantra, but without the antidotes of mindfulness and diligence, you run the serious risk of damaging your vows and breaking the sacred commitments of the samayas.

Meditating without sufficient study and contemplation is like casting stones in the dark—you are unlikely to hit your target. As the saying goes, "Foolish meditation is like blindly throwing stones."

Those who engage in the practice of Secret Mantra without keeping perfectly pure samayas, and breaking them as well, will not achieve any results. As the saying goes, "You try to bring rain, but provoke drought; you perform rituals for prosperity, but find yourself a hungry ghost."

Like a captain setting sail on the vast ocean in search of precious gems, he may succeed, but he may also lose his life, thus taking great risks.

Carefully examining these perilous behaviors, make sure you succeed instead of losing everything.

–213–

Implementing the Lessons

Six instructions to put into practice:
Whatever appearances arise, let them dissolve in their own nature.
Whatever comes in the field of your awareness, let it be naturally purified in spontaneous arising.
Whatever the movements of your thoughts, let them vanish without leaving traces like a bird crossing the sky.
Allow awareness to unfold in the vast, primordially liberated, inseparable state, free of extremes.
Look at the subject who is liberated and you will see the ultimate emptiness of samsara and nirvana.
Dismantling duality brings you to the fundamental nature of the universal ground.
Those who know this are wise in the meaning of the supreme vehicle.

Six instructions to put into practice through direct experience:

Whatever appearances arise, whatever your perceptions might be, do not attempt to apply antidotes, block them, or encourage them. Let the outer appearances be liberated and dissolve on their own. In this way, delusion brought on by appearances will no longer taint your experience of awareness, and grasping at appearances will cease to accompany your mind stream.

Whatever good or bad perceptions enter your field of consciousness, if you let all conceptual thoughts arise and come to rest in their natural state, they will not affect you in any way and will dissolve by themselves.

Whatever positive or negative thoughts arise in your mind, do not try to analyze them, just let them vanish, leaving no more trace in your mind than a bird in the sky.

Realizing the meaning of the indivisible union of appearances and emptiness, of awareness and emptiness, you will be free from the extremes of eternalism and nihilism, leading to a view that is vast and primordially free.

By investigating "who" is liberated, you will come to see that the subject and object of liberation merge into one, as they do not exist separately. This realization brings you to the essence of the emptiness of samsara and nirvana.

Having correctly ascertained the uncontrived simplicity of the fundamental nature in which the delusion of duality is unmasked, you will reach the universal primordial ground. At this point, dualistic clinging will collapse of its own accord.

Those who understand all these points are true experts in the meaning of the Great Perfection of the supreme vehicle.

–214–

Lacking Authenticity

Distinguish six situations that lack authenticity:
A spiritual master who aspires to good fortune and fame is not authentic.
A Dharma practitioner who gives priority to wealth and possessions is not authentic.
A monastic who gives priority to worldly dharmas is not authentic.
A yogi who entertains self-clinging and partiality is not authentic.
A practice of the Secret Mantra that emphasizes treading the path gradually for eons is not authentic.
A practice of the Great Perfection that falls into extremes and discriminations is not authentic.
I urge you to recognize the great and vast sameness.

There are six ways to pretend to be genuine when you are not. It is crucial, therefore, to discern between attitudes that are improper and should be abandoned and those that are correct and should be cultivated in your mind:

Making large offerings, particularly to the virtuous community of the sangha, with the hidden motive of enhancing your reputation, is not in keeping with the conduct of an authentic spiritual teacher.

Placing excessive value on accumulating wealth, boasting about it, and relentlessly pursuing more is a clear indication of a disingenuous practitioner.

Those who have embraced the monastic life are meant to embody renunciation of the three worlds of samsara. If, instead, they devote themselves primarily to the concerns and schemes of worldly life, they do not embody the spirit of true renunciants.

Those who are fixated on their own ego, viewing everyone on their side as divine and everyone on the opposite side as demonic, are not authentic yogis.

Spending three eons or more traveling the path gradually is not the swift and authentic path of the Secret Mantra of the Adamantine Vehicle.

Discriminating between your philosophical views and those of others, between allies and adversaries, and thus falling into biased, sectarian views, does not represent the true meditation and conduct of the Great Perfection.

Accordingly, I urge you to cultivate a broad and open mind that no more differentiates between good and bad than space cares about the whirling of a spear within it.

–215–

Stay in the Ultimate Nature

Six ways to abide in the state of dharmatā:
Do not let the five sense consciousnesses become fixated on objective phenomena.
Do not let the clinging mind engage in emanating and withdrawing mental fabrications.
Do not become attached to bliss or clarity and do not let your thoughts wander.
Relax in spontaneous presence without dressing it in the clothes of conceptual elaborations.

Be vast and open like the dharmatā without being chained by mental fixations.
Let the mind be at ease and spacious without being bound by the tether of perceptions.
Those who understand these points will be close to the supreme meaning.

To remain in the simplicity and authenticity of the ultimate meaning of the true nature, the dharmatā, requires six special qualities:

The eye and the other sense organs naturally fixate on external objects, leading to attachment to what is perceived as "good" and aversion to what is seen as "bad." Thus, the external objects will lure the inner senses as the interaction of objects, sensory organs, and consciousness gives rise to delusion.

Within, the clinging mind is rife with desires and aversions. One thought begets a second one, a third and so on. Mental constructs proliferate endlessly and delusion pervades the whole mental landscape. Stop making these fabrications!

Whatever experiences of bliss, clarity, and the absence of discursive thoughts and concepts may occur, do not cling to them in any way. Otherwise, you will be lured into the rainbow-like shimmering phantasmagoria of the mind. This is how even great meditators are caught in the web of thoughts. Just leave it as it is!

Contemplating without elaboration in the naked simplicity of the Great Perfection, relax in meditative equality within spontaneous presence. In contrast, if you tell yourself: "My mind is luminous," or "My mind is emptiness," or "My view and meditation are of a high order," thus indulging in conceptual evaluations, you are obscuring your awareness as if you were wrapping yourself in layers of conceptual clothing.

Within the ultimate, vast, and open true nature, if you keep attempting to master your mind through calm abiding and focusing your attention, remember these words, "Do not stagnate in the pond of inner stillness." Clinging will render such practices ineffective.

Adopt a broad and open attitude in which the extremes of eternalism and nihilism dissolve and remain at ease in a vast understanding, free from the snares of concepts.

Those who know how to do this, come closer to an authentic understanding of the Great Perfection.

–216–

MISUNDERSTANDINGS ABOUT THE GREAT VEHICLE

Six indications of not having understood the meaning of the Great Vehicle teachings:

All migratory beings are sublime bodhisattvas,
Considering them as inferior and denigrating them shows that you have not understood the meaning of the Great Vehicle.

All those who come to beg are kind in encouraging you to virtue,
Being paralyzed by miserliness shows that you have not understood the meaning of the Great Vehicle.

Enemies and demons that harm you are the supreme objects of your patience,
Becoming angry and hating them shows that you have not understood the meaning of the Great Vehicle.

Criticism of your flaws and mistakes are instructions to amend your defects,
To be irritated out of self-cherishing shows that you have not understood the meaning of the Great Vehicle.

Gain and respect, name and fame are the source of ruin and division,
Infatuating yourself with the eight worldly dharmas shows that you have not understood the meaning of the Great Vehicle.

Blessings and spiritual powers can attract the demons,
To become proud of these and arrogant shows that you have not understood the meaning of the Great Vehicle.

These misunderstandings lead many practitioners to wander in the cycle of existences.

Not understanding the true nature of the teachings of the Great Vehicle leads to erroneous practice and six misconceptions:

Benefiting as much as possible beings who err in samsara brings about the same accumulation of merit as making offerings to the buddhas. Without taking support of others,[154] it is impossible to attain buddhahood. As all beings have the nature of bodhisattvas, heirs of the victorious ones, to harbor animosity and contempt toward some of them shows that you have not understood the meaning of the Great Vehicle

When approached by beggars, fulfilling their needs aids you to progress toward the transcendent perfection of generosity. Those who ask you for alms are thus showing you great kindness. Failing to understand this, reacting with irritation, your hands tied by the demon of greed is a clear sign of failing to grasp the meaning of the Great Vehicle.

By practicing patience with those who harm you—the eight classes of harmful spirits and other perverse samaya-breaking entities, such as the "spirit kings,"[155] who harass you with their malice—you can perfect the accumulation of merit associated with patience and purify your obscurations. Failing to acknowledge that these enemies are the best supports for your patience, hating them to the point of wanting to destroy them, reveals a lack of understanding of the Great Vehicle.

Repeatedly proclaim your faults and shortcomings. When slandered or maligned, use the opportunity to recognize your own flaws. Failing to bring such unpleasant vilification onto the path, will obstruct your progression to enlightenment. If you do not see those who attack you as teachers and teachings, if you become angry and resentful, you will have missed the essence of the Great Vehicle.

Being concerned with gain, respect, reputation, and other aspects of the eight worldly dharmas, is like inviting the demon of ruin into your home, bringing all kinds of trouble. From the perspective of pure Dharma practice, gain, privilege, and fame are all ominous demons. If you do not give up these worldly concerns, you will keep trying to obtain what attracts you and avert what repels you. You should know, however, that if you succeed to some extent in these worldly endeavors, you will keep on wanting more. This endless pursuit shows that you have not understood the meaning of the Great Vehicle.

Having developed great powers and abilities, obtained signs of accomplishment, and received the blessings of the body, speech, and mind of your yidam deity, can lead to pride and vanity. You will then engage in many activities motivated by attraction and aversion, thus inviting the obstacles of the demon. Unaware that these are obstacles set by Māra, you might convince yourself that, now possessing great powers, you should attempt to exorcise evil spirits and other entities causing harm to others, believing this will aid them. However, in truth, by doing so, you have failed to grasp the true meaning of the Great Vehicle.

Many mistake these defects for qualities and keep wandering in samsara.

–217–

What to Give Up and Where to Stay

Six situations to leave and six to abide in:
Abandon the objects of distraction and busyness and stay in solitude.
Abandon group partiality and keep to yourself.
Abandon worldly activities, including farming, and stay quiet.
Abandon socializing and remain in solitary places.
Abandon your many worldly projects and activities and stay in solitary places.
Abandon negative and neutral actions and abide in virtue.

Having dispelled misunderstandings about the meaning of the Great Vehicle, it is then important to live simply and quietly. There are six ways to do this:

The distractions of a busy life are significant obstacles to contemplative practice and the path to enlightenment. Leaving all this behind, stay alone in a secluded place, like a wild animal.

Harboring sectarian feelings, fueled by attachment and aversion, discriminating between "us" and "them," you will accumulate innumerable faults. Stay clear of social entanglements and hide away like a wounded deer.

Devoting yourself to farming, commerce and other worldly activities, keeps you in a constant rush, unable to sit still during the day and hardly sleeping at night. Clear your mind of all these concerns and remain in a state of perfect ease, with a vast, open mind.

If you need to coordinate with many people, you will never be able to please everyone and will even fail to accomplish your own goals, creating endless difficulties. It is better to stay peacefully in the solitude of a mountain hermitage.

Focusing on one goal and one activity, you are likely to succeed in accomplishing it fully. But if you undertake all kinds of projects simultaneously, you may never complete any of them. Put aside such restlessness and remain in nonaction in a secluded place.

Above all, avoid negative actions, and even neutral: dedicate yourself diligently to positive deed alone.

–218–

Six Things to Do

While abiding in the above situations, there are six things to do:
Recognize the naked face of pristine awareness.
Establish the fundamental nature of mind.
While knowing [the nature], remain free of any conceptual notion of knowing.
Do not deliberately fixate upon concrete reference points.
Cut off the tendency to make deliberate efforts [by letting it subside] in its own place.
Look at the nature of the agent of these actions and bring it to the state of exhaustion [in the dharmatā].

In keeping with what was said earlier, once you have severed all ties and entered a mountain retreat, there are six things to do:

When awareness is wrapped in the cocoon of the ordinary mind, you are far from the Great Perfection. It is therefore crucial to clearly distinguish awareness from the ordinary mind and to recognize the nature of this awareness in its pristine nakedness.

It is not enough to recognize that the ordinary mind, made of conceptual thoughts, is deluded. You must establish its true nature through your own direct experience, with certainty, unmistakably.

Having glimpsed the view to some extent, if you still harbor attachments, merely believing that you have understood the Great Perfection will not help you. Relying on attentive presence and vigilance, you must apprehend your own awareness and the true nature of mind without engaging in intellectual analysis.

If attachment to name, fame, gain, and respect becomes entrenched within you, leading to the rejection of some things and the pursuit of others, true peace will remain elusive. Abandon these pursuits, and allow events to unfold naturally.

For those committed to unwavering diligence in Dharma practice, complete dedication is essential. At the same time, they should examine the nature of the subject who endeavors and understand that all activities and practices are never separated from the nature of dharmatā. In doing so, one brings them to their point of exhaustion.

–219–

Six Qualities of Awareness

Six qualities of the contemplative state of awareness:
Appearances manifest unceasingly, utterly vivid.
Awareness is never hazy, but pristinely clear.
Naturally clear and transparent, it is not tainted by the proliferation of thoughts or by excitement.
It is not carried away either by this proliferation and excitement, but is utterly stable and majestic.
It is not dull and cloudy, but utterly lucid.
It does not lean toward any of the four extremes and remains perfectly relaxed in its natural openness.
If these six qualities are present, you will not stray from the path.

Recollecting the simplicity of awareness has six qualities:

While remaining in meditative rest in the evenness of the ultimate nature of reality, your perceptions of appearances will not cease. Consider the way stars reflect on the surface of the ocean: they sparkle with clarity, without the ocean reacting with attachment or aversion. Meditate with this same clarity.

The clarity and radiance of this awareness must be perfectly vivid. If this open presence fades into a vague, indistinct state, it will become clouded by confusion and ignorance. Preserve its radiant clarity, totally free from the veils of delusion.

When thoughts proliferate and you feel that they are disrupting your meditation, alternating between hope and doubt will not help. Simply remain in the transparent lucidity of the natural liberation of thoughts as they arise.

As conceptual thoughts proliferate, as the mind becomes restless and destabilizes your concentration, remain in a vast and majestic openness.

As luminosity shines from within, if you do not let the mists of confusion and bewilderment thicken, they will dissipate on their own, revealing pristine clarity.

Without being drawn into any of the four extremes—especially the belief in the solid existence of reality or the nothingness of nonexistence—leave things in their natural openness.

Understanding awareness with these six qualities, you will not deviate from the path.

–220–

Practicing View and Meditation

Six ways to practice the view and meditation (of the Great Perfection):
Whatever appears, if you realize it within the view, you are free from grasping to philosophical tenets.
Whatever thought arises, if you experience it as meditation, you are free from the division of meditation and post-meditation.
Whatever actions you perform, if you remain without attachment, you are free from all kinds of fixation and grasping.
Whatever appears, if you recognize it as realization, your experiences will be liberated (in primordial wisdom).
If you travel the paths with certainty about the nature of reality, all paths and stages are liberated into valid yogic cognition.
If all practices are accomplished as the five kāyas, you are free from grasping to the fruition.
Such a yogi is like space.

If you gain a firm conviction in the ultimate view and meditation of the Great Perfection, you will understand intimately that this same view apprehends all phenomena as the union of appearances and emptiness. Prejudices such as "This is my view, and these are the views of others that must be refuted," will vanish by themselves.

When you recognize the original nature of the mind's fundamental simplicity, everything that arises becomes meditation. The line between meditation and post-meditation will blur and you will no longer differentiate between formal practice sessions and the seamless extension of meditation into everyday life.

If all your physical, verbal, and mental activities are free from attachments and infatuation, you will continuously rest in the natural presence of mind, where attachments and fixations spontaneously dissolve in their natural state. Then will come a state free from overconfidence that prides itself on practicing virtue and accomplishing the Dharma.

Whatever the spontaneous efflorescence of awareness—the ultimate reality—might be, if you perceive it to be nothing other than the realization of dharmatā, clinging to meditative experience will be liberated in its natural state.

Thus, once you have impeccably established the view that makes no distinction between meditation and pauses, every stage of the path you undertake will unfold within the continuum of dharmatā. You will effortlessly traverse the paths and levels, unburdened by the hope of reaching the bhūmis or the fear of failure to do so.

Whatever you do with your body, speech, and mind is taking place within the five dimensions, or "bodies," of buddhahood. Thus, imbued with the qualities of these five kāyas, you will be free from grasping to the fruit. A yogi who has realized this is like space.

–221–

Six Mistakes to Eliminate

Six faults to be abandoned after examination:
Though you have faith and diligence, if you prematurely part from your teacher,
Like a young bird separated from its mother, you will not perfect the path.

Though you understand the law of cause and effect, if you do not let go of grasping,

Like being lured by a deceitful person, you will be carried away by circumstances.

Though you are highly intelligent, if you do not practice,
Like a weapon lost in the battle, this will not help at the time of need.

Though you recognize the nature of your mind, if you do not familiarize yourself with it,
Like a child in a war, you will be conquered by the enemy of conceptual thoughts.

Though you have meditated for a long time, if you do not give up grasping,
Like a famous person without heirs, your effort will be wasted.

Though you know what is real and what is not, if you do not discriminate,
Just as when an arrowhead remains in an injured body, the infection of negative emotions will surge.

Therefore, not being carried away by these faults is crucial.

These are six faults you must abandon if, on examination, you discover them in your mind stream:

You might be confident that you see the excellence of all your spiritual master's actions, and diligently practice the supreme Dharma, but if you part from your master before having your practice is firmly established, you will not reach the highest point of the path. Without completing the entire journey, you will resemble a fledging whose feathers have not yet grown and who, separated from its mother, will not survive.

You may understand and remain aware of the infallibility of the laws of cause and effect, but if you do not dispel your craving for desirable things, the Dharma practitioner you think you are, will remain under the sway of circumstances. Your mind will be little more than a swindler fooling others, an impostor who mimics excellence.

No matter how knowledgeable you might have become through study, reflection, and meditation, if you have neither integrated the vital points of practice nor intimately blended the Dharma with your mind, faced with life's circumstances, good or bad. Bereft of the ultimate antidote, you will be like a warrior who loses his weapons in the midst of battle and is left helpless, bare-handed to confront his enemies.

If you have been introduced to the dharmatā, the ultimate nature of reality, without sufficient familiarity and stability in recognizing the manifestations of awareness, a single discursive thought may become the enemy that annihilates your recognition of this ultimate nature. You will be no different from the young son of a soldier sent to the battlefield before he has completed his training: too frail, he will succumb in no time.

No matter how many days, months, or years you have spent meditating, unless you have radically severed your attachment and conceptualization concerning the true nature of all things, you will be like an old marmot huddled in his burrow. Your efforts will have been as futile as those of an aging, childless woman who, despite her success in worldly affairs, finds herself at the end of her life with nothing more than the vicissitudes of long labor and no one to inherit her accumulated wealth.

If you can discern right from wrong regarding the view, meditation, and action, yet fail to attune your conduct to your spiritual level, you may imagine that you have overcome your afflictive mental states, while the dormant poison of these afflictions awaken eventually. This is like being struck by a weapon and neglecting to remove the bullet or arrowhead lodged in your flesh, leaving the wound to fester until it ultimately proves fatal.

Do whatever is necessary to abandon these six mistakes.

–222–

Six Useless Things

Six unnecessary situations if you realize the fundamental nature:

If your stainless awareness remains in your mountain-like body,
You need not rely upon solitary mountain retreats.

Whatever happens if you do not waver from the state of dharmatā,
You need not experience the hardship of staying in time-bound retreat.

If you experience all appearances and sounds as the display of primordial wisdom,
You need not divide your practice into meditative and post-meditative sessions.

If your fixation upon abandonment and attainment is naturally purified in the ground,
You need not plan to accumulate merit based on characteristics.

If you perceive all that appears as the pure realm of the three kāyas,
You need not apply antidotes in your meditation.

If you experience your realization to be limitless and unrestricted,
You need not entertain thoughts of hope and fear.

Whoever has these qualities will grasp the meaning of primordial wisdom.

These are six things that you need not pursue assiduously once you have realized the fundamental nature:

If your mind rests undisturbed and without distraction in [the hermitage of] your mountain-like body, you need not go to a mountain solitude.

If you can maintain a practice where all your actions of body, speech, and mind never leave the continuum of the ultimate nature, the dharmatā, there is no need not endure the hardships of long retreats, telling yourself, "I am going into retreat for these many years or that many months." It is enough to ensure that your mind never strays beyond the ultimate nature of reality, whether during practice sessions or in the intervals between them.

If all appearances manifest as wisdom deities, all sounds as mantras, and all thoughts as the play of primordial wisdom, there is no need to divide your days into meditative sessions and intervals in which you engage in all the activities you set aside from during formal sessions.

Nothing needs to be abandoned and nothing needs to be newly obtained. Once the realization of the dharmatā, from which nothing can be either subtracted or added, has dawned in your mind, you no longer need to accumulate a vast store of merit nor entertain hopes for great fame. All the appearances related to your three doors—body, speech, and mind—will manifest as the play of the three bodies, the dimensions of buddhahood. Deliberately engaging in all kinds of meditations, sadhanas, and mantra recitations will no longer be necessary.

If the realization of dharmatā, vast and free of all polarity, is born within your mind, you will be free of any form of hope for a "fruit," such as buddhahood and of all other concerns, such as worrying that someone may surpass you in knowledge.

Anyone who abides in this continuum will grasp the meaning of primordial wisdom in all its naked truth.

–223–

Six Consequences

Instructions to achieve six types of outcomes:
Whoever abandons negative actions naturally becomes a hero.
Whoever destroys the six poisons within becomes a powerful being.
Whoever is free from fixation and grasping becomes virtuous.
Whoever has vigilant introspection and carefulness becomes wise and learned.
Whoever renounces harming others is like someone protected by natural armor.
Those who surround themselves with oath-bound protectors will have many followers.
The supreme instruction is to do whatever you can to achieve these qualities.

These are six essential instructions which, when practiced, will be effortlessly accomplished:

If you do not commit a single negative action while being vigilant and circumspect, you are truly brave. If you do not succumb to negative behavior and free yourself from your enemy, samsara, in all your future lives, you become the greatest hero.

You can rightly be called a powerful person if, at the very moment one of the five poisons arises, you immediately apply the appropriate antidote to prevent such a poison from proliferating.

If you abide in the continuum of the nature of reality, free from mental representations, you will bring your spiritual practice to its highest point. By consistently examining your actions and thoughts without ever lowering your guard, you will avoid falling into delusion and wrongdoing under any circumstances, thus becoming wise and virtuous—the epitome of mastery.

If you are entirely devoid of malice and return good for evil, you will be as though protected by armor.

If you never fail to make restorative offerings to the oath-bound Dharma protectors, you will naturally be surrounded by disciples and benefactors.

The supreme instruction is to ensure that you embody these principles in every way possible.

–224–

Six Misleading Circumstances

Six deceptive situations to avoid:
If you fail to recognize your own awareness, you will be deceived by the ordinary aspects of consciousness.
If you fail to give rise to luminosity, you will be deceived by lethargic śamatha.
If you fail to cut through (all appearances) once and for all, you will be deceived by a state of perpetual indeterminacy.
If you do not let all concepts purify themselves naturally, you are deceived more than ever by mental fabrications.
If you do not realize the state of union, you will be deceived by repeated talk about nonaction.
If you do not abide in the natural state, you will be deceived by grasping to single-pointed concentration.
These states are deceptively similar, so do not waste your time in meaningless practices.

If you fail to recognize the nature of your own awareness, the ultimate reality, the dharmatā in its essential nakedness, whatever else you may be introduced to will be nothing but an imitation.

If the realization of the clear light of the dharmatā does not arise from within, the nature of the mind will remain trapped in a state of mental stillness that will drift into an amorphous and undetermined state.

"The antidote that frees all" refers to the recognition that the nature of appearances is sufficient to eliminate all that needs to be eliminated. Without this, your one-pointed concentration will drift into an undefined state, neither virtuous nor unvirtuous.

Failing to know how to purify your mental fabrications through the spontaneous liberation of thoughts is the pinnacle of delusion.

Without uniting skillful means and wisdom, speaking of the Great Perfection's nonaction is nothing more than hollow and misleading words.

No matter how long you meditate on inner stillness or strive in other forms of meditation, if you do not recognize the wisdom that is primordially present within you, you will remain unable to cut the afflictive mental states at their root and will only delude yourself.

Many meditative states look alike, so focus on the correct ones. If you find yourself drifting into a mere likeness, beware of falling under its influence.

–225–

Six Ways to Go Astray

Showing the six situations where you go astray:
If you do not realize the nature that transcends representations,
engaging in the ten virtuous actions turns into bondage.
If you do not reverse clinging to the self, unelaborated practices
become subject to acceptance and rejection.
If, beyond phenomena, you do not elucidate [the nature
of mind] within absolute space (emptiness), even if you
meditate, your practice will stray into mental constructs.
If you do not realize the true face of whatever [appearances] you
encounter, your meditation will remain fabricated.
If you do not apprehend the naturally clear ultimate reality,
your meditation will be conceptual.
If you do not realize the primordial freedom free from fixation,
your meditation will be a conceptual construct.
Avoid these six ways of going astray.

What are these six deviations?

If you do not realize the meaning of emptiness free of representations, then no matter how diligently you perform the ten virtuous actions, they will remain in the realm of virtue bound with characteristics. Vanity and pride will prevail in your mind and liberation will elude you.

If a sincere revulsion for the three worlds of samsara does not arise from the depths of your being, merely proclaiming that you are going to a mountain solitude or that you are abandoning all activities to dedicate yourself to a practice free of elaboration is nothing more than an attempt to enhance your reputation.

If you do not correctly elucidate absolute space—the true nature of reality that transcends conditioned phenomena—you may meditate for as many years as you like without escaping mental constructs. Claiming that you have mastered the development phase and passed the completion phase will only further entangle your mind instead of liberating it.

When negative emotions arise, if you do not eliminate them by applying the antidotes at the very moment you encounter them, all the practices and meditations that you undertake will remain artificial.

If you recognize the ultimate nature of reality, the understanding of clear light will flourish on its own accord. But until you apprehend this fundamental nature, your diverse conceptual meditations will remain mere mental fabrications.

If you do not grasp the ultimate nature of reality, which is primordially free and without fixation of any kind, even if you persevere in countless meditations on the stillness of mind, on concentration (*dhyāna*), and the phases of development and completion, you will not extricate yourself from the views tainted with characteristics.

Make sure you are not sidetracked by such deviations.

–226–

Six Things to Slay

Instructions on six things to slay:
If you wish to pacify evil spirits and negative forces, slay attachment to your body and life.
If you wish to be in harmony with the world, slay pride and arrogance.
If you wish to pacify suffering, slay dualistic fixation.
If you wish to realize the ultimate reality, slay grasping to the supremacy of antidotes.

> **If you wish to actualize the nondual primordial wisdom, slay (attachment to) meditative mind as an antidote.**
> **If you wish to achieve enlightenment in one life, slay procrastination and laziness.**
> **If you can accomplish this, you will be victorious over your enemies, the four demons.**

What do these six instructions truly convey? In general, if you wish to pacify evil spirits and negative forces, you must first understand that what is called "evil spirit" is not something external. It is nothing more than the expression of an exaggerated attachment to your own mind and body. By freeing yourself from this self-clinging, the disease-bearing spirits will lose their power to steal your life force.

If you seek harmony with those around you, adopt a humble posture and discard pride and arrogance. In doing so, you will find yourself at peace with everyone.

If you wish to alleviate the suffering that plagues your mind, eliminate the concept of the duality of subject and object, for the very root of your suffering lies in dualistic thinking.

If you are striving to realize the fundamental nature of all things, as it truly is, do not seek an antidote separate from what needs to be eliminated and avoid clinging to the belief in the supremacy of any particular view that needs to be fostered.

If your aim is to meditate on the nonduality of skillful means and wisdom, you must cast off any form of meditation that clings to intellectually constructed antidotes.

If your goal is to achieve enlightenment in one lifetime, be diligent day and night, without distraction. Dispel the nonchalance that whispers, "Later, later. Not today . . ." or "When you are old . . . This is not the time yet; you are still young."

By putting these instructions into practice, you will conquer your enemies—the four demons.

–227–

Six Essential Attitudes

Showing the nature of six indisputable realities:
Apart from doing whatever pleases sentient beings, there is no other way of making offerings to the buddhas.
Apart from eagerly benefiting beings, there is no other path to liberation.
Apart from realizing the absence of division or exclusion, there is no other state of equality.
Apart from realizing the nonduality of object and subject, there is no other dharmatā to be realized.
Apart from realizing samsara to be devoid of intrinsic existence, there is no other nirvana.
Apart from realizing your own lack of inherent nature, there is no other need to clear mistakes and obscurations.
One who realizes these principles actualizes the dharmakāya present in him.

What is the nature of these six indisputable realities?

If you dedicate yourself wholeheartedly to benefiting others and bringing them happiness, there is no need to make other offerings to the Buddha, for this is the highest offering one can make.

If you prioritize altruism and devote yourself to it with all your strength, while eradicating any sense of self-importance, there is no need to seek another path to enlightenment.

If you fully realize the ultimate reality, the dharmatā, which knows no divisions or distinctions, this is the view of the equality of samsara and nirvana. There is no need to seek any other view.

If you perceive subject and object as two hands clutching each other, you will go astray. The object is emptiness, the subject is emptiness, and the mind is also emptiness. Yet, if you realize the nonduality of the mind and its objects, you need not look for another form of realization of the ultimate reality, the dharmatā.

Whatever the appearances of the three worlds of samsara, if you perceive them as devoid of true existence, like illusions, samsara will no longer delude you and you will not need to seek nirvana on the opposite shore of a samsara that must be abandoned.

We often speak about "someone" achieving buddhahood, but in truth if you examine the nature of that "someone," you will find neither a subject who accomplishes nor anything to be accomplished. Moreover, if you apprehend the ultimate reality, the dharmatā, the very notions of "deviations" and "obscurations" become irrelevant.

If you understand all this, the realization of the natural presence of the dharmakāya in your own mind will arise effortlessly.

–228–

Six Challenges

The characteristics of the six challenges are:
Entering the Dharma is a challenge, but even more challenging is to persevere in it without going back.
Understanding the Three Baskets of teachings is a challenge, but even more challenging is to apply them to your mind.
Receiving the samayas is a challenge, but even more challenging is to keep them perfectly.
Encountering the profound teachings is a challenge, but even more challenging is to practice them.
Giving birth to the wisdom mind is a challenge, but even more challenging is to maintain the realization.
Benefiting others is a challenge, but even more challenging is not to be discouraged.
If you aspire to enlightenment, strive to accomplish these aspects despite the challenges.

Having the good fortune to enter the Dharma path, rather than one of the hundreds of other paths that present themselves, is extremely rare and difficult. Even more difficult is to persevere on the path to its highest point, the point of no return.

Grasping the meaning of the Three Baskets through study, reflection, and meditation is no small feat. While you may acquire a reasonably good knowledge of their contents, fully assimilating them and merging the Dharma with your mind is an even greater challenge.

Receiving and observing the sacred commitments of the Adamantine Vehicle of the Secret Mantra, is difficult. Once these bonds are established, preserving them perfectly until the end of the path is an even greater challenge.

Encountering the deep meaning, the essential instructions of Mahāmudrā and the Great Perfection is difficult. Fully integrating these teachings in the field of your experience is an even greater challenge.

Cultivating the correct understanding of the ultimate reality is difficult. Nurturing this understanding through practice and bringing it to its ultimate point through direct experience is an even greater challenge.

Benefiting others is very difficult, but maintaining patience when those you have helped show no gratitude and repay your kindness with harm is an even greater challenge.

If you wish to attain buddhahood, you must embrace these difficulties as part of your practice, no matter how daunting the challenge may seem.

–229–

Six Wonders

Six truly wonderful instructions:
How wonderful, if you have faith and diligence,
To receive the teachings and to use them in times of need.
How wonderful, if you have devotion and respect,
To receive instructions from your master who is the Buddha in person.
How wonderful, if you implement the profound methods,
To enjoy the five sense objects without abandoning them and yet achieve liberation.
How wonderful, that an ordinary person practicing diligently
May attain enlightenment in one lifetime.
How wonderful, if you abide in the state of realization without distraction,
To actualize the deep yet clear dharmatā.
How wonderful, if you always familiarize yourself with the three mandalas,
To experience the primordial wisdom of the three kāyas.

Here are six instructions, sources of wonder, provided as you successfully navigated the six previous challenges:

If you possess faith and diligence, both of which are essential to the Dharma, over time you will be able to apply the teachings you have received in all circumstances. How wonderful to have them at your disposal when you need them most!

If you have true devotion, combined with respect, you will soon meet a spiritual master and receive the essential instructions that are more valuable than the treasures of a universa monarch accumulated over kalpas. This is truly wonderful!

If you associate the skillful means with the profound path and perceive the experiences of the five senses as dreams and illusions, you will be able to use them as supports on the path, finding liberation by experiencing them rather than by rejecting them. How marvelous are these skillful means of the Secret Mantra!

By practicing diligently and wholeheartedly, even an ordinary person can attain buddhahood in one lifetime and with one body. How wonderful is this direct path!

If you meditate continuously, never being distracted from realizing the ultimate nature of reality, the luminosity of dharmatā will shine from within. What a wonder to actualize the ultimate meaning, deep and luminous, from which the purest qualities spontaneously arise!

If you train in perceiving all forms, sounds, and thoughts as the mandalas of the body, speech, and mind of the buddhas, you will not need to seek elsewhere for the primordial wisdoms associated with these three kāyas. How wonderful it is when this realization of the true nature of forms, sounds, and thoughts arises from within!

–230–

Six Defects of Practitioners

Six defects of Dharma practitioners:
Not knowing the distinctions, they lack the eye of the view.
They cut themselves off from meritorious activities, the friend who is always needed.
They lack teachers who, like those who guide the blind, can lead them to liberation.

The walking stick of listening and contemplation that they hold is broken.
They are influenced by the undesirable demon of negative emotions and dualism.
Unable to free themselves from samsara, they plunge from a precipice into the lower realms.
Thinking of those beings who have these six defects,
Unbearable compassion brings me to tears,
But until their negative karma is exhausted, there is no way to rescue them.

Here are six defects that Dharma practitioners should identify:

Regarding the view, not knowing how to distinguish wisely between right and wrong, you will be unable to recognize the authentic view, the very eye that guides you to advance on the path to liberation.

Furthermore, the support of meritorious activities is always indispensable. However, if one's view is inwardly distorted, even the performance of outward meritorious deeds will fail to keep one on the perfect path.

Moreover, the help of meritorious activities is always indispensable. But if your view has been inwardly distorted, even the performance of all kinds of meritorious deeds will fail to keep you on the perfect path.

Like a blind person yearning for liberation, if you find a guide who knows the right path, he or she can lead you to your destination. But if you become separated from this guide—your spiritual master—you will inevitably lose your way.

An elderly person can get around without much difficulty by using a stick to walk. On the path to liberation, this stick represents study and reflection. If it breaks, you will be unable to move forward.

If you fall under the sway of the unwanted demon of subject-object duality which clouds and obscures the mind and must be eliminated, bewitched by this demon, you will remain unable to escape the three worlds of samsara and fall into the abyss.

Observing the behavior of all beings driven mad by these six defects, my mind fills with unbearable compassion, and tears come to my eyes. Yet, alas, until their accumulated karma is exhausted, they cannot be helped!

–231–

Do Not Become Confused

Six instructions to avoid a mistaken path:

Even if you cannot serve the Three Jewels,
Fearing the lower realms, do not commit negative actions.

Even if you fail to develop devotion and respect for your supreme lama,
Considering the defects of wrong views, do not slander or denigrate him.

Even if you lack love and affection for your spiritual brothers and sisters,
Considering the defects of breaking samaya, do not be jealous of them.

Even if you fail to practice the teachings of your lineage as the scriptures prescribe,
Considering the defects of bad karma, do not speak badly of Dharma practitioners.

Even if you fail to dismantle grasping at the true existence of delusive appearances,
Considering how outer and inner phenomena change, do not fixate on things as permanent.

Even if you fail to actually benefit others,
Considering the interdependent nature of cause and effect, at least do them no harm.

Now come six instructions to avoid following the wrong path:

Even if you do not serve and respect the Three Jewels in manifold ways, with respect and trust, at least refrain from accumulating bad karma by committing negative acts related to them.

Lacking faith in the Three Jewels, if, among other things, you engage in trading the sacred objects that symbolize their enlightened body, speech, and mind [statues, books, and stūpas], you will go straight to the lower realms. It would be wise to fear such an unfortunate fate!

Even if you do not feel the respectful fervor that makes you see the sublime master as the Buddha in person, at least avoid slandering and discrediting him. Once distorted views take root in your mind, they will render you impervious to transformation by the Dharma, even if you were to meet the Buddha in person. Contemplate the flaws of such a situation.

Even if you do not feel the same affection and affinity for your spiritual brothers and sisters as you would if you were children born of the same parents, at least avoid envying their qualities and accomplishments. Think of the harmful consequences of transgressing the samayas, which will swiftly lead you straight to the underworld.

Even if you are unable to practice the teachings of your main lineage in accordance with the corresponding texts, take care not to criticize and belittle practitioners of other traditions, considering that your Dharma is supreme and others' defective. Such an attitude is tantamount to rejecting the Dharma itself. Contemplate the flaws of such an attitude.

Even if you cannot dismantle attachment to the true existence of deceptive appearances, realizing that they are like illusions and dreams, at least avoid taking as permanent the activities connected with such deluded perceptions. Do not squander your entire life in worldly occupations—defeating adversaries and protecting kin—when everything, within and without, is subject to perpetual change.

Even if you do not succeed in directly benefiting others through your actions, words, and thoughts, at least avoid harming them. Otherwise, be certain that the laws of cause and effect will ensure you will pay the price for the harm you have inflicted on others.

–232–

Six Relevant Considerations

Six instructions worth listening to:
Looking at the frustration of not accomplishing even a small task,
Shouldn't you be more unhappy about neglecting your virtuous practices?

Looking at the pain caused by the changing nature of conditioned happiness,
Isn't it appropriate to be concerned when your meditative experience stalls?

Looking at the pain of lacking food and drink for one day,
Isn't it appropriate to worry about failing to accomplish your four daily practice sessions?

Looking at the discontent of failing to defeat your enemies in this life,
Isn't it appropriate to worry about being defeated by the enemies of negative emotions?

Looking at the pain of the death of your illusory life partner,
Isn't it appropriate to worry about being separated from Dharma, your ultimate partner?

Looking at the frustration of failing to accomplish minor activities,
Isn't it appropriate to be more saddened about the failure to accomplish spiritual activities when you have the freedom and advantages of this human existence?

Contemplating these appropriate considerations is utterly virtuous.

What are these six instructions that are worth listening to?

In everyday life, when you are at work or involved in public affairs, if even one of your activities fails, when carving stone for instance, you are very upset and exclaim, "Oh no! My work is ruined!" Shouldn't you grieve far more when your daily practices are interrupted, since these virtuous practices deserve all your diligence?

Material satisfactions, however intense, will eventually fade and dissipate. All that has been momentarily gathered will be dispersed. Compared to these frustrations, more appropriate is to be saddened if the continuity of your meditative experiences and your realization is interrupted, for if this occurs, you are moving away from the path to liberation.

After a day without food or drink, you feel the pangs of hunger and thirst. Shouldn't you feel a much greater sense of loss if you haven't done your four daily sessions, because you would be jeopardizing your aspirations for your future existence?

In this life, if someone harms you and you fail to subdue that enemy, everyone bemoans your lack of bravery. Control yourself and avoid giving free rein to the enemies of the five mental poisons. If they get out, you should really lament letting these far more formidable foes escape.

At present, you are full of the joy and satisfaction of sharing your life with your spouse, your companion in delusion. But soon he or she will be swept away by the agony of death, which inevitably follows birth. Shouldn't you grieve even more at the prospect of being separated from the Dharma, your lasting and supreme partner?

If your activities of body, speech, and mind are in any way thwarted, you are racked with worry. But more appropriate is to grieve for failing to take advantage of the favorable freedoms and conditions of human life to practice the Dharma.

By contemplating these six logical reasonings, you will quickly travel the path to liberation, the most meritorious of undertakings.

–233–

Six Attachments to Give Up

Six things to abandon for those who want to practice Dharma properly:
Abandon worldly activities, the mire of samsara.
Abandon all plans for marriage and children, the fetters that bring misfortune.
Abandon the childish attachment to the reality of illusory appearances.
Abandon enjoying deceptive sense pleasures.
Abandon honors that earn the respect of others; they are like the lasso of Māra.
Abandon the disastrous parents of ignorance and dualism.
Doing so, you will be liberated from samsara

Thus, there are six unnecessary things from which you should detach your mind if you want to practice Dharma properly.

As long as you remain stuck in the vast swamp of samsara's three worlds, ultimate liberation will remain out of reach. Therefore, give up all worldly activities.

Setting up a home with a spouse and many children creates bonds that keep you from fully practicing the supreme Dharma and that bring about countless troubles and calamities. Cut through such hindrances.

All the trivial activities of ordinary people, driven by animosity or attachment, are like childish games. Better to eliminate the attachment that makes you apprehend delusory appearances as real.

Deceiving others by boasting of qualities that you lack, while concealing your flaws, are all tricks born of a mind disturbed by sense pleasures. Instead, you should cut the rope of clinging to deceptive attractions.

Strong attachment to the things of this life and constantly postponing the pursuit liberation are the lassos of māra. If others respect you and place themselves at your service, these conditions can lead you to adopt inappropriate means of livelihood and misuse spiritual wealth. Forsake all this.

Ignorance and afflictive mental states are the most calamitous of parents. To free yourself from them, you must sever attachment to the notions of subject and object. In doing so, you will interrupt this recurring disaster. This is the only way to escape samsara.

–234–

Six Guidelines

Six instructions as guidelines:
Without knowing how to liberate instantly all encounters (with objects), you will be unable to destroy your grasping to appearances.
Without knowing how to liberate nakedly by looking nakedly, you will be unable to cut the roots of dualism.
Without apprehending the luminous depth of your meditative experiences, you will stagnate in the absence of concepts.
Without realizing dualistic appearances to be delusive, you will be unable to cut through the bonds of desire and attachment.
Without awareness of life's transience, your spiritual practice will be lax.
Without familiarizing yourself with the display of awareness, you cannot avoid falling from a precipice into the six realms.
Therefore, perfectly training in these crucial points is essential.

Six essential instructions should serve as your guidelines.

As soon as an afflictive mental state arises, you must annihilate it by bringing it into direct contact with its antidote. Otherwise, you will be unable to overcome your enemies—the discursive thoughts—and eliminate them.

By staring nakedly at the nature of these mental fabrications, they will free themselves in the emptiness of their true nature, at the very moment they appear.

Without mastering the vital point of liberation, you will be unable to end the delusion caused by the dualistic perception of subject and object and will remain strongly attached to these concepts.

By bringing awareness directly into the field of your experience, the realization of the luminous nature of reality will shine from within. This experience is very different from sinking and stagnating in an opaque mental stillness.[156] Without making this distinction, you will wander down side roads into a mental stillness that is merely a temporary suspension of discursive thoughts.

Without abandoning the fixations generated by the subject-object duality, which are all various forms of delusion, you will remain entangled in the bonds formed by the ordinary activities of this life and by attachment to the eight worldly concerns.

If you fail to revive your diligence by contemplating the impermanence of life, you will alternate periods of application to virtuous practices and periods of slackness when you neglect your practice.

Let the creativity of awareness express its full potential. Otherwise, you will not close the roads leading to the precipice from which you fall into rebirths in the six realms of samsara.

Therefore, practice these six vital points in the best way possible.

–235–

Six Extreme Situations

Six ultimate situations when you need to make crucial decisions:
The worst position is to become a leader. Abandon this!
The ultimate well-being is to be free from worldly activities. Abandon them!
The ultimate ruin is to engage in unvirtuous actions. Give them up!
The ultimate satisfaction comes from engaging in virtuous actions. Strive in them!
The ultimate goodness is to avoid worldly affairs. Abandon them!
The ultimate negativity is to turn away from Dharma activities. Stop this!
Acting in this way is most excellent and the highest nobility.

There are six key points to heed in extreme situations.

Deceiving others, notably by assuming leadership, is a source of much suffering. As it is said: "Where power is, there is sin." Power is unnecessary; avoid it.

Ultimate happiness comes from freeing your mind of all clinging to the ordinary concerns of this life. By doing so, you will save yourself from countless failures, vain hopes, and needless anxieties. Letting go of worldly occupations is wiser.

The ultimate calamity is continuing to commit negative acts that keep you bound to the lower realms. Avoid this at all costs.

If you apply yourself wholeheartedly to the virtuous activities of studying, reflecting, and meditating, you will secure your happiness in this life and in lives to come. Ultimate satisfaction comes from practicing virtue with your body, speech, and mind.

The ultimate excellence is to leave worldly affairs far behind and dedicate yourself to the Dharma. In doing so, all good qualities will spontaneously manifest. Discard ordinary pursuits.

The ultimate scourge is to turn away from Dharma practice. If you postpone practice or reject it, your observance of the precepts will degenerate, and your sacred bonds will be torn apart. Avoid such behavior!

Adhering to these injunctions represents the pinnacle of excellence

–236–

Six Detachments That Support Your Practice

Taming your mind stream with the six abandonments:
Cut through craving for food; it becomes impure, excrement and urine.
Give up concern for worldly fame, for renown is like an echo.
Give up attachment and aversion to delusive appearances lest they arise as enemies.
Give up dualism and self-grasping. If you do not, you risk being pierced by the weapons of the five poisons.
Do not emulate worldly leaders, for mundane achievements and power can undermine sublime Dharma.
Abandon gathering and increasing your wealth, for this will increase nonvirtue and diminish virtuous actions.
If you act like this, Dharma practice will flourish.

Six behaviors to eliminate:

Overindulgence in food merely amasses the ingredients of your own excrement. Stop coveting food.

Reputation and fame are little more than the empty echoes of conversations reverberated off a rocky cliff. Abandon the pursuit of worldly recognition.

If you take for real all delusory appearances, the whole world will appear hostile; attachment as well as animosity will grow in your mind. Stop clinging to your loved ones and hating your enemies.

If you stab yourself with the weapons of the five poisons, you will end up severing the vital artery of liberation. Uproot the "I," the ego, forged by the duality of subject and object.

Consider the lives of influential figures; their worldly responsibilities leave them with little time to practice the sublime Dharma. Do not be tempted to emulate them.

What fuels the proliferation of negative actions and the decline of virtuous ones? It is none other than the thought, "If only I could amass great wealth!" This thought leads you to hoard more and more and to do business or trade. Cut it off at the root.

If you follow these instructions, the accomplishment of the supreme and authentic Dharma will flourish.

–237–

Six Benefits of Accomplishment

Six qualities resulting from seeing the ultimate nature of reality:
You nakedly see and recognize the face of dharmatā and
spiritual experience arises from the depths of your heart.
Attachment to spiritual experience naturally dissipates and
appearances vanish without leaving imprints.
You are free from ordinary conceptual thoughts and primordial
wisdom arises unhindered.
Whoever has these six qualities will experience dharmatā.

Understanding the meaning of the ultimate reality translates into six signs of the "heat," symbolizing progress on the path of realization.

If you recognize the nature of awareness in all its nakedness, this is the introduction to the view.

If the direct experience of this recognition arises from within, you will be freed from the chains of doubt forged by a divided mind.

If you remain unattached to all experiences, whether good or bad, you will naturally be liberated from the obstacles posed by māra.

When all phenomena leave no more trace in your mind than a bird in the sky, vanishing before any notion of good or bad can take hold, you will dwell in perfect ease and serenity.

Freed from the fixations that drive the pursuit of the eight worldly concerns, the all-embracing primordial wisdom will naturally manifest within your mind stream.

With these six qualities, you will experience the dharmatā.

–238–

Six Analogies

Six instructions in the form of analogies:
Divide the three periods [of the day and the night] into sessions and pauses, and meditate on impermanence.
Think of friends and relatives as travelers.
Think of wherever you stay as a guesthouse.
Think of food, wealth, and riches as entertainment.
Think of all your activities as dreams.
Wherever you go, near or far, meditate on death.
If you follow these instructions, you will be liberated from the abodes of samsara.

Practitioners must integrate six modes of perception.

To allow your virtuous practices to flourish, it is recommended to divide your daytime practice into three sessions, interspersed with three breaks. By meditating diligently and repeatedly on impermanence, you will gain stability in the Dharma.

You might be together for now, but time will relentlessly separate you from your parents and loved ones. Instead of imagining that you will spend your whole life together, think that you are all visitors.

As for where you live, think of wherever you stay not as a place to be cared for in the long run, but as a hostel you are merely passing through.

Do not attach more importance to food and material goods than to children's games. Meditate on their ephemeral and illusory nature.

Whatever your activities might be, perceive them as dreams, fantasies. Avoid cherishing and becoming attached to them.

Regard all your journeys, whether near or far, as steps bringing you inexorably closer to death.

If you adopt these six ways of perceiving things, you will swiftly free yourself from the places of suffering within samsara.

–239–

Six Points to Take to Heart

Instructions on six points to take to heart:
Cherish the experience of seeing the ultimate nature of mind.
Cherish the wisdom that helps you identify your hidden defects with the help of instructions.
Cherish the understanding of philosophical views that unravel the crucial points.
Cherish the pure discipline that protects you like armor.
Cherish the stainless wisdom that cuts through delusion.
Cherish the nongrasping conduct that liberates from goal-oriented attitudes.

Take the following six instructions to heart:

The expression "seeing" the true nature of mind refers to the introduction to the nature of ordinary mind (*sems*), or to pristine awareness (*rigpa*). This introduction can be understood on various levels: as mere intellectual understanding, as a meditative experience, or as the full realization of the mind's true nature. It is the latter—the full realization—that truly matters.

When speaking of the discernment that allows you to identify your defects, it refers to the instructions that put the finger on your deepest flaws and thus help you eliminate them. It is not enough to spend your time discussing scriptures. You need to pay special attention recognizing and addressing your own shortcomings.

You may have mastered the views of the various philosophical schools at their different levels and elucidated the essential points of view, meditation, and action associated with them. You have understood, for instance, that the view of the listeners still harbors a sense of attachment to self, while the view of ordinary people is governed by attachment to the eight worldly concerns. The bodhisattvas' view is free from contamination by self-attachment, the enemy par excellence. The Middle Way presents various approaches, including the Svātantrika and Prāsaṅgika. It is important to examine closely the qualities and defects of each of these views.

Then, when reaching the views of the Mahā, Anu, and Ati yogas, one eliminates all residual defects and amplify all qualities. Great masters like Gyalwa Longchen Rabjam and Mipham Rinpoche have refuted some philosophical views, clarified others, invalidated those not in accordance with the Buddha's ultimate vision, and refined those that are, just as gold is refined by hammering, rubbing, and melting. Most philosophical debate today consists of extolling the excellence of one's own spiritual lineage and venting animosity toward others, the way people bicker with their claws out. This is not how to get to the heart of the matter.

Pure discipline must be worn like armor. The most important point is to be free of hypocrisy. If you behave blamelessly in full view of everyone, observing the rules of the virtuous community just outwardly while unknown to anyone else you give free rein to your mental poisons, you cannot claim to possess "pure discipline."

As for severing the attachments that lead you astray, if you have a sound discernment born of study, reflection, and meditation, you will be able to cut off delusion at its root. Otherwise, if you remain full of grasping and merely proclaim far and wide you have realized the view, your spiritual practice or affiliation with the vehicle of Secret Mantra will be quite pointless.

What does it mean to cherish conduct without fixation on a goal? A conduct that is naturally liberated and without targets can bring great progress in the view, meditation, and action if it is appropriate to your level of practice. If not, this will do you no good.

–240–

Six Principles

Six general practices to take on the path:
Blocking the river of defilements that leaks down, observe cause and effect extremely carefully.
Climbing the peak (of view, meditation, and conduct), aim for the pinnacle of vehicles.
At mid-height, carefully engage in virtuous activities.

For the preliminary, abandon the motivation of the lower vehicles, and develop bodhicitta, the altruistic mind of enlightenment.
For the main practice, counteract grasping to phenomena as real by understanding their lack of inherent existence.
For the conclusion, transform the path by dedicating with the purity of the three spheres (of subject, object, and action).
If you follow this advice, your practice of virtue will be successful.

To make the most of your Dharma practice, consider the following analogy: Imagine you must carry a valuable object over a long distance. You would take every possible precaution to ensure it arrives undamaged and in perfect condition. In the same way, here are six vital instructions to guide your spiritual journey.

"Leaking down" refers to errors and moral downfalls that may occur to you. Just as a vessel with a pierced bottom slowly empties, so too will your spiritual progress if you pride yourself in having a lofty view while disregarding the law of cause and effect. This is known as the "dark evil's view," which results in the proliferation of negativity. That is why you must pay the utmost attention to the law of cause and effect, even in its most minute aspects, accumulating even the smallest virtue, avoiding the smallest fault, and confessing the slightest negative thought.

"Climb the peak" refers to the view, which should be as high as possible, while the conduct should be as down-to-earth and scrupulous as possible. Thus, if you reach the summit of the view, the Great Perfection, by reaching up to the sky you will be able to touch the firmament of Trekchö* ("cutting through solidity") and Thögal* ("direct crossing").

When "crossing at mid-height," you must find a good balance in your practice of virtuous activities, which means that you must persevere as best you can in the ten virtuous Dharmic activities. Like a person who gradually build wealth by first acquiring a needle and thread, you must set to work day and night, without interruption, finding the proper rhythm and balance in practicing the ten virtuous activities, combining periods in which virtue is accumulated through the body, other periods when it is accumulated through speech, and others when accumulated through the mind.

To begin with, you should abandon the limited attitude of the lower vehicle of the listeners, who focus mainly on themselves. Then, take the bodhisattva vows and develop bodhicitta—the vast altruistic mind that aims to achieve enlightenment for the sake of others.

As for the main practice, when we speak of "clinging to the reality of things" this refers to our strong belief that our environment, our body, and our mind truly exist. No matter how many times we hear that they have no intrinsic existence, they continue to seem real to us. Similarly, we keep on hearing about impermanence and yet, even if we are struck with a fatal illness, we continue to cling to the permanence of things. You must interrupt this grasping at reality's solidity and recognize that all actions within the phenomenal world are like dreams and illusions and are, by nature, empty of intrinsic existence.

At the conclusion of your practice, you must purify the three spheres [the perception of a subject, an object, and an action endowed with true existence], thus integrating your practice with the path. This corresponds to the triad formed by the preparation, the main practice, and the conclusion.

If you can transmute in this way all your action of body, speech, and mind, great benefits will follow. But for this transmutation to take place, it is imperative to realize the lack of intrinsic existence of things within the purity of the three spheres.

If you master these six elements, your practice of virtue will be crowned with success, just as it is easy to gallop a good horse over flat terrain and arrive quickly at your destination.

–241–

Expand Your Perspective

Six great qualities that expand the ability to explain:
Limited mental scope will not do. You need to know how to explain the baskets of the teachings.
Focusing endlessly on knowing the words will not suffice. You must know how to explain the instructions.
Fearing the profound (meaning) will not do. You must know how to explain the classes of tantras.
Merely following the words will not suffice. You need to know how to elucidate them through practice.
Knowing philosophical systems partially is not enough. You must know how to explore them all.

> **Doubt and confusion will not do. You must develop certainty in explaining.**
> **Whoever has these qualities gathers all the teachings into one point.**

These are six points to expand your mind to embrace the essential points of the teachings:

Avoid being narrow-minded, fainthearted, and focused entirely on yourself. Broaden your perspective by studying and integrating the various meanings of view, meditation, and conduct as explained in the Three Baskets, and then keep them in mind.

Yet, mastering the ten traditional sciences through extensive study is not enough. You must receive the essential instructions on the practice of the profound meaning, through which you can achieve buddhahood. This is what Lord Atiśa pointed out to the great translator Rinchen Sangpo.[157]

Regarding the meaning of profound emptiness, the ultimate certainty will be found in the Great Perfection, which is conveyed through the "eight wondrous phrases" and the "twelve adamantine laughters."[158] If you understand these, you will simply laugh, free of fear.

It is crucial to comprehend the deeper meaning within the various classes of tantras of the Secret Mantra. If you remain confined to the literal words of the texts, you will never reach the true end of understanding. Instead, delve into the inner meanings of view, meditation, and action, allowing spontaneous understanding to arise relying on words only.

Holding your own philosophical tradition in high regard while dismissing others is a mistake. You must recognize all the scriptures as profound instructions and understand that the diverse aspects of the Buddha's teachings are not contradictory. In doing so, whatever view, meditation, and action you may practice, you will be free from doubts and hesitations. As stated in the *Adamantine Verses on True Nature*,[159]

> Even if you met a hundred virtuous scholars, a thousand realized beings,
> Ten thousand translators and pandits, one hundred thousand instructions,
> And a billion treatises,
> You would not have the slightest doubt to clear up.

This is the goal you must set for yourself. After the omniscient Jigme Lingpa had grasped the meaning of the Great Perfection, he reported that even if he had met the mahāsiddha Saraha in person, he would not have needed to for any further clarification since perfect certainty had arisen within him. One who understands this has gathered all Dharma into a single essence.

–242–

Committed to Excellence

Six ways of engaging in the sublime practices:
Engage yourself for the benefit of others in whatever training you undertake.
Out of compassion, take the suffering of others into your own experience.
Whatever wealth you acquire, devote it to virtuous activities.
Protect the purity of the three vows and samayas.
Do not part from the ultimate nature of reality in any action.
Supplicate out of devotion, respect, and longing,
This is the life of perfect liberation of sublime ones. Follow their example!

If you really want to practice the Dharma to perfection, adopt these six behaviors:

Whatever your activities of body, speech, and mind might be, if you benefit others, you will walk the path of the bodhisattvas, the source of immense benefits.

Whatever suffering you endure, understand that many other beings are experiencing similar pain. Therefore, care for their suffering with great compassion, just as you would if their pain were your own.

If you happen to have wealth and possessions, do not hoard them for the long term. Instead, be generous, make offerings, contribute to the construction of shrines, and support the monastic community. In short, use your riches to accumulate merit.

Once you have taken vows and precepts, and established sacred bonds—pertaining respectively to individual liberation, the bodhisattva path, and the Secret Mantra—guard them with vigilance and circumspection, avoiding any fault that might tarnish them.

Whatever activities you engage in, physically, verbally, and mentally—whether eating, moving, sitting, or sleeping—never separate yourself from the view of the dharmatā and vigilantly keep your mind free from distraction.

In all the above activities of daily life, whether in joy or in sorrow, keep in mind your spiritual master and invoke him.

These six essential instructions characterize the life of perfect liberation of the exalted beings; let them guide your own path.

–243–

Taking Disease on the Path

Six ways of taking sickness on the path:
Sickness exhausts the negative karma that keeps you in samsara.
Sickness cleanses the stains of negative emotions.
Sickness prompts you to supplicate out of devotion, respect, and longing.
Sickness encourages you to strive in virtuous activities.
Sickness empowers you to meet with the path of liberation.
Sickness reminds you to develop proficiency and intensify your (practice).
Thus do wise ones take sickness on the path.

If you are struck by illness, six instructions will help you integrate it on the path:

When you experience physical or mental illness, remind yourself, "Alas! These are the afflictions that plague the three worlds of samsara! Far greater are the sufferings of extreme heat and cold endured in the hell realms, the pangs of hunger and thirst suffered by the pretas, and the bondage and hard treatment that afflict the animals. Through the sickness I experience, may the obscurations related to the bad karma of all beings be purified!" By doing so, you can powerfully purify the defilements associated with illness.

It is said that illness helps to cleanse and exhaust the mental toxins of animosity, desire, and ignorance—especially desire. Keep this in mind.

Illness motivates us to pray to the spiritual master and the Three Jewels. For the carefree who feel they are flying over the difficulties of life, illness can inspire them to perform ceremonies, receive the blessings of a master's empowerment, and pray with intense fervor. The fear of dying from their sickness can drive them to engage in virtuous practices with their body, speech, and mind.

Understanding that depending on your behavior, according to the laws of causality, "This will happen and that will not happen" can spur your diligence in practicing virtue. In his youth, Jetsun Milarepa caused the death of eighteen people and horses. These misdeeds led him to meet Marpa the translator and receive his teaching. Similarly, adverse circumstances can induce you to embrace the path of liberation. In this way, a serious illness can eventually bring you onto the spiritual path.

If illness leads you to realize the meaning of ultimate reality (*dharmatā*), and you master such a realization, your practice will make great progress. Therefore, bring sickness onto the path and engage in practice with your whole heart and mind.

–244–

Six Things to Know

Instructions on the six kinds of knowledge:
Know your harmful enemies and demons to be as beneficial as the gods.
Know an excess of affection and longing for your relatives and friends to be detrimental, leading to downfalls.
Know your negative emotions to be as harmful as thorns.
Know this attachment to the self that you protect, to be as harmful as a malicious spirit.
Know that adverse circumstances enhance the path of liberation.
Know praise and name and fame to be an evil nest of flaws.
These six kinds of knowledge are extremely important.

Now come six instructions on what should be known but can only truly be known through direct experience and practice:

There are times when an enemy or negative force seeks to harm you. You expect them to hurt you and feel animosity toward them. Don't be motivated by such a destructive feeling. In reality, this hostility offers you the opportunity to practice patience, which will allow you to progress on the path to liberation and enlightenment. Therefore, it is wise to see your enemies as helpful guides.

You may also think that your loved ones are, by definition, beneficent. You tell yourself that they will assist you if you fall ill and perform virtuous deeds in your memory after death. However, the deep attachment you form toward them can actually pull you into the lower realms of samsara's three worlds. Therefore, it is better to regard them as potential antagonists to be guarded against.

A thorn piercing your body will bother you until you pull it out. Consider as equally pernicious the afflictive mental states, the five poisons, that have lodged themselves in your mind stream.

Attachment to the "I" and the tendency to cherish this "I" are nothing but harmful influences. If an evil spirit enters people or settles in their homes, they will go hungry, resort to begging, fail to find work, and be afflicted with all sorts of calamities. If you examine this so-called malignant influence, it is none other than the grasping to the "I," the belief in an autonomous, permanent self. You must eliminate self-centeredness, which is truly the demon of indigence.

When faced with adverse circumstances—physical illness, mental suffering, slander, or hostile schemes—if you can integrate them into the path, as explained in the seven-point mind training,[160] they become catalysts for progress toward liberation. Consider them in this light.

As your fame and notoriety grow and praise is heaped upon you, your vanity and pride will swell. Your misuse of religious goods will increase and drag you down. All this is a nest of vices.

Know this and take it to heart!

–245–

The Definitive Meaning

Six instructions on the essential definitive meaning:
Abiding in the unborn nature, recognize the foundation of delusion.
When (appearances) arise unceasingly, cut delusion from the root.
Realizing the lack of duality, you avert the army of samsara.

When the intellect, taken as real, naturally frees itself, the obstacles of the four extremes are eliminated.
The view must be established on the peaks by unraveling the inner essence of samsara and nirvana.
The conduct must be established by descending to the bottom of the valley and following the path [of the laws of cause and effect].
These represent the ultimate essential profound meaning.

What are the instructions that point to the essential and definitive meaning? If you fully realize the emptiness of phenomena, which have never really been "born," you will apprehend the origin and foundation of delusion—namely, the failure to recognize this empty nature.

The primordial nature of all phenomena being "unborn," phenomena can manifest themselves unceasingly and without hindrance. Emptiness arises in the form of interdependent manifestations whose display unfolds infinitely.[161] But where does this display come from in the first place? Where does it reside in between? Where does it finally disappear? These deceptive appearances must be examined conclusively.

If you then realize the true nature of the unborn and the unceasing, you will have repelled the hordes of samsara. From that point on, you will no longer have to wander in the circle of existences.

Regarding the spontaneous liberation of thoughts and the intellect, if you practice in this way, the deluded mind will soon be spontaneously liberated and the four conceptual extremes—existent, nonexistent, both existent and nonexistent, and neither existent nor nonexistent—will be dispelled.

Having thus perfected and refined the view, you will have elucidated the foundation of both samsara and nirvana. Understanding their origin will also clarify the right conduct and all your actions will be directed to virtue.[162] This is the ultimate profound and essential meaning.

–246–

Striking the Vital Points

Six actions that strike the vital points:
Keeping an unchanging attitude, do not abandon Dharma.
Do not be deceptive so that others will not be ashamed of you.
Do not allow devotion and respect to diminish so that they become intermittent.
Be extremely careful about the three trainings so that you are not stained by faults and downfalls.
Always think of death so you do not give in to laziness.
Use the antidotes to naturally free your mind at the very moment you encounter negative emotions.
If you carry out these actions, all your aspirations will be fulfilled.

These are six practices to put into action.

You need to have a stable character that does not sway like wild grass in the wind. If so, once you commit yourself to the supreme Dharma, you will never turn back.

If your attention and alertness do not waver and you behave impeccably, you will be free of hypocrisy. Thus, no one will find fault with your conduct, and you will have no reason to be ashamed in front of others.

If you feel faith and respect one day and not at all the next day, these fluctuations will prevent the blessings of the spiritual master and the Three Jewels from entering your mind. Since such blessings result from complete trust and devotion, make sure they are unwavering.

Take the same constant care of the three trainings as you would of an injured eye that must be protected with continuous attention. In this way, the three trainings will not be contaminated by faults and downfalls.

If you do not constantly keep death and impermanence in mind, you will continue thinking of new things to do and will be carried away by ordinary activities. Do not succumb to carelessness.

If you do not use the proper antidote at the very moment a negative emotion arises, the antidote will not be useful after the emotion has affected you. However, if the antidote is applied immediately, the emotion will be naturally freed.

Master these six points, and all your aspirations, both immediate and ultimate, will be fulfilled.

–247–

Igniting Primordial Wisdom

Six instructions to cause your primordial wisdom to blaze forth:
In the state of nongrasping, all appearances are clear.
In the state of nonduality, you maintain stability in equanimity.
In purity and clarity, you abide in the naturally pristine state.
In the luminous nature of mind, you abide in the naturally lucid state.
Abiding in the ultimate nature of reality, your smile of joy shimmers.
In the expanse of reality beyond conceptual mind, you experience spacious vastness.
In these ways, you will accomplish the unfabricated natural Great Perfection.

If the primordial wisdom that realizes the true nature is present in your mind, as a sign of this presence, when fixations related to desire or aversion no longer occur, the appearances perceived by the six aspects of consciousness manifest vividly.

Realizing the true nature does not mean that phenomena cease to manifest. In fact, they appear like stars clearly reflected on the surface of the ocean. There is then no attachment or aversion born from belief in the reality of an object, but there is no absence of phenomena either. While phenomena appear distinctly, the notions of "good" and "bad" are appeased in the serenity of equal taste.

In the ultimate nature of reality, the dharmatā, pristine awareness is primordially luminous. One speaks of natural radiance because it does not need to be newly illuminated.

If you rest continuously in this dharmatā, a smile of joy will illuminate your mind now free of all narrowness and rigidity.

When you remain in the equanimity of the continuum of the absolute expanse, beyond the intellect, everything is liberated into an expansive vastness.

In this way, you will realize the natural simplicity of the Great Perfection.

–248–

The Natural State

Six instructions to mix with the crucial points (of meditation) in the natural state:
Naturally abiding meditation on the great luminosity
In the self-cognizing, innate primordial wisdom beyond the intellect,
Concentrate where focus is needed and relax where leniency is needed.
Not giving in to distraction, remain undistracted and equipped with mindfulness.
Abide in unbiased equanimity making no distinction between movement and stillness.
In the limitless sky-like naturalness,
The Great Seal of dharmakāya is spontaneously accomplished.

The practice of the "natural state" pertains to the true nature of phenomena. It is important to associate this practice with whatever spiritual practice you currently follow.

Your own awareness transcends the domain of the intellect. It is the timeless, unaltered simplicity of primordial wisdom. Nothing needs to be fabricated anew. If you meditate while leaving everything in its natural presentation, within this primordial wisdom, clear light will shine forth uninterruptedly.

In doing this, do not be too tense, so as not to get tangled up in mental fabrications. Do not become too lax either, which would result in slipping into an amorphous neutrality. Should you drift into blind distraction without even realizing it, you will wander in the dark. Therefore, collect yourself, mindful that you have a task to which you must unwaveringly give your full attention.

The nature of discursive thoughts is none other than pristine awareness; do not try to block them. If the mind remains still, do not allow yourself to be enveloped by this stillness; instead, remain in the continuum of equanimity free of fragmentation, resting in the space-like dharmakāya. In this way, the Great Seal will be spontaneously accomplished.

–249–

Immutable Awareness

Six qualities of (pristine awareness), that which neither abides nor changes:
Pristine awareness is empty, clear, and unelaborate.
Not being altered by the stains of subject-object dualism and hope and fear,
Abide in its natural, fresh, and naked state,
Without thought, action, meditation, or conceptuality,
Vivid, lucid, open, and brilliant.
Liberation upon arising, unbiased, original mind
Is what pacifies all suffering and conceptual elaborations.

What is the nature of these six qualities of that which neither remains nor changes?

Can the empty and luminous nature of awareness be considered "existent"? No, for it is not a permanent entity.[163] Could it be "nonexistent"? Neither, for it is not mere nothingness. It is neither both—a perpetual nothingness—nor neither. If you grasp this, you will be free from the obscurations of subject-object duality, hope and fear.

In its spontaneous presentation, this nature is the fundamental state of mind. If you avoid becoming entangled in meditative experiences and mental fabrications, you will realize the continuum of this nature in its pristine nakedness.

This nature, free from deliberate reflection, is untouched by mental fabrication. Since there is no need for analysis, it transcends deliberation. In the absence of an object and the act of meditation, it is not conceived by a "view" and does not become an object of investigation. In a continuum that is not "meditated" upon by the ordinary mind, it remains clear, lucid, bright, and fluid. This "ordinary," or natural, mind is liberated as it unfolds and does not fall into any bias. Thus, all the torments of samsara and conceptual elaborations are pacified.

–250–

The Great Equality

Six features of the great equality of dharmatā, the ultimate nature of reality:
The space-like awareness that is free from all extremes
Is beyond the division of samsara and nirvana and the label of abandonment or adoption.
In the state of the view of dharmakāya that is liberated from the ground and free from action,
You are free from fixation, grasping, and mental activity.
The ultimate reality and nature as the *prajñāpāramitā*, the transcendence of wisdom,
Cuts through attachment and clinging and is free from the mind's conceptuality.
When these are present, the domain of all the victorious ones will be spontaneously accomplished.

Six remarkable points about the perfect equality of dharmatā:

Awareness free from the two extremes of realism and nihilism is like space—untouched by the karmic actions and afflictive mental states of the three realms of samsara. It is neither diminished by these conditions nor enhanced by the kāyas and primordial wisdoms at the time of nirvana. Transcending the divide between samsara and nirvana, it remains beyond distinctions of rejecting one or attaining the other.

Continuously abiding within the continuum of the primordially free dharmakāya, there is, in truth, no virtue to be performed. This view, being utterly free from any conceptual representations, leads to the purest meditation, which is to become intimately familiar with this complete absence of references. This will free you from any preconceived idea that such a state could be anything less than perfect.

The expression of this true nature is none other than the perfection of transcendent wisdom, the prajñāpāramitā. You will be free from the kind of hesitations that make you question, "Have I truly realized the ultimate nature of reality?" or "Perhaps I have failed"?

At this point, you will have severed all attachments that bind you to the concerns of this life, and the qualities belonging to the domain of the victorious ones will spontaneously manifest.

–251–

Remaining in Awareness

Six indications of pristine awareness abiding in the dharmatā:
In the state of devotion, you experience pristine awareness as radiantly alive.
In the state of ultimate reality, you experience pristine awareness as completely majestic.
In the state of concentration, you experience pristine awareness as steadfastly magnificent.
In the state of spiritual experience, pristine awareness is brilliantly clear.
In the state of dharmatā, you experience pristine awareness as immaculately limpid.
In the state of self-cognizing pristine awareness, awareness is sharpness and vivid.
By meditating in this way, primordial wisdom remains in the expanse of pristine awareness

Six criteria indicating that pristine awareness remains immutably within ultimate reality, dharmatā:

When you have developed fervent devotion to the master, all experiences of happiness and suffering will unravel into their true nature, leaving the mind perfectly at ease, radiating joy, overflowing with felicity.

Remaining in equanimity in the simplicity of the true nature of mind, you will sit in majesty. like a mountain that no gale can shake, like Dathong Tulku.[164]

You will rest in an unruffled, unchanging calm abiding and deep concentration.

As your meditative experience blossoms within, your inner realization will illuminate the outer world.

The ultimate nature of reality, dharmatā, being free of all obscuration, you will experience a transparent radiance.

Pristine awareness that knows itself will become vivid and clear and, never losing strength, will triumph.

By meditating in this way, you will be liberated into the vast expanse of pristine awareness.

–252–

Authentic Disciples

Six qualities of fortunate disciples who are appropriate vessels:
Devotion and respect have been perfected so you do not lose faith no matter how your teacher acts.
Having faith in Dharma, you are careful about the cause and effect of virtuous and unvirtuous deeds.
With pure samaya, you have strong love and affection for your vajra kin.
Imbued with Dharma, you cherish virtuous activities.
Having applied antidotes vigorously, you naturally liberate adverse circumstances in the natural state.
Having gained inspiration, you practice meditation diligently.
Those with these (qualities) are supreme vessels of the precious and sublime Dharma.

If you bring to its ultimate point the devotion that sees the master as the Buddha in person, no matter what the master does to pacify, increase, attract, and subjugate, your confidence will only grow stronger, never wavering.

Having gained deep confidence in the master's instructions and being eager to put them into practice, you will be able to transform your mind stream and will be attentive to the laws of cause and effect—what to adopt and what to avoid—as dearly as you would guard your own eyes.

Keeping perfectly pure samaya, considering your vajra brothers and sisters as members of the same family, with whom you will practice until enlightenment, you will be filled with affection for them.

Uniting your mind with the Dharma, you will develop an aversion to the ordinary, scattered activities driven by the eight worldly concerns and will engage only in virtuous practices.

By continually applying antidotes on the path, these antidotes will gain strength while the defects they counteract will weaken. Whatever adverse circumstances and obstacles arise, they will be liberated at their source and will be unable to overwhelm you.

As you keep progressing on the path of liberation, you will experience a great joy that will stimulate you to practice without wavering, with strength and diligence. In so doing, you will become a precious vessel, as if made of the purest gold, for the supreme Dharma.

–253–

Unsuitable Vessels

Six characteristics of an unsuitable and useless vessel:

Even if you have meditated for a long time, if you have not freed your mind,
Staying in solitude like a wild animal will be meaningless.

Although you know the categories of teachings, unless they serve as antidotes (to negative emotions),
Like a parrot, knowing a lot through listening and contemplation will be less meaningful.

Even though you rely on spiritual guides, if you do not receive their instructions,
You lack purpose and are like someone who remains thirsty in front of a large lake.

Even though you have received instructions, without applying them to your mind,
Like merely holding a medical prescription, having instructions will be less meaningful.

Even though you achieved signs of the warmth of spiritual experience, without realizing the nature of mind,
Like tīrthikas entering their paths, your meditation practices will be less meaningful.

Even though you undertake great hardship in Dharma practice, without developing positive qualities,
Your efforts are no more fruitful than a marmot hibernating in its burrow.

Therefore, you must accomplish the crucial points.

These six instructions emphasize that if you do not transform your mind through the practice of the supreme Dharma, you are a poor vessel for the teachings and will only accomplish minor worldly goals.

If you spend days, months, and years meditating in the solitude of the mountains without freeing yourself from the bonds of afflictive mental states, even if you end up spending your whole life there, you will be little different from the animals that inhabit the wilderness.

If you have extensive knowledge of the Three Baskets of the Buddha's teachings and even teach them to others, but have not used this knowledge as an antidote to your negative emotions, all your learning and reflection amount to little more than a parrot's talk. Consider the monk Good Star, who memorized the twelve sections of the (Three) Baskets, while Devadatta mastered a vast quantity of scriptures, equivalent to the load of an elephant. Despite their learning, both conceived wrong views of the Buddha and slandered him. Although they lived in the Buddha's presence, they ended up in the hell realms.

Even if you accompany your spiritual master like his shadow for months and years, if you do not properly receive the instructions that embody the quintessence of his wisdom, it is like sailing the vast ocean for a long time in search of the wish-fulfilling jewel, only to leave empty-handed and end up starving.

Having received instructions and tried to assimilate them, if the signs of the warmth of direct experience do not manifest, these instructions will not have served as an antidote to your afflictive mental states. This is like, consulting an expert physician, yet ignoring the prescribed treatment, taking, for instance, a useless remedy for headaches when you suffer from tuberculosis or a disease of the humors.

Even if you have signs of the warmth of progress on the path, such as clairvoyance, miraculous powers, and other marks of accomplishment, if you do not realize the nature of mind as it is, what is the point of having meditated so long? Tīrthikas can fly in the sky, manifest inconceivable miracles, and endure harsh asceticism, living naked and fasting. Yet, if spiritual qualities do not take birth in their mind streams as a result, they are only inflicting unnecessary torment upon themselves.

If you do not wish to end up like a marmot hibernating in its burrow, your Dharma practice must touch on the crucial points.

–254–

The Supreme Master

Six signs of a supreme master:
While relying on a master, if you experience cheerful warmth and are drawn to Dharma,
This is a sign of the cloud of blessings arising from practice.

If (the master) encourages students to practice and possesses numerous qualities,
This is a sign that he holds a great wealth of profound aural transmissions.

If (the master) feels no jealousy or fear of losing his followers and wealth to others,
This is a sign he has exhausted desire and attachment to worldly dharmas.

If (the master) is knowledgeable in leading students with various mental capacities,
This is a sign he has compassion and skill in benefiting others.

If (the master) greatly benefits suffering beings,
This is a sign he has trained in the immeasurable bodhicitta and compassion.

If (the master) has a spacious, carefree mind and is free from worldly activities,
This is a sign he has the confidence associated with realizing the fundamental nature.

Thus, search for such a master and then rely upon him.

What are these six signs of a spiritual teacher's excellence?

When you fully entrust yourself to a teacher and your body, speech, and mind become peaceful and controlled, naturally inclined to the supreme Dharma, this is a sign that the blessings of the teacher and of the spiritual lineage have gathered like clouds and penetrated your mind.

When a disciple relies on a teacher who explains that a particular teaching has certain qualities and how it can be practiced, if the disciple follows these instructions step by step, the related qualities will gradually unfold in his or her mind. This is a sign that the teacher holds the profound instructions of the oral tradition.

If the teacher does not show the slightest jealousy or resentment when others attract his disciples or take his belongings, regardless of their value or quantity, and if there is no enmity among those around him, with everyone seeing each other as children of the same family, this is a sign that the teacher has completely exhausted all attachment to worldly affairs and is free from craving and aversion.

If the teacher knows how to guide all his disciples on the path of liberation and omniscience according to their individual capacities, it is a sign that he is full of benevolence and compassion and excels in transforming beings.

If the teacher dispels the suffering of others on a large scale, discerning who is burdened with thick obscurations, who has committed negative acts, or who is suffering from illness, and if, above all, he is overflowing with immense tenderness and compassion toward all beings, this is a sign that he has developed bodhicitta.

If those around him sometimes behave inappropriately, quarrel, or engage in undesirable actions, and in such situations, the teacher shows a broad and serene mind and avoids engaging in the activities of worldly affairs, it is a sign that he is firmly established in the realization of the true nature of things.

Seek out and find a teacher who displays these signs of authenticity.

–255–

Six Things to Avoid

Six signs showing what Dharma practitioners should avoid:
If you are filled with partisan prejudices and bigotry, this is a sign of attachment and aversion.
If you feel animosity toward others for whatever they do, this is a sign of wrong views arising.
If you are greatly attached to delusive appearances, this is a sign of your spiritual practice waning.
If you accumulate material possessions in your native land, this is a sign of turning away from Dharma.

If you take interest in ordinary life, this is a sign of demonic obstacles.
If you lack certainty about Dharma, this is a sign you have lost the path to liberation.

Dharma practitioners must avoid six pitfalls that can hinder their practice:

If you prioritize worldly intrigues, you will be caught up in a whirlwind of activities driven by attachment to your clan and animosity toward rivals. This indicates a lack of commitment to impartiality.

If all your actions, words and thoughts are filled with animosity, you will fail to see the excellence in your teacher's deeds. This is the sign of holding wrong views.

As for the deceptive pursuits of this life—fame, wealth, possessions, power, pomp, and splendor—if your inclinations toward them increase, your virtuous practice will decline.

If you are busy accumulating possessions in your native land, you will turn away from the Dharma. This is a sign that your vocation as a renunciant will be swept away by ordinary activities.

If you are solely concerned with the ordinary affairs of this life and neglect to consider your future lives, this a sign that Māra, the demon who creates obstacles, has infiltrated your mind.

If you have not arrived at clear certainty in your understanding of the Dharma, through study, reflection, and meditation, this is a sign that you have lost the path of liberation.

–256–

Six Mistakes to Avoid

Six errors to avoid:

Instead of making offerings to your spiritual master who is the object of refuge in this and the next lives,
Taking care of those near and dear ones who do everything to please you is a great error.

Instead of reciting mantra, the root of siddhis,
Engaging in endless gossip is a great error.

Instead of accumulating the seven noble riches of faith and so forth,
Gathering wealth, the root of suffering, is a great error.

Instead of meditating on the ultimate reality and nature of mind,
Engaging in distracting activities and bustle is an error.

Instead of taming self-grasping, the source of evil deeds,
Being proud of your reputation is an error.

Instead of listening and contemplating that dispels the darkness of ignorance,
Engaging in murky and ignorant meditation based upon assumptions is an error.

Those who avoid these errors will approach nearer to the path of liberation.

Why is it desirable to avoid six things that are inherently wrong?

Your root master is a reliable refuge, both in this life and in future lives. It is therefore appropriate to appreciate the excellence of all his actions for the benefit of beings, to offer him your respect, serve him faithfully, and avoid anything that might sadden his heart. If, instead, you give preference to your kin and friends, it is a serious mistake.

The recitation of mantras of your tutelary deity is the source of both ordinary and supreme siddhis. But if, instead of committing to such practices, you multiply idle chatter that fuels worldly attachments and animosities, discussing wars, and indulging in all sorts of gossip, you are making a serious mistake.

Instead of generating the seven noble qualities or riches, such as faith, when they are not yet born in your mind, and magnifying them once they are born, if you occupy yourself with amassing gold, silver, possessions, and land, you are making a serious mistake.

If, instead of meditating properly on the fundamental nature of mind, you allow yourself to be carried away by distraction and busyness, you are making a serious mistake.

The ego, attachment to the self, is the source of all flaws. If instead of unmasking it, you become infatuated with your social rank, wealth, and fame, you are making a serious mistake.

If, instead of devoting yourself to study, reflection, and meditation on the supreme Dharma, which dispels the darkness of ignorance, without the slightest regard for the laws of cause and effect, you prioritize the affairs of this life and sink into foolish meditation, you are making a serious mistake.

Avoiding all these mistakes, follow the path to liberation without further delay.

–257–

Crucial Points of Conduct

Six instructions that strike the vital points:
A broken canal cannot maintain the flow of water. Therefore, rely upon a wise teacher.
As they cause you to fall into delusion, abandon frivolous and evil activities.
As you will be stained by their negative conduct, do not accompany ordinary people.
Do not debate about words as this is a distraction, a thorn for meditative concentration.
There is no end to the busyness of worldly activities, so immediately leave all your unfinished tasks.
Do not discuss your yidam practice with others as siddhis will remain far distant.
Craving for food and drink is bound to increase, so sustain yourself on whatever comes your way.
If you follow these instructions, virtuous activities will expand.

To reach the essence of Dharma practice, observe these six vital instructions:

Just as water cannot reach its destination if the pipe that channels it is broken, so too must you rely on a learned and accomplished master; otherwise, the flow of blessings [from the spiritual lineage] will not reach you.

When you observe the behavior of those childish beings lost in the three worlds of samsara, you find little more than negative actions and conduct contrary to the Dharma. Thus, you should abandon the deluded ways of ordinary beings.

In particular, if you indulge in the company of evil friends and those who are fond of distraction and entertainment, or if you spend your time with people who have no interest in practicing the Dharma, their poor behavior will inevitably contaminate you. Instead, seek solitude in a mountain retreat.

When you rest in the continuity of contemplation free from torpor and excitement, words become thorns that distract your mind, making it unfit for concentration. If you engage in arguments driven by attachment or aversion, discussing wars and conflicts, or involving yourself in endless polemics, your mind will become feverish, and these disturbances will act as many thorns to your concentration. In short, avoid controversies.

The more activities you undertake, the more your agitation will grow, leaving you without a moment's rest. Abandon all unnecessary occupations and adhere to nonaction.

If you reveal to others the identity of your tutelary deity, the yidam, and transmit empowerments and blessings indiscriminately, ordinary and extraordinary siddhis will flee from you. Therefore, keep the identity of your yidam a closely guarded secret.

If you get into the habit of eating and drinking a lot, your appetite for food and drink will only increase. It is better to live only on what comes to you, content with what is necessary for your vital needs and consider anything beyond that as superfluous.

By following these instructions, all your activities will naturally lead to the increase of virtue.

–258–

Crucial Contagious Defects

Six contagious defects of flawed teachers:
Students who rely upon bad teachers,
Are infected with the extreme views of eternalism and nihilism due to the teachers' limited philosophical views.
Because of the teacher's negative conduct, the students are led to a wrong and harmful path.
Because of the teacher's negative signs of accomplishment, the students' animosity and viciousness increase.

> **Because of the teacher's incorrect meditation, the students stick to their deluded habitual tendencies.**
> **Because of the teacher's mistaken Dharma practices, the students are led astray to worldly activities.**
> **Because of the teacher's erroneous results, the students fall into samsara, in particular in the lower realms.**
> **Therefore, those who are interested in the path of liberation,**
> **Should examine and abandon those flawed teachers**
> **Who, in how they create obstacles, are like great demons.**

Six defects that characterize bad teachers or spiritual masters and the disciples they contaminate, who exude the foul odor of someone whose body has been smeared with filth:

Teachers consumed by anger or dominated by desire will instill the same defects in their disciples. Others fall into the extreme views of nihilism or eternalism, entrapping themselves in the grip of dualistic thinking. They take pride in their erroneous views and disdain all other philosophical positions. By relying on such guides, you will only accumulate bad karma. If, in addition, these so-called guides behave like hypocritical charlatans, you will be drawn into their misconduct—a highly undesirable situation.

Until realization of the ultimate nature of reality is truly born in your mind, do not be tempted to develop extraordinary powers—such as flying in the sky, displaying clairvoyance, and seeing gods and demons—which will only heighten your irritability and aggression.

Even if your practice is imperfect, you might achieve various levels of śamatha. But without understanding the ultimate nature of reality, these superficial meditative experiences will merely reinforce your habitual tendencies.

A teacher who has not attained stability in his experience of the view and in his realization will become lost in the wanderings of the eight worldly concerns. Relying on such a teacher will only lead you deeper into the three worlds of samsara and, more especially, to a fall into the lower realms.

For those sincerely committed to the path of liberation, an unworthy guide is the most formidable of demonic obstacles. Therefore, you must carefully examine the qualifications of a teacher before placing your trust in him or her, avoiding at all costs those who fail to meet the proper requirements and behave in reprehensible ways.

–259–

Bad Company

Six types of negative influences resulting from the behavior of inappropriate friends:
If you accompany thoughtless and childish people, you will be influenced by their careless conduct.
If you join a party of young people, you will be influenced by their unbridled amusements and laughter.
If you accompany laypeople, you will be influenced by their interest in farming, business, and fame.
If you accompany businesspeople, you will be influenced by their interest in profit-making and accumulating wealth.
If you accompany hateful people, you will be influenced by their cruel behavior.
If you accompany those who emphasize taking care of their friends and relatives, you will be influenced by their eagerness to earn a livelihood.
Therefore, abandon such inappropriate friends and rely upon noble friends who are committed to Dharma.

In addition to bad guides, you should also be wary of bad friends who behave inappropriately. What defines such harmful company?

They are shallow, interested only in the worldly pursuits of this life, with no consideration for their future lives. If you associate with them, you will be influenced to engage in activities such as subduing enemies, protecting relatives, farming, trade, and similar endeavors, leading you further away from the Dharma.

If you involve yourself in the frivolous entertainments of the young, you will be swept away by distractions like songs, dances, and games that incite desire. Your mind will become inflamed with passion, setting the stage for your discipline to decline.

If you share the life of the laypeople, you will be interested only in their mundane activities—farming, profit-seeking, and the thirst for fame—and neglect the practice of Dharma.

Particularly, if you associate with businesspeople and traders, you will be drawn into deceptive practices aimed at securing maximum profit and amassing wealth.

If you associate with irritable people filled with animosity, their toxic influence—like the venom of a poisonous snake—will infect you, making you irascible.

If you surround yourself with people strongly attached to their kin ones, you will be consumed by the pursuit of food and clothing, leaving no time for spiritual practice, and your spiritual life will deteriorate.

Therefore, avoid bad company and seek the companionship of those who live in accordance with the Dharma.

–260–

Undesirable Spouses

Six flaws of relying upon a spouse who is a source of mishaps:
Even though you develop the thought of impermanence, your practice strays into laziness.
Even though you have faith and discernment, you do not find time to manifest them.
Even though you know that this ordinary life is meaningless, you cannot abandon worldly activities.
Even though you have profound instructions, your practice remains just a wish.
Even though you are greatly learned through listening and contemplation, you are unable to benefit yourself and others.
Even though you understand the ultimate view, you die an ordinary death.
You should be extremely careful not to end up in such circumstances.

If you choose to live with someone who behaves poorly, you will be contaminated by his or her conduct. What are the signs of such bad manners?

When the thought of death and impermanence arises in your mind, it should naturally lead you to practice the Dharma. However, if you [become caught up in household affairs and] fail to truly engage in practice, merely acknowledging impermanence without acting on it, you will find yourself mired in distraction and procrastination.

Even if you possess faith and intelligence, without diligent study, reflection, and meditation, these qualities will remain dormant and ineffective. Consequently, you will not find the path to liberation.

Ordinary activities focused on this life are futile. If you do not distance yourself from them, recognizing them as dreams and illusions, you will not taste the fruits of your practice.

You may have received many profound instructions, listening to them attentively and benefiting from the great kindness of your lama, but if you merely keep on telling yourself, "One day I will put all this into practice!" these teachings will remain mere aspirations. You will not enable you to dispel your deluded perceptions in this life, at the time of your death, or in the bardo, the intermediate state leading to your next existence.

All your study, all this pondering, all this knowledge of yours, will be of no value if it is not deeply integrated with your mind: you will be unable to free yourself from obscurations and afflictive mental states, and you will be of no help to others.

Even if you have some intellectual understanding that tells you, "This is the view of the true nature," without deep certainty in this view, you will die an ordinary death. There are so many who merely appear to be practitioners! In such cases, when the Dharma does not fulfill its function, it could even lead one to the lower realms. Pay close attention to all this!

–261–

The Traps of the Demons

Six aspects of the devious activities of demons:
The demon of possessions betrays those who crave wealth.
The demon of erudition betrays those who are learned.
The demon of privilege betrays those who are born into higher social classes.
The demon of past merit betrays those who gather wealth.
The demon of adverse circumstances betrays those who are filled with negative karma.
The demon of good repute betrays those who wish for fame.
Many are deceived in this way. You should not be carried away by these demons.

In this context, deception refers to deceiving oneself. This is what is meant by the traps set by the demon, Māra. Six of them are described here.

If you are strongly attracted by wealth and aspire to opulence, you will be dominated by greed for possessions. If, to achieve this, you engage in all kinds of deceit, dishonestly appropriating what has not been given to you, this is a trap of the demon.

If you have become very learned in the five traditional sciences and the demon of pride creeps into you because of these qualities, you will be led astray and be reborn in the lower realms.

If you are born into an influential family or one of high lineage and become convinced of your greatness and privilege over common people, to the point of exploiting them, this too is a trap of the demon.

If you are accompanied by a whole entourage, a plethora of disciples, or if you are in charge of a monastic community or lead a group of any kind, and become renowned for your knowledge and your power, becoming infatuated with it, the demon has infiltrated your past merit.

If you behave recklessly, taking the lives of others or jumping off a cliff yourself, the demon of adverse circumstances is at work. It can also manifest as disease, evil influences, and obstructive spirits.

Last, if you place great importance on worldly fame and seek notoriety, you have fallen into yet another of Māra's traps, for fame is nothing more than the hollow echo of worldly chatter.

Guarding against these six demons and many others is eminently desirable.

–262–

Becoming Impervious

Six pitfalls of becoming impervious to the Dharma caused by defective training:
Your mind remains ordinary with excessive activities and chatter.
Negative actions caused by delusion arise incessantly and repeatedly.
Holding the view that clings to a self, you engage in all kinds of actions of attachment and aversion.
Meditating on negative thoughts, wrong views arise continuously.

Regarding your conduct, you engage in various unvirtuous and non-Dharmic activities.
Your mind being resistant to Dharma, you are always carried away by this life's pursuits.
Impervious people like this squander their path to liberation.
Hence, abandon such bad habits caused by defective training.

Although you strive to perfect the qualities derived from the three trainings, if you do not do so properly, this flawed approach will lead you to become jaded in your Dharma practice.

If you persist in spinning myriads of ordinary thoughts in your head, accompanied by chatter, talking about politics and the like, your illusory activities will roll in like waves on the surface of water and your life will be exhausted before you see the end of these activities.

As for the view, unless you have realized emptiness, you will be caught up in self-grasping, attachment to your philosophical positions and hostility to other opinions, all of which will contaminate your view with fixation. You will find yourself in a dead end.

As for meditation, if you fall into a spirit of competition with others, genuine meditation cannot arise in your mind and you will wonder why you have no signs of accomplishment, why you do not feel any of the master's blessings. Doing so, you will constantly conceive adverse views.

Your conduct will be tainted with negativity and flaws, and you will commit all kinds of actions irreconcilable with the Dharma.

If all these imperfections infect your view, your meditation, and your behavior, no matter how many teachings you receive, you will simply say to yourself, "Well, the teacher said this and that" and not pay much attention. Falling into the grip of ordinary habits that only concern this present life, you will waste the path to liberation and omniscience, and remain resistant and impervious to the Dharma. These flaws create bad habits, and it is important to get away from them.

–263–

Avoid Mixing Vice and Virtue

Six situations mixing virtue with nonvirtue to be abandoned:
Do not rely upon a teacher who lacks the essence (of the pith instructions) and who fuels attachment and aversion.
Do not lead students who are unreceptive (to Dharma) and always look for (others') negativity and faults.
Do not accumulate nonvirtue and negative karma in the name of virtue.
Do not practice generosity while expecting respect and other benefits in return.
Do not make offerings of food and wealth to nurture friends and relatives instead of making offerings [to the Three Jewels].
Do not give Dharma discourses for the sake of deceptive interest in wealth.
If you listen to these pieces of advice, you will be in accord with the Dharma.

Mixing nonvirtue with virtue is like mixing poison with delicious food, or preparing barley or rice still full of small pebbles that make it inedible. Six undesirable mixtures are explained here:

With a guide who inwardly lacks the essence of the qualities of scholarship, virtue, and good nature, and outwardly is possessive of his disciples and hostile to other teachers and students, your character will never become pacified and controlled and you will remain impervious to any transformation by the Dharma. Do not follow such a guide!

If you accept unqualified disciples who, at gatherings in particular, constantly look for shortcomings in their teacher and fellow students, attachment, enmity, and futility will flourish, while the sacred commitments will be damaged. Beware of accepting such disciples.

Accumulating vices and faults means, for example, slaughtering large numbers of animals to celebrate a feast where meat and alcohol are offered in abundance. This might look like a righteous celebration, but in truth, it is pure negativity.

You might be generous, but with the aim to be praised or to receive a thousand after having given a hundred. Many gifts are thus made in the hope of receiving much more in return. Do not practice generosity in this way.

If you enjoy an abundance of goods and food and use it only to repeatedly cater to your relatives and friends, you will never disengage from your family ties and will not be able to practice the path of liberation. Abstain from such offerings.

Refrain from fooling others with various lies and dissimulation, from scheming to obtain favors from patrons to shamelessly using spiritual offerings made to you during empowerments or teachings.

If you follow these instructions and avoid these six ways of mixing nonvirtue and virtue, you will remain in harmony with the Dharma.

–264–

Contradictions

Six assumptions that contradict reality:
Assuming you are a Dharma practitioner although your mind has not turned away from ordinary worldly ways,
Assuming you are relying on a spiritual master despite lacking faith, respect, and service,
Assuming you are a great teacher without applying the Dharma to your own mind,
Assuming you are staying in solitude despite not abandoning clamor, distraction, and laziness,
Assuming you are practicing meditative concentration despite making no progress in inner development,
Assuming you are benefiting others although you have not assimilated the crucial points of Dharma practice,
Wise people should cast off these six contradictions.

There are six ways of pretending to behave in accordance with the Dharma when one is actually turning one's back on the path to liberation:

If your mind has not changed profoundly, if you have not engendered an unyielding determination to extricate yourself from the three worlds of samsara after having acquired a firm conviction on the inescapability of the laws of cause and effect, what is the point of posing as a Dharma practitioner, settling in a hermitage, and wearing monastic robes?

If you claim to follow a spiritual master, without faith and respect, without the desire to serve, without having developed the pure vision that perceives him as the Buddha in person and without the devotion that allows you to apprehend the excellence of all his actions, the master's blessings will not penetrate your mind, and you will be little more than a puppet practitioner.

You may have listened to hundreds of volumes of teachings and studied them, but if you have not integrated the qualities of the Dharma and they have not served as antidotes to the five poisons and other afflictive mental states that govern your mind, what is the point of posing as a learned scholar or great teacher?

If, without having rid yourself of distractions and laziness, you go to retreat centers or isolated monasteries, or surround yourself with disciples, you will continue to accumulate a host of desires and aversions. Such a hermit is nothing more than a vain facade.

You boast of having meditated for years, while not a single meditative experience or spiritual realization has blossomed in your mind, and you brag of having sealed the entrance to your retreat with mud: all of this is just pretense.

When practice has reached its goal, attachment to the self is cleared from the mind and the desire to benefit others arises from the depths of your being. If this is the case, the time has come to put yourself at the service of others. But until then, pretending to benefit others in various ways boils down to deceiving yourself and practicing hypocritical Dharma.

These six pretenses are all facades of a false Dharma. Wise practitioners will avoid them as much as possible.

–265–

Six Fallacies

Six fallacies that deceive you:

A false view deceives your mind;
Proclaiming [the view of] nonelaboration without confidence
to conform to what others say, is tantamount to deluding
yourself.

A false meditation deceives your mind;
An ignorant meditation based on assumptions cannot strike the crucial points.

False conduct deceives your mind;
Unrestrained and erratic behavior lacks carefulness.

False samaya deceives your mind;
It is hypocritical in observing precepts and does not restrain from negativities and downfalls.

False study and contemplation deceive your mind;
Their goal is to become a famous scholar and not to reach enlightenment.

A false fruition deceives your mind;
Not realizing the nature of mind, it expects a future fruition.

Therefore, not being carried away by these deceptions is crucial.

There are six ways a Dharma practitioner can pose, but they are just ways to fool the world.

Without having in the least realized the view of emptiness, to act as if this were the case and to open your eyes wide while staring into space, to pose as a great meditator or as a follower of the Great Perfection to acquire worldly notoriety, and to imitate others when talking about nonelaboration—all these actions amount to deceiving yourself and ensuring yourself a painful future in the three lower realms of samsara.

To boast of the number of months and years you spent in a mountain hermitage, without having integrated the crucial points of the practice, is to have indulged in foolish meditations like someone throwing stones or shooting arrows in the dark with little chance of hitting the target. You are only fooling yourself and this is not how meditative experiences and authentic realization will come about.

You are mistaken in both view and conduct if your attitude takes on the appearance of a virtuous scholar with a good character, giving the impression of being a renunciate free of activities, who has pacified his mind and mastered his emotions, and pretending to act with circumspection. Or worse still is if you get drunk and chase women or men under the pretext that you are a follower of the Secret Mantra, thus behaving in a wanton and reckless manner. This is called the "view of the dark demon let loose."

If you do not guard your samayas with sincere vigilance, you will conceive adverse views toward your teacher, doubt his instructions, and lack circumspection about faults and downfalls. If you pretend to observe the precepts of body, speech, and mind when you do not, you will only be deluding yourself.

Having studied much and elucidated the various philosophical tenets through reflection, if you do not engage in the practice that leads to buddhahood, you will not attain enlightenment. To aspire to fame for your learning will only result in deluding yourself.

The fruit of the view, meditation, and action is realization of the nature of the tathāgatagarbha, the essence of buddhahood, the ultimate nature of reality and of the mind. Lacking such realization, to pass as an accomplished being while leaving the realization as a mere wish, you go astray.

All these ways of deceiving yourself look like child's play. Be careful not to go in these directions!

–266–

Six Inappropriate Modes of Conduct

Six inappropriate actions to abandon:
Do not deceive others by making assumptions about the meaning of Dharma as this betrays the past masters' legacy.
Do not argue with your vajra kin as this will pollute your relationship with them.
Fearing the general laws of the land, do not engage in unvirtuous activities.
Do not accept bribes from others since this is like spreading poisonous vomit.
Do not ridicule Dharma and Dharma practitioners by making rules that are beyond your competence.
Stop engaging in worldly pursuits unless your master encourages you.
Accomplish buddhahood with Dharma for which you have received transmission and permission.

There are six behaviors in which it is inappropriate to engage and which therefore must be abandoned:

If your spiritual lineage is excellent, but you do not use that heritage in accordance with the teachings, if you neglect to make offerings to the master and the Three Jewels, if you do not practice virtue and instead behave in a reprehensible manner, these are all blameworthy behaviors.

Concerning your vajra brothers and sisters, your spiritual companions, disciples of the same master who share the same samaya, if you do not like them, if you slander them or speak to them in an unfriendly way, or if, even worse, you rob or kill them, as can be the case when two communities fight, all the inhabitants of the land, including insects, will go straight to hell, as the Buddha taught.[165] In essence, do not quarrel.

In a kingdom or state, the king or ruler establishes laws that must be respected. The same is true of the supreme Dharma: if you disregard it and do as you please, you will inevitably be in contradiction with it. Avoid these transgressions at all costs!

If an ill-mannered individual vomits in front of everyone, no one will think to eat that vomit. Similarly, soliciting or accepting bribes or any other form of enrichment related to corruption is like swallowing poisonous rejects. In general, it is best not to hope for rewards: if you have given a gift or done a favor for someone, do not blame them for not showing gratitude, and do not blame them for not doing you a favor in return.[166]

If you possess some legal knowledge, but lack sufficient expertise proficient in the laws of your land and, without gauging your own capacities, you impose new rules indiscriminately within your community, you will cover yourself and the Dharma with ridicule.

If someone beseeches you insistently, calling out your friendship, or if you are given no choice, you may have to put aside your practice of the path of liberation for a while, but do not let just anyone who tries interfere.

"Accomplish buddhahood with the teachings that have been transmitted to you and for which you have received permission" means that to practice the Dharma authentically, you must have been instructed to do so by your teacher and must have received the necessary empowerments. It is important to do this if your aim is to attain buddhahood.

–267–

Six Consequences of Remaining in Populated Places

Six disadvantages of going to crowded places for sincere Dharma practitioners:
Defiled by samaya violation, spiritual experience and blessings will evaporate.
Because negative emotions proliferate, you will break your vows and precepts related to the three trainings.
Because you break your promise, abundant adversities and obstacles will arise.
Tainted by delusive appearances, you will lose the dynamic energy of your view and meditation.
Debased by worldly dharmas, your mind will become resistant to the Dharma.
Influenced by past bad karma, you will end up as an ordinary householder.
Therefore, do not frequent laypeople's homes but live in solitary places.
Even if you occasionally visit, consider them to be prisons
And remain extremely cautious not to let your senses be distracted by objects.

Those who wish to practice the Dharma authentically must consider six harmful consequences of frequenting densely populated places.

If you stay alone in a mountain hermitage, you will be spared the obscurations that veil your meditative experiences. If you leave to go to places frequented by all kinds of laypeople, both good and bad, you may accumulate deteriorations of samaya. The blessings of the supreme yidam attainments and the ordinary attainments will vanish. Therefore, avoid cities and villages.

If you talk with many people, some will be happy to see you, others will not get along with you. As a result, all the qualities related to the observance of the precepts of the three trainings will be shattered. Avoid this!

What's more, if after promising to observe four periods of practice during the day, you mingle with many people, you will not be able to continue your practice, and obstacles and unfavorable circumstances will multiply. Don't fall victim to this!

If you are carried away by the deluded perceptions connected with the mundane aspects of ordinary life, you may find yourself in the grip of a household and distraction of all kinds, discussing business, setting up housekeeping, eating meat, and drinking liquor. The prosperity of your view, your meditation, and your conduct will vanish. Beware of all this! Otherwise, it is like ruining a brocade by dragging it in the dust. The Dharma and your mind will drift farther and farther apart.

Staying in such places for a long time, dragged by your bad karma, you will eventually get married and end up like an ordinary layperson without any practice of the sutras and the mantras. Therefore, avoid remaining in crowded places and stick to solitary sites. If by any chance you must go to a populated area, consider that you are in the king's prison, remain vigilant and beware of letting your senses be distracted. Proceed with caution.

–268–

Six Key Points of Practice

Aspects of practice summarized in six principles:
The fundamental nature of the view should culminate in buddhahood.
Regarding Dharma practice, skillfully strike the crucial points through the instructions.
Primordial wisdom-awareness should be established with essential logical reasoning.
The vital point of generating (spiritual experience) must rest with liberation when subject meets object.
Bring all practice together within the unchanging continuum of mind's nature.
Embrace all phenomena within the Great Perfection.
When these decisive points are struck, enlightenment is accomplished in this life.

These six instructions summarize all aspects of the path for those engaged in the practice of the supreme Dharma.

The view, first of all, is the Buddha's vision as it is. The view is said to be pure and perfect if it is free from misunderstanding and delusion. You must see whether you are able to realize it.

As for the essential instructions on practice, they are intended to dispel all obstacles [to realization], to facilitate all forms of progress, and to enable you to move quickly through the paths and bhūmis. So, you must identify them and go straight to the crucial points.

If you correctly understand the nature of the primordial wisdom of awareness and if your understanding contradicts neither the words of the Buddha nor the essential instructions of the masters nor the textual sources and logical reasoning of the scholars, that is excellent! You will then be in conformity with the decisive demonstrations based on the scriptures and on reason.

As your meditative experience develops, you must beware of complacency and pride. You should liberate other afflictive mental states at the very moment your mind encounters them.

The root of all phenomena is the unchanging nature of mind. Everything must be brought back to the continuum of this nature. It is important to integrate this vital point.

Whatever teachings you practice, the ultimate point of all of them is comprehended in the Great Perfection.

If you strike the vital points of these instructions, you can attain buddhahood in this very life.

–269–

Laying the Foundation

Instructions on laying the six foundations:
To lay the foundation of wisdom, engage in listening and contemplation.
To lay the foundation of Mahāyāna, train in bodhicitta.
To lay the foundation of blessings, look for a pure practice lineage.
To lay the foundation of realization, recognize the nature of mind.
To lay the foundation of positive qualities, unite devotion with diligence.
To lay the foundation of happiness, abandon samsara.
In this way, follow the enlightened activities of the noble ones.

If you plan to build a beautiful house, you must start by building solid foundations. Likewise, for Dharma, laying sound foundations in a proper way is crucial.

To begin with, when you engage in the Dharma, lay the foundation of knowledge by thoroughly studying the content of the teachings that you are going to put into practice. Then clarify your doubts and misunderstandings through reflection until perfect certainty takes shape in your mind.

When you approach the path of the Great Vehicle, its root is benevolence magnified by bodhicitta, the altruistic wish to attain enlightenment for the sake of all beings. You must maintain the continuity of this practice without fail.

If you practice correctly, you will surely be filled with blessings. Now, the foundation of these blessings is found in an excellent spiritual lineage, at each step of which the samayas have remained undamaged.

To lay the foundation for meditative experiences and realization, you must realize the empty nature of mind. The life force of all practice lies in this point.

Spiritual qualities will flourish only if you combine confidence and diligence, the two legs that allow you to walk easily on a path. If such is the case, this life will be happy and the following ones as well. As the omniscient Jigme Lingpa said,

> Well-being in this life results from the compassion of the Three Jewels.
> A good destiny in future lives results from your spiritual practice.[167]

Practice in an authentic way, in accordance with these words, forsaking the activities of the three worlds of samsara and following the example set by the masters of the past, such as Jetsun Milarepa and many others.

–270–

Do Not Hoard

Six shortcomings of hoarding wealth and property:
As the support of the five poisons, wealth and property increase negative emotions of attachment and aversion.

Bound by stinginess, you will accumulate negative karma that leads to rebirth in hungry ghost realms.
Carried away by worldly dharmas, you will be separated from the path to enlightenment.
Your life will be wasted in worries about increasing and protecting your wealth and property.
You will stray from practicing Dharma and invite blame from gods and humans.
It is a demonic obstacle that can cost your life.
Therefore, those who practice sublime Dharma
Should abandon accumulating and increasing wealth.

A practitioner of the sublime Dharma should avoid accumulating many possessions and hoarding wealth. Otherwise, six defects will ensue.

The more wealth you accumulate and hoard, the more your grasping for your own possessions will grow and the more envy and animosity you will feel toward those who are richer than you. The defects also result from poor judgment that leads to cheating others in various ways and feeding the five mental poisons. The stains of greed and hostility will only spread. One characteristic of wealth is that the more it grows, the more torment it creates. Wealth also causes you to accumulate the karma that leads to rebirth among the spirits suffering from greed and neediness, the pretas. Once rich, you will be tied to the ordinary world and entangled in the eight worldly dharmas, tormented by avarice and the desire for deference from others. All this amounts to turning your back on the path of enlightenment.

Moreover, you will never have enough, and the endless pursuit of wealth will prevent you from learning the Dharma. You will use all sorts of schemes to increase your possessions, and you will fear that enemies or wrongdoers will acquire them. You will also suffer from not getting some particularly coveted good, or from losing anything to others. In this way, you will exhaust your life without enjoying the opportunity to practice the Dharma.

If you wish to integrate the Dharma into your mind, you will have to be careful and vigilant, the same vigilance that, when applied to the accumulation of wealth, turns your back on the Dharma and makes men and gods say of you, "How greedy! How covetous and belligerent! You look like the beast that guards the treasures of tortured spirits!"[168]

What is more, the richer you are, the more numerous your enemies will be. Your wealth can even endanger your life, as thieves and other types of criminals might kill you. You could also be the target of sanctions enacted by the rulers.

In short, if you aspire to practice the Dharma, stay as far away as possible from activities related to acquiring, preserving, and increasing wealth.

–271–

A Sublime Family

Six family members to be perfectly chosen:
For a sublime father, look for the unchanging dharmadhātu.
For a sublime mother, look for the naturally arising primordial wisdom.
For a sublime child, look for the child of naturally arising pristine awareness.
For a sublime partner, look for the state of union and inseparability.
For sublime wealth, look for the precious gem of the mind's nature.
For a sublime dwelling, look for the pure realms of the Three Kāyas.
If these are gathered, you will reach the ultimate land of pristine awareness.

If you are going to have a family, you might as well make it flourish by including members as perfect as possible. These verses compare the various family members to six aspects of the sublime Dharma.

Look for an ideal father in the true nature of unchanging absolute space, emptiness. Such a father will never let you down!

As for your sublime mother, you will find her in the luminous wisdom that has spontaneously arisen. She will never leave you.

The sublime child is none other than the spontaneously born infant, in whom wisdom and compassion are united. Take good care of him.

The sublime companion is found in the nondual union, which ignores all decline.

Sublime wealth is the jewel of the true nature of mind. Once you become familiar with it, all your aspirations will naturally be accomplished.

The sublime abode will be found by securing rebirth in the pure lands of the three kāyas—the dharmakāya, the saṃbhogakāya, and the nirmāṇakāya—where you will go from bliss to bliss.

If you gather all the members of such a family, you will have reached the citadel of awareness and if you maintain this same family, you will never again stray into the three worlds of samsara but will go from bliss to bliss.

–272–

Following the Tradition

Six ways to anchor your practice within the tradition:
As an escort in samsara, practice taking refuge.
As the activity of cultivation, engage in virtuous activities.
As a swift mount of horse, engage in the practice of method.
As precious treasures, engage in gathering the two accumulations.
To increase profit, practice the qualities of the (stages and paths).
As nutritious food and drink, enjoy the instructions.
Whoever acts like this will uphold the lineage of the past masters.

Establishing your practice within an authentic tradition in six ways is like forming an excellent estate, surrounded by vast fertile land.

First of all, to protect yourself from the enemies and thieves of the three worlds of samsara, take refuge. This will allow you to free yourself from the sufferings of the cycle of existences, those of the lower realms in particular.

As for working the land, cultivate the field of the ten Dharmic activities, doing prostrations, circumambulations, and meditating on the certain and deep meaning of samādhi. By doing so, your spiritual qualities will increase.

On your estate, you may have a very fast horse. Similarly, by practicing the path of the Secret Mantra of the Adamantine Vehicle, you will be galloping on the fast track [to enlightenment].

For the supreme wealth that ensures you will never be destitute, carry out the dual accumulation of merit and wisdom. These two accumulations will never leave you and will allow your spiritual qualities to increase throughout your future lives.

Instead of profit and income from ordinary commerce, enjoy the abundance generated by Dharma practice. At best, you will be able to reap it every day, in the middle case every month, and at least every year.

Just as you have an appetite for nutritious and delicious food and wish to quench your thirst, if you aspire to put the instructions of your spiritual master into practice daily, your qualities will blossom with each passing day.

Those who practice in this way uphold the lineage of the victorious ones of the past and will become equal to the masters of old.

–273–

Integrating Awareness on the Path

Six instructions for taking pristine awareness onto the path:

Sometimes, consider your favorable conditions and friends;
Understand that they reflect your subjective perceptions, and they will enhance your meditative experience.

Sometimes contemplate the appearance of adverse and harmful conditions;
They are crucial for developing disenchantment with delusion.

Sometimes examine your friends' and other people's teachers;
If you know what is positive and negative, you will be encouraged to practice.

Sometimes look at the magical display of the four elements within space;
You will realize that all efforts collapse within the nature of mind.

Sometimes observe the mansions and wealth in your locality;
By knowing them to be illusory, disenchantment toward delusive appearances will arise.

Sometimes note the entourage, wealth, and properties of others;

By perceiving others as objects of compassion, you will abandon attachment to samsara.

In short, by examining the nature and multiplicity of phenomena that appear,
Your grasping at intrinsic existence and your delusion will be dismantled.

This is followed by six instructions for integrating the experience of awareness into the path and bringing it to a culmination. It is also known as "reading in the book of phenomena."

Sometimes examine how you perceive favorable conditions, the sublime masters, and your vajra brothers and sisters. As their blessings enter you, if you can recognize that this is your own phenomenal world, your contemplative experience will progress.

As you contemplate the deeds of a supreme master, you will keep his life of perfect liberation clearly in mind. Likewise, by witnessing the spiritual practice of your excellent spiritual companions, your practice will benefit as well.

Contemplate adversity, those who harm you through enmity, the negative forces that create interruptions, and other troubles. See how all that has been accumulated ends up being dispersed and that which was high falls to the lowest point; see how all birth ends in death and how all that was united becomes separated. Tell yourself that the delusory appearances of the three worlds of samsara are entirely devoid of substance. In disgust, you will have no other aspiration than to escape from them.

Sometimes consider your virtuous friends and those who are less virtuous, observe the qualities of the genuine masters of other disciples and the defects of those who lack these qualities. When you see excellent qualities in others, say to yourself, "This is the way of liberation," and you will strive to achieve such qualities. Noting their faults, tell yourself, "These are the faults to avoid," and this will spur you to practice.

Sometimes imagine the transformations of the elements within space, the formation of Mount Meru and the four continents, and their destruction by water and fire. Contemplate the specific changes of each season, the transformations of spring, summer, fall, and winter. Despite all these transformations, space itself never changes. Likewise, whatever the fantasies of deluded thoughts may be, as soon as the struggles associated with them dissolve into the continuum of the ultimate reality, you will know their true nature.

At other times, observe the homes and riches of your land: how were they in the time of your youth, in your middle age, and how are they today in the time of your old age? The well-being of yesteryear is no more, and what was suffering then has also changed. You will understand that the things of this life are but illusions. If you stop paying attention to these deceptive perceptions, you will feel a deep revulsion for delusion.

Sometimes contemplate the wealth and the possessions of others. Some people strive relentlessly to accumulate so much! But they fail and die before reaching their goals. See these people as objects of compassion and abandon all attraction to samsara.

Others are dominated by the greed and animosity of acquiring wealth and sometimes end up losing their lives for it. Others try to become rich dishonestly and are punished by rulers. Others have all their possessions violently stolen by brigands and are plunged into despair.

Contemplating the plight of all these lost beings, and filled with great compassion for them, you will no longer feel the slightest attraction for the three worlds of samsara and will abandon all craving.

In short, as it is said, "The true book is not written in ink on paper but on the phenomena of the outer world." If you grasp that the vast multiplicity of phenomena arises as an illusion through the interplay of interdependence, the mistaken attachment to the reality of things cannot but collapse.

–274–

Observe with Lucidity

Instructions for observing clearly:
Look at the changing four seasons, the outer appearances;
Sadness due to impermanence will arise, and you will only be making short-term worldly plans.[169]

Look at benefit being repaid with harm;
You will develop extraordinary revulsion from the heart.

Look at others who engage in acts driven by attachment and aversion;

You will develop intense renunciation and see the futility of all efforts.

Look at children who were nurtured, not repaying their parents' kindness;
You will expect less from others.

Look at the rich who passed away naked;
You will develop weariness with material possessions and friends.

Look at the kindness of your lama who is your guide on the path to liberation;
Devotion and respect from the heart will arise and lead to the welling of tears.

In this way, examine carefully the delusive conditions of pleasure and pain
And generate renunciation and disenchantment.

Here are six instructions to help you advance your practice by carefully examining the nature of external phenomena.

Contemplating the passage of the four seasons, you can see how when one season arrives the features of the previous one change or disappear, pointing out the impermanence of all things. If, for example, some of your activities are linked to spring or any another season, you will realize that you can only continue them for three months in that season. This will help you to make only short-term plans and to destroy your attachment to the permanence of things.

Sometimes, you help your parents and relatives, while leaders come to the aid of their fellow citizens, but in return, the recipients show nothing but hostility. It happens that people rebel violently against their rulers, children kill their parents. Meditating on the madness of the activities of the three worlds of samsara, a powerful feeling of renunciation will arise from the depths of your heart like never before.

For no sensible reason, nations become overly focused on their own affairs and become hostile toward other countries. This leads to wars and conflicts.

Consider how many people have died prematurely before they could accomplish their goals. With an overwhelming sense of renunciation, understand that you do not need all the things and activities of ordinary life.

Too often, children whose parents have taken great care of them since their early childhood turn against them and do not show the slightest tenderness toward them. It is therefore better not to entertain too much hope by expecting that your children, your parents, your relatives, and your friends will treat you well simply because you have shown them affection.

As for the wealthy, at the time of death, they will have no choice but to leave behind the body they pampered so much, while their consciousness will leave for an unknown destination like a poor, lonely, naked man who crosses his arms over his chest, his hands under his armpits. What is the point of forging so many attachments to your loved ones and possessions that you will have to leave behind and that will not be of any help to you on the day you die?

Contemplate, in contrast, the immense goodness of the spiritual master, your guide on the path to liberation. Those who have integrated the qualities of the supreme Dharma are noble guides. When they abide in the lower realms of samsara, their qualities do not decline in any way, and they accomplish the good of beings. The most benevolent person, the one to whom we should be most grateful, is the lama, the noble spiritual friend who inspires you to virtue and is the source of all qualities. Thinking of the kindness of the spiritual master, tears of fervent devotion will come to your eyes.

Do the conditions that cause the joys and sufferings of the three worlds of samsara last? Have you been able to fulfill all your aspirations? Ask yourself these questions and you will become weary and disillusioned with samsara.

–275–

Six Observations to Consider from Time to Time

Six things to carefully consider from time to time:

Sometimes consider the physical actions of yourself and others;
You will perceive them as illusory as the performance of actors.

Sometimes listen to the sounds of your words;

You will hear them as inexpressible and resounding yet empty,
like an echo.

Sometimes reflect on the joy and pain that arise in your mind;
You will see them as the play of pristine awareness, and reality
will dawn within.

Sometimes look directly at the face of moving conceptual thoughts;
You will see them vanish, and naked dharmakāya will appear.

Sometimes observe the nature of mind in its unwavering state;
You will see it empty of all mental activity, and the realization of
the exhaustion (of phenomena) will dawn.

Sometimes gaze at open presence free from deliberate seeking;
You will see nonaction and joy will spring from your inner
depths.

Those who know all this are adepts in the profound meaning.

Now come six instructions for carefully examining your own mind, which favor meditative experiences and realization:

Think back to what you did in your youth, middle age, and old age; then similarly consider the actions of others: Does it not all look like a play? Little has been accomplished in accordance with your wishes. In fact, the events of this world have no more reality than dreams!

Try to think of everything you have said from childhood to the present. Remember the praise you have received. What are the fruits of that today? Remember the criticisms that you have received. What are the consequences today? All these sounds will appear to you as the resonance of emptiness, as echoes. Then move on to the practice that leads you to realize the ineffable.

Sometimes, think of all the joys you have had since your mother gave you birth; then all your sufferings. Have your joys been a source of lasting satisfaction? Have your sorrows tormented you forever? If, at the end of this examination, you perceive all these joys and sorrows as the unfolding of awareness, the understanding of the simplicity of the unchanging nature of all things will emerge.

At other times, contemplate the spectacle of thoughts swarming in all directions; notice how you are influenced by your habitual tendencies and how you project yourself into the future. Then look at the nature of pure awareness of the present moment, the very awareness you have lost in distraction. These mental constructs, as many as they are, vanish as soon as they are formed. In truth, they have no intrinsic power to do you any good or harm. The seat of their birth, presence, and disappearance is the nature of mind, the unchanging nature of the absolute dimension, the dharmakāya. Contemplate this nature in all its nakedness.

Sometimes, look at the natural presentation of the mind, as it is, in its fundamental nature, without wavering. The comings and goings of discursive thoughts will vanish like clouds in space and the realization of the exhaustion of phenomena in the dharmatā will manifest.

At other times, rest imperturbably in the equality of natural simplicity and contemplate the perfect absence of action. Aware of the futility of endless activities, abide in the perfect rest of the pristine nature, and a serene ease will emerge.

Those who grasp these points will become experts in the deep meaning of the Great Perfection.

–276–

Six Points to Contemplate Conscientiously

Six points to perfectly ponder:
Be ready for the battle with birth, old age, sickness, and death.
Repay your past karmic debts today.
Flee the fearful narrow ravines of subject and object.
Cast off the burden of sin and its ripening effect.
Accomplish the path of liberation and enlightenment within this life for it is certain to be exhausted.
Prepare to cross the great mountain pass of death.
If you do all of this, you will reach the shore of liberation.

There are six points that you need to ponder, clarify, and implement.

How much suffering have the battles of birth, old age, illness and death inflicted on you to this day? You must therefore prepare for those coming ahead, and then ultimately reach the state that transcends them.

In your past lives, you harmed others and stole their property. As a result of your karma, you are now subject to illness, negative influences, obstacles, theft, and other difficulties. All these trials are nothing but payments for your karmic debts. If, instead of doing harm in return, you engender bodhicitta and exchange their suffering for your happiness, you will purify these debts.

The duality of subject and object and the clinging to these notions are transitory and dreamlike. Once you have entered the ravines of subject and object, getting out is very difficult. Do everything possible to escape these dreaded gorges.

From time immemorial until now, through a myriad of existences, you have carried the burden, as heavy as a mountain, of the ripening of your past misdeeds. Apply the antidote of the four powers of confession and see if you can rid yourself of this persistent burden once and for all.

Life is destined to run out and from the moment you are born from your mother's womb, each day you live brings you closer to death. In vain do you wish to lengthen it at will. But if, from now until the day of your death, you use this existence to advance on the path of liberation and enlightenment, your life will have taken on its full meaning. Do not be distracted, do not get scattered! When the day of death arrives, you will have to pass this great milestone, like crossing a high mountain pass while carrying a heavy load. You will be rightly distraught. That is why you must ask yourself morning, noon and evening what method you will be able to use when death comes. This is how you will reach the firm ground of liberation.

–277–

Let It All Go

Six sublime dharmas for all becoming clear [in ultimate reality]:
Driven by revulsion, let go entirely of samsara [in absolute space].
Relying on diligence, let go entirely into the practice [of the natural state].
Praying with respectful devotion, let yourself go entirely [into the ultimate dimension] of the spiritual master.
Within the samaya, let yourself go fully [into the essence of] the approach and accomplishment of the yidam.

> **Diligently offering tormas and gaṇacakra, let yourself go entirely [into the absolute space] of the ḍākinī.**
> **With the help of the profound instructions, let yourself go entirely [into the unique sphere of] view and meditation.**
> **By doing so, you will quickly attain the ultimate siddhi.**

The expression "letting go" applies, for example, to a thief who, suffering from being bound hand and foot, finally "let go" or gives up, confesses his misdeeds, and tells the truth.

Here you should forsake samsara by regarding all the ordinary activities of the three worlds with as much disinterest and disgust as vomit. Once you have thus let samsara go from your sphere of concern, you will no longer have any attraction to it.

If driven by diligence, you continuously stimulate your body, speech, and mind, you will never part from spiritual practice.

If the respectful fervor that perceives the spiritual teacher as the Buddha himself keeps arising in your mind, you will completely let yourself go in the nature of the teacher. It is said that "the master cannot resist the call of devotion." Indeed, if you are filled with devotion, the blessings of the master are bound to come to you.

If, while preserving a perfectly pure samaya, you continuously devote yourself to the approach and accomplishment [belonging to the practices of visualizations and recitation of the development stage], you will surely receive the ordinary and extraordinary siddhis of the yidam.

If you persevere in offering tormas and sacred feasts (*gaṇacakras*), the activities of the ḍākinīs and Dharma protectors cannot fail to be accomplished.

If you integrate, repeatedly, the crucial points of the view and of the meditation instructions, especially those of the Great Perfection, the understanding of the ultimate reality, the dharmatā, will arise without error in your mind.

Those who practice in this way will quickly attain accomplishment.

–278–

Six States of Equality

Six states of equality to be perfectly known:
Knowing all beings of the six realms to be your parents, equalize your enemies and your children.
Knowing the delusive appearances of wealth, equalize gold and a lump of clay.
Knowing the lack of true existence of cause and effect, equalize merit and nonmerit.
Knowing the ultimate nature of the six consciousnesses, the dharmatā, equalize the meditative and post-meditative states.
Knowing the negative emotions to be primordial wisdom, equalize the nonexistence of abandoning and adopting.
The ultimate nature being primordially pure, know the equality of samsara and nirvana.
The recognition of these equalities is the great yoga.

Recognizing the perfect equality of all phenomena is the ultimate realization. This ultimate meaning of equality is realized through direct experience. According to the path of the vehicle associated with characteristics, it is only when reaching the eighth bhūmi that the sameness of all phenomena is fully realized.

In the Adamantine Vehicle of the Secret Mantra, one speaks of the view of the indivisibility of "great purity" and "great equality."[170] What exactly does the great equality refer to? As soon as you stop discriminating between the notions of enemies and dear ones when considering all beings of the six realms and when you see them all as your mothers and fathers, you will be free from excessive attachment to your children and aversion to harmful enemies. This is the equality that you must actualize.

On the other hand, whatever possessions come to you, remain free of attachment, considering them to be delusory perceptions; persevere until you no longer make any distinction between a bar of gold and a pile of pebbles or dirt.

Within the ultimate nature of reality, there is no such thing as cause and effect. At this level, virtue is no more beneficial than vice is harmful, since the ultimate reality, the dharmatā, is like space.

The perceptions formed by the various aspects of consciousness that apprehend forms, sounds, smells, tastes, and textures should not lead to attachment if they seem good to you or to aversion if they seem bad. You must make sure that this "good" and "bad" cannot deceive your pristine awareness, nor thwart your vigilance and balance, in which meditation and post-meditation are united.

If you understand the true nature of the five mental poisons, the five primordial wisdoms will shine through. It is therefore important to know the equality of acceptance and rejection.

When you consider the primordial purity of the dharmatā, you will realize that the habitual tendencies and the afflictive mental states of samsara need not be eliminated as imperfections, and that the nirvana-related dispositions, kāyas, and wisdoms are not to be acquired as something new. Indeed, nirvana, the state beyond suffering, is primordially perfect in our nature. The basis of samsara and nirvana is never corrupted. One who realizes this equality is a yogi of the Great Perfection.

–279–

Disengagement

Six instructions on disengagement:
When you realize the lack of intrinsic existence in whatever appears, you will not be engaged with delusive appearances.
When you realize the meaningless nature of whatever you do, you will not be engaged with worldly dharmas.
When you realize selfish interests to be deviations, you will not be attracted to the lower vehicle.
When you realize the unborn nature of the ground, you will not care about arising and ceasing.
When you realize the nonreferential nature of mind, you will not be fixated on conceptual attributes.
When you realize the dharmatā to be beyond action, you will not be engaged with effort and achievement.
These signs of realization appear naturally when you apprehend the ultimate nature of reality.

If you realize that everything that appears is of an illusory and dreamlike nature, you will not be inclined to engage in deceptive worldly activities and will not be interested in what concerns this present life only.

To carry out all the activities, words, and cogitations motivated by the eight worldly concerns is impossible. If you understand that such concerns are meaningless, you will not toil to defeat your enemies and protect your kin.

If you continually think just about yourself and remain polarized on your fate, this is the attitude of the listeners and solitary realizers. Do not deviate from the path of the Great Vehicle.

The basis of the ultimate nature of reality, the dharmatā, is unborn. Having realized this, you will avoid engaging in fabricating concepts of origin and cessation that serve no purpose.

If you grasp the view of the dharmatā free of representations, you will avoid entangling yourself in all sorts of concepts such as "mind is permanent" or "mind is empty," since the ultimate reality is not something that can be manufactured in any way. If you understand "nonaction," you will not engage in the laborious search for accomplishment.

The sign of having realized the fundamental nature of all is that you will naturally avoid engaging in these six ways of going astray.

–280–

Avoiding Sheepish Conformity

Six instructions on not being carried away by sheepish conformity with others:

Do not let your (practice of) bringing everything on to the path sheepishly conform to that of others, but instead, subdue your gross and subtle conceptual thoughts.

Do not let your (journey on) the paths and bhūmis sheepishly conform to that of others, but instead remove the two obscurations.

Do not let your (practice of) cause and effect sheepishly conform to that of others, but instead adopt virtue and discard nonvirtue.

> **Do not let your meditation sheepishly conform to that of others, but instead (abide in) natural clarity free from grasping.**
> **Do not let your conduct sheepishly conform to that of others, but instead direct your activities to Dharma.**
> **Do not let your conduct sheepishly conform to that of others, but take as your example the life of perfect liberation of the sublime masters of the past.**
> **Those who succeed at this will accomplish the essence of sublime Dharma.**

As has just been taught, it is very valuable to correctly realize the view of the true nature of things, not merely by hearsay or approximation.[171] So now come six pieces of advice not to rush into what others say and just pretend to understand what it is about, which is a faulty way of practicing.

When it comes to bringing afflictive mental states as well as joy and suffering onto the path, if you merely proclaim that you are bringing them onto the path when actually you are not, you are just sheepishly imitating others without understanding what you are doing. Instead, strive to bring all thoughts, gross and subtle, onto the path without falling under their power. By doing so, you will remain in control.

Telling yourself, "I have completed the five paths and reached the tenth bhūmi; I have insight and have obtained the signs of accomplishment," when these are merely impressions on your part, will not do you much good. What you must do is evaluate how thoroughly you have removed the veil of afflictive mental states and the veil that obscures all that can be known.

You may also imagine that you are paying attention to the laws of causality, when this is only empty words, for at the slightest alarm you tremble with fear. You had better avoid negative acts and never abandon virtue even at the cost of your life, clearly distinguishing between what must be done and what must be avoided.

"I have meditated for so many years, I had such and such a meditative experience and I have reached realization." Do not give in to this kind of inflated caricature of your practice. What you need to achieve is the realization of the true nature, spontaneously luminous and free from grasping.

As for your conduct, it must be adapted to time and circumstances. If you engage in worldly activities in the most ordinary way, without checking whether they truly catalyze progress in your spiritual experience, they will not help you. As recommended in the root verses, your actions must therefore be in accordance with the supreme Dharma.

As for the spiritual masters, telling yourself that their manners seem to be those of the exalted beings is not enough. You must make sure that this is indeed the case and that their conduct and way of being conform with the life of perfect liberation of the supreme masters of the past.

If you follow this advice, you will be practicing the essence of the Dharma.

–281–

Six Mistakes

Six instructions to avoid six faults:
There is nothing more to do than to realize the view,
But be aware of the flaws of a practice that is nothing more than words.
Identify (and avoid) the fault of stagnating complacently in a meditation that merely abides in ordinary clarity.
Identify (and avoid) as well a concentration that, even if stable, lacks clarity and sinks into drowsiness.
Strongly holding to (a mental object of concentration) may generate the warmth of spiritual experience,
But it is important to recognize its partial nature.
While focusing on an object, many subtle thoughts may swarm in the background:
Be alert to the danger posed by the thieves that are conceptual thoughts.
You may stem the five negative emotions while meditating,
But if they resurface with force once your meditation is over, the defect lies in not having uprooted them.
Moreover, recognize that you have not realized the nature of mind.
After identifying these faults, use the antidotes to free yourself from them.

Next come instructions on six mistakes to avoid. What are they?

First, if you understand the view correctly, the meaning of emptiness, that is enough. Once you understand emptiness, there is nothing else to do.

But if your realization of emptiness amounts to mere words and you bask in "nonaction," you will waste your human life in vain. You need to identify such a misconception.

You may relax into meditation as it presents itself, but you must also prevent the demon of conceit from creeping into you and detect the rise of self-importance that makes you think, "Meditative experiences and realization have taken birth in me; I have achieved accomplishments, including the gift of clairvoyance."

If, failing to identify the clarity aspect of meditation, you sink into the turbidity of śamatha and stagnate in the daze of an inert calm abiding, you will not transcend the sphere of the ordinary world. Therefore, you must identify the deviation associated with the wandering of discursive thoughts that brings forth mental grasping.

If you do some practice, observe the discipline and obtain satisfaction from it. Even if you experience some signs of progress on the path, such as "warmth," acquiring approximate qualities is not enough. Develop spiritual perfections to their fullest extent, not only "fragments" of them, which is the meaning of the word *kortse.*[172] Identifying this defect is important.

If you contemplate the view of the equality of dharmatā, you need not make efforts to acquire something more nor to discard anything else. All phenomena belong to a single essence. If dual thoughts proliferate, however, you will be carried away by mental fabrications: these are the thieves you should be wary of.

When you remain in the equanimity of meditation, you might be merely hushing the five poisons so they remain silent for a while, only for these afflictive mental states to reappear with force as soon as you leave your meditation, revealing that you have not eradicated them. Keep checking to see if they are still present in your mind. Otherwise, merely remaining in meditative evenness will not enable you to eliminate disturbing emotions once and for all. In fact, until all phenomena are exhausted in dharmatā, you need to guard yourself against these afflictive mental states and call upon the appropriate antidotes to free yourself from them.

–282–

Six Decisive Experiences

Six decisive experiences that can free you from samsara:

The fundamental nature is beyond the conceptual mind,
At the time of the ground, you conceptualize mind's phenomena.

When the mind fixates upon an object and grasps it, it falls into samsara,
On the path, do not cultivate conceptual experience.

In the state of purity, one cannot speak of "benefiting" sentient beings at the time of fruition,
As samsara and nirvana are not two separate entities.[173]

Awareness, the foundation of the true nature, is not contaminated by the conceptual mind,
Being free from elaboration, it is not an object of knowledge.

Beyond knowing and grasping, it is the authentic path,
Free from all reference points of recollection, thinking, and seeking.

The ultimate fruition does not fixate on reference points,
It is free from obscuration, unadulterated, naturally clear, and does not lean in any direction.

The one who realizes this is a supreme yogi with a vast mind.

The term *decisive* (*ladawa, la bzla ba*) refers to gaining a clear conviction through direct experience. Here are presented six decisive experiences that enable you to free yourself from the three worlds of samsara:

If you fully realize the fundamental nature of all things, you will transcend the realm of the intellect and attachment to the notions of subject and object.

If you examine what happens at the level of the ground, you will find that mental phenomena are the product of intellectual fabrications. When meditative experiences arise in your mind, check to see if you have any attachment to them. If you do, you are in the three worlds of samsara, which is undesirable.

On the path, do not fixate on meditative experiences. It is realization that should be actualized within the great sameness.

To adopt faultless, perfectly pure behavior of body, speech, and mind, realize the nonduality of samsara and nirvana.

At the time of the fruition, you cannot strictly speak of "accomplishing" the good of sentient beings.

This fundamental nature of your own pristine awareness uncontaminated by the intellect is not knowable through words and writings, for it is free from mental elaborations.

From the general point of view of the Great Vehicle, the mind confined to samsara cannot know the crucial points of the perfect path, which is free from grasping, from cogitations, and from any target or goal.

The supreme goal is free from all characteristics and representations. Therefore, if you realize the meaning that transcends all references, you will dwell in the immaculate and perfect authenticity, luminous and unbiased.

Whoever understands these points is a great yogi with a vast mind, endowed with all the signs of the Great Perfection.

–283–

Six Realizations

The nature of six realizations:
Realization induced by the words of others, like the instructions of your spiritual teacher.
Realization of the lack of intrinsic existence, of the illusory nature, induced by objects the mind apprehends.
Realization of absolute, baseless expanse induced by mind, the apprehending subject.
Realization of the unobscured and naked state induced by the true face of pristine awareness.
Realization that the mind is free from all extremes induced by seeing the ultimate meaning.

Realization that the ground is the state of resolution induced by confidence in meditation and exhaustion [of an object and act of meditation].
Whoever possesses these realizations will achieve the space-like wisdom.
Free from the notion of action and actor, you will be spontaneously accomplished in the primordial nature.

What are those six realizations?

Listening to the sound of Dharma allows you to truly understand the ultimate nature of reality, especially when a spiritual master describes the nature of your mind and instructs you to observe it for yourself. If, at that time, his words enable you to understand the nature of mind as it is, these are called "essential instructions" (*upadeśa*).

If you understand the nature of external phenomena, after examining them repeatedly, you will naturally realize that they are devoid of true existence and are like illusions.

If you realize the nature of the mind that grasps onto these objects, you will see that it is similar to space, devoid of any root, birth, abiding, and cessation.

If you realize the true nature of pristine awareness, you will see the open presence of *rigpa*, the mind in its original nakedness, stripped of all veils.

If you repeatedly apprehend what "seeing" means here, you will transcend the realm of conceptual thinking and fixation on the notions of subject and object.

When you grasp the meaning of meditation, the notions of birth and death will be exhausted in the dharmatā.

For whoever realizes this, the wisdom mind will be spontaneously accomplished in the space of its original nature, beyond action and actor.

–284–

Six Obstacles of the Demons

Six obstacles created by demons:
Abandoning your spiritual master, you rely on bad friends.
Abandoning enlightenment, you follow the paths of samsara.
Abandoning your own good, you pretend to accomplish that of others.

Abandoning renunciation—needing nothing—you engage in the eight worldly dharmas.
Abandoning solitary places, you become lost in clamor and distraction.
Abandoning nonduality, you cling to reference points and words.
Such a practitioner is blessed by the demons.
These obstacles will lead to suffering in this and future lives, and to the loss of the ultimate purpose.

What are those six obstacles of the demons?

If you abandon an authentic teacher to spend time with friends who indulge in bad behavior, you are turning your back on the path to liberation.

If you cannot make yourself diligently pursue the Dharma that achieves liberation and enlightenment but instead follow the path of ordinary samsaric activities, you will be deluded.

If you neglect the accomplishment of your own good, under the pretext of apparently devoting yourself to benefiting others, even before you have acquired the qualities that result from eliminating all aspects of delusion and realizing all accomplishments, you will only destroy your own good.

If you do not abandon the ordinary activities of this world, truly convinced that they are perfectly vain, and direct your efforts to the eight ordinary concerns, you will forsake your own good.

If you do not dwell wholeheartedly in a solitary place but become enmeshed in all manner of distractions, your samādhi will not last long.

If you abandon the realization of the nonduality of all phenomena and are carried away by words and characteristics, you will fall under the power of Māra.

Anyone who behaves in such ways is blessed by the demon and will lose, in suffering, the ultimate goal of this and future lives.

–285–

VIGILANT INTROSPECTION

Six means of vigilant introspection:
Your conduct resembles that of an elephant on the loose,
Watch out: Is it stuck in the mire of suffering?
The nature of the view should be the inseparability of appearances and emptiness,
Watch out: Is it carried away by self-grasping?
The natural clear and luminous awareness, still in infancy,
Watch out: Is it carried away by delusion?
The crop of devotion and respect, the root of blessing,
Watch out: Is it destroyed by the frost of wrong views?
The lamp of the path that leads to liberation and enlightenment,
Watch out: Is it in danger of being blown out by the wind of desire?
The master's instructions are like the nectar of immortality.
Watch out: Are they mixed with the poison of doubt?
Scrutinizing without distraction is therefore crucial.

There are six means of vigilant introspection. You should continually post the sentinel of attention and circumspection to watch your own mind. Such a sentry must always be on the alert to scrutinize your way of being. Why? If your behavior is like that of a crazed, uncontrollable elephant on the loose, doing anything and everything, you will end up sinking into the dreaded swamps of karma and afflictive mental states. Thus, you must constantly check whether your mind is vigilant and circumspect. This is essential!

The view is understanding the fundamental nature of the union of appearances and emptiness. You must constantly check whether this view has been carried away by the demon of attachment to the "self." If that is the case, the view of the indivisibility of appearances and emptiness is lost!

The spontaneously luminous nature of awareness is like a young child. Ensure that it does not rush after delusion. When it wanders off in pursuit of the objects of delusion, deprived of landmarks, like a child, it may fall into a crevice or over a cliff if not cared for by an older protector.

The root of blessings is respectful fervor toward the spiritual master. This devotion and respect are like a harvest to be watched carefully: Is it threatened by the frost of wrong views or not? If devastated by such a frost, meditative experiences and realization will have a very hard time to bloom.

The master's instructions are like torches that light the path to liberation and enlightenment. Watch carefully: Is their flame in danger of being blown out by the gusts of the passions of ordinary life?

If you practice your teacher's instructions, which are like an elixir of immortality, with all your heart, you will first attain liberation [from samsara] and eventually the omniscience [of buddhahood]. Be constantly alert to check whether poisonous doubts such as asking yourself, "Could the master be misleading me?" are creeping into your mind. Be attentive to all these points and keep yourself free from distraction.

–286–

Ignorance of the Sublime Meaning

Six states of ignorance of the sublime meaning:
The mind that conceives an origin will not know the unborn
because the unborn is beyond the realm of concepts.
The mind that grasps at existence will not know emptiness
because emptiness is beyond any object.
The acting mind does not know the nonacting mind, which is
free from all activities.
The speculating mind will not know nonduality, which is free
from thought.
The mind that grasps will not know freedom from extremes,
which transcends all directions.
The mind that conceptualizes conduct will not know
nonelaboration, which transcends mental elaborations.
Do not grasp at the characteristics of a substantial reality
For the ultimate nature of reality is simple, unadulterated,
natural, and free from all speculation.

There are six states of ignorance of the perfect meaning.

The intellect according to which things are born, remain, and cease, cannot grasp the unborn, since the meaning of the absence of birth, existence, and cessation eludes the domain of the intellect.

The grasping that keeps becoming attached to the characteristics of a solid reality cannot conceive of emptiness, since emptiness escapes the intellect that clings to the characteristics of what it takes as real.

Whoever engages in incessant activity does not grasp the meaning of nonaction, the nature of which is perfect relaxation.

If you perpetuate countless cogitations and fixations such as "This is it; no, this is not it," and so on, you will not understand the meaning of nonduality that is free from all discursive thinking and formulation.

As long as you harbor desire and attachment for the affairs of this life, you will not grasp the meaning of freedom from extremes, which is totally free from grasping and bias.

If you keep discriminating between what is to be rejected and what is to be accomplished, you will not grasp the meaning of the fundamental simplicity of mind, which transcends all mental constructs.

If you focus on solid reality and its characteristics, you will not grasp the meaning of the fundamental nature, which is not an object of conceptual thought, but is the ultimate simplicity devoid of all representations and conceptualization.

–287–

The True Face of Ultimate Reality

Six features that establish the fundamental nature's true face:
Awareness that knows itself in its transparent simplicity, free of fabrications and alterations,
Is neither ordinary nor indeterminate.
Nonconceptual, free from subject and object,
It is not a mental antidote since it is free from all abandonment and correction.
Not perceived by others but realized by oneself.
Beyond all reference points and subjective experiences, there is no reference to the self.
Although always present, knowing its secret is difficult.
Beyond realization and nonrealization, it is all-pervasive.
Whoever knows this is expert in the ultimate reality.

If you recognize the fundamental nature of dharmatā, six points make this nature explicit. What are they?

When we speak of pristine awareness knowing itself in all its transparent simplicity, this refers to a state unaltered by any kind of fabrication, a state that does not lean in any direction, toward neither being nor nonbeing.

This awareness is not the mere experience of a calm abiding (*śamatha*) left in an ordinary neutrality. It should be much more than an amorphous indeterminacy.

What you are meditating on is not a set of elaborations governed by discursive, deluded thoughts, but the primordial wisdom free from subject-object duality.

Nor is the mind a mere antidote to afflictive mental states, for the ultimate nature of mind transcends all notions of discarding and remedy.

Your awareness is never known by someone else, since it belongs to the realm of your own primordial self-knowing wisdom.

Awareness ignores the concepts of "self" and "other," as it is beyond any form of experience based on representations.

The meaning of dharmatā, the nature of reality, is never separate from your mind, yet the secret of dharmatā is difficult to penetrate, as its omnipresence transcends all notions of realization and nonrealization.

Those who recognize this fundamental nature have fully understood the ultimate nature of all things.

–288–

Manifestations of the Ultimate Reality

Six signs of the natural manifestation of ultimate reality:
When you realize it, it is naturally clear and lucid.
When concepts cease, appearances unfold unceasingly and transparently.
When appearances manifest, they shine vividly.
Whenever occasional moments of dualism arise, everything shines in a distinct way.
In meditative balance, you experience clarity free of extremes.
The movement of thoughts and quiescence are equalized in pristine clarity.
Whoever knows these crucial points traverses to the highest yoga.

When the natural Great Perfection is spontaneously actualized, six qualities can describe this realization.

If you realize the meaning of pristine awareness, of dharmatā, that awareness is self-luminous just as the sky is naturally clear and luminous. There is no need to look for something else that might illuminate it from outside.

Of the three meditative experiences of bliss, clarity, and absence of conceptual thoughts, if the latter occurs, you need not interrupt the perceptions of the six aspects of consciousness: it is enough to simply remember the nature of pristine awareness (*rigpa*). Then, the sense organs and their objects will be perceived distinctly, unmixed, in a perfectly transparent way.

In this state, whatever perceptions of the six aspects of consciousness manifest, you will remain in a continuum free of grasping and all phenomena will naturally shine like stars reflected on the ocean's surface.

Although you clearly distinguish between the mind as a subject on the inside and the objects it grasps on the outside, in the absence of grasping to the notions of subject and object, no karma can be accumulated, and everything will shine forth clearly and distinctly.

When abiding in meditative evenness, there is no form or substance, yet it is also not a pure nothing: this is a vividly clear state, free from all extremes.

Even if thoughts keep arising, as long as awareness does not fall into distraction, its vast and open presence will never be interrupted.

Those who understand these key points have reached the summit of yogic practice.

–289–

Six Things to Let Go Of

Six things you should not pay any attention to when practicing the Dharma:
Disregard the torments of tiredness, hunger, and thirst.
Give up connections with people and places, as well as farming and similar activities.
Give up attachment to friends and aversion to foes, as well as the desire for notoriety.
Give up grasping and desire for the five sense objects.
Give up accepting praise and challenging blame.

> **Let your conceptual thoughts vanish by themselves and let go of antidotes to eliminate them.**
> **Acting like this, you will accomplish the path of liberation and enlightenment.**

Six things that practitioners of the sublime Dharma should not care about.

If you practice the supreme Dharma resolutely, your aim should be to attain buddhahood. To do so, you must bear asceticism, fatigue, hunger, thirst, or any other hardship with resilience. Making yourself comfortable will not lead to enlightenment. Do not fear these austerities.

If you leave for other places, be content with the amount of food you need to survive and clothing to protect you from the weather. Do not seek the company of benefactors and do not surround them with excessive and inappropriate attention. Refrain from engaging in farmwork and similar activities. If you leave your native land, go to another place, and end up socializing with all sorts of people and engaging in farming and similar activities, you might as well have stayed home.

If you harm the enemies who are hostile to you and favor those you are attached to, or if you strive to be recognized as a scholar throughout the world, you will be totally distracted by the eight worldly concerns. Pay no attention to any of these!

If you seek visual, auditory, and other sensory experiences, and as a result—motivated by attachment and envy—you yearn to see all sorts of sights and images, long to hear your fame celebrated, to achieve a high rank and receive many compliments and other gratifications, all this will hinder your practice. Disregard it all!

If you are praised, you are delighted and feel good; if you are criticized, you become upset. You should pay little attention to the good and bad things said about you. Otherwise, if you react to praise and criticism, this reveals your attachment to worldly concerns. Ignore all this!

Pay little heed to your ruminations as well; let them fade away of their own accord without resorting to antidotes. Usually, a practitioner is supposed to be vigilant, to remember what to do and what to avoid, and to be very circumspect at all times. Here you must let the mental constructs fade away and be liberated naturally, without having to laboriously apply antidotes to counteract what is to be eliminated.

By practicing in this way, you will accomplish the path to liberation and enlightenment.

–290–

Continuously Practice the Six Pāramitās

Practice without departing from the six pāramitās:
Do not surrender your generosity to its enemy, miserliness.
Do not let the thief of immorality ransack your morality.
Do not let the weapons of anger pierce your patience.
Do not let laziness shackle your diligence.
Do not let the poison of distraction mix with your meditative concentration.
Do not let the darkness of ignorance obscure your wisdom.
In this way, practice the pāramitās by thwarting these six enemies.

If the six transcendental perfections are not present in your mind stream, you cannot attain buddhahood. Therefore, you should eliminate six factors that are contrary to these perfections.

If generosity succumbs to avarice, its opposite and enemy, you will just accumulate possessions and not use them for offerings or to give away. Do not fall under the power of stinginess!

In order to preserve your discipline, you should master your mind with vigilance and caution. Otherwise, drinking without control and indulging in sense pleasures will be like putting weapons in the hands of bandits who will steal your moral discipline. Do not surrender to them!

Continually cultivate patience. No matter what undesirable circumstances arise, you must maintain your forbearance. Otherwise, the weapons of anger will penetrate your mind. Guard yourself against this!

You must remain diligent with complete focus. Otherwise, your inclination to the most worthless worldly activities will take over and if, in addition, you relax with the sole aim of remaining idle and cozy, while being distracted, you will fall under the yoke of indolence.

As for perfectly peaceful meditation, the one-pointed and deep concentration, it is important not to mix this with the poison of distraction.

Finally, the wisdom acquired through listening, reflecting, and meditating must not be obscured by the darkness of ignorance and lack of discernment.

Therefore, strive to eliminate those inclinations that are contrary to practicing the six transcendental perfections.

–291–

Lacking Karmic Connections with the Dharma

Illustrating the nature of six situations that lack karmic potential:
Those who wear [the causes of] suffering as an ornament have no karmic link with liberation.
Those who calculate their conduct according to the opinion of others have no karmic link with dismantling delusion.
Those who engage in listening and contemplation for a good reputation have no karmic link with spiritual practice.
Those who commit negative actions have no karmic link with rebirth in the higher realms.
Those who procrastinate and are lazy have no karmic link with meditative experience.
Those who are egocentric, with strong attachment and aversion, have no karmic link with Dharma practice.
Not being hindered by the lack of karmic links is crucial.

There are six types of individuals who are not connected with the Dharma:

Those who endure suffering in the three worlds of samsara, without recognizing suffering for what it is, and actively rush toward it have no karmic link to attain liberation and omniscience.

Those who conduct themselves with hypocrisy and obsequiousness have no karmic link to destroy the delusion of the eight worldly dharmas.

Those who, having become learned through study and reflection, thirst for fame and prestige, and feel justified in displaying their pride have no karmic connection with spiritual practice.

Those who constantly act in a deplorable manner contrary to virtue have no karmic connection with the higher realms of samsara.

Those who are afflicted with a heavy dose of indolence have no karmic connection with meditative experiences and realization.

Those who grasp to the self and constantly harbor thoughts of desire and aversion have no karmic connection with liberation and the accomplishment of Dharma.

Take this to heart and do not to fall prey to these disconnections.

–292–

Observe the Mind

Six ways to observe the mind during meditation:
Sometimes look at the mind remaining calm and stable.
Whoever knows it to be unborn, unceasing, and non-abiding
Has the key point of mastering the nature of mind.
Sometimes look at the true face of these spiritual experiences.
Whoever knows them to be non-abiding and lacking an object of attachment
Has the key point of realizing the unborn nature of self-experienced joy and bliss.
Sometimes look at the increase of inner qualities.
Whoever knows them to be naturally liberated unceasing magical displays
Has the key point of conduct that develops qualities arisen from the unborn nature.
Sometimes look at dharmatā in meditative equipoise.
Whoever knows it to be naturally arising, primordially pure, and great bliss
Has the key point of integrating all phenomena on the path of evenness.
Sometimes look at the naturally abiding outer and inner aspects of pristine awareness.
Whoever knows samsara to be free from subject and object
Has the key point of having established the one and only ultimate meaning.
Sometimes look at the nonmeditative state of the naturally abiding pristine awareness.
Whoever knows the unobstructed transparency of view and meditation, beyond all action,
Has the key point of seeing the natural face of dharmakāya nakedly.
Fortunate yogis and yoginis who actualize these six crucial points
Rest in the blissful state where all minds and mental objects have been exhausted in the dharmatā.

When you meditate on the meaning of the Great Perfection, six essential instructions allow you to observe your mind.

Sometimes observe your mind while it is quiet, free from excitement or torpor, and when your attention and alertness are stable. You will discover that this mind was not really born in the first place, so it cannot truly cease either, and that it resides nowhere in between. It is thus devoid of origin, dwelling, and destination. If you do not examine the mind, you will be content with a blissful ignorance, but if you examine it, you will find that, like a dream or an illusion, it has no solidity whatsoever. Once you have achieved full control over your mind, your meditation will become stable.

Sometimes, while meditating on the mind, you will experience many fluctuations. So, it is important to examine the nature of what we call "mind" [*sems*]: It does not sit still for a moment, like a prayer flag fluttering in the wind. But when you recognize that the objects of mind's attachments and desires lack intrinsic existence, and that the mind is itself insubstantial, whatever meditative experiences and spiritual qualities arise from removing [the veils] and from realization, you will not take any pride in the satisfaction associated with those experiences. This is an important point to deepen your understanding of the unborn.

Sometimes contemplate the flourishing of spiritual experience and realization on the path, as well as qualities such as clairvoyance, and understand that all these experiences are nothing other than the limitless magical play of the mind. Do not harbor any attachment to these manifestations and allow them to be liberated spontaneously. When you notice signs of progress, without letting the demon of infatuation seep into your mind, if you understand that these qualities arise from the unborn nature, you will have struck the vital point of practice.

At other times, during meditative equipoise, contemplate the meaning of dharmatā. Practitioners who understand that the ultimate nature of reality, dharmatā, is the primordial wisdom of great bliss arising of its own accord, originally free from all veils, will be able to bring the meaning of the equality of all phenomena of samsara and nirvana onto the path.

At times, contemplate outer appearances related to the five sense objects and your own awareness as well as the perceptions of the six aspects of consciousness within. If you subject them to scrutiny, you will find that samsara, which is never separate from attachment and grasping, is a mere appearance and you will have struck the crucial point that resolves everything in the light of the single essence of absolute truth.

At other times, without meditating deliberately, look at the natural presentation of awareness. If you understand that what is called view, meditation, and action are but transparent simplicity free from the fabrications of the intellect, this is the vital point of the introduction to the dharmakāya in all its nakedness.

If you have the good fortune to master these six vital points and to put them into practice, you will soon have the joy of seeing your intellect dissolve in the exhaustion of phenomena that transcends such intellect.

–293–

Six Attitudes to Abandon

Abandoning six negative attitudes:
Tightfisted and miserly people make little provision for their future lives.
Those without faith neither rely upon spiritual masters nor gather the wealth of instructions.
Those who are knowledgeable yet do not practice diligently what they have learned will not find the path to enlightenment.
Those who are strongly attached to friends and relatives will not find companions in the bardo.
The dharma of self-grasping and ego cannot ward off the army of the four māras.
Those who are slaves of desire will fail to conquer the citadel of ultimate happiness.
Those who indulge in these negative attitudes will bring about their own ruin.
Therefore, training in positive actions is crucial.

Six pernicious attitudes that are important to leave behind:

Stingy people, even though they are rich and have many possessions, keep food and clothing for themselves and are incapable of largesse. Such stinginess causes rebirth among the tortured spirits, the pretas. This is not the proper way to provide for future lives!

Devoid of faith, not taking a teacher as your guide, you cannot gather the treasure of instructions, which can only be received from a qualified master whom you trust.

No matter how much you know about the Dharma, without practicing diligently to blend this knowledge with your mind, attaining enlightenment and buddhahood will be very difficult.

If you are attached to your family and friends to the point of committing all sorts of negative actions on their behalf, you will not find any allies to help you through the bardo.

If you are attached to the notion of a "self" and cherish yourself excessively, you will not be able to defeat the hordes of the four māras and will fall under their power.

If you harbor strong inclinations for the pleasures of five senses and become their servant, the lasting good of the path to liberation will elude you.

If you persist in perpetuating these six harmful attitudes, you will suffer from their undesirable consequences and will not gain any spiritual quality. Cultivate virtuous behavior!

–294–

Six Objectives

Explaining the nature of the six objectives:

At first, you must give rise to disenchantment and the mind of renunciation
Because you need to focus on Dharma rather than sense objects.

Then, know how to let the mind rest in natural ease,
As it should be perfectly relaxed in the enlightened body, speech, and mind of the buddhas.

After that, you must bring great relief to the mind,
As you need to be fearless due to your confidence in realization.

Following that, you must achieve the supreme mind of great bliss
And, to this end, actualize the state of primordial purity.

Then, you must spread your bliss to others,
And for that you must lead beings through the fourfold enlightened activities.

Finally, you must remain in the irreversible state
And, to do this, actualize the mudra of spontaneous accomplishment.

Aim to reach the ultimate point by using these six objectives.

Practitioners of the sublime Dharma must accomplish six goals.

As a beginner, since your mind is burdened by the sufferings of the three worlds of samsara, you must generate a deep sense of renunciation in which you no longer have any appetite for samsaric existence. Otherwise, your mind will be chronically seduced by the pleasures of the five senses, and you will fail to keep the Dharma constantly in mind. So, it is said.

Then, while abandoning fascination with the pleasures of the five senses, devote yourself with perfect concentration to the study, contemplation, and assimilation of the teachings.

After that, you must know how to release all efforts related to listening, reflection, and meditation. To do this, let your body, speech, and mind rest inseparably in the enlightened body, speech, and mind of the victorious ones.

This relaxation should give rise to a vast feeling of relief, born of a perfectly serene ease that will deliver you from all your torments. For this, you need the total, fearless confidence associated with realization of the dharmatā.

Then bring this realization to the point of exhaustion [of phenomena] so that at that very point the mind reaches the level of supreme bliss and you actualize the state of primordial purity.

Then, impart this bliss that has become yours to others, and to do so, guide them with the four enlightened activities.

Finally, establish yourself in the state of no return and actualize the mudra of the five spontaneously accomplished kāyas.

Take this to heart to reach the ultimate end of the path through accomplishing these six goals.

–295–

Six Methods to Bring Everything onto the Path

Six methods of bringing everything onto the path:
While not in meditation, look directly at the moving thoughts.
When you know the true face of whatever thoughts arise in their own nature,
All that appears will certainly be liberated in the field of the unborn.
Look at the mind that struggles to enter into meditation.
When you know to equalize pleasure and pain, which have only one origin [emptiness],
You will certainly realize the equality of what to abandon and what to accept and will liberate them in their inseparability.
Contemplate until the immaculate main practice is born:
When you know that the nature of mind can appear in infinite ways,
Gradually, all movements of thought can be definitively incorporated in the unborn nature.
When you arise from meditative equipoise, look at the nature of the post-meditation state,
You will know how to blend that with the ultimate state of the nature of mind.
This will certainly enable you to incorporate everything in the inseparability of meditation and post-meditation.
After this, look directly at the flow of conceptual thoughts.
You will know that whatever negative emotions arise subside on their own.
This will definitely bring all appearances and experiences into the primordial ground.*
Look at the unity of the preliminary, main, and concluding practices.
You will know all three to be traceless like the paths of birds
And will certainly realize the crucial point of the single nature of past, present, and future.
If you know this, you will experience post-meditation as dharmatā.

Whatever qualities and defects, joys and sorrows, manifest, there are six instructions for transforming them into allies on the path. How is that done?

Without intentionally engaging in mental stillness or deeper insight, without being affected by clinging to representations, understand that the movement of the myriad thoughts passing through your mind results from giving free rein to their whims. But if you recognize their true face, whatever these thoughts might be, they will be liberated into their own place and the perceptions of the six aspects of consciousness will be established in the field of the unborn.

If you then engage in meditation, know how to approach the stillness of mind and the deeper insight. As these two meditations blossom in your mind stream, cultivate equal taste for joys and sorrows. Without craving well-being or abhorring suffering, equalize them. Then, attraction and rejection will be liberated in perfect equality.

At the time of the main practice, contemplating the meaning of dharmatā, unaltered and unborn, recognize that all phenomena, both samsara and nirvana, manifest from the nature of mind, and are devoid of any essence and existence of their own. As this understanding permeates your mind, you will enter the unborn.

When emerging from meditative equipoise, preserve the experience of it and recognize the nature of post-meditation. Thus, know how to blend meditation and post-meditation within the realization of the nature of mind.

Once you have brought meditation and post-meditation into a seamless state of indivisibility, without giving free rein to the proliferation of thoughts, look at their very nature, and you will know how to naturally quiet the afflictive mental states, all of them—desire, animosity, ignorance—by letting them be liberated at the very moment they arise. In this way, it is certain that appearances and experience will return to the primordial ground.

As for the three phases of preparation, main practice, and post-meditation, it is important to blend them so they are present at every stage. Thus, at the time of the preliminaries, the main practice and the post-practice are already present; at the time of the main practice, the preparation and the post-meditation are also present; and at the time of the post-meditation, the two others remain fully present so that these three phases are never separated.

In general, whatever virtuous practices you engage in, remain free of fixations, like a bird that passes through the sky without a trace. In doing so, you will understand with certainty that the nature of the three times—past, present, and future—falls under a single vital point, and you will experience post-meditation in the sphere of dharmatā.

–296–

Practitioners with Six Qualities

Explaining the nature of those with six positive qualities:
Frightened by the suffering of samsara, they take refuge.
Taming their minds with devotion, they follow the path of the victorious ones.
Valuing merit, they are generous and strive in gathering the two accumulations.
Striking the whip of joyous effort, they persevere in accumulating merit day and night.
With a sense of shame and modesty, they are willing to sacrifice their life for Dharma practice.
Using wisdom, they analyze the ultimate reality and can merge all appearances and experiences into dharmatā.
Those who have these qualities will go to the other shore of samsara.

If you are going to practice, strive to have all of these six qualities:

Frightened by the suffering of samsara, you seek the protection that the refuge of the Three Jewels can give you.

Once you have fully generated clear faith, ardent faith, and consummate trust, and have mastered your mind stream with the help of mindfulness and vigilance, you will practice taking the example of the victorious ones, the perfect buddhas.

If you have accomplished the accumulation of merit, you will understand it as the source of all happiness. Having perfected this accumulation of merit and displayed great generosity, you should also engage in the accumulation of wisdom, thus completing the two accumulations.

Constantly urging yourself to the task with the spur of diligence, devote yourself always and solely to virtue, day and night.

Adopting a perfectly pure attitude, endowed with moral awareness toward yourself and others, you will be ready to risk your life for the sake of the supreme Dharma and for your spiritual teacher.

Able to analyze the vast and profound meaning of knowledge gained through study and reflection, naturally liberating the six aspects of consciousness with the help of the insight gained through meditation, allowing the mental constructs to undo themselves in the primordial wisdom of emptiness—the nature of reality, you will abide in the enlightened vision of the integration of the three kāyas on the path.

Whoever has these six qualities in full will be able to reach the other shore of samsara in this very life.

–297–

Six Indispensable Objectives

Six indispensable objectives:
Like a swamp of filth, abandon the activities of this life.
Like a sun, let the primordial wisdom free from extremes shine forth.
Like darkness, dispel as much as possible the murk of ignorance.
Like a sprout, cultivate as much as possible spiritual experience and realization, though they are still projections of the mind.
Like a dream, abandon as much as possible the delusion of subject and object.
Like a wish-fulfilling gem, gather as much as possible the fruit of the three kāyas.
Keep in mind this instruction of the sublime beings.

Six indispensable objectives for practicing the supreme Dharma:

All activities related to the ordinary aspects of this life, the eight worldly dharmas, are like a filthy quagmire: do everything you can to escape from them.

Primordial wisdom, free from all extremes, is like a torch, a sun that dispels the darkness of the world. Let it shine and dissipate as much as possible the dark opacity of lack of discernment and ignorance.

Meditative experiences and [what you consider to be] "realization" are all ephemeral, illusory, and deceptive manifestations, entirely devoid of permanence and true existence. But these varied experiences are also signs that you are practicing, so it is desirable to cultivate them assiduously.

The misleading perceptions created by attachment to the notions of subject and object are like dreams: do your best to dispel them.

Develop as much as possible in your mind the qualities of the fruition, the three bodies (*kāyas*) of buddhahood.

These six objectives are the actual instructions of the supreme masters.

–298–

Qualities of the Training

Six natural qualities of supreme training:
Abandoning the activities of the deluded body;
Abandoning the worthless chatter of speech;
Abandoning the comings and goings of conceptual mind;
Abandoning the ordinary desire for sense objects;
Abandoning the inclination and attachment to distraction and dispersion;
Abandoning the concern with fulfilling others' expectations;
Whoever combines these qualities will be able to practice Dharma perfectly.

There are six qualities in which you should train:

Abandon as much as possible the worldly activities of this deluded body.

Abandon as much as possible vain chatter and the endless stream of words; choose silence.

If you indulge in all sorts of cogitations and sustain the kingdom of the intellect, you will go astray. Abandon discursive thoughts as much as possible.

Turn away as much as possible from thirst for and attachment to sense pleasures.

Cut off as much as possible the many social connections you have made amid distractions and activities that sidetrack your mind.

Forsake as much as possible the habit of acting according to the opinion of others.

If you succeed in all these points, the supreme Dharma will be correctly accomplished.

–299–

The Traps of Desire

Six things that bind us with the trap of desire:
The desire to be free from the mind's conceptual elaborations;
The desire to achieve the union of bliss and emptiness;
The desire to achieve the space-like nonreferential state of purity;
The desire to achieve the state of emptiness with the essence of primordial wisdom;
The desire to achieve the pristine awareness in the form of a tent of light;
The desire to achieve the primordially liberated self-originating primordial wisdom.
As in the description of an elephant by those who touch only parts of it,[174]
Such perceptions grasp on to things based on the view of the reality of the self.
Therefore, abandon the trap of this biased view of self,
And establish your own unbiased awareness that is neither existent nor nonexistent,
In the vast expanse free from all extremes.

Six mental attitudes that ensnare you in the trap of your expectations:

If, for example, you strongly desire to be free of the conceptual mind, you will not succeed in eliminating it.

The same applies to the desire to realize the view of the indivisible union of bliss and emptiness, to the desire to realize the view free of references and representations—immaculate as space, to the desire to actualize the realization of emptiness imbued with the essence of primordial wisdom, to the desire for the realization of awareness manifesting as pavilions of light, or for the accomplishment of the primordial wisdom arising of its own accord and free from its origin.

If you try to fathom the view, emptiness, and other subjects in partial ways, you will be like those [six blind men] who tried to describe an elephant. [Each one touched a different part of its body and mistook it for the pachyderm itself.] All these attempts pertain to grasping at the characteristics of a self-entity considered to be real. Doing this, your realization will be partial and incomplete. Therefore, you should abandon the fixation on a narrow view that holds the self as real and establish yourself in the pristine awareness free of partiality, which cannot be said to "exist" or "not exist," and resolve everything with certainty in the vast expanse free of extremes.

–300–

Six Types of Cessation

Six types of natural cessation that result from practice:
Externally, perception of outer objective phenomena naturally ceases.
Internally, perception of inner subjective phenomena naturally ceases.
Secretly, reference to perceptions naturally ceases.
At the level of suchness, recollections naturally cease.
Ultimately, spiritual experiences naturally cease.
Awareness that alternates between meditative and post-meditative states naturally ceases.
Whoever perfects these types of cessation will establish their realization in the state of exhaustion [of phenomena in dharmatā].

These six instructions belong to the view of the Great Perfection, which I do not understand much about. They refer to six experiences that will cease as your practice progresses.

First, concerning the outer world, the objects to which the mind grasps, all clinging will cease of its own accord, without having recourse to antidotes.

Inwardly, the moment you realize the view, the thoughts that grasp through the play of attraction or repulsion will cease within their own nature.

Secretly, whatever perceptions of things as "good" or "bad" might occur, hopes that arise from attachment to desirable objects and fears associated with the repulsion of undesirable objects will naturally cease.

The reference-free attentive presence that allows you to recognize the fundamental nature of phenomena, their suchness, and ultimately all meditative experiences will be brought to the point of exhaustion and cease within their own nature.

When you understand that the perceptions of meditative equipoise and the perceptions of post-meditation are not truly separate, they will both naturally cease.

When these six cessations reach their consummate point, the vision [of relative phenomena] will be brought to exhaustion [in the space of the dharmatā].

–301–

Six Practices You Should Never Give Up

How to practice without departing from six attitudes:
Never fail to perceive your body as the mandala of the victorious ones.
Never fail to use your speech as enlightened speech to benefit beings.
Never fail to realize your mind as the dharmakāya.
Never fail to perceive food and drink as offerings of ambrosia.
Never fail to perceive moving and remaining as illusory enlightened activities.
In your practice, never lose sight of the ultimate nature of reality.
Whoever trains in these attitudes
Will enjoy the supremely secret royal treasure.

Once you have realized the meaning of dharmatā, you will never be separated from it, just as fire is never separated from heat. There are six practices to train in this.

Your body never becomes different from the mandala of the purity of the three seats.[175] Avoid considering it as ordinary.

The expressions of your speech are none other than the enlightened speech of the buddhas, unborn and free from fabrication, which enables all who hear it to spontaneously achieve liberation.

Once you have realized the wisdom of the spontaneous liberation of your mind, you will never stray from the understanding of the dharmakāya, the experience of self-awareness.

If you perceive food and drink as offerings to the mandala of the three pure seats, they will never be different from offerings of ambrosia.

In all your physical activities, such as walking or sitting, if you never separate yourself from the view of the dharmatā, you will continually perceive your movements as walking from one point of the mandala to another,[176] all your movements as mudras, and all your words as the recitations and performance of the practices associated with your tutelary deity.

In meditation and in post-meditation, whatever your practice might be, never stray from the understanding of the nature of reality.

Whoever trains in these six ways of not straying from the view will enjoy the royal, supreme, and secret treasure of the Great Perfection.

–302–

Six Analogies for Samsara

Six analogies showing the nature of samsara:
Like a magical illusion of people, all phenomena lack true existence.
Like dreams, all appearances are delusory.
Like the reflection of the moon on water, samsara appears while devoid of intrinsic existence.
Like clouds, good and evil and pleasure and pain are transitory.
Like dewdrops, phenomena that are perceptible to you and those that are not, are all ephemeral.
Like water bubbles, phenomena naturally arise and cease.
Meditate on these analogies and integrate them into your mind stream.

Six analogies show the transitory nature of samsara:

The experiences of this life, good and bad, do not have even a trace of real existence, just like the appearance of horses, cattle, men, and women conjured by a magician with magic formulas.

Similarly, delusive perceptions, pleasant or unpleasant, are like last night's dream. There is no point in pursuing them.

Whatever perceptions of the six aspects of consciousness you might experience, if you examine their true nature, you will realize that they have no intrinsic existence, just like reflections of the moon on water.

The best moments you have experienced, as well as the most difficult, the joys and sorrows, are like clouds in the sky: present one moment, gone the next, sometimes pristine white, sometimes starkly dark.

What is clearly perceptible, such as the sensations of well-being and suffering, as well as what you cannot perceive, everything is impermanent like dewdrops on the tips of grass.

If you clearly understand the natural characteristics of these phenomena, you will know that they appear like bubbles forming in water and disappear naturally without having to apply antidotes.

Try to integrate these analogies into your thought process.

–303–

Six Analogies for Nirvana

Six analogies indicating the nature of nirvana:
Like the sun's rays radiating from the essence of the sun, the diversity of phenomena radiates from the nature of mind.
Like a lotus that grows in the mud, the nature of mind is unstained by negativities.
As though by a wish-fulfilling jewel, enlightened qualities are spontaneously accomplished.
Like the sun and moon in a cloudless sky, the natural clarity of the mind is unobscured by conceptual thoughts.
Like an empty yet clear sky, the nature of mind is all-pervasive and unbiased.
Like the great ocean, the nature of the mind is beyond the increase and decrease of the relative mind.
Whoever knows these analogies will be liberated in the inseparability of samsara and nirvana.

Six analogies illustrate the nature of nirvana:

The multiple perceptions that fill your mind, the diversity of the pure and impure appearances of samsara and nirvana, are all manifestations of the mind's creativity, just as rays naturally emanate from the sun when it is present and darkness reigns in its absence.

To understand the fundamental true nature of mind is to understand its emptiness. The emptiness of mind-in-itself is not tainted by karma and afflictive states of mind, like the pristine lotus that grows in the mud.

The kāyas—the dimensions of buddhahood—and the primordial wisdoms are originally present within the nature of mind like oil in a sesame seed. These qualities are spontaneously accomplished, just as wishes are by a wish-fulfilling gem.

Like the sun in a cloudless sky, the vast and deep luminosity of the mind cannot be obscured by karma and afflictive mental states.

Like space, both empty and luminous, the mind embraces the whole of samsara, without leaning in the direction of emptiness alone.

Just as a vast ocean [remains equal to itself], since all qualities are present in the nature of mind, nothing new can improve or increase it, nor can any defect make it decline or deteriorate.

Whoever recognizes these points is free from the duality of rejecting samsara and striving to attain nirvana.

–304–

How to Motivate Yourself

Six important points to motivate yourself:
It is important to follow the Dharma after setting your own goals.
It is important to exhort yourself to engage in virtuous activities.
It is important to guide yourself in the use of antidotes.
It is important to act on your own and to strive tirelessly to practice the Dharma.
It is important to take the reins of your practice and bring it to its ultimate point.
It is important to take care of your loved ones—that is, to free all beings from the six worlds.
This is a general instruction to be kept in your mind.

Now come six instructions worthy of consideration, which will encourage you to practice.[177]

First of all, the decision to enter the Dharma is yours alone. Do not listen to your parents, relatives, or friends who attempt to persuade you to engage in ordinary activities.

Keeping the imperfections of samsara clearly in mind, you must encourage yourself, shake off your chronic languor, be your own mentor, and focus entirely on spiritual practice.

At all times, you must be your own guide. Having realized the vanity of the desires and aversions you have harbored in samsara from time immemorial, from now on resolve to devote yourself to the supreme Dharma.

Examine at every moment whether you are engaging in positive or negative actions, and in the latter case apply the antidotes of study, reflection, and meditation. If you have undertaken positive actions, enhance them.

It is up to you to give yourself sound advice and it is up to you to prompt yourself. If you must do something for your own good, it is for you to decide whether to do it or not. Do not act out of concern for the opinions of others or under compulsion from a potentate or in order to conform to monastic discipline.

You must do your own work and take on all difficulties in earnest, without ever turning away from the Dharma, whether you are hungry or cold, with no warm coat to wear, whether you give up eating meat, and so on.

If you do this, you will succeed on your own. You will begin by listening to the teachings, then expand your understanding through reflection, and finally devote yourself to practice. If the duration of your practice is that of your life, you will have truly brought it to its fullest potential while doing your best to conquer the citadel of realization.

Once this is done, it is time to take care of your parents and loved ones. By "parents," here we do not mean your father, your mother, and other family members or friends in this life: we are talking about all sentient beings of the six realms of existence, whom you should benefit as much as possible. With great compassion, you must do everything to pull them out of samsara's ocean of suffering.

These are general teachings that you should keep in mind.

–305–

Blending the Mind with Virtue

Six methods of blending your mind with virtuous activities:
Repeatedly examine whatever actions you do, positive or negative.
Tame your ordinary conceptual thoughts.
At all times, make single-pointed supplication prayers respectfully.
Whatever you do, make persistent efforts to keep your actions in accord with the words of the Buddha and the commentaries.
With the confidence of realization, understand all appearances to be subjective experiences.
Whatever you do, make sure that your intention is unbiased.
If you act like this, you will accomplish the path of liberation and enlightenment.

If you succeed in blending your mind with the teachings the best you can, your practice will serve its purpose.[178] To do this, whatever practice you are engaged in, unite it with the Dharma. What does this mean?

From the moment you wake up in the morning until the moment you go to bed at night, you must be vigilant, aware at all times of the virtuous or unvirtuous nature of your thoughts, words, and actions. If you have accomplished any virtuous, beneficial act, rejoice, amplify it, cultivate bodhicitta, and dedicate your merits. If it is a negative act, feel regret and confess your wrongdoings.

You must control ordinary thoughts. To this end, examine them repeatedly and see if you are carried away by the whims of the ordinary mind, which must be avoided at all costs. Tone your thoughts down. This being done, you must keep watching to ensure that your undesirable mental habits do not reappear and avoid accumulating negative karmic acts under the power of delusion.

If you poke an irascible pig in the snout when it runs at you, it will immediately turn around. This is how you should tame the vagaries of your wandering mind through mindfulness and vigilance.

Whatever your joys and sorrows, whatever favorable or unfavorable circumstances you may face, in all situations, mingling your mind stream with the spiritual lineage, repeatedly invoke your spiritual teacher and the supreme Dharma.

While praying respectfully in this way, at all times in your practice check whether you are able to conform your thoughts, words, and deeds with the words of the Buddha and with the commentaries composed by his successors, the *śāstras*. Strive to gradually integrate the supreme Dharma into your mind stream.

If you persevere in this way, a time will come when you gain stable confidence in your realization of the view of dharmatā and you will perceive all circumstances, favorable or adverse, as nothing other than the magical display of your own perceptions. From then on, all your perceptions of the phenomenal world will arise not as enemies but as allies of your practice, and they will further clarify the path [to enlightenment].

Whatever you do, whatever you say, whatever you think, be free from partiality and from the infatuation that boasts, "I have done great virtuous deeds!" Guard yourself against the pride that relishes admiring your own qualities. Do meritorious deeds, but perceive them as illusions, as dreams. In this way, perform as many positive actions as you can, without attachment, and aspire to magnify them further. Think of the countless buddhas and bodhisattvas whose beneficial acts are immensely vast and tell yourself that if you persevere, you will quickly travel the path of liberation and enlightenment.

–306–

Six Paths to Avoid

Six paths Dharma practitioners should not follow:
Without the fertile soil of faith, the fruit of happiness will not ripen.
Without a learned and virtuous master, the darkness that obscures pristine awareness will not be cleared.
Without Dharma practice, the source of joy and happiness, the lake of suffering will swell.
Without the ten virtuous actions guiding your spiritual path, you will lose the foundation of Dharma.
Without disentangling yourself from ordinary ways, you will be bound by the rope of laziness.
Without the eyes of insight, you will plunge from the precipice of samsara.
Do not go down such paths; practice with perseverance. This is crucial.

All Dharma practitioners should avoid engaging in six situations contrary to the Dharma. What are they?

Even if you have seeds of barley, rice, and so on, without a field to plant them in, these seeds will not bear fruit. Similarly, if you do not possess the fertile ground of faith, the fruits of virtue will not ripen.

If you are not guided by a learned and virtuous master endowed with excellent human qualities, you will not be able to dispel the veils of ignorance that obscure pristine awareness.

If you do not practice the Dharma properly, with joy and happiness, when you have the opportunity to do so, and if you only think of practicing Dharma when the lake of suffering of birth, old age, sickness, and death overflows, it will be too late.

If your path is not guided by the ten virtues, the root of the Dharma will be lost and degenerate.

If you do not travel far from your native land as you think of doing so, you will find it difficult to turn to the Dharma, study it, reflect on it, and practice it. You will keep telling yourself that you will come to it slowly, but in so doing you will be hindered by the chains of laziness and will let too much time pass without practicing the Dharma.

If you lack the eyes of wisdom born from studying, reflecting, and meditating, you will eventually fall off of a precipice into the three worlds of samsara.

Therefore, you must practice with utmost effort not to go down these unfavorable paths.

–307–

SIX VAIN HOPES

The nature of six false hopes:
Hoping to avoid the suffering of the lower realms while engaging in negative actions;
Hoping to attain the higher realms of existence without engaging in virtuous actions;
Hoping to purify delusions without abandoning negative emotions;
Hoping to attain buddhahood without making efforts to gather the two accumulations;
Hoping to attain happiness in the next life while devoting oneself to all kinds of activities for the sake of this life;
Hoping not to wander in samsara without engaging in Dharma practice, the path of liberation—
Entertaining such hopes will lead to disappointment.

If you hope to obtain a result without having generated its causes, your hopes will be disappointed.

If you behave in inherently negative and unvirtuous ways, you cannot escape the sufferings of the lower realms. Even if you aspire to avoid suffering at all costs, it will be your lot.

If not having done a single virtuous deed, you nevertheless hope to reach the relatively happier realms of gods and men without having generated the causes for it, you will resemble an inept person who wishes to start a large enterprise without having gathered the appropriate conditions.

If you do not deliberately remove afflictive mental states from your mind, you have no chance to escape delusion.

If you have not gathered the two accumulations of merit and wisdom, it is like trying to walk without your two legs: your hopes of reaching buddhahood will be dashed.

If you devote all your actions, words, and thoughts to the eight worldly concerns, such as praise, fame, gain, and consideration of others' opinions, you will have no means of obtaining a higher rebirth in your future lives. You may have obtained honors and gains, but in doing that, you have accumulated nothing but negative actions.

If you do not practice the supreme Dharma of the path of liberation, although you entertain hopes to disentangle yourself from the three worlds of samsara, you will have no choice but to wander in the cycle of rebirths.

In short, wishing to enjoy the fruit of seeds that have not been planted just leads to disappointment.

–308–

Toward a Happy Rebirth

Six causes for birth in the happier and higher realms:
You have a karmic potential resulting from virtue accumulated in the past.
In this life, the three doors of your body, speech, and mind remain unwaveringly honest.
You cause no harm to sentient beings.
With faith in cause and effect, you distinguish virtuous actions from unvirtuous ones.
You are interested in the perfect and noble view of the definitive teachings.
You endeavor in Dharma practice with faith and respect.
Such individuals hold the happiness and bliss of higher rebirths in the palms of their hands.

There are six causes for rebirth in the higher realms of existence.

If in your past lives you accumulated positive deeds such that today you have been born in a land where the Buddha's teachings have flourished, if you are endowed with the freedoms and favorable conditions of a human existence, if you are accepted and guided by a spiritual master and you put his instructions into practice, all this represents the actualization of favorable karmic predispositions.

If you deceive others in action, in speech, or in your thoughts, while acting as if nothing was wrong, or if you pretend to possess qualities that you are totally lacking, you are deceiving everyone. Don't do that! Behave with integrity and you will progress on the path to liberation.

Avoiding the slightest harm to any sentient being, abandoning all hostility to others, and the very basic foundation of malevolence toward others are all signs that you are on the bodhisattva path. Above all, refrain from all forms of violence.

With faith and trust in the laws of causality, you practice virtue to the best of your capability while carefully avoiding negative actions. You distinguish clearly between the two and devote yourself to benefiting others and abandoning all conduct detrimental to them.

While doing so, you yearn to understand the view, meditation, and conduct of the definitive meaning, and you develop a sincere aspiration to grasp the view of the great Middle Way, or the view of the great purity and equality of the Adamantine Vehicle of the Secret Mantra, or to attain deep conviction in the view of the Great Perfection through the ways of letting the mind rest in its natural state like a mountain,[179] and you practice with confidence, perseverance, and reverence in the supreme Dharma.

If you act like this, you hold in your hands the joys and bliss of gods and men associated with the higher realms of samsara.

–309–

The Causes of Rebirth in the Lower Destinies

Six causes for birth in the lower realms:
Rude and irascible, you get angry without any reason.
You denigrate virtue and praise unvirtuous actions.
Dishonest, you deceive others by any means.
You are jealous of others' success and prosperity.
You are extremely attached to wealth and possessions, a prisoner of stinginess with no inclination to give to others.
Proud and arrogant, you despise others.
Whoever acts in these ways, the lower realms await them,
Where they will experience immeasurable suffering without any hope of liberation.

There are six defects that, if they take root in your mind, will definitely lead you to the lower destinies of samsara.

If, when confronted with the slightest difficult circumstance, you lose your temper and your character resembles a thornbush, your harsh ways will prevent you from getting along with anyone.

You criticize those who practice virtue and praise those who keep committing negative actions, such as so-called heroes who kill a large number of enemies, or thieves and other wrongdoers. Moreover, while indulging in various misdeeds yourself, you deceive your fellow human beings by using all sorts of stratagems. You denigrate those who are endowed with many qualities, such as strength, abundance, power, fame, and knowledge, declaring that all this is nothing at all: this shows that jealousy has gone to your head.

Strong attachments to your wealth and possessions make you stingy, and you are not inclined to make offerings or to exercise generosity.

If someone very learned is endowed with vast qualities, you do not recognize these for what they are and show nothing but contempt for them, while boasting of having great qualities yourself when you have none. In all these cases, you are definitely inviting the lower destinies. In the three lower realms, you will experience extreme suffering without ever seeing the time of liberation coming.

Be very careful to avoid these defects.

–310–

Achieving Liberation

Six Dharma practices that enable you to accomplish the path of liberation:

With intense devotion and respect, rely upon a wise teacher
So you can expand the activity of listening and contemplation and cut the root of samsara.

In an empty gap without blessings and protection,
You may be deceived by the obstacle-creating māras.
Therefore, rely upon the Three Jewels.

Without developing disenchantment toward friends and foes,
You will be unable to escape from the mire of negative emotions.
Therefore, liberate yourself from the māras of attachment and aversion.

If you lack vigilant introspection,
You might fall off of a precipice into the lower realms.
Therefore, always be careful.

Without the support of the army of virtuous activities,
You will be unable to avert the warfare of samsara.
Therefore, make efforts in restoration and purification practices.

Without being equipped with the nonreferential view,
The conditioned virtues fail to accomplish enlightenment.
Therefore, combine virtues with wisdom.

If you strive in this way, enlightenment will be swiftly gained.

Six crucial points of supreme Dharma practice that will enable you to accomplish the path of liberation:

If you rely upon spiritual masters and, with intense and respectful fervor, see them as the Buddha himself, they will guide you unerringly on the path to liberation.

You have received teachings in the presence of your master: reflect on them and expand your knowledge, without ever becoming satiated, like a hungry yak grazing on one tuft of grass with its eyes fixed on the next. In this way, you will be able to perfectly clarify the view, meditation, and action.

When you find yourself in a vulnerable situation that is like a no-man's-land, without refuge and blessings from your protectors, you will be lured by the māras, who will create obstacles in the bardo. Therefore, pray to the Three Jewels at all times, visualizing them above your head.

When you feel animosity toward an enemy, convince yourself that this feeling is devoid of any essence and put it out of your mind. When you feel irrepressible attachment for a loved one, tell yourself that this feeling is devoid of all essence. Without becoming weary of such feelings, you will fail to extricate yourself from the mire of attraction and repulsion. You must therefore free yourself from the demons of attachment and hostility.

Fully aware of what to adopt and reject regarding positive and negative behaviors, continuously monitoring your state of mind, perform virtue and abandon nonvirtue. If you do not distinguish between these two, you will fall into the abyss of the lower realms. Therefore, you must, at all times, exercise the utmost circumspection in your actions, words, and thoughts.

Apply yourselves to the various practices and methods of the supreme Dharma—prostrations, circumambulations, listening to the teachings and writing them down, and so on. Without the allies of these spiritual practices, you cannot repel the hordes of the three worlds of samsara. Thus, constantly enhance your virtuous practices; be diligent to increase the smallest virtue and purify the smallest negative act.

You should imbue all this with the understanding of emptiness free of representations, perceiving all things as like dreams and illusions. Otherwise, all your virtuous deeds will remain vulnerable to a single moment of anger, your meritorious acts will mature only once without being renewed, and you will fail to attain enlightenment. It is therefore crucial to develop the wisdom that is free of the three conceptual spheres [subject, object, and action]. If, once again, you understand the dreamlike and illusory nature of phenomena and strengthen all your practices by dedicating them to the benefit of beings, as bodhisattvas do, with diligence you will quickly attain enlightenment.

–311–

Accumulate Merit

Six virtuous efforts to accumulate merit:

There is great merit in respecting noble and exalted beings.
Thus, making offerings to the spiritual master, yidam deity, and ḍākinīs is important.

There is great merit in benefiting those who are less fortunate.
Thus, taking care of the destitute and downtrodden with immeasurable compassion is important.

There is great merit in practicing internally the sublime Dharma in an unbiased way.
Thus, persevere in listening, contemplation, and meditation.

Turning to others, there is great merit in benefiting them.
Thus, with bodhicitta, teach them the Dharma, protect them and support them.

Turning inward, there is great merit in being free of reference points.
Thus, abandon self-grasping, pride, and fixation on characteristics.

More than anything else,[180] there is great merit in actualizing the ultimate reality.
Thus, accomplish the ultimate meaning of the Three Jewels.

Practicing in this way, you will swiftly accomplish buddhahood.

There are six ways to gather a vast accumulation [of merit and wisdom] with little effort.

Looking upward, respect and serve the Three Jewels and the spiritual masters and you will accumulate infinite merit. To this end, make offerings to the masters, the tutelary deities, and the ḍākinīs.

Gazing toward all beings, cultivate a good heart, the powerful desire to benefit them. This is a major source of merit and the unquestionable cause of achieving buddhahood. Therefore, with unconditional compassion, protect all who suffer, whether friend or foe, and extend your care and compassion to the helpless.

Inwardly, devote yourself correctly and the best you can to listening, reflecting, and meditating on the supreme teachings of the different traditions without any sectarianism. Inwardly, practice the supreme teachings of the various traditions correctly and to the best of your ability, without sectarianism. By doing so, the qualities of learning will arise naturally in your mind stream. Thus, be diligent in practicing the Dharma.

Outwardly, benefit others as much as possible in deeds, words, and thoughts. Benevolence is a major source of merit. Having generated bodhicitta, explain the Dharma to inspire others to practice it; be the protector, refuge, and ally of all.

As for yourself, to be free from characteristics and representations, if you have performed some virtuous acts and acquired some qualities, consider them as dreams and illusions. Being free of reference points is a major source of merit.

Abandon your attachment to yourself, your sense of self-importance and attachment to reference points that lead you to proclaim, "I have accumulated so much merit. I am truly incomparable."

Of all practices, the most meritorious are to preserve the simplicity of the fundamental nature of all things and to understand the ultimate meaning of the Three Jewels—the ultimate nature [emptiness], its expression or character [luminosity], and [all-pervasive] power to know. In this way, you will quickly attain buddhahood.

–312–

Causing Your Own Downfall

Six[181] situations where you bring about your own downfall:
When you do not listen to instructions given with love,
You will be ruined, like the turtle that fell from the sky when it opened its mouth and lost its grip on the stick.
When you wish for happiness after committing unvirtuous actions,
You will be ruined as by eating poison and wishing for pleasure.
You will be ruined by abandoning your spiritual master and relying upon evil friends
As this is like abandoning your escort and running among your enemies.
You will be ruined by moving downward from the divine path of Dharma and engaging in worldly pursuits,
As this is like leaving the royal life to graze cattle and horses.
Thus, avoiding these situations is crucial.

These are six situations in which you hasten your own downfall.

In a past existence, the Buddha and Ānanda were born as two geese, while Devadatta was born as a turtle, a friend of the geese. The pond where they lived had dried up, and the turtle was about to die. It suggested to the geese that they take in their beaks a stick that it could hold with its mouth and two legs, so they could carry it to a place with fresh water. The geese agreed and advised the turtle to hold on tight and never open its mouth. As they flew over a village, people exclaimed, "Look, those two geese had such an ingenious idea for carrying the turtle!" and everyone praised the geese. The turtle couldn't resist opening its mouth to say, "It was *my* idea!" As it did so, it let go of the stick and fell to its death. This story illustrates what happens when you do not listen to good advice.

Committing multiple negative actions, while expecting everything to go well, is similar to ingesting poison and expecting to live long, while, in fact, you will die within an hour, thus causing your own demise.

If you do not follow a spiritual master properly and do not apply his instructions, but prefer the company of thugs, murderers, or prostitutes, this is like being offered an escort to cross a country infested with thieves but preferring to go alone, at the risk of being robbed of all your belongings and even losing your life.

If you turn away from the sublime Dharma to engage in the ordinary activities of fighting your enemies, protecting your friends, trading, and seeking fame, you are like a king abdicating so he can herd people's cattle and tend to their horses. Everyone would laugh at him for giving up his kingdom and royal prerogatives.

Be very careful not to fall into these ways.

–313–

Six Situations to Avoid

Six things you should advise yourself to avoid:
Do not stay in crowded places, but rely upon solitary retreats.
Do not be trapped by worldly activities,[182] but keep your three doors tamed and relaxed.
Do not let your mind run wild, but bring it back to the Dharma.
Do not be immodest, but keep your promises and commitments.
Do not let your samayas be broken, but honor your master and vajra kin.
Do not let your mind be depressed and withdrawn, but develop expansive openness.
Sleeping in the bed of comfort and ease is crucial.

Six pieces of advice you should give yourself regarding the paths not to take.

Don't go to villages. Stay in mountain retreats and all spiritual qualities will flourish.

You might fall into the trap of unbridled behavior, pretending to be an accomplished yogi, doing your best to impress others, making divinations about the rebirth of the dead and predictions about people's life spans, and so forth. Do not do any of this! Instead, strive to pacify and control your body, speech, and mind.

Do not give free rein to your impulsive mind, engaging in all sorts of distractions and excitement. Instead, direct all your thoughts to the Dharma alone.

If you commit even the slightest negative action, tell yourself that the buddhas and bodhisattvas are ashamed of you. Instead, cultivate faith and understand that if you show no restraint, you will inevitably break all the promises and commitments you have made.

If you do not keep your sacred commitments, free from the slightest hypocrisy, you will never achieve the ultimate spiritual accomplishments. Therefore, respectfully place your spiritual master and companions above your head and sincerely guard your sacred commitments as if they were your most precious treasure, without any duplicity.

Do not withdraw into suffering, exclaiming in a plaintive voice, "Ah, I have been practicing for so long, so many months and years. What more am I supposed to do?" Instead, cultivate a vast and free mind.

Give priority to bringing forth the realization that makes you feel at ease on the pleasant couch of the ultimate nature of reality.

–314–

Six Unfortunate Losses

Carefully ponder the six situations of losing something precious:

Your spiritual master is your most kind old father.
What a loss to forget him or her!
Rather serve and supplicate him.

Beings of the six realms are your kind old mothers.

What a loss to let them suffer!
Rather lead them on the path of great bliss.

The body, speech, and mind of this human existence endowed with freedom and advantages are difficult to find.
What a loss to leave them in idleness!
Rather employ them in the virtue of benefiting others.

The supreme friends and the yidam deity are the sources of siddhis.
What a loss to be separated from them!
Rather accompany them with respect.

What a loss to let fall into delusion the supreme child, the beautiful child of awareness,
Rather ensure that he upholds the secure citadel of dharmatā.

The precious gem of the nature of mind is your inherited wealth.
What a loss to lose it!
Rather care for it without distraction.

These six instructions are extremely important if you want to uphold the ultimate kingdom.

In ordinary life, when parents take care of their children, they show great tenderness toward them. But the benevolence of a spiritual master is even greater. Properly put into practice, his or her instructions will enable you to free yourself from samsara, especially from the lower realms, and to actualize the qualities resulting from the elimination [of obscurations] and the realization. Therefore, considering the loss incurred when you forget your teachers even for a moment, serve them and supplicate them continually.

Considering the infinity of beings in the six realms—all of whom were your mothers and fathers in past lives—with the firm intention to establish them in a bliss that is free from an instant of suffering, even the prick of a needle, have no other concern than to benefit them in deeds, words, and thoughts.

As for your body, your speech, and your mind—endowed with the freedoms and favorable conditions so difficult to obtain—without wasting a single hour of your time, dedicate them entirely to benefit others and practice virtue.

Your vajra brothers and sisters are your supreme friends and your yidam, your tutelary deity, is the source of all siddhis. To part with them would be a terrible loss! Therefore, always cherish them as your most precious companions. You should accompany them without the slightest attachment or animosity, intimately blending your mind with theirs.

The sublime offspring is the beautiful child of the naturally arising wisdom, your own pristine awareness. What a loss if you let him go astray! Protect him in the citadel of dharmatā, preventing him from wandering off.

If the wealth of the parents falls to their children, they will live in opulence. What wealth are we talking about? Here we are talking about the recognition of the nature of mind, which is like a precious wish-fulfilling jewel. To prevent it from slipping away—this would be such a loss!—cherish mindfulness and vigilance, free from distraction.

To reach the unchanging citadel of liberation and omniscience and the bliss it bestows, consider these six instructions to be crucial.

–315–

Six Calamities

Six calamities resulting from not bringing Dharma practice to its ultimate point:

Even though you do not want the suffering of birth in samsara,
You will experience it like a gush of water that cannot be stopped by covering it with earth.

Even though you do not want the pain of old age,
You will experience it like the frost that withers flowers.

Even though you do not want the torment of sickness,
You will experience it like a golden fish wriggling on hot sand.

Even though you do not want the grief of separation,
You will experience it like a mother camel who loses her calf.

Even though you do not want the harm inflicted by enemies and demons,
You will experience it like a small bird being chased by a hawk.

Even though you do not want the agony of death,
You will experience it like a flame being blown out by the wind.

Thinking of these calamities, please persevere in Dharma practice.

Failure to reach the ultimate point of Dharma practice results in six calamities:

Not a single person yearns for the sufferings of the three worlds of samsara. Yet you cannot avoid them until you rid yourself of the obscurations formed by your karma and your afflictive mental states, just as you cannot block a powerful upsurge of water that breaks through the ground, simply by attempting to cover it with earth.

When you grow older, your vision becomes blurred, your organs no longer function normally, and many other discomforts afflict you. Not a single person calls for this decay, yet it is the lot of all beings in the three worlds of samsara, just as in winter flowers are withered by frost.

As for the ordeal of illness that strikes the body, you do not want that either, but it will come as inexorably as the torments of a fish caught on a hook and thrown on hot sand.

In the course of your life, you have made connections with many people, some beneficial, some harmful. But in all cases, separation comes with its share of unwanted suffering, which recalls the inconsolable distress of a mother camel separated from her calf. You, too, have forged strong attachments with your friends and loved ones.

No one wishes for the calamities caused by enemies and evil spirits. Yet karmic retribution created by negative actions during your past lives will pursue you like a hawk chasing a small bird.

Aside from those who suffer the intolerable torments of the hell realms, who would wish for the agony of death? And yet, not a single being in the world has ever escaped death, which plays with life like wind with a flame.

Thus, fully aware of the imminence of these sufferings, zealously practice the Dharma.

–316–

Vain Wishes

Six instructions on wishes that will never be fulfilled:

Even though you wish to never separate from your spouse and relatives,
You will certainly be separated.

Even though you wish to never leave your comfortable home and bed,
You will certainly have to leave.

Even though you wish to never lose your pleasures and possessions,
You will certainly lose them.

Even though you wish to never lose this precious human life with freedoms and advantages,
You will certainly die.

Even though you wish to never separate from your noble masters and stop receiving sublime teachings from them,
You will certainly be separated.

Even though you wish to never separate from your noble friends,
You will certainly be separated.

Therefore, wear the armor of diligence from now on,
Since now is the time to visit the island of great bliss that is beyond separation.

To those friends who develop heartfelt sadness,
I, the mendicant who lacks Dharma, encourage you with this advice.

You imagine you can enjoy the company of your spouse, family, and friends for your whole life. Yet, all that has been gathered is doomed to be separated, and the day will come when the Lord of Death, Yamarāja, will tear you apart.

You may have a beautiful home and the most comfortable bed and expect to enjoy them forever. But you will inevitably be dispossessed of them—by enemies who destroy them or because you must leave.

You also think you would like to enjoy forever an abundance of food, clothing, possessions, and other pleasures. Nevertheless, when the time of decline comes, you are sure to suffer.

You may hope that this human body endowed with freedoms and favorable conditions will be yours forever, but all compounded phenomena are subject to impermanence, and death will certainly come.

You have met an excellent spiritual master and hope to remain forever in his presence, receiving his teachings. But the spiritual master, too, will pass into parinirvāṇa or go elsewhere. In any case, you will surely be separated from him.

You may expect to share the company of excellent spiritual friends forever, but you will have to part. This is certain.

Thus, from today onward, redouble your diligence, spurred on by the thought of death and impermanence, and if you reach the island of unchanging bliss, all these perfections will be yours.

Therefore, to my spiritual friends who are deeply saddened and weary of the three worlds of samsara, "I, a beggar without Dharma (Longchenpa), urge you to follow this advice."

–317–

Six Results That Occur on Their Own

Six outcomes that naturally occur without seeking them:

Leave behind the things of samsara—you do not need them at all,
And you will naturally experience the happiness of nirvana even though you did not wish for it.

Without bias, engage in virtuous activities with faith and diligence,
And you will naturally meet with joy and happiness and the sublime Dharma even though you did not wish for them.

Whatever you do, follow the instructions of your noble master,
And you will automatically receive profound instructions even though you did not ask for them.

Train your mind in the four immeasurables
And you will naturally benefit sentient beings without even having wanted to.

Give up stinginess and offer whatever you have to gather the accumulations,
And wealth and prosperity will come to you even though you did not wish for them.

Meditate upon the wisdom mind of the buddhas beyond meeting or separation
And deluded appearances and self-grasping will naturally cease.

If you practice according to the scriptures, these outcomes will certainly occur.

Without being filled with hopes and worries about a "goal," if you diligently create the causes for it, it will be naturally accomplished.

Deciding that you have no need for the deceptive experiences of the three worlds of samsara, as many as they are, leave them behind and clear them from your mind. Then, even if you do not seek it, the bliss of buddhahood, nirvana, will arise of its own accord.

With faith and without partiality, if you are diligent in virtuous practices, unremittingly, day and night, even without coveting them, joy, bliss, and the sublime Dharma will come to you.

If, no matter what you do, say, or think, you sincerely conform to your spiritual master's instructions, you will receive all the profound instructions without even needing to ask for them.

If you cultivate the four immeasurable attitudes—benevolence, compassion, rejoicing, and impartiality—and familiarize yourself constantly with bodhicitta, the altruistic intention of attaining enlightenment, you will benefit others naturally, without having planned for it.

Abandon any desire to obtain this or that through countless activities, to secure your means of living, to quench your thirst for gain, status, and entourage. Devote all your possessions to making offerings and accumulating merit. Then, prosperity will come to you naturally without having sought it.

Realize that the wisdom mind of the buddhas is perfectly present in your mind, beyond separation and reunion, and this will naturally serve as an antidote to deluded perceptions created by self-clinging, which will fade away by themselves.

If you practice in accordance with the scriptures, all this will happen spontaneously, just as when someone is carried away by the current of a great river; even without intending to be swept away, it will happen anyway. Similarly, if you practice the Dharma in a perfectly pure way, spiritual qualities will arise without your seeking them.

–318–

Six Recommendations

Think carefully about the six essential requirements:
To be disgusted with the delusory appearances of samsara,
You must feel the same revulsion as on seeing a swamp full of rotten corpses.
To refrain from evil and unvirtuous activities,
You must be careful like a newly married bride.
To give rise to remorse for unvirtuous activities,
You must be like someone who is terrified after ingesting poison.
To be able to overpower the negative emotions to be abandoned,
You must have an antidote as strong as the king of wild animals.
Your ability to release into their own sphere all thoughts that arise
Must be as immediate as the dissolution of salt in water.
To be able to perfectly distinguish what is in accordance with the Dharma and what is not,

> **You must have wisdom like the beak of a swan (that can separate milk from water).**
> **With these requirements, you will be in accord with all the sublime Dharma.**

If you wish to practice a perfectly pure Dharma, six things are necessary.

To reverse your grasping to the delusion that prevails in the three worlds of samsara, you must generate a deep sense of revulsion, as if seeing a swamp full of rotting corpses. The feeling of renunciation is the root of the Buddha's teachings.

You must be very careful with negative behavior, just as a young bride arriving in her new home is attentive and cautious. Likewise, if you are vigilant and thoughtful, you will gain a stable mind.

If you happen to commit even the smallest negative action contrary to the Dharma, do not neglect this, but regret it immediately, just as someone who has just swallowed a glass of poison is terrified by imminent death and the agonies he is about to endure.

All afflictive mental states without exception should be eliminated. As soon as one arises in your mind stream, you must overpower it, just as the roar of the lion, the king of animals, causes all other animals to tremble with fear.

Whatever thoughts arise, you must know how to free them into their own sphere. Any other outcome will not be beneficial. If you put salt in water, it can only dissolve into it. Likewise, liberate your thoughts as soon as they come in contact with your mind stream.

You must also differentiate wisely between virtuous actions that are in accordance with the Dharma, and negative ones that contradict it, just as when a swan drinks milk mixed with water, its beak can extract the milk and leave the water. Similarly, you must be able to forsake behaviors that are contrary to the Dharma and practice those that accord with it.

If you abide by these six requirements, you will remain in harmony with the entire supreme Dharma.

–319–

Qualifications of a Yogi

Six indispensable qualifications of supreme yogis:
Their view should be like a king, unchanging and stable.
Their conduct should be like a minister, timely and appropriate.
Their observance of vows should be like a guard, enduring all adversities.
Their discernment should be like an attendant who has an eye for everything.
Their conceptual thoughts should be like clouds, naturally dissipating.
Their spiritual qualities should be like a treasure-house, containing everything one may need.
Whoever has these qualifications will spontaneously accomplish the two purposes [of self and others].
What are the qualifications of a yogi endowed with the highest capacities?

How should the perfect view be? If in this world, a benevolent king (or ruler)[183] is endowed with power, the country will be happy, the king will have no difficulty ruling, and both his entourage and his subjects will live in harmony. Likewise, the view must be a source of certainty and rule your mind without the slightest error.

If such a king, whose acts accord with the Dharma, is assisted by a wise minister, the administration of the kingdom will be easy, and the people will live in harmony. In the same way, you should adjust your conduct appropriately to the times and circumstances, just as a wise minister will righteously punish wrongdoing and reward good deeds, thus earning the approval of all subjects.

As far as conduct is concerned, one distinguishes the conduct of the listeners, of the bodhisattvas, and of the followers of the Secret Mantra. You must conform your conduct to the level of your view and realization. To do this, it is important to protect the precepts of individual liberation, the bodhisattva vows, and the sacred commitments of the Secret Mantra with the same vigilance that characterizes the guards of a great king. To achieve this, you must avoid being overpowered by afflictive mental states and be able to bring all circumstances onto the path.

You must also be discerning: if the king has a clever and resourceful attendant who is able to carry out his intentions faithfully, all will be well with the people. Similarly, with the help of wisdom, you must be able to put into practice, through experience, the teachings of the nine vehicles.

If discursive thoughts do not vanish of their own accord like clouds in the sky, they will reinforce grasping to the self and accumulate innumerable samsaric seeds.

As for the supreme qualities of listening, pondering, and meditating, they are like the royal treasury in which everything one may possibly need can be found. In the same way, no matter what quality you might consider, there is not a single one that you do not need.

If you have all these qualifications, the twofold benefit of others and of yourself will be spontaneously accomplished.

–320–

Six Ways to Achieve Excellence

Six ways of practicing Dharma that accomplish goodness:
If you want to become the king of kings and leaders, encourage yourself in Dharma.
If you want to become the king of warriors, defeat the army of the enemies, negative emotions.
If you want to become the king of ministers, make decisions according to the Buddha's words.
If you want to become the king of the powerful, tame the evil spirit of self-grasping.
If you want to become the king of the rich, accomplish the prosperity of the two accumulations.
If you want to become the king of doctors, treat the chronic ailments of your own weaknesses.
If you know these methods, you will be the sovereign of gods and humans.

Everywhere in the world, someone gifted with many qualities will be considered to be learned, virtuous, and benevolent. Here, we are talking about six ways necessary to accomplish the best qualities of Dharma practice.

If you want to become a king among kings, act in accordance with the supreme Dharma and become an object of respect throughout the three worlds. Urge yourself to practice the Dharma.

If you wish to become the king of the brave, annihilate the horde of your true enemies—negative emotions. Thus will you repel the armies of samsara once and for all and thereby become a supreme hero.

If you wish to be sovereign among humans, conform to the teachings of the Buddha and make the necessary preparations so that everything you do accords with the Dharma.

If you wish to be king of the mighty, subdue the evil mind that clings to the self and apprehend the nature of the nonego. If you do so, you will have mastered everything.

If you wish to be king of the wealthy, hoard the twofold accumulations and you will be replete with merits not only in this life but also in all your future lives.

If you wish to be the king of therapists, apply appropriate antidotes to your defects at all times and you'll be cured of your disruptive states of mind.

If you do these things, you will become the ruler of devas and humans.

–321–

Fearsome Enemies

Six types of enemies to be wary of:

While practicing Dharma, when the mind of renunciation and faith occurs,
The fondness, affection, and advice of friends and relatives can arise as enemies.

When you give up all samsaric activities,
Attachment and craving arise as enemies.

When Dharma practitioners engage in offering food and wealth,
The enemy of pride arises as others shower words of praise.

When you practice the profound instructions,
Divided mind, doubt, and hesitation will arise as enemies.

When the signs of progress, the warmth of spiritual experience occur,
The enemies of joy and excitement and grasping upon references arise.

When the door of various positive qualities opens,
The enemies of pride and arrogance and strong self-regard arise.

Therefore, you must be wary of these enemies arising.
The supreme armor of meditation is to develop loving-kindness and patience.

Six enemies endanger the attainment of liberation. You must confront them.

When you enter the path of Dharma and consider giving up all samsaric activities to devote yourself to spiritual practice, while you are developing faith and renunciation, your parents and other relatives might tell you, "Stay at home; enjoy the wealth accumulated by your parents instead of devoting yourself to spiritual practice." This kind of advice is a true enemy. Don't heed it!

When you fully abandon ordinary, mundane activities, you will understand that the attachment to the eight worldly considerations, for food, clothing, power, status, and the like are your enemies. Conquer them!

When you genuinely practice the Dharma, instead of accumulating possessions and food, you give them away generously. At that time, people will tell you that if you live a long time you will need these things. They will tell you this and that and give you all kinds of advice that act in fact as your enemies. Don't listen to them!

When you practice the profound instructions received from your spiritual teacher, others might instill doubts in your mind, saying that your teacher is not qualified, that his instructions are not authentic, or that you are not capable of practicing such instructions anyway. You may harbor doubts of your own. Such doubts manifest as your enemies.

As your meditative experiences and your realization blossom, if you think, "Oh, I have attained a high realization and thanks to it I have become clairvoyant, I had such and such signs of accomplishment," and become very pleased with yourself, developing a good deal of infatuation, know that this is an obstacle, an enemy that stands in your way.

If various spiritual qualities arise as a consequence of your study, reflection, and meditation, you might tell yourself that no one else has such qualities. Pride and vanity will arise in your mind, and you will fall into narcissism. As it is said, "The water of qualities does not dwell on the peak of pride." Your existing qualities will wither, and you will not acquire new ones.

Therefore, you must be extremely wary about these various enemies. It is also said, "Practicing bodhicitta and resilience is the supreme armor." Accordingly, meditate on loving-kindness to all beings, and develop fortitude in the practice of Dharma, just as when you don armor, helmet, and other protection on the battlefield you will not be pierced by the enemy's weapons. Cultivate fortitude against all these foes.

–322–

Six Designations for Practitioners

Six designations for Dharma practitioners:
Those who can stand upright in their spiritual practice are capable.
Those who can lead their body, speech, and mind to virtue are faithful.
Those who are neither deceitful nor cunning are noble.
Those who can avoid falling into wrong paths are wise.
Those who spend their lives according to Dharma are prudent.
Those who are kind to others and greatly compassionate are followers of the Great Vehicle.
In these ways, you should follow the conduct of the noble ones.

Six designations are given to different types of Dharma practitioners:

Those who can stand on their own feet after having practiced the Dharma are resilient. When they encounter adversity, among the four activities that can overcome such obstacles—pacification, augmentation, attraction, and subjugation—they excel in the latter.

Those who are diligent in the practice of virtue, in actions, words, and thoughts, are genuine disciples.

Those who never deceive others and are free from deceit are good human beings.

Those who never engage in the wrong ways and who never give an ear to pernicious guides who teach evil are insightful.

Those who succeed in devoting their whole lives to the Dharma and thus know how to accomplish their own good are wise.

Those who are filled with benevolence and compassion, having fully integrated the instructions, are true practitioners of the Great Vehicle.

Such is the conduct of noble beings: strive to emulate them.

–323–

Free from the Trap of Suffering

Six situations where you will be free from the trap of suffering:
Having attained the difficult-to-find human existence, you have met the Dharma.
Having met authentic spiritual masters, you have developed devotion and respect.
Having abandoned samsaric activities, you are free from distraction and clamor.
Having received profound instructions, you are free from the obscuration of errors.
By always engaging in virtuous activities, you are free from laziness.
By spontaneously accomplishing great bliss, you are free from conceptual representations and grasping.
Whoever possesses these six qualities will be spared pain.

When a wild animal is caught in a trap, it has little chance to escape and will soon be killed. This will happen to you if you are caught in the net of suffering. But if you enjoy the difficult-to-attain human existence and meet with the supreme Dharma, you will use this opportunity to free yourself from suffering.

If you meet a genuine master, you will develop the respectful fervor that sees him or her as the Buddha in person.

If you abandon the activities of the three worlds of samsara, you will not stray into futility and distraction.

If you receive your teacher's profound instructions and keep them in mind, you will be spared the obscurations associated with obstacles and the deviations related to wrong views and incorrect meditation.

If you apply yourself with continual diligence to virtuous conduct and practice, you will be free from the influence of laziness and indolence.

If you spontaneously accomplish great bliss, you will be free from conceptual references and fixations.

If you possess these six qualities in full, you will be spared the torments of the three worlds of samsara.

–324–

Identify Your Defects

Instructions on knowing your own six failings:

If you are unable to stay in secluded places because of loneliness,
Know that you lack practice of one-pointed concentration and other capacities.

If you are unable to get along with most people,
Know that you lack tact and your mind is wild by nature.

If you are unable to abandon non-Dharmic activities even after relying upon spiritual masters,
Know that their blessings and positive qualities have not penetrated you.

If you are proud, untamed, and haughty,
Know that you lack the essence of spiritual experience and are ignorant of the ultimate reality.

If your knowledge of instructions is limited and you are extremely lazy,
Know that you have not entered the path of liberation but are wandering in samsara.

If you give preeminence to your own interests before those of others and lack compassion,
Know that you are not following the Mahāyāna path and lack bodhicitta.

Based on the outer signs, you can infer the inner attitude.
Therefore, abandon what is contrary to the Dharma and avoid entering a mistaken path.

Six instructions to identify some of your faults.

If, when you find yourself in a secluded place, you cannot stand solitude and are depressed because you have no one to talk to and no distractions, this is a clear sign that you lack the focus needed for calm abiding and deeper insight.

If, when you find yourself in a group, you cannot get along with anyone and give free rein to attachment and repulsion, you lack the life skills that allow you to maintain harmonious relationships with others. If that is the case, you must acknowledge your difficult character and your rough ways.

If, while following a spiritual teacher, you indulge in all kinds of negative actions contrary to the Dharma, you should know that the master's blessings and qualities have not entered your mind.

If you have not cured your arrogance and overflow with pride, you lack the essence of spiritual experience and therefore have not realized the fundamental nature of things.

If you have received little instruction and are very lazy, the time for attaining supreme liberation has not yet come and you will keep wandering in the three worlds of samsara.

If you think only of yourself and lack benevolence and compassion, you are in contradiction with bodhicitta and with the path of the Great Vehicle.

It is by examining signs that things reveal themselves. Accordingly, by examining external signs you can check whether what lies inside you does not accord with the Dharma. Strive to eliminate these six flaws that are contrary to the Dharma.

–325–

Six Types of Squandering

Six types of squandering:

If, without fear of the lower realms, you accumulate the negativity of nonvirtue,
You are squandering the difficult-to-find human existence with its freedoms and advantages.

If, even after entering the door of Dharma, you develop attachment and aversion due to partiality,
You are squandering your confidence in the ultimate and perfect meaning.

If you hold your head high with arrogance[184] in your knowledge of words gained through listening and contemplation,
You are squandering the wisdom that realizes the ultimate truth.

If you abandon practicing the profound Secret Mantra teachings,
You are squandering your perseverance by enduring vain austerities.

If you abandon the supreme wisdom of the nondual unity,
You are squandering your meditation on the extremes of either appearance or emptiness.

If you abandon your Dharma practice in mountain retreat places,
You are squandering your accomplishments by wandering in villages and monasteries.
It is therefore crucial that you do not go down such paths.

There are six ways to waste this precious human body endowed with freedoms and favorable conditions.

If you have no fear of the suffering of the lower realms and keep committing negative actions, you are wasting your human existence endowed with freedoms and favorable conditions.

If you have crossed the threshold of the teachings of individual liberation, the bodhisattvas, and the Secret Mantra, but remain full of partiality, attachment, and aversion, considering those on your side as gods and those opposed as demons, you are only wasting your faith.

If you have studied and reflected a lot, but your mind becomes infected with pride, even meeting the Buddha in person, you will not develop faith. This is a sign of having wasted the wisdom that realizes the true nature of everything.

If you forsake the practice of the deeper meaning of the Secret Mantra to invest great effort in the mundane activities of ordinary life, you are wasting your perseverance and the hardships you endure.

If you forsake the nondual unity of the primordial wisdom, which is present in the nature of your mind, you will cling either to the extreme of existence or to the extreme of emptiness, thus wasting your meditation.

If you stop practicing the Dharma on a secluded mountainside to wander in villages, mingling with many people and multiplying attachments and aversions, you are wasting the ordinary and extraordinary siddhis.

Avoid going down these paths.

–326–

Walking in the Footsteps of Previous Masters

Six means to follow in the footsteps of the past masters:

If you want to cut the root of negative actions, obscurations,
and habitual tendencies,
Look at the groundless and rootless nature of the mind.

If you want to search for the wish-fulfilling jewel that fulfills all
aspirations,
Make continuous efforts on the profound path.
If you want to realize the dharmatā, the ultimate nature of
reality,

Abide in your own nature because you will not find it by searching elsewhere.

If you want to integrate the instructions through practice,
First, tame your mind and then practice.

If you want to practice the sublime Dharma authentically from the heart,
Give up the concerns of this life and cut the bonds of attachment.

If you want to swiftly follow in the footsteps of the great noble ones,
Look at their conduct and make it the heart essence of your practice.

This advice is the essence of the crucial pith instructions.

There are six ways to follow in the footsteps of previous masters by taking the example of their great deeds and their lives of perfect liberation.

If you wish to purify your negative actions, obscurations, and habitual tendencies at their root and aspire to undertake an inner journey to liberation, you must contemplate the nature of your mind, which is rootless and without any [truly existing] foundation. Then your negative acts and obscurations will be purified by themselves.

If you wish to obtain the miraculous wish-fulfilling gem, devote yourself to listening, contemplating, and meditating on the profound instructions of your supreme master and all your aspirations will be fulfilled.

If you aspire to unmistakably realize the meaning of the fundamental nature [of your mind], you need not exert yourself in all kinds of efforts: simply leave your mind in its natural state, remain in the continuum of contemplation, and you will understand.

If you wish to intimately blend your mind stream with the direct experience of all the instructions you have received, tame your afflictive mental states and you will know how to integrate these instructions into your practice.

If you wish wholeheartedly to be in conformity with the sublime Dharma, put aside all preoccupation with the ordinary activities of this life and cut the bonds of whatever makes you cling to them.

If you aspire to follow in the footsteps of the learned and accomplished masters of the past, contemplate [accounts of] their behavior and extract the quintessence of spiritual practice.

This advice covers the ultimate vital points of supreme Dharma practice. Implement it diligently.

–327–

Six Ways of Acting Contrary to the Teachings

Six actions that are in disharmony with the general Buddhist teachings:

Engaging in all kinds of negative activities,
Yet still hoping to fulfill the aspirations of others is not the way of a genuine practitioner.

Being hypocritical, deceptive, and deceitful,
Yet still hoping to please the Three Jewels is not the way of a genuine practitioner.

Not striving hard to practice in solitude,
Yet blaming the Dharma is not the way of a genuine practitioner.

Speaking of compassion while acting selfishly,
Yet still hoping to benefit others is not the way of a genuine practitioner.

Nurturing self-grasping while speaking of emptiness,
Yet still hoping to tread the path of liberation is not the way of a genuine practitioner.

Clinging to your own views while speaking of going beyond the extremes,

Yet still hoping to realize the ultimate truth is not the way of a genuine practitioner.

Therefore, abandon such actions for this is how the Buddhist tradition degenerates.

There are six ways of being that contradict the tradition of a Dharma practitioner in general: If you engage in all kinds of negative behavior—taking life, consuming intoxicating beverages, chasing sensual pleasures, and participating in all kinds of inappropriate conduct—while fancying yourself to be practicing Dharma, you are just deluding yourself. Behaving in this way does not conform at all with the tradition of a Dharma practitioner.

If you deceive others with hypocrisy, deception, and duplicity, while hoping to please the Three Jewels and the spiritual masters, this does not conform at all with the tradition of a Dharma practitioner.

If you live in lonely places without seriously practicing, being constantly distracted and scattered, and after a while tell yourself with bitterness, "I've been practicing for so long and yet I do not see any meditative experiences and realizations coming," this kind of expectation is not in keeping with the tradition of a genuine Dharma practitioner.

If, just paying lip service you proclaim, "Oh, poor things! How worthy of compassion they are!" while in practice you are exclusively pursuing your own interests, yet still pretend to be dedicated to the good of others, you are clearly not in accord with the tradition of a Dharma practitioner.

If you firmly tie the knot of self-clinging in your mind while proclaiming, "It is all emptiness," and yet still hope to attain the ultimate level of the path of liberation, such hope is hardly in keeping with the tradition of a Dharma practitioner.

Whatever view you entertain, be it nihilism or eternalism, if you consider it supreme while continuing to speak of the "emptiness free of extremes" and hope nevertheless to realize the fundamental nature of all, you are not in accord with the tradition of a Dharma practitioner.

In all these cases, the authentic tradition of the Buddha's teaching can only degenerate.

–328–

Six Great Things to Do

Six exceptionally virtuous and excellent things to do:

When the teachings are accessible and you have obtained the freedoms and advantages,
This is the time to quickly escape the pit of samsara.

When you are practicing the essence of what you have heard and contemplated,
This is the time to fully merge your mind with Dharma.

When you are experiencing many forms of suffering and adverse circumstances,
This is the time to invigorate your diligence in Dharma practice.

When six types of objects appear at the doors of your six consciousnesses,
This is the time for the dualistic appearances of subject and object to be liberated in their true nature.

While meditating upon the essence of the view, meditation, and conduct,
This is the time to become familiar with the creativity of pristine awareness in an unbiased way.

While striving to accomplish your ultimate objective now,
This is the time to work hard to practice the instructions given with kindness.

If you do not apply the antidotes according to your capacities,
At the moment of death, the Lord of Death will laugh at your wasted life.

There are six extremely virtuous actions that will initially ensure that you are reborn in the higher worlds of samsara and that, ultimately, you attain the omniscience of buddhahood.

To begin with, since the Buddha's teachings still exist in this world and you have obtained a precious human existence endowed with freedoms and favorable conditions, you are like a traveler who wishes to depart for a distant country and has gathered all the necessary conditions for his journey. Now is the time for him to move forward to the best of his capacities. Likewise, now is the time for you to apply all your energy and use all possible means, large and small, to escape the pit of the three worlds of samsara.

As you practice the essence of study, reflection, and meditation, this is the time to blend your mind with the Dharma intimately and to constantly position yourself to check whether you are in accord with the teachings.

When various obstacles arise, bringing about diverse types of suffering—disease, famine, conflict, etc.—while greed, animosity, lack of discernment, and jealousy rage, it is high time to resolve to focus your efforts on Dharma practice.

As the objects related to the six aspects of consciousness appear—forms, sounds, smells, tastes, textures—avoid all behavior driven by desire or aggression: the time has come to untie the knot of dual appearances related to subject and object in its own nature.

As you meditate upon the meaning of view, meditation, and action, you should perfect the qualities associated with these three, while refining your understanding of the creativity of awareness.

Now that you hold in your hands the ready-to-use opportunity to practice the supreme Dharma that will ensure your long-term benefit, you must put into practice the precious instructions that your glorious teacher has so kindly bestowed upon you: this is the time to be diligent like a beggar who just received some food.

Using antidotes wisely, in accordance with your abilities, if you gather all the favorable conditions and practice, at the time of death you will avoid abject desperation and will not find yourself facing the Lord of Death's ridicule.

–329–

Six Situations Doomed to Failure

Six contradictory situations that lead to failure and are unfounded[185]:

Without gaining mastery over yourself,
Wishing to gain mastery over others is illogical and senseless.

Unable to benefit and help yourself,
Wishing to help others is contradictory and premature.

Not being an authentic student yourself,
Wishing to become a teacher is incongruous and rash.

If you appear like a piece of stiff leather and have not succeeded in transforming yourself,
Wishing to transform others is paradoxical and senseless.

Lacking the confidence of realization that allows you to aim correctly,[186]
Trying to teach meditation to others is illogical and premature.

Without abandoning your ordinary conduct,
Trying to lead others on the path of Dharma is inexplicable and foolish.

Freedom from such defects is thus crucial.

"Thoughtless conduct" refers to unsuitable conduct that can in no way lead to the desired result. Six such types of conduct are explained here.

If, right now for instance, you have no self-control whatsoever, do not even appreciate enjoying all the conditions for practicing the Dharma, and instead want to serve a powerful ruler, you are completely deluded.

If you have been unable to achieve your own good and even lack the ability to do so, the idea of your accomplishing the good of others is rather incongruous.

If you do not have all the qualities of a genuine disciple, trying to play the role of a qualified spiritual guide is absurd.

If your mind is as stiff as uncured leather, offering teachings to others and claiming to transform them is thoughtless and contradictory.

If you do not enjoy the confidence born from the realization that allows you to aim correctly, wanting to impart meditation instructions to others based on your nonexistent experience is incomprehensible.

Since your conduct is no different from that of ordinary beings, your ability to establish them in the supreme Dharma is no greater than that of a shepherd who believes he is capable of herding *garuḍa*s.

Do whatever it takes to avoid contamination by these defects.

–330–

Six Incentives

Six ways to perfectly encourage yourself to practice the sublime Dharma:

If you want to give up the meaningless activities of this life,
The moment you feel faith, drop all your unfinished tasks,
For activities are endless like ripples in water.

If you wish to go to a solitary place to practice Dharma,
As soon as the intention arises, go there without putting it off.
If you do not go then, you will face many obstacles that can discourage you.

When you rely upon your teachers, follow whatever they say.
You will never rejoice their hearts if you merely boast about serving them.

When you look at the nature of your mind, rest in its natural state without fabrication.
If you do not let your mind rest, you will not see its natural face by generating thoughts endlessly.

When you seek spiritual qualities, be perpetually diligent.
Impatience and sporadic zeal will never allow you to perfect your spiritual qualities.

When you reach the exhaustion (of phenomena) in the dharmatā, you will achieve the stronghold of the fundamental nature.
Seeking it elsewhere, you will never find it.

The vain activities of the world are nothing but delusions. If you happen to consider abandoning them and develop some confidence in the Dharma, then is the time to give up all your ongoing projects. If you perpetuate useless activities, they will not cease any sooner than will ripples on the surface of water: one after another, they will continue without end.

If you happen to think, "I must head to a solitary place, free myself from ordinary activities and devote myself one-pointedly to Dharma practice. I must practice in a mountain retreat!" Do not hesitate! Leaving as soon as this thought arises in your mind is much better. If you tell yourself, "Oh, not right now, sometime later, when I am free," time will pass and the opportunity for dedication to the practice will never arise, for many adverse circumstances will keep you from leaving.

When you follow a spiritual master, carefully do all that he advises. Otherwise, you may boast, "I serve my master," or "I did so much!" but that is not how to fulfill your master's vision.[187]

When you contemplate the nature of your mind, you must leave it in its natural simplicity. If you keep scattering your mind in all directions, you will not behold the face of the ultimate nature of reality, the dharmatā.

When you seek to acquire spiritual qualities, you must work diligently day and night, with the same perseverance and continuity as a bee gathering nectar from flowers. These qualities will not flourish in your mind stream in a day or two. Nor will you succeed in perfecting such qualities by relaxing your efforts every time you move a mere step forward.

Moreover, you must experience the exhaustion of phenomena in the dharmatā and thus conquer the citadel of the fundamental nature of all things. Otherwise, if you do not know that the ultimate nature of reality resides in your own mind and keep looking for it elsewhere, you will never find it.

–331–

Six Antidotes

Six antidotes to apply if you want to realize the fundamental nature.
Do not occupy a high and prominent place but sit in a lowly seat.
Do not be a leader of many but follow those who have noble qualities.
Do not chase fame spurred by the wish to excel but dismantle the mountain of ego.
Do not seek victory that satisfies your ambitions, but accept defeat and develop contentment.
Do not scrutinize the qualities and faults of others but check whether or not your own mind stream is virtuous.
Do not be distracted by the objects of the six consciousnesses but look at the nature of your mind.
Whoever applies these six antidotes will strike the crucial points of practice.

If you wish to apprehend the ultimate nature of all things, you must begin by applying these six remedies.

First, do not put yourself in a prominent position just because you have a higher status, come from a good family, or are wealthy. Being humble, adopting the lowest position, and behaving as if you had no qualities whatsoever is much preferable.

Moreover, do not seek to lead a large number of people. Much better is to persevere in doing well what you do.

In your behavior, do not seek fame and the consideration of others; dismantle the mountain of pride that you may conceive about your activities.

Do not seek to emerge victorious in accordance with your desires and ambitions. Accepting defeat and being content with what comes your way is far better.

Do not be constantly looking for the qualities and faults of others. It is better to be vigilant and circumspect about your own positive or negative actions, and to accomplish the former while avoiding the latter.

Without being distracted by perceiving the objects of the six aspects of consciousness, contemplate the nature of your mind. Thus, by applying these six remedies, you will strike the key points of spiritual practice.

–332–

Six Points of Certainty

Essential instructions on six points of certainty:

If you are able to supplicate with devotion, respect, and longing,
You will certainly realize the nature of mind and receive blessings.

If you know how to release and relax in the natural state of nonaction,
The self-cognizing, nondual primordial wisdom will certainly shine naturally.

If you know how to look directly at dualistic and conceptual characteristics,
They will certainly be liberated in their natural state without fabrication or corruption.

If you know how to let deluded thoughts of subject and object rest in their natural state,
They will certainly be purified naturally, and nonconceptual primordial wisdom will dawn.

If you activate your pristine awareness with skillful means, from the ultimate nature and primordial ground,
Unwavering, unelaborate, and spontaneously present luminosity will certainly manifest.

If you are persistently diligent and free of laziness or procrastination,
The qualities of the bhūmis and paths and the signs of warmth will certainly manifest from within.

Once you have generated the causes, six kinds of results will manifest without fail.

If you perceive your spiritual master as the Buddha himself, if you generate the fervent devotion that enables you to apprehend the excellence of all his actions and turn your prayers to him—if you are capable of all this, you are bound to realize the nature of the mind.

If you can relax while leaving things as they are,[188] without engaging in action, the experience of primordial wisdom, your nondual awareness, will undoubtedly shine forth in your mind.

If, while contemplating the true nature of discursive thoughts related to duality, you allow for their spontaneous liberation and let awareness rest without fabrication or alteration, thoughts of attachment and rejection will be liberated by themselves in their natural state.

You must first understand that the delusory perceptions associated with grasping to subject and object are not really born; second, these perceptions do not dwell anywhere; and finally, they do not go anywhere. If, with this understanding, you leave them in their own nature, the natural radiance of the dharmatā, the primordial wisdom free of concepts, will surely shine forth.

If, with the help of the appropriate physical postures, recitations, and meditations, you strike the crucial point of awareness, it is certain that the true nature of all things, the primordial and unchanging ground free from conceptual fabrication, will spontaneously arise within your mind.

If you are not prone to indolence or laziness and keep practicing the supreme Dharma with perseverance day and night, in the best case the qualities of the bhūmis and paths will grow daily, in the middle case monthly, and in the worst case yearly.

–333–

Six Truths

Listing six truths:
If you deceive others, you are deceiving yourself.
If you give victory to others, you are giving victory to yourself.
If you oppress others, you are harming yourself.
If you help others in any way, you are helping yourself.
If you blame others out of jealousy, you are blaming yourself.
If you accumulate merit for the sake of others, you are accumulating merit for yourself.

Rare it is to find anyone who understands these truths and even rarer to find those who integrate them into their mind stream.
Therefore, train your mind on these points.

Six truths are listed:

If you deceive others with hypocrisy, deceit, and duplicity, in truth you are deceiving yourself, since the stain of deceit is yours and you are, therefore, the loser.

If, on the other hand, imbued with bodhicitta, you allow others to win, you will naturally be the true winner.

If you are full of animosity, constantly perceiving others as enemies and harming them with cruelty and malice, you are in fact harming yourself, for the maturing of such behavior will cause rebirth in the lower realms.

If you benefit others, both spiritually and in everyday life, these acts will bring benefits for many lifetimes to come.

If you are constantly jealous of others and denigrate them, you are woefully lacking in pure vision. Your jealousy will eventually come back to bite you in the face.

If you gather both merit and wisdom for the sake of others, your own accumulations will be perfected as well.

Yet, people very rarely understand all these pith instructions and even more rarely do they integrate them into their mind stream. That is why it is important to practice mind training, which consists essentially in caring less about yourself and more about others.

–334–

Lack of Support

Six situations where you are not supported:
Those who lack faith and respect will not be supported by compassion.
Those who lack insight will not be supported by listening and contemplation.
Those who neglect their samayas will not be supported by siddhis.

Those who do not follow what they are taught will not be supported by advice.
Those whose minds are evil will not be supported by Dharma.
Those who are ungrateful will not be supported by mutual help.

Six ways of lacking support are identified. What are they?

Those who are totally devoid of faith and respect are not receptive to the compassionate support of spiritual masters, buddhas and bodhisattvas.

Those who do not gain wisdom through listening, reflection, and meditation will not be supported by the indispensable knowledge of the view, meditation, and action in accordance with the key points of the supreme Dharma.

Those who do not keep the samayas properly will never obtain the supreme and ordinary accomplishments.

If those who are told, "These are the excellent qualities of the supreme Dharma that are indispensable," do not heed these teachings to the best of their abilities, no one will be able to give them good advice.

For those whose mind streams are filled with craving and animosity, the time of being supported by the qualities of the supreme Dharma will not come.

Those who do not know how to express gratitude by returning good for good are not ready to be supported by benevolence.

–335–

When the Dharma Becomes Inoperative

Six situations where Dharma loses its effectiveness:

Inwardly, if you do not see negative emotions as enemies,
Outwardly, the instructions of the spiritual master will be ineffective.

If you do not leave behind the activities of this life,
The time to practice Dharma will never come.

If you do not let go of the urge to plan for your old age out of fear of the declines inherent in aging,

Your heartfelt and diligent practice of the sublime Dharma will be ineffective.

If you do not develop certainty from within,
Your devotion and respect for the Dharma and your teacher will be ineffective.

If you do not abandon negative actions in samsara,
The compassion of the noble ones will be unable to save you.

If you do not abandon strong grasping to inherent existence,
The instructions free from partiality will be ineffective.

Even if you try to practice the Dharma to the best of your ability, your practice may not fulfill its function [if certain conditions are missing]:

If, inwardly, you fail to let the afflictive mental states subside, after having come to regard them as enemies; outwardly, the sharpness of the instructions you have received will not cut through these afflictive states of mind and will not serve their purpose.

If you do not leave behind the eight worldly concerns, which are limited to this life's affairs, even if you feel that you are practicing well, the time of ripening will not come in your practice.

If you practice the supreme Dharma as well as you can now, it will help you at the time of death. But, if you make only material preparations for your old age related to food, clothing, and finances, when death approaches, all this will be useless in alleviating your agony. Sincere diligence in practicing the Dharma, that fails to keep death in mind, will only be a cause for hardship.

If certainty is not established in your mind about the view, meditation, and action, confidence and respectful devotion to the Dharma and the spiritual master will not arise.

If you do not move away from the negative acts of samsara and unvirtuous behavior, the compassion of the buddhas and bodhisattvas will be powerless to lead you on the path to liberation.

If you think only of yourself, are strongly attached to the tangible reality of things, are convinced of the true existence of activities related to the eight worldly concerns, and are unable to eliminate this conviction, receiving instructions free of bias will not help.

–336–

Six Tragicomedies

Six tragicomedies:

Unsure whether you will live or not,
Planning to own a home is a tragicomedy.

Unsure whether you will be able to use it or not,
Collecting and hoarding wealth is a tragicomedy.

Unsure whether you will be able to wear it or not,
Making efforts to gather clothing is a tragicomedy.

Unsure whether you will have the power to eat or not,
Engaging in preparing food is a tragicomedy.

Unsure whether you will be able to remain together or not,
Becoming acquainted[189] with friends is a tragicomedy.

Unsure whether you will be repaid with gratitude,
Raising children is a tragicomedy.

When I observe the deluded attitude of worldly beings,
I see many such tragicomedies.

If you place your hopes in the ordinary pursuits of the three worlds of samsara, this leads to tragicomic delusion. Why?

You have no idea whether your life will be short or long, the time of death being unpredictable and the circumstances that will cause it uncertain. You are not in control. Nonetheless, you build dwelling places and erect imposing mansions. If a noble being saw you, he or she would burst out laughing.

As for your possessions and wealth, who knows whether you will be able to use them or not? If you collect and hoard a large amount of property, the day will come when it will either be snatched away by a ruler or annihilated by enemies, a tragicomic situation indeed.

What is the point of searching for and storing all kinds of clothing? Who knows if you will be able to wear it or not? Such a quest is another tragicomic situation.

What is the point of searching for and hoarding so much food? Will you be able to eat it or not? This is not in your power, and food is likely to be wasted, a tragicomic situation.

Regarding your father and mother, your family, friends, and acquaintances, who knows how long you will be able to enjoy their company? Hoping to keep them around forever is tragicomic.

Who knows whether your children will show you gratitude in return for the care you have taken of them? Raising many children is therefore tragicomic.

Such samsaric behavior and situations are deluded and tragicomic. Better to abandon them all.

–337–

Six Necessary Actions

Explaining six necessary actions:
At all costs, you must abandon worldly activities.
At all costs, you must dispel the darkness of ignorance.
At all costs, you must dismantle the stronghold of subject and object dualism.
At all costs, you must increase your qualities of experience and realization.
At all costs, you must actualize the unity of primordial wisdom.
At all costs, you must obtain the gem of the three kāyas.

Six indispensable actions:

Whatever your occupations in the samsaric world, the day will come when you must give them up. There is nothing you can continue doing throughout your entire life.

The darkness of ignorance is the root of all delusion: dispel it!

You have kept reinforcing the bastion of dualistic grasping to subject and object: dismantle it now!

The qualities of meditative experiences and realization depend on relying upon spiritual masters and following their instructions: continually augment them!

Having understood the instructions that unite skillful means with wisdom, integrate them into your mind stream!

The ultimate nature of your own mind being like a jewel, you must apprehend and care for it, as it will fulfill all your aspirations.

–338–

Six Pathetic Situations

Explaining six pathetic states:[190]

Even though many years have passed since your ordination,
You still do not know the vows to be protected and the precepts on what should be followed and what discarded. How pathetic!

Even though many years have passed since you entered the path of Dharma,
You still need to distinguish virtue and nonvirtue. How pathetic!

Even though many years have passed since you entered the Mahāyāna path,
You are still not close to following the precepts of bodhicitta. How pathetic!

Even though many years have passed since you began to engage in listening and contemplation,
You still have no inclination to practice. How pathetic!

Even though many years have passed since you began practicing,
You are still not developing qualities as signs of the warmth of practice. How pathetic!

Even though many years have passed since you realized the view,

> **You have still not dismantled the delusion of clinging to substantiality. How pathetic!**
>
> **All of these are like first constructing a building's walls**
> **And later laying the foundation. How ludicrous!**
> **If you look at these attitudes, they are laughable and if you reflect upon them, they are depressing.**
> **Therefore, rely on noble beings and engage in listening, contemplation, and meditation.**

My life of so-called perfect liberation is perfectly summarized in these instructions!

As it is said, if many years after taking monastic vows, you still do not know what is allowed and what is forbidden regarding the precepts of prātimokṣa, bodhisattvas, and the Secret Mantra, shame on you.

If many years have passed since you crossed the threshold of the supreme Dharma and you still haven't learned what is to be accomplished, positive actions, and what is to be abandoned, negative actions, you should be ashamed.

If many years have passed since you embarked on the path of the Great Vehicle and you have barely come close to knowing the precepts and the training of bodhicitta, you should feel embarrassed.

If you have spent many years listening to, studying, and reflecting on the Dharma, but have not put the meaning of the teachings into practice, you have much to be ashamed of.

If you have spent many years meditating without noticing any signs of "warmth" indicating the birth of the spiritual qualities associated with meditation, that is truly pathetic.

If, many years after you have intellectually understood the view, you still cannot dismantle your stubborn attachment to the reality of phenomena, remaining in such delusion is pathetic.

You are like someone who builds a house up to the roof, including the walls, and then later worries about laying a foundation—a very strange way of proceeding!

When you look at all these situations, you at first laugh, but when you think about the flaws, after laughing, you become depressed. Therefore, trusting in the noble beings, engage in study, reflection, and practice, and avoid such pathetic and embarrassing behavior.

–339–

The Presence of the Dharmatā within You

Six crucial points on how the dharmatā is naturally present within you:
Without examining and analyzing, you see your true nature.
Without speculating and purifying, samsara is primordially pure.
Without cutting and untying, the conceptual characteristics are liberated naturally.
Without searching and accomplishing, the five kāyas are spontaneously present within you.
Without abandoning and adopting, you are free from the extremes of virtue and nonvirtue.
Without action and effort, enlightened activities are spontaneously accomplished.
Whoever knows these truths is adept in the crucial points.

The ultimate nature of reality, the dharmatā, is present within your mind stream. Six key points emphasize this.

To know this, you need not engage in all sorts of investigations: it is up to you to see the ultimate nature of reality, there is no point looking for it outside.

Samsara is pure from the beginning. Since nothing should be considered rejectable, you need not speculate about this and, consequently, there is nothing to purify.

Nor is it necessary to cut through notions of eternity and nothingness or any other concepts, as though you were cutting a rope: if you see the actual nature of the dharmatā, everything is liberated into its true nature.

As for qualities that are meant to be obtained, there is no point in seeking them since they are spontaneously present in the five dimensions of buddhahood. Nor must you intentionally remove veils either: simply transcend the extremes of "desirable qualities" and "undesirable defects."

The enlightened activities of the buddhas are continuous and pervasive. They do not require deliberate effort, for they are spontaneously accomplished.

Whoever apprehends these six points is an expert in the quintessential meaning of the ultimate nature of reality. When someone realizes the view of the dharmatā, this is what happens. So it is said.

–340–

Six Qualities of a Wise Spiritual Master

Six instructions describing a wise master:
A master who is wise in generating faith in the faithless,
A master who is wise in showing what to adopt and what to discard,
A master who is wise in teaching the crucial points of practice,
A master who is wise in protecting disciples from obstacles and hindrances,
A master who is wise in providing hearing transmissions in unified ways,
A master who is wise in transforming adverse circumstances on the path.

Six instructions indicate how a supreme master, expert in the essential instructions, shows the way to liberation.

When people who come from distant lands—who are ignorant of the Dharma, whose customs are barbaric, and who harbor wrong views—meet a spiritual master, a "friend in good" (*kalyāṇamitra*), behold his face, and hear his teachings, faith arises in their minds, reflecting such a master's wisdom.

Such a master is also wise in explaining what should be done and what should be avoided, and in knowing how to inspire disciples to put this into practice.

He wisely helps those who are trying to untie the knots of self-clinging in their mind stream and inspires them to abandon their preoccupations centered on ordinary life.

A wise spiritual master is expert in dispelling the obstacles that may arise during practice and in protecting disciples, showing them how to turn any obstacle into support on the path.

In accordance with the disciple's abilities, he provides with insight the instructions from the oral tradition that unite favorable conditions.[191]

If slander, backbiting, and other sources of suffering arise, he is expert in helping the disciples bring them onto the path of enlightenment.

These are six signs of a wise and expert spiritual guide.

–341–

Six Good Reasons to Follow a Spiritual Guide

Showing six appropriate reasons (to rely upon a master):

Since you rely upon a doctor when you have an ordinary sickness,
Relying upon a master to cure the sickness of samsara is appropriate.

Since you rely upon an escort while traveling on dangerous paths,
Relying upon a master to protect yourself in the bardo is appropriate.

Since you rely upon elders for guidance,
Relying upon a master for guidance on the ultimate aim is appropriate.

Since you rely upon a leader when mired in dispute,
Relying upon a master to pacify adverse circumstances is appropriate.

Since a sailor relies upon a skillful captain,
Relying upon a master to cross the ocean of suffering is appropriate.

Since merchants rely upon experienced seafarers,
Relying upon a master to achieve enlightenment is appropriate.

Here are six kinds of valid reasoning:

If you suffer from an ordinary illness and must undertake a long and arduous journey, consulting an expert doctor is essential. Even more so is consulting a spiritual guide to overcome the ills of the three worlds of samsara.

Likewise, if you are about to travel to a distant land and your route is full of bandits and fraught with dangers from the four elements, relying on a reliable escort is essential. By the same logic, you should entrust yourself to a spiritual guide when embarking on the long journey though the perilous paths of the bardo, the intermediate state between death and rebirth.

If you need guidance to conduct worldly affairs, relying on the advice of your elders is appropriate. Likewise, you should practice in accordance with the reliable instructions of a spiritual guide.

You need the support of a leader who protects his people. In the same way, to pacify adverse circumstances and obstacles, rely on a spiritual master.

If you aspire to cross an ocean, you should trust an expert navigator who knows the sea routes well. Similarly, to free yourself from the ocean of suffering of the three worlds of samsara, trust in a spiritual master.

Merchants who set out to find the jewel island on the high seas do well to entrust themselves to a seasoned captain. Likewise, to reach enlightenment, entrusting yourself to a spiritual guide is highly desirable.

–342–

Six Comparisons

Six types of comparisons:

Look at the pain of sickness that you experience now:
How will you bear the suffering of the three lower realms?

Look at the effort people make to escape imprisonment:
Are you not ruining your life by remaining in the prison of samsara?

Look at the hardship people experience to earn their livelihood:
Are you losing this life's ultimate harvest?

Look at the defects of negative friends you occasionally spend time with:
Can you bear the difficulty of getting along with unruly sentient beings?

Look at the ordinary precautions people take to avoid falling into ravines:
Consider the distress of sentient beings who fall into the abyss of the three lower realms.

Look at the grief people experience over the death of their spouse in this life:
Can you bear the pain of separation from the everlasting friend of Dharma?

Contemplating these comparisons, you will reach the other shore.

Six comparisons are here taught.

When you experience some physical or mental suffering, you find it hard to bear and seek out an expert and benevolent doctor for treatment. Think carefully: Will you be able to endure the unbearable torments of the three lower realms?

Look at the efforts that those who are thrown into prison by a powerful ruler make to escape: By remaining in the prison of the three worlds of samsara, are you not destroying your own good? Ask yourself if there is any way to break out.

You toil without respite during the day and hardly sleeping during the night just to provide for yourselves and to obtain food and clothing. Will you be able to endure the hardship of practicing the supreme Dharma, the sole provider of the unsurpassed harvest?

If you associate even briefly with bad friends, you will forge all kinds of attachment and aversion. Many disputes, and much slander and backbiting will ensue. Considering this, can you endure the vast majority of sentient beings whose behavior is contrary to the Dharma and who are very difficult to get along with?

Knowing that if you fall off of a precipice, you will be destroyed, you are extremely careful. Think then of the suffering that awaits as you are about to plunge into the abyss of the lower realms.

When your spouse in this life dies, you beat your chest, overwhelmed with grief. But if you are cut off from the Dharma, your perennial friend, you do not even feel the mere scent of his presence in your mind stream.

If you know how to think about all this correctly, you will safely cross to the other side.

–343–

Essential Instructions on Spiritual Practice

Six pith instructions on practice:

Just as the sun illuminates the sky,
Establish the crucial point of the self-arising primordial wisdom that is clear yet empty.

Just as from Mount Meru's peak you see all the smaller mountains,
Understand everything from the perspective of the nature of mind, the pinnacle of all realizations.

Just as on an island of gold, you find no ordinary stone,
Apprehend all objects that lead to distraction as being the true face of dharmatā.

Just as wind freely flows within space,
Let all conceptual characteristics naturally vanish.

Just as the hosts of weapons flung (at the Buddha) turned into a shower of blossoms,
Take all appearances on the path as dharmakāya.

Just as when a lion's three capacities are fully matured,[192]
The view of equality subjugates all characteristics of hope and fear.

Whoever knows these instructions is skillful in the crucial points of the profound meaning.

Now come six special instructions experienced through practice.

When the sun shines in the sky, its rays dispel the darkness on the four continents. Likewise, self-arising primordial wisdom in which luminous awareness and emptiness are united is your inner sun. Having established this crucial point, see whether or not this sun rises.

If you see the vista from the top of Mount Meru, the queen of mountains, the lower mountains are clearly visible. Likewise, if you contemplate the true nature of mind, you will embrace the meaning of all the teachings of the sutras and the Secret Mantra.

If you come to an island made entirely of gold and jewels, you will not find any ordinary stones even if you search. This is what happens if you succeed in no longer discriminating between meditation and post-meditation, having been introduced to the ultimate nature of reality, the dharmatā.

When a light breeze blows through space, it does not affect the sky, neither benefiting nor harming it. Similarly, if you leave conceptual thoughts in their own clarity, they will have no impact at all.

When, filled with animosity, Māra and his armies of demons hurled a rain of weapons at the Buddha, he was fully absorbed in the samādhi of love, so the weapons turned into a rain of flowers. The same will happen if you know how to bring all appearances onto the path of dharmakāya.

Once a lion has fully developed its three capacities, it fears no other animal. Similarly, if your expertise in the view of the nature of reality, the dharmatā, has reached its peak, you will be able to overcome all attributes related to hope and fear.

One who knows all this is expert in the vital and profound points [of practice].

–344–

Integrate the Different Vehicles onto Your Path

Six condensed instructions for integrating the various vehicles onto your path:
Being introduced to the universe and its contents as delusory perception, take pure perception onto your path.
Being introduced to the suffering of samsara, take compassion onto your path.
Being introduced to the beings of the six realms as your parents, take loving-kindness onto your path.
Being introduced to the interdependence of cause and effect, take the three vows onto your path.
Being introduced to the three doors [of your body, speech, and mind] as the support of the four empowerments, take the generation and completion stages onto your path.
Being introduced to appearances and sounds as the nature of mind, take dharmatā onto your path.
Following these instructions, you will remain free from obscurations and will never stray from your path.

Six instructions integrate the methods of different vehicles:

If you are introduced to the understanding that all deceptive appearances—the joys and sufferings of the world—are illusory and dreamlike, you will understand that these are only the empty forms of voidness, and the perception of the infinite purity of phenomena will arise.

If you become aware of the sufferings of the three worlds of samsara, you cannot but feel immense compassion for suffering beings, who all have been your parents.

If you have been introduced to the understanding that all of these beings have indeed been your mothers and fathers, and that it is therefore natural not to discriminate between enemies and friends, the love that wishes beings to find happiness and the determination to benefit them will arise spontaneously.

If you realize the inescapability of the laws of cause and effect that operate within interdependence, you will avoid transgressing the precepts of individual liberation, bodhicitta, and the Secret Mantra Vehicle.

If you know that the four empowerments—the vase, the secret, the wisdom, and the word empowerment—are focused on your body, your speech, your mind, and its ultimate nature, you will be able to bring the development and the perfection phases onto the path.

If you recognize that all appearances and sounds are the play of the nature of mind, you will understand the ultimate nature of reality.

If you understand all this, you will be free from deviations and obscurations on the path.

–345–

Six Procrastinations to Be Banished

Six crucial points not to be put off because of laziness:

Spending a lot of time looking for an ideal place to do a solitary retreat will delay your practice;
What is crucial is to remain in the solitude of mind free from subject and object.

Searching for instructions merely in words can delay your practice;
What is crucial is to seek the profound practice relying on skillful means.

Accumulating and hoarding means of livelihood can delay your practice;
What is crucial is to develop contentment with whatever you have and to search for sustenance in the manner of birds.

Being overly busy preparing for future meditative practice can postpone it;
What is crucial is to leave aside all unfinished tasks and projects.

Engaging solely in accumulating merit and purifying negativities to give rise to spiritual experience and realization can delay them;

What is crucial is to go radically to the heart of the profound practice.

Gradually reaching the stages and paths can delay your practice;
What is crucial is to develop stability and familiarity in the nature of the mind as being the three kāyas.

If you practice in these ways, you will accomplish enlightenment, the state of bodhi.

Now here are six crucial points to avoid letting your practice stray into laziness:

Don't put off practicing until you find a suitable solitary place as you may end up never finding one. You should rather settle into the solitude of a mind free of dualistic clinging to subject and object. The time to seek inner solitude is now.

Spiritual instructions that rely only on words will be of little use at the time of death. Thus, you must gather all the instructions needed to practice the path of skillful means and the path of liberation, so that you can find the depth that lies within your own mind.

Hoping to live for a very long time, you accumulate and hoard food and possessions. Busy with this, you postpone Dharma practice. Instead, learn to be content with the food and clothing you have.

If you are thinking of undertaking meditative practices that lead to attainment quietly and at your convenience, your life may succumb to impermanence. Therefore, whatever activities you are engaged in, leave them, and concentrate all your energy on the vital points of meditative practice.

If you think of the progress of your meditation and realization as a slow, easygoing journey, telling yourself things like "The day I am rich, I will make offerings and donations" or "When I am a little older, I will retire to a mountain hermitage," this will not do. What you need is, starting today, to use the most energetic means to get to the deepest level of practice.

Nor will it do to plan to progress leisurely along the five paths and the ten bhūmis, hoping to perfect your realization gradually. You must go to the crucial point and, through your practice, stabilize the recognition of the nature of your mind within the three dimensions of buddhahood, the kāyas.

If you practice in this way, you will quickly attain enlightenment, buddhahood.

–346–
Six Commitments

Six types of commitments in six types of training:
Remain in bodhicitta without letting it degenerate.
Never feeling you have enough of the two accumulations, persist in practicing the six pāramitās.
To train your wisdom, engage in Dharma conversations.
To develop meditative concentration, remain in solitary places.
To avoid worldly activities, maintain ascetic virtues.
To attain the supreme stages of the path, honor your lama continuously.
Whoever acts like this will enter the great path of the supreme vehicle.

There are six ways to train in abiding in the practice:

Constantly nurturing the mind of enlightenment, bodhicitta, and never letting it wane constitutes the most crucial point of all Dharma teachings.

Never be satisfied with what you have accomplished regarding the two accumulations. By persevering unceasingly in their practice, the six transcendental perfections will naturally come to completion.

To refine the insight born from listening, reflecting, and meditating, continually and exclusively engage in conversations centered upon the Dharma. Then, your insight will blossom.

To develop contemplation and samādhi in your mind stream, always remain in mountain retreats, away from all and everything.

To give up the countless occupations you are engaged in, redirect all your efforts to the practice of the twelve ascetic virtues.[193]

To achieve the supreme bhūmi, buddhahood, respectfully serve your spiritual master.

Whoever acts in these ways will travel the royal path of the Great Vehicle.

–347–

Six Beds for Resting

Perfectly explaining the six types of beds on which to rest:[194]
To avoid distraction of body and mind, rest on the bed of solitude.
To avoid tormenting oneself and others, rest on the bed of celibacy.
To naturally avoid feeling regret, rest on the bed of the perfect Dharma path.
To gather positive qualities, rest on the bed of the path of abiding in excellence.
To succeed in your endeavors, rest on the bed of the path of the siddhas.
To manifest the perfectly purified state, rest on the bed of spontaneous presence.
Whoever rests on these six beds will experience joy and happiness.

Here, the six ways of resting on a bed are excellently explained.

What is taught is that you must dwell in mountain solitudes to overcome agitation related to the restlessness of your body and mind.

To avoid being obsessed with your self-centered interests and hostile to the interests of others, abiding on the pure bed [of chaste conduct] is essential.

To avoid regretting your actions, remain on the excellent bed of the supreme Dharma of liberation.

To actualize spiritual qualities, establish yourself on the pure and perfect bed of listening, reflecting, and meditating.

To bring the practices you have undertaken through body, speech, and mind to culmination, you should settle on the bed of the ordinary and supreme siddhis.

What was perfectly refined in the past does not need be obtained again: rest on the bed of spontaneous presence.

If you recline in these six beds at the appropriate time and rest in them blissfully, you can sleep in peace.

–348–

Six Destinations

Six destinations for Mahāyāna followers:
Aspiring for the qualities of buddhahood, they head to the ultimate nature of reality.
Aspiring to benefit sentient beings, they seek to teach according to beings' needs.
Aspiring to realize the nature of mind, they seek freedom from the three poisons.
Aspiring to achieve wisdom, they seek to achieve the meditative concentration of the stream of Dharma.
For the sake of beings, they seek (to benefit them) in all their rebirths.
Aspiring for the path of liberation, they rely upon their teachers.
Whoever aims for these destinations is training in the Buddha's teachings.

Six teachings describe the destinations of Great Vehicle practitioners.

If you wonder whether you will be able to obtain the qualities of abandonment [of all obscurations] and realization that lead to buddhahood, you must advance toward the ultimate nature of reality. To do so, you have to familiarize yourself with the meaning of dharmatā.

If you aspire to benefit beings, you need to make progress in expounding the Dharma in accordance with their abilities—high, medium, or low.

If you wish to realize the fundamental nature of your own mind, do your best to eliminate the three poisons and other afflictive mental states.

If you wish to acquire the insight born from listening, reflecting, and meditating, you must continually abide by the supreme Dharma without a moment's distraction.

If you are determined to transform beings by all possible means and according to their propensities and aptitudes, you must pursue this endeavor throughout your successive lives.

If you wish to accomplish the path of liberation, it is important to continually rely on a spiritual friend, a teacher. If this is the case, you will achieve liberation effortlessly.

Whoever engages in these directions will be truly training in the Buddha's teachings.

–349–

Paying Attention

Six types of attention that you should maintain:
Pay attention to strive in the roots of virtue.
Pay attention to earnestly work hard in Dharma practice.
Pay attention to direct your mind toward unsurpassable buddhahood.
Pay attention to cultivate bodhicitta for the sake of others.
Pay attention to heed the meaning of dharmatā day and night.
Pay attention to develop the mind of renunciation and disenchantment.
Whoever does this enters the noble path of the bodhisattvas.

Six points on which you should carefully set your mind:

When you endeavor to develop the root of your virtuous practices, remain in mindful presence, vigilantly monitor your mental state, and be circumspect in your conduct. The three aspects of any practice—namely, the preparation, the main phase, and the conclusion, or follow-up—must be fully present.

When you are earnestly engaged in the Dharma, your mind must be fully engaged in listening, reflecting, and meditating.

If you wish to attain unsurpassed and perfect enlightenment, here too you must maintain your attention, vigilance, and concern.

To generate the mind of enlightenment aimed at benefiting all beings, you must remain in the continuum of altruistic love and compassion.

To abide unwaveringly in the dharmatā day and night, during the day you must bring appearances onto the path and during the night you must bring clear light onto the path.

If at any time you are filled with great weariness toward samsara and a strong desire to escape it, renunciation—the flame of practice—will light in your mind by itself. You should preserve this state of mind.

Whoever acts in this way will advance on the excellent path of the heirs of the victorious ones.

–350–

On the Proper Use of Speech

Perfectly indicating six types of speech:
The speech judiciously adapted to the infinite variety of the conduct of beings,
The speech that perfectly explains the ocean of Dharma,
The speech that exalts the qualities of the buddhas,
The speech that perfectly exposes the inexhaustible qualities of the Mahāyāna path,
The speech that fills space in all ten directions with the sound of Dharma,
The speech that dismantles samsara and presents nirvana,
Whoever has these kinds of speech is a great bodhisattva.

One can distinguish six qualities regarding the use of speech.

In all circumstances, aim to use speech as do the bodhisattvas, experts in the methods of compassionately helping beings.

Seek to teach the vast and deep ocean of the various aspects of the Dharma with speech free of limitations or obstructions.

Use your speech to continually praise the qualities of buddhahood, which are born from eliminating all obscurations and bringing all qualities to maturity.

You must also employ the speech that perfectly expounds the profound emptiness of the Great Vehicle together with the qualities of the five paths and ten levels [that lead to buddhahood].

You must manifest the speech that causes the sound of the Dharma to resound throughout space in the ten directions.

Those who use speech in this way are great bodhisattvas able to destroy the three worlds of samsara and show the path of liberation that leads to nirvana, beyond suffering. They are the great heirs of the victorious ones.

–351–

Six Emanations

Perfectly showing the six types of body emanations:
To mature [the minds of] human beings, great bodhisattvas manifest with human bodies.
To tame the lower realms, they manifest with nonhuman bodies.
To mature the gods and demigods, they manifest with bodies that resemble theirs.
To tame beings of lesser capacities, they manifest as listeners and solitary realizers.
To lead beings on the Mahāyāna path, they manifest as bodhisattvas.
To fully confer the empowerment,[195] they manifest in sambhogakāya form.
Those who have attained perfect mastery manifest spontaneously.

Buddhas manifest in multiple appropriate ways to transform the diversity of sentient beings. To do so, they adopt six kinds of physical forms.

To mature human beings who have not had the good fortune to meet in person the Buddha or the bodhisattvas who were his spiritual heirs, they manifest as friends in virtue, the spiritual guides.

To help beings of the lower realms enter the path of liberation, our guide, the Muni, manifested in infinite ways. As recounted in the jātakas, the record of his past lives, he manifested as a deer, a *sharawa* lion,[196] a golden peacock—the king of birds—and in many other forms.

For the sake of nonhumans, buddhas manifest in various forms according to their perceptions.

To transform the devas (the gods), and the asuras (the demigods), he will take the form of the seventy-five glorious Dharma protectors,[197] who are all bodhisattvas on the path of accumulation and the path of joining.[198]

To transform beings with lesser capacities, he will take the form of arhats, the listeners. The dark ages are deprived of the light of Dharma and then the solitary realizers appear. They do not teach the Dharma by word of mouth but perform innumerable miracles through which they establish beings on the path of liberation.

To set these beings on the path of the Great Vehicle, the buddhas manifest in the pure lands as bodhisattvas like Avalokiteśvara, Mañjuśrī, and many others.

To perfect and transmit the empowerment of the vase, the secret empowerment, the empowerment of wisdom, and the empowerment conveyed by words, they act in tangible reality or, on the saṃbhogakāya level, in the aspect of Vajrasattva or the buddhas of the five families.

As for those who have attained ultimate mastery, including miraculous powers, they spontaneously manifest in various forms in the ways best suited to transform sentient beings.

–352–

Six Heads of the Bodhisattvas

The six "heads," or principles, of the bodhisattvas:

To gather beings, including those in the god realm,
The principle is to pay homage to the spiritual teacher with supreme qualities.

To prevent the continuity of the lineage of the Three Jewels from breaking,
The principle is to observe the precepts of the buddhas and assimilate [the crucial points of the] practice.

To become lord of the billionfold universe,
The principle is to focus on profound purity.

To guide all beings on the path of enlightenment,
The principle is to mature them perfectly.

To accomplish the unsurpassable qualities,
The principle is to abide in the transcendent perfection of wisdom.

To become the object of respect in the three realms of existence,
The principle is to perfectly dedicate all merits.

Those who possess these qualities will accomplish the supreme bhūmi of the enlightened mandala.

Now come the six "heads," or principles, of the bodhisattvas, the heirs of the victorious ones.

To gather all beings throughout the world, including the devas, the first "head" or principle, is to honor the supreme spiritual masters endowed with the highest qualities, at whose lotus feet even the mighty ones of this world, Brahmā, Indra, and others prostrate.

To ensure that the lineage of enlightened activities of the Three Jewels continues uninterruptedly, the second "head," or principle, is to abide by the precepts of the buddhas and bodhisattvas.

In order for Mahā Brahmā [Great Brahmā] to manifest as a bodhisattva to rule over the billions of universes, this immense multiverse, the third principle is to aspire to deep purity.

To establish all beings on the path of liberation and enlightenment, the fourth principle is to manifest in whichever forms will provide the greatest good for sentient beings and will mature them, whether this means taking the form of a wild animal, a beggar, or any other form.

In order to accomplish the perfect and unsurpassable Dharma, the transcendent perfection of wisdom, the supreme mother of the four types of noble beings, the fifth principle is to engender this transcendent perfection, as the listeners, solitary realizers, bodhisattvas, and buddhas have gradually done.

By perfectly performing the dedication of accumulated merit, the sixth principle, bodhisattvas achieve the supreme mandala, buddhahood, and become objects of veneration for the beings of the three worlds.[199]

These six "heads," or principles, fall within the domain of activity of the bodhisattvas who have attained the bhūmis.

–353–

The Six Ears of the Bodhisattvas

The six ears of bodhisattvas:
Ears that neither reject unpleasant words nor desire pleasant ones.
Ears that do not despise and reject unpleasant words.
Ears that delight to hear about the deeds of the bodhisattvas who have appeared in this world.
Ears that wear the armor of compassion when they hear of beings born in states deprived of freedom.
Ears that, on hearing praise of the qualities of the buddhas, are inspired and incited to diligence.
Ears that know that all the sounds of the world, in the ten directions of space, are like echoes.
Make sure you have these six kinds of ears.

Six types of ears that are specific to bodhisattvas:

When bodhisattvas hear derogatory words, whether they come from those called demons or vile persons, they should be like the Buddha, whose mind was not at all disturbed when slandered by Devadatta and disparaged by the tīrthikas. Similarly, when gods and men sang his praises, he did not relish this nor did he congratulate himself for being the object of such praise.

Likewise, bodhisattvas may hear praise or, conversely, criticism. In the latter case, if someone belittles them with animosity, they will not say to themselves, "Oh, he slanders me! But he himself has many defects." They will refrain from any resentment toward their slanderers and will not accuse nor belittle them in return.

There is also the ear that welcomes news that a bodhisattva has appeared in this world and rejoices in the accomplishment of bodhisattvas who, throughout their past lives, have practiced generosity and meditated in samādhi. They delight in hearing the stories of the Buddha's past lives, the jātakas. While rejoicing wholeheartedly, they make the aspiration prayer "May I do the same!"

When the ear of a bodhisattva hears of beings who are born in conditions that deprive them of freedom [to practice the Dharma], an ever-greater compassion is conceived. To benefit people in remote countries [where the

Dharma is unknown], far from grieving, it is more than ever important to don the armor of bodhicitta. This is what the Buddha did when he manifested listeners, such as Kātyāyana.[200] This is also what the Master, the disciples, and the Abbot[201] did in the Land of Snows, Tibet, in order to transform the people of that place where the Dharma had not yet spread.

Hearing praise of the wisdom and qualities of the Buddha, ask yourself, "When will I be able to obtain such qualities?" When a ready source of wealth is mentioned to one who faces severe financial difficulties, he surely thinks, "Oh, I must have it!" and makes every effort to obtain it.

In any case, when hearing the countless praises and criticisms that resound in this world throughout the ten directions of space, as Patrul Rinpoche said,

> "All talk is like an echo," said the buddhas,
> But these days it is more like the re-echo of an echo.
> What the echoes say and what they mean are not the same,
> So do not take any notice of those insidious echo words.[202]

Accordingly, you have no reason to be elated when hearing praise nor depressed when hearing criticism.

These are the six ears that are appropriate to have.

–354–

The Six Eyes of the Bodhisattva

Six types of eyes enable bodhisattvas to see:
To see the forms of the world, they have eyes of flesh.
To look at different kinds of beings, they have divine eyes.
To see the faculties of beings, they have wisdom eyes.
To know the diversity of the teachings (dharmas) as they are, they have the eyes of Dharma.
To dispel obscurations, they have eyes of nonattachment.
To look at dharmadhātu, they have eyes of omniscience.
Having these eyes enables them to benefit beings perfectly.

Bodhisattvas use six kinds of eyes to contemplate the realms of sentient beings.

First, they are able to see all the billions of worlds without rocks and mountains obstructing their vision. In ordinary life, for example, we can explore our country by driving around it. A clairvoyant rishi of India will see much more, while a clairvoyant listener or solitary realizer will see even farther, and a clairvoyant bodhisattva will see immensely farther yet. An all-knowing buddha who contemplates things with the eyes of primordial wisdom sees a buddha on every atom and apprehends without the slightest obstruction all the pure and impure fields in the universe with his eyes of flesh.

When it is time to teach beings, the divine eyes of bodhisattvas enable them to see who has the superior abilities to receive the teachings of the Great Vehicle or the vehicle of Secret Mantra, or whether it is more appropriate to give a particular disciple teachings meant for listeners or solitary realizers. In this way, they will fathom the abilities, dispositions, and aspirations of these beings, as their insight reveals to them all that is normally invisible to ordinary beings.

With the eye of wisdom, they can distinguish between beings with superior, average, or limited faculties.

With the eye of Dharma, by examining the eighty-four thousand sections of the doctrine, they will correctly distinguish what belongs to the conventional meaning and what to the definitive meaning, what is to be understood literally and what requires interpretation.

Through the eye free of grasping, they know without hindrance all that is to be known in the past, present, and future.

Through the eye of self-knowing and omniscient awareness, they will behold the inconceivable dharmadhātu.

Thus, through these six eyes, bodhisattvas know both the multiplicity and the nature of all things and are able to benefit sentient beings.

–355–

Six Hands of the Bodhisattva

Six types of hands of bodhisattvas:
To be devoted to the victorious ones and to have trust in them, they have the hands of faith.
To meet the needs of the destitute according to their wishes, they have the hands of generosity.
To dispel doubt, they have the sublime hands of learning.
To free sentient beings [from suffering], they have hands that bring happiness.
To offer teachings to sentient beings, they have hands free from stinginess.
To gather the accumulations and make offerings, they have the hands of service.
Those with these six kinds of hands will make the light of Dharma shine.

Bodhisattvas have six supreme hands, which means six kinds of actions:

They have the hands of faith that enable them to generate the aspiration to attain the state of buddhahood. Consequently, they know how to expound the qualities of the victorious ones with perfect clarity.

They are endowed with the giving hands of the transcendent perfection of generosity to give their bodies, eyes, heads, and all that is precious to them to the needy, to all who implore them, in accordance with their desires.

They have the supreme hands of study to cut through the distortions of doubts of those who engage in listening, reflection, and meditation.

They employ the hands that free all beings from the multiple sufferings of samsara and lead to happiness on the path of liberation.

They have hands free from stinginess to teach the Dharma, indifferent to fatigue and difficulties.

Having perfected the double accumulation of merit and wisdom, they have hands that are skilled and quick to serve the buddhas, make offerings to them, support the virtuous community and monasteries, and perform other meritorious work.

Those who possess these hands that benefit beings shine the light of Dharma.

–356–

The Six Legs of the Bodhisattva

Six kinds of legs of bodhisattvas:
To fulfill aspiration prayers, they have the legs of ethical discipline.
To gather the qualities of enlightenment, they have the legs of joyful effort.
To complete the tasks undertaken, they have the legs of commitment.
To follow the instructions of their teacher, they have the legs of proper conduct.
To avoid feeling that they have learned enough, they have the legs of discernment.
To engage in virtuous activities, they have the legs of earnest persistence.
Those who have these six types of legs will impeccably reach the state of perfect buddhahood.

The heirs of the victorious ones, the bodhisattvas, have six types of legs.

When bodhisattvas make a vow, wishing for instance, "Let fire turn into water" or "Let water turn into fire," when they utter words of truth, things happen accordingly. Through the power of their prayers, they also have the capacity to generate in an instant the equivalent of merit that normally takes kalpas to accumulate. To acquire such power, bodhisattvas have brought the transcendent perfection of ethical discipline to its highest point. They are thus endowed with the legs of moral discipline.

The legs of unwavering diligence enable buddhas to perfect their eminent qualities, such as the ten strengths, the four kinds of fearlessness, the eighteen distinct qualities, the seven branches of enlightenment, the eightfold noble path, and other qualities, by obtaining those they do not yet have and enhancing those they have already.

Bodhisattvas also possess the legs of commitment, for once they have made a resolution, they will never abandon it.

To fulfill their spiritual master's instructions, bodhisattvas possess the legs of harmony, through which they know how to preserve harmony among their vajra brothers and sisters and with their teacher's entourage.

Bodhisattvas also have the legs of insight, for they are never satisfied with what they have already learned, like someone who has not yet quenched his thirst after drinking the equivalent of a vast lake.

Bodhisattvas further stand on the legs of sincere commitment to conduct that in all respects accords with the Dharma.

Thus, those who are endowed with these six types of legs will travel the path of the bhūmis of the victorious and will eventually reach the level of buddhahood.

–357–

Six Types of Armor of the Bodhisattvas

Six types of armor that the māras' weapons cannot pierce:
To protect sentient beings, bodhisattvas don the armor of loving-kindness.
To complete the tasks they have undertaken, they don the armor of aspiration.
To liberate sentient beings, they don the armor of compassion.
To dispel ignorance, they don the armor of wisdom.
To maintain the Mahāyāna attitude, they don the armor of patience.
To perfectly accomplish virtue, they don the armor of skillful means.
Whoever has donned these six types of armor will reach the perfect state of buddhahood.

When an army prepares for battle, the soldiers don armor and necessary protection to avoid injury from the enemy's weapons. Similarly, bodhisattvas wear six types of armor to shield them from Māra's obstacles.

First, there is the armor of benevolence, which allows bodhisattvas to protect beings from suffering. Indeed, for the sake of even a single being, a bodhisattva does not hesitate to work diligently for many kalpas, thus wearing the armor of the freedom from discouragement and weariness. Whatever task bodhisattvas set themselves, from the moment they begin until they complete it, they never relax their determination, thus donning the armor of aspiration to bring their actions to completion.

In all their actions, bodhisattvas have nothing else in mind than the benefit of others, not their own interests, thus putting on the armor of compassion.

Donning the armor of the altruistic mind of enlightenment, they take upon themselves the suffering of sentient beings, display the strength of mind associated with certainty in the Dharma, and manifest the other aspects of the six types of patience.

They also wear the armor of insight acquired through listening, reflecting, and meditating, which enables them to dispel the darkness of ignorance and delusion in the minds of beings.

Bodhisattvas show sagacity in using methods to attain the highest virtues and to accomplish in an instant what would take others months or years. They thus don the armor of skillful means.

These various kinds of armor allow bodhisattvas to carry out their enlightened activities.

–358–

Six Types of Weapons of the Bodhisattvas

Six types of weapons bodhisattvas hold:
The weapon of equality to cut dualism,
The weapon of insight and primordial wisdom to cut afflictive mental states,
The weapon of right livelihood to cut inappropriate ones,
The weapon of pure morality to cut the stream of unethical behavior,
The weapon of generosity to cut the snare of stinginess,
The weapon of tirelessness to mature the minds of beings—
Whoever possesses these weapons will sever the vines of samsara.

Warriors arm themselves with guns, knives, bows and arrows, spears, and other arms. Bodhisattvas have six types of weapons.

To cut through the delusion of the duality of the object and the subject of attachment, they have the weapon of the realization of the ultimate sameness of phenomena.

To tear the net of afflictive mental states, they wield the weapon of deeper insight that realizes the absence of identity. In so doing, they fully uproot afflictive mental states.

To cut off inappropriate means of living, which include wrongly using religious wealth, they have the weapons of virtuous livelihood, which accords with the Dharma.

To stem the tide of reprehensible activities resulting from letting mental toxins have free rein, they hold the weapon of pure moral discipline.

Stingy people are unable to give anything to others and are trapped in their avarice. To overcome this flaw, bodhisattvas have recourse to the weapon of daring to give, which allows them, if necessary, to give away their eyes, their bodies, and many other things without feeling any sense of loss.

Finally, bodhisattvas use the weapon of fortitude in working tirelessly to mature the minds of sentient beings and to benefit them, without ever being discouraged by fatigue or by feeling helpless, a weapon that will allow them to cut through the vines of samsara's three worlds.

–359–

Six Extraordinary Instructions

Six types of extraordinary instructions:

Though you know that all sentient beings are primordially enlightened,
To liberate them, you must gather the two accumulations extensively.

Though you might know that the buddhas' pure realms are as vast as space,
To be born in a such a realm you must engage in purification with unmatched diligence.

Without becoming weary of maturing sentient beings,
Do not abandon the characteristics of selflessness.

With clairvoyance, engage in miraculous deeds
Without wavering from the state of dharmadhātu.

Do not give up the aspiration to achieve supreme enlightenment
And make sure to accomplish the all-knowing primordial wisdom.

Bring satisfaction to all beings by turning the wheel of Dharma
Without ever leaving the state of dharmatā, the ultimate nature of reality.
Whoever possesses these qualities will attain the state of *sugata*, "One who has gone to bliss."

Then come six instructions for bodhisattvas, which go beyond the instructions given to listeners, solitary realizers, and ordinary beings.

A bodhisattva knows that all beings are primordially enlightened and are actual buddhas within the sphere of the tathāgatagarbha, the buddha nature. But to be able to introduce these beings to their true nature, bodhisattvas must accumulate abundant merit and wisdom over many kalpas without ever becoming discouraged, as did the precious Mañjuśrī and Avalokiteśvara. Although they are already buddhas, they continue to manifest as tenth bhūmi bodhisattvas for the sake of beings.

Like space, the various pure lands of buddhas are all equal—there are no good or bad ones. Even though bodhisattvas know this, they do not abandon the armor of persevering in the purification that leads to rebirth in a pure land such as the Land of Great Bliss (Sukhāvatī) in the western direction or the pure field of the bodhisattva Mañjuśrī [in the east].

To mature all beings who are on the path by teaching them the Dharma throughout the three times, bodhisattvas accomplish all that is necessary without ever becoming weary and while recalling the characteristics of the great and small vehicles, mainly the meaning of the equality of the nonexistence of the self.

As for benefiting beings, without being satisfied with mere assumptions, whatever the ways of accomplishing this good may be, bodhisattvas have a sound knowledge of what can truly help, and to do so, they have the capacity to deploy vast miraculous manifestations.

Moreover, if, for the sake of others, they must give their limbs or their heads, their realization never waivers from the absolute expanse, the dharmadhātu.

As for generating the altruistic thought of enlightenment, even if they must give away their bodies hundreds of times for the sake of others, in their hearts they will never abandon the mind of enlightenment dedicated to the benefit of all beings. The direct experience of buddhahood, the all-knowing primordial wisdom, prompts them to free all beings by turning the wheel of Dharma. While doing so, they never leave the sphere of the absolute expanse, the dharmadhātu.

Whoever possesses these qualities will attain the state of a sugata, "One who has gone to bliss."

–360–

Māra's Influence

Six influences of Māra that should be identified and averted:
Becoming discouraged from benefiting others and having a disturbed mind.
Being satisfied with the accomplishment of minor goals [such as the selflessness of the person], while being unable to handle major ones.
Doubting the Dharma path and abandoning it.
Being interested only in your own liberation instead of working for the maturation of all sentient beings.
Forsaking the [bodhisattvas'] vast conduct for fear of the samsaric suffering.
Not focusing on high aspirations but wishing merely to appease negative emotions.
These are all the influences of Māra and must be discarded.

Avoid succumbing to the following six obstacles created by Māra:

No matter how hard a bodhisattva tries to help others, he will never lose heart. Do not think, "I will not be able to benefit others." Also, if you have helped some people transform themselves, including your disciples, do not be disturbed if they return evil for good.

Without being satisfied with accomplishing minor goals, persevere on the vast [Mahāyāna] path and do not confine yourself to pursuing a narrow goal [nonexistence of the individual self].

Another trap to avoid is to tell yourself, "If I can attain buddhahood myself, without worrying about transforming all sentient beings, that will suffice," or to think, "I'm not the kind of person who can benefit beings."

Already frightened at the mere mention of the pains of the six realms, you might think, "If I am to devote myself without limit to the altruistic conduct of the bodhisattvas, I will have to be reborn time and again in the three worlds of samsara to work for the sake of beings. This is too much for me!" Don't think like this!

The best and most inclusive aspiration prayer is that of the bodhisattva Samantabhadra.[203] Instead of striving for higher goals, with the help of the Prayer of Excellent Actions in particular, if you only aspire to appease your own negative emotions in the ultimate sphere of dharmadhātu, this is again one of the traps set by the demon.

It is important to recognize that all these obstacles are the work of Māra and to cast them as far away as possible.

–361–

Blessings from Past Masters

Six indications of having received the blessings of the sublime beings:
You develop the supreme mind that aspires to attain unsurpassable perfect enlightenment.
You thoroughly abandon the activities of Māra on recognizing them.[204]
You listen to the Mahāyāna teachings and practice them diligently.
You never tire of benefiting others in samsara.
You teach the listeners and solitary realizers and never take pride in this.
Though you realize the view, you persevere in embodying appropriate conduct.
These are the ways of the bodhisattvas as they journey on the sublime path.

There are six signs that the blessings of past masters have entered your mind.

As the unsurpassed and perfect mind of enlightenment gradually grows within you, everything you do will benefit others.

Having recognized that distractions and dispersion prevent you from progressing on the path of liberation and are the work of Māra, you move away from them.

After hearing the teachings of the Great Vehicle, you make sincere efforts to practice their view, meditation, and action.

No matter how arduous your efforts to benefit beings across the three worlds of samsara, even if this means undergoing rebirth for many kalpas, you never succumb to discouragement.

If you expound the Dharma to listeners and solitary realizers, you avoid being filled with the condescension that makes you think, "I teach such people really well," or "I excel at imparting the instructions of the bodhisattvas."

Although you are striving toward the realization of perfect equality—the ultimate nature of reality, dharmatā—you keep acting in conformity with the Dharma, while avoiding distractions and involvements.

These are the ways of those who wholeheartedly dedicate themselves to the supreme path of the bodhisattvas.

–362–

How Māra Influences Teachers

Six types of Māra affecting those who teach Dharma:
Not teaching those who lack protection is the work of Māra.
Neglecting students who are worthy recipients of the teachings is the work of Māra.
Teaching sublime Dharma for the sake of wealth is the work of Māra.
Giving profound teachings to unworthy students is the work of Māra.
Teaching the Fundamental Vehicle to those who are interested in the Supreme Vehicle is the work of Māra.
Giving a mere overview of the teachings instead of teaching on what students are interested in is the work of Māra.
One must not be deceived by these works of Māra.

Māras affect those who aspire to teach the Dharma in six ways:

If you withhold teachings from those who lack any form of refuge or protection, using the pretext of secrecy, you succumb to Māra's influence.

If you disregard dedicated disciples who possess a profound aspiration to practice the sublime Dharma and fail to fulfill their aspirations, you become an instrument of Māra.

If you teach Dharma with the desire to collect as many offerings as you can, this is the work of Māra.

If your motivation for teaching the Dharma is solely to amass as many offerings as you can, you fall under Māra's influence.

If you impart profound teachings on emptiness to disciples whose mental dispositions belong to the lower vehicles and who are not suitable vessels for such teachings, their minds being unprepared to comprehend them, you are facilitating the work of Māra.

If you say to those who wish to receive the teachings of the supreme vehicle: "This does not suit you, you will find it easier to assimilate the teachings of the lesser vehicles," and lead them solely toward the path of the basic vehicle, it is the influence of Māra that operates.

If, instead of bestowing upon disciples the teachings they earnestly seek to transform themselves, you offer only superficial and general teachings, you fall into the snares laid by Māra.

Exercise utmost caution to avoid being caught by these traps Māra sets.

–363–

How Māra Influences Disciples

Six perverted influences of Māra that students must avoid:

Forsaking spiritual masters and relying on evil friends
Indicates that you are ensnared by Māra and will be deprived of guidance and protection.

Listening to the teachings of the lower vehicle after having abandoned those of the greater vehicle
Reveals that you are influenced by Māra, causing deviation from the true path.

Abandoning the path of liberation to pursue worldly knowledge
Shows that you are enthralled by Māra as your actions and conduct become misguided.

Intending to attain nirvana solely out of aversion to the idea of rebirth
Reveals that you adhere to Māra, as that destroys the armor of bodhicitta.

Denigrating the sublime Dharma without possessing sufficient knowledge yourself
Demonstrates an obsession with Māra as you are confused about what to adopt and what to discard.

Not distinguishing between virtue and nonvirtue, what is compliant with the Dharma and what is not, resulting in confusion about how to conduct yourself,

Clouded by the darkness of ignorance, you are gripped by Māra.
Qualified students must abandon these activities.

When it comes to students and disciples, we must also consider six māras, each representing erroneous approaches incompatible with the path to liberation.

If, instead of relying on an authentic spiritual master, you choose to keep bad company, heeding their words and engaging in activities that revolve solely around this present life, striving to benefit only your loved ones and to vanquish your enemies, you succumb to the influence of Māra. In essence, neglecting the shelter of a protector, an ally who guides you toward liberation, keeps you under Māra's yoke.

To forsake the teachings of the Great Vehicle, instead immersing yourself in the study of the lesser vehicle of the listeners and solitary realizers, is a path that leads you astray and ensnares you in Māra's trap.

If, instead of devoting yourself to the path of liberation and enlightenment, you divert your focus to worldly endeavors, crafts, magic, clairvoyance, and other ordinary skills, you are deceived by Māra.

If you loathe the idea of repeatedly being reborn in the three worlds of samsara for the sake of benefiting sentient beings, and instead aspire, like the listeners, to confine yourself solely to the tranquility of nirvana, Māra has stripped you of the armor of bodhicitta.

If you have not properly assimilated qualities derived from the study of Dharma, and content yourself with vague hearsay—like the rabbit who had merely heard the sound of a branch falling into the water[205]—neglecting the supreme Dharma, you will confuse what is to be embraced and what is to be avoided and will be lured by Māra.

If you reverse what needs to be accomplished and what should be discarded, failing to discern what is contrary to the principles of Dharma, you will remain cloaked in the darkness of ignorance, yet another trap set by Māra.

Disciples worthy of the teachings will strive to forsake these demons and transcend their influence.

–364–

Protecting Yourself from the Māras

Six ways to be immune to Māra's activities:
Shunning pride, serve your teacher with respect.
Shunning hatred, shower praise on others.
Shunning laziness, work hard in practicing the profound meaning.
Shunning sectarian prejudice, explore the full range of Buddha's teachings.
Shunning bias, enter the path of union.
Shunning worldly activities, put practice at the heart of your life.
Whoever acts in these ways will defeat Māra's army.

Six instructions enabling Dharma practitioners to protect themselves from the influence of the māras and avoid obstacles:

Even if you possess certain qualities, do not dwell on them or harbor pride. Instead, wholeheartedly serve an authentic spiritual guide who imparts the profound and supreme teachings.

In all circumstances and at all times, let go of anger, fostering harmonious relationships with others and expressing genuine appreciation for their qualities.

Forsake the distractions and trivial amusements of ordinary life, casting off indolence, and devote yourself to study, contemplation, and meditation on the profound meaning.

Relinquish all biases and prejudices: if you devote yourself to spiritual practice, do not think that you need not study the various fields of knowledge, and if you are versed in these fields of knowledge, do not deem practice as pointless. Explore all the Buddha's teachings with the zeal of a bee relishing the nectar of flowers.

Abandon any sectarian mindset that discriminates between "your" tradition and that of others. If you practice the Great Perfection that transcends all effort, refrain from dismissing the development phase that requires effort. However, should you diligently commit yourself to the development phase, avoid proclaiming that practices deemed "effortless" cannot lead to liberation. Instead, advance along the path by recognizing the seamless integration and harmony of all teachings.

Finally, renounce favoritism toward your kin and close acquaintances, as well as the urge to vanquish adversaries. Abandon involvement in mundane activities, such as working in the fields or any other ordinary pursuits that yield only transient advantages in this fleeting life. Instead, devote yourself to secluded places and immerse yourself in the very essence of practice.

Those who unwaveringly follow these instructions will triumph over the obstacles generated by the legions of Māra.

–365–

Six Behaviors Harmful to the Precepts of the Mahāyāna

Six behaviors that harm the Mahāyāna precepts:
Abandoning the Three Jewels, deceiving those worthy of veneration,
Giving up superior intention for deceptive conduct,
Insulting bodhisattvas,
Inducing regret in those who perform virtuous acts,
Hating and being jealous of those who enter the supreme vehicle,
And embarking on a path that lacks either wisdom or skillful means.
Persistently strive to abandon these six behaviors.

There are six ways to err by veering from the path of the Great Vehicle:

Rejecting the three precious jewels instead of placing your trust in them, and deceiving those who are worthy of veneration, your spiritual masters in particular.

Misleading others after abandoning the best of motivations, the precious bodhicitta. With duplicity, feigning to possess qualities you do not have and concealing the defects that afflict you.

Rudely criticizing the bodhisattvas, heirs of the victorious ones.

Inducing regret in those who diligently pursue virtue by saying, for example, to those who devote themselves to textual studies that their efforts would be better spent on profound meditation, as the texts miss the essence, or dissuading those committed to meditation by saying that it is futile without the necessary knowledge.

Being disturbed when someone surpasses you on the path of the Great Vehicle, harboring animosity and jealousy toward that person.

Separating the skillful means of compassion from the wisdom of emptiness, rather than harmoniously uniting them.

Remain vigilant, perpetually watchful for these six attitudes that can lead you astray from the path of the Great Vehicle.

–366–

Antidotes to Discouragement

As you strive to benefit others, you will be confronted with jealousy and slander.
To overcome discouragement, apply six antidotes:[206]
Jealousy and slander are karmic retribution from having blamed others in the past.
This provides an excellent way to exhaust the negative karma generated by your afflictive mental states.
Blame is a teaching that exposes your hidden flaws
But it can also be like a dog that barks indiscriminately at everyone, high or low,
Providing you with opportunities to exercise patience, which increases virtue and brings appreciable benefits.
Blame is the magical display of emptiness: elusive, it leaves no trace.
Considering all this, let go of painful resentment, grief, and weariness
To devote yourself to the benefit of others.

When you dedicate yourself to benefit others, it is inevitable that jealous people will attempt to belittle and demean you. Here are six ways to dispel your discouragement:

If you denigrate others, you can be sure that you yourself will be the object of criticism in your future lives. Use the criticisms that afflict you now as antidotes to the bad karma associated with your disturbing states of mind.

Others may expose your hidden faults and admonish you, saying, "You have such and such a fault; do not act like that!" Consider their words akin to the senseless barking of dogs who make no distinction between excellence, which is to be praised, and villainy, which is demeaning.

Your detractors present you with the opportunity to cultivate patience. By doing so, your virtues will only flourish.

Understanding that all sounds are no different from transient echoes that are the magical display of emptiness and leave no more trace than a bird in the sky, you will avoid falling into the trap that inspires this saying, "The angry man is miserable, beset by countless troubles," just like someone who throws himself naked into a thornbush.

Abandon all aversion and sadness and devote yourself with all your strength to benefit others.

–367–

Coping with Ingratitude

Six ways to be resilient in the face of ingratitude from those around you:
Surround them with even more compassion,
Give up any expectations you may have of the people in your circle,
Think about everything that happened in the past,
Consider your own karma and circumstances,
And be ready for ingratitude from whoever accompanies you.
See all phenomena as dreams and illusions.
Apply these antidotes when you are saddened by the negativity of your loved ones.

If you have followers, an entourage, and subordinates, and they show you ingratitude, a few ways are taught to avoid succumbing to anger and to cultivate patience.

Regardless of the extent of ingratitude shown by those around you, be even more compassionate toward them. Remind yourself that their behavior stems from their instinctual irascibility or personal suffering.

Do not harbor any hopes or expectations concerning the actions and attitudes of those around you.

Recognize that much of what you experience today is the result of your past lives: it is a process of reaping the consequences of negative actions accumulated in previous existences, intertwined with current circumstances.

When you examine your relationships with others, see them as dreams and illusions.

It is important to apply these antidotes to the discouragement and hurt engendered by an unfortunate entourage.

–368–

Aspiration Prayers for All Times

Six aspiration prayers always to remember:

Wherever I am born and in all rebirths,
May I obtain the seven qualities of the higher rebirths.

Let me encounter the Dharma from birth,
And be free to practice it to perfection.

May I practice Dharma night and day,
Fulfilling the wishes of my sublime master.

When the accomplishment of Dharma and its essential ends
Has enabled me to cross the ocean of samsara in this life,

Then may I never tire of helping others
Nor of spreading the Dharma in this world.

May the deep wave of benevolence free of partiality
Lead all beings to enlightenment!

Make this prayer the king of your aspirations,
For its merits and benefits are as limitless as space.

The seven qualities of the higher rebirths that are desirable in all your existences include longevity, good health, harmonious physical appearance, good fortune, honorable lineage, abundance, and discernment.

Wherever you are born, may you encounter the supreme Dharma soon after you enter life, and then give yourself appropriately to study, reflection, and meditation, remaining the master of your destiny and free from constraining influences.

To practice Dharma, first entrust yourself to a qualified master, then delight his heart by practicing day and night without being distracted or endlessly busy.

Once you have grasped the meaning of the supreme Dharma, do not waste your life in vain; do your utmost to extract its quintessence.

Strive to cross, in this very life, the vast ocean of existence. When you reach the other shore, expound the breadth and depth of Dharma to all beings wandering in samsara.

Never feel the slightest weariness in helping others and, relying on the twofold accumulation [of merits and wisdom], ensure that the waves of benevolence, free from any partiality, carry you and all sentient beings together to the state of buddhahood!

This prayer condenses the crucial points of all bodhisattva aspirations. Its benefits are as limitless as space, so recite it at any time and in any circumstance.[207]

–369–

Taking Possession of the Dharma Treasure

Six instructions to uphold the treasure of Dharma:
Seek the Dharma without hypocrisy.
Practice it persistently, with reverence.
Expose it to others and praise it.[208]

Regard those who bestow the teachings as guides:
Respect them, offer them your service, and rely upon them with veneration.
Thus, tirelessly preserving and nurturing the treasure of Dharma
Embodies the extraordinary conduct of bodhisattvas.

Here are six instructions for those who hold the treasure of supreme Dharma.

With the utmost sincerity, impartially explore the diversity of the vast and profound teachings and constantly seek them out.

Having thoroughly investigated and understood the teachings, diligently apply them with unwavering commitment, recognizing that even a simple verse encompasses the essence of the Buddha's wisdom, akin to discovering a precious gem.

Expose the qualities of the Dharma to others and sing its praises, expressing your admiration.

Regard those who expound and elucidate the teachings as if they were the Buddha himself: honor them with profound respect and offer them unwavering service.

Hence, be tireless holders of the sublime Dharma, day and night. When sharing and teaching it, align yourself with the noble tradition of the bodhisattvas, the true heirs of the Buddha.

–370–

Guiding Beings

Guide beings with six boundless qualities:
Cultivate compassion, driven by the aspiration to alleviate the suffering of others.
Nurture loving-kindness, aspiring to bring them happiness.
Practice boundless rejoicing, wishing that they are never separated from their present happiness.
Practice impartiality, free from any discrimination based on closeness or distance.
Engage in the practice of the transcendent perfections.
Practice the state without representation, free from the concepts of the three spheres.
This is why the development of bodhicitta is so important.

If we consider the bodhisattvas' determination, their merits are boundless, and so are the objects of their meditation and their altruistic attitude. It is crucial to constantly nurture the altruistic intention of bodhicitta, the determination to free all beings in the six realms of existence from suffering, and to familiarize yourself with compassion.

Moreover, you must establish in happiness beings who are suffering, and wholeheartedly rejoice in the happiness of those who enjoy it, wishing that, not only does their happiness not decline, but that it continues to flourish. Without harboring any jealousy, genuinely celebrate the well-being of those who are currently born in the higher realms and in the bliss of Dharma.

Altruistic love, compassion, and rejoicing must encompass all beings, yourself included, without any exception, in the way that space encompasses all beings.

When you have fully developed these four immeasurable attitudes, they lead to the altruistic commitment to attain enlightenment for the sake of all beings, bodhicitta, and to actualize this commitment through the conduct of a bodhisattva [practicing the pāramitās].

While engaging in this practice, endeavor to perceive the dreamlike and illusory nature of the meditator, the object of meditation, and the act of meditating. Beware of fixations that may cause thoughts such as "I am meditating on compassion; I am a bodhisattva." Practice free from the three spheres—subject, object, and action—and from all other conceptual constructs.

Thus, accord great importance to the expansion of supreme bodhicitta.

–371–

Six Qualities of the Buddhas

Six qualities of the buddhas to embody flawlessly:
Look at all sentient beings with the eyes of kindness.
Discern the nature of every karma-forming action, both those to be adopted and those to be rejected.
Realize the nature of the primordial wisdom of the great enlightenment.
In pursuit of benefiting beings, do not abandon the cycle of existences,

Freeing yourself from conceptual thoughts, remain untainted by the influence of samsara.
If you aspire to attain buddhahood, diligently practice these instructions.
Such is the perfect conduct of bodhisattvas.

Here are six instructions for attaining buddhahood:

Contemplate all beings with a tenderness and compassion as powerful as that of parents looking upon their child.

With the help of mindfulness, vigilance, and discernment, recognize virtuous actions to be adopted and unvirtuous actions to be abandoned. Align your conduct accordingly.

"When will I realize the primordial wisdom of the buddhas?" Embrace this quest with the intensity of a thirsty person seeking water.

If you aspire to endeavor to benefit beings, be prepared to remain in samsara for as long as it takes, if only to accomplish the good of a single being. Never think that you would be better off forsaking the good of others to focus on your own.

Understand, too, that the three worlds of samsara are not fundamentally corrupted: all samsaric appearances are, by nature, akin to dreams, illusions. Does not a lotus emerge immaculately from the mud?

If you aspire to buddhahood, persevere steadfastly, guided by these instructions. Such is the flawless conduct observed by the bodhisattvas, the heirs of the victorious ones.

–372–

Six Obstacles

Six types of obstacles that you should strive to avoid:
Those who have not dedicated much time to studying the teachings should avoid villages, crowded places, and other settings filled with commotion.
Those who do not uphold their vows must avoid accepting respect and service from others.
Those who cannot control their senses should avoid gazing at women or men.

Those who do not know how to meditate should guard themselves against indulging in sensual pleasures.
Those who have little control over their bodies and minds should avoid the company of people with whom they do not get along.
Those who depend on unwholesome livelihoods should guard against hypocrisy.
Those who succumb to these obstacles will be deceived by Māra.

Dharma practitioners are susceptible to six obstacles.

Lack of study: If you have not dedicated much time to studying the teachings, you would be wise to avoid busy places like villages and instead seek mountain retreats.

Neglected vows: If you are unable to uphold your vows and precepts with utmost vigilance and care, beware of accepting offerings from benefactors. Otherwise, you risk becoming one of those old renunciants who hoard possessions while claiming to have renounced worldly attachments.

Uncontrolled senses: If you have not mastered your senses, avoid cohabiting with a woman [or man].[209] Failure to do so may lead you to establish a household and become entangled in samsara.

Restless mind: Maintain your mind in meditative evenness, without letting it wander to external stimuli.

Discordant relationships: If you tend to be impulsive or even aggressive, in thought and deed, avoid the company of individuals who are like thornbushes[210] and get along with no one.

Unwholesome livelihood: Abstain from seeking impure means of sustenance, especially religious goods and offerings, by pretending to be a Dharma practitioner while engaging in hypocrisy. This includes suggesting that you are gifted with clairvoyance or any other extraordinary powers.

If you do not avoid these traps, you will fall prey to the influence of Māra.

–373–

Six Types of Unwholesome Company

Instructions on six types of unwholesome company to avoid:
Do not associate with worldly people, materialistic *Cārvākas and other tīrthikas.**
Do not mingle with ordinary people who are only interested in mundane matters.
Do not keep company with listeners, who are only concerned with themselves and lack altruistic intentions.[211]
Do not associate with solitary realizers, who have little inclination to engage in benevolent actions for the welfare of others.
Do not socialize with those who are caught up in accumulating wealth and possessions.
Do not mix with those who crave gain, respect, recognition, and fame, and surround themselves with a large entourage.
If you mingle with such negative people, you will become just like them.

Six types of undesirable company to avoid:

Do not associate with those who are concerned only with matters limited to the present life, those who hold views that question the law of cause and effect, and who deny the succession of states of existence, such as the adepts of Cārvāka.

Avoid spending your time with ordinary people who dedicate themselves solely to accumulating possessions, seeking social status, and overcoming their enemies.

Nor is it desirable to adopt the attitude of listeners, lacking compassion and solely concerned with personal well-being, or to embrace the views of solitary realizers, who show little interest in the welfare of others.

Avoid associating with those who have amassed significant possessions and squander their lives on endless distractions.

If, driven by a desire for wealth, respect, and fame, you associate with a vast entourage, you will find yourself spending your time trying to please them and will be trapped by the eight worldly considerations.

Engaging with these undesirable influences will only lead to a worsening of your situation.

–374–

Six Qualities of Prime Importance

Elucidating the six important qualities:
Nurturing compassion for sentient beings is essential for those desiring to realize selflessness.
Having firm confidence in the law of causality is essential to comprehend emptiness.
Not remaining trapped in samsara is essential for those who wish to establish themselves in nirvana.
Not expecting anything in return is essential for those who practice generosity.
Abandoning pride is essential for those who comply with moral discipline.
Minimizing possessions is essential for those who remain in solitude.
Possessing these six qualities will enable you to authentically practice the sublime Dharma.

Six spiritual qualities should be considered as essential.

Cultivating compassion for all beings is the key to attaining the wisdom that recognizes the absence of self-identity and will allow the realization of emptiness to naturally emerge in your mind stream.

Deepening your conviction in emptiness enhances your discernment and increases your attention to the laws of cause and effect.[212]

Aspiring to nirvana, in which suffering comes to an end, requires not lingering within the confines of the three worlds of samsara.

When practicing great generosity toward others, avoid anticipating, "As a result of this benevolence, I shall enjoy material comfort in future lives." Do not cling to the notion of a reward for your actions.

As you uphold virtuous moral discipline, avoid indulging in thoughts such as, "When it comes to a pure observance of the precepts of individual liberation, the bodhisattvas, and the Mantrayāna, I surpass all others!" Abandon any sense of superiority.

Should you choose a life of seclusion amid the mountains, living in solitude, cultivate contentment with minimal possessions. Do not let it be said that hermits like you accumulate wealth, including gold and silver, from the offerings bestowed upon you!

Possessing these six qualities will enable you to practice the Dharma in accordance with its fundamental principles.

–375–

Six Teaching Objectives

Six reasons for imparting the sublime Dharma:
Teaching helps you refine both your own wisdom and that of others.
Instructing disciples helps eliminate their uncertainties and doubts.
Teaching ensures the preservation of the Buddha's teachings and upholds the sublime Dharma.
Teaching enables others to discern what to adopt and what to avoid, preventing them from straying onto the wrong path.
Teaching enables others to know the differences between the higher and lower philosophies and to enter the profound path.
Teaching enables others to learn and understand philosophical principles while countering deviations and dispelling obscurations.
These are the goals that teachers must set for themselves.

Six reasons are found for teaching the Dharma, benefiting both oneself and others:

Teaching involves cultivating knowledge through listening, reflection, and meditation.

Teaching serves to dispel doubts among the community of disciples, instructing them in the meaning of view, meditation, and action.

Furthermore, it contributes to preserving the Buddha's instructions and safeguarding the treasure of scriptural transmission and realization.

Teaching assists others in correctly discerning what to adopt and what to avoid, preventing them from falling into the erroneous paths followed by listeners and tīrthikas.

Teaching also helps in distinguishing the various levels of the view, in engaging in the path of accomplishment, and in establishing both the preliminaries and the main practice of the profound path.

In the pursuit of mastering philosophical views, both your own and those of others, the teachings provide the means to rectify any erroneous perspectives, attain the genuine qualities of an authentic view, avoid deviations, and dispel obscurations.

Those who teach the Dharma diligently will engage in these multifaceted endeavors.

–376–

Six Practices for Meeting the Buddhas

Six practices for encountering the buddhas:
Undertake the three trainings by observing pure moral discipline and
Practicing single-pointed meditative concentration on the physical form of the Buddha.
Persevere in making offerings, singing praises, and reciting prayers and mantras, with reverence and devotion.
Remaining undistracted by ordinary activities, look at the nature of mind.
Even if freed from afflictive mental states, eagerly continue to take birth in the cycle of existences [for the benefit of others].
Demonstrate joyful, tireless diligence in performing virtuous actions.
Make aspirational prayers with a pure altruistic intention.
If you strive in these six actions, the buddhas will watch over you.

Six practices will enable you to meet the Buddha and never be separated from him again throughout your lives.

If you impeccably practice the three trainings of ethical discipline, concentration, and wisdom, the buddhas will accept you as their disciple throughout your lives.

With your mind completely involved in meditation, practice calm abiding and deeper insight. In particular, engaging your mind fully in meditation, achieve mental calm by concentrating on the Buddha's physical form and maintaining awareness of the Buddha during your meditation.

Express respect and devotion by making offerings, paying homage to buddhas and spiritual masters, and diligently reciting mantras associated with their names.

Let go of worldly activities, sources of distraction and delusion, and contemplate the nature of the mind.

Even if you have liberated your mind from afflictive mental states, willingly return to the three worlds of samsaric existence to fulfill the noble purpose of guiding beings on the path to liberation, as expressed in *The Prayer of Aspiration to Excellent Action*,

> As far as karma and negative emotions prevail,
> That far my prayers of aspiration will reach.

Continuously and tirelessly, train your body, speech, and mind in virtue. With the purest form of altruism, the best of attitudes, formulate prayers such as "May the Buddha's teachings spread! May I bring about the welfare of all beings! May I emulate the bodhisattvas Mañjuśrī and Samantabhadra in all my actions!"

If you persist in these six practices, the victorious ones will take you under their protection and ensure that you will meet them in all your future lives.

–377–

Six Essential Principles to Remember and Never Forsake

Six principles not to forsake, even at the cost of your life:
Do not forsake your commitment to achieving perfect enlightenment for the sake of others.
Do not forsake the sublime teachings of the Buddha.
Do not forsake sentient beings who wander in samsara.
Do not forsake virtue, which is vital for purifying [the mind of its] obscurations.
Do not forsake your guide—your spiritual master—and the yidam deity.
Do not forsake the noble path of training until you reach the exalted state of supreme beings.

Six instructions outlining what you should never forsake under any circumstances, even if it costs you your life:

Never relinquish bodhicitta, the selfless aspiration to attain enlightenment in order to establish all beings in buddhahood. Just as one would prioritize saving an entire city engulfed in flames over a single house, so too should you prioritize the liberation of all beings over your individual concerns.

If the supreme Dharma is threatened with destruction, be ready to sacrifice your life to save it. Never abandon it!

Never turn away from sentient beings who wander in samsara. Regard them all as your own family and strive to accomplish their ultimate welfare, both directly and indirectly.

Hold fast to the practice of virtue, the vital force that, in conjunction with the three supreme practices,[213] enables the purification of mental obscurations.

Above all, cherish more than your own life the spiritual guide who shows you the way and your chosen wisdom deity, the yidam, and never abandon them.

To train for the supreme path, never neglect the practice of cultivating a calm mind, deeper insight, and bodhicitta.

–378–

Six Powerful Antidotes

Six powerful antidotes:
No matter how poor you are, do not give up on virtuous activities.
Regardless of your own excellence, refrain from belittling those who display shortcomings.
Even when not prompted to do so, lead others toward the path to liberation.
Help others without any expectation of receiving something in return.
Even if you are harmed, resist the temptation to retaliate with negative intentions.
Apply these antidotes with mindfulness and vigilant introspection.
Now, let us explore instructions on six powerful antidotes:

Even if you lack food and clothing, do not abandon your virtuous practices under any circumstances.

However excellent your qualities might be, beware of showing contempt for those who lack them.

Even if no one urges you to practice Dharma, engage in listening, reflection, and meditation to enable you to guide others onto the path of liberation.

Think of all beings as kin whom you do not yet know, and continually benefit them.

When you do something good for others, do not entertain hopes that they will treat you the same way in return. And even if they wrong you and display unpleasant behavior, resist the urge to respond with anger or an urge for revenge. Instead, use mindfulness and vigilance as antidotes to such negativity.

–379–

Six Clever Ways

Six skillful means to accomplish the qualities of enlightenment:
Embrace all sentient beings with boundless love and compassion.
Comprehend the profound implications of karmic deeds.
Even if you are liberated from afflictive mental states, willingly take rebirth in samsara
Without ever neglecting the welfare of others.
Aspire to the primordial wisdom of the buddhas and strive diligently to attain it.
Understand that, like space, all phenomena transcend definite attributes.
Dedicating your merits toward the realization of enlightenment, practice skillful means.
Six skillful ways of attaining enlightenment, buddhahood:

Altruistic love desires that all beings, friends and enemies alike, find happiness. Compassion wants them to be free from suffering. Nurture love and compassion!

Having understood how positive and negative actions shape the karma of sentient beings, constantly be diligent in practicing Dharma.

Although you are free from afflictive mental states, willingly take rebirth in any realm where beings endure suffering, for the sole purpose of benefiting them.

Maintain a benevolent state of mind toward all beings, at all times, day or night, without ever relinquishing it.

Formulate the wish, "May all beings, including myself, attain the primordial wisdom of the buddhas!" Foster this aspiration within your mind.

Dedicate any merits generated through the accumulation of positive deeds and wisdom, transforming them into the causes of bodhicitta—the supreme enlightened mind. Employ skillful means by associating them with aspirational prayers emulating those expressed by Mañjuśrī and Samantabhadra.

–380–

Six Great Ways

Explaining six major methods bodhisattvas use:

Dedicating even the smallest merits [to the welfare of sentient beings], and rejoicing in those of others
Allows small merits to transform into great ones.

Remaining near and serving exalted beings, and guiding fellow sentient beings onto the path,
Accumulates great merit with little effort.

Practicing the four enlightened activities in accord with the dispositions of others
Will dispel their anger and animosity.

Speaking kindly and generously, providing sustenance, clothing, and material goods
Helps bring ordinary beings onto the path of Dharma.

Guiding beings according to their aspirations and praising the path of the Mahāyāna
Ripens those who are already on the path.

Teaching the crucial points of the vast and the profound teachings
Liberates those who are already matured.

Equipped with these skillful methods, you will encounter no difficulty in accomplishing the welfare of others.

Wise bodhisattvas use six remarkable methods:

To transmute small merits into large ones, dedicate it to others and rejoice in their merits.

To effortlessly accumulate vast merit, have faith in the noble beings who have attained the stages of the bodhisattva path, direct your prayers to them, and guide beings through those bhūmis.

To alleviate animosity and anger in others, discern their dispositions, abilities, and aspirations, then, to promote their welfare, employ the four enlightened activities: pacification, augmentation, attraction, and subjugation.

To introduce to the Buddha's teachings ordinary individuals who have not yet been transformed by the Dharma, start by talking to them in a way that suits their mental dispositions, and once their interest is sparked, guide them along the five paths to liberation. Provide them with their material needs, such as food and clothing, rallying them toward the path of liberation by hoisting the flag of generosity. Practice what you preach. These are the four ways of gathering beings to be benefited.*

To gradually bring to maturity disciples who have already entered the path, wisely praise the teachings of the Mahāyāna in accordance with their inclinations and aspirations.

Finally, to fully liberate those who have reached maturity, impart the complete Dharma instructions, both the profound teachings on emptiness and the extensive teachings encompassing the five paths and ten bhūmis.

By employing these diverse means, accomplishing the welfare of sentient beings becomes an effortless endeavor.

–381–

Bringing the Most Resistant to the Path

Six strategies for bringing those with adverse views onto the path:

Behaving in a peaceful, controlled way, in tune with their mental dispositions, will allow you to lead them toward the path.

Praising them and rejoicing in their positive qualities will facilitate bringing them onto the path.

[If this proves ineffective], give them teachings that will address their aspirations,
And assure them that if they practice sincerely, you will provide them with assistance and support.
In this way, lead them onto the path of Dharma.

Alternatively, [in case previous attempts fail], you can try a more forceful approach by momentarily displaying wrath, to shake them off their wayward path.
You may cause them some slight misery, and then open the path for them.

Regarding people who behave badly,
With a kind heart, intimidate them by assuming a wrathful attitude.
[This combination of firmness and compassion] can help guide them toward the path.

Another effective way to bring them on the path involves showing kindness that evokes gratitude in others.

A perfectly pure approach to benefit beings is to display miraculous abilities.
In these ways, bodhisattvas employ various skillful means to benefit others.

Six methods aligned with the principles of Dharma can be employed to bring onto the path individuals whose views and actions are in conflict with the teachings.

First and foremost, you must exemplify the teachings yourself by pacifying [negative emotions] and mastering [your mind]. By doing so, you will naturally inspire others to follow suit. Furthermore, praising their positive qualities and rejoicing in them also serves as a means to bring others onto the path.

Another approach involves explaining the meaning of the Dharma, which is deeply ingrained in your own mind, and promising that if they embrace the practice and cultivate spiritual qualities, you will provide them with sustenance and other forms of support to facilitate their journey on the path.

To eradicate the undesirable aspects of their minds, it may be necessary to adopt an appearance of anger and admonish them. In some cases, causing temporary hardship can direct them toward the path.

For those who have committed severe misdeeds, maintaining benevolence toward them while assuming a wrathful demeanor can serve as a wake-up call. Remind them of the consequences of their wicked actions, evoking a sense of worry within them.

Alternatively, by relying on the gratitude they feel toward the goodwill you have shown them, you can guide them back onto the right track.

The most profound method is to manifest miracles for the benefit of all beings.

These are extraordinary methods that bodhisattvas skillfully apply to work toward the welfare of others.

–382–

Training for Major Tasks

Six practices to undertake in preparation for major tasks:
Aspire to benefit beings throughout the duration of samsara.
Extend your loving-kindness toward all beings, without any form of hatred or malice.
Aspire to liberate beings using skillful means that are free from ignorance.
Without jealousy, aspire to establish them in the bliss of evenness.

Harboring no pride or arrogance, devote yourself solely to benefit others.
Relinquishing stinginess, be inclined to share with others all your merit.
Providing benefit and happiness with these practices is crucial.

To effectively accomplish the welfare of beings, there are six ways to employ skillful means, as practiced by bodhisattvas:

Do not let your bodhicitta commitment degenerate. Emulate the noble Mañjuśrī and Avalokiteśvara by vowing to benefit beings until samsara, the world conditioned by suffering, is empty.

Free from even the slightest trace of hatred or animosity, embrace nonviolence and constantly cultivate the altruistic love that wishes beings to find happiness.

Having dispelled the darkness of ignorance for those who lack discernment in choosing what to adopt and what to discard, use the skillful means employed by the bodhisattvas to liberate these beings from being trapped in the extremes of samsara or nirvana.

When you witness admirable qualities in others, regard them as embodiments of bodhisattvas. Free yourself from all forms of jealousy and wish to establish all beings in the bliss of perfect evenness.

If you possess beneficial qualities yourself, guard against pride and conceit. Instead, focus exclusively on serving others and working for their benefit.

Should you possess material wealth, free yourself from the grip of avarice. Make offerings to the Three Jewels and donations to those in need. Also, dedicate the merits you have accrued to the welfare of all beings. Strive to bring happiness to those around you through these means.

–383–

Severing Self-Grasping

Six resolutions to eradicate self-grasping:

In the same way that the victorious ones protect me,
I shall protect sentient beings to the best of my abilities.

Just as the assembly of bodhisattvas protects me,

Likewise, to support their endeavors, I shall benefit others.

Just as my sworn protectors watch over me,
I shall, in turn, assist them by upholding the samayas.

Just as buddhas and the Dharma are the protectors of beings,
I will likewise be an ally to the Dharma and practice it perfectly.

Just as those naturally endowed with compassion have become my companions,
I shall likewise be their ally and strive in virtue.

Just as the noble spiritual masters became my protectors,
I will likewise be a guardian of beings and aid them.

Embrace these attitudes and practice accordingly with reverence.

Buddhas, who possess unconditional compassion, take under their protection beings who, like me, are vulnerable to suffering and are yet to become vessels for the teachings. They thus become their refuge and protector. In the same way, to the best of my abilities, I will assist the buddhas in safeguarding sentient beings.

The assembly of bodhisattvas, heirs of the victorious ones, extend their protection and refuge to all who suffer, particularly those who have fallen into lower realms. I commit myself to supporting them and working for the benefit of others.

Seeing that I behave in accordance with the Dharma, the oath-bound protectors become my allies: they remove obstacles and adverse circumstances while arranging favorable conditions. For my part, I will present them with offerings and praise and facilitate their work by upholding my sacred commitments properly.

Buddhas possess pure qualities such as the ten forces, the four kinds of fearlessness, and the eighteen distinct qualities, making them the refuge and protectors of beings. I will accompany them by cultivating spiritual qualities to the best of my abilities.

Those individuals with a loving nature are my companions. I, in turn, will become their ally and strive to establish sentient beings on the path to liberation.

The supreme spiritual masters are the protectors and refuges who free me from the three worlds of samsara. I will in turn become a protector and refuge for others, and I resolve, without hypocrisy, to devote myself to their welfare.

–384–

The Nature of the Six Purities

Elucidating the nature of the six stainless purities:
Perfectly pure and impartial listening and contemplation lead you to the attainment of ultimate knowledge.
Perfectly pure view allows you to master the meaning of the union [of appearances and emptiness].
Perfectly pure meditation dissolves duality into its true nature.
Perfectly pure conduct safeguards your mind stream from all defilements.
Perfectly pure meditative experiences and realization allow for the ceaseless manifestation of enlightened qualities.
Perfectly pure accomplishments enable you to grasp the essence of dharmatā.
Those who embody these qualities are experts in understanding the Mahāyāna.

Even if you already practice the supreme Dharma, there are six ways to avoid being tainted by defects.

To ensure the utmost purity of your view, immerse yourself in exhaustive listening, contemplation, and meditation, so that your view faithfully reflects the Buddha's enlightened wisdom. By doing so and remaining on the continuum where skillful means and wisdom are united, you become expert in the ultimate meaning.

In perfectly pure meditation, the knots of duality completely unravel in their true nature.

Perfectly pure conduct is devoid of afflictive mental states and deluded actions.

Meditative experiences and realization are perfectly pure when you have mastered the limitless creativity of awareness. Then, your experiences and realizations will arise while you remain free of grasping and bias.

Accomplishments are perfectly pure when both ordinary and supreme siddhis unfold in the expanse of realizing dharmatā, the ultimate nature of reality.

If you have all these qualities, you are an expert in the meaning of the Great Vehicle.

–385–

Cherish Others More than Yourself

Six practices for cherishing others more than yourself.
If you prioritize yourself while disregarding others, practice the following:

Pay little attention to your own suffering,
Strive joyfully to alleviate the suffering of others.

Pay little attention to your own happiness,
And strive joyfully to bring happiness to others.

Pay little attention to the five mental poisons within yourself,
And strive joyfully to dispel negative emotions in others.

Pay little attention to arousing primordial wisdom within yourself,
And strive joyfully to awaken such wisdom in others.

Pay little attention to your own purification of the two obscurations,
And strive joyfully to purify those of others.

Pay little attention to gathering the two accumulations for your own good,
And strive joyfully to enable others to perfect them.

Whoever adopts such conduct will swiftly accomplish their own well-being.

Bodhisattvas are those who give more importance to the welfare of others than to their own. Unlike ordinary individuals who predominantly focus on personal well-being with little concern for the welfare of others, bodhisattvas place paramount importance on others' well-being and pay minimal attention to their own.

When confronted with physical or mental suffering, a bodhisattva adopts a mindset of acceptance, stating, "If it goes, let it go; if it remains, let it remain," thus attaching little significance to their own suffering. Instead, they wholeheartedly commit themselves to relieving the present and ultimate suffering of others.

Similarly, concerning personal happiness, a bodhisattva declares, "If I experience the bliss of higher states of existence and of liberation, so be it; if I do not, so be it as well," assigning little importance to their own fate. Instead, they enthusiastically engage in sustained efforts to bring immediate happiness to others and guide them toward bliss in the long term, the ultimate excellence of enlightenment.

Regarding afflictive states of mind, the five poisons may or may not pass through the bodhisattvas' minds, but their primary focus lies in transforming the mental afflictions of others. They will surround with benevolence those harboring animosity and extol the qualities of those who envy them.

Furthermore, a bodhisattva internally resolves, "Whether or not the penetrating insight of wisdom, which discerns the absence of a personal self, arises within my own mind stream, I will tirelessly and cheerfully strive for its emergence in the minds of others."

Regardless of whether they succeed in purifying their own minds from the veils created by afflictive emotions and the cognitive veils that obscure the entirety of knowable phenomena, a bodhisattva cheerfully endeavors to dispel these veils that obscure the minds of others.

Bodhisattvas do not confine their efforts solely to perfecting their own accumulation of merit and wisdom. Above all, they ardently endeavor to inspire and support others in their pursuit of such accomplishments, finding joy in the progress of their achievements.

When you shift your focus away from yourself and wholeheartedly dedicate yourself to the well-being of others, your own welfare is naturally accomplished.

–386–

Six Awakened Aspirations

Six unfathomable enlightened aspirations:

I aspire to unite all the activities
Of the bodhisattvas and accomplish them entirely.

I aspire that upon attaining buddhahood,
I shall carry out all enlightened activities, just as the sugatas have done.

For the welfare of all sentient beings,
I am prepared to endure hardship for immeasurable eons.

I aspire to accomplish whatever benefit of sentient beings
The bodhisattvas have yet to accomplish.

I aspire to carry out the unfathomable activities of the buddhas
In each and every one of the infinite pure realms.

If I fail in fulfilling these aspirations,
I would be deceiving the victorious ones and their heirs.

Accordingly, I shall constantly don these six mighty suits of armor.

As described in the sutras, the beneficent activities of the great bodhisattvas, the heirs of the buddhas, such as Mañjuśrī and Samantabhadra in particular, are beyond ordinary comprehension. Aspiring to follow in their footsteps, I offer my prayers, yearning,

> May I manifest the same profound wisdom as Mañjuśrī, the same boundless compassion as Avalokiteśvara, the same noble aspirations as Samantabhadra, and more.
>
> When I reach enlightenment, may I unite and embody the realization of wisdom, benevolence, and capabilities of all the victorious ones.

With unwavering devotion to the welfare of every individual being, I am ready, if needed, to endure boundless eons of hardships within the cyclic existence of samsara for their sake.

I will transform all those restless beings who live in this age of dregs and whom past bodhisattvas have been unable to free. I will guide them onto the path of liberation, with the resolve to accomplish what the bodhisattvas of the past could not achieve, with unwavering fortitude in the face of any challenge and difficulty.

In every pure land—Sukhāvatī, the Land of Great Bliss; Sandok Palri, the Glorious Copper-Colored Mountain; Abhirati, the Land of Pure Joy, and many others—buddhas engage in unimaginable activities. May I unite all their noble activities with mine.

If I fail to perfectly perform the enlightened activities of the buddhas and bodhisattvas, I will deceive those in whose presence I have vowed to diligently practice the teachings of the Great Vehicle. Therefore, at all times, I must don the impenetrable armor of equal taste.

–387–

Six Suits of Armor

Six shields that the māras cannot overcome:
To pursue their livelihood, fishermen, butchers, farmers, soldiers, merchants, and laborers,
Endure heat, cold, hunger, thirst, even risking their lives,
Ever engaged, never idle.
Contemplate these six examples and, with unwavering determination,
Strive to attain enlightenment, which is so hard to find, for the sake of limitless beings.

Six kinds of fortitude, six types of protective armor to shield yourself against the adversities encountered on the path of practicing the Dharma: if you don these six, the obstacles of Māra shall find no opening.

Ponder the plight of Indian fishermen, for example, naked in quagmires, killing fish as they toil in scorching heat. Should you not devote at least equal energy to practice Dharma?

How many horrors are the butchers who perpetually slaughter animals engaged in! How hard is the life of peasants laboring in the fields! What hardships soldiers endure while training for battle! How many difficulties face merchants setting out for distant lands, suffering from hunger and exhaustion! How many frustrations face the servants and employees who must constantly put on a brave face in front of their masters merely to secure their basic needs!

All must endure scorching heat in summer, chilling cold in winter, hunger, and thirst. Some even lose their lives. . . .

If only a fraction of such efforts could be channeled into the pursuit of the supreme Dharma! Then liberation and omniscience would draw near. Ponder deeply and guard against indolence. Practice unswervingly!

Bearing in mind the determination of fishermen, peasants, and the others cited above, be equally determined to achieve the enlightenment so difficult to obtain for the sake of the infinite number of beings. The aspiration for buddhahood must be driven by the welfare of all, transcending selfish interest. This is what you must keep in mind.

–388–

Six Demons to Avoid

Six demons (māras) to be cast aside:

The demon of fame entices you to egotistically seek notoriety
While abandoning the altruistic training, bodhicitta, vital on the journey to liberation.

The demon makes you jaded by dint of quibbling about what the supreme beings have abandoned and realized,
Although you have not transcended your ordinary mind.

The demon of procrastination lures you to postpone the practice of single-pointed concentration,

While leaving the fruition of your practice in the realm of wishful thinking.

The demon of greed that drives you to leave your solitary mountain retreat
To go out and conduct business, practice usury, and toil in the fields.

The demon of ignorance that drives you to engage in foolish meditation based on mere speculation,
While abandoning study and reflection on the Buddha's words, logical reasoning, and pith instructions.

The demon of jealousy that makes you conceal your own flaws,
While falsely attributing faults to others to belittle them.

It is crucial not to be ensnared by these demons.

Six activities of the demon that must be counteracted.

Having engendered the supreme mind of enlightenment on the path to liberation, it is essential to nurture this commitment for the benefit of beings by meditating according to the texts. Abandoning this resolve, as well as the aspiration to perfect the accumulation of merit and wisdom, and instead seeking personal gain while craving fame through attaining high status—all these are nothing but obstacles of the demon.

While you are in no way different from ordinary beings, engaging in endless discussions about the qualities of those who have realized the ultimate truth of dharmatā and speculating on what they have eliminated and realized indicates that you have succumbed to the demon that makes you jaded.

If, instead of devoting yourself right now to the practice of single-pointed meditation, you keep postponing and leave the fruition of meditation in the realm of wishful thinking, you are faced with the demon of procrastination.

After retiring to a mountain solitude, if, instead of remaining there, you begin to wander around inhabited places, participate in village ceremonies, and conduct business resorting to cunning methods for personal gain, you have fallen prey to the demon of greed.

While you should be assiduously devoting yourselves to study, reflection, and meditation, to logical reasoning and practicing essential instructions, if you are forsaking them to indulge in inane, approximate, and conceptual meditations, while persuading yourself that you are meditating on inner calm and deeper insight, this is merely an obstacle of the demon.

Should you conceal your own shortcomings while unjustly attributing nonexistent faults to others, using every opportunity to criticize and disparage them, this is the work of the māra of jealousy.

Exercise great caution to avoid becoming ensnared by these demons.

–389–

Six Immutabilities

Six qualities that grant you stability and freedom from faults:
Like Mount Meru, you remain unshaken by the mindset of listeners and solitary realizers.
Like space, you remain unperturbed by thoughts and negative emotions.
Like the noble beings, you stand firm, unaffected by the allure of material gain and reputation.
Like the earth, you remain unwavering, undisturbed by the trials of illness and suffering.
Like the ocean, you remain unperturbed by hunger, thirst, heat, and cold.
Like an unstoppable inferno, you persist, undeterred by the harms of spirits and obstacles.
Whoever is endowed with these qualities stays firmly on the path of the supreme vehicle.

By emancipating yourself from your shortcomings, you attain six kinds of immutability that will spare you being swept away or destabilized by obstacles and falling under their power.

Your benevolence stands firm like Mount Meru, unaffected by the mindset of the listeners and solitary realizers who primarily seek their own well-being, with little concern for others.

Your mind remains unalterable, like space, not succumbing to the role of a servant to afflictive states such as hatred, desire, and ignorance.

You do not place your hopes in transient worldly gain and respect, concerns confined to this life. As the saying goes, "Those who are free from the eight worldly concerns are supreme beings, those who reduce these eight concerns are supreme beings in the making." A bodhisattva must cultivate equal taste with regard to such worldly considerations.

Unfazed by illness and suffering, your dedication to the supreme Dharma stands unwavering like the earth.

Like the vast ocean, you are impervious to hunger, thirst, heat and cold, and diligently pursue the path of study, reflection, and meditation.

Confronted with the nuisance of evil spirits and obstacle creators, you do not succumb to their influence but instead resemble a raging fire consuming everything that threatens to smother it.

Whoever possesses these qualities is firmly established on the path of the supreme vehicle.

–390–

Six Crucial Practices

Highlighting six paramount practices:
Nurturing the well-being of yourself and others is crucial.
For the powerful to work toward uplifting the humble and oppressed is crucial.
To gratefully acknowledge the kindness of others as the wellspring of happiness and goodness is crucial.
Repaying harm with aid and benefit is crucial.
To benefit sentient beings as an offering to the victorious ones is crucial.
To prioritize dispelling the suffering of others even at the expense of your own well-being is crucial.
These are the great traditions of the Mahāyāna.

When embarking on the path of the Great Vehicle, six points are of crucial importance:

Setting aside self-centered pursuits and directing your attention toward the welfare of others is of paramount importance.

It is essential that noble beings endowed with great spiritual qualities strive to fully free themselves from delusion and, consequently, liberate from the lower realms of samsara all beings who, lacking such qualities, are clouded by ignorance.[214]

Recognizing that your present happiness and ultimately the qualities of enlightened excellence arise from the benevolence and the very existence of sentient beings, it becomes essential to cultivate a deep sense of gratitude toward all, without discrimination or attachment to those close to you or aversion toward those distant.

When ill-intentioned individuals cause harm, seize your possessions, or even resort to violence, responding with compassion and benevolence by repaying harm with goodness is crucial.

Making offerings to the victorious ones is the source of the accumulation of vast merit. Above all, working for the welfare of beings to fulfill the true intention of the buddhas is the most essential endeavor.

Without dwelling on the thought "I am well, I feel fine!" turn your full attention to promoting the welfare of others.

These six crucial points epitomize the great Mahāyāna tradition.

–391–

Gratitude

Six expressions of my gratitude:[215]

Afflicted by troublemakers, I encountered the Dharma and
found the path to liberation.
My gratitude goes to those who wronged me.

Afflicted by suffering, I discovered the Dharma and attained
ultimate happiness.
My gratitude goes to suffering.

Tormented by nonhuman spirits, I found the Dharma and
transcended fear.
My gratitude goes out to evil spirits and demons.

Having been the target of animosity from humans and other
kinds of beings, I encountered the Dharma and attained
goodness and happiness.
My gratitude goes to those who attacked me.

Thanks to unfavorable circumstances, I met the Dharma and found the path toward the immutable.
My gratitude goes to adversity.

Encouraged by others, I met the Dharma and found the quintessential meaning.
My gratitude goes to those who have inspired me in this way.

To repay their kindness, I dedicate my merits to them!

Six ways to express your gratitude:

The punishments inflicted by kings and the violence perpetrated by armies are all cause for dread. If, to evade them, you have relocated and earnestly devoted yourself to the Dharma, you will have encountered the teachings and embarked on the path to liberation and enlightenment. Ultimately, those who have harmed you will have exerted a beneficial influence by spurring you to practice the Dharma.

You may also come across the Dharma after being disheartened by the suffering that has befallen you. These afflictions will have provided you with the conditions conducive to the discovery of unchanging bliss, as was the case with Jetsun Milarepa. Ultimately, suffering will have done you a great service.

The malevolent influence of nonhuman beings has affected your vital force, resulting in numerous illnesses and other detrimental effects. To protect yourself, you have turned to the Dharma and found the bliss that transcends fear. Therefore, you can express gratitude to the evil spirits and harmful influences for their kindness toward you.

If you have experienced ill-treatment from your parents or have been expelled from a home where you are no longer welcome, or endured any other form of abuse, and if these difficult circumstances have led you to encounter the Dharma, derive immense benefit from it, and find bliss, those who mistreated you turn out to have been a source of good.

If, faced with illness, pernicious influences, adversity, and numerous obstacles, you diligently engage in the practice of the Dharma and join the path of the great unchanging bliss, these difficulties will have served you well.

On the other hand, if a spiritual friend tells you, "You should practice the Dharma, rely on a spiritual master for guidance, and immerse yourself in listening, contemplation, and meditation," and you follow their advice, you will encounter the Dharma and its quintessential meaning. Great then is the benevolence of those who have thus incited you to move toward the Dharma!

Whatever virtuous deeds you perform, dedicate them repeatedly to the authors of these six forms of benevolence, just as Gyalwa Longchenpa dedicates his own merits here.

–392–

Bringing Difficulties onto the Path

Six reasons to take harmful situations onto the path:
Seeking refuge from harm leads you to meet your spiritual guide.
Out of fear of suffering, you wholeheartedly embrace the path of Dharma.
Moved by immeasurable compassion, you magnify your bodhicitta.
Training in benefiting others, you are motivated to accumulate (merit) and purify (obscurations).
Observing the nature of your mind leads you to attain spiritual realization.
Accepting difficulties wholeheartedly encourages you to act virtuously
And allows you to cultivate the qualities of the bhūmis and paths.

Six logical reasons for accepting hardships and bringing them onto the spiritual path:

Nightmares, illnesses, or the influence of evil spirits can lead you to seek refuge and rely on a spiritual master who takes you under his protection. These difficulties ultimately serve a beneficial purpose.

Frightened by the suffering of samsara, particularly that of the three lower destinies, you will enter the path of supreme Dharma. You can thank that suffering for it!

Cultivating the four immeasurable attitudes of love, compassion, joy, and impartiality will give rise to bodhicitta and will allow it to continue to grow.

You owe it to all beings, so difficult to transform, to persevere in accumulating merit and purifying the two obscurations.

It is through your efforts to apprehend the ultimate nature of reality that spiritual realization blossoms within you. Such efforts bear fruit.

These six logical reasons show that when you embrace the adversities and challenges you encounter, the practice of virtue inspires and empowers you to amplify the qualities of the paths and bhūmis.

–393–

Benefits of Doing Good for Others

Six advantages of working for the benefit of others:
Like an escort, it protects you from all fears.
It shields you from malevolent spirits and disruptive influences.
Like a skilled physician, it heals your physical ailments.
Like a valiant hero, it repels the demons who create obstacles.
It severs the root of karma and afflictive mental states.
It enables you to perfect the two accumulations that allow for the attainment of enlightenment.
Its benefits are as infinite as space!

Altruism has six advantages and qualities:

Practicing benevolence toward others acts as an unwavering escort, safeguarding you from potential threats posed to your life by enemies and thieves.

In the face of malevolent spirits and disruptive influences, it shields you from their harmful effects.

When afflicted by ailments stemming from elemental imbalances, altruism acts as a potent remedy.

It assumes the role of a fearless champion, able to surmount the obstacles created by Māra.

Altruism cuts karma and afflictive mental states at the root.

It provides the means to perfect the accumulation of both merit and wisdom, resulting in qualities and benefits as vast as space and culminating in the attainment of enlightenment.

–394–

Six Other Commendable Advantages

Six remarkable benefits [of accomplishing the welfare of others]:
You will triumph over the most negative deeds.
You will garner the praise of the holders of the Buddha's teachings.
You will liberate yourself from samsara and attain abundant benefits and bliss.
You will ascend through the bodhisattva levels and be revered by all.
You will become the captain of innumerable beings.
You will flawlessly accomplish both the immediate and ultimate goals of yourself and others.

What are the main benefits of altruistic actions?

Eliminating the negative states of mind that afflict sentient beings, you will generate immeasurable benefits and qualities.

When, for the sake of others' welfare, you completely dispel this negativity within yourself, the enlightened buddhas express their appreciation and acknowledge those who thus carry on their lineage by benefiting sentient beings.

By renouncing all activities associated with cyclic existence across the three worlds, you will experience immediate benefits and eventually attain ultimate bliss.

As you ascend through the levels of the bodhisattvas, you become an object of reverence and offerings from all beings, be they human or celestial.

With unwavering dedication toward the well-being of an infinite number of beings, you resemble a captain embarking on a vast ocean and discovering the wish-fulfilling gem on the jewel island.

Through this journey, you attain first the states of gods and humans and finally the ultimate excellence of buddhahood.

–395–

Six Analogies on the Fundamental Nature of All Things

Six analogies that unequivocally establish the fundamental nature of all things:
The fundamental nature is as unchanging as space,
Like the ocean, it is unwavering and ceaseless.
Like the wish-fulfilling gem, it grants all wishes without deliberation.
Like camphor, its properties vary according to circumstances.
Like a mirror, it is clear, empty, and unaltered.
Like sesame oil, it permeates everything equally, without discrimination.
It is crucial to assimilate these analogies.

When you examine the fundamental nature of all things accurately, it resembles space: unperturbed by lethargy or excitement.

By abiding in the continuum of this nature, your realization will not sway from the dharmatā.

The perceptions and appearances of the six aspects of consciousness manifest themselves boundlessly, unhindered, like myriad stars reflected on the surface of the ocean.

If you are free from discursive thoughts, your ultimate aspirations will be fulfilled as by a wish-granting gem.

Camphor soothes illnesses related to "heat" but aggravates those related to "cold." Similarly, the ultimate nature of reality manifests differently in diverse circumstances.

Meditate unwaveringly on the ultimate nature, the dharmatā, the luminous emptiness akin to a pristine mirror.

Such meditation must encompass all phenomena, without any bias, akin to oil present in every single sesame seed without exception, irrespective of the quantity or size of the seed.

To elucidate these six points, regarding the first aspect, the fundamental nature is analogous to space in six aspects:

Like space, it does not lean in any direction.
Like space, it is boundless.

Like space, it is neither wide nor narrow.
Like space, it has neither a top nor a bottom.
Like space, it lacks color and shape.
Like space, it is the source of everything, both samsara and nirvana.

These six points concern the ultimate nature of reality, the dharmatā.

When we say that the fundamental nature is akin to space in not leaning in any particular direction, it implies that the sphere of dharmatā cannot be delineated to include or exclude this or that. Being all-pervading like space, the dharmatā remains unbounded.

When referring to space, it is inappropriate to speak of "dimensions," "up" or "down," as space transcends any form of measurement and orientation.

Furthermore, even when the universe takes shape within space, space does not become cluttered, and when that universe is destroyed and disappears, space does not expand either. Similarly, regardless of the circumstances affecting the ordinary body and mind, awareness remains unburdened and unaffected.

Can we assert, "This is the top, or the bottom, of space"? If you comprehend the meaning of the ultimate nature of reality, you will realize that it has neither form nor color. Just as space allows for the unfolding of the universe and its contents, the fundamental nature of mind allows for the emergence of both samsara and nirvana, depending on whether or not this ultimate nature is realized.

Second, six aspects of the ocean analogy:
Like the ocean, the fundamental nature is expansive and spacious.
Like the ocean, it is fluid, transparent, and deep.
Like the ocean, it is unfathomable and cannot be grasped by intellectual faculties alone.
Like the ocean, it remains clear and undisturbed by the two extremes [of nihilism and eternalism].
Like the ocean, it is vast, open, and naturally limpid.
Like the waves in the ocean, discursive thoughts naturally subside [in the fundamental nature].

As these six analogies elucidate, when you realize the fundamental nature, you comprehend its vastness and openness, akin to the ocean that encompasses the four continents.[216] Attempting to pinpoint any specific entity and proclaim, "This is the nature of mind," will prove to be an impossible endeavor.

The fundamental nature resembles the profound, transparent depths of the ocean, characterized primarily by its fluidity. Like the ocean, the fundamental nature remains unfathomable to ordinary minds, which fail to grasp its immensity. As does the ocean, the true nature remains limpid, undisturbed by the fluctuations between the extremes of samsara and nirvana. Like the ocean, the vast expanse of ultimate realization is a clear, boundless immensity, wherein the waves of mental fabrications naturally dissolve.

> **Third, six aspects of the analogy with a wish-fulfilling-gem:**
> **Like a wish-fulfilling-gem, the fundamental nature fulfills all aspirations without the need for deliberation.**
> **Like a wish-fulfilling-gem, the fundamental nature provides for all needs, without partiality.**
> **Like a wish-fulfilling-gem, it is naturally pure.**
> **Like a wish-fulfilling-gem, its creativity manifests as ornaments.**
> **Like a wish-fulfilling-gem, its luminous clarity is free of conceptual elaboration.**
> **Like [the radiance of] a wish-fulfilling-gem, all phenomena belong to the same absolute space.**

As portrayed by these six analogies of the wish-fulfilling-gem, the miraculous jewel bestows every wish without the need for conscious deliberation such as "I must provide clothing to this person and nourishment for that one." Spontaneously, effortlessly, and without conceptual thoughts, the wish-fulfilling-gem fulfills the wishes of all, granting them everything they long for—attire, sustenance, possessions. Similarly, upon attaining the realization of the ultimate nature of reality, ordinary perfections such as longevity, prosperity, and fame naturally manifest without the need to seek them out.

The bounteousness of the wish-fulfilling-gem is entirely impartial, granting the wishes of both the humble and the affluent or powerful. Likewise, when meditative experiences and realization arise in your mind stream, they transcend biases and prejudice.

The wish-fulfilling-gem possesses an inherent clarity akin to crystalline purity. Similarly, the fundamental nature of the mind reveals its pristine clarity when recognized, causing the spontaneous dissolution of the two veils.

This gem spontaneously fulfills every wish, thus adorning the land where it dwells. Similarly, the creativity of awareness accomplishes every aspiration and thus becomes an ornament [of enlightenment].

The luminosity and transparency of a jewel do not stem from any fabrication, just as the radiant nature of your mind remains untouched by conceptual constructs.

When the jewel emits rainbow rays of light, its brilliance remains inseparable from the jewel itself, innately belonging to its natural space. The same is true when the miraculous gem fulfills every wish [within its own natural realm].

Fourth, six points concerning the analogy with camphor [which exhibits medicinal or toxic properties depending on circumstances].
In the way that camphor has varying [applications and] effects, when the fundamental nature is misunderstood, it becomes the very source of samsara.
The example of camphor's effects illustrates how beings consequently endure suffering in the six realms of samsara.
Similar to camphor's diverse effects, when the fundamental nature is comprehended, it becomes the source of buddhahood,
Just as camphor acts in various ways, the realization of the primordial ground leads you to obtain the peace and bliss of the three kāyas.
Like camphor (in and of itself), at the level of the primordial ground, neither samsara nor nirvana exist as separate entities.

Instead, as in the case of camphor, the fundamental nature manifests in various ways depending on the circumstances.

In the fourth analogy, akin to the diverse effects of camphor, the nature of the primordial ground can manifest itself in six different ways. When unrecognized, this nature becomes the source of the three worlds of samsara. However, when realized, it becomes the source of nirvana. It is like camphor, which can be regarded as divine ambrosia for treating heat-related illnesses and as a harmful substance when administered to a patient suffering from a cold-related illness, thus demonstrating its capacity to manifest differently depending on the situation.

Like camphor, which is therefore not a remedy good for all illness, the universal ground can also manifest as the source of suffering experienced by beings in the six realms of existence. Indeed, in the absence of recognition of the true nature of the primordial ground, the six main afflictive mental states lead to habitual tendencies and consequently suffering. Conversely, upon realizing the nature of this ground, it becomes for these beings the very source of buddhahood.

Returning to the analogy of camphor, its mere fragrance can alleviate heat-related ailments. Likewise, realization of the nature of the primordial ground ensures the attainment of peace and bliss in the three kāyas. Just as the detrimental effects of camphor can be entirely dissipated, with the wind carrying away its scent, the nature of the primordial ground allows for the emergence of both samsara and nirvana. This depends on whether the mind succumbs to delusion within the three worlds of samsara or liberates itself from such delusion. In essence, the primordial ground transcends identification with samsara or nirvana, delusion or realization. Its manifestation depends solely on circumstances.

Fifth, let us explore the six aspects of the mirror analogy:
Like a mirror, the fundamental nature is primordially luminous.
Like a mirror, this nature remains untainted and unobscured.
Like a mirror reflecting an infinite array of images, the manifestations of this nature are limitless.
Like a mirror, its essence is nondual.
Like a mirror, it abides in a luminous state, untouched by conceptual constructs.
Like a mirror, its inherent clarity remains immaculate and retains its original purity.

The nature of the primordial ground resembles a mirror in six ways.

This nature is pristinely pure, vivid, luminous, and untarnished, much like a mirror. Just as morning mist is created by the dampness of earth, haze can settle on a mirror adventitiously. Simply wipe it off and the mirror is restored to its pristine radiance, never fundamentally impaired.

A mirror impartially reflects all forms, regardless of their beauty or ugliness. It neither takes pleasure in beauty nor is repelled by ugliness. The unlimited manifestations of samsara and nirvana exhibit similar qualities.

Although the mirror faithfully reflects both the good and the bad, it remains untouched by the dualistic concepts of good and bad itself.

Resting in the continuum of lucidity, freed from the delusion created by discursive thoughts, evokes the mirror's innate purity, akin to the natural luminosity of the mind.

> **Sixth, let us explore six aspects of the sesame seed analogy.**
> **Just as oil pervades every sesame seed, the fundamental nature permeates both ordinary beings and buddhas alike.**
> **Like sesame seeds, causes and effects, births and deaths proliferate.**
> **Comparable to sesame oil [in a lamp], the mind illuminates all phenomena.**
> **Similar to sesame oil [which is consumed as it fuels a lamp], concepts related to objects are liberated in the mind itself.**
> **Just as oil is extracted from sesame seed, the dharmakāya is revealed through meditation.**
> **As when the oil [is extracted] from sesame seeds, once the fruit [of enlightenment] is actualized, the result never returns to its cause.**
> **Those who comprehend these points have truly mastered the understanding of ultimate reality.**

Every single sesame seed, irrespective of its size, contains oil. Similarly, the fundamental nature of the universal ground is omnipresent in both buddhas who have realized it and ordinary beings who are unaware of it.

A single sesame seed can give rise to an infinite number of seeds. In the same way, the interconnected chain of cause and effect expresses itself in unlimited births and deaths.

Sesame oil can fuel a lamp that illuminates its surroundings. Likewise, when your experience of the mind's true nature illuminates external phenomena, if you fall into delusion, you will apprehend the multitude of things as good or bad.

Once the concepts attached to objects are liberated within the single continuum of the primordial nature of mind, the duality between delusion and liberation dissipates like oil that is exhausted in a lamp.

When sesame seeds are pressed, the oil contained within them is extracted. Similarly, through dedicated meditation and familiarization with the pristine nature of mind, the manifestations of the dharmakāya become apparent.

Once extracted, sesame oil does not revert to the seed. Similarly, upon achieving the fruit of buddhahood, it never returns to samsara.

If you realize all this, you become proficient in mastering the meaning of the fundamental nature.

–396–

Severing Attachment to Duality

Six instructions for severing attachment to duality:

Using the analogy of a dream, recognize that what you perceive is born of the mind:
Just as you awaken from dreams, illusory appearances cease to exist.

Similarly, appearances [of the waking state] are also empty by nature and cease as soon as you awaken from ignorance,
Grasping to outer objects as inherently existent will also be undermined.

Using the analogy of an illusion, understand that appearances are potent projections of the mind:
Whatever appears is devoid of intrinsic existence and recognized as being delusory perceptions shaped by habitual tendencies.

Using the analogy of a reflection, recognize that [all appearances] are [manifestations of] the nature of mind:
Understand that they are empty in themselves, devoid of clinging to the notions of subject and object.

With the analogy of mist, realize that appearances are akin to the play of the mind:
[Upon scrutiny], what appears as seemingly tangible "objects" naturally vanish, revealing their emptiness.

> **Using the analogy of a rainbow, perceive (appearances) as ornaments of the nature of mind:**
> **Just as a rainbow dissolves into space, the experiences of the mind dissolve into primordial wisdom.**
>
> **Using the analogy of a crystal, recognize appearances as the natural radiance of the mind:**
> **The true nature of this mind and its natural expression are liberated in primordial wisdom, inseparable from one another.**

These six instructions enable you to cut through fixations on dualistic perceptions.

All the appearances of samsara and nirvana are akin to dreams, nothing more. They are devoid of true existence. This shows that all these dreams are mere creations of the mind. Whether you experience pleasant dreams or nightmares, everything vanishes upon awakening. Similarly, upon purifying delusion, the appearances of samsara and nirvana reveal their emptiness. When you recognize the innate emptiness of phenomena, the veils of ignorance effortlessly dissipate.

Usually, you are attracted by pleasant forms, sounds, scents, tastes, and tactile sensations, while repelled by unpleasant ones. Yet, allowing these attachments to unravel in emptiness, they will naturally be purified by themselves.

Phenomena that initially appear real are best understood through the analogy of magical illusions. They take the form of horses, oxen, or battling armies and other phantasmagoria created by a magician using small pebbles and other tricks. Likewise, the mind has the capacity to generate countless "pure" and "impure" perceptions. Whatever appears, know that it lacks inherent existence. Thus, you will understand that all appearances of samsara and nirvana arise from delusions caused by habitual tendencies.

Using the analogy of reflections, recognize the nature of mind and understand that appearances lack inherent existence. Understand the union of appearances and emptiness—primordial wisdom—free from any attachment to the notions of subject and object.

Just as wreaths of mist envelop a mountain when heat combines with the humidity of the ground, the mind's displays unfold when the perception of external objects meets consciousness. This play undoubtedly appears but lacks a true beginning, existence, and cessation. Realizing that perceptions and appearances of objects are devoid of independent existence allows you to comprehend the meaning of emptiness.

When a rainbow shines in the sky, it is undeniably present, yet you cannot use it for anything. Similarly, if you perceive appearances without grasping onto them, they adorn the mind like a rainbow ornamenting space. When the rainbow fades, it dissolves into space. Likewise, when the dualistic subject-object perception and the perception of the external world fade away, they are liberated into the continuum of primordial wisdom.

When sunlight strikes a crystal, a multitude of five-colored lights radiate from it. These shimmering lights certainly appear, but they are merely emanations from the crystal: remove the crystal and the rainbow lights vanish.

These various analogies illustrate the mind's natural luminosity. The true nature of mind is emptiness and its radiance manifests in the form of countless appearances, some deemed good and others bad. Whatever they may be, all these appearances are primordially liberated in nonduality.

–397–

Six Concise Introductions

Six condensed introductions:

The ultimate, universal ground is nondual and free from orientation.
Delusion about the ground is the defining characteristic of samsara.

Delusory perceptions and your attachment to them are nothing but deceptions of your own mind.
To counteract this, you must train in recognizing the absence of any inherent foundation in these appearances.

For appearances associated with the mind to return to their true nature, they should be liberated within primordial wisdom:

Thus, you will reach the primordial citadel through the naturally radiant wisdom.

These six instructions represent the quintessence of all teachings;
To realize them brings the deepest fulfillment.

Six instructions that introduce you to the fundamental nature of the mind:

The universal, primordial, and ultimate ground refers to the primordial state where the distinction between samsara and nirvana has not yet arisen. In this nonduality, there is no specific orientation, dimension, or fragmentation.

When the creative potential of the ground, of pristine awareness, unfolds, the mind perceives it as an external object and defines itself as the perceiving subject, thus falling into the trap of duality. This is how delusory appearances of samsara manifest.

If you sever these delusions at the root, you can avoid being caught in the grasping associated with attraction and repulsion. You will realize that nothing is there but the magical creations of your mind, and that external objects lack inherent existence.

Once you bring these delusory perceptions to an end, you come to understand that they were nothing more than dreams, illusions devoid of true origin, existence, and cessation. Then, appearances will dissolve into the ultimate nature of mind, devoid of any foundation or root.

Thus, the grasping mind within and the outer objects of attachment without both arise and are liberated spontaneously into primordial wisdom, the nature of which is naturally free within dharmakāya.

These six points encompass the entirety of the Dharma and correspond to the fundamental nature of the Great Perfection at the level of the universal ground. The mere realization of this nature brings profound fulfillment and causes the delusion that characterizes samsara to vanish.

–398–

The Three Kāyas

The ultimate and profound meaning, the introduction to the three kāyas, is elucidated in six points.
First, the spontaneously present (three kāyas)
Resemble a crystal, a mirror, and the sun's rays
And are respectively innate purity, luminous expression, and manifestation.

The nature of the dharmakāya is perfectly pure,
Like a pristine crystal that is limpid from the very beginning.
The character of the saṃbhogakāya is luminous,
Like a reflection in a stainless mirror.
The manifestations of the nirmāṇakāya, which do not truly exist within or without,
Radiate in all the ten directions like the rays of the sun and moon.
These three kāyas are spontaneously and primordially present within yourself.
Recognize that they are an integral part of yourself, and do not seek them elsewhere.

Second, the introduction to the ceaseless aspect of the three kāyas similar to a precious gem:
The nature of the dharmakāya is natural purity.
The character of the saṃbhogakāya is unceasing luminosity.
The nirmāṇakāya is unimpeded primordial wisdom—that is, the cognizant power.[217]
Similar to a precious gem [found inside the head] of a mighty wrestler,[218] these three kāyas are your birthright.

Third, the introduction to the three kāyas using the analogy of a rising sun:
Just as the essence of the sun is open and unimpeded, free of discursive mind,
Self-cognizing primordial wisdom is the dharmakāya free of discursive mind.
Just as a cloudless sun is pure and luminous,
Wide-open and luminous [perceptions of] the five sense doors are the saṃbhogakāya.
Just like the sun's radiant light makes everything appear,
The ceaseless manifestation of the six objects of the senses is the nirmāṇakāya.
Self-cognizing awareness is like the sun shining at twilight.
Recognize that the three kāyas are present in your awareness, that they are an integral part of yourself.

Fourth, the introduction to the three kāyas by using the analogy of the sun rising in space:
The space-like utterly pure ultimate reality is the dharmakāya.
Its natural luminosity similar to the sun is the saṃbhogakāya.
The nonduality of awareness and emptiness is the nirmāṇakāya.
Recognize that these three kāyas are your birthright.

Fifth, the introduction to the three kāyas by using the trio of analogy, its meaning, and evidence:
The analogy for the dharmakāya is a perfectly pure sky,
Which transcends all delimitations and directions.
Its meaning is the saṃbhogakāya, the naturally pure luminosity,
Primordially present in itself and uncompounded.
The evidence consists in luminosity that manifests outwardly as the nirmāṇakāya.
Thus, similar to an all-illuminating lamp,[219] conviction is gained concerning the three kāyas.

Sixth, the introduction to the three kāyas as the ultimate union of absolute space and awareness:
The primordially pure, space-like dharmadhātu is the dharmakāya.
The character of this space—that is, its luminosity, is the saṃbhogakāya.
The union of awareness and emptiness, beyond all extremes, is the nirmāṇakāya.
These three kāyas are primordially present in your pristine awareness.
Do not search for them elsewhere—you will never find them.

Ignoring these (six) points is akin to attempting to extract gold from ordinary stones,
To a blind person seeking gold, to the sun obscured by clouds,
To a legless person trying to climb a ladder, to a blind person visiting a temple,
And to a new moon rising in the night:
Although [mind's nature] might be visible, it remains veiled by ignorance.

> **Therefore, decide on the correct practice, free from error,**
> **And give priority to attaining stability in the recognition of the nature of mind**

The profound meaning, the introduction to the three kāyas, is explained in six points:

First, the introduction to the spontaneous presence of the three kāyas by using three analogies—a crystal, a mirror, and the sun's rays:

When the sun shines on a crystal or a mirror, rainbow lights radiate from them. Similarly, when the appearances of samsara, nirvana, and the path (which are the natural luminosity of awareness) manifest, they embody the ultimate nature, luminous character, and cognizant power.

The nature of the dharmakāya may be illustrated by a crystal or a mirror. When these two are free from any obscuring overlay, they are perfectly pure and clear. In the same way, the nature of the dharmakāya is primordially unaffected by adventitious impurities. Its luminous quality, similar to that of a mirror, refers to the saṃbhogakāya endowed with the five primordial wisdoms. And just as reflections may appear on an immaculate mirror, the nirmāṇakāya refers to the mirror's capacity of manifestation. These three kāyas are an omnipresent fundamental state wherein there is no distinction between outside and inside.

Just like the sun and moon radiate rays of light, the three kāyas emanate the pure and impure perceptions of beings[220] to be guided in the ten directions of space. These three kāyas are primordially and spontaneously present within you. They are not something new to discover, something you did not have before. You should understand that they are your birthright and need not be sought elsewhere.

Second, the introduction to the ceaseless aspect of the three kāyas by using the analogy of a precious gem:

The crystalline nature of the gem gives it a transparency that evokes the naturally pure dharmakāya. Countless rays of light emanate from this gem that never loses its ability to radiate even when it is enclosed within a box—its luminous character is the saṃbhogakāya. These rays of light are all-pervading and this illustrates the unceasing primordial wisdom, the cognizant power—in other words, the nirmāṇakāya. The rays of light of the three kāyas are primordially present and need not be produced anew; they are your birthright. They are like the gem found inside the body of a mighty wrestler, which gives him unrivaled strength.

Third, the introduction to the three kāyas by using the analogy of the rising sun:

When the sun rises, its light makes all the four continents naturally appear. Since its luminous core is all-pervading, it is open and unimpeded. You cannot think that the sun's radiance of light illuminates only pure and elevated places like the summits of the mountains and does not reach low and impure places. This analogy illustrates the self-cognizing primordial wisdom, the dharmakāya free of ordinary mind.

Just like the sun unobscured by the clouds is naturally luminous and pure, when [the perceptions of] the five senses of the eyes, ears, nose, tongue, and body are not sidetracked by attachment or aversion to their respective objects but are wide open and clear—this constitutes the saṃbhogakāya.

In the same way that the sun's radiance of light makes everything appear, awareness's creative power makes the objects of the six senses appear. It is not necessary to block the objects that manifest, they will remind you of awareness. This refers to the nirmāṇakāya.

The essential instructions of your master, like the sun rising at dawn, enable you to understand and see awareness. If this happens, you will find that the three kāyas are an integral part of yourself. Their natural presence within you actually refers to their presence within the dharmadhātu, the expanse of the ultimate nature of reality, free of all mental elaboration.

Fourth, the introduction to the three kāyas using the analogy of the sun:

The sky-like utterly pure ultimate reality illustrates the dharmakāya. Its natural luminosity similar to the sun and moon illustrates the saṃbhogakāya. And just as the sky together with the sun and moon is the union of emptiness and luminosity, the nondual nature of awareness and emptiness constitutes the nirmāṇakāya. You must recognize that the three kāyas are within yourself, otherwise this fact will not bring you any benefit.

Fifth, the introduction to the three kāyas by means of example, meaning, and evidence:

What is the analogy for the fundamental nature of the ground devoid of all contrivance? Like the sky, it is utterly pure, vast, immense, and does not fall into the side of materiality. This nature is the dharmakāya. This dharmakāya pervades the whole of samsara and nirvana. It is not that it is present here and absent there, it is beyond all delimitations and directions. Though omnipresent in samsara and nirvana, it transcends them both and does not pertain exclusively to one of them.

The meaning (of this analogy) is the luminosity, the five primordial wisdoms pure by nature and spontaneously present since the very beginning. Their accomplishment is the accomplishment of the saṃbhogakāya. Primordially present in itself, this luminosity is of an uncompounded nature and need not be contrived as something new.

What is the evidence that it is so? Just as the presence of a gem implies its radiant light, the unceasing luminosity taken in its own right constitutes the nirmāṇakāya. This luminosity need not be produced anew. Just like a lamp dissipates darkness in a house, when luminosity is recognized with self-cognizing primordial wisdom, you naturally gain the conviction that it is so.

Sixth, the introduction to the three kāyas as the ultimate union of space and awareness:

According to its aspect of emptiness, the ground is the primordially pure dharmadhātu similar to space. This is the dharmakāya. The nature of this dharmakāya is not a mere voidness. The appearing aspect of the ultimate expanse refers to its character of luminosity endowed with the five primordial wisdoms. And this is the saṃbhogakāya. Appearance and emptiness are not separate, and their union is the nirmāṇakāya. When you recognize that awareness has been present within you since the very beginning, you will not search for it elsewhere. If you look for it, you will never recognize it.

Ignoring these six points, you will resemble (1) someone who, mistaking a pile of pebbles for gold, attempts to extract the nonexistent gold by heating the pebbles over a fire. But they are just ordinary stones that contain no trace of gold. You will resemble (2) a person born blind who desires to amass vast amounts of gold despite his blindness preventing him from locating it. You will look like (3) a veiled sun or (4) a person lacking legs who aims to climb the stairs to reach the roof of the house but faces unsurmountable odds or (5) a visually impaired person in a temple. As a final example, (6) if the moon rises in the dark of night, it illuminates the landscape, but appearances remain indecisive. Similarly, even with a seemingly clear understanding of the fundamental nature of phenomena, ignorance remains present.[221] Therefore, it is crucial to realize the primordial ground with certainty and unmistakably and to achieve stability in recognizing the nature of your mind.

–399–

Uniting Meditation and Post-Meditation

Six states of realization in which meditation and post-meditation merge seamlessly
Will be understood with the help of six analogies.

First, the analogy of the wind freely flowing through space:
In the state of clear and pure pristine wisdom akin to the vast expanse of space,
Experience the movement of thoughts as pure, free, and naturally lucid.
By doing so, you will realize a state of transparent awareness devoid of grasping.
If you fail to understand this, your single-pointed meditative concentration
Will be as fragile as the flame of a butter lamp exposed to the wind.

Second, the analogy of the rising sun:
Experience pristine awareness, free from [the duality of] brightness and dimness, and from all extremes,
And you will also experience the naturally pure, luminous, and lucid primordial wisdom.
Lacking this understanding is similar to being afflicted with a contagious disease:
Drowsiness and torpor, distraction and agitation will obscure your understanding of the fundamental nature of phenomena.

Third, the analogy of a flame protected from the wind:
Practice without letting your mind be carried away by appearances.
By doing so, you will experience the great evenness in all its simplicity.
Failing to understand this point, you will resemble a child with a bad temper,

And your meditation arranged in sessions will not help in critical moments of need.

Fourth, the analogy of the vast immensity of space:
Practice the omnipresent lucidity, free from all extremes.
This will lead you to the realization that transcends hope and fear, and grasping as well.
If you fail to understand this, you will resemble a little bird with a broken wing:
Despite all its efforts to fly, it ends up plunging off of a precipice.

Fifth, the analogy of the ocean and its waves:
Practice dissolution into the expanse of the naturally arising [awareness].
Through this, you will experience the union of arising, abiding, and ceasing within the expanse of the ultimate nature of reality.
If you fail to understand this and uphold the primordial ground as dual,
You will never be freed from affirmation and negation, subject and object.

Sixth, the analogy of streams merging into the ocean:
Practice bringing all discursive thoughts within the continuum of the nature of mind.
By doing so, you will experience the equal taste of the diversity of phenomena within the single sphere.
Without this understanding, you will struggle to employ the essential means to master the manifold conceptual thoughts,
Which will spread like sesame seeds scattered on the ground.
If you can strike the crucial points of the instructions in these ways,
You will become like those great yogis whose meditation is continuous like a flowing river.

Lacking this knowledge, like drying streams,
Your view, meditation, and action will not withstand circumstances.

These six instructions, drawing on six analogies, seamlessly unite the meditation experience and the periods that follow.

The first analogy is that of the breeze that arises and flows freely without disturbing the atmosphere. Similarly, the natural creativity of awareness is expressed through the unrestricted movement of thoughts within the pure, luminous, space-like continuum of primordial wisdom. Although thoughts are in motion, they become liberated by themselves, thus forestalling the accumulation of karma. Train yourself in this way to embrace the natural radiance [of pristine awareness].

As this primordial wisdom is omnipresent, one refers to it as "unimpeded transparency." To experience this, guard yourself from clinging to the desire to make this state even clearer than it already is. However, without understanding the crucial point of uniting luminosity and emptiness, free from grasping, if you achieve one-pointed concentration in the practice of calm abiding as stable as a flame protected from the wind, you will undoubtedly reduce afflictive states of mind. But to eradicate them, you need to cultivate deeper insight. Without it, you will never be able to eliminate these afflictive states entirely and you will continue to succumb to circumstances.

The second analogy is that of the rising sun that naturally shines. Likewise, the radiance of the nature of mind shines spontaneously, without alternating between brilliance and opacity, transcending all extremes. Experience it for yourself with a perfectly focused mind. Such is the introduction through direct experience to the naturally pure and clear primordial wisdom.

If you fail to recognize this pristine, luminous wisdom, it is akin to being afflicted with a contagious disease. Sometimes you will sink into lethargy, at other times into opacity. Thoughts may overwhelm you and your mind will run wild. If that is the case, the time to contemplate the fundamental nature of mind will not come.

The third analogy is that of the flame of a lamp in the absence of wind. When we speak of the immutability of appearances and mind, it means remaining unaffected by the appearances of the world, while inwardly practicing at the heart of pristine awareness, experiencing the simplicity and great evenness of the fundamental nature [of the mind]. Failing to comprehend this great evenness, you will resemble a capricious child: even if you dedicate yourself to regular practice sessions, you will lack the effective antidote when it is most needed, rendering it useless.

The fourth analogy, that of the immensity of space, concerns deep contemplation, or samādhi. It corresponds to the practice of limpid lucidity, which is omnipresent, devoid of all extremes and equal at all times. If you know how to experience it, you will apprehend a realization free of the grasping associated with hope and doubt. Otherwise, you will resemble a bird with a broken wing that takes off hoping to fly far away, but soon finds itself in dire difficulty and, despite all its efforts, eventually falls into an abyss, unable to reach its destination and doomed to suffer.

The fifth analogy relates to the ocean waves that are inseparable from the ocean. It encompasses everything that arises from the creativity of self-emerging primordial wisdom. Experience these manifestations as the display of awareness. If you can practice in this manner—the nature of awareness being emptiness—blend the appearances that arise from the natural radiance of this awareness with the expanse of dharmatā, which transcends all notions of beginning, abiding, and ceasing. However, if you are unable to do so and, from this primordial ground, you conceive a duality between a knowing subject and a known object, you will be entangled in dualistic attachment, oscillating between attraction and rejection.

The sixth analogy is that of rivers flowing effortlessly into the vast ocean. Similarly, experiencing deluded thoughts within the nature of the mind is what we call the unique flavor of view and meditation. You may argue endlessly about the view, meditation, and action, but in truth they should not be considered separate because they are all part of the dharmatā. Likewise, experience the nature of the ground, the path, and the fruition within the equal taste of the single essence.

If you disregard these crucial points, imagine throwing a large quantity of sesame seeds on the ground and hitting them with a stick: the seeds will scatter in all directions eluding your grasp. Similarly, you will not be able to tame the proliferation of thoughts through the essence of practice. Conversely, when you comprehend these vital instructions, you will become a great yogi whose practice resembles the continuous flow of a river.

If you understand how to meditate appropriately on these essential points, the evenness of meditation will merge with post-meditation, becoming like the course of a great river. This is what we call the "yoga like a continuously flowing river." If you are unable to practice in this way, just as streams dry up during summer heatwaves, your view, meditation, and conduct will be vulnerable to circumstances. Faced with both good and bad conditions, you will succumb to them because you do not know how to naturally liberate whatever arises.

–400–

Remain in Your Own Nature

Six key points about the view dwelling in its own nature:
First, within the view free of attachment to subject and object,
As for keeping your awareness in its natural, nondual state:
The six objects of consciousness being empty by nature, [the view] is free from the extreme of the object.
The primordial wisdom being naturally clear, [the view] is free from the extreme of the subject.
In the absence of the dualistic notion of subject and object, you simultaneously transcend both extremes.
Since "liberation from extremes" is a mere figure of speech, you are also liberated from the extreme of nonduality itself.
If you realize all this, you are emancipated from any form of attachment or grasping.

There are six crucial points to consider when it comes to conquering the [primordial] "citadel," which refers to dwelling in the very nature of dharmatā, having embraced the view of the Great Perfection as it is.

First and foremost, it is essential to remain within the continuum of the view of dharmatā, free from fixations on both the external object of attachment and the inner subject that conceived this attachment.

Having contemplated the nature of awareness, and reclaimed your true nature, disregard the duality of subject and object. Then, subjecting the five objects of the senses—shapes, sounds, smells, tastes, and textures—to careful analysis, you will discover their emptiness of inherent existence. Consequently, attachment to external objects loses its foothold.

Likewise, within, the aspects of consciousness related to the five senses—visual, auditory, olfactory, gustatory, and tactile—being liberated at the very moment of their arising, primordial wisdom transcends the extremes of subject and object.

Furthermore, the nondual nature of outer objects and inner subjects goes beyond the notions of existence and nonexistence. The expression "free of extremes" is simply a way of speaking. Thus, you even become free from the very concept of "nonduality."

If you realize this, you will harbor no attachment or grasping toward the phenomena of samsara and nirvana, regardless of their nature.

> **Second, the pith instruction for remaining in your own nature by realizing the view**
> **Free from the notions of existence, nonexistence, eternalism, and nihilism:**
> **With primordial wisdom naturally arising, the view is free from the extreme of nonexistence;**
> **As it is uncontaminated by conceptual thoughts, it is free of the extreme of existence.**
> **Devoid of object and name, it is free of both extremes simultaneously.**
> **As the play of manifestations may appear [deceptively] as dual, the view is even free from the extreme of neither existent nor nonexistent.[222]**
> **Recognize this great and perfect primordial freedom!**

Second, the view pertaining to the ultimate nature of reality will free you from the grip of eternalism, a notion supported by the tīrthikas who assert the existence of a fundamental substance known as *prakṛti*[223] and of truly existing entities such as Indra and Vishnu. The view also liberates you from the nihilistic beliefs upheld notably by the cārvākas, who deny the karmic laws of causality.

This second vital instruction enables you to realize your own nature through the view of dharmatā, the ultimate nature of reality. This view is timeless and not newly produced from causes and conditions; rather, as primordial wisdom arises spontaneously, it is thus devoid of the extreme of nonexistence, or nihilism.

Being free from the contamination of mental constructs, this view of dharmatā also transcends the extreme of inherent existence, the notion of permanence in things, known as eternalism.

Since dharmatā ignores the subject-object duality, the view transcends the concepts of object and name and is thus free from being "both existent and nonexistent."

As the unfolding of dharmatā manifests itself through the appearance of an object and a subject, it is liberated from the extreme of "neither existent nor nonexistent." However, it is crucial to recognize that this liberation is not a newfound state but an original liberation. This is what you should recognize to be the great and flawless liberation.

Third, dwelling in the natural state devoid of beginning and cessation:
As with space, the notion of a beginning lacks any foundation; [dharmatā] is therefore free from the extreme of an origin.
Since its manifestations are ceaseless, it also transcends the extreme of a cessation.
In the very moment it manifests, it is free from both existence and nonexistence.
The agent that conceives this also lacks true existence, thereby freeing oneself from the extreme of nondualism.[224]
Recognize that the ultimate nature [of phenomena emanating from awareness] belongs to dharmadhātu alone—the pure and ultimate sphere.

Third, the view of dharmatā is not something that is actually "born," that newly appears. Consequently, it is also not subject to true cessation. How do you behold the natural state free from both birth and cessation? You may ask: "Where does space come into existence? Where does it come to an end?" In truth, space lacks any foundation from which it could originate. Similarly, when contemplating the ultimate nature of reality, you cannot ascribe to it a point of origin, or identify any hypothetical causes that would bring it into being. Consequently, this ultimate nature, the dharmatā, transcends the extreme of origin.

However, the manifestation of dharmatā is boundless and you can witness the unceasing display of phenomena. Just as a rainbow appears in the sky without obstructing it, and the sky also does not disturb the rainbow, the mind's manifestations are limitless and not subject to cessation. Just as space is uncompounded, these manifestations occur unhindered, freeing them from the extreme of cessation.

Moreover, the very moment of "birth" or beginning is indistinguishable from the unborn,[225] and the dharmas (phenomena) transcend the extremes of existence and nonexistence. As the object apprehended by the intellect does not possess true existence either, you are liberated from existence and nonexistence, as well as the very notion of their nonduality.

Understand that the ultimate nature [of phenomena and awareness] belongs to the single absolute space.

> **Fourth, maintain the natural state that transcends both emptiness and appearances:**
> **[The ultimate nature], being naturally luminous, is free from the extreme of emptiness.**
> **Being nonconceptual, it is free from the extreme of manifestation.**
> **As it implies neither division nor exclusion, it is simultaneously free of both extremes.**
> **Devoid of targets and fixations, it is free from the extreme of nonduality itself.**
> **Recognize this to be the natural freedom of great evenness.**

Fourth, the view of dharmatā is free from both the extreme of gross phenomena, such as a pillar or a vase, and the extreme of nothingness, devoid of all things. While the ultimate nature of reality is emptiness, it also manifests as luminosity, thereby avoiding the pitfall of the other extreme, nihilism. This luminous expression remains free from the concepts of subject and object, thus transcending the extreme of manifestation. The radiant nature and the absence of concepts being inseparable, [the view of dharmatā] transcends both extremes simultaneously. Moreover, this view is also untainted by any form of conceptualization—"it is this, it is that"—and objectives. Therefore, it is liberated from the extreme that nonduality may entail. Recognize the spontaneous liberation, the great evenness!

> **Fifth, upholding a state of freedom from eternalism and nihilism:**
> **Everything that appears, being empty by its very nature, is free from the extreme of eternalism.**
> **Emptiness manifesting in diverse ways is free from the extreme of nihilism.**
> **Appearances and emptiness being inseparable, they transcend both extremes.**
> **The subject who experiences this view being pure by nature, the extreme of nonduality is also transcended.**
> **Consider that everything is primordially pure and devoid of birth.**

Fifth, how does the nature of dharmatā transcend both permanence and nothingness? Whatever manifestations arise within the realm of dharmatā, their fundamental essence is none other than emptiness. Thus, it remains liberated from the extreme of permanence or eternalism, which posits an unchanging reality with immutable existence—a viewpoint upheld by non-Buddhist tīrthikas who assert the existence of permanent entities like *puruṣa*, said to be a conscious Self.

From the sphere of this emptiness, all phenomena appear—an infinite and unimpeded unfolding of the diverse manifestations of samsara and nirvana. The nature of reality is thus emancipated from the extreme of nothingness, the absence of anything.

Therefore, emptiness and phenomena are not separate entities that occasionally merge or separate; rather, they are indivisible and transcend both extremes of eternalism and nihilism. Upon recognizing the inseparability of appearances and emptiness, the distinction between a subject that perceives and an object that is perceived dissolves. This liberates you even from the extreme of the mere concept of nonduality. Acknowledge that all phenomena are originally unborn and primordially pure.

Sixth, abiding in the nature of liberation from good and evil:
Awareness transcends the confines of elevation, thus dispelling the craving for excellence.
Not confined by degradation either, it dissipates the urge to eliminate what is perceived as bad.
As awareness does not confine itself to the separation between these two perspectives, it remains free from duality.
Since it does not confine itself to nonduality either, it is free of extremes.
Failing to master the fortress of this view
Will result in lack of stability. Deviations and obscurations will arise,
Hindering progress beyond the lower views.
Therefore, it is of utmost importance to treasure the instructions on these crucial points that enable you to dwell in the natural state.

Sixth, by nature, both good and bad are self-liberating. What does this mean? The ultimate nature of reality does not succumb to pride when elevated to the highest heights, for it transcends the vain infatuation with excellence.

When, on the other hand, you encounter illnesses, malevolent spirits, obstacle makers, or any other adversities, there is no cause for despondency or discouragement. Remain untethered from the extreme of perceiving these circumstances as inherently bad.

Furthermore, the dualistic grasping that distinguishes between good and bad also finds liberation within its own essence. Finally, the nature of nonduality itself is not confined to the intellectual concept of nonduality. It transcends the notions of existence, nonexistence, both, and neither.

Failure to truly grasp these six pivotal points, which form the formidable fortress of the great view, will hinder your ability to abide steadfastly in the ultimate nature of reality. This can result in various deviations and obscurations, such as clinging to dharmatā as a tangible entity or being unable to progress beyond the perspectives of lower spiritual paths. Therefore, it is imperative to assign utmost significance to these essential instructions.

–401–

Making Thoughts Your Ally

Six methods for turning discursive thoughts into allies:
Learn to let discursive thoughts dissipate by themselves like the wind in space,
And primordial wisdom will emerge naturally from within.

Train yourself to allow the movement of thoughts to become pure of its own accord, akin to a flash of lightning illuminating the entire sky;

Then all the movements of the mind will manifest as naturally radiant primordial wisdom.

Allow your attentive presence to naturally become clear, just as murky water settles on its own;
Consequently, mental constructs will arise as the spontaneous realization of the victorious ones.

Let all arising thoughts dissolve in the dharmatā and they will become your allies;

Doing so, the realization that transcends appropriation and rejection will be born from within.

Allowing grasping to naturally dissipate, the absence of an object will manifest as an ally;
And the primordial, groundless wisdom in which the perceiving subject has vanished will emerge within you.

Allow for the clear and natural purity to shine by itself, and luminous space will become your ally;
As thoughts unfold and leave no trace, primordial wisdom will arise from within.

For the yogi who practices in this manner,
Original wisdom will emerge from the discursive thoughts themselves,
Just as a great fire grows out of dry wood.
Therefore, it is crucial to allow all appearances to manifest as allies.

What are the roots of delusion? Discursive thoughts. However, if you recognize the nature of these thoughts, they can become allies in meditation. Ignoring their nature, they will not serve as such. Here are six instructions on how to make friends of these thoughts.

When a thought arises in your mind, as soon as it has arisen, let it vanish like a gentle breeze dissipating in space. Become familiar with this process. Just as once the breeze settles, all that remains is the radiant expanse of the sky, once thoughts have dissolved, all that remains is primordial wisdom, naturally arising from within.

At present, many thoughts are flowing through your mind. This is the moving aspect of the mind. Instead of focusing on any specific movement, take the example of a lightning bolt that illuminates the sky for one instant, only to vanish the next. Initially, a thought of attraction—a surge of faith or any another virtuous thought—or of repulsion emerges in your mind like lightning in the sky. At the very moment it arises, if you know how to purify it within the emptiness of dharmatā, whatever thought arises will not proliferate but will manifest as primordial wisdom. Thus it is said.

Maintaining a vigilant presence allows you to discern and remember what is to be embraced and what is to be avoided. However, this vigilance must be devoid of attachment and must occur within natural freedom. Just as when you stop stirring muddy water, it naturally settles and becomes clear, if you cease stirring up your mind and allow it to rest without further feeding it, thoughts are bound to fade away. In this manner, whatever emerges in your mind will manifest as the self-realization of the buddhas.

Whatever thoughts form in your mind, they have no option but to dissolve in dharmatā and have no intrinsic capacity to obscure or veil it. As a wispy cloud cannot conceal the vastness of the sky, the dharmatā remains transparent.

If you realize this, a level of accomplishment that transcends the pursuit of virtue and the rejection of nonvirtue will dawn in your mind. The grasping of thoughts, whether deemed good or bad, will be exhausted. Conversely, when discursive thoughts and objects tightly grasp each other like two intertwined hands, these thoughts will proliferate. Avoid such entanglement and thoughts will become your allies. You will recognize that they are devoid of any roots or foundation, and primordial wisdom will flourish within you.

Ultimately, thoughts are nothing but the radiant expression of dharmatā. If you know how to engage with them as allies of pure, luminous space, they will continue to arise, yet leave no imprint, much like a bird flying across the sky. Essentially, when thoughts arise and purify themselves without leaving any imprint, primordial wisdom will arise from within.

A yogi who knows how to befriend thoughts in these ways will experience these very thoughts as primordial wisdom. But be cautious! As it is said, "Do not prematurely label thoughts as dharmakāya: most important is to liberate them." This is a fundamental point. If you liberate them, they will all become your allies, just as a large amount of dry wood feeds a great fire. Reflect deeply on this.

–402–

Remaining in the Ultimate Nature of Reality

Six crucial points for abiding in the state of dharmatā:

By assuming the six-point body posture during meditation,
Establish subtle channels, wind-energies, and essences in their natural state.

By recognizing the universe and its contents as the mandala of the victorious ones,
Liberate ordinary, deluded perceptions.

By sealing the lower door and pressing down the upper breath
Embrace the great bliss in its natural state.

By turning the tip of the tongue upward, almost touching the roof of the mouth,
Rest without conceptualization in the state of the ultimate nature.

By gazing into space, one cubit in front of you
Purify the naturally luminous primordial wisdom within the expanse [of emptiness].[226]

Preserving the original simplicity of the nature of mind, relaxed and limpid,
Is the crucial point of the spontaneously present primordial wisdom.

With these skillful means, remain in the state of dharmatā.
Those with the proper predisposition will implement these essential points with perseverance.

There are six essential points for steadily abiding in the ultimate nature of reality, the dharmatā.

Allow the various elements of the body—the subtle channels (*nāḍīs*), the wind-energies (*prāṇa* or *vāyu*) and essences (*bindus*)—to rest in their natural state, without contrivance or fabrication. If you do so, they will function as wisdom channels, wind-energies, and essences. To facilitate this functioning, it is important to adopt the seven-point [or six-point] physical posture.*

When it comes to speech, excessive talk becomes a source of distraction. Therefore, it is wiser to speak sparingly, maintain silence, and abide in the continuity of the natural state.

Recognize the universe and all its contents—the entirety of phenomena—as the mandala of the victorious ones.

Concerning the vital point that allows the emergence of great bliss in your body, do not let the lower breath escape, seal the lower door, and press the upper breath downward while bringing the lower breath upward so that they meet at the level of the navel. Abide in this manner.

For the crucial point of resting in the continuum of dharmatā free from discursive thoughts, turn the tip of the tongue upward, almost touching or lightly touching the palate.

The crucial point that purifies the naturally luminous primordial wisdom within the expanse [of emptiness] is to place your gaze straight ahead in space, at a distance of about the length of your forearm.

The crucial point in the spontaneous accomplishment of primordial wisdom is to relax your mind in perfect simplicity, allowing its natural radiance to manifest.

With the diligent application of these six crucial points, all fortunate beings who abide in the continuity of dharmatā will witness the dawning of the fundamental nature within themselves.

–403–

Methods for Remaining in the Ultimate Nature of Reality

Six instructions on methods to stay in the continuum of dharmatā:
First, the instruction on the inseparability of the three times
Frees the mind from the constraints of dualistic, conceptual thinking:
Do not dwell on the past or anticipate the future;
Relax in the present moment, without the slightest fixation.

There are six essential instructions for allowing the mind to rest without fabrications, as it is, in its natural simplicity, the continuum of dharmatā.

First, past, future, and present thoughts merely appear while being entirely devoid of inherent existence. They never depart from dharmatā, the ultimate nature of reality, emptiness. Understanding this allows you to transcend the dualistic fixations that momentarily grip the conceptual mind. To accomplish this, do not ruminate in the wake of past thoughts, do not invite or anticipate future thoughts, and rest perfectly at ease in the state of nongrasping. This is the essential instruction that unifies the three times in an indivisible manner.

The instruction akin to a swallow entering its nest
Dispels the extremes of hope and doubt.
The present moment is beyond emergence and fixation:
Without falling into distraction, relax into the state of evenness.

Before building her nest, a swallow carefully examines the surroundings, to check whether it presents any dangers. Once she finds the ideal location and has built her nest, she will swoop in without the slightest hesitation. However, if you keep telling yourself that your meditation is on the right track or that it is not there yet, breeding all sorts of hesitations, hopes and doubts, these will build the cage that traps the parrot of your mind.

Conversely, when you transcend the limitations of conceptual thoughts, the duality between the emergence of thoughts and their fixation on objects dissolves. At that moment, you will gain access to the continuity of the true nature of mind, originally devoid of any fabrications that proclaim "it is so" or "it is not so." In this state, your task is simply to abide, undistracted, in perfect evenness.

The instruction akin to a person who abandons all endeavors,
Dispels the confines of fixation on targets and objectives.
In the state of the evenness of ultimate, unfabricated reality, the fundamental nature of mind,
Rest in equanimity after letting go of everything in the great liberation from grasping.

If you surrender all your occupations to rest in perfect serenity, you will discover a perfect ease within. When thoughts of faith and devotion arise, you will most probably congratulate yourself. Conversely, when thoughts of attraction or aversion spring forth, you will deem them undesirable and strive to suppress them. These are all self-imposed objectives, however. What matters most is dispelling fixation on such objectives and finding rest in the unbroken flow of unconstructed simplicity—the fundamental nature of your mind. Leave all preoccupations in nongrasping.

The instruction akin to a garuḍa soaring through the sky
Liberates the mind from the constraints of dualistic, conceptual doubts.

Sever the ties of the ordinary mind's limitations and rest in the spontaneously arisen natural state,
Letting go of everything in the vast expanse.

When a garuḍa soars in the skies, he is never afraid of falling. Like him, rid yourself of the webs of doubt and duality that entangle the mind. To do this, guard against perpetuating past thoughts and inviting future ones. This will free your mind from the grip of present thoughts and allow it to abide in a state devoid of mental fabrications and to rest in the naturally arisen fundamental nature. Leave all things in the continuum of this nature that encompasses both samsara and nirvana.

The instruction resembling the rising sun that dispels darkness at dawn
Transcends the limitations of conceptual thinking that perceives the diverse array of objects.
Without retracting your senses inward or obstructing the movement of thoughts,
Serenely relax after liberating the six aspects of consciousness.

At the break of dawn, the sun naturally rises. It is inconceivable that it could do otherwise. Similarly, when perceptions of sensory objects—shapes, sounds, scents, tastes, and textures—arise, refrain from superimposing mental constructs upon them. It is impossible not to perceive the six objects of the senses and consciousness, so there is no point in withdrawing your sensory faculties or bemoaning the fact that your thoughts escape toward sense objects. When your thoughts tell you "This object is excellent, so attractive" and "This other one is so repulsive," do not attempt to halt the flow of thoughts. However, do not indulge either in craving attractive objects or feeling aversion for those you deem detestable. Instead, fully relax your perceptions of the six aspects of consciousness and allow them to rest in their natural state.

The instruction for purifying mental constructs into their true nature
Transcends the constraints of proliferating thoughts.
Irrespective of your perceptions, do not succumb to the duality of attraction and rejection.

Let everything rest in the freshness of pristine simplicity.
Abide in the continuum of nonduality,
And realization of the limitless expanse will surely manifest.

The vital instruction aimed at relinquishing the mental constructs of eternalism and nihilism in the natural state [of the mind] allows you to dispel conceptual limitations, even as thoughts of all kinds—positive and negative—continue to arise. To succeed in embracing this essential point, resist the inclination to favor virtuous and desirable thoughts or to reject unvirtuous and undesirable ones, regardless of their nature. Instead, let them all rest in the freshness of simplicity. By doing so, you will remain in the primordial, nondual wisdom that has always resided within you. Subsequently, the realization of the vast expanse free from the limitations of eternalism and nihilism will spontaneously arise within your mind.

–404–

Six Shortcomings of Meditation

Six common flaws in meditation:
If you lack lucidity and clarity, the nonconceptual state of mind may sink into lethargy.
Placing excessive emphasis on clarity during meditation may limit your experience of primordial wisdom.
Attempting to contain the formation of thoughts may result in narrow-mindedness.
Without realizing deep clarity, mere discussions [on emptiness] prove to be futile.
Lacking deep trust, you will be vulnerable to doubt.
If your actions, words, and thoughts are contrived, the grip of delusion will only strengthen.
Each of these six shortcomings contributes to obscuring your mind.
Therefore, those who aspire to realize the ultimate meaning must address these flaws through meditation.

Six general flaws of meditative evenness are recognized:

Neglecting the luminous aspect of the mind and being content to merely calm thoughts, in the absence of deeper insight, your meditation on calm abiding will remain imperfect.

If you insist that your meditation must incorporate the luminosity of dharmatā and artificially fabricate such clarity, your experience of primordial wisdom becomes increasingly narrow.

In your pursuit of suppressing the proliferation of thoughts at any expense, if you confine your mind too tightly within itself, your meditation may become excessively constricted. Placing too much emphasis on achieving mental tranquility runs the risk of fixating on a limited aspect, which is a flaw that must be avoided.

Merely engaging in eloquent discussions about the Great Perfection and the luminosity of the mind, without grasping the profound luminosity of dharmatā—the quintessential nature of reality—will ultimately prove futile. Understanding the nature of dharmatā is of paramount importance.

If you have not acquired a deep conviction, doubt will permeate your mind. Cultivating a clear inner certainty about the view of dharmatā thus becomes crucial. Mere empty words cannot engender unwavering certainty regarding such a view.

Leave your three doors—body, speech, and mind—in their natural state, without fabrication. Otherwise, your initial delusion will only increase.

Each of these six flaws clouds the mind. Therefore, those aspiring to comprehend the ultimate, immaculate meaning must engage in practices that dispel these shortcomings.

–405–

Six Deviations

Presentation of six types of deviation:
Engaging in meditation on the four infinite spheres of perception [of the formless world];[227]
Adopting the nihilistic view that denies the principle of causality even at the level of relative truth;
Adopting the view of "great permanence," or eternalism,

believing in the immutable nature of the subject-object duality;
Viewing the whole world as an enemy, akin to thorns;
Considering that phenomena are nothing other than the mind, focusing on self-illuminating consciousness;[228]
Regarding ordinary thoughts as deities, thereby straying from the ultimate meaning.
Be cautious not to fall into these six deviations, but instead remain in the vast and directionless space of the ultimate nature of reality
And never wander away from the great equality.

Your meditation can go astray in six ways. First, you may become lost in conceptual views by absorbing yourself in one of the four states of infinite perception of the formless world—infinite space, infinite consciousness, absolute nothingness, and neither truly existing nor completely nonexistent.

When you dismiss the ineluctable nature of the law of causality, which is inescapable on the level of relative truth, and claim to have transcended it, you fall into nihilism.

If you cling to the dualistic notion of immutably existing subject and object—the concept of "great permanence"—you deviate into the realm of non-Buddhist tīrthikas, who posit the existence of eternal entities like Īśvara and Indra.

Considering all your perceptions of the outside world as obstacles to your samādhi, as enemies or thorns, will disrupt your concentration.

If you reduce everything to the mind-only perspective and focus your meditation solely on the self-knowing, self-illuminating consciousness, it ultimately amounts to meditating on the basic consciousness, ālayavijñāna.[229]

When, without having mastered the essential points of the development phase, you imagine that all discursive thoughts are wisdom deities, you are far from the ultimate accomplishment.

Do not get lost in these six deviations and wander away from the continuum of great evenness, the boundless expanse of the ultimate nature of reality.

–406–

Correct Six Defects

Six methods for rectifying six defects, should they arise:
Rectify them as if they were clouds vanishing into space:
Whatever fantasies come to mind,
Rectify them by letting them naturally dissolve in the expanse of dharmatā.
Rectify them like a thief entering an empty house:
The essence of discursive thoughts being devoid of inherent existence,
At the moment a thought arises, it has not truly come into being and is elusive.
Simply liberate it to rectify it without having to remove it.
Rectify them like a fire spreading through a dry forest in winter:[230]
Whatever thoughts grasp onto objects, if you examine their nature,
Their blaze will enhance your understanding of dharmatā and you will amend them in this way.
Rectify them as you would blow on a poison while reciting a mantra,
Dissolving discursive thoughts in their unborn state.
Rectify them like a subject who beholds his king:
When the five poisons appear, recognize them and release your grip; they will vanish in their own nature
And the meaning of dharmatā will reveal itself. Thus, everything will be rectified.
Correct them like a bird that always returns to the boat:
All the distractions and agitations that arise
Have no choice but to return to dharmatā and are thus ultimately rectified.
In this way, with the help of these six key points, whatever thoughts are formed,
Allow them to be purified, cleared, and liberated by themselves.

When faced with six types of defects during meditation, it is important to rectify them. When, for example, clouds form in the sky, the sky leaves them as they are: it does not rejoice if there are clouds, nor does it grieve at their absence. As for clouds, it is in their nature to vanish suddenly. In the same way, whatever phantasmagoria, good or bad, arise in your mind, if you leave them as they are in the expanse of dharmatā, without intervening or altering them, you will remedy them at the same time.

A thief can search every corner of an empty house: he has nothing to gain, and the owner has nothing to lose. Likewise, whatever thoughts enter your mind, from the very moment they appear, they are devoid of inherent existence. If you become aware of this, no matter how many thoughts arise, they bear the seal of the view of dharmatā. They will not persist, and will vanish without giving rise to attachment. By relaxing into this state of nongrasping, you eliminate all defects.

When a fire breaks out in a forest during the dry season of winter, it spreads very easily. Similarly, whatever thoughts are associated with the five sense objects, if you contemplate the nature of the attraction or repulsion they generate, they manifest as allies of dharmatā, without harming it.

Blowing on poison while reciting mantras[231] not only prevents the poison from causing your death but also extracts a beneficial essence from it. Similarly, if you eradicate thoughts by letting them free themselves naturally in the unborn nature, they will become allies of your meditation and will not hinder it in any way.

When subjects catch sight of the king, they prepare to serve him deferentially and instantly feel respect for him. Similarly, when any of the five mental poisons originate in your mind, simply recognize them, without grasping, without intentionally meditating on them, and without engaging in dualistic thinking. Relax into this state and the meaning of the ultimate nature of reality, the fundamental nature of the five primordial wisdoms, will reveal itself.

If you release a bird from a boat and it soars over the ocean, apart from perching on a whale, it will find nowhere to land and will eventually return to the boat. Similarly, whatever thoughts arise, if you are certain that they proceed from the unborn dharmatā, they will have no other destination than to return to dharmatā itself. In this way, you will be able to amend these thoughts, leaving them with no escape.

In this manner, no matter what thoughts are set in motion, they will be cleared in their own nature through these six key points and will not lead you astray if you let them rest in their natural state.

–407–

Confidence Born of Perfect Realization

Six signs of confidence arising from perfect realization:
You will not be disheartened by your shortcomings nor infatuated with your qualities.
You will understand that your mind resides within your perishable body as the dharmakāya.
Without being attached to samsara, you will never tire of benefiting others who dwell there.
Deviations and obscurations, regardless of their nature, are encompassed within the perfection of the single sphere without privileged direction.[232]
Realizing that demons are expressions of dharmatā, which is their ultimate nature, you will fear no obstacle.
Within the immensity of space, you will experience the sensations of pleasure and pain without acceptance or rejection, hope or fear.
Those who attain such realization will achieve a perfect understanding of the fundamental nature.

If a perfectly pure realization arises in your mind, it will manifest as six forms of confidence:

Should anything appear as a flaw, you will not be discouraged by the notion that your meditation is defective. Should anything appear as a virtue, you will not succumb to the attachment that whispers, "Behold, a great quality!" Thus, such judgments will neither elate nor discourage you.

Even though you inhabit a human body of flesh and bone, if you recognize that the ultimate nature of your mind is none other than the dharmakāya—the absolute dimension of buddhahood—as it is said, you possess "the body of a human, the mind of a buddha." This is a crucial point.

Whatever endeavors you undertake with your body, speech, and mind across the three realms of samsara, remain free from attachment and never grow weary of dedicating yourself to the well-being of those caught in the cycle of existence.

The ultimate nature of reality eludes the definitions of "existence" or "nonexistence." It does not lean toward any extreme—neither the naive realism of eternalism nor nihilism—rather, all remains flawless within the expanse of the single sphere.

Instead of regarding māras as obstacles to be cast aside, perceive them as adornments of dharmatā, which only illuminate your spiritual qualities. Having no reason to fear them, welcome them with serenity. Similarly, there is no need to deliberately repel suffering since both happiness and unhappiness will nurture the blossoming of your experience of the ultimate nature. By comprehending this, your realization of the fundamental nature will reach its ultimate point.

–408–

Achieving Perfect Stability

Six criteria of having achieved perfect stability:

All phenomena, appearances, and existence are perceived as illusory manifestations,
And, as a sign that they lack inherent existence, they continually manifest.[233]

The essence of afflictive mental states is primordially pure:
Unshaken by the five poisons, it manifests as the naturally radiant primordial wisdom.
Flaws and qualities both manifest as the great primordial wisdom,
While the inclination to reject or accept naturally vanishes.

When you realize that the essential meaning is not outside you,
Thoughts appear limpidly in the state of dharmatā.

Upon discovering the precious jewel that is the nature of the mind,
When faced with death and the bardo [between one state of being and another], neither fear nor torment will arise.

When you perceive the Buddha in the very nature of your own mind,
You are liberated from the bonds of reliance on effort and of hope and fear.

Such a yogi has achieved perfect buddhahood.

A practitioner who has attained stability in assimilating the pure and perfect meaning of dharmatā understands that all phenomena, the realm of appearances and existence, are akin to dreams and illusions. Since this manifestation [of the very nature of dharmatā] clearly lacks inherent existence, the shadows of attachment and aversion are dispelled.

The nature of afflictive mental states is originally pure. Recognize that they possess the nature of the five wisdoms, and they will be instantly liberated upon arising, causing no disturbance to your mind. At that time, primordial wisdom will arise from within.

Having arisen primordially, the great wisdom, free from the notions of rejecting flaws and adopting qualities, requires no elimination of imperfections or addition of qualities. Consequently, the tendency to attract or repel naturally dissipates.

When the essence of dharmatā is no longer perceived as external by those on the path of transformation, discursive thoughts dissipate into the continuum of dharmatā.

Similar to a miraculous gem granting all desires, understanding the fundamental nature of the mind serves as the source of all qualities associated with eliminating veils and realizing the excellence of buddhahood. Accomplishing these qualities ensures that even if death were to approach tomorrow, you would be free from fear, traversing death and its ensuing transition without torment or distress.

By recognizing that the ultimate nature of your mind is buddhahood itself, you will reach such a level of realization that you will be free of all effort, hope, and doubt.

Such a yogi embodies perfect buddhahood.

–409–

Six Kinds of Confidence

When realization becomes as vast as space, six forms of inner confidence emerge:
[The confidence born of] the realization of the Middle Way free from extremes.
[The confidence born of] the realization of perfect unity within the realm of great luminosity.
[The confidence born of] the realization of perfect equality within the realm of great bliss.
[The confidence born of] the realization of the nonduality of the single essence.
[The confidence born of] the realization of spontaneous presence, the great freedom devoid of any orientation.
Once the realization of the natural state of primordial purity has reached its pinnacle,
There is no longer a "person" who claims to have achieved it.
Free of any pride associated with this attainment,
Incomparable is the yogi of illusion!

When the realization of the ultimate nature of reality becomes as vast as space, six forms of confidence manifest:

The first arises from the realization of the Middle Way, wherein all phenomena are free from the extremes of existence and nonexistence, eternity and nothingness.

This Middle Way, transcending the extremes of eternalism and nihilism, is not a mere void, and confidence is born from the realization of the union [of appearances and emptiness] within the great luminosity.

From the expanse of the realization of this great luminosity emerges the understanding of the equality between samsara and nirvana, together with the great bliss that unfolds as the manifestation of primordial wisdom.

Within the single essence, confidence also arises from the realization of nonduality, where the rejection and adoption of samsara and nirvana come to an end.

The luminous and spontaneously present nature of this sole essence corresponds to the realization of the omnipresent enlightened view, unbound by any orientation.

As the realization of the nature of primordial purity reaches its peak, there is no pride that arrogantly declares, "I have achieved the realization of dharmatā." Realization ignores vanity.

Such is the incomparable yogi of illusion.

–410–

Six Modes of Liberation

Six modes of liberation are associated with these realizations:

When external objects appear,
These appearances are instantly liberated like ice melting in water.

Internally, when awareness apprehends phenomena,
They are instantly liberated, as a bubble bursts in water.

In between the two, the movement of thoughts that oscillates between name and meaning within the dualistic aspect of the mind
Is instantly liberated, like lightning crossing the sky.

When you hear the sound of words used to designate things,
This sound is instantly liberated like a fading echo.

When you uphold a philosophical standpoint,
That view is instantly liberated like a rainbow vanishing into space.

When spiritual accomplishment, the fruit of your practice, manifests,
It is liberated as swiftly as the King of Jewels grants wishes.

Liberation occurs spontaneously, and remedies dissolve into their own nature.
Transcending names and objects, liberation happens naturally.

In this way, beings endowed with higher capacities will be liberated in this life; if not, at the moment of death; or, at the very least, during the bardo.

How does a yogi of illusion achieve realization? When the external sense objects—shapes, sounds, smells, tastes, and textures—are perceived by the corresponding faculties, the appearances and your experience of awareness, which have been corrupted, are liberated the very instant they manifest, just as ice melts into water during the summer. Consequently, attachment and repulsion will not crystallize upon these objects.

Internally, mental formations arise from awareness. At the very moment you perceive them, they are liberated into this awareness, just as a bubble forms and dissolves inseparably in water.

In between, all the oscillations between objects of attachment and the subject that clings—the constant fluctuations of duality—dissolve in the realm of dharmadhātu. This instant liberation of the mental movement resembles the swift passage of lightning across the sky.

When you utter the names *pillar*, *vase*, and so forth, at the moment these names resonate, they are liberated like fleeting dreams or illusions, or akin to the fading of echoes.

Your philosophical views—whether they align with Cittamātra, Svātantrika, or Prāsaṅgika—are liberated at the very moment you conceive them, much like a rainbow dissolving into space.

The fruits of spiritual practice, the kāyas and wisdoms, are liberated as soon as they are attained, as naturally as the miraculous gem fulfills wishes. Antidotes dissolve into their own nature, and the realization that transcends names and objects arises spontaneously. The most accomplished practitioners will thus find liberation in this life; otherwise, at the moment of death; or, at least, during the bardo.

Now come two sets of six-point instructions,
Which show how individuals with average faculties
Can achieve liberation during the bardo of dharmatā.

For individuals with average faculties who have been unable to achieve liberation during the transitional states of the present life and of death, there are two sets of six-point instructions concerning liberation in the bardo of dharmatā, the ultimate nature of reality.

–411–

Abandoning the Physical Body

Six ways to let go of your bodily envelope:

When the outer and inner (elements) dissolve in the mind,
This is the moment when you stop apprehending "objects."

When the mind is governed by primordial wisdom,
This is the moment when you naturally part from a grasping "subject."

When your experience of the primordial wisdom of awareness withdraws into the cocoon of habitual tendencies,
When the subtle energy (the breath, *prāṇa*) of the earth dissolves into that of water, and you are no longer able to carry your body,
This is the moment to practice the transference of consciousness (*phowa*). You excrete and urinate uncontrollably, and your body gives off a foul odor.

When the subtle energy of the water element dissolves into that of fire, your limbs lose their strength.
Your face is sweaty;[234] saliva and mucus flow from your mouth and nose.

When the subtle energy of the fire element dissolves into that of wind, your mouth and nostrils dry up.
The heat leaves your body; your mouth and nose lose their shine.

At this stage, if your body heat is concentrated in the soles of your feet, you will be reborn in the infernal realms.

If it accumulates in the secret center, you will be reborn in the realm of hungry spirits.
If it is concentrated at the navel level, you will be reborn in the animal kingdom, while if it is at the heart level you will be reborn as a human being;

At the throat level, in the realm of the demigods; at eye level, in the realm of the gods.
And if the heat dissipates through the crown of your head, you will obtain the unsurpassable fruition (of enlightenment).

When the subtle energy of the wind element dissolves into consciousness,
Your breath becomes laborious, impeding full inhalation.
The natural brilliance in your eyes fades away;

Your outer breath ceases and consciousness dissolves into luminosity;
The inner breath ceases and the mind separates from the body.
The body is abandoned, while primordial wisdom arises into absolute space.
These are the initial phases of dissolution, pertaining to the elements.

First, relinquishing the body, the physical vessel of the mind, occurs in six stages.

Initially, the outer elements merge into the inner ones, and subsequently, the inner elements merge into the mind. At this juncture, perception of external objects—form, sound, smell, taste, and touch—ceases.

As the mind enters the domain of primordial wisdom, you are separated from the objects it perceives in its embodied state. In fact, at this moment, the mind transcends the dualistic apprehension of subject and object, and the notion of a grasping subject fades away.

Having disengaged from these two aspects of the mind, when, while based on wisdom-awareness, the mind withdraws into the cocoon of habitual tendencies,[235] the subtle energy of the earth element absorbs into that of water. Consequently, you no longer have the strength to stand up nor to move your limbs. It is time to perform the transfer of consciousness. The body becomes incontinent, excreting and urinating, emanating a nauseating odor.

As the subtle energy of the water element is absorbed by that of fire, your limbs lose all vigor and your face sweats, while saliva and mucus flow uncontrollably.

When the subtle energy of the fire element is absorbed in the wind element, heat dissipates from your body. Your mouth and nose dry up, losing their luster and taking on a corpse-like color.

At this point, depending on where the heat concentrates within your body, distinct rebirths await you: in hell if the heat concentrates at the soles of your feet, among the tortured spirits if at the secret center, as an animal if at the navel center, as a human if at the heart, among the demigods if at the throat level, and among the gods if at eye level. Finally, if the heat dissipates at the top of your head at Brahmā's opening (fontanelle), you will reach the unsurpassable fruition and be reborn in a pure land.

As the subtle energy of the wind element dissolves in your consciousness, your breathing becomes labored. After exhaling deeply, you struggle to breathe in again and your breath becomes increasingly tenuous. You struggle to hold the air in your lungs. The "lamp" in your eyes goes out. Normally, when pressing on your eyeballs, you see various luminous circles, but now they no longer appear.

The outer breath ceases and consciousness dissolves into clear light. The inner breath ceases, and the unity of mind and body disintegrates. With the body abandoned, primordial wisdom manifests in the absolute expanse of the bardo.

These are the first stages [of death], the gradual dissolution of the elements.

–412–

Various Modes of Liberation according to the Faculties of Beings

The second set of six-point instructions deals with the various modes of liberation available to each individual, according to their faculties.

The first of these six points applies to those with the sharpest faculties among individuals with superior faculties[236]

For whom the bardo does not occur. As soon as their corporeal envelope is destroyed,
The deeper insight of dharmatā shines forth spontaneously,
And they rest in a state free from the extremes of conceptual elaborations.

Thus, there exist six distinct paths leading to liberation, each aligned with the particular abilities of individuals. Those endowed with profound insight engage in practice right now, in this very life, meditating upon the luminosity of the path. At the very moment when the ground luminosity manifests, the "mother" luminosity unites with the "daughter" luminosity. As soon as the body envelope disintegrates, the great penetrating insight of the ultimate nature of reality becomes spontaneously clear, and they rest in a state free from conceptual limitations. From then on, such practitioners do not have to continue through the intermediate state, the bardo that follows after death.

Second, beings possessing medium faculties among the noble beings
Attain liberation in the third instant.
In the initial moment, when body and consciousness part ways,
The natural radiance of the dharmakāya, the absolute body, the great [wisdom] devoid of concepts manifests.
In the second instant, the saṃbhogakāya, the body of supreme enjoyment, manifests as rays of light.
In the third instant, the clear light is perfectly liberated [in primordial wisdom].
And they abide in the equality of the dharmakāya, the space-like absolute body.

Second, the less gifted among beings of higher faculties obtain liberation at the third instant of the bardo.

In the first instant, that of the separation of body and consciousness, the luminosity of the primordial ground naturally shines forth, perfect liberation occurs, and the nonconceptual dharmakāya manifests.

In the second instant, the appearances associated with the saṃbhogakāya—such as sounds, light, and rays—arise during the bardo of the dharmatā.

In the third instant, after the clear light has reached its peak, it fades away and they enter the state of dharmakāya equality.

> **Third, noble beings among those of average faculties**
> **Linger in an unconscious state, devoid of discursive thoughts, for a duration of one to three days.**
> **Upon emerging from this state, the primordial wisdom appears in the form of light.**
> **The natural radiance of the enlightened body, the spontaneous resonance of the enlightened speech, and the natural luminosity of the enlightened mind manifest for five days.**
> **By recognizing that they possess the enlightened body, speech, and mind, they reach liberation.**

Beings of average ability among the higher beings remain as if unconscious for one to three days in the basic consciousness, without the slightest discursive thought.[237] When this state dissipates, appearances arise from the fundamental ground and the luminosity of primordial wisdom manifests. During five "days of concentration"[238] the natural light of the enlightened body, the natural resonance of mantras—enlightened speech—and the radiance of awareness manifest. Remaining in the state of meditative equality in which they recognize that these are manifestations of the three bodies, they are liberated.

> **Fourth, the least gifted among beings with moderate faculties**
> **Abide in a state of unconsciousness for a span of three to five days.**
> **When they wake from it, the five wisdoms display their radiance.**
> **Unperturbed, they attain liberation, for they recognize these as manifestations of their own [awareness].**

The least capable of those with average faculties lose consciousness for three to five days, depending on the case. At the very moment they awaken, the five primordial wisdoms radiate five supreme colors within the clear light. Confronted with these manifestations, they are not frightened, understanding that it is the creativity of their own awareness.

> **Fifth, for the most adept among those with limited faculties,**
> **Their experience of awareness descends into a state of oblivion for three days.**[239]
> **When this state dissipates, the clear light of the five primordial wisdoms**
> **Glows for five days before waning.**
> **From this effulgent radiance, various objects materialize,**
> **Sounds emanate rays of light, and thoughts generate waves of luminosity.**
> **At that moment, they recall the places, possessions, and individuals they once knew.**
> **Subsequently, they remember the Dharma teachings, prompting them to reactivate the antidotes.**
> **Primordial wisdom, free from grasping and naturally luminous, arises spontaneously,**
> **Liberating them from the manifestations of the bardo.**
> **Finally, they attain perfect enlightenment within the absolute expanse of dharmadhātu.**

Fifth, for the most capable ones among those possessing limited faculties, the experience of awareness will first sink for three days into basic consciousness (*ālayavijñāna*). Upon emerging from this state, they encounter the radiant luminosity of the five primordial wisdoms for five days, after which the manifestations of these wisdoms dissipate.

Phenomena such as shapes, sounds, smells, flavors, and touch emerge from this light, accompanied by sounds emanating from light rays, as well as discursive thoughts arising from these sounds.

At this juncture, they perceive the places where they have lived, their possessions, relatives, and friends from the life they just left. They wonder if these people can see and hear them when they speak to them. They find themselves reminiscing about memories from their previous existence and the realization dawns that they have entered the bardo of existence, the intermediate state leading toward their next life.

Then, as they remember the Dharma, the antidotes are reactivated and the primordial wisdom, unbound by any form of grasping, naturally arises. Thus, they are delivered from the apparitions of the bardo and attain perfect enlightenment within the absolute expanse of the dharmadhātu.

Sixth, concerning those less gifted among beings with limited faculties,
For a single day, their experience of awareness plunges into a state of oblivion.
When this state dissipates, primordial wisdom manifests for a day, only to fade away thereafter.
They have the impression of dwelling within the body of their recent existence,
With their senses fully functional and the ability to travel anywhere they wish, without hindrance.
Yet, as their consciousness lacks a physical support, they seek an environment and a place to live.
Driven by the force of karma, they enter a specific womb.
Reborn as humans endowed with seven remarkable qualities,
They encounter the profound teachings and attain liberation in this very life.

Sixth, beings possessing very limited faculties first spend a day in a state where their experience of awareness vanishes. Upon emerging from this state, primordial wisdom appears to them for a day then again disappears. At this juncture, they have the impression of still inhabiting the bodily form they had in their previous life, enjoying sight and all other sensory faculties. They have the ability to transport themselves to any place they think of, traversing mountains and rocks without hindrance.

Yet, the fact that their consciousness is deprived of a physical support renders them deeply uncomfortable. Like a feather blown by the wind, they are unable to stop for a moment, wondering where they might find a place to stay. In fact, they are carried along by their karma: if they have accumulated positive deeds, they are reborn with a body that offers them a foundation for practicing the Dharma. Conversely, if their misdeeds outweigh their virtues, they head for the underworld. In such ways, they enter various matrixes or other doors of rebirth.[240]

If they obtain a human body endowed with the seven qualities of the elevated modes of being,[241] they will reunite with their spiritual guide from their previous life, who will give them the teachings of the Great Perfection and other profound teachings through which they will attain liberation in a single lifetime.

For those who have done much evil,
The bardo does not even appear: as soon as body and mind separate,
Carried away by their own hallucinations, they experience the hell realms.
As for those who have perpetrated negative acts of moderate gravity, they remain briefly in the bardo,
Before experiencing either of the other two lower destinies,
While those who have committed as much good as evil remain in the bardo for a longer period
And forty-nine days later take on a body in keeping with their karma.

Those who have behaved in a very negative way, without seeking to transform themselves through the Dharma and the teachings, do not experience the manifestations of the dharmatā bardo described above. As soon as their consciousness separates from the body, caught up in hallucinations that are the product of their own minds, they sink into the infernal realms. This applies particularly to those who have committed the five heinous crimes with immediate effect[242] and to those who have degraded the sacred commitments with their vajra master.

On the other hand, those who have committed negative acts of moderate severity pass briefly through the bardo, a week for instance, before being reborn in one of the other two lower realms, that of the tormented spirits (*pretas*) or that of the animals.

As for those who have performed an equal measure of positive and negative acts, they remain in the bardo for a longer period, up to forty-nine days, and are reborn in situations specifically determined by their past actions.

Upon completion of the bardo of dharmatā,
The bardo of becoming unfolds for beings of the two lower levels of faculties.
It is therefore of utmost importance to abandon all unvirtuous actions right now,
To engage in virtuous actions, and conquer the imperishable citadel of the nature of mind.
These are highly beneficial instructions! Take them to heart!

Once the manifestations of the bardo of dharmatā have ceased, the two categories of beings with average abilities enter the bardo of becoming and experience an (insubstantial) body resulting from the union of the mind and the subtle energy of the breath, the prana. Thus, it is at this very moment, while you have the opportunity, that you must earnestly strive to discard all forms of negativity and accomplish what is positive. This is how, having recognized with certainty the fundamental nature of mind, you will conquer the immutable citadel.

These instructions are most beneficial. Take them to heart!

–413–

The Ultimate Fruition

When ultimate fruition is achieved,
Six qualities of perfect enlightenment manifest:
Upon dispelling the subject-object duality and deluded inclinations,
Deceptive perceptions and grasping onto them[243] dissolve into the absolute expanse.

Like the pure radiance of the sun and sky when clouds dissipate,
First arises the absolute body, the dharmakāya, pure in two ways:
The radiant primordial wisdom emerges in the expanse of dharmatā.
Unelaborated, luminous, omnipresent vastness,
This spontaneous manifestation is liberated in primordial purity.[244]

Second, regarding the pure body of perfect enjoyment, the saṃbhogakāya,
Within this state (of dharmakāya), the five families of the Buddha Immense Ocean,
Embodied with the splendor of all the major and minor marks of perfection,
Appear like rainbows to bodhisattvas of the tenth bhūmi.

> **Third, akin to the reflection of the moon upon any surface of water,**
> **The nirmāṇakāya manifests wherever the water of the beings to be transformed is found,**
> **Taking the form of [sacred or useful] objects, reincarnations, supreme emanations, and more,**
> **Appearing to beings to transform them according to their needs.**
> **As long as there are sentient beings in the six realms of samsara,**
> **These manifestations will benefit them through inconceivable activities.**

Whether we attain liberation in this present life, like beings of superior ability, or in the bardo, like beings of average ability, when we achieve the ultimate fruit, perfect enlightenment has six qualities. What are they?

Once liberated from the habitual tendencies formed by the delusion entangled in the duality of subject and object, all deceptive perceptions, along with your clinging to them, dissolve into the absolute expanse, just as when clouds dissipate, the sun shines brightly in a pristine sky.

First and foremost, regarding the nature of the absolute body, the dharmakāya, it possesses a dual purity: it is both primordially pure and pure through the elimination of adventitious veils. In this state of twofold purity, radiant primordial wisdom shines forth in the expanse of the ultimate nature of reality. This luminosity transcends conceptualization. It is an omnipresent vastness and the manifest aspect of the spontaneously present clear light, which should not be reduced to [the emptiness aspect of] primordial purity alone.[245]

Second, concerning the body of perfect enjoyment, the saṃbhogakāya, while remaining within the expanse of the realization of the absolute body, the buddhas of the five families appear to bodhisattvas who have progressed from the first to the tenth stage (*bhūmi*) like a rainbow shining in space. These buddhas known as the Immense Ocean[246] are measureless and radiate with the splendor of thirty-two major and eighty minor marks.

Third, concerning the body of manifestation, the nirmāṇakāya, just as the moon is reflected wherever there is a surface of water, the nirmāṇakāya will manifest wherever beings reside. There exist various forms of nirmāṇakāya: handcrafted objects—such as the material supports of the body, speech, and mind of buddhas [statues, books, stūpas, etc.]—rebirths, supreme emanations incarnated in this world [such as Buddha Śākyamuni], as well as birds, wild animals, and other manifestations that facilitate the transformation of sentient beings according to their abilities and mental dispositions. These manifestations will continue to appear as long as there are beings in the six realms of samsara and will spontaneously benefit them through inconceivable ways.

Six primordial wisdoms are based on the kāyas:
The wisdom of the absolute expanse (*dharmadhātu*) is the unchanging, ultimate nature.
The mirror-like wisdom, naturally radiant, is the source of all appearances.
The wisdom of equality is indivisible and of equal taste.
The wisdom of perfect discernment apprehends the multiplicity of phenomena as well as their nature.
The all-accomplishing wisdom performs unimaginable deeds.
The spontaneously present wisdom is uncompounded,
Incomparable, it is the epitome of all the wisdoms of the victorious ones.
Like the wish-fulfilling gem, it grants all aspirations without discursive thought.

There are six primordial wisdoms based on the three bodies of the buddhas. Among these, the wisdom of the absolute expanse (*dharmadhātu*) is the realization of the unchanging, ultimate nature.

The mirror-like wisdom is the vast and profound luminosity. It thus becomes the support and source of the emanation of the other four primordial wisdoms.

The wisdom of equality unites samsara and nirvana indivisibly in a single taste, without rejection or attraction.

The wisdom of perfect discernment concerns the second of the two kinds of supreme knowledge—the knowledge of the ultimate nature of phenomena and the knowledge of their multiplicity.

The all-accomplishing wisdom accomplishes deeds beyond ordinary comprehension for the benefit of beings, employing the most appropriate means.

These five primordial wisdoms are not newly produced by causes and conditions. In addition, the primordially and spontaneously accomplished wisdom is uncompounded. It is ineffable, representing the epitome of all the primordial wisdoms of the victorious ones. It transcends all representations and does not rely on chains of conceptual thought, just as the miraculous gem grants all aspirations spontaneously and without deliberation.

The fourth aspect concerns the manner in which compassion arises for the benefit of sentient beings:
It awakens by arousing bodhicitta, the mind of enlightenment, through aspiration prayers and by virtue of the two accumulations,
And, essentially, within spontaneous presence through the power of primordial wisdom.

Fourth, you may wonder how the buddhas' compassion, both relative and ultimate, arises for the welfare of beings. First, while on the path of training, the bodhisattvas generated the supreme aspiration of enlightenment, known as bodhicitta. Our Teacher, Buddha Śākyamuni, in particular, made five hundred great vows, and these aspirational prayers were fulfilled in the same manner that reciting the dhāraṇī containing the name of the protector Amitābha grants rebirth in the Pure Land of Great Bliss. Compassion is also nurtured through the twofold accumulation of merit and wisdom. As a result, effortlessly and naturally, the buddhas possess the profound understanding of all phenomena and of their fundamental nature, arising from the state of spontaneous presence.

Fifth, how compassion unfolds:
It unfolds naturally through its inherent potency,
As well as through contact with beneficiaries
And in response to exhortations and supplications.

Fifth, how does compassion manifest? What we refer to as "natural compassion arising spontaneously" corresponds to the way in which the buddhas generate the mind of enlightenment for the sake of others. This cultivation of the enlightened mind leads buddhas to continuously hold beings in their wisdom mind, making their compassion both spontaneous and potent. When an object of their compassion presents itself, even if it is just one being open to transformation, and that being fervently prays with faith, compassion will embrace them all the more readily. Compassion arises when coming in contact with those who will benefit. It is also evoked through prayers and supplications: when individuals pray and recite the Buddha's name, the Buddha envelops them in his compassion.

Sixth, the benefit of beings can be realized in three distinct ways:
With support, without support, and by virtue of the ultimate nature.
Furthermore, if we include those who fall into partiality, it can be envisaged in four aspects that must be known with certainty.

The dharmakāya opens up a realm of possibilities[247] and bestows benefits upon beings without tangible support.
The obscurations of beings having been cleansed by the power of their aspirations and bodhicitta,
The form body, the rūpakāya, manifests itself.
Compassion inseparably united with the primordial wisdom of the sambhogakāya is a self-experience,[248]
Benefiting beings using a support, purifying the obscurations of the bodhisattvas of the tenth bhūmi.

The welfare of beings is achieved by virtue of the ultimate nature, the kāya of dharmadhātu,
In a state where the concepts of existence and nonexistence, exaggeration and denigration, subside.
Appearing before beings according to their aspirations,
The manifested body, the nirmāṇakāya, benefits beings through various emanations.

Some philosophical traditions speak of benefiting beings always with a tangible support,[249]
Affirming that the ultimate state of perfect buddhahood
Benefits beings through the kāyas and wisdoms endowed with real existence.
However, even without tangible support, the activity [of kāyas and wisdoms] is unbounded.[250]
Furthermore, akin to stūpas blessed by the sages, the rishis,

The welfare of beings can be achieved [without deliberation] by the sheer power of past aspirations.
Regarding the accomplishment of the twofold goal [the welfare of others and of oneself] through the kāya of the ultimate nature, the svabhāvikakāya, they acknowledge,
Unlike the other two perspectives, that it transcends the notions of existence and nonexistence, exaggeration and denigration.
The indivisible svabhāvikakāya benefits beings in ways tailored to their needs.
In conclusion, these three approaches [to benefiting beings] must ultimately converge into one,
And they should be understood in accordance with the first approach.
Thus, one will be emancipated from the dichotomy of existence and nonexistence. Some philosophical traditions speak of benefiting beings always with a tangible support,

How do buddhas bring about the welfare of beings? They do so in three distinct ways: with support, without support, and by virtue of the ultimate nature. Those who fail to grasp these three approaches form a fourth category and exhibit intellectual bias. It is therefore essential to identify these various approaches unequivocally.

The absolute body, the dharmakāya, creates a realm of possibilities for beings to acquire the full range of immaculate qualities. As the dharmakāya does not constitute a tangible support—unlike the form body, the rūpakāya—it benefits beings without any concrete foundation.

Moreover, as the obscurations of beings are purified by the power of aspiration prayers and by awakening the mind of enlightenment, the form bodies of the saṃbhogakāya and nirmāṇakāya of the buddhas appear to them.

The primordial wisdoms and the power of knowing are perceived solely by the saṃbhogakāya buddhas. These form a support endowed with major and minor marks and enable the gradual purification of the bodhisattvas' obscurations, from the first to the tenth bhūmi.

The ultimate nature also accomplishes the welfare of beings. As the kāya of dharmadhātu, in a state where the notions of existence and nonexistence are pacified, these buddhas bring about the immediate welfare and ultimate bliss for beings in the process of being transformed. They manifest in diverse emanations according to the aspirations and needs of these beings, including as emanated objects, various incarnations, and supreme manifestations.

According to other philosophical views, perfect buddhas benefit beings not only by relying on the support of the form body but also, on the ultimate level, through the indivisible union of kāyas and wisdoms to which these views attribute intrinsic existence. Nonetheless, the buddhas' activities can be carried out without hindrance even in the absence of any such tangible support. Furthermore, such activities can also be expressed through the power of past aspirations, just as an offering stand blessed by the rishis offers enduring protection against the disturbance of *nāgas*.[251]

Although one might argue that the ultimate nature accomplishes the dual purpose of benefiting others and oneself, and this may seem plausible, this nature remains devoid of the notions of existence and nonexistence. Thus, the indivisible body of the ultimate nature, the svabhāvikakāya[252] benefits beings in the process of being transformed according to their aspirations and mental dispositions.

In truth, these three (manners of benefiting others) are ultimately one, and it is inappropriate to assume that when one of these ways is accomplished, the others are absent, since the first two [with and without support] are encompassed within the first (the Madhyamaka view). Thus, the welfare of beings is not achieved with partiality and is liberated from the conceptual entanglements of existence and nonexistence.

A Heart Advice

To reach the unsurpassable enlightenment
Ordinary individuals with excellent aspirations
Rely on three paths–the common, the special, and the supreme.
With diligent effort, they ascend the path gradually,
And spiritual qualities spontaneously emerge in accordance with their aspirations.

So, take it to heart to persistently practice the path to liberation in harmony with your true nature.

To attain the unsurpassable enlightenment, ordinary beings will engage in various practices in harmony with their mental dispositions and aspirations. By relying on the common, extraordinary, and supreme activities, step by step, these beings can traverse the entire path. Persevering with earnest diligence, they will naturally achieve all spiritual qualities in accordance with their aspirations.

As I contemplate the decline of these dark times, sadness overwhelms me.
Life passes swiftly, yet we squander it in the wanderings of distraction.
The domains of knowledge are boundless, and the web of conceptual elaborations endless:
Day and night, practice the essence of the teachings!

In these dismal times, the five degenerations are steadily worsening. Reflecting on this fills me with sadness. Life is fleeting: it may end at twenty, at thirty. It passes without respite. Moreover, rather than utilizing it for earnest Dharma practice, we allow it to be frittered away in distractions.

If you think you should master the vast domains of knowledge, you will never reach their end. Therefore, in every moment, day and night, persist in the practice of Dharma!

You will die before you have achieved everything you wish to do in this life.
One thing invariably begets another, akin to the endless rolling waves of the ocean.
Do you reckon all these will be of any avail when you die? Ponder this thoughtfully,
And henceforth devote yourself to practice, striving to achieve liberation and enlightenment.

In the ordinary world, you endeavor to conquer your adversaries in this life, protect your loved ones, amass possessions, and engage in all kinds of pursuits. Yet, even if you toil ceaselessly until your final breath, you will never see the end of these countless efforts. One will follow another, then another, cascading like ripples on the surface of wind-swept water. Take a pause to ask yourself, "Will this be of any use to me on the day I die?" Right now, abandon all these activities, both great and small, and devote yourself to attaining liberation and enlightenment.

Where will you go when you depart from here? What fate awaits you?
Who will help you? How assured are you of attaining happiness and freedom from fear?
While you still possess the capacity to do so,
It is high time to set forth toward the reliable and enduring state, the safe abode of liberation.

If you die suddenly, where will you go after that? What joys and sorrows will you encounter? You can imagine anything you wish, but you cannot be sure. When death comes, will your loved ones, friends, wealth, and possessions be of any help to you? What assurance do you have of finding happiness in this life and of living your future lives without fear? Think about it, and now that you have some control over the situation, it is time—more than time—to hasten toward the refuge of liberation, the steadfast and enduring abode where you can be certain to be free from fear.

You will leave behind your body, possessions, friends, and kin,
And all the experiences of this life without exception.
Alone will you go, with no one to aid you.
Now, right now, is the right time to seek refuge and allies.

At the hour of death, you will leave behind this body you care so much for, which can hardly bear even the slightest thorn's prick. All your accumulated possessions, caring parents, spouse, and beloved ones, the joys and delights of this life, fame, power, and influence, all these experiences, without exception, shall be left behind. Like a hair plucked from a lump of butter, you shall depart alone.

Consider now: At that very moment, will these loved ones and possessions offer any aid or comfort? Now, without delay, is the right moment to seek refuge and allies in the supreme Dharma.

Such an opportunity will not last forever,
And when heaven and earth reverse, when your world is turned upside down by the arrival of the Lord of Death,
What will you do? Upon whom will you rely?
From this very moment, practice the sublime Dharma.

At present, you may enjoy good health and experience joy and happiness, but that cannot endure forever, and you are not immortal! At the moment of death, your world will be turned upside down. You will ponder: "What can I do? I have no refuge or protector, and I have not practiced Dharma." If you want to have a source of hope in that moment, you must practice the supreme Dharma now, without delay!

Who is truly smart? Who is wise, discerning, or heedless?
At the time of death, this will become clear. Hence, muster the army of virtue,
Meditate on the fundamental nature of mind,
And the delight of ascending toward higher destinies filled with bliss will arise spontaneously.

Are you wise in your choice of objectives? Indeed, if you approach the moment of death with confidence and fearlessness, you will have been wise enough to give yourself sound advice. Therefore, at this very moment, gather the army of virtue and meditate with unwavering focus on the fundamental and quintessential nature of mind. Then, the joys of higher modes of being and the splendor of ultimate bliss will effortlessly manifest and become yours.

The victorious ones will invite you into the jeweled palace of the magnificent abode of liberation,
There, [upon actualizing] the supreme, primordial wisdom, your own awareness,
You will attain enlightenment and, in this infinite expanse,
Continuously abide in the unchanging great bliss.

If you engage in authentic Dharma practice, you will reach the resplendent jeweled palace of liberation, the perfect abode attained through the path of the three vehicles. The victorious ones, the perfect bhagavān buddhas, will invite you to this pure land, calling to you, "Come here!"

Once you have actualized the primordial wisdom of awareness, you will attain enlightenment and enjoy the ten forces, the four freedoms from fear, the twenty-one immaculate dharmas, and other sublime qualities. At all times, you will experience the great, unchanging, and supreme bliss.

Therefore, I, the Dharma-less vagabond, implore you:
Keep these heartfelt and beneficial pieces of advice close to your mind!

This Dharma-less vagabond (as the omniscient Longchenpa refers to himself) thus kindly encourages the beings he is yet to guide and transform. He gives these heartfelt counsels from his heart, trusting in their beneficial nature, and urges us to seize the opportunity of this life to integrate them within our minds.

Conclusion

Even a single six-point set from this precious treasure of teachings brimming with spiritual qualities
Will enable you to achieve the ultimate goal.
I have explained this wish-fulfilling jewel, these essential instructions

For the benefit of sincere practitioners aspiring for liberation. Thus, this treasure of essential instructions that are in accordance with the Dharma has been presented in a series of six points. Even without considering the entire set of these instructions, practicing just one of them encompasses everything perfectly. Composed as a quintessential elixir of deathlessness (*amṛta*), these instructions are intended to be useful for future disciples with faith who aspire to attain liberation.

Dedication

Through this merit, may all sentient beings without exception, myself included,
Come to rediscover their inherent buddha nature.
May they be endowed with the perfect qualities resulting from letting go [of all defects] and realizing [all enlightened qualities].

As a result, may they become Dharma sovereigns,
spontaneously benefiting others and themselves as well.

Through the merit of having composed this treatise, may all beings without exception, including myself, realize the fundamental and essential nature of buddhahood, tathāgatagarbha. May we attain mastery over the ocean of kāyas and wisdoms, dispelling the two veils—the veil formed by afflictive mental states and the veil that conceals the knowable. Consequently, may we realize the wisdom that comprehends the nature of all things and the wisdom that discerns the manifold aspects of phenomena. Having brought spiritual qualities to perfection, accomplishing spontaneously the twofold benefit of others and ourselves, may we become Dharma kings and reign over the three worlds.

From now on and throughout all my lives,
May I never tire of working for the sake of sentient beings within the cycle of existence,
May I hear the treasure of Dharma from the mouths of noble beings
And delight the victorious ones by practicing it authentically.

From this day forth and throughout my future lives, I vow not to shy away from remaining in the three worlds of samsara, nor shall weariness deter me when contemplating the cycle of existences, so that I can devote myself entirely to benefiting all beings without exception.

May I meet with many eminent guides and receive their teachings, the treasure of supreme Dharma. By practicing these authentic teachings according to my spiritual master's instructions, may my actions become clouds of offerings delighting the victorious ones!

Even upon attaining enlightenment, may I never forsake my commitment to sentient beings,
And as I remain in samsara, may I never be stained by its flaws.
May I bring to the path of liberation all those with whom I am connected by sight, hearing, thought, and touch,
And, in so doing, greatly delight the victorious ones and their heirs.

Even if you attain buddhahood, do not forget sentient beings. Instead, with unwavering diligence, dedicate yourself solely to the welfare of others, emulating the eight bodhisattvas, the Buddha's spiritual heirs.

Just as a lotus emerges immaculate from muddy waters, abide in the three worlds of samsara, untouched by negative emotions and imperfections linked to karmic obscurations.

Lead on the path to liberation all the beings you see, hear, think about, and touch. Indeed, the most profound offering you can present to the victorious ones is boundless benevolence bestowed upon sentient beings. This is the essence that truly delights the enlightened beings and their spiritual heirs.

May I expound the profound Dharma to beings with the right predispositions
And sow the seeds of Dharma for those unfortunate enough not to have it.
May I ardently practice the Dharma until I reach its highest point,
Thus delighting my revered spiritual teachers, my glorious protectors!

To those blessed with excellent karmic predispositions, impart the profound Dharma, and they will behold the qualities of a noble spiritual guide. For those whose predispositions are yet to mature, sow the seeds of Dharma in accordance with their mental dispositions, capabilities, and aspirations.

However, as far as you are concerned, merely hearing the Dharma is insufficient. You must zealously practice its essence, letting the spiritual qualities associated with meditative experiences and realization flourish within you. May your practice reach its ultimate point. By practicing thus, you will fill the hearts of all the venerable and supreme spiritual masters with joy.

Colophon to the Root Text

Thus concludes the text titled ***The Precious Treasury of Essential Instructions*** composed by Longchen Rabjam, the yogi of the supreme vehicle, holder of the treasure of the supreme words of "He Who Has Gone into Bliss," the Sugata, that he heard many times, and who has excellently cultivated the wisdom born through listening, reflection, and meditation on the vast and profound meaning.

Colophon to the Commentary

In the year of 1985, our supreme refuge Dilgo Khyentse Rinpoche gave oral explanations of this precious treatise to Kyabje Shechen Rabjam Rinpoche, Jigme Khyentse Rinpoche, Datong Tulku, Gelong Konchog Tenzin (alias Matthieu) and a few other disciples in Bhutan, in the palace called Heap of Great Bliss (Punakha) and in other places. Konchog Tenzin recorded these teachings and preserved them in the Shechen archives. In 2020, I, Gyurme Dorje, bearing the name of Khenpo of Shechen Monastery, who had the immense fortune to behold the face of the sublime protector (Khyentse Rinpoche) and to hear his voice, transcribed these teachings in written form. Subsequently, Shechen Rabjam Rinpoche, our refuge, and I again read the transcription while listening to the teachings in their entirety. Rabjam Rinpoche provided essential corrections and clarifications, particularly concerning expressions from the Kham dialect. I humbly confess that any errors and imperfections that may remain are solely due to my own ignorance, and wholeheartedly seek your forgiveness.

Acarya Dongak Tenzin, who possesses faith, pure samaya, and an excellent motivation, carried out the input of the text. The work was completed in the fourth month of the lunar calendar, Saga Dawa, in the year of the Iron Ox (2021).

May the merit generated by this work fulfill the enlightened aspirations of our glorious master. May the waves of blessings emanating from this text benefit the teachings of the victorious ones in general and, more specifically, all those who hold faith in the teachings of our master and protector.

Colophon to the English Translation

The translation of Gyalwa Longchen Rabjam's root verses was carried out in English by Khenpo Sönam Tsewang and Gelong Konchog Tendzin (Matthieu Ricard), and in French by the latter, who also translated Khyentse

Rinpoche's commentaries into English and French. The text was edited by Judith Amtzis and Anna Wolcott Johnson. This work of transcription, translation and editing was generously supported by the Tsadra Foundation.

May these precious teachings turn toward the Dharma the minds of those who read, reflect, and meditate on them. May they enable them to practice these teachings authentically and reach the ultimate goal of the path for the benefit of all beings in the vast expanse of space.

Glossary

abandoning and realizing, qualities of (*spangs rtogs kyi yon tan*). The two major qualities of a buddha: (1) having abandoned the two veils (emotional and cognitive) and (2) realization, knowing the ultimate nature of reality as it is.

accomplishment (*siddhi, dngos grub*). There are two categories of accomplishments resulting from Dharma practice. The "supreme accomplishment" refers to reaching complete enlightenment, which is the goal of the path, while the "common accomplishments," achieved by advanced practitioners and bodhisattvas, are used for the sole purpose of benefiting others. They include clairvoyance, clairaudience, flying in space, becoming invisible, perpetual youth, or the ability to transform things. Yet, the most significant achievements on the spiritual path are renunciation, compassion, unwavering faith, and realizing the correct view.

afflictive states of mind *(kleśa, nyon mongs).* These are also known as the "five mental poisons" *(dug lnga)*: animosity, desire/attachment, ignorance, pride, and jealousy. The equivalent Tibetan term, *nyonmong (nyon mongs)*, denotes that which "upsets" and "clouds" the mind. *Nyonmong* is often translated as "negative" or "destructive" emotions, but it should be noted that ignorance cannot be counted as an emotion. In Western languages and in modern psychology, emotions are considered to be transient states of mind that are accompanied by specific facial expressions and physiological reactions, while ignorance is a cognitive state, not an emotion per se.

aggregates, five (*pañca skandha, phung po lnga*). Psychosensory components on the basis of which the mind constructs the illusory notion of an individual, autonomous, and truly existing self, which can only bring suffering. These are the aggregate of forms (*gzugs kyi phung po*), of sensations (*tshor ba'i phung po*), of representations or perceptions (*'du shes kyi phung po*), of compositional factors (*'du byed kyi phung po*), and of consciousness (*rnam shes kyi phung po*).

arhat (*dgra bcom pa*). According to Theravāda, the main school of the Fundamental Vehicle, arhats are individuals who have conquered the four main enemies—

namely, birth, disease, old age, and death, as well as the afflictive states of mind (animosity, attachment, ignorance, pride, and jealousy) causing the sufferings of samsara. They attain the cessation of suffering by realizing the emptiness of the individual self.

awareness (*vidyā, rig pa*). The mind's awareness of its own fundamental nature, luminous, vast, and free from delusion and grasping.

bardo (*bar do*). This means "in between" and refers to an intermediate state. The different bardos are commonly described as six, though the number can vary according to different tantras. Generally, bardo is used to signify the transitional phase between death and the subsequent rebirth.

bhagavān (*bcom ldan 'das*). This means "divine" (in Hindu literature) or "blessed," while the Tibetan translation refers to one who has "conquered" (*bcom*) the four māras, possesses (*ldan*) the perfect qualities of enlightenment, and has transcended (*'das*) the extremes of samsara and nirvana.

bhūmis. Literally "grounds," which refers to ten spiritual stages (*sa bcu*) through which a bodhisattva passes before attaining full buddhahood, the eleventh *bhūmi*. These are (1) Perfect Joy (*Rab tu dga' ba*), (2) Immaculate (*Dri ma med pa*), (3) Illuminating (*'Od byed pa*), (4) Brilliant (*'Od 'phro ba*), (5) Hard to Conquer (*Sbyang dka' ba*), (6) Manifest (*Mngon du gyur pa*), (7) Far-Reaching (*Ring du song ba*), (8) Immutable (*Mi g.yo ba*), (9) Excellent Intelligence (*Legs pa'i blo gros*), and (10) Cloud of Dharma (*Chos kyi sprin*).

bodhicitta (*byang chub kyi sems*). The "thought, or mind, of enlightenment." This is defined as the intention to achieve buddhahood for the sake of all beings. There are both relative and absolute aspects. Relative bodhicitta (*kun rdzob byang chub kyi sems*) is itself divided into two stages: the wish to attain ultimate perfection in order to be able to free all beings from suffering (*smon pa'i sems bskyed*) and the actual entry into spiritual practice in order to actualize this wish (*'jug pa'i sems bskyed*). Absolute bodhicitta (*don dam byang chub kyi sems*) is the realization of emptiness and the recognition that buddha nature abides in every sentient being.

bodhisattva (*byang chub sems dpa'*). "Hero of enlightenment." A distinction is made between "ordinary" bodhisattvas, simple practitioners of the Great Vehicle who do their best to free themselves from the circle of death and rebirth and achieve enlightenment, and "sublime" bodhisattvas who have attained one of the ten bhūmis.

bodies, see *kāyas*.

buddha nature (*tathāgatagarbha, bde gshegs snying po*). Literally, the "essence of buddhahood" that is present in all sentient beings as oil is present in every sesame seed. It also refers to the fundamental nature of mind, luminous yet empty of intrinsic existence.

Calm abiding, see *śamatha*.

Cārvāka (*Rgyang 'phen pa*). A Hindu philosophical school that traces its origins to the sixth or seventh century B.C., with Bṛhaspati and Cārvāka often considered to be its main founders. What distinguishes Cārvākas from other Hindu schools is their materialistic, atheistic, hedonistic, and skeptical standpoint. According to Cārvākas, the material world is the only real existence. They reject the idea of karmic causality, deny the existence of past and future lives, and recognize only perception as a valid source of knowledge. Buddhism categorizes this viewpoint as metaphysical nihilism.

conceptual extremes, see *four conceptual extremes*.

consciousness (*ṣat vijñāna, saptavijñāna, aṣṭavijñāna, rnam shes tshogs drug/bdun/brgyad*). Depending on the texts, six, seven, or eight aspects of consciousness are considered. The six main aspects include the five aspects related to sense organs and the conceptual consciousness (*manovijñāna, yid kyi rnam shes*). The seventh is intellectual consciousness associated with afflictive states of mind (*kleṣavijñāna, nyon yid kyi rnam shes*). The eighth is the basic consciousness or (*ālayavijñāna, kun gzhi rnam shes*) characterized by a mere awareness "that the world exists out there." It gathers habitual tendencies and constitutes the source of the other aspects of consciousness.

ḍākinī (mkha' 'gro ma). Literally "she who moves in space." "Space" here refers to the absolute space of the dharmadhātu, and the feminine principle is associated with wisdom. There are several levels of ḍākinīs: the ḍākinīs of wisdom, who have attained complete realization, and the worldly ḍākinīs, who possess certain supernatural powers. The word is also used as a title for great female teachers and as a respectful form of address for the wife of a spiritual master.

Dharma (*Chos*). In its broadest sense, Dharma designates all that is knowable and, more specifically, all the teachings formulated by buddhas and realized masters that show the way to enlightenment. It includes both the Dharma of transmission (*rlung gi chos*) transmitted through scriptures, and the Dharma of realization (*rtogs pa'i chos*) referring to spiritual qualities born from practicing these teachings. The Dharma is described as "sublime" because it delivers beings from suffering. The Sanskrit word has ten different meanings, including "phenomena" as well as "objects of knowledge." Vasubandhu defines *Dharma* as a "protection" (*chos skyobs*) because the Dharma can repel our adversaries (ignorance and the afflictive mental states) and also protects us from lower destinies.

dharmatā (*chos nyid*). Dharmatā is used (1) to designate the specific, relative characteristics of phenomena, such as the heat of fire and the wetness of water and (2) to designate the ultimate nature of reality, emptiness, which cannot be expressed in conceptual, dualistic terms. In *The Precious Treasury of the Supreme Vehicle* (*Theg mchog rin po che'i mdzod*), Gyalwa Longchen Rabjam defines dharmatā as "unfabricated, causeless, primordially pure, and free from obscuration" (*ma byas rgyu med ye dag sgrib byed dang bral ba'i chos nyid ces bya bar 'dod do*) and also as the emptiness aspect of pristine awareness (*rig pa'i stong cha chos nyid*). According to an oral explanation by Jigme Khyentse Rinpoche, "Dharmatā corresponds to the establishment of the final and ultimate nature of phenomena, without distortions or superimpositions, beyond concepts, when nothing more can be said about it and there is nowhere further to go."

eight freedoms (*dal ba brgyad*) and **ten favorable conditions** (*'byor ba bcu*) **conducive to practicing the Dharma.** First are the freedoms from eight obstacles to practicing the Dharma, which are (1) birth in a hell realm, (2) among the pretas, or tormented spirits, (3) as an animal, (4) among savages, (5) as a long-living god, (6) as one who holds erroneous views, (7) in a dark kalpa during which no buddha has appeared in the world, and (8) with impaired sense faculties. Second, among the ten favorable conditions, five depend on ourselves (*rang 'byor lnga*): (1) being born as a human being, (2) in a place where Dharma flourishes, (3) with complete sense faculties, (4) not living in a way that contradicts Dharma, and (5) having faith in what deserves it. Five conditions that depend upon others (*gzhan 'byor lnga*) are (1) a buddha has appeared in the world, (2) and taught the Dharma, (3) the Dharma has remained until our time, (4) we have entered the Dharma, (5) and have been accepted by a spiritual teacher who can guide us on the path.

eight worldly concerns (*'jig rten chos brgyad*). Gain (*rnyed pa*) and loss (*ma rnyed*), happiness (*bde ba*) and suffering (*sdug bsngal ba*), renown (*snyan grags*) and infamy (*mi snyan pa*), praise (*bstod pa*) and criticism (*smad pa*).

elements, four or five (*catvāri bhūta, pañca, 'byung ba bzhi*). Earth, water, fire, and air, as the principles of solidity, moisture, heat, and movement, to which is added space, without which the other four elements could not unfold.

five degenerations (*snyigs ma lnga*). The "age of the residue" or "of dregs" (*snyigs dus*) is characterized by degeneration in (1) the life span (*tshe*), (2) the general karma (*las*), (3) the view (*lta ba*), and (4) the faculties of beings (*sems can*), as well as by (5) an increase in the obscuring emotions (*nyon mongs*).

five kinds of clairvoyance (*pañca abhijñā, mngon par shes pa lnga*). Direct mental perceptions (*mngon sum*) resulting from meditative practice. These are (1) the mental ability to display miraculous powers (*rdzu 'phrul gyi mngon shes*); (2) divine vision (*lha'i mig gi mngon shes*), which confers the ability to see phenomena hidden by time or space; (3) divine hearing (*lha'i rna ba'i mngon shes*), which enables one to hear distant coarse or subtle sounds; (4) reminiscence of past lives, one's own and those of others (*sngon gnas rjes dran gyi mngon shes*); and (5) precise perception of others' thoughts (*gzhan sems shes pa'i mngon shes*).

five paths (*lam lnga*). According to the Great Vehicle, the five gradual paths to buddhahood are (1) the path of accumulation (*tshogs lam*), on which one accumulates the causes that make the path to liberation possible; (2) the path of joining (*sbyor lam*), which prepares one for the path of vision; (3) the path of vision (*mthong lam*), where the bodhisattva actually sees the two absences of identity (of the individual self and of phenomena); (4) the path of meditation (*sgom lam*), on which the bodhisattva deepens his or her realization of the ultimate nature of reality, largely through the merits engendered by the practice of compassion; and (5) the path of no more learning (*mi slob pa'i lam*), which culminates in perfect buddhahood (*rdzogs pa'i sangs rgyas*).

five poisons (*dug lnga*) that disturb our minds and those of others. See *afflictive states of mind.*

five traditional sciences (*rig gnas lnga*) that a learned person must master. They include arts and crafts (*bzo rig gnas*); medicine (*gso ba'i rig gnas*); grammar, or philology (*sgra' rig gnas*); logic, or valid knowledge (*gtan tshigs kyi rig gnas*); and Buddhist philosophy (*nang don rig gnas*).

five wisdoms (*ye shes lnga*). The five wisdoms of buddhahood corresponding to the five Dhyāni buddhas, or five buddha families: mirror-like wisdom (*me long lta bu ye shes*, Vajrasattva, Vajra family); wisdom of equality (*mnyam nyid ye shes*, Ratnasambhava, Jewel family); all-discerning wisdom (*so sor rtog pa'i ye shes*, Amitābha, Lotus family); all-accomplishing wisdom (*bya ba sgrub pa'i ye shes*, Amoghasiddhi, Action family) and wisdom of dharmadhātu (*chos dbyings ye shes*, Vairocana, Tathāgata family).

four activities (*las bzhi*). Performed for the sake of others by accomplished yogis: (1) pacifying (*zhi ba*) sickness, obstacles, mental obscurations, and ignorance; (2) enriching (*rgyas pa*) merit, life span, glory, prosperity, and wisdom; (3) bringing under control (*dbang*) the good qualities, life force, and powerful energies of the three worlds; and (4) subjugating wrathfully (*drag po*) outer and inner negative forces.

four boundless thoughts (*catvārapramāṇa, tshad med bzhi*). Boundless loving-kindness, boundless compassion, boundless sympathetic joy, and boundless equanimity. They are boundless because the number of beings to whom they apply is boundless, the motivation to benefit them is boundless, the virtues of doing so are boundless, and the excellence of the result is boundless.

four conceptual extremes (*caturanta, spros pa'i mtha' bzhi*). These consist of conceiving reality in terms of existence (or eternity), nonexistence (or nothingness), both at the same time, and neither one nor the other.

four empowerments (*dbang bzhi*). (1) The vase empowerment (*bum dbang*), (2) the secret empowerment (*gsang dbang*), (3) the wisdom empowerment (*shes rab ye* *shes kyi dbang*), and (4) the precious word empowerment (*tshig dbang rin po che*). Within Atiyoga (*Rdzogs chen*), the four empowerments are (1) elaborate (*spros bcas*), (2) unelaborate (*spros med*), (3) very unelaborate (*shin tu spros med*), and (4) utterly unelaborate (*rab tu spros med*).

four kinds of faith (*dad pa bzhi*). These develop gradually as you progress in your practice and gain confidence in the teacher and the teachings. (1) Clear faith (*dang ba'i dad pa*) arises when you hear about the qualities of the buddhas, bodhisattvas, and enlightened beings, and about the qualities of the Dharma. Then, (2) yearning faith (*'dod pa'i dad pa*) inspires you to strive to acquire such qualities for yourself, and (3) confident faith (*yid ches kyi dad pa*) in the validity of the teacher and the teachings will take birth in your mind. Finally, (4) irreversible faith (*phyir mi ldog pa'i dad pa*) is such that you could not conceivably give up confidence in the Dharma even at the cost of your life.

four samayas related to the practice of Great Perfection. (1) Those who have been perfectly introduced to the nature of the mind, are able to abide in it, realize that outer appearances are groundless, and that inner awareness is object-free. [. . .] Such practitioners have transcended the discrimination between what is to be accepted and what is to be rejected. For in the fundamental nature of awareness, obscurations and faults (to be abandoned) are absent—indeed, are wholly nonexistent. This is the so-called samaya of nonexistence (or of absence) (*med pa'i dam tshig*). (2) Dualistic phenomena, such as vow and absence of vow, thing and non-thing, origin and cessation—and all thoughts and assumptions—share a single ultimate nature. Were you to name this state of resting in the one nature, which cannot be seen by watching, and which is the singular ineffable primordial wisdom without affirmation or denial, you could call it the samaya of the one [nature] (*gcig pu'i dam tshig*). (3) When you settle in the one ultimate nature, when awareness of the five sense perceptions is left open and nondiscursive in the realization that outer and inner phenomena lack existence, all phenomena are decisively settled in the vast spaciousness of the ultimate nature. This is called [the samaya of] all-embracing evenness (*phyal ba'i dam tshig*). (4) Furthermore, in the radiance of the primordially pure awareness of ultimate reality, qualities of knowledge are spontaneously present. [If you remain in this nature], you constantly experience phenomena in terms of the "four visions," considered to be the samaya of "spontaneous presence" (*lhun grub kyi dam tshig*). (Excerpts from Jigme Lingpa, *The Treasury of Precious Qualities*, 2:205–7.) The four samayas also correspond to four vajra principles (*rdo rje' i chings bzhi*) according to which phenomena are presented—that is, their nonexistence (*med pa*), their evenness (*phyal ba*), their spontaneous presence (*lhun grub*), and their single nature (*gcig pu*).

four visions of Thögal practice (*Thod rgal kyi snang ba bzhi*). (1) The vision of the absolute nature becoming manifest (*chos nyid mngon sum*), (2) the vision of the increase of meditative experiences (*nyams gong 'phel*), (3) the vision of awareness reaching its peak (*rig pa tshad phebs*), and (4) the vision of the exhaustion of phenomena in dharmatā (*chos nyid zad pa*).

four ways of gathering beings to be benefited, or **four attractive qualities of a bodhisattva** to inspire beings to engage in the practice of Dharma (*bsdu ba'i dngos po bzhi*). (1) To practice generosity (*sbyin pa*), (2) to please beings by saying gentle words suited to their minds and offer them teachings in accordance with their needs and capacities (*snyan par smra ba*), (3) to indicate practices that lead to liberation (*don spyod pa*), (4) to behave and practice in accordance with what one teaches (*don mthun pa*).

ground (*gzhi*). Primordial (*gdod mai'i gzhi*), also called "universal," "fundamental," "ground of all," in which samsara and nirvana are not yet differentiated. It is associated with the notion of primordial purity (*ka dag*). This primordial ground spontaneously manifests (*lhun grub*) through the creative power of awareness (*rig pa*).

guru yoga, see *Yoga*.

interdependence, see *twelve factors of interdependent production*.

kalpa (*skal pa*). An eon or cosmic era subdivided into four periods, a phase of formation, maintenance, destruction, and emptiness. Countless kalpas follow one after the other.

kāyas (*sku*). Three or five aspects of buddhahood. The three kāyas are the absolute body (*dharmakāya, chos sku*), the body of perfect enjoyment (*saṃbhogakāya, longs sku*), and the body of manifestation (*nirmāṇakāya, sprul sku*). They correspond to the empty nature (*ngo bo*) of mind and of all phenomena, the luminous character (*rang bzhin*) of the five wisdoms, and the ceaseless cognizant power (*thugs rje*). When five are considered, the immutable adamantine body (*vajrakāya, mi 'gyur rdo rje'i sku*) and the body of perfect enlightenment (*abhisaṃbodhikāya, mngon par byang chub pa'i sku*) are added. The five bodies correspond to the awakened body, speech, mind, qualities, and activity of a buddha.

listeners (*śrāvaka, nyan thos*). Practitioners of the Fundamental Vehicle, who listen to the Buddha's teachings and put them into practice with the main intention of attaining liberation for themselves.

mandala (*maṇḍala, dkyil 'khor*). Sanskrit term literally meaning "center and circumference." The center is primordial wisdom, and what surrounds it are the central wisdom deity and the other deities dwelling in a "measureless palace" (*gzhal yas khang*). Every element of the mandala, down to the smallest detail, has a symbolic meaning linked to the accomplishment of the path and the fruit.

mantra (*snags*). Derived from the Sanskrit root *man*, "to think," to which is added the instrumental suffix *tra*. According to this etymology, it's an "instrument of thought." According to another etymology found in Tibetan commentaries, the word *mantra* combines *man* (to think) and *tra* (which protects) and thus means "which protects the mind" from distraction, wandering, and deluded perceptions. In a meditative retreat, during the period one is focusing on reciting a large number of mantras, it's advisable to take a vow of silence.

Māra (*bdud*), or demon. In the context of Buddhist practice, anything that stands in the way of enlightenment is called a demon. In particular, Māra personifies ego-clinging and fixating on the true existence of phenomena, as well as all our defects and negative tendencies. The *Prajñāpāramitā* texts list forty-six types of māras, the four main ones being the māra of aggregates (*skandhamāra, phung po'i bdud*), symbolizing our attachment to forms, perceptions, and mental states as "real"; the māra of destructive emotions (*kleśamāra, nyon mongs kyi bdud*), symbolizing our addiction to habitual patterns of negative emotions; the māra of the Lord of Death (*mṛtyumāra, 'chi bdag gi bdud*), symbolizing both death itself, which shortens our precious human lives, and also our fear of change, impermanence, and death; and the māra of the sons of the gods (*devaputramāra, lha'i bu'i bdud*), symbolizing our thirst for pleasure and comforts. The three daughters of Māra, who after their father's failure, tried in turn to distract the Buddha when he was on the eve of attaining enlightenment are Taṇhā (thirst, greed), Ārati (aversion), and Rāga (desire, passion).

Middle Way (*Madhyamaka, Dbu ma*). The philosophical system expounded by Nāgārjuna (first to second century A.D.) and his contemporaries or successors. The Middle Way transcends the extremes of existence and nonexistence, eternalism and nihilism.

mind of enlightenment, see *bodhicitta*.

nine graded vehicles (*theg pa rim pa dgu*). The three vehicles of the sutras—those of the listeners, solitary realizers, and bodhisattvas—followed by the six vehicles of the tantras, subdivided into the three classes of outer tantras (Kriyā, Upā, and Yoga) and three classes of inner tantras (Mahā, Anu, and Ati). The vehicles can also be grouped into three: the Hīnayāna, or Fundamental Vehicle, which comprises the first two; the Mahāyāna, comprising the third; and the Vajrayāna, the last six.

nirvana (*mya ngan las 'das pa*). Lit. "beyond suffering." Each vehicle has a different notion of nirvana, the opposite of samsara. For the Fundamental Vehicle, nirvana is the peace of cessation attained by an arhat, but for the Great Vehicle, nirvana—the perfect enlightenment of a buddha—transcends (the suffering of) samsara and (the peace of "little") nirvana.

Nyingma (*Rnying ma*), "ancient." The earliest of the four main schools of Tibetan Buddhism. It was the first Buddhist school established in Tibet by the great

Indian master Guru Padmasambhava, assisted by the Abbot Śāntarakṣita, at the request of King Trisong Detsen, in the eighth to ninth centuries. The disciples of this school study and practice the teachings stemming from the first spread of Buddhism in Tibet—the complete sutra, vinaya, and abhidharma; the Mahāyāna treatises; and the tantras, including those specific to the Great Perfection—from the eighth century until the time of the new translations, which began with Rinchen Zangpo (*Rin chen bzang po*, 958–1051) and gave rise to the Kadam (which later became the Geluk), Sakya, and Kagyu schools.

perceptions (*snang ba*), also translated as "appearances" or "phenomena." This is what appears to individuals' eyes according to their mental dispositions and inner development. Patrul Rinpoche speaks of three categories of perception: (1) deluded perceptions (*'khrul snang*), which arise to the consciousness of beings who are caught up in samsara; (2) interdependent perceptions (*rten 'brel*), which are illustrated by the eight analogies of illusion (*sgyu ma*) that are not to be taken as real (the perceptions of the bodhisattvas of the ten bhūmis, in their post-meditation state, *rjes thob*); and 3) the perfectly correct perceptions (*yang dag*) associated with wisdom, when one realizes the true nature of the mind and of the external world, which then appear as the display of bodies (*kayā*) and wisdoms (*jñāna*). We also speak of pure perceptions (*dag pa'i snang ba*) in relation to understanding the union of appearances and emptiness, or impure appearances (*ma dag pa'i snang ba*) linked to deluded perceptions.

piṭaka, see *Three Baskets*.

posture, seven-point, see *seven-point posture of Vairocana*.

prātimokṣa (*prātimokṣa, so sor thar pa*). "Individual liberation." The goal of Fundamental Vehicle practitioners. The term refers to the eight categories of vows related to individual liberation that the vinaya teaches, ranging from (temporary) twenty-four-hour vows to those of fully ordained monks.

samādhi (*ting nges 'dzin*). A state of perfect concentration. In Tibetan, *ting* (deep), *nges* (certain), *'dzin* (hold, focus) indicates a "focus on that which is deep and certain."

śamatha (*zhi gnas*, "calm abiding"). The foundation of all concentrations. After calming (*zhi*) the distraction of the mind caused by external stimuli, the mind remains (*gnas*) stable, without wavering, in the concentration it has deliberately chosen.

samaya (*dam tshig*). Often described as the sacred bond, or commitment,established between a master and a disciple following a Vajrayāna initiation or "transmission of power" (*dbang skur*). It is also the sacred bond established between the disciple and the teachings he or she has received, and between vajra brothers and sisters who are disciples of the same spiritual master. (The various types and levels of samayas are described in detail in many texts, including the tenth chapter of Jigme Lingpa, *The Treasury of Precious Qualities*, 2:179–228.) According to oral clarifications given to the translator by Jigme Khyentse Rinpoche, samaya is often presented as a kind of contract between the master and the disciple, or as a way of fulfilling one's duties to the master, of being faithful to him, or even of satisfying him. In reality, the role of the spiritual master being exclusively to benefit beings, by observing the samayas you benefit yourself. If, for example, you are affected by a serious illness and scrupulously follow the recommendations and prescriptions of a doctor, it is not to please or honor him, but to heal.

samsara (*'khor ba*). The Tibetan word means "circle" or "going round in circles." It refers to the succession of existences during which each being endures suffering resulting from his negative actions and emotions. In its unawakened state, the mind, enslaved by the poisons of hatred, desire, and ignorance, transmigrates uncontrollably from one existence to the next. This cycle of existences includes the three lower realms of hell, hungry spirits, and animals, as well as the three higher realms of men, demigods, and gods. The qualification of these worlds of existence in terms of inferior and superior is a reflection of the intensity of suffering that prevails in them. The human condition is considered to be the only state where suffering is sufficiently felt to motivate us to break free from the circle of death and rebirth, while at the same time enabling us to follow the spiritual path leading to liberation.

sangha (*dge 'dun*). One of the Three Jewels. In its broadest sense, this term designates the community of Buddhist practitioners, both religious and lay. Depending on the context, it may have a more restricted meaning, designating only the monastic community or the ideal community of realized beings.

self (*ātman, bdag*). Autonomous and permanent identity of the individual (*gang zag*) and of phenomena (*chos*). For Buddhism, belief in such entities, and the resulting grasping to the "self" or "ego" (*bdag' 'dzin*), are at the heart of ignorance, constituting the root cause of suffering and wandering in samsara.

seven riches or qualities of noble beings (*'phags pa'i nor bdun*). Faith, discipline, generosity, listening to the teachings, decency, moral awareness of oneself, and fear of others' justified disapproval. Beings described as "noble" or "supreme" (*'phags pa, āryas*) are those who have attained the first bhūmi.

seven-point posture of Vairocana (*Rnam snang chos bdun*). (1) Cross the legs in the Vajrāsana, the so-called lotus posture, right foot over left thigh. (2) Close the hands into fists with the thumb pressing the base of the fourth finger, and place them on the thighs where they join the pelvis, with the elbows locked straight. (One variation is to place the hands palms up, right over left, on the lap, with elbows bent out to the sides; another is to place both hands palms down, relaxed, on the knees.) (3) The shoulders should be raised and rolled slightly forward. (4) The abdomen should be pushed forward. (5) The spine should be kept straight and erect, "like a pile of golden coins." (6) The chin should be slightly tucked in. (97) The eyes should remain without blinking, focused unwaveringly at a distance of twelve fingers' breadth beyond the tip of the nose. See Shechen Gyaltsap, *A Chariot to Freedom* (Boulder: Shambhala, 2022), 41.

siddhi, see *accomplishment*.

solitary realizers (*pratyekabuddhas, rang sangs rgyas*). Those who attain the cessation of suffering by meditating on the twelve links of dependent arising without relying on a teacher. Solitary realizers realize the emptiness of the personal self and go halfway to realizing the emptiness of phenomena. Thus, they realize the emptiness of perceived phenomena.

spiritual stages, see *bhūmis*.

supreme being (*'phags pa'i gang zag*). Someone who has attained the first of the ten bhūmis of the bodhisattva path that leads to perfect buddhahood at the end of the tenth bhūmi, the ultimate point of the five paths.

sutra and **śāstra** (*sūtra*; *mdo* and *bstan bcos*). The sutras are a collection of the Buddha's sayings, while the śāstras (treatises) are commentaries written by the eminent holders of the Buddha's teachings, including the eighteen great panditas of India. The Buddha's sayings translated from Sanskrit into Tibetan make up the 101 volumes of the Kangyur (*Bka' 'gyur*), while the śāstras, composed in India and translated into Tibetan, are collected in the 213 volumes of the Tengyur (*Bstan 'gyur*).

ten Dharma activities (*chos spyod bcu*). (1) Writing commentaries and spiritual instructions, if you are qualified to do so; (2) making offerings (of the mandala, the seven branches, etc.); (3) giving to the needy; (4) listening to the teachings; (5) reading the holy scriptures; (6) committing their meaning to memory; (7) explaining this meaning to others; (8) reciting your daily prayers; (9) pondering the teachings you have received; (10) assimilating them through contemplation and meditation.

ten unvirtuous actions (*mi dge ba bcu*). The three of body are (1) killing, (2) stealing, and (3) sexual misconduct. The four of speech are (1) lying, (2) gossiping, (3) divisive speech, and (4) speaking harsh words. The three of mind are (1) envy, (2) ill will, and (3) erroneous views. These three categories comprise the wrongdoings of body, speech, and mind, respectively.

ten virtuous deeds (*dge ba'i las bcu*). The three of body are (1) protecting life, (2) being honest, and (3) maintaining proper sexual conduct. The four of speech are (1) speaking the truth, (2) avoiding gossip, (3) avoiding slander, and (4) speaking gentle words that bring happiness to others. The three of mind are (1) rejoicing in others' good fortune, (2) having only thoughts that are beneficial to others, and (3) having correct views.

Thögal (*Thod rgal*). Together with *Trekchö*, this is the most profound practice of the Great Perfection. Literally meaning "leap over," insofar as this method enables you to reach your goal directly and immediately by "leaping over" the intermediate stages. The term is also translated as "direct crossing."

three bodies, see *kayā*.

three lower destinies (*durgati, ngan song gsum*). These include that of the infernal realms, where rebirth results from actions motivated by hatred; that of spirits tormented by destitution, hunger, and thirst, where rebirth is engendered by attachment; and finally, that of animals, where rebirth results from lack of discernment.

three trainings (*bslab pa gsum*). Ethical discipline (*śīla, tshul khrims*), contemplation (*samādhi, ting nge 'dzin*), and wisdom (*prajñā, shes rab*).

three types of suffering (*trilakṣaṇa, sdug bsngal rnam pa gsum*). Suffering upon suffering (as when losing your parents and falling very ill); suffering of change (as when going to a pleasant picnic and being bitten by a snake); and the all-pervading, latent suffering inherent in all forms of conditioned existence as long as it remains under the sway of ignorance.

three vehicles (*theg pa gsum*). The lesser vehicle of listeners and solitary realizers and the Great Vehicle of the bodhisattvas.

three ways of rejoicing a spiritual master (*mnyes pas gsum*). For disciples, the supreme way is to attain spiritual accomplishment through their practice, the middle way is to serve the teacher in various useful ways, and the lesser way is to make material offerings.

three worlds of samsara (*khams gsum*). The world of desire (*kāmadhātu, 'dod khams*), of which human beings are a part; the world of form (*rūpadhātu, gzugs khams*); and the formless world (*arūpadhatu, gzugs med khams*). These three worlds each have numerous subdivisions.

transcendent perfections (*pāramitā, pha rol du phyin pa*), **six or ten.** (1) Generosity (*sbyin pa*), (2) ethical discipline (*tshul khrims*), (3) patience (*bzod pa*), (4) effort (*brtson 'grus*), (5) concentration (*bsam gtan*), (6) insight (*shes rab*), (7) method (*thabs*), (8) aspirations (*smon lam*), (9) strength (*stobs*), and (10) primordial wisdom (*ye shes*).

Trekchö (*Khregs chod*, "to cut through solidity"). This refers here to a practice that totally and at once cuts through our belief in the solidity of things, our fixations on afflictive mental states, and the real existence of external phenomena.

Three Baskets (*Tripiṭaka, Sde snod gsum*). The Three Baskets, or collections, of the words of the Buddha (vinaya, sutra and abhidharma), which were compiled at the first Buddhist council held shortly after the nirvana of Lord Buddha in the Nyagrodha cave at Rājagṛha under the aegis of King Ajātaśatru. Ānanda recited from memory all the Buddha's teachings (sutra), Kāśyapa all his metaphysical teachings (abhidharma), and Upāli all the rules of ethical discipline (vinaya). The collection was supplemented and completed at the third council held at the behest of King Kaniṣka. The Tibetan translation of the Three Baskets, known as the Kangyur, "Translated Words," made during the first period of translation of Sanskrit texts into Tibetan (*Snga 'rgyur*) at Samye Monastery, fills 103 volumes.

twelve ascetic virtues (*sbyangs pa'i yon tan bcu gnyis*). (1) To wear discarded clothing (*phyag dar khrod pa*), (2) to possess only three monastic robes (*chos gos gsum pa*), (3) to wear clothes and boots made of felt (*phying pa*), (4) to eat one's daily meal in one sitting (*stan gcig pa*), (5) to live on alms alone (*bsod snyoms pa*), (6) not to eat after midday (*zas phyis mi len pa*), (7) to live in secluded places (*dgon pa ba*), (8) to dwell under the shelter of trees (*shing drung ba*), (9) to live outdoors (*bla gab med pa*), (10) to live in charnel grounds (*dur khrod pa*), (11) to sleep in a sitting position (*tsog pu ba*), and (12) to remain wherever one happens to be (*gzhi ji bzhin pa*). See *Bod rgya tshig mdzod chen mo* (Beijing: Nationality Publishing House, 1985), p. 2023.

twelve factors of interdependent production (*pratītyasamutpāda, rten 'brel bcu gnyis*). These can be considered either in the order of their progressive appearance, or in the reverse or regressive order. The progressive order describes the process of production of samsara beginning with ignorance. On the other hand, the regressive order describes the process of cessation of samsara starting with old age and death, all the way back to the root cause of samsara—namely, ignorance. The twelve factors of interdependent production are as follows:

1. Ignorance (*avidyā, ma rig pa*) refers primarily to the belief in the identity of the individual self and the real existence of phenomena, arising from ignorance of the Four Noble Truths and karmic causality.
2. Compositional factors (*saṃskāra, 'du byed*) consist of the accumulation of three types of virtuous, unvirtuous, and "non-transferring" actions (*mi g.yo ba'i las*). The latter engender rebirth in the higher spheres of samsara and are so called because they mature in their respective spheres of existence but do not allow access to other spheres.
3. Consciousness (*vijnana, rnam shes*).
4. Name and form (*nāmarūpa, ming gzugs*) correspond to the formation of the five aggregates after consciousness has entered the matrix and also designate the five aggregates themselves.
5. The sources of perception (*āyatana, skye mched*) refer to the six psychosensory faculties: sight, hearing, smell, taste, touch, and mental awareness.

6. Contact (*sparśa, reg pa*) is the detection of phenomena occurring when external objects and consciousness come together through the sensory faculties.
7. Sensation (*vedanā, tshor ba*) results from the detection of an object; it can be pleasant, unpleasant, or neutral.
8. Thirst (*tṛṣna, sred pa*) is the impulse to welcome and desire what is pleasant and to repel what is unpleasant.
9. Appropriation or attachment (*upādāna, len pa*) is the movement that "appropriates" the object of thirst; the main object of thirst being attachment to existence.
10. Becoming (*bhava, srid pa*) is the fulfillment of thirst and appropriation, resulting in the emergence of the next life.
11. Birth (*jāti, skye ba*) consists in returning to a sphere of existence as a consequence of acts committed in the past.
12. Old age and death (*jarāmaraṇa, rga shi*)—that is, aging that begins from the moment of birth and ends with death.

The twelve factors of interdependent production (*rten 'brel bcu gnyis*) can be considered according to the direct order of their appearance or in a reverse order. The direct order describes the process of the production of samsara starting with ignorance, and the regressive, or reverse, order describes the cessation of samsara starting with old age and death and going back to the root cause of samsara, ignorance.

two accumulations (*tshogs gnyis*) of merit and wisdom. These are the two wheels of the chariot that leads to enlightenment. When you perform positive deeds, you accumulate the merit needed to progress along the path; and when you recognize the ultimate, empty nature of these merits and of all phenomena, you develop wisdom.

two veils or obscurations (*sgrib gnyis*) that cover the buddha nature present in every being are (1) the emotional veil formed by afflictive states of mind (*nyon mongs pa'i sgrib*) and (2) the cognitive veil that obscures all that can be known (*shes bya'i sgrib*). The former stands in the way of liberation from samsara and the latter in the way of accomplishing ultimate buddhahood.

ultimate nature of reality, see *dharmatā*.

Vajarayāna (*Rdo rje theg pa*). The Adamantine Vehicle refers to the aspects of Tibetan Buddhism that are based on the tantras. But it also allows for practice in a seamless way of the teachings of the Fundamental Vehicle, those of the Mahāyāna and those of the Secret Mantra. One of the extraordinary features of the Vajrayāna is to provide skillful means that enable the practitioner to swiftly attain liberation from suffering and ultimate enlightenment.

vehicle, see *nine graded vehicles*.

vipaśyanā (*lhag mthong*), "deeper insight." The practice of śamatha helps calm and stabilize the mind but does not by itself uproot ignorance and delusion. For this, it is necessary to cultivate deeper insight, which leads to the realization of the ultimate nature of phenomena and of our own mind, both of which appear while being devoid of intrinsic existence.

yidam (*iṣṭadevatā*, *yi dam* or *yid dam*). The wisdom deity to whom a practitioner dedicates (*dam*) his mind (*yid*) and who constitutes the focal point of the development stage (*bskyed rim*). The yidam represents various aspects or qualities of buddhahood (wisdom, compassion, enlightened activities) in masculine or feminine, peaceful or wrathful forms. As a tutelary deity, the yidam corresponds to the practitioners' particular dispositions, enabling them to remedy their shortcomings and take advantage of their particular qualities. According to Shechen Gyaltsab Pema Namgyal (*Zhe chen rgyal tshab 'gyur med padma rnam rgyal*, 1871–1926) and Dilgo Khyentse Rinpoche, for such a practice to be fully meaningful, it is essential to consider that the yidam is none other than the expression of the creativity of our own awareness (*rig pa'i rtsal*) and that it is inseparable from our root master.

yoga (*rnal 'byor*). Lit. "union with the natural state." This term designates the spiritual practice that enables us to unite with the fundamental nature of our mind and with the ultimate nature of reality. Guru Yoga in particular enables us to unite with the ultimate nature of the spiritual master, which is none other than the buddha nature originally present in every sentient being.

yogi, yoginī (*rnal 'byor pa*, *rnal 'byor ma*). Disciples, men and women, who practice the spiritual path assiduously and authentically, who have carried out many years of retreats in secluded places and are experts in the various practices of the Vajrayāna.

Abbreviations

Dg.K.	Derge Kangyur (*Bka' 'gyur*)
DKR	Dilgo Khyentse Rinpoche. *Man ngag mdzod kyi don khrid rab gsal zla ba'i bdud rtsi* [*The nectar of brilliant moon*: A meaning-commentary on *The precious treasury of essential instructions*]. New Delhi: Shechen, 2021.]. New Delhi: Shechen, 2021.
JDL	Khenpo Jamyang Drupa Lodrö. *Man ngag mdzod kyi 'bru 'grel don gsal me long* [The mirror that illuminates the meaning, a word-to-word commentary on *The Treasury of Essential Instructions*], vol. 7 (*ja*). Chengdu: Snga 'gyur mthun lung dgon, 2015. BDRC W3CN3329 I3CN10791.
TK	Tulku Pema Kalsang. *Man ngag rin po che'i mdzod kyi zab gsang snying po'i don rdo rje'i ljags kyis bkral ba skyud byang du bsdus pa gdams zab nor bu'i gter mdzod*, [The treasure chest of the profound jewel-like instructions] vols. *E* and *wam*). Transcribed by Khenpo Tenzin Dralha (*Mkhan po bstan 'dzin dgra lha*). Gansu: Ken su'u mi rigs dpe skrun khang [Gansu minorities press], n.d. An identical edition (with a slightly different pagination) was published in 2011 by Bod ljongs bod yig dpe rnying dpe skrun khang. BDRC W1KG18488 I1KG18502 (vol. 1) and I1KG18503 (vol. 2).
Toh.	Tōhoku University Complete Catalogue of the Tibetan Buddhist Canons (Bkaḥ-ḥgyur and Bstan-ḥgyur)

Notes

1. *Kun mkhyen klong chen rab 'byams pa'i gsung rab mdzod bdun la blta bar bskul ba* [*Exhortation to read the Seven Treasuries, the supreme writings of the omniscient Longchen Rabjam*], vol. 1 of Patrul Rinpoche's Collected Works (Chengdu: Si khron mi rigs dpe skrun khang, 2009), pp. 179–87.
2. *Man ngag mdzod kyi 'bru 'grel don gsal me long* [The mirror that illuminates the meaning, a word-to-word commentary on *The Treasury of Essential Instructions*], in *Mkhan chen dam pa 'jam dbyangs grub pa'i blo gros kyi gsung 'bum*, vol. 7 (*ja*) (Chengdu: Snga 'gyur mthun lung dgon, 2015), f. 357a.
3. Dilgo Khyentse Rinpoche, *Man ngag mdzod kyi don khrid rab gsal zla ba'i bdud rtsi* [The precious treasury of essential instructions, a meaning-commentary on *The nectar of brilliant moon*] (New Delhi: Shechen, 2021).
4. The most important source is a list drawn up by Longchenpa himself when he was at Tharpa Ling, *Dkar cha rin po che'i mdzod khang, which includes his works composed until at least 1356 (the date of birth of his son* Jamyang Trakpa Özer), which is the basis of the list given by his early biographer and disciple, Chödrak Zangpo. See Chödrak Zangpo, *Kun mkhyen dri med 'od zer gyi rnam thar mthong ba don ldan,* in *Bi ma snying thig,* in *Snying thig ya bzhi,* vol. 6, part 4 (*ya*) (Taklung Tsetrul Rinpoche, Darjeeling, 1975), 499–590. This is translated into English with the Tibetan text included in Shinichi Tsumagari, ed., *Meaningful to Behold: A Critical Edition & Annotated Translation of Longchenpa's Biography* (self-pub., CreateSpace, 2016). For a contemporary compilation of Longchenpa's works, see Stéphane Arguillère, *Profusion de la vaste sphère: Klong-chen rab-'byams (Tibet, 1308–1364): Sa vie, son oeuvre, sa doctrine* (Leuven: Peeters Publishers and Department of Oriental Studies, 2007).
5. The four parts of the latter, the Heart Essence in Four Parts are (1) the *Heart Essence of the Ḍākinīs* (*Mkha' 'gro snying thig*), given by Guru Rinpoche to Yeshe Tsogyal and found as a terma by Pema Ledrel Tsal (*Padma las 'brel rtsal, Rin chen tshul khrims rdo rje,* 1291–1315); (2) *The Quintessence of the Ḍākinīs* (*Mkha' 'gro yang tig*), which is the essence of the former, formulated by Longchenpa; (3) *The Essence of Vimalamitra* (*Bi ma snying thig*), revealed by Dangma Lhungyal (*Ldang ma lhun grub rgyal mtshan*, eleventh to twelfth centuries) and Chetsun

Senge Wangchuck (*Lce btsun seng ge dbang phyug*, eleventh to twelfth centuries); and (4) *The Quintessence of the Guru* (*Bla ma yang tig*), which is the essence of *The Essence of Vimalamitra*, written by Longchenpa. Finally, there is *The Profound Quintessence* (*Zab mo yang tig*), in which Longchenpa elucidated the very essence of all the four preceding texts, so it is not counted as a fifth part. According to an oral explanation by Dilgo Khyentse Rinpoche, the spelling *thig* is used in most cases, while the spelling *tig* applies to the most essential teachings. See *Snying thig ya bzhi* (Darjeeling: Taklung Tsetrul Pema Wangyal, 1975).

6. Mipham Gyatso, *Mdzod chen bdun spar du bsgrubs pa'i dkar chag rin chen me long*, in *Gsung 'bum Mi pham rgya mtsho*, vol. 9, pp. 1–40 (Chengdu: Gangs can rig gzhung dpe rnying myur skyobs lhan tshogs, 2007).
7. Shechen Rabjam, Gyurme Kunzang Namgyal, founded Shechen Tennyi Dargyeling Monastery in 1735. See Shechen Rabjam, *Zhe chen Rab 'byams pa 'gyur med kun bzang rnam rgyal, rgyal ba gnyis pa kun mkhyen ngag gi dbang po'i gsung rab mdzod bdun ngal gso gsang tik rnams rmad byung 'phrul gyi phyi chos ji ltar bsgrub pa'i tshul las brtsams pa'i ngo mtshar gtam gyi gling bu skal bzang rna ba'i dga' ston. A detailed dkar chag to the Rdzogs-chen redaction of the Mdzod bdun and other works of Klong-chen-pa Dri-med-'od-zer including historical accounts of the Rnying ma pa tradition and Rdzogs-chen Monastery by the Second Ze chen Rab 'byams pa 'Gyur med kun bzang rnam rgyal* (Gangtok: Dodrup Sangyay Lama, 1978).
8. Various exhaustive attempts have been made to place in time the composition of each of the Seven Treasuries, using some indications and occasional references made by Longchenpa himself to his earlier writings in various texts. One may consult in particular Dorji Wangchuk, "Cross-Referential Clues for a Relative Chronology of Klong Chen Pa's Works," *Contributions to Tibetan Buddhist Literature* 14, no. 3 (2008): 195–244 and Arguillère, *Profusion de la vaste sphère*. As for the places where Longchenpa composed these treatises, only four of the *Seven Treasuries* clearly identify the place of their composition as Gangri Thökar, Longchenpa's hermitage in the mountains above the valley of the Kyichu River.
9. See note 5.
10. As noted by the translators of *The Precious Treasury of the Fundamental Nature*, "It must be understood that the word 'samaya' is used here in a special sense. Generally speaking, on the level of the tantras, samaya is understood as a pledge and refers to the attitudes and behavior to which masters and disciples commit themselves once empowerment has been bestowed and received. In the present context, however, the four 'samayas' are in fact four principles, four ways of understanding phenomenal appearance, that flow from the realization cultivated by the practitioner of the Great Perfection." See Longchenpa, *The Precious Treasury of the Fundamental Nature*, trans. Padmakara Translation Group (Boulder: Shambhala, 2024), xxi.

11. Tsumagari, *Meaningful to Behold,* 30.
12. According to Chödrak Sangpo, his birthplace was Draphu Tödrong (*Gra phu stod grong*) in Yoru (*G.yo ru*), but other sources vary. See Tsumagari, *Meaningful to Behold,* 3n4.
13. Throughout his life, Longchen Rabjam used various names to sign his writings. He received some of these names while taking vows, as in the case here of Tsultrim Lodrö (*Tshul khrims blo gros*), to which he would sometimes add the epithet Samyepa (*Bsam yas pa*) to indicate that he spent many years in retreat around Samye Monastery in Chimphu (*Mchims pu*). Some were given to him when he was receiving empowerments, and others were bestowed upon him in visions. He used some of these names to sign his writings, including Longchen Rabjam (*Klong chen rab 'byams*), Natsok Rangdrol (*Sna tshogs rang grol*), a combination of both (*Klong chen rab 'byams sna tshogs rang grol*), and Ngagi Wangpo (*Ngag gi dbang po*). When he had a vision of Guru Padmasambhava and his consort Yeshe Tsogyal giving him empowerments and entrusting him with the lineage of the Khandro Nyingthig, Guru Padmasambhava gave him the name Orgyen Drime Özer (*O rgyan dri med 'od zer*), and Yeshe Tsogyal gave him the name Dorje Ziji (*Rdo rje gzi brjid*). Distinguished authors such as Tulku Thondup have connected the use of these various names to the level of the teachings expounded in the corresponding treatises. For a discussion on this, see Tsumagari, *Meaningful to Behold,* 7n11.
14. Most sources speak of Kumārāja (see, among others, the Treasury of Lives, s.v. "Kumāradza," and Wikipedia, s.v. "Kumaradza"), but as Khenpo Dorji Wangchuk rightly pointed out, "One would expect the name to read Kumārarādza (for *Gzhon nu rgyal po*) instead of Kumārādza, which has become a standard, a phenomenon that is sometimes described as "Tibskrit" (i.e., a kind of hybrid Tibetan-Sanskrit) name. The change from Kumārarādza to Kumārādza may have been due to haplology. See Dorji Wangchuk, "Cross-Referential Clues for a Relative Chronology of Klong Chen Pa's Works," *Contributions to Tibetan Buddhist Literature* 14, no. 3 (2008): 206n37.
15. The most widely accepted list of the eight main places of Longchenpa in Bhutan (*gling brgyad*) includes the following: (1) Paro Samtenling (*Spa gro bsam gtan gling*), (2) Shar Kunzangling (*Shar kun bzang gling*), (3) Khothang Rinchenling (*Mkho thang rin chen gling*), (4) Ngenlung Drechaling (*Sngan lung 'bras bcags gling*), (5) Bumthang Tharpaling (*Bum thang thar pa gling*), (6) Tang Ogyencholing (*Stang o rgyan chos gling*), (7) Shingkhar Dechenling (*Shing mkhar bde chen gling*), (8) Kurtö Kunzangling (*Skur stod kun bzang gling*). See Sangay Dorji, *Kun mkhyen long chen pa'i gdan sa chags rabs* (Thimphu: KMT, 2019). We are grateful to Lopön Karma Phuntsok for providing us with this text.
16. Karma Ura, *Longchen's Forests of Poetry and Rivers of Composition in Bhutan* (Thimphu: The Centre for Bhutan Studies and GNH Research, 2015).
17. Two texts by Longchenpa, titled *Immaculate Radiance* (*Zhal chems dri ma med pa'i 'od*) and *The Mirror of Crucial Points* (*Zhal chems gnad kyi me long*), bear the

name of "spiritual testament." However, they are included in *The Quintessence of the Ḍākinīs* (*Mkha 'gro yang thig*), which, according to some sources, might have been written around 1350–1351 (Arguillère, *Profusion de la vaste sphère*, 157). One may therefore speculate, without any certainty, that they were written many years before Longchenpa's parinirvāṇa, unless he wrote them shortly before his passing away, which the biography of Chödrak Zangpo seems to indicate (Tsumagari, *Meaningful to Behold*, 53), and they were subsequently added to the *The Quintessence of the Ḍākinīs*. See *Mkha' 'gro yang tig*, vol. *hung*, in *Snying thig ya bzhi*, vol. 7, pp. 261–81 and pp. 283–85 (Darjeeling: Taklung Tsetrul Pema Wangyal, 1975).

18. See *Mkha' 'gro yang tig*, p. 559.
19. Khenpo Shenphen Chökyi Nangwa (*Mkhan po gzhan phan chos kyi snang ba*, 1871–1927), best known as Khenpo Shenga (*Gzhan dga'*).
20. Bathur Khenpo Thupten Chöphel (Ba thur mkhan po thub sten chos dpal, 1886–1956), commonly known as Khenpo Thupga (*Thub dga'*) who mostly lived at Changma hermitages (*Lcang ma ri khrod*) in Dzachukha.
21. These spiritual treasures fill five of the twenty-five volumes of Dilgo Khyentse Rinpoche's writings. See *Gsung 'bum rab gsal zla ba* (New Delhi: Shechen, 1994).
22. Trans. Ani Jinpa Palmo (Boston: Shambhala, 2008).
23. New York: Aperture, 1996.
24. Khenpo Jamyang Drupai Lodrö (*'Jam dbyangs grub pa'i blo gros*, 1939–2015), commonly known as Khenpo Tepa (*Mkhan po Te pa*), was from Domang Monastery (*Mdo mang dgon*) in Golok. He studied with Khenpo Pema Wangchen (*Mkhan po Padma dbang chen*, d.u.), himself a student of the great Khenpo Kunpel (*Mkhan chen Kun bzang dpal ldan*, 1870/2–1943) and Khenchen Ngakyi Wangpo (*Mkhan chen ngag gi dbang po*, 1879–1941). Jamyang Drupai Lodrö also studied with Khenpo Jigme Phuntsok (*Mkhan po 'jigs med phun tshogs*, 1933–2004). He himself became a teacher at Larung Gar Philosophical College, at Domang, and at Palyul monasteries in eastern Tibet. He visited Namdroling Monastery in South India, where he transmitted several of his eight volumes of writings, including the commentary on *The Treasury of Precious Instructions*, to Khenchen Pema Sherab and gave him permission to give the reading transmission of any of his writings.
25. Tulku Pema Kalsang, *Man ngag rin po che'i mdzod kyi zab gsang snying po'i don rdo rje'i ljags kyis bkral ba skyud byang du bsdus pa gdams zab nor bu'i gter mdzod*, 2 vols. (*e* and *wam*), transcribed by Khenpo Tendzin Dralha (*Mkhan po bstan 'dzin dgra lha*) (Gansu: Ken su'u mi rigs dpe skrun khang, n.d.). An identical edition (with a slightly different pagination) was published in 2011 by *Bod ljongs bod yig dpe rnying dpe skrun khang*.
26. Although this treatise was not originally composed in Sanskrit, it is traditional to begin a Tibetan text by mentioning the name of the text in Sanskrit to affirm that it comes from authentic sources and attest that it is based on the teachings

of Buddha Śākyamuni and on the commentaries of the great panditas of India. It is also a way to invoke the blessings of the Buddha and the great masters of India in order to remove any obstacles in composing and studying the text. It serves as a way to become familiar with Sanskrit, the original language from which the Indian scriptures were translated into Tibetan, and to remember the kindness of the Buddha and the Indian masters.

27. In Sanskrit, *upadeśa* refers primarily to the instructions a spiritual master confers on a disciple.
28. The two Tibetan terms *ngotsa* (*ngo tsha*, "shame") and *trelyö* (*khrel yod*, "modesty") are often associated. *Ngotsa* is about feeling a sense of shame within ourselves regarding our own inappropriate thoughts, words, and actions, whether or not others are aware of them. *Trelyö* is related to the shame we feel when thinking about how others, especially those we respect like the Buddha and our spiritual mentors, might view our objectionable behavior. TK (p. 157) adds that *ngotsa* can also involve feeling ashamed when comparing our flawed behavior with what the Dharma teaches, while *trelyö* is the shame we feel when comparing the same behavior with the societal norms in the ordinary world.
29. The Tibetan original reads *mi go sa*, but this should be corrected to *migs*.
30. *Drenpa* (*dran pa*, *smṛti*) is a Tibetan term variously translated as "mindfulness" or "attentive presence." In Buddhist texts, it primarily means "remembering" the teachings of the Buddha in every situation and checking whether thoughts, words, and deeds align with these teachings. It involves staying present in the moment, preventing the mind from dwelling on the past and anticipating the future, and avoiding being carried away by current thoughts. Practitioners need to maintain *dranpa* consistently, both during meditation and in everyday life. It includes an ethical aspect that helps us determine whether any specific state of mind is beneficial and should guide our actions. *Dranpa* also enables us to identify the appropriate antidotes to various afflictive mental states. *Dranpa* should be associated with *shezhin* (*shes bzhin*, *saṃprajanya*), "vigilant introspection," which acts as a constant guard, checking for distraction, and *bakyö* (*bag yod*, *apramāda*), "circumspection," which involves being concerned with the consequences of our actions.
31. Munīndra literally means "a superior sage," one of Buddha Śākyamuni's names.
32. This example is taken from Jigme Lingpa's (*Rig 'dzin 'jigs med gling pa*, 1729–1798) *Treasury of Precious Qualities* (*Yon tan rin po che'i mdzod*). See Jigme Lingpa, *The Treasury of Precious Qualities*, vol. 1, trans. Padmakara Translation Group (Boston: Shambhala, 2011), 41, 191.
33. According to TK (vol. 1, p. 159), it is difficult to have such a conviction before having realized the self-cognizing primordial wisdom (*so sor rang rig pa'i ye shes*).
34. *snying rlung*. It is said that when *prāṇa*, the breath, settles in the heart, the mind is disturbed to varying degrees, even to the point of madness.
35. *Bsam gtan ngal gso*, one of the three texts of the Trilogy of Rest (*Ngal gso skor*

gsum), composed by Gyalwa Longchen Rabjam, the author of *The Precious Treasury of Essential Instructions*. This text has been translated into English as Longchenpa, *Finding Rest in Meditation, The Trilogy on Rest,* vol. 2, trans. Padmakara Translation Group (Boston: Shambhala, 2018). As Khyentse Rinpoche was referring to this text, following Rabjam Rinpoche's instructions, we have slightly harmonized the oral teaching with the original text.

36. *Ḍākinī* (*mkha' 'gro*) means "who travels in space" and refers to the feminine principle associated with wisdom that moves in the absolute space of dharmadhātu. A distinction is made between ordinary, worldly ḍākinīs (*'jig rten mkha' 'gro*), who have a few spiritual powers, and wisdom ḍākinīs (*ye shes mkha' 'gro*), who possess full realization.
37. Jetsun Milarepa (*Rje btsun Mi la ras pa*, 1040–1123) was one of Tibet's greatest yogis and poets, whose biography and spiritual songs have inspired generations of practitioners to this day. A supreme disciple of Marpa, he is one of the main masters at the source of the Kagyu tradition.
38. Vajrakīlaya (*Rdo rje phur ba*) is a major yidam deity of the Nyingma tradition, embodying the enlightened activity of all buddhas. This practice is said to be particularly powerful in removing outer, inner, and secret obstacles on the path to enlightenment. Vajrakīlaya is one of the eight principal yidams (*sgrub pa bka' brgyad*) of the Nyingma tradition. He appears in wrathful form, indicating the indomitable power of compassion to benefit beings. His peaceful form is Vajrasattva.
39. According to TK, "respectable people" refers not only to those who come from a respectable background or those who are not associated with wrongdoers, cheats, or people who harm other human beings. It also includes people who adhere to the compassionate vision of the Great Vehicle.
40. The texts describe three or four aspects of faith (*dad pa*), or confidence. See the glossary, "four kinds of faith."
41. *Cakravartin* (*'Khor lo bsgyur ba'i rgyal po*) literally translates to "one who turns the wheel." In Buddhist and Tibetan literature, it refers to a universal monarch of great virtue and wisdom, who is invested with authority over the territories reached by his golden wheel. There are several levels of cakravartin depending on the number of continents touched by this wheel, which can be one, two, three, or all four continents surrounding Mount Meru.
42. The translation of this verse follows the interpretation of Dilgo Khyentse Rinpoche. According to JDL (p. 8a), "high or low level" refers to the different levels of the teachings, and the verse would then be translated as follows: "[The] lower and higher views must be integrated into the ultimate view free from extremes."
43. The Three Sentences That Strike the Vital Points (*Tshigs gsum gnad brdeg*) were spoken by Garab Dorje, the first human master of the Great Perfection lineage, and constitute a direct and profound presentation of view, meditation, and action based on the realization of pristine awareness (*rig pa*). Patrul Rinpoche

composed a famous commentary on these three sentences titled *Extraordinary Teachings of the Wise and Glorious Dharma King* (*Mkhas pa shri rgyal po'i khyad chos*), in *Gsung 'bum o rgyan 'jigs med chos kyi dbang po*, vol. 5 (Chengdu: Si khron mi rigs dpe skrun khang, 2009), pp. 416–18.

44. Literally "to remain in equality" (*mnyam par bzhag pa), means to remain without wavering with the object of one's meditation, perfectly concentrated, or to remain in a state of perfect equality without discriminating between samsara and nirvana, pleasure and pain. By extension, this term often designates seated meditation, in which the body, gaze, and mind remain calm and poised.*

45. These are the four activities (*las bzhi*) accomplished practitioners undertake to benefit beings: pacifying (*zhi ba*) disease, obstacles, mental confusion, and ignorance; increasing (*rgyas pa*) merit, lifespan, glory, and prosperity; mastering (*dbang*) spiritual qualities, vital force, and the energies of the three worlds; and subjugating through compassionate wrath (*drag po*) external and internal negative forces.

46. Equal taste (*samarāsa*, *ro snyoms*). One of the results of practicing the path is that practitioners become able to maintain their equanimity and inner freedom whatever of life's circumstances and obstacles they might encounter on the spiritual path. "Equal taste," or "one taste," is associated with perceiving the ultimate nature of phenomena and of the mind, emptiness united with appearances, awareness united with luminosity, and wisdom with compassion. Equal taste is also one of the Six Yogas of Naropa. There are numerous teachings on this subject based on the Six Cycles of Equal Taste (*Ro snyoms 'khor drug*), revealed by Tsangpa Gyare Yeshe Dorje (*Gtsang pa rgya ras ye shes rdo rje*, 1161–1211), founder of the Drukpa Kagyu lineage.

47. The "male or female malignant spirits" (*pho 'dre* and *mo 'dre*) refer to a range of entities, often harmful, sometimes benign, such as the local deities said to inhabit mountains, lakes, trees, and so on. When Guru Padmasambhava came from India to Tibet, via Nepal, along the way he subjugated and swore an oath to the main "gods and demons" who wanted to prevent him from establishing Buddhism in Tibet so that, from now on, these forces would no longer harm beings and would protect the Dharma and those who practice it. There are eight main classes of gods and demons (*lha srin* [or *'dre*] *sde brgyad*), of which there are also eight subcategories. See Dudjom Rinpoche, *The Nyingma School of Tibetan Buddhism: Its Fundamentals and History*, 2nd ed. (Boston: Wisdom, 2002), 2:158–59.

48. Here, "noble being," or "exalted beings" (*ārya*, *'phags pa'i gang zag*), refers to a person who has attained the first of the ten bhūmis of the bodhisattva path, which leads to perfect buddhahood at the end of the tenth bhūmi, the ultimate point of the five paths.

49. It is said that Patrul Rinpoche received, no less than twenty-five times, from his root master, Jigme Gyalwai Nyugu (*'Jigs med rgyal ba'i myu gu*, 1765–1842), the teachings on the preliminary practices (*sngon 'gro*) according to the cycle

of Jigme Lingpa's Heart Essence of the Vast Expanse (*Klong chen snying thig*). He wrote down these teachings in *The Words of My Perfect Teacher* (*Kun bzang bla ma'i gzhal lung*), an essential work for practitioners of Tibetan Buddhism, written in a style that combines classical Tibetan with the picturesque language of everyday life. Revered by all four schools of Tibetan Buddhism, it has been translated into many languages. See *The Words of My Perfect Teacher*, rev. ed., trans. the Padmakara Translation Group (New Haven, CT: Yale University Press, 2010).

50. It is said that Chekawa Yeshe Dorje (*'Chad kha ba ye shes rdo rje*, 1101–1175) studied and practiced mind training (*lojong*) for twelve years before summarizing it in his *Seven-Point Mind Training* (*Blo sbyong don bdun ma*). These teachings spread widely and numerous commentaries were written on them, including one composed in the nineteenth century by one of the luminaries of Tibetan Buddhism, Jamgön Kongtrul Lodrö Thaye (*'Jam mgon kong sprul blo gros mtha' yas*, 1813–1899), one of the key figures in the nineteenth-century revival of Buddhism in eastern Tibet. Several other commentaries are frequently taught within Tibetan Buddhism, notably the succinct commentary by Gyalse Ngulchu Thogme Zangpo (*Dngul chu rgyal sras thogs med bzang po*, 1295–1369), which was orally explained by Dilgo Khyentse Rinpoche in Tibetan and then translated into English as *Enlightened Courage* (Ithaca, NY: Snow Lion, 1993), as well as detailed commentaries by Shabkar Tsogdruk Rangdrol (*Zhabs dkar tshogs drug rang grol*, 1781–1851) called the *The Emanated Scriptures of the Bodhisattva* (*Rgyal sras sprul pa'i glegs bam*), in *The Collected Works of Zhabs dkar tshogs drug rang grol*, vol. 7 (New Delhi: Shechen, 2003, BDRC W23893), and Shechen Gyaltsab Pema Namgyal, called *Theg pa chen po'i blo sbyong gi man ngag zab don sbrang rtsi bum bzang*, in *The Collected Works of Zhe chen rgyal tshab padma rnam rgyal*, vol. 7 (New Delhi: Shechen, 1975–1994). An English translation of the latter volume is available as Zhechen Gyaltsab, *Path of Heroes, Birth of Enlightenment*, trans. Deborah Black, 2 vols (Cazadero: Dharma Publishing, 1995).

51. The great Indian sage Paramabuddha, better known by his Tibetan name Padampa Sangye (*Pha dam pa sangs rgyas*, d. 1117) studied with 150 masters. He visited Tibet four times and China three times, and he spread the teachings of the Pacification of Suffering (*Zhi byed*), one of the eight great traditions of Tibetan Buddhism still practiced today. These teachings are based on transcendent knowledge (*prajñāpāramitā*), which dispels ignorance, the root cause of suffering. Padampa lived for many years in the high valley of Tingri, on the borders of Nepal, where he composed his famous *Hundred Verses of Advice to the People of Tingri* (*Ding ri brgya rtsa ma*), translated into English as *The Hundred Verses of Advice*, with commentary by Dilgo Khyentse Rinpoche and translated by Padmakara Translation Group (Boston: Shambhala, 2006). This verse appears in that translation on p. 78.

52. The Tibetan transcript reads *tha ka*, though this should be corrected to *tha ma*.

53. Rigdzin Jigme Lingpa (*Rig 'dzin 'Jigs med gling pa*, 1729–1798) was considered to be an incarnation of Avalokiteśvara, as well as of Vimalamitra and King Trisong Detsen. At the age of six, he entered the monastery of Palgi Riwo and received the name Pema Khyentse Özer. At the age of thirteen, he met his root guru, Rigdzin Thukchok Dorje (*Skyid grong rig 'dzin thugs mchog rdo rje*, d.u.). He also received instructions on the Kama and Terma traditions from many other teachers. Without arduous study, but rather due to his inner realization, he was able to assimilate and express the whole of the Buddhist doctrine. At the age of twenty-eight, he did a three-year retreat in the hermitage near Palri Monastery and had many signs of accomplishment. He had visions of Guru Padmasambhava and his consort Khandro Yeshe Tsogyal in which the terma cycle known as the Longchen Nyingthik was revealed to him. He did another three-year retreat in the Metok Phuk (Flower Cave) at Chimphu above Samye. He had three visions of Gyalwa Longchen Rabjam, thus receiving the blessings of Longchenpa's body, speech, and mind. At Tsering Jong in Southern Tibet, Jigme Lingpa established the hermitage of Pema Ösel Thekchok Chöling, where countless disciples were to come from all over Tibet. Jigme Lingpa's immediate incarnations were Jamyang Khyentse Wangpo (1820–1892), his body incarnation; Patrul Rinpoche (1808–1887), his speech incarnation; and Do Khyentse Yeshe Dorje (1800–1866), his mind incarnation.
54. A sacred feast (*gaṇacakra*, *tshogs kyi 'khor lo*) is a ritual during which the five sense objects and various foods and drinks are blessed as wisdom ambrosia, which is offered to the deities of the Three Roots, as well as to the mandala of one's own body.
55. Known editions of this text have only five verses instead of six here, as is also the case on a few other occasions throughout the text. It is conceivable that omissions may have occurred in the early calligraphic versions of the root text, but as the original manuscripts of Gyalwa Longchen's Seven Treasuries have not been found, it is impossible to know more. This happens a number of times in the root text.
56. Perfect mastery of body and mind comes only with the realization of the first bhūmi, at which level the mind knows ultimate reality as it is and the adamantine body transcends any notion of decline.
57. According to Buddhism, actions, words, or thoughts are virtuous if they help ease suffering and its causes and free oneself from their grip. On the other hand, actions that contribute to the continuation of suffering are considered unvirtuous.
58. The great panditas of Buddhist India include the Six Ornaments of the Buddha's teachings—namely, Nāgārjuna and Āryadeva, the ornaments of Madhyamaka; Asaṅga and Vasubandhu, the ornaments of Abhidharma; and Dignāga and Dharmakīrti, the ornaments of Pramāṇa. The Two Supreme Ones are Guṇaprabha and Śākyaprabha.
59. There are only five points in this verse in known editions.

60. See Patrul Rinpoche, *The Words of My Perfect Teacher*, chap. 3.
61. The four powers (*stobs bzhi*) of confession enable one to purify negative acts. They are those of regret, of the support, of the antidote, and of the resolution. (1) The power of regret is inspired by one's negative actions. It is essential to fully acknowledge one's faults and wish to make amends for them with deep regret. (2) We also need a support for our confession—namely, the refuge (the Three Jewels); our spiritual master; or more specifically, Vajrasattva, the buddha of purification. Along with the refuge, it is also essential to engender the mind of enlightenment. (3) The power of the antidote is the practice of purification itself, in particular the meditation and visualizations centered on Vajrasattva. For more details, see Patrul Rinpoche, *The Words of My Perfect Teacher*, 265–71. (4) At the end of the practice, it is essential to resolve firmly never to fall into the same errors again, and this is the power of resolve. It is said that there is no negative act that cannot be purified by these four powers.
62. *Trīskhandhadharmasūtra*, *Phung po gsum pa'i mdo* (Toh. 284, Dg.K. mdo sde, *ya*), ff. 57a–77a. This is the sutra of the confession for the bodhisattvas. The three heaps correspond to confession, rejoicing in the virtuous deeds of others, and pleading with those who transmit the Dharma to remain in this world.
63. The ten virtuous, or Dharmic, activities (*Chos spyod rnam pa bcu*) are copying the scriptures, making offerings, being generous, listening to the teachings, retaining them, reading them, explaining them to others, reciting them, reflecting on them, and meditating on their meaning. An alternative is also given by Jamgön Kongtrul Lodrö Thaye: (1) writing commentaries and spiritual instructions, if one is qualified to do so; (2) making offerings (of the mandala, the seven branches, etc.) (3) giving to the needy; (4) listening to the teachings; (5) reading the holy scriptures; (6) committing their meaning to memory; (7) explaining this meaning to others; (8) reciting one's daily prayers; (9) pondering over the teachings one has received; (10) assimilating them through contemplation and meditation. See Jamgön Kongtrul Lodrö Thaye, *Gsung 'bum 'Jam mgon kong sprul blo gros mtha' yas* (New Delhi: Shechen, 2002), vol. 12, p. 238.
64. The three supreme practices (*dam pa gsum*) concern the excellent preparation, the excellent main part and the excellent conclusion. This means that for any practice, it is important to (1) begin with generating of the altruistic mind of enlightenment (*bodhicitta*); (2) accomplish the main practice by maintaining the view of the emptiness of phenomena and the recognition of the nature of mind, or, if this is beyond one's present capabilities, to at least be perfectly concentrated on the practice; and (3) conclude by dedicating the merits to the immediate and the ultimate benefit of all beings.
65. In the various editions available today, this verse has only five points.
66. The bodhisattva Dharmodgata (*Chos 'phags*), or Noble Dharma, is said to have been born in a palace located in the City of Perfume (Gandhavatī) and to have become renowned for his teachings of the *Prajñāpāramitā*. In particular,

he guided Sadāprarudita ("He who always cries," so called because he was so moved by beings' suffering) to enlightenment in one lifetime.

67. Here, in the available editions, there are only five verses instead of six.
68. This thornbush, also known as goat's head (*gze ma ra mgo*) is a thorny plant, *Acanthospermum hispidum*, found in South Asia; South America, where it originated; and elsewhere. It strikingly resembles a goat's head with its horns.
69. Among the four māras, or demons, this is the one associated with pride.
70. The three methods of liberating thoughts are generally described as (1) freeing thoughts through naked attention (*gcer grol*), (2) the spontaneous liberation of thoughts at the very moment they arise (*shar grol*), and 3) the spontaneous liberation of thoughts (*rang grol*). Other methods are also described, such as the primordial liberation of thoughts (*ye grol*), which consists of recognizing through direct experience that delusion has no more tangible reality than a bad dream and that thoughts are manifestations of pristine awareness.
71. Padampa Sangye, *The Hundred Verses of Advice*, v. 12.
72. This is a mythical weapon that never stops spinning and that nothing can stop.
73. According to Khenpo Sönam Tsewang, the Tibetan here, *bslu mi thub pa min*, should be corrected to *bslu mi thub pa min*. (DKR, f. 44b.)
74. Taken literally in its condensed form, the expression *zhing khams sbyong ba* would mean "to purify" or "to practice the pure lands." It refers to the purification of our impure perceptions into experiencing the pure lands, which, according to Dilgo Khyentse Rinpoche, refers to becoming familiar with one's own pristine awareness. This expression could therefore be rendered as "training for the pure lands." These are also the prayers made by bodhisattvas to bring about the appearances of a particular pure land for the sake of beings, prayers that are spontaneously realized when these bodhisattvas reach enlightenment. See also TK (p. 56) for a similar explanation.
75. Dilgo Khyentse Rinpoche often gave the example that a grain of rice will not yield wheat.
76. This is usually a large rock that is said to be the home of a protector. It can also be a precious or semiprecious stone, such as a turquoise, that has been blessed by a spiritual master as a support for the presence of a person's protector(s).
77. The commentaries interpret these verses in two complementary ways. In the first verse, for example, a great dwelling is described both as being similar to an iron house burning in the underworld and as the cause of being reborn in such a place.
78. The six hollow organs (*lus kyi snod drug*) are counted as the stomach, large intestine, gallbladder, bladder, small intestine, and prostate. The five viscera (*don lnga*) are the heart, lungs, kidneys, liver, and spleen.
79. The Tibetan text should be corrected to *tshong gi khur ma gtogs*.
80. Some yogis spend time practicing in charnel grounds, which are strong reminders of impermanence and where they are often challenged at night by frightening displays conjured by harmful spirits. Charnel grounds mainly

refer to places where sky burials are performed. In a sky burial, customary in Tibet, the body of a deceased person is taken to a consecrated place where an officiant cuts it up in a precise manner while monks, nuns, or yogis recite the relevant prayers. Once the funeral rituals have been completed, the body is left for the vultures to swiftly dispatch. Cremation is generally reserved for the bodies of spiritual masters or respected practitioners. In rarer cases, depending on astrological calculations or death due to certain illnesses, bodies are buried.

81. Mamos (*mātṛ* or *mātṛkā*) are wrathful female deities. They embody the main natural forces that react to human violence and environmental depredation by creating obstacles, epidemics, and diseases. They are also known to gather in cemeteries and other burial grounds.
82. Lochen Rinchen Sangpo (*Lo chen rin chen bzang po*, 958–1055) was the first translator (*lotsāwa*) of the second period of translation of Buddhist texts from Sanskrit into Tibetan. He traveled twice to India, mainly to Kashmir, where he learned Sanskrit. He translated the *Prajñāpāramitā* in eight thousand and twenty-five thousand verses, as well as its famous commentary, titled *Abhisamayālaṅkāra*. According to tradition, he built around a hundred temples in the Himalayan valleys of Lahul, Spiti, Kinnaur, and in western Tibet.
83. Kecara (*Bka spyod*) is the celestial field of Vajrayoginī. Practitioners who obtain this accomplishment go with their physical body to this pure land. According to Dilgo Khyentse Rinpoche's oral explanations, this accomplishment differs from the accomplishment of the Rainbow Body, in which a practitioner who has attained the ultimate and unparalleled realization of the Great Perfection dissolves his body into light and leaves behind only the dead parts of his body—the hair and the nails.
84. The renowned Kadampa master Kharak Gomchung (*Kha rag sgom chung*, 1040/45–1100) was a most perfect example of renunciation of any activity other than spiritual practice. Aware of the unpredictability of death, he did not even carve steps in and out of his cave or remove the thorny bushes at the entrance, thinking it would be a waste of time if he were to die that day. He was famous for his boundless compassion. His seventy counsels (*ang yig bdun bcu pa*) are said to contain the very essence of the Kadampa teachings. He was the main disciple of Geshe Gonpa Wangchuck Gyaltsen (*Dge bshes dgon pa dbang phyug rgyal mtshan*, 1016–1083), and his own pupils included Ngul Tön (*Rngul ston*) and Dharma Kyab (*Dhar ma skyabs*).
85. Dilgo Khyentse Rinpoche repeated the explanation of instruction of verse fifty-six twice, within a day of each other, in a very similar way, so we have merged the two commentaries.
86. According to the vinaya, one-third of the stomach should be filled with solid food, one-third with liquids, and one-third should remain empty.
87. These are the precepts of prātimokṣa, the bodhisattvas, and the Secret Mantra.
88. See note 52.
89. There are in fact five instructions in this series.

90. The four changes of attitude (*blo ldog rnam bzhi*) are reflection on the rarity and value of human existence, on the impermanence of all things, on the law of cause and effect, and on the imperfections of samsara.
91. The objects perceived by the six main aspects of consciousness: the basic consciousness (*ālayavijñāna*) and the five aspects related to the sense organs. One often adds to these six the conceptual consciousness and the consciousness tainted by the afflictive states of mind (*kleśa*). See the glossary under "consciousness."
92. This refers to the vast (*rgyas*) aspects of the teachings, which include the description of the five paths and the ten bhūmis, compared with the profound (*zab*) aspects, which deal in particular with emptiness and absolute truth, the understanding of which requires engaging in the direct experience acquired through practice.
93. *Karmaśatakasūtra*, *Mdo sde las brgya pa* (Toh. 340, Dg.K. mdo sde, *ha*, ff. 1b–309a).
94. *Saddharmasmṛtyupasthāna*, *Dam pa'i chos dran pa nye ba bzhag pa* (Toh. 287, Dg.K. mdo sde, *ya*, ff. 82a–318a).
95. The Tibetan here, *lang gong 'og*, should be corrected to *lam gong 'og*.
96. This refers to Vajrasattva's pure land, *Abhirati* (*Mngon par dga' ba*).
97. A *dhāraṇī* is a Sanskrit formula, usually longer than a mantra, that derives from the Sanskrit root *dhṛ* translated to *gzungs* in Tibetan, referring to the capacity to "hold" and "retain" some spiritual power that comes about when reciting a dhāraṇī.
98. In this series, Longchenpa sets out seven instructions instead of the usual six.
99. The four conceptual extremes (*spros pa'i mtha' bzhi*) are to conceive reality in terms of existence, nonexistence, eternity, or nothingness.
100. It is very rare indeed, within samsara, to gather the causes that enable human rebirth, principally the observance of the ten virtuous actions and of the perfection of moral discipline. The texts also explain the rarity of human existence using images or analogies. In particular, it is said that it is more difficult to obtain a human existence than it is for a blind turtle that rises once every hundred years from the bottom of the ocean to pass its head through the orifice of a yoke floating on the surface agitated by waves. Finally, this rarity is also underlined by numerical comparisons that show the low probability of obtaining a human body: the texts say that there are as many beings in the underworld as there are dust particles on Earth, as many hungry ghosts as there are grains of sand in the Ganges, as many animals as there are tiny grains in a millet-beer barrel, and as many demigods as there are snowflakes in a storm, but as few gods and humans as there are dust particles on a fingernail. For more detailed explanations, see Patrul Rinpoche, *The Words of My Perfect Teacher*, chap. 1.
101. This refers to the four classes of demons, or māras (*bdud*). The māras personify the attachment to the ego and to the reality of phenomena, somewhat similar

to the meaning given to the word *demon* in English as the personification of temptations, vices, and instincts. See the glossary under "māra."

102. In this verse, the Tibetan *dgos* must be corrected to *dogs* in the Shechen edition.

103. Here, verb that is used, *'bur 'joms*, "to level down" or "to smooth out" illustrates the practice of leveling down thoughts as soon as they begin to appear, as one would level down a bubble that just formed on the surface of water.

104. Approach (*bsnyen pa*) and accomplishment (*sgrub pa*) are the two main stages of the creation or development phase (*bskyed rim*), during which the wisdom deities are visualized and their mantras recited. First, we "approach" the deity by familiarizing ourselves with the practice. Next, we "accomplish" the deity by uniting with its wisdom nature. After the development phase comes the perfection phase (*rdzogs rim*), which may or may not be accompanied by formal representations.

105. These include the concentrations or absorption in the four levels of the formless world: infinite space (*nam mkha mtha' yas skye mched, ākāśānantyāyatana*), infinite consciousness (*rnam shes mtha' yas skye mched, vijñānānantyāyatana*), absolutely nothing (*ci yang med pa'i skye mched, ākiācanyāyatana*), and neither existing nor nonexisting (*'du shes med 'du shes med min skye mched, naivasājñānāsamjñāyatana*).

106. Five buddha families (*rgyal ba rigs lnga*). Vajrasattva represents the Vajra family and possesses the wisdom of perfect equality (*mnyam nyid ye shes*). Ratnasambhava represents the Jewel family and possesses the mirror-like wisdom (*me long ye shes*). Amitābha represents the Lotus family and possesses the wisdom of perfect discernment (*so sor rtog pa'i ye shes*). Amoghasiddhi, of the Action family, possesses the all-accomplishing wisdom (*bya ba sgrub pa'i ye shes*). And Vairocana, of the Tathāgata family, possesses the wisdom of the absolute expanse (*chos dbyings ye shes*).

107. JDL (p. 69b) offers another explanation: "There is no better reflection than to cut [the mind] at the root"—that is to say, to understand that the mind is without a base or a root.

108. Sacred arts (painting, sculpture, music, etc.), crafts, and traditional sciences are highly esteemed in the Buddhist world and can be closely integrated with the spiritual path, but for those who wish to devote themselves entirely to the quest for liberation and enlightenment, these activities take up a significant part of their time, attention, and determination that could be allocated to this quest.

109. This advice does not mean that we shouldn't take care of loved ones who are in difficulty if they are ill, elderly, or in need. It is addressed to people who, because of strong emotional and affective ties, carry on indefinitely with ordinary activities and end up never practicing the Dharma.

110. Willow leaves shake and rattle in the slightest wind and show their dark-green tops and pale-green undersides.

111. The king of the desire gods, Kāmadeva (*Dod pa'i lha*; in Sanskrit, *kāma* means "passion," and *deva*, "celestial") is traditionally depicted as a green-skinned warrior carrying a bow and arrows with five types of flowers. In the texts of the Pali Canon, he becomes Māra, who tried to distract Siddhārtha Gautama, the night before his enlightenment, when he was seated under the bodhi tree at the diamond throne of India, the vajrāsana, the present Bodh Gaya. Among the various means Māra employed that night, he sent his three (sometimes five) daughters—Taṇhā, or thirst; Ārati, aversion; and Rāga, desire-attachment—to seduce the one who was about to become Buddha Śākyamuni.

112. *Āryabhadracaryāpraṇidhānaraja, Bzang po spyod pa'i smon lam gyi rgyal po* (Toh. 1105, Dg.K. phal chen, *cha*, ff. 336b–341a). This text is taken from the last part of the *Gaṇḍavyūha Sūtra*.

113. "Leaving a small home for a large one" is a traditional saying about the pitfalls of leaving a small home with the idea of renouncing worldly life and finding yourself busy in a large monastery or a community of retreatants. However, the wisdom of the saying extends to those who leave a spacious worldly home for a smaller hermitage, since even in a secluded place, one may engage in many ordinary activities, thus defeating the purpose of being there.

114. In the development stage (*bskyed rim*) practice, before visualizing the main deity and entourage within the mandala, one visualizes a series of "protective tents" (*srung gur*) or "domes" made of symbols of the buddhas of the five families. These vast domes are impervious to any form of obstacle that might disturb the spiritual practice.

115. These words, often quoted by Dilgo Khyentse Rinpoche, are usually attributed to Jetsun Milarepa, but we were not able to locate this quote in his biography or in the collection of his spiritual songs.

116. The solitary realizers understand a person's lack of self-existence. As for the nonidentity of phenomena (dharmas), they understand the nonidentity of gross phenomena, but take the indivisible particles at the subtle level as real.

117. Life stones (*bla rdo*) are used as material support for the protective deities of the Dharma. They are often obsidian or black tourmalines that form a natural triangle, cubic pyrite crystals, but also turquoise and other semiprecious stones.

118. At the moment of death, when the light of the dharmakāya, the ultimate dimension of buddhahood, shines and the meeting between the mother luminosity of the dharmakāya and the daughter luminosity of the buddha nature within each of us occurs, an accomplished yogi can seize this brief moment to unite with the dharmakāya and thus attain a "lesser" buddhahood. This has the same nature as the "great" buddhahood, but its realization is still limited, like the sky that we see through the eye of a needle: it is the true sky but only a tiny glimpse of that sky. (According to oral explanations given by Dilgo Khyentse Rinpoche when he was teaching on this particular stage of death.) See also verses 412–413 of the present text.

119. The triad of "protect, repel and annihilate" (*srung ldog gsad gsum*) refers to activities that can and must only be performed by yogis who have reached a high level of spiritual realization. The sole purpose of these three acts is to benefit beings by protecting them (from famine, conflict, epidemics, and any other obstacle), by repelling anything that might threaten their physical and mental integrity (invasions, persecutions, etc.) and by eliminating ("annihilate" should here be understood figuratively) malignant forms and evil spirits while liberating their consciousness in the absolute space of dharmadhātu.
120. Throwing pebbles into water in this way is a gratuitous exercise that is useless for the lake into which they are thrown and to the person throwing them. Another interpretation proposed by Khenpo Sönam Tsewang is, "If you lack instruction, you will meditate as foolishly as one who throws stones in the dark," without knowing what you are throwing stones at and without seeing what they land on.
121. See note 91.
122. In Asia, farmers pierce the nostrils of certain animals, especially water buffaloes, and attach rings to them. When they want to take the animals somewhere, they attach lanyards to the rings, which allows the animals to literally be led by the nose.
123. At the end of a thread-cross-ransom (*mdos glud*) ritual, offerings topped by an effigy made of colored threads crisscrossing on a frame are thrown with great pomp in a place where obstacle-making spirits are believed to have gathered. For removing obstacles to the life of a spiritual master or another person, an effigy of the person is offered along with the other articles as a ransom to replace the master him or herself. But if one has no idea where to throw this ransom and to whom one is giving it, the ritual will have no meaning or effect.
124. The mountain spirits (*btsan*; lit. "powerful") belong to the eight classes of gods and demons (*lha srin sde brgyad*, see note 49), who are spirits that inhabit the mountains and rivers. The regal spirits (*rgyal po*; lit. "kings"), who also belong to these eight classes, are entities that are a priori evil but brought under oath to protect the Dharma by a qualified master.
125. Skillful means (*upāya, thabs*) are the means used in Buddhist practices, particularly those pertaining to the Mahāyāna and the Vajrayāna to progress swiftly on the path of liberation and enlightenment. Skillful means must always be associated with wisdom and with an unconditional compassion for all sentient beings.
126. Enunciated by Sachen Kunga Nyingpo (*Sa chen kun dga' snying po,* 1092–1158) one of the founding patriarchs of the Sakya lineage, this sentence belongs to the famous teachings that urge one to free oneself from four fundamental attachments (*gzhen pa bzhi brel*) and that have given rise to numerous commentaries, one of the most renowned being the one formulated by Jetsun Trakpa Gyaltsen (*Rje btsun Grags pa rgyal mtshan,* 1147–1216):

> If you are attached to this life, you are not a true spiritual practitioner,
> If you are attached to samsara, you do not have renunciation,
> If you are attached to your own self-interest, you have no bodhicitta,
> If there is grasping, you do not have the view.

127. The Tibetan *btang gro bzhag sdod*, translated here as "mastering" (the mind) literally means "goes where you send it and stays where you put it."
128. According to Khenchen Pema Sherap, these are like nails as they are used to fix something firmly in the right position.
129. In the vocabulary of the Great Perfection, the expression *rangbab* (*rang babs*), which can be translated as "leave as is," "let rest in its natural state," refers to leaving our perceptions and our thoughts as they are in their natural state, without interfering with, altering, or modifying anything. Dilgo Khyentse Rinpoche gave the example of a leaf that falls from a tree and is left on the ground as it fell.
130. It is a matter of using afflictive mental states as catalysts to advance on the path, just as, to take an example given by Jigme Khyentse Rinpoche, someone who falls into the water takes support of the water itself to swim and avoid drowning. However, this does not mean that one will experience mental poisons in ordinary ways, with attachment or repulsion, which will surely cause suffering.
131. See note 49.
132. The "ultimate truth in itself" (*rnam grangs ma yin pa'i don dam*), which is ineffable and transcends all conceptual elaboration, as opposed to the approximate absolute truth (*rnam grangs pa'i don dam*), which is conceived within the distinction between relative and ultimate truth. For a profound and detailed explanation of this topic, see Mipham Rinpoche's commentary on Śāntarakṣita's *Madhyamakālaṃkāra*: Jamgön Mipham, *The Adornment of the Middle Way*, trans. Padmakara Translation Group (Boston: Shambhala, 2008).
133. Longchen Rabjampa Drime Özer, *Dpe don nges don rdo rje'i mgur*, in *Gsung thor bu* [Miscellaneous writings] (Paro, Bhutan: Lama Ngodrup and Sherab Drimey, 1982), vol. 2, f. 9. In the original verse of the few editions available, the last line reads *zab mo'i de nyid sgoms na legs* instead of *'gyur med btsan sa bzung na legs*, cited in the present commentary.
134. The recommendation to abandon your "native country," which is found in many texts, does not mean that the country of your birth is bad in itself, but after having decided to devote yourself to spiritual practice, if you remain where you have lived for a long time, there is every chance that you will have difficulty extricating yourself from the attachments and aversions that have been forged in the past with people, places, and possessions.
135. These are the words of the Buddha and the śāstras, the commentaries written by the eminent holders of the Buddha's teachings, such as the eighteen great panditas of India. The words spoken by the Buddha translated from Sanskrit into Tibetan are collected in the 101 volumes of the Kangyur (*Bka' 'gyur*) and

the śāstras composed in India and translated into Tibetan are collected in the 213 volumes of the Tengyur (*Bstan 'gyur*).

136. The qualities of nirvana stem from recognizing that phenomena are nothing more than the manifestations of awareness and the delusions of samsara stem from failing to do so.

137. The second point begins with the Tibetan word *kho*, which literally means "he" or "she" but can be explained in various ways. According to Khenchen Pema Sherap, here *kho* refers to phenomena at large. When they appear, we have this tendency to grasp them as being intrinsically existing in an autonomous way. In this context, the meaning of the phrase is "eliminate from the back of your mind the grasping to the independent existence of all phenomena." It is indeed the grasping to phenomena as being truly existent that must be eliminated. It is, for example, futile to boast about a reasoning that makes you think that the pillar in front of you truly exists because you can perceive it with your eyes and because it supports the beam and therefore functions. There is no need to boast about such understanding because if you analyze the phenomena correctly, nothing exists independently and nothing is endowed with solid existence. So do not cling to phenomena as truly existing.

138. This verse appears in slightly different ways in numerous texts and commentaries related to the lojong practice and is often quoted in oral teachings but is generally not attributed to one source in particular.

139. In the context of the Great Perfection, "cognitive potency" (*thugs rje*) is considered to be the union of the empty "nature" (*ngo bo*) and the luminous "character" (*rang bzhin*). In their translation of Jigme Lingpa's *Treasury of Precious Qualities*, Wulstan Fletcher and Helena Blankleder note the difficulty of accurately translating the trio *ngo bo*, *rang bzhin*, and *thugs rje*, which are constantly cited in the Great Perfection texts in connection with the fundamental mode of being of the mind. For the first term, *ngo bo*, they have stuck to the usual translation, "nature," while pointing out that C. S. Lewis devotes no less than fifty pages of his *Studies in Words* to a discussion of the history and meanings of this word. Here, the word "nature" is taken in its descriptive aspect: "What is this or that like?" Thus, to the question, "What is mind like?" the Great Perfection answers, "It is empty in nature; it precedes all attribution and is free from it." *Rang bzhin* is practically synonymous with *ngo bo*, but in this case it refers to a quality of the mind that is as inherent and fundamental as its emptiness—namely, its character of luminosity and knowledge. In order to remain close to the descriptive dimension of this word, the translators of *The Treasury of Precious Qualities* chose "character." From then on, we will say of the mind that it has "emptiness as its nature and luminosity as its character." The third term in this trio, *thugs rje* is usually translated as "compassion." *Thugs rje* is the honorific equivalent of *snying rje* (*nyingje*). In contexts where the word denotes the inability to bear the suffering of others, its proximity to the word "compassion" is not in doubt. But the Tibetan word denotes not

only the ability and willingness to simply sympathize and share in the suffering of others but the heroic intention to eradicate it. However, even if one adopts the word *compassion*, the etymological meaning of the Tibetan words ("lordship" or "power of the mind") gives them a number of meanings that the word *compassion* cannot cover. According to Khenpo Yonten Gyatso, in his expanded commentary of Jigme Lingpa's *Treasury of Precious Qualities* (*Yon tan rin po che'i mdzod kyi 'grel pa zab don snang byed nyi ma'i 'od zer, hung*, in *Rnying ma bka' ma rgyas pa, vol. thi [Kalimpong: Dupjung Lama, 1982–1987]*, f. 311), in the context of the Great Perfection, *thugs rje* means, "pure and natural awareness that has not yet departed from its true state or condition of purity" but has the potential to do so. In this case, *thugs rje* could be translated as "cognizant power" or "power to know." In his *Clear Explanation of the Two Truths* (*Bden gnyis bsal bzhad*), Shechen Gyaltsab Pema Namgyal sums up these three points as follows: "The nature of the ground being emptiness, it is primordially pure, free from all conceptual elaborations and characteristics. Its character being luminosity, it is the source of all phenomena, which are spontaneously accomplished. The ceaseless and omnipresent power to know is the creative power that is spontaneously present in the base. These are the three aspects of the primordial wisdom that are present in the ground." See *Zhe chen rgyal tshab 'gyur med pad+ma rnam rgyal gyi gsung 'bum* [Collected works of Shechen Gyaltsab Pema Namgyal] (Zhe chen dgon: Khams zhe chen bstan gnyis dar rgyas gling, 2014), vol. 9, p. 332.

140. The transcendent perfections, or *pāramitās*—generosity, discipline, patience, diligence, focus, and wisdom—become "perfect" when they "transcend" attachment to the notions of subject, object, and action.

141. The three supreme points concern the excellent preparation, the excellent main part and the excellent conclusion (see note 66). TK (p. 483) interprets this verse as follows: "Make offerings to the three supreme ones [Buddha, Dharma, and Sangha], and constantly strive to perfect the two accumulations."

142. There are several ways of listing the precepts of this sixfold training (*bslab pa'i mtha' drug*). According to the way presented here by Gyalwa Longchen Rabjam, the six trainings relate to (1) the view (*lta ba*); (2) the samaya (*dam tshig*); (3) the conduct (*spyod pa*); (4) the practice (*nyams len*); (5) the experience (*nyams myong*); and (6) the pith instructions (*man ngag*). According to the *Ultimate Instructions on the Secret Mantras* (*Gsang sngags bka'i tha ram*), one of the five sections of *The Union of Eight Pronouncements of the Sugatas* (*Bka' brgyad bde gshegs 'dus pas*), a major treasure text (*gter ma*) of the Nyingma tradition, revealed by Ngadak Nyang Ral Nyima Özer (*Sngags bdag nyang ral nyi ma 'od zer*, 1136–1204), one of the first great tertöns, the six trainings include: (1) the samayas (*dam tshig*), which lay the foundations and delight the spiritual master; (2) the view (*lta ba*), which establishes with certainty that all phenomena of samsara and nirvana pertain to the mind (*sems*); (3) forsaking ordinary experiences and activities (*la spyod pas dor ba*), which allows one to focus on

meditative evenness (*mnyam bzhag*), to maintain it in the post-meditative state, and to no longer differentiate between rejection and acceptance; (4) progressing through the stages of the path after having received an empowerment (*dbang*) and freeing oneself from emotional afflictions; (5) without distraction, taking into experience (*nyams su blang*) the wisdom of samādhi; and (6) ultimately, attaining the siddhis thanks to the pith instructions (*man ngag*).

143. On life stones (*bla rdo*), see note 119.

144. Exhaustion of phenomena in the ultimate nature of reality, dharmatā (*chos nyid zad pa*), is the last and ultimate stage of the four visions (*snang ba bzhi*) associated with the Thögal (*thod rgal*) practice of Great Perfection. All phenomena are thus "exhausted," or purified, in the single essence (*thig le nyag gcig*), beyond formulations and concepts.

145. In his commentary, Dilgo Khyentse Rinpoche explains the meaning of the expression *ya re cha*. We have therefore included its phonetic transcription in the translation.

146. As DKR and other commentators explain, the Tibetan word *dred* can mean "jaded" or "waterproof" (like the stiff leather of a butter skin, which has held butter for years without the butter penetrating the skin and without this skin losing its stiffness), but also, depending on the context, "slipping" as on a slab of ice or on muddy ground, for example.

147. This applies for example to becoming rich for having been generous in a past life and then being distracted by wealth and attached to it.

148. The archetypal example of someone who attained ultimate realization at the very moment he received the empowerment and corresponding instructions is King Indrabodhi. As reported in Jigme Lingpa's *Treasury of Precious Qualities* (vol. 2, note 660), "Only exceptional beings like King Indrabodhi, who received the Guhyasamāja [Secret Assembly Tantra] from the Buddha, or King Candrabhadra, who received the Kālacakra [The Wheel of Time], attain the complete realization of the Mahāmudrā at the very moment they receive the initiation. In the case of ordinary people, abhiṣeka (in Tibetan *dbang*, "empowerment") literally meant "cleansing and filling," as it cleanses or removes the veils that cover and obscure one's wisdom and fills the mind with the seeds of the four kāyas. Thus, it causes to appear what has always been present but has remained concealed from beginningless times. It is hard for ordinary people to gain liberation right away. Nevertheless, if one receives the seeds of the four kāyas by means of the four empowerments, and if one gradually implements the stages of the practice, these seeds will start to burgeon (just as happens when the farmer plows and plants his fields, tending and fertilizing them). And, by and by, the power of the empowerment will make itself felt—though for this to happen, one must practice the stages of generation and perfection."

149. JDL gives *mnyam* for both the root verse and the commentary, while other editions, including Dilgo Khyentse Rinpoche's commentary, write *mnyan*.

150. This practice falls under the stage of perfection with representations (*dmigs*

bcad rdzogs rim) and consists of holding the breath in the "vase" formed in the abdomen after retracting upward the lower prāṇa and compressing downward the upper prāṇa, all accompanied by the relevant visualizations.

151. Here the presentation of the ground Great Perfection as being perfectly pure at the level of the ground, as being none other than the tathāgatagarbha, is made from the perspective of the very nature of the universal ground, not from the perspective of the practitioner who is at the beginning of the path, and from whom, as mentioned earlier, the ground Great Perfection is obscured.
152. See the detailed explanations given in verse 412.
153. The comparison here does not indicate that those who are in this great bliss have totally lost control of their minds; it relates to the fearlessness aspect of some intoxicated people.
154. Those whom you might benefit and those who criticize or harm you are both helping you to correct your faults, perfect patience, and accumulate merits.
155. The spirit kings, or *gyalgong* (*rgyal 'gong*), are male malevolent spirits usually depicted in the form of a monk. Those who entertain adverse views about their spiritual master may be reborn as one of these demons.
156. This instruction refers to a potential deviation when doing śamatha practice, not to śamatha itself.
157. Atiśa (*Jo bo rje dpal ldan a ti sha*, 982–1054), also known as Atiśa Dīpaṃkara Śrījñāna, came to Tibet in 1042 and met the great translator Lochen Rinchen Zangpo (*Lo chen rin chen bzang po*, 958–1055). Atiśa was very impressed by the extent of Rinchen Zangpo's knowledge. However, when he asked how he practiced the different teachings he knew, Rinchen Zangpo replied that he practiced each of them separately. Disappointed by this reply, Atiśa told the translator, "You should find the essential point common to all the teachings and practice that way." For more details on this story, see Patrul Rinpoche, *The Words of My Perfect Teacher*, 258.
158. The eight great wondrous phrases (*go mtshar ba'i tshig chen po brgyad*), expressing the realization of the Great Perfection, are found in the tantra called *The Mound of Jewels* (*Rin po che spung ba'i rgyud*), in *Rdzogs chen rgyud bcu bdun* [Seventeen Nyingmapa tantras of the Pith Instructions Class of Atiyoga], vol. 1, pp. 424–39 (Chengdu: Si khron mi rigs dpe skrun khang, 2016). The twelve adamantine laughters (*rdo rje gad mo bcu gnyis*) are also enumerated in *The Mound of Jewels Tantra* and refer to the twelve bursts of laughter expressing the ultimate nature of the Great Perfection that is primordially present in all phenomena.
159. In the conclusion of the *Gnas lugs rdo rje tshig rkang*, from the *Klong chen snying thig* (*Heart treasury of the vast expanse*), in *The a 'dzom redaction of the gsung 'bum of 'jigs med gling pa*, vol. 12 (New Delhi: Shechen, 1999), pp. 461–62.
160. See note 52.
161. One of the central tenets of the Prajñāpāramitā literature is that while appearing, things are empty and being empty, they can appear. Accordingly, emptiness is not just the ultimate nature of phenomena, but the very potential that allows

these phenomena to unfold infinitely. This understanding is summed up in Nāgārjuna's famous phrase, "Because all is emptiness, all can be." See *Mūlamadhyamakakārikā* (Toh. 3824, Dg.T. rgyud 'grel, *wi*), ff. 1–56, 14. For a separate Tibetan edition of the root text see Nāgārjuna, *Prajñā nama Mūlamadhyamaka-kārikā, Dbu ma rtsa ba'i tshig le'ur byas pa shes rab ces bya ba* (Varanasi: The Pleasure of Elegant Sayings Press, 1974). It is precisely because phenomena are devoid of intrinsic existence that they can manifest themselves infinitely. A universe made up of autonomous entities endowed with real existence would be frozen forever, as it would prohibit the process of cause-and-effect laws, which is linked to the interdependent nature of phenomena and their lack of intrinsic reality. Among other commentaries on this crucial subject, see Jamgön Mipham, *The Wisdom Chapter: Jamgön Mipham's Commentary on the Ninth Chapter of The Way of the Bodhisattva*, trans. Padmakara Translation Group (Boulder: Shambhala, 2017).

162. This image, which compares the view to a lofty peak and the conduct to the bottom of the valley, is in line with Guru Padmasambhava's phrase, "The view must be higher than the sky and the conduct finer than flour." The conduct must therefore be very down-to-earth, carefully observing the most minute aspects of the laws of causality. TK (vol. 2, p. 122) comments in a similar way.
163. The luminous emptiness is the ultimate nature of all phenomena, but it does not constitute any autonomous, truly existing, and permanent entity, unlike, for example, the concept of ātman of Hinduism. This nature is not fluctuating for all that. It is therefore "immutable" while transcending the notions of past, present, and future that belong to conventional truth.
164. Dathong Tulku is a close disciple of Khyentse Rinpoche who received these teachings with Rabjam Rinpoche, Jigme Khyentse Rinpoche, and myself. He is a strongly built and jovial Bhutanese lama with whom Khyentse Rinpoche liked to joke.
165. According to Khenchen Pema Sherab (explanation given to the translator), this point is mentioned in the sutras. This does not mean that the bad karma of the samaya breakers can be transferred to others, including insects, but that they have the karma to be reborn in a place thus defiled by schism in the sangha. It is also said that no one can attain the first bhūmi in these places and that even the crops fail.
166. This passage is inaudible in the recording of these teachings, and so this sentence was completed by Rabjam Rinpoche.
167. We have been unable to locate the source of this quotation.
168. Although they are constantly suffering from lack of something (food, drink, etc.), some pretas are holders of great treasures, which they can hardly enjoy, while being very worried about these treasures being stolen from them. They therefore have watchmen who jealously guard these useless treasures.
169. The term *blo sna bstungs*, often translated as "having nothing but short-term plans," refers to avoiding all kinds of worldly plans as if we had countless years

to live. Seasoned practitioners, however, may commit themselves to engaging in meaningful activities for the sake of sentient beings and the Dharma over the long term. They do so while remaining acutely aware that impermanence and death may manifest at any time, and reminding others of this reality.

170. For a detailed explanation of this union of "great purity" and "great equality," see Mipham Rinpoche, *Gsang 'grel phyogs bcu'i mun sel sbyi don 'od gsal snying po* (*The general meaning of the quintessence of secrets*), in *The Expanded Redaction of the Complete Works of 'Ju Mi-pham Series*, vol. 19, ff. 1–120 (New Delhi: Shechen, 1984–85).

171. According to TK (vol. 2, p.189), *g.yom rgyug* is synonymous with *hol rgyug*, which refers to a thoughtless approximation or imitation.

172. This explanation is given by Dilgo Khyentse Rinpoche.

173. From the point of view of the true ultimate nature of all things, since saṃsāra and nirvāṇa are not fundamentally different, there is no real "accomplishment" of the good of beings because they have, from the beginning, the nature of Buddha. On the other hand, on the relative level, it is certainly possible to help beings dispel their ignorance and realize their Buddha nature.

174. This refers to the story of six blind men who each touch a different part of an elephant and describe the elephant according to their partial perceptions of the animal. We have translated this line according to spelling found in this volume, *glang chen mras ba bzhin* (DKR, f. 294b), while TK (vol. 2, p. 230) has *glang chen smos pas*, which has a similar meaning. JDL (f. 229a), however, has *glang chen smyos pa*, which can be translated as "like a mad elephant that sees things only partially."

175. The purity of the three seats of the mandala (*gdan gsum tshang ba'i dkhyil 'khor*) refers to the five aggregates (*skandha*) and the five elements (*dhātu*) that are the "seats" of the male and female buddhas. The internal and external sources (*āyatanas*), the faculties and their objects, are the seats of the male and female bodhisattvas. The four limbs are the seats of the wrathful guardians of the mandala gates.

176. A Vajrayāna practitioner must cultivate pure vision and perceive the environment in which he or she lives as the mandala of his or her tutelary deity and all beings, men and women, as wisdom deities.

177. Khyentse Rinpoche commented twice on these verses, as he returned to verse 304 after commenting on verse 305. We have therefore merged the two commentaries by introducing elements of the second into the first.

178. Khyentse Rinpoche also commented twice on these verses, and we proceeded as above.

179. According to the teachings of the Great Perfection, one speaks of four ways of leaving everything as it is in its natural state, free from any alteration (*cog bzhag bzhi*): (1) the mountain-like view where everything is left as it is (*lta ba ri bo cog bzhag*), (2) the ocean-like meditation where everything is left as it is (*sgom pa rgya mtsho cog bzhag*), (3) the action in which appearances are left as they are

(*spyod pa snang ba cog bzhag*), and (4) the result that is the awareness left as it is (*'bras bu rig pa'i cog bzhag*).

180. The word *bar du* usually means "between" or "in the middle of," but in some rarer cases, as here, it can also mean "beyond" or "more than anything else."
181. Gyalwa Longchenpa speaks of six situations, but the text only contains four. It can be tentatively assumed that they were lost when the original manuscripts were copied in the fourteenth century. They are missing in all known editions of Longchen Rabjam's works.
182. Most editions have *gdos chos*, while TK (vol. 2, p. 249) has *gdol chos*, "rude," "barbarian," "outcast."
183. The root text, which was composed in the fourteenth century, as well as the commentary, refer to a time when power rested in the hands of kings. This verse naturally also applies to today's forms of governance.
184. According to JDL (f. 250b), the expression *rdo 'jong* refers to the image of a tall pillar with an ornate capital on which your head rests, which is an analogy for a haughty attitude.
185. According to TK (p. 292), *blab rtsol* is equivalent to *bab rtsol*, which can be translated as "unexamined," "nonsense," "thoughtless," "inconsiderate," or "hasty."
186. "Aiming right," or "hitting the target," refers here to giving the disciple instructions that are perfectly suited to his abilities and aspirations.
187. JDL (f. 256b) comments in a slightly different way: "This is not the way the essence of the master's heart will penetrate the mind of the disciple."
188. *Rang babs*, see note 131.
189. According to JDL (f. 262b), *nyes kha* is a colloquial expression in his region (Domang in Kham) for gathering or arranging a meeting between future friends or spouses. According to Tulku Kalsang, it would be an abbreviation of *nyes cha* (defect) + *nyen kha* (danger). He then comments on the verse as follows: "Since we cannot know whether our relationships with others will be lasting or not, we must beware of committing faults and incurring dangers to satisfy these ephemeral acquaintances."
190. The expressions *ya cha*, *ya re cha*, and *yi re mug* indicate a situation that is dismaying, pathetic, and depressing.
191. That is, which unites the instructions of the entire lineage from the primordial Buddha, Samantabhadra to the root master, according to JDL (f. 265a) or, according to TK (p. 313), "which unites the view and the practice."
192. The three capacities of the lion (*seng ge'i rtsal gsum*) are miraculous transformations (*rdzu 'phrul*), swiftness (*myur mgyogs*), and wings made of wind (*rlung gshog*). According to another explanation, these three masteries refer to the lion's ability to judge distances perfectly when jumping from one mountain to another (*tshad dzin thun ba'i rtsal*), his ability to hold his breath for a long time when crossing space (*ring bar bsgangs pa'i rtsal*), and his ability to leap through the air (*bar nang du spar ba'i rtsal*).

193. The twelve ascetic practices (*sbyangs pa'i yon tan bcu gnyi*) are as follows:

1. Wearing clothes made of rags thrown away by others (*phyag dar khrod pa*),
2. Possessing only the three monastic robes (*chos gos gsum*),
3. Wearing clothes made of felt (*phying pa*) rather than clothes made of expensive materials, like silk, brocades, etc.,
4. Begging for food (*bsod snyoms pa*),
5. Eating once a day (*stan gcig*),
6. Limiting your amount of food (*zas phyis mi len*) to what is necessary to survive in good health,
7. Living in secluded places (*dgon pa*),
8. Residing at the foot of a tree (*shing grung pa*) rather than in a built dwelling,
9. Residing in areas exposed to the weather (*bla ga' med*),
10. Residing near mass graves and in cemeteries (*dur khrod pa*),
11. Sleeping while seated (*tsog pu*),
12. Staying always in the same place (*gzhi ji bzhin*).

194. In this section 347, the opening and concluding verses speak of six "beds" (*mal*) that serve for the analogies developed in the six main points. Alternatively, six attitudes or ways of practicing are compared to resting on a comfortable bed. A number of editions, among those available, do use the word *mal* in the intermediary verses. This is true in particular of JDL (ff. 271b and 272a). Others, such as the Adzom edition (BDRC W1PD8, vol. 3, ff. 60a and b), and the Derge edition (BDRC W00EGS1016299–I1CZ5001-1029-1140, ff. 42b and 43a), generally considered reliable, switch to the word *lam* (path) in these six intermediate verses. TK (vol. 2, p. 324) uses *mal* consistently both in the root verses and in his explanations. JDL (f. 69a) remarks in his commentary that this is certainly a textual error but that no one having corrected the root verses so far, he has left them as they were, while opting for *mal* in his commentary, which is consistent with the meaning of the analogies. Moreover, a manuscript in Tibetan cursive (*dbu med*; BDRC BW3CN2890-I3CN2892, f. 74a) shows traces of corrections where *lam* has been rectified to *mal*. It should be noted that in the most widely used cursive script used for manuscripts, *mal* and *lam* look very similar, which make them prone to calligraphic mistakes. For these various reasons, we have adopted *mal* in our translation.

195. This translation is in line with Dilgo Khyentse Rinpoche's commentary. JDL (f. 274b) interprets this verse as follows: "In order to acquire the infinite ocean of qualities resulting from the elimination [of obscurations] and maturation [of the qualities of enlightenment], they manifest in the form of the buddhas of the saṃbhogakāya." According to this latter interpretation, the root verse could then be understood as follows: "To fully master [the qualities of enlightenment], they manifest in the form of the saṃbhogakāya."

196. *Sha ra bha*, king of the animals, an eight-legged lion.
197. *dpal mgon bdun bcu rtsa lnga*, important Dharma protectors, considered to be manifestations of the great protector Mahākāla.
198. The path of accumulation (*tshogs lam*) and the path of joining (*sbyor lam*) are the first two of the five paths that lead to buddhahood through the ten bhūmis.
199. According to JDL (f. 276a), "In order to achieve the Buddhadharma and become the supreme object of offering for all beings residing in the three worlds, the sixth priority is the dedication of the merits accumulated by oneself and others in the three times, within the continuum of emptiness, free of representation. In making the dedication, the bodhisattvas vow that the strength of these merits will enable all beings to attain unsurpassable enlightenment."
200. The Mahāyāna texts mention that some arhats, like this Kātyāyana, are emanations of the Buddha himself (*sprul pa'i snyan thos*). Their purpose is to guide beings and benefit them in various ways according to their mental dispositions and abilities. The question of the contemporaneity of certain arhats with the Buddha who manifested them has given rise to debate among scholars.
201. Guru Padmasambhava, King Trisong Detsen (and the other main disciples of Padmasambhava, twenty-five in number), and the Abbot Śāntarakṣita.
202. Dilgo Khyentse Rinpoche, *The Heart Treasure of the Enlightened Ones*, trans. Padmakara Translation Group (Boston: Shambhala, 1993), 43.
203. The prayers and aspirations mentioned are those of the bodhisattva Samantabhadra.
204. The texts of the Prajñāpāramitā, in particular, describe up to forty-six types of māras.
205. The story told in the sutras is that one day a rabbit heard the sound of a large branch breaking off and falling into the water, producing a resounding "Tcha-tcharr!" Frightened by the noise, the rabbit darted away in fear. Observing the rabbit's hasty escape, other animals questioned him: "Why are you running away like that?" The terrified rabbit could only respond by uttering, "Tcha-tcharr!" Hearing his anxious words, the other animals, now alarmed, began to flee, and soon, as the cry of "Tcha-tcharr!" spread from mouth to ear, all animals in the vicinity found themselves swept up in a frenzied flight.
206. In the available editions, this section has only five instructions instead of six.
207. Practitioners of the Nyingma tradition, among others, commonly use this prayer to conclude practice sessions, ceremonies, and aspiration prayers.
208. Translated in accordance with Adzom Drukpa's edition of the Seven Treasuries and Khyentse Rinpoche's commentary (DKR, f. 357b), which both have *gzhan la ston cing / yon tan bsnags pa brjod*. The version of the root text used by JDL (f. 289a) has *bstod cing*, in which case the verse should be translated as "Appreciate and extol the virtues of others, acknowledging their admirable qualities."
209. This advice, intended for men who have taken a vow of chastity, applies equally to women, and concerns any situation that might lead to a deterioration in the precepts they have pledged to follow.

210. See note 70.
211. According to JDL (f. 291a), it is important not to think that listeners and solitary realizers lack benevolence and compassion. The negation means here that their degree of compassion and loving-kindness is comparatively less.
212. While the root verses and the commentary might seem different at first sight, they both convey the same teaching: those who truly understand emptiness won't behave recklessly, especially by harming others, claiming that "everything is empty." In his oral teachings, Dilgo Khyentse Rinpoche gave the example of such a misguided practitioner who, while cutting the head of a sheep in a nomadic area of Eastern Tibet, declared, "The one who kills is empty, the one who is slaughtered is empty, the act of killing is empty." Khyentse Rinpoche emphasized that this was a typical example of the conduct that has "fallen" into the side of emptiness and that this kind of statement opens the door to the boundless activities of Māra.
213. On the three supreme practices (*dam pa gsum*), see note 66.
214. In DKR (f. 364b), *ma yon tan med pa* should read *mar yon tan med pa*, and *ya bsgral ba* should read *yar bsgral ba*.
215. Gyalwa Longchen Rabjam speaks here on his own behalf.
216. According to Buddhist cosmology, itself inherited from the Hindu cosmology that prevailed at the time, our universe (one among billions of other universes) has a central mountain called Mount Meru surrounded by four main continents, with each continent being bordered by two smaller continents. The continent we live on, called Jambudvīpa, is situated to the south of Mount Meru.
217. On the meaning of "cognizant power" (*thugs rje*) in this context, see note 141.
218. The *Mahāparinirvāṇa Sūtra*, chapter 12, tells the story of a mighty wrestler who had a gem inside his head between his eyebrows, without being aware of it. The sutra goes on to say that similarly, we all have the buddha nature, without realizing it.
219. This refers to the four "lamps" (*sgron me bzhi*) that shine during the practice of Thögal.
220. Beings gifted with pure perception can perceive the saṃbhogakāya, while those with impure perception perceive only the nirmāṇakāya.
221. In several editions of the root text, as well as in DKR (f. 392b) and TK (vol. 2, p. 450) one reads *yul med ming dang bral*, whereas JDL (f. 325b) has *yod med ming dang bral* ("free from the denominations of existence and nonexistence").
222. This second point emphasizes the freedom from the four conceivable extremes (*mu bzhi*), which are (1) existent, (2) nonexistent, (3) both existent and nonexistent, and (4) neither existent nor nonexistent. "Neither existent nor nonexistent" also implies, in this context, "neither without object nor without name," in continuation of the line above that says "devoid of object and name."
223. In Indian Sāṃkhya philosophy, prakṛti is the primordial nature, the first cause of material phenomena. She unites the potentialities of energy and matter, embodying the unconscious, dynamic feminine principle. She associates with the static masculine principle, puruṣa, which is pure consciousness.

224. JDL (p. ff. 325b–326a) gives the following commentary: "When it comes to clinging to the extremes of conceptual elaborations, in the absence of grasping to something that would really exist through a "birth" and of grasping to the complete nonexistence of things, there is no conceivable third option to be an object of grasping for the intellect. Hence, you are also liberated from the extreme of nonduality." See also TK, vol. 3, p. 450.

225. "Since what appears is devoid of its own existence" (JDL, p. 653).

226. The point here is not to purify primordial wisdom itself but to purify that which prevents us from fully realizing it.

227. These are meditations related to the four levels, or "infinite" states, of the formless gods that are at the highest level of samsara. These four levels correspond to the four formless absorptions (*gzugs med pa'i snyoms 'jug bzhi*): infinite space (*nam mkha mtha' yas*), infinite consciousness (*rnam shes mtha' yas*), absolutely nothing (*ci yang med pa*), and neither existing nor nonexisting (*'du shes med 'du shes med min*).

228. In so doing, we limit ourselves to the view of the Cittamātra (*Sems tsam pa*), the philosophical system of "mind only." According to this system, phenomena are no more than projections of the mind and are thus illusory in nature. On the other hand, the Cittamātrins consider that awareness, which illuminates and knows itself in a nondual mode (*gnyis med rang rig rang gsal*), exists in an ultimate way, which is refuted by the proponents of Madhyamaka.

229. As Dudjom Rinpoche and Dilgo Khyentse Rinpoche frequently reminded us, the disciple may have the impression of having a very clear meditation and experiencing awareness (*rig pa*), whereas this is only a limited clarity within the basic consciousness, ālayavijñāna, which remains under the empire of ignorance. Similarly, for a disciple, it is easy to confuse ordinary mind (*sems*) with primordial wisdom (*ye shes*). For further explanations, see in particular the *The Tantra of the Great All-Illuminating Sphere* (*Thig le kun gsal chen po'i rgyud*) in *The One Hundred Thousand Nyingma Tantras Rnying ma rgyud 'bum* or the *The Mirror of the Essential and Profound Meaning* (*Zab don gnad gi me long*) in Gyalwa Longchen Rabjam's *The Profound Quintessence* (*Zab mo yang tig*).

230. In India and Tibet, winter is the dry season, while summer brings the monsoon rains.

231. It is believed that reciting specific mantras while blowing on a poison will neutralize its harmful effects.

232. *Thig le nyag gcig* is an expression from the vocabulary of the Great Perfection that literally means "single drop" or "single sphere" and, by extension, "single essence." It indicates the fact that the totality of the phenomena of samsara and nirvana are embraced within the single sphere of the ultimate nature of reality, dharmatā. Phenomena are the natural radiance, or manifestation, of the same unchanging nature in which the three kāyas are united.

233. This statement may seem paradoxical, but in *The Root Stanzas of the Middle Way* (*Mūlamadhyamakakārikā*; see translation published by the Padmakara Trans-

lation Group, 2008), Nāgārjuna explains that it is precisely because phenomena are devoid of intrinsic existence that they can manifest infinitely. Nāgārjuna demonstrates that if there were entities possessing intrinsic existence, the chain of cause and effect could not function. He concludes (in chapter 24, stanza 14):

> Where emptiness is granted
> Everything is likewise granted.
> Where emptiness is unacceptable
> All is likewise unacceptable.

234. Azom Drukpa's edition of the root verses and Khyentse Rinpoche's commentary use *rngul* (sweat), while JDL and TK have *rdul,* in which case the phrase would mean "your face takes on an earthy appearance."
235. According to Shechen Khenpo Gyurme Dorje, *rig pa ye shes kyi steng du,* which literally means "upon, on the basis of, wisdom-awareness" refers to the fact that even when the mind is obscured by ignorance, it is still grounded on primordial wisdom, which is its true and ultimate nature. According to TK (vol. 2, p. 479), "As the habitual tendencies of the creative power of the awareness of primordial wisdom reabsorb into the cocoon of clear light, the five wind-energies reabsorb into the absolute expanse" (*rig pa ye shes kyi rtsal gyi bags chags 'od gsal gyi bubs su 'dus pa'i tshe*).
236. In these sets of instructions, the categories of beings endowed with superior, average, or inferior faculties are in turn subdivided into two categories each, high and low, leading to six categories in total.
237. They are as if "vanished" in ālayavijñāna. According to Dilgo Khyentse Rinpoche, in ālayavijñāna, one has no other discursive thought except the vague feeling that the "world exists out there," without any other attribute or concept.
238. Bardo days are not ordinary days, but rather "days of concentration" (*bsam gtan gyi zhag*). According to Dilgo Khyentse Rinpoche, one of these days corresponds to the length of time we have been able to maintain a stable state of concentration (dhyāna) during the life we have just left. Consequently, the forty-nine days traditionally attributed to the bardo, the intermediate state between a death and rebirth, do not necessarily correspond to our usual days.
239. Awareness (*rig pa*) cannot itself be obscured in its own nature, but we can cease to experience it directly.
240. Beings of samsara take birth through four "doors," or forms of birth (*skyes gnas bzhi*): from a womb, from an egg, from moisture, or in a miraculous way.
241. Various enumerations of these seven qualities of beings of the higher destinies of samsara are found. According to one of them, the qualities are (1) long life, (2) freedom from disease, (3) pleasing physical appearance, (4) auspicious conditions, (5) respectable ancestry, (6) material ease, and (7) keen intelligence.
242. The five crimes with immediate effect (*mtshams med lnga*) are (1) killing one's father, (2) killing one's mother, (3) killing an arhat, (4) dividing the spiritual community, and (5) spilling the blood of a buddha with the intention of

harming him. Those who commit any of these crimes are reborn directly into the "Hell of unsurpassable torments" immediately after their death, without passing through the intermediate state of the bardo.

243. According to JDL (f. 346b), misleading perceptions pertain to imputed ignorance (*kun btags ma rig pa*), while grasping to these perceptions pertains to coemergent ignorance (*lhan skyes ma rig pa*).

244. According to JDL (f. 347a), the absence of elaborations corresponds to the dharmakāya, the luminosity corresponds to the saṃbhogakāya, and the omnipresent vastness corresponds to the nirmāṇakāya. Since this spontaneously present manifestation is devoid of intrinsic existence, it is naturally liberated in its primordial purity.

245. According to JDL (f. 347b), the primordial wisdom associated with dharmakāya leans neither toward primordial purity (*ka dag*) nor toward spontaneous presence (*lhun grub*). The emptiness aspect of primordial purity expressed by the spontaneous presence is thus not a mere "emptiness" and is therefore "liberated" from the extreme of emptiness within spontaneous presence. As for the spontaneous presence, since it is also devoid of existence of its own, it is liberated in unborn primordial purity.

246. Mahāhimasāgara Vairocana Buddha (*Rnam par snang mdzad gangs chen mtsho*), a buddha of the body of perfect enjoyment (*saṃbhogakāya*) who manifests in five families. In Sanskrit, *mahāsāgara* means "great ocean," which Tibetan translators have rendered as *gangs chen mtsho*, "ocean of the snowy mountains." According to Buddhist cosmology, in the midst of countless buddha fields, Mahāhimasāgara Vairocana Buddha is seated on a vast lotus in the adamantine posture. Immense, he remains perfectly still, while from the pores of his body flows a stream of fragrant water in which countless buddha fields are laid out for the benefit of beings. In both his hands, in the *mudrā* of equanimity, rests a begging bowl containing an ocean of fragrant water from which emerges a lotus with twenty-five stamens tiered one atop the other. On each stamen are pure lands of the buddhas of the five families, associated respectively with the enlightened body, speech, mind, qualities, and activity of the buddhas. Each of these is subdivided into five sub-aspects, such as "body-body," "body-speech," "body-mind," and so on. Śākyamuni Buddha's pure land, the Saha world, resides on the thirteenth stamen, corresponding to the "mind-mind" aspect, and is located at the heart of the Buddha Immense Ocean.

247. *Go 'byed*, "to open possibilities," is a translation of the Sanskrit *ākāśa*, "space," which offers the possibility for the whole phenomenal world to unfold. This is the case with the dharmakāya, which opens up infinite possibilities without constituting a concrete support, as is the case with the rūpakāya, the form body.

248. In the case of the saṃbhogakāya, "self-experience" (*rang snang*) means that those at the saṃbhogakāya level perceive this primordial wisdom themselves, but it is not perceived by beings at the nirmāṇakāya level, with the exception of bodhisattvas who have attained the tenth bhūmi.

249. According to JDL (f. 351a), "the 'other' philosophical views" refers to differences between proponents of Rangtong (*Rang strong*, "emptiness of self" or "emptiness in itself") and Zhentong (*Gzhan strong*, "emptiness of something else"—that is, emptiness of that which is not buddha nature) views. According to some holders of the Cittamātra view, primordial wisdom is a real support for the accomplishment of the welfare of sentient beings, a position refuted by the Madhyamaka, according to which no entity, even ultimate, is endowed with intrinsic existence. However, according to the Madhyamaka, even if the kāyas and wisdoms have no intrinsic existence and provide no tangible support, this does not prevent the activity of buddhas from manifesting unhindered.

250. JDL (f. 351a) suggests, with due caution, that a textual error may have crept into the available editions of Gyalwa Longchenpa's work, since with "*gags med*," the sentence seems to mean the opposite of what the context indicates. By correcting "*gag pa med*" to "*ga' yang med*," the sequence of ideas seems easier to understand. The sentence could then mean: "Even though, in accordance with the Madhyamaka philosophy, we do not adhere to the notion of a concrete existence of the kāyas and wisdoms that could provide a foundation for the buddhas' actions, it does not hinder the boundless manifestation of this very activity."

251. These are offering stands (*mchod sdong*) that refer to an altar, or stūpa, where offerings are made for a specific purpose. In this context, allusion is made to an altar where sages, or rishis, perform a sādhana and the recitation of mantras focused on the practice of garuḍas, traditionally considered the enemy of nāgas, who are responsible for leprosy and other skin diseases.

252. Although counted as a fourth kāya, the svabhāvikakāya does not constitute a separate body but indicates the indivisible union of the three bodies.

Bibliography

Tibetan texts

Chödrak Sangpo (*Chos grags bzang po*). *Kun mkhyen dri med 'od zer gyi rnam thar mthong ba don ldan* [Meaningful to behold: A biography of the omniscient Drime Özer (Longchenpa)]. In *Bi ma snying thig*, part 4 (*ya*), in *Snying thig ya bzhi*, vol. 6, pp. 499-590. Darjeeling: Taklung Tsetrul Rinpoche, 1975. BDRC MW12827_D41341.

Dilgo Khyentse Rinpoche (*Dil mgo mkhyen rtse rin po che*). *The Collected Writings of Skyabs-rje Dil-mgo Mkhyen-brtse Rin-po-che. gSung 'bum rab gsal zla ba*. New Delhi: Shechen, 1994. BDRC W21809.

———. *Man ngag mdzod kyi don khrid rab gsal zla ba'i bdud rtsi* [The precious treasury of essential instructions, a meaning-commentary on *The nectar of brilliant moon*]. New Delhi: Shechen, 2021.

Jamgön Kongtrul Lodrö Thaye (*'Jam mgon kong sprul blo gros mtha' yas*). *Rgya chen bka' mdzod* [Collected works, expanded edition]. New Delhi: Shechen, 2002. BDRC W23723.

Jamyang Drupai Lodrö (*'Jam dbyangs grub pa'i blo gros*). *Man ngag dzod kyi 'bru 'grel don gsal me long* [The mirror that illuminates the meaning]. In *Mkhan chen dam pa 'jam dbyangs grub pa'i blo gros kyi gsung 'bum* [Collected works of Khenchen Jamyang Drupai Lodrö], vol. 7. Chengdu: Snga 'gyur mthun lung dgon, 2015. BDRC W3CN3329.

Jigme Lingpa (*Kun mkhyen 'jigs med gling pa*). *The A 'dzom redaction of the gsung 'bum of 'jigs med gling pa*. Paro: Lama Ngodrup and Sherab Drime, 1984. BDRC W7477.

Ju Mipham Gyatso (*'Ju mi pham rgya mtsho*). *The Expanded Redaction of the Complete Works of 'Ju Mi-pham Series*. Paro: Lama Ngodrup and Sherab Drimey, 1984–85. BDRC MW23468.

Khenpo Yonten Gyatso (*Mkhan po yon tan rgya mtsho*). *Yon tan rin po che'i mdzod kyi 'grel pa* [A commentary on the Treasury of Precious Qualities], in *Rnying ma bka' ma rgyas pa*, Vols. 37–39. Edited by Dudjom Jikdral Yeshe Dorje. Kalimpong: Dupjung Lama, 1982–7. BDRC W19229.

Longchen Rabjam (*Klong chen rab 'byams dri med 'od zer*). *Gsung thor bu*. Paro: Lama Ngodrup and Sherab Drimey, 1982. BDRC W23504.

———. *Mdzod bdun* [Seven treasuries]. Adzom edition. Dkar mdzes bod rigs rang skyong khul, a 'dzom chos sgar, 1999. BDRC W1PD8.

———. Snying thig ya bzhi [The heart essence in four parts]. Darjeeling: Taklung Tsetrul Pema Wangyal, 1975. BDRC W12827.

———. *Snying thig ya bzhi* [The heart essence in four parts]. Darjeeling: Taklung Tsetrul Pema Wangyal, 1975. BDRC W12827.

Patrul Rinpoche (*Dpal sprul o rgyan 'jigs med chos kyi dbang po*). *Gsung 'bum o rgyan 'jigs med chos kyi dbang po* [The Collected Works of Patrul Rinpoche]. Chengdu: Si khron mi rigs dpe skrun khang, 2009. BDRC MW1PD107142.

Rdzogs chen rgyud bcu bdun [Seventeen Nyingmapa tantras of the Pith Instructions Class of Atiyoga]. Chengdu: Si khron mi rigs dpe skrun khang, 2016. BDRC W3CN7084.

Sangay Dorji. *Kun mkhyen long chen pa'i gdan sa chags rabs* [Dwelling places of Kunkhyen Longchenpa in Bhutan]. Thimphu: KMT, 2019.

Shabkar Tsogdruk Rangdrol (*Zhabs dkar tshogs drug rang grol*). *The Collected Works of Zhabs dkar tshogs drug rang grol*. New Delhi: Shechen, 2003. BDRC W23893.

Shechen Gyaltsab (*Zhe chen rgyal tshab padma rnam rgyal*). *The Collected Works of Zhe chen rgyal tshab padma rnam rgyal*. New Delhi: Shechen, 1975–1994. BDRC W3916.

———. *The Collected Works of Zhe chen rgyal tshab padma rnam rgyal*. Khams zhe chen bstan gnyis dar rgyas gling: Zhe chen dgon, 2014. BDRC W1PD133163.

Tulku Pema Kalsang (*Rdzogs chen sprul sku padma skal bzang*). *Man ngag rin po che'i mdzod kyi zab gsang snying po'i don rdo rje'i ljags kyis bkral ba skyud byang du bsdus pa gdams zab nor bu'i gter mdzod* [The treasure chest of the profound jewel-like Instructions], 2 vols. Transcribed by Khenpo Tenzin Dralha (Mkhan po bstan 'dzin dgra lha). Gansu: Ken su'u mi rigs dpe skrun khang, n. d. [See also an identical edition with a slightly different pagination. Lhasa: Bod ljongs bod yig dpe rnying dpe skrun khang, 2011. W1KG18488.]

Texts in Western Languages

Arguillère, Stéphane. *Profusion de la vaste sphère: Klong-chen rab-'byams (Tibet, 1308–1364) Sa vie, son oeuvre, sa doctrine*. Leuven: Peeters Publishers and Department of Oriental Studies, 2007.

Barron, Richard. *The Precious Treasury of Pith Instructions*. Junction City: Padma, 2006.

Dilgo Khyentse Rinpoche and Padampa Sangye. *The Hundred Verses of Advice: Tibetan Buddhist Teachings on What Matters Most*. Translated by the Padmakara Translation Group. Boston: Shambhala, 2006.

Dilgo Khyentse Rinpoche. *Brilliant Moon: The Autobiography of Dilgo Khyentse.* Translated by Ani Jinpa Palmo. Boston: Shambhala, 2008.

Dorji Wangchuk. "Cross-Referential Clues for a Relative Chronology of Klong Chen Pa's Works." *Contributions to Tibetan Buddhist Literature* 14, no. 3 (2008): 195–244.

Dudjom Rinpoche. *The Nyingma School of Tibetan Buddhism: Its Fundamentals and History*. 2nd ed. Boston: Wisdom, 2012.

Jamgön Mipham. *The Adornment of the Middle Way*. Translated by the Padmakara Translation Group. Boston: Shambhala, 2008.

Jigme Lingpa. *The Treasury of Precious Qualities*, with commentary by Longchen Yeshe Dorje, Kangyur Rinpoche, 2 vols. Translated by Padmakara Translation Group. Boston: Shambhala, 2011–2013.

Karma Ura. *Longchen's Forests of Poetry and Rivers of Composition in Bhutan.* Thimphu: The Centre for Bhutan Studies and GNH Research, 2015.

Longchenpa. *Finding Rest in Meditation. The Trilogy on Rest.* Translated by the Padmakara Translation Group. Boston: Shambhala, 2018.

Longchenpa and Khangsar Tenpa'i Wangchuk. *The Precious Treasury of the Dharmadhātu.* Khangsar Tenpa'i Wangchuk's Collected Works. Translated by the Padmakara Translation Group. Boulder: Shambhala, 2025.

———. *The Precious Treasury of the Fundamental Nature*. Khangsar Tenpa'i Wangchuk's Collected Works. Translated by the Padmakara Translation Group. Boulder: Shambhala, 2024.

Nyoshul Khenpo Jamyang Dorje. *A Marvelous Garland of Rare Gems: Biographies of Masters of Awareness in the Dzogchen Lineage.* Translated by Richard Barron. Junction City: Padma, 2005.

Padampa Sangye and Dilgo Khyentse Rinpoche. *The Hundred Verses of Advice.* Translated by the Padmakara Translation Group. Boston: Shambhala, 2006.

Patrul Rinpoche. *The Words of My Perfect Teacher*. Rev. ed. New Haven, CT: Yale University Press, 2010.

Ricard, Matthieu. *Journey to Enlightenment: The Life and World of Khyentse Rinpoche, Spiritual Teacher from Tibet*. New York: Aperture, 1996.

Tsumagari, Shinichi. *Meaningful to Behold: A Critical Edition & Annotated Translation of Longchenpa's Biography*. Self published, CreateSpace, 2016.

Tulku Thondup. *Masters of Meditation and Miracles: Lives of the Great Buddhist Masters of India and Tibet.* Edited by Harold Talbott. Boston: Shambhala, 1999.

———. *The Practice of Dzogchen: Longchen Rabjam's Writings on the Great Perfection.* Edited by Harold Talbott. Boston: Snow Lion, 2014. [First published in 1989 under the title *Buddha Mind: An Anthology of Longchen Rabjam's Writings on Dzogpa Chenpo*].

Zhechen Gyaltsab. *Path of Heroes, Birth of Enlightenment.* Translated by Deborah Black. 2 vols. Cazadero: Dharma, 1995.

The Padmakara Translation Group Translations into English

The Adornment of the Middle Way, Shantarakshita and Mipham Rinpoche. Boston: Shambhala, 2005, 2010.

Counsels from My Heart, Dudjom Rinpoche. Boston: Shambhala Publications, 2001, 2003.

Enlightened Courage, Dilgo Khyentse Rinpoche. Dordogne: Editions Padmakara, 1992; Ithaca, NY: Snow Lion, 1994, 2006.

Enlightened Vagabond: The Life and Teachings of Patrul Rinpoche. Boulder: Shambhala, 2024.

The Excellent Path to Enlightenment, Dilgo Khyentse. Dordogne: Editions Padmakara, 1987; Ithaca, NY: Snow Lion, 1996.

A Feast of the Nectar of the Supreme Vehicle, Maitreya and Jamgön Mipham. Boulder: Shambhala, 2018.

Finding Rest in Illusion, Longchenpa. Boulder: Shambhala, 2018.

Finding Rest in Meditation, Longchenpa. Boulder: Shambhala, 2018, 2020.

Finding Rest in the Nature of the Mind, Longchenpa. Boulder: Shambhala, 2017, 2020.

A Flash of Lightning in the Dark of the Night, The Dalai Lama. Shambhala, 1993. Republished as For the Benefit of All Beings. Boston: Shambhala, 2009.

Food of Bodhisattvas, Shabkar Tsogdruk Rangdrol. Boston: Shambhala, 2004.

A Garland of Views: A Guide to View, Meditation, and Result in the Nine Vehicles, Padmasambhava and Mipham Rinpoche. Boston: Shambhala, 2015.

A Guide to the Words of My Perfect Teacher, Khenpo Ngawang Pelzang. Translated with Dipamkara. Boston: Shambhala, 2004.

The Heart of Compassion, Dilgo Khyentse. Boston: Shambhala, 2007.

The Heart Treasure of the Enlightened Ones, Dilgo Khyentse and Patrul Rinpoche. Boston: Shambhala, 1992.

The Hundred Verses of Advice, Dilgo Khyentse and Padampa Sangye. Boston: Shambhala, 2005.

Introduction to the Middle Way, Chandrakirti and Mipham Rinpoche. Boston: Shambhala, 2002, 2004.

Journey to Enlightenment, Matthieu Ricard. New York: Aperture Foundation, 1996.

Lady of the Lotus Born, Gyalwa Changchub and Namkhai Nyingpo. Boston: Shambhala, 1999, 2002.

Lion of Speech: The Life of Mipham Rinpoche, Dilgo Khyentse. Boulder: Shambhala, 2020.

The Life of Shabkar: The Autobiography of a Tibetan Yogin. Albany, NY: SUNY Press, 1994; NY: Snow Lion, 2001.

Nagarjuna's Letter to a Friend, Yeshe Dorje, Kangyur Rinpoche. Ithaca, NY: Snow Lion, 2005.

The Natural Openness and Freedom of the Mind, Deshek Lingpa and Khangsar Tenpa'i Wangchuk. Boulder: Shambhala, 2024.

The Nectar of Mañjuśrī's Speech, Kunzang Pelden. Boston: Shambhala, 2007, 2010.

Nyingma, Part Two. The Treasury of Precious Instructions 2. Compiled by Jamgön Kongtrul Lodrö Taye. Boulder: Snow Lion, 2024.

Practicing the Great Perfection: Instructions on the Crucial Points, Shechen Gyaltsap Gyurme Pema Namgyal. Boulder: Shambhala, 2020.

The Precious Treasury of the Fundamental Nature, Longchenpa and Khangsar Tenpa'i Wangchuk. Boulder: Shambhala, 2021.

The Root Stanzas on the Middle Way, Nagarjuna. Dordogne: Edition Padmakara, 2008; Boulder: Shambhala, 2016.

A Torch Lighting the Way to Freedom, Dudjom Rinpoche, Jigdrel Yeshe Dorje. Boston: Shambhala, 2011.

Treasury of Precious Qualities, Book One. Longchen Yeshe Dorje, Kangyur Rinpoche. Boston: Shambhala, 2001. Revised version with root text by Jigme Lingpa, 2010.

Treasury of Precious Qualities, Book Two. Longchen Yeshe Dorje, Kangyur Rinpoche. Boston: Shambhala, 2013, 2020.

The Way of the Bodhisattva (Bodhicharyavatara), Shantideva. Boston: Shambhala, 1997, 2006, 2008.

White Lotus, Jamgön Mipham. Boston: Shambhala, 2007.

The Wisdom Chapter: Jamgön Mipham's Commentary on the Ninth Chapter of the Way of the Bodhisattva. Jamgön Mipham. Boulder: Shambhala, 2017.

Wisdom: Two Buddhist Commentaries. Khenchen Kunzang Pelden and Minyak Kunzang Sönam. Dordogne: Editions Padmakara, 1993, 1999.

The Wish-Fulfilling Jewel, Dilgo Khyentse. Boston: Shambhala, 1988.

The Words of My Perfect Teacher, Patrul Rinpoche. Sacred Literature Series of the International Sacred Literature Trust. New York: Harper-Collins, 1994; 2nd ed. Lanham, MD: AltaMira Press, 1998; Boston: Shambhala, 1998; New Haven, CT: Yale University Press, 2010.

Zurchungpa's Testament, Zurchungpa and Dilgo Khyentse. Ithaca, NY: Snow Lion, 2006.